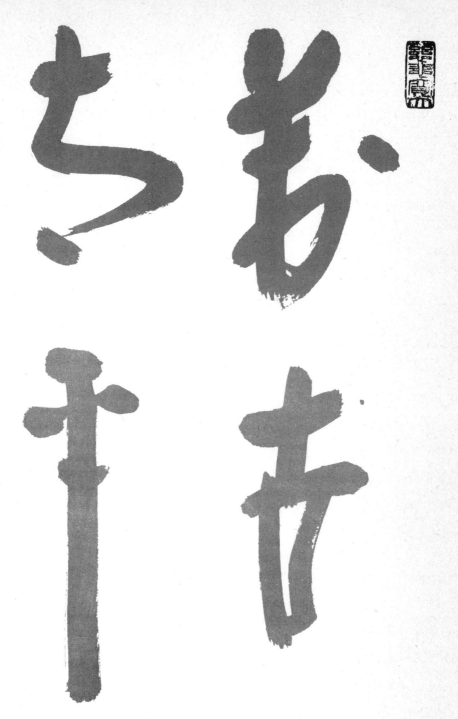

Japanese characters (written by Hisatsune Sakomizu) from the Emperor's rescript announcing Japan's surrender.

BOOKS BY THOMAS M. COFFEY

AGONY AT EASTER • IMPERIAL TRAGEDY

IMPERIAL TRAGEDY

JAPAN IN WORLD WAR II

THE FIRST DAYS AND THE LAST

THOMAS M. COFFEY

THE WORLD PUBLISHING COMPANY

NEW YORK AND CLEVELAND

Published by The World Publishing Company
Published simultaneously in Canada
by Nelson, Foster & Scott Ltd.
First Printing—1970
Copyright © 1970 by Thomas M. Coffey
All rights reserved
Library of Congress catalog card number: 73–136600
Printed in the United States of America

WORLD PUBLISHING
TIMES MIRROR

SOURCES AND ACKNOWLEDGMENTS

Imperial Tragedy is the story of Japan's involvement in World War II, told within the framework of the first days of conflict and the last. It is a scrupulously factual story. Each incident in it, each conversation, even the inner motives and feelings of the participants which the book records whenever possible, have been authenticated. Yet it might be better for the reader to approach the book as if it were a work of imagination rather than fact because he can then follow the sweep of the story and the development of the people in it without being distracted by the question of whether all this actually happened. He can look beyond the events and get to know the Japanese themselves, thereby most deeply appreciating the enormous proportions of Japan's tragedy and more easily understanding the singular behavior of its leaders as the nation's crisis grew. Contrary to widespread supposition, those who decided Japan's fate in the closing days of the war were not just frightened men trying to escape doom. They were men who had been trained in an extraordinary tradition, and who sought to solve a cataclysmic dilemma without betraying that tradition, without being unfaithful to their beliefs or to themselves. It is because a number of them did keep faith with their beliefs, even in extremis, that their story can be called, in the most classical sense, a tragedy, and deserves to be seen first in such a light.

However, if after reading this book as a story, one then wonders about its historical accuracy (and anyone might well be so astonished as to wonder), let him be assured that he has read no fiction here. All the events and conversations are presented the way careful research and inquiry indicate they happened. Though the conversational exchanges could not be recorded word-for-word since almost all of them were in Japanese, which does not lend itself to literal translation, their sense and tone in English have been preserved as closely as possible. Every incident has been substantiated. In cases where the time of an incident could not be determined exactly, the approximate time is indicated. Wherever a person's thoughts or feelings are described, evidence of authenticity is available. The story of *Imperial Tragedy* comes largely out of the minds and mouths of the Japanese themselves. This is how they saw World War II. Below are the major sources of the material in the book:

Extensive interviews and conversations in Japan during the years 1968 and 1969 with the following people: Sadao Akamatsu, Mrs. Aya Anami, Professor Tsunesaburo Asada, Mitsuo Fuchida, Masaru Fujimoto, Saiji Hasegawa, Zenshiro Hoshina, Naoki Hoshino, Masao Inaba, Eimei Kato, Professor Kumihiko Kigoshi, Tei Koyama, Shigeharu Matsumoto, Ian Mutsu, Leslie Nakashima, Yoshio Nasu, Susumu Nishiura, Junnosuke Ofusa, Sogen Ohmori, Masanori Otagiri, Esho Saito, Saburo Sakai, Mr. and Mrs. Hisatsune Sakomizu, Tatsuo Shibata, Ryutaro Shibuya, Mr. and Mrs. Hajime Suzuki, Dr. Eizo Tajima, Sadao Takai, Mrs. Yukie Tojo Takamori, Masahiko Takeshita, Fumihiko Togo, Mrs. Katsuko Tojo, Yoshihiro Tokugawa, Yasuji Watanabe, and Mrs. Sumi Yokoyama.

To each of these people the author extends sincerest appreciation, as he does also to Mrs. Haruyo Suzuki Onoda, who translated most of the interviews, and to Miss Mihoko Okamura, whose insights were of exceptional value.

Also very helpful were Makoto Kuwabara of Japan's National Diet Library; Kumao Toyota and Tadashi Ohikata of the Japanese Ministry of Justice; Colonel Atsuhiro Okamura, and Major Kameo Abe of the Japanese Self Defense Forces; Kazutoshi Hando of the Pacific War Research Society; Masaru Ogawa of the *Japan Times*; Robert Krauskopf and John E. Taylor of the U.S. National Archives in Washington; and Dr. Stetson Conn, Miss Hanna Zeidlik, and Ditmar Finke of the U.S. Army Military History Department, also in Washington.

The following is a list of the books and documents most useful in research:

BOOKS

ARGALL, PHYLLIS, *My Life with the Enemy*, Macmillan, New York, 1944.

BARBER, NOEL, *A Sinister Twilight*, Houghton Mifflin, Boston, 1968.

BENEDICT, RUTH, *The Chrysanthemum and the Sword*, Houghton Mifflin, Boston, 1946.

BERTRAM, JAMES, *Beneath the Shadow*, John Day, New York, 1947.

BROOKS, LESTER, *Behind Japan's Surrender*, McGraw-Hill, New York, 1968.

BROWNE, COURTNEY, *Tojo: The Last Banzai*, Holt, Rinehart and Winston, New York, 1967.

BUSH, LEWIS, *The Road to Inamura*, Robert Hale, London, 1959.

BUTOW, ROBERT J.C., *Tojo and the Coming of War*, Princeton University Press, Princeton, 1961.

———, *Japan's Decision to Surrender*, Stanford University Press, Stanford, 1954.

CHINNOCK, FRANK W., *Nagasaki: The Forgotten Bomb*, World, New York, 1969.

CRAIG, WILLIAM, *The Fall of Japan*, Dial Press, New York, 1967.

CRAIGIE, SIR ROBERT, *Behind the Japanese Mask*, Hutchinson, London, 1945.

CREWE, QUENTIN, *A Curse of Blossom*, Weidenfeld and Nicolson, London, 1960.

FEIS, HERBERT, *The Atomic Bomb and the End of World War II*, Princeton University Press, Princeton, 1966.

———, *The Road to Pearl Harbor*, Princeton University Press, Princeton, 1950.

FUCHIDA, MITSUO AND OKUMIYA, MASATAKE, *Midway: The Battle that Doomed Japan*, U.S. Naval Institute, Annapolis, Maryland, 1955.

GAYN, MARK, *Japan Diary*, William Sloane, New York, 1948.

GIBNEY, FRANK, *Five Gentlemen of Japan*, Farrar, Straus & Young, New York, 1953.

GIOVANNITTI, LEN, AND FREED, FRED, *The Decision to Drop the Bomb*, Coward-McCann, New York, 1965.

GREW, JOSEPH C., *Ten Years in Japan*, Simon and Schuster, New York, 1944.

———, *Report from Tokyo*, Simon and Schuster, New York, 1942.

———, *Turbulent Era*, Houghton Mifflin, Boston, 1952.

GUILLAIN, ROBERT, *Le Peuple Japonais et la Guerre*, R. Julliard, Paris, 1947.

HANDO, KAZUTOSHI AND OTHERS, PACIFIC WAR RESEARCH SOCIETY, *Japan's Longest Day*, Kodansha International, Tokyo, Japan, and Palo Alto, California, 1968.

HARA, TAMEICHI, *Japanese Destroyer Captain*, Ballantine Books, New York, 1961.

HAYASHI, SABURO AND COOX, ALVIN D., *Kogun*, Marine Corps Association, Quantico, Virginia, 1959.

HERSEY, JOHN, *Hiroshima*, Alfred Knopf, New York, 1946.

HIGASHIKUNI, PRINCE NARUHIKO, *Ichi Kozoku No Senso Nikki*, Nihon Shuhosha, Tokyo, 1957.

HOSHINO, NAOKI, *Jidai to Jibun (An Era and Myself)*, Diamond Publishing Co., Tokyo, 1968.

HOUGH, RICHARD, *Death of the Battleship*, Macmillan, New York, 1963.

IKE, NOBUTAKA, *Japan's Decision for War*, Stanford University Press, Stanford, 1967.

INOGUCHI, RIKIHEI, AND NAKAJIMA, TADASHI, WITH ROGER PINEAU, *The Divine Wind*, U.S. Naval Institute, Annapolis, Maryland, 1958.

IRIE, SUKEMASA, *The Imperial Palace*, Hoikusha, Tokyo, 1962.

ITO, MASANORI, *The End of the Imperial Japanese Navy*, W.W. Norton, New York, 1962.

JAMES, DAVID H., *The Rise and Fall of the Japanese Empire*, George Allen and Unwin, London, 1951.

KASE, TOSHIKAZU, *Journey to the Missouri*, Yale University Press, New Haven, 1950.

KATO, MASUO, *The Lost War*, Knopf, New York, 1946.

KAWAI, MICHI, *Sliding Doors*, Keisen-jo Gaku-en, Tokyo, 1950.

KODAMA, YOSHIO, *I Was Defeated*, Booth and Fukuda, Tokyo, 1951.

KONOYE, PRINCE FUMIMARO, *Lost Politics*, Asahi Shimbun, Tokyo, 1946.

LORD, WALTER, *Day of Infamy*, Holt, Rinehart and Winston, New York, 1957.

LORY, HILLIS, *Japan's Military Masters*, Viking, New York, 1943.

MARSHALL, BYRON K., *Capitalism and Nationalism in Prewar Japan*, Stanford University Press, Stanford, 1967.

MORISON, SAMUEL E., *History of United States Naval Operations in World War II*, Little, Brown, Boston, 1948.

MORRIS, IVAN, *Japan, 1931–1945—Militarism, Fascism, Japanism?* D.C. Heath, Boston, 1963.

MOSLEY, LEONARD, *Hirohito, Emperor of Japan*, Prentice-Hall, Englewood Cliffs, New Jersey, 1966.

NITOBE, INAZO, *Bushido, The Soul of Japan*, Charles Tuttle, Rutland, Vermont, and Tokyo, Japan, 1969. (First published by Putnam's Sons, New York, 1905.)

OGATA, TAKETORA, *Ichi Gunjin no Shogu (Life of a Soldier)*, Bungei Shinju-sha, Tokyo, 1954.

OKUMIYA, MASATAKE, AND HORIKOSHI, JIRO (with Martin Caidin), *Zero! The Story of Japan's Air War in the Pacific: 1941–45*, Dutton, New York, 1956.

OSADA, DR. ARATA, *Children of the A-Bomb*, Putnam's Sons, New York, 1959.

OWEN, FRANK, *The Fall of Singapore*, Michael Joseph, London, 1960.

POTTER, JOHN DEANE, *Yamamoto*, Viking, New York, 1965.

————, *The Life and Death of a Japanese General,* New American Library, New York, 1962.

REISCHAUER, EDWIN O., *Japan, Past and Present,* Knopf, New York, 1964.

ROTH, ANDREW, *Dilemma in Japan,* Little, Brown, Boston, 1945.

RUSSELL (LORD RUSSELL OF LIVERPOOL), *The Knights of Bushido,* Cassell, London, 1958.

SADLER, A.L. *The Beginner's Book of Bushido* (a translation of *Budo Shoshinshu* by Daidoji Yuzan), Kokusai Bunka Shinkokai, Tokyo, 1941.

SAKAI, SABURO, WITH MARTIN CAIDIN AND FRED SAITO, *Samurai,* William Kimber, London, 1959.

SAKOMIZU, HISATSUNE, *Secret History of the End of the War,* Jikyoku Geppo, Tokyo, 1946.

————, *The Prime Ministry Under Attack,* Kobun-sha, Tokyo, 1965.

SANEMATSU, YUZURU, *Yonai, Mitsumasa,* Kojin-sha, Tokyo, 1966.

SHIGEMITSU, MAMORU, *Japan and Her Destiny,* Dutton, New York, 1958.

————, *Showa no Doran* (Showa, Years of Upheaval), Chuo Koron-sha, Tokyo, 1952.

SHIMOMURA, HIROSHI, *A Secret History of the War's End,* Kodan-sha, Tokyo, 1950.

SIMPSON, COLIN, *Japan, An Intimate View,* Barnes, New York, 1959.

SUZUKI, DR. DAISETZ T., *Zen and Japanese Culture,* Pantheon, New York, 1959.

SUZUKI, KANTARO, *The Autobiography of Kantaro Suzuki* (edited by Hajime Suzuki), Jiji Tsushin-sha, Tokyo, 1968.

TAKAMI, ZYUN, *Diary of Zyun Takami,* Imuru Hisaji, Tokyo, 1965.

TOGO, SHIGENORI, *The Cause of Japan,* Simon and Schuster, New York, 1956.

TOKUGAWA, MUSEI, *Musei Senso Nikki,* Kurimoto Kazuo, Tokyo, 1960.

TOLISCHUS, OTTO, *Tokyo Record,* Reynal and Hitchcock, New York, 1943.

TOYODA, SOEMU, *Saigo No Teikoku Kaigun,* Sekai No Nihon-sha, Tokyo, 1950.

TREFOUSSE, HANS LOUIS, *What Happened at Pearl Harbor?* College and University Press, New Haven, Connecticut, 1958.

TSUJI, MASANOBU, *Singapore: The Japanese Version,* St. Martin's Press, New York, 1961.

WAKATSUKI, REIJIRO, *Kofuan Kaikoroku,* Yomiuri Shimbun-sha, Tokyo, 1950.

YOSHIDA, SHIGERU, *The Yoshida Memoirs.* Heinemann, London, 1961.

DOCUMENTS

ANAMI, GENERAL KORECHIKA—*Diary,* unpublished, courtesy of Japanese Self Defense Forces, translated by Colonel Atsuhiro Okamura, Major Kameo Abe, and Mrs. Haruyo Suzuki Onoda.

Biographical Notes on Japanese Cabinet Appointed in April, 1945, United States Office of Strategic Services, Washington D.C., April, 1945.

The Brocade Banner: The Story of Japanese Nationalism, United States Army Intelligence Section.

Dai To-A Senso Shusen ni Kan Suru Shiryo (Source Materials Pertaining to the Termination of the Greater East Asia War), Japanese Government, Tokyo, 1945.

A Functional Index to the Proceedings of the International Military Tribunal, Far East. Dull, Paul S., and Umemura, Michael T., University of Michigan Press, Ann Arbor, 1957.

International Military Tribunal, Far East—Exhibits, records, and transcript of Proceedings.

Interrogations of Japanese Officials on World War II, United States Army, Military History Section, unpublished.

Japanese Land Self Defense Forces Historical Division's publications, records, and documents concerning August, 1945.

KIDO, KOICHI—*Diary,* United States National Archives, unpublished.

Mission Accomplished, Interrogations of Japanese Military, Industrial, and Civic Leaders of World War II, United States Air Force.

National Broadcasting Company Transcript of interviews of the following prominent Japanese: Seizo Arisue, Genki Abe, Marquis Koichi Kido, Hisatsune Sakomizu, Saburo Hayashi, Shunichi Matsumoto, Prince Naruhiko Higashikuni, Naotake Sato, Tsunesaburo Asada, and Tsunezo Wachi. (These interviews conducted in 1965 during preparation of the television program: "NBC White Paper—The Surrender of Japan.")

Secret History of the Pacific War, Japanese War Ministry—1941–45, by various staff members, translated by Mrs. Haruyo Suzuki Onoda, unpublished.

Shusen Shiroku (Historical Record of the Termination of the War),

Japanese Foreign Ministry, Tokyo, 1952.

Statements of Japanese Officials on World War II, U.S. Army Military History Section, unpublished.

Strategic Bombing Survey, United States Government, various booklets on conditions in Japan during the war, mostly published in 1946 and 1947.

Translation of Japanese Documents, U.S. Army Military History Section, unpublished.

What the Atomic Bomb Did in Hiroshima, published by the Hiroshima Peace Memorial Museum, Hiroshima, 1969.

PERIODICALS

Japan Times (newspaper) for the war years.

Kaizo (magazine), Tokyo, February, 1951. "Togo, Shigenori, A Tragic Character," by Motojiro Mori.

Mainichi (newspaper), Tokyo, for the war years.

Maru (magazine), Tokyo, September, 1949, "Mitsumasa Yonai and Korechika Anami," by Masazo Sakonji.

New York Times for the war years.

Sekai (magazine), Tokyo, August, 1951, "General Anami at the End of the War."

Time, New York, August, 20, 1945, for a description of the end of the war.

OTHER SOURCES

National Diet Library, Tokyo.

Japanese Ministry of Justice, Tokyo.

United States Embassy, Tokyo.

U.S. Library of Congress.

U.S. National Archives.

U.S. Army Military History Section.

New York Public Library.

Columbia University Asian Studies Library.

University of California (Berkeley) Library.

International House of Japan (Tokyo) Library.

Tokyo Foreign Correspondents' Club Library.

SOME PERSONS
PROMINENT
IN THE STORY

Abe, Genki (Á-bay). In 1941, a member of the government Planning Board. In 1945, home minister.

Akamatsu, Colonel Sadao. In 1941, a private secretary to Prime Minister Tojo. In 1945, with the Japanese Army in Shanghai, China.

Anami, General Korechika. In 1941, commander of the Eleventh Army in Central China. In 1945, minister of war.

Arao, Colonel Okikatsu (A-rá-o). In 1941, commander of an infantry training camp at the foot of Mount Fujiyama. In 1945, chief of the War Ministry's military affairs section.

Arisue, Lieutenant General Seizo (A-rí-su-ay). In 1945, director of army intelligence.

Asada, Dr. Tsunesaburo. Professor of physics, Osaka University.

Fuchida, Captain Mitsuo. In 1941 (as a commander), led the air strike against Hawaii. In 1945, navy air operations officer.

Hara, Yoshimichi. In 1941, president of the Privy Council. In 1945, retired.

Hasegawa, Saiji. In 1941, London correspondent for Domei News Agency. In 1945, Domei foreign editor.

Hasunuma, General Shigeru. The Emperor's chief military aide-de-camp.

Hata, Field Marshal Shunroku. In 1941 (as a general), commanded the army in China. In 1945, commanded the Second General Army, headquartered at Hiroshima.

Hatanaka, Major Kenji. In 1941, a staff officer in China. In 1945, on the staff of the War Ministry's military affairs section.

Hayashi, Colonel Saburo (Hy-ash-ee). In 1945, secretary to General Anami.

Hiranuma, Kiichiro. In 1941, the recently-resigned home minister in Prince Konoye's Cabinet. In 1945, president of the Privy Council.

Hirohito, Emperor of Japan.

Hoashi, Ensign Masato (Ho-ash-ee). In 1941, the first navy flier to find British battleships *Prince of Wales* and *Repulse*. Later killed in action.

Hoshina, Vice Admiral Zenchiro. In 1941 (as rear admiral), chief of naval logistics. In 1945, director of the Bureau of Naval Affairs.

Hoshino, Naoki. In 1941, chief secretary of Tojo Cabinet. In 1945, retired.

Ida, Lieutenant Colonel Masataka (Eé-da). In 1945, a staff officer of the War Ministry's military affairs section.

Inaba, Lieutenant Colonel Masao. In 1941, a staff officer in charge of infantry training with the Kwantung Army in China. In 1945, chief of the budget subsection of the War Ministry's military affairs section.

Kido, Marquis Koichi (Keé-do). Lord keeper of the Emperor's privy seal.

Koga, Major Hidemasa. In 1941, a member of General Tojo's staff. In 1945, a staff officer of the Imperial Guards, and husband of Tojo's daughter, Makie.

Koiso, General Kuniaki. In 1941, retired. In 1945, again retired after being prime minister from July, 1944, to April, 1945.

Konoye, Prince Fumimaro. In 1941, prime minister until October, when he was succeeded by General Tojo. In 1945, retired, but active in attempt to secure peace through Russia.

Matsumoto, Shunichi. In 1941, a Foreign Ministry official. In 1945, vice minister of foreign affairs.

Mori, Lieutenant General Takeshi. Commander of the First Imperial Guards Division.

Nagano, Admiral Osami. In 1941, chief of the navy general staff. In 1945, supreme naval advisor to the Emperor.

Nagumo, Admiral Chuichi. In 1941, commander of the task force which attacked Hawaii. Later, on June 6, 1944, committed suicide at Saipan, just before American forces completed the conquest of the island.

Nakashima, Leslie. In 1941, until December 8, a reporter for the American news agency, United Press. In 1945, a reporter for Domei and the *Nippon Times*.

Nasu, Major General Yoshio. In 1941 (as a colonel), led the infantry landing at Kota Bharu, Malaya, which began the war. In 1945, director of the War Ministry's Military Regulations Bureau.

Nishina, Dr. Yoshio. Nuclear physicist at the Institute for Physical and Chemical Research in Tokyo.

Nishiura, Colonel Susumu. In 1941, a private secretary to Prime Minister Tojo. In 1945, with the Japanese Army in Nanking, China.

Ofusa, Junnosuke (Oáf-sa). In 1941, until December 8, a reporter for the *New York Times* in Tokyo. In 1945, a reporter for the *Nippon Times.*

Ohmori, Sogen. Master of kendo (Japanese swordsmanship), and operator of Jikishin Dojo (The Direct Mind School) in Tokyo.

Ohnishi, Vice Admiral Takajiro. Originator of the navy's kamikaze suicide squadrons. In 1945, navy vice chief of staff.

Okada, Admiral Keisuke. Retired prime minister. Near-victim of assassination by army extremists during his term as prime minister in 1936.

Osaki, Zenjiro. In 1941, a greengrocer with a small shop in the Nihonbashi district of Tokyo. In 1945, an army private.

Sakai, Saburo. Naval fighter pilot. In 1941, a participant in air battles over the Philippines. In 1945, the leading Japanese fighter ace still alive during the last days of the war.

Sakamaki, Ensign Kazuo. In 1941, commander of one of five midget Japanese submarines which tried to invade Pearl Harbor as part of the December 8 attack against Hawaii. In 1945, a prisoner-of-war in America.

Sakomizu, Hisatsune (Sá-ko-mee-zu). In 1941, an official of the government Planning Board. In 1945, chief secretary of the Kantaro Suzuki Cabinet.

Shiizaki, Lieutenant Colonel Jiro. In 1945, a staff officer of the War Ministry's military affairs section.

Shimada, Admiral Shigetaro. In 1941, navy minister in the Tojo Cabinet. In 1945, retired.

Shimomura, Dr. Hiroshi. In 1941, editor of Japan's largest newspaper, the *Asahi Shimbun.* In 1945, president of the government Information Board under Prime Minister Suzuki.

Sugiyama, Field Marshal Gen. In 1941 (as a general), chief of the Army General Staff. In 1945, commander of the First General Army.

Suzuki, Baron Admiral Kantaro. In 1941, vice-president of the Privy Council. In 1945, prime minister.

Takai, Lieutenant Commander Sadao. In 1941 (as a lieutenant), a participant in the attack against British battleships *Prince of Wales* and *Repulse*. In 1945, a bombing and torpedo instructor on the southern Japanese island of Kyushu.

Takeshita, Lieutenant Colonel Masahiko (Ta-késh-ta). In 1941 (as a major), a staff officer in the army's Military Personnel Bureau. In 1945, a staff officer in the military affairs section of the Military Affairs Bureau.

Togo, Shigenori. In 1941, foreign minister under Prime Minister Tojo. In 1945, after a period of retirement which resulted from a disagreement with Tojo, again foreign minister under Prime Minister Suzuki.

Tojo, General Hideki. In 1941, prime minister. In 1945, retired.

Tokugawa, Yoshihiro. A chamberlain at the Imperial Palace.

Tolischus, Otto D. In 1941, until December 8, chief of the *New York Times* bureau in Tokyo. Repatriated to the United States in 1942.

Toyoda, Admiral Soemu. In 1941, commander of the Kure Naval District. In 1945, chief of the Navy General Staff.

Ugaki, Vice Admiral Matome. In 1941, chief of staff of the Japanese Combined Fleet under Admiral Isoroku Yamamoto. In 1945, commander of the Fifth Air Fleet stationed on Kyushu.

Umezu, General Yoshijiro. In 1941, commander in chief of the Kwantung Army in China. In 1945, chief of the Army General Staff.

Watanabe, Captain Yasuji. In 1941 (as a lieutenant commander), staff gunnery officer of the Combined Fleet under Yamamoto. In 1945, senior staff officer of the Combined Fleet under Yamamoto. In 1945, senior staff officer on the merchant marine control board, in charge of the dwindling Japanese merchant fleet.

Yamamoto, Admiral Isoroku. In 1941, commander in chief of the Japanese Combined Fleet. On April 18, 1943, killed in an American aerial ambush over the South Pacific island of Bougainville.

Yokoyama, Mrs. Sumi. Secretary to physicist Dr. Yoshio Nishina.

Yonai, Admiral Mitsumasa. In 1941, retired after a term as prime minister. In 1945, navy minister.

Yoshizumi, Lieutenant General Masao. In 1945, director of the army's Military Affairs Bureau.

PART I

DECEMBER
1941

DECEMBER 8,
A HALF-HOUR
AFTER MIDNIGHT

A S T H E American ambassador's long black automobile came to a sharp stop, he quickly emerged from it into the midnight air of Tokyo, which was clear and chilly, though not severe for December. Scarcely taking time to close the car door behind him, he hurried up to the door of the official residence (a term which denotes office but sometimes also means home) of the Japanese foreign minister and, being admitted almost immediately, continued to hurry through the central hall, up a staircase to a second floor reception room which he knew well. The ambassador, Joseph Clark Grew, had been received in that room on countless occasions during his more than nine years of service in Japan. Never before had he entered it with an expression as grimly serious as the one he wore tonight.

He was greeted uneasily by a Japanese Foreign Office functionary named Toshikazu Kase who spoke good English and sometimes acted as interpreter for the foreign minister, though the present foreign minister, Shigenori Togo, had little need of an interpreter, having been stationed for three-and-a-half years, during the 1920s, at the Japanese embassy in Washington. Ambassador Grew, declining to sit, filled the awkward moments before Mr. Togo's entrance by bringing forth copies of the urgent document which was the subject of his visit. The document, telegraphed from Washington the previous day, had not reached him until less than two hours before, at 10:30 P.M., Tokyo time, December 7, though its markings showed it had been received in Tokyo at noon, more than ten hours earlier. Grew would have to suppress his anger at the delay in delivering the telegram because he could not prove who was responsible for it.

Foreign Minister Togo entered the room directly, approaching the tall American with quick, precise steps; and the two men, both lean and spare, both fastidiously dressed, both carefully groomed but with almost comical mustaches on their serious faces, appraised uneasily each other's moods. Grew, having found Togo at all times difficult to

3

fathom, could see no promise in his face tonight and wondered anxiously if this most crucial call he had ever made upon a Japanese foreign minister had any chance at all of being productive. Togo, aware of the general purpose of the ambassador's visit, but aware, too, of a whole pattern of contrary events which were at this moment already in motion, wished fervently that he could have been spared this meeting with the impeccable American who stood staring down at him.

Ambassador Grew, indicating the paper in his hand, began stiffly, "I have here a personal message from President Roosevelt to His Imperial Majesty, Emperor Hirohito. It is a message of such momentous importance that I respectfully request the opportunity to deliver it in person to His Majesty at the earliest possible moment."

Togo, though he had been apprised the previous day that a message from President Roosevelt could be expected, was nevertheless taken aback by the ambassador's demand for an audience with the Emperor. Under such circumstances and at such an hour it was unthinkable. Glancing at his watch, he said, in a loud voice meant to compensate for the fact that the ambassador was hard of hearing, "An immediate audience with His Majesty would be most difficult, I'm afraid. It is now a half hour after midnight. And of course such an audience would have to be arranged through the Imperial Household Ministry. I cannot possibly say when it would be granted."

Grew's face, becoming even more intense, indicated his determination. It was his responsibility not merely to get the president's message to the Emperor, but to get it to him quickly, and he felt he could hope to do so only by insisting on an immediate personal interview. "I know you must be aware," he said, "that the matter is of most urgent importance."

Togo glanced toward the document in Grew's hand. "The question of an audience," he said, "would also depend upon the contents of the president's message."

"With your permission," Grew said, "I shall read you the message." And when Togo nodded, he began to read: "From Franklin Delano Roosevelt, President of the United States, to His Imperial Majesty, Emperor Hirohito of Japan. Washington, December 6, 1941.

Almost a century ago the President of the United States addressed to the Emperor of Japan a message extending an offer of friendship of the people of the United States to the people of Japan. That offer was accepted, and in the long period of unbroken peace and friendship which has followed, our respective nations, through the virtues of their peoples and the wisdom of their rulers have prospered and have substantially helped humanity.

Only in situations of extraordinary importance to our two countries need I address to Your Majesty messages on matters of state. I feel I should now so address you because of the deep and far-reaching emergency which appears to be in formation.

Developments are occurring in the Pacific area which threaten to deprive each of our nations and all humanity of the beneficial influence of the long peace between our two countries. Those developments contain tragic possibilities.

The people of the United States, believing in peace and in the right of nations to live and let live, have eagerly watched the conversations between our two governments during these past months. We have hoped for a termination of the present conflict between Japan and China. We have hoped that a peace of the Pacific could be consummated in such a way that nationalities of many diverse peoples could exist side by side without fear of invasion; that unbearable burdens of armaments could be lifted from them all; and that all peoples would resume commerce without discrimination against or in favor of any nation.

I am certain that it will be clear to Your Majesty, as it is to me, that in seeking these great objectives both Japan and the United States should agree to eliminate any form of military threat. This seemed essential to the attainment of the high objectives.

As Grew read on, Togo listened carefully, looking for surprises, but up to this point he had found none. What could be the purpose of such a message? Had the president sent a personal telegram to the Emperor simply to restate all the impossible demands the United States had been making upon Japan during the last several months in the negotiations at Washington? The message could only be insulting if it offered no concessions. Ambassador Grew continued:

More than a year ago, Your Majesty's government concluded an agreement with the Vichy government by which five or six thousand Japanese troops were permitted to enter into northern French Indochina for the protection of Japanese troops which were operating against China further north. And this Spring and Summer the Vichy government permitted further Japanese military forces to enter into southern French Indochina for the common defense of French Indochina. I think I am correct in saying that no attack has been made upon Indochina, nor that any has been contemplated.

During the past few weeks it has become clear to the world that Japanese military, naval and air forces have been sent to southern Indochina in such large numbers as to create a reasonable doubt on the part of other nations that this continuing concentration in Indochina is not defensive in its character.

What was he about to propose? That Japan withdraw entirely from Indochina? Togo could not imagine that the president of the United States had drafted this long and urgent message just for that. America had already made such a demand back in July, shortly after Japan had moved into southern Indochina, and the demand had been rejected at that time. Why should it be accepted now? Would the United States accept a demand that it withdraw from the Philippines? Grew went on reading:

Because these continuing concentrations in Indochina have reached such large proportions and because they extend now to the southeast and southwest corners of that peninsula, it is only reasonable that the people of the Philippines, of the hundreds of islands of the East Indies, of Malaya and of Thailand itself are asking themselves whether these forces of Japan are preparing or intending to make attack in one or other of these many directions.

I am sure that Your Majesty will understand that the fear of all these peoples is a legitimate fear inasmuch as it involves their peace and their national existence. I am sure that Your Majesty will understand why the people of the United States in such large numbers look askance at the establishment of military, naval and air bases manned and equipped so greatly as to constitute armed forces capable of measures of offense.

It is clear that a continuance of such a situation is unthinkable.

None of the peoples whom I have spoken of above can sit either indefinitely or permanently on a keg of dynamite.

There is absolutely no thought on the part of the United States of invading Indochina if every Japanese soldier or sailor were to be withdrawn therefrom.

I think that we can obtain the same assurance from the Governments of the East Indies, the Governments of Malay and the Government of Thailand. I would even undertake to ask for the same assurance on the part of the Government of China. Thus a withdrawal of the Japanese forces from Indochina would result in the assurance of peace throughout the whole of the South Pacific area.

I address myself to Your Majesty at this moment in the fervent hope that Your Majesty may, as I am doing, give thought in this definite emergency to ways of dispelling the dark clouds. I am confident that both of us, for the sake of the peoples not only of our own great countries but for the sake of humanity in neighboring territories, have a sacred duty to restore traditional unity and prevent further death and destruction in the world.—Signed, Franklin D. Roosevelt.

Togo, who understood the telegram without having to listen to Kase's translation, continued to look expectant as Ambassador Grew finished reading. Did the president have nothing more than that to propose? The neutralization of French Indochina seemed to Togo the only concrete subject touched upon in the entire document, and even in the matter of Indochina Roosevelt's suggestion could hardly be called a proposal. It was simply the restatement of another insulting demand, unaccompanied by an offer of concessions on the American side. Rather than concessions, indeed, it offered threats. The United States will not invade Indochina *if* every Japanese soldier is withdrawn. Could that be construed as anything but an American invasion threat? Did the president actually believe that Japan, having already suffered a series of American insults—last summer's seizure of Japanese assets in the United States, the refusal to sell Japan any more oil, the demands that Japan withdraw immediately from China—would now accept one more insult as the price of peace?

Grew, having finished, paused to await a reaction, then, seeing no expression in Togo's impenetrable face, handed him a copy of the document he had just read.

Togo, after glancing at the long telegram, looked up and said, "I assure you, Mr. Ambassador, I shall give the president's message the most thorough study."

Grew could not conceal his sudden alarm. "Does that indicate some doubt," he asked, "as to whether you will request an audience for me?"

The ambassador could not imagine how embarrassing were the difficulties he had created for the foreign minister. Togo's relations with Grew had previously been cordial and diplomatically candid. It was painful for him now to have to withhold from the ambassador the overwhelming reasons why their conversation seemed so futile. But Togo was not the kind of man who, after a lifetime in the service of his country, would let personal considerations govern him in such a critical situation. Useless as the president's telegram might be, he was aware that even at the cost of appearing to lack personal candor, he must keep the matter open, at least for a short time. If he were to send Grew away now with a straightforward refusal of his request for an audience with the emperor, he might endanger the most important state secret in the history of Japan.

Offering his hand to indicate the interview was at an end, Togo said, in a tone of concern, "I understand your deep feeling, Mr. Ambassador. I promise you I shall quickly present the matter to the Throne."

Ambassador Grew reluctantly departed, no more certain of the fate of President Roosevelt's telegram than he had been when he arrived.

DECEMBER 8,
1 A.M. IN TOKYO,
5:30 A.M. IN MID-PACIFIC

C O M M A N D E R Mitsuo Fuchida, clutching the rail to balance himself against the upheavals of a rough sea, made his way carefully along the flooded deck of the huge aircraft carrier *Akagi* and entered the briefing room, which was dimly lit in accordance with the strict blackout imposed when the task force left homeland waters. Steadying himself against the furniture, Fuchida gazed for a moment at elderly, fatherly Vice Admiral Chuichi Nagumo who stood before a long table, surrounded by his staff, concentrating on ocean charts as if he were unaware of the storm which battered his proud flagship. Admiral Nagumo was, in fact, painfully aware of the storm, and had, for that reason, summoned Fuchida earlier than he had intended. With the waves outside rising as high as the flight deck, it would be foolish to waste time hoping for calm. If he must launch this doubtful operation, he had better do it now, a half-hour early, since it might take that much longer for the planes to get away in weather like this.

As to the wisdom of launching the operation at all, Admiral Nagumo remained only partially convinced. It was Yamamoto's idea, not his. Nagumo had never been an air admiral. He was a torpedo specialist. But since he was senior in rank, the command of this most daring enterprise in Japan's naval history had been offered to him and the Samurai tradition into which he had been born would not allow him to consider refusing it, however much he might question its prospects of success. Japan's most vital need was oil. He believed that if her precious ships must be risked, they should be risked in the battle for the oil-rich lands of Southeast Asia and the Netherlands East Indies, rather than in Hawaii, where the dangers of American counterattack were overwhelming. He was not, however, the commander in chief of His Imperial Majesty's Combined Fleet. That honor had fallen to Admiral Isoroku Yamamoto; and Yamamoto had clung stubbornly to his belief that if war came, the navy should begin it with an attack against America's Pacific Fleet at Pearl Harbor. Yamamoto had not been impressed by Nagumo's argument that even the largest of carriers, even the incomparable 34,000–ton *Akagi* itself, could be disabled by a few bombs. Yamamoto had insisted that to ensure the conquest of the oil lands in the south, the U.S. Pacific Fleet must first be neutralized. That was Nagumo's mission; and to accomplish it, despite his fear of enormous losses, he led his great force (including six carriers, two battleships, three cruisers, and nine destroyers) steadfastly southward through pounding seas toward Hawaii, which was now only about 250 miles away.

It was 1:15 A.M., December 8, Tokyo time; 5:45 A.M. the previous day, December 7, in mid-Pacific. Admiral Nagumo turned from the charts to Commander Fuchida, who had been chosen to lead the aerial attack against Hawaii and was now awaiting the order to take off. Fuchida was wearing a red shirt, like all the fliers who served under him, to indicate his indifference to bloodshed. One might not even notice a wound if the blood were absorbed by a red shirt. He was also perfumed, and with his red shirt, wore his best uniform in the tradition of Samurai entering battle. His ancestral origins were, however, only partially Samurai. His father was a farmer in the vicinity of Kashiwabara, about 35 miles from Kyoto in southern Honshu. But his mother's father had been a Samurai, and it was therefore natural that his boyhood hero should be a fighting man. When Fuchida was not quite four years old, in 1905, Admiral Heihachiro Togo returned from the war with Russia after leading the Japanese fleet in a climactic battle which destroyed almost the entire Russian navy, including six battleships and five cruisers. Like millions of other little boys in Japan at the time, Mitsuo Fuchida decided immediately to become an admiral. Unlike most of the others, he had clung to his resolve. After middle school, he had applied for admission to the naval academy and was accepted shortly after the end of World War I. Upon graduation in 1924, he visited Hawaii, then in January of 1925, San Francisco, on his first cruise as an officer. While in San Francisco, he and some of his fellow officers were invited aboard the U.S. battleship *Maryland*, which happened to be docked there. Above the deck of the *Maryland*, Fuchida saw three scout planes poised on catapults. At that moment he decided to become a naval aviator, and on his return to Japan enrolled immediately as a student pilot at the Kasumigaura Naval Air Base.

At this moment, Fuchida was aware from intelligence reports that the *Maryland* was probably one of the American ships awaiting him in Pearl Harbor. He was aware also that the tattered, 36-year-old battle flag of his boyhood hero, Admiral Togo, was flying from the mast of the *Akagi*.

As Admiral Nagumo looked at Fuchida, a faint smile deepened the lines of his face. Nagumo was still a handsome man, though he had the settled look of age and his white, close-cropped hair was sparse on top. He had very little to say to the comparatively tall, slender aviator who stood before him. Fuchida needed no instruction about his mission. He and another of the navy's young aviation experts, Commander Minoru Genda, had developed most of the detailed plans of the attack, and they had trained the fliers who would execute it. Nagumo seemed about to speak, then hesitated and checked the time. They were still a half-hour ahead of schedule, perhaps an unfortunate circumstance inasmuch as the Navy had promised Foreign Minister Togo that the attack would not take place until at least a half-hour after Ambassador Nomura in Washington broke off relations with the United States. Because the storm had not abated, that extra half-hour would probably be used in getting the planes into the air. If, however, the planes got off early despite the weather, they could not be expected to dissipate their fuel by circling until the proper diplomatic moment to strike. It was too late now for any more diplomacy.

Admiral Nagumo held out his hand to Fuchida. "There is no further information," he said. "Take off according to plan."

Fuchida saluted, retired from the briefing room, and hurried back along the wet, rolling deck to the operations room where his pilots were awaiting him.

Five minutes later Fuchida watched with fierce pride and satisfaction as his flight crews ran shouting to their planes. Here were the best-trained and most disciplined pilots in the world. He had no doubt of it. Most of them, like himself, were veterans of air combat in China. They averaged about 2,000 hours of flight time. And they were completely ready for their mission. He was certain of that. Since late October, at Kagoshima Bay on the southern Japanese island of Kyushu, he and Commander Genda had subjected them, day after day, to the most rigorous and precise training any fliers had ever undergone. It was a measure of their skill that they had survived without a single casualty. And just yesterday afternoon they had performed flawlessly in a full-scale rehearsal of the operation they were now about to undertake.

On deck, Fuchida watched the planes emerge from the darkness below into the dim light of the flight line, listened to the engines cough and roar. Though the sea had not abated, the fog had lifted slightly, and as the *Akagi's* green signal light flashed on, he was able also to see the green light of the carrier nearest to it. The six large carriers, turning into the north wind to facilitate takeoff, proceeded in parallel columns of three, with the two battleships protecting them at the corners astern and two heavy cruisers at the corners in front. A light cruiser led the formation. Nine destroyers hovered around it. A fleet of supply ships followed it, and almost 200 miles ahead, three submarines acted as its forward eyes. There had been no attempt to camouflage or conceal the identity of the ships. It would have been pointless. If anyone reported seeing such a flotilla, the U.S. Navy would know it had to be Japanese. The Rising Sun, therefore, flew openly from the masts of all the ships and was painted prominently on the wings and fuselages of all the planes. To avoid being seen, the task force had sailed north from the homeland, then descended toward Hawaii along a rarely traveled southerly route. If it had encountered any ship or airplane along the way, up to one day before the planned attack, Admiral Nagumo's orders had been to abandon the operation and return home. But as far as he knew, good fortune had held and the presence of his fleet in Hawaiian waters was still undetected.

It was 1:30 A.M. of the 8th, Tokyo time (6 A.M. of the 7th in mid-Pacific), when the planes began taking off from the pitching, rolling decks of the six carriers. Though Admiral Nagumo might be worried about them getting away safely, Commander Fuchida felt no such concern. Before the day was over he expected to lose half his planes, but he expected to lose them to the Americans, not to the weather. He had no illusions about the power of America, and no confidence in the likelihood of surprise. He had great confidence, however, in the ability of his pilots. They would succeed in their mission. But it was not realistic to suppose that more than half of them would return.

Despite his belief that so many of his men would die, and perhaps himself among them, Fuchida felt little fear. This made him in no way unusual. He didn't suppose there was very much fear among his men, either. Japan, by the very nature of its culture, had come closer than any other nation to breeding fear out of its fighting men. A warrior learned from the Samurai tradition that he must be prepared to live with suffering, and at all times be aware of death as a part of life. Samurai soldier-poet Daidoji Yuzan Shigesuke wrote in the seventeenth century:

One who is a Samurai must before all things keep constantly in mind, by day and by night from the morning when he takes up his chopsticks to eat his New Year breakfast, to Old Year's night when he pays his yearly bills, the fact that he has to die. That is his chief business.

There was a certain peace of mind to be found in embracing this dictum, and thanks to its constant reiteration in one form or another, an amazing percentage of Japanese fighting men were able to embrace it. Instead of fear, Fuchida felt a flood of excitement as his own airplane rolled forward (a Mitsubishi Type 97 high-level bomber), and a man in his maintenance crew presented to him a white cloth headband which is the Samurai symbol that one must be ready to die. He felt the same kind of excitement now as he had felt in October when his friend, Minoru Genda, had informed him that the Hawaiian operation was being considered, and that if it came to pass, he would lead it. Fuchida's excitement had little to do with thoughts of His Majesty the Emperor, or the destiny of the nation. He was excited, rather, at the realization of his role in such a momentous event.

He gave his plane a quick, once-over inspection, then glanced up at his pilot, a brilliant young lieutenant named Mitsuo Matsuzaki, and his radio operator, Petty Officer Shigenori Mazuki, who were already aboard and ready to go. Fuchida would not be flying the plane since he would have more than enough to do commanding the operation. He stepped onto the wing, climbed into the middle seat behind Matsuzaki, and as the plane taxied to takeoff position, glanced up toward the bridge where Admiral Nagumo and his staff, including Minoru Genda, were anxiously watching the operation. Fuchida's plane was one of the last to leave the carrier. As it sped down the flight deck and into the stormy air, he glanced at his watch. Not yet 1:45, Tokyo time; 6:15 here in mid-Pacific. A few minutes later, the plane emerged above the heavy clouds, and in the early light of dawn kept its rendezvous with the others. In perfect formation, with Fuchida leading the way, the first attack wave of 183 planes (49 level bombers, 40 torpedo planes, 51 dive bombers, and 43 fighters) turned and flew at 125 nautical miles per hour toward the Hawaiian island of Oahu, slightly more than 200 miles away.

DECEMBER 8,
ABOUT 1:20 A.M.

THE PRIME MINISTER of Japan, General Hideki Tojo, replaced the telephone on the table beside his Western-style bed and
threw back the covers. Having been awakened by a call from Foreign
Minister Togo, he now stood up, put on round, light-rimmed glasses,
and dressed quietly in a high-collared general's uniform, being careful not to awaken his wife, Katsuko, and two small daughters, Yukie
and Kimie, who were asleep in adjoining bedrooms. The Tojos had
several children between the ages of 31 and eight, but since there was
room for only two of them in this house behind the prime minister's
official residence, the others—except for the two oldest sons,
Hidetaka and Teruo, who were married—lived three blocks away in
the war minister's official residence, which was available to them
because their father was also war minister in his own cabinet. (He
was, incidentally, home minister as well.) General Tojo walked silently downstairs and outside, through the immaculate gardens, to his
office in the main building of the prime minister's official residence.
He was ready now to greet his subordinate with proper military
dignity. Tojo had been a military man all his life. He had been prime
minister for only seven weeks.

Those seven exhausting weeks had begun when, on the afternoon
of October 17, General Tojo, then war minister, had been called to
the Imperial Palace and charged by His Majesty, Emperor Hirohito,
to form a new cabinet and replace the resigning prime minister,
Prince Fumimaro Konoye, who had been unable during six months
of negotiations to resolve the nation's disagreements with the United
States.

The Emperor had said to Tojo: "We believe that an extraordinarily
grave situation confronts the nation. Bear in mind that cooperation
between the army and navy should be closer than ever before."

Tojo, never an immodest man, had been so genuinely surprised and
overwhelmed by the Imperial mandate that he had asked for a few
moments alone to think about his fitness for it. While he was meditat-
ing in a large vestibule off the imperial receiving room, Admiral
Koshiro Oikawa, the navy minister, had a short audience with the
Emperor, after which he, too, retired to the vestibule. The Lord
Keeper of the Privy Seal Marquis Koichi Kido had entered and,
finding them together, had laid another charge upon both of them.

"I presume you have just received Imperial words regarding cooperation between the army and navy," the marquis said in his formal

court style. "As regards the fundamental line of national policy I am commanded to convey to you the Imperial desire that careful consideration be taken by studying the internal and external situation more comprehensively and more deeply than ever, regardless of the resolution of September sixth."

It was not for Tojo to wonder why the Emperor had declined to say this himself. If it came from Marquis Kido, then it came from the Emperor, since Kido, being the Emperor's political adviser, had more influence over him than any other public official. Kido had recommended Tojo as prime minister, and though several senior statesmen, all former prime ministers, had opposed the choice, Kido had prevailed.

The resolution to which the Emperor referred, through Marquis Kido, had been adopted after an imperial conference on September 6. It was a secret policy statement which placed a late October time limit on the negotiations then in progress with the United States and directed the military to prepare for immediate hostilities in the event the negotiations failed. Though Tojo, as war minister in the Konoye cabinet, had strongly supported the resolution, he had, as prime minister and war minister in his own cabinet, bowed to the Emperor's desires, exploring all the possibilities he thought acceptable in an effort to avoid war. At a series of eight liaison conferences attended by the cabinet and the Supreme Command between October 23 and November 1, he had argued consistently, against his military colleagues, in favor of extending the deadline for negotiations and avoiding precipitate action. With the support of Foreign Minister Togo, he had managed to get the negotiation deadline pushed forward to November 30, but he had not, in that time, stemmed his country's military momentum, nor had he solved the basic differences with the United States. Secretary of State Cordell Hull's uncompromising note of November 26 proved that. There wasn't even a mention in the Hull note of Japan's offer, a week earlier, to withdraw from southern Indochina and from large parts of China in exchange for the lifting of America's oil and steel embargo and the release of Japanese assets frozen in the United States. How could the Americans have ignored a proposal which proved the Japanese government's desire for peace, a proposal which would virtually have restored the situation to the status of the previous summer, before the Japanese Army entered southern Indochina and America retaliated with its economic sanctions? The Americans were demanding even more now than they had demanded then: complete withdrawal from all of Indochina and all of China; renunciation of all the hard-fought gains Japan had made in the last ten years; and on top of it, recognition of the hateful Chungking government of Chiang Kai-shek. Was any more proof needed of America's insincerity? Roosevelt and Hull had simply decided that under no circumstances would they resume sending oil and steel to Japan. Oil! That was the crux. Japan, already using stockpiled oil, had only enough to last two years under peaceful conditions, and much less than two years in case of war. This meant that if there must be war, it could not be long postponed because the stockpile of oil in Japan diminished with every passing moment. The navy alone was using about 10,000 tons per day.

As a result of these considerations, the cabinet and the Supreme Command, during the liaison conferences between October 23 and November 1, had been forced to choose between three alternatives: one, caution and compliance with American demands, which Tojo and everyone around him equated with national suicide; two, immediate war, which the army favored but the Emperor desired to avoid; three, continued negotiations accompanied by preparations for war and a determination to fight if necessary. Tojo had espoused the third alternative, which seemed to him the most reasonable, and it had prevailed. But the continuing negotiations had not persuaded the United States to soften its demands. Indeed, Secretary of State Hull's November 26 note had been so hard as to make further talks pointless. It was annoying, therefore, that at this most irretrievable juncture, the American president should be by-passing the Japanese government to send a message direct to His Majesty. If the president had concessions to make, why had he not made them earlier? If he was still pressing his impossible demands, it was unfortunate that he had bothered to communicate with the Emperor at a time like this. General Tojo glanced at his watch. It was 2 A.M. The army must already be preparing to land in Malaya. The carrier planes should by this time be ready to take off for Hawaii.

Foreign Minister Togo, dressed in a Western-style business suit, entered the prime minister's office carrying in his hand a Japanese version of President Roosevelt's message, which his foreign office staff had hastily translated. Though he moved with his customary quickness, Togo appeared tired.

General Tojo stood erect, then bowed to greet him. Five feet, four inches tall, so slender he might almost be considered frail, so short-sighted he had to wear thick glasses, so bald the only hair showing on him was his neat black mustache, Tojo did not look like a man about to lead his nation into the most ambitious amd perilous war in its 2,600-year history. In his high-pitched voice, he said to Togo, "You have the message there, I suppose. Are there no concessions in it?"

Togo said, "None that I can see."

"What does the president say?"

"He says he has heard that Japanese troops are being concentrated in French Indochina. The Powers are very uneasy about it. The United States regards it as a matter of great concern. Therefore, it is his desire that our troops be withdrawn from Indochina, and if we do withdraw our troops, the United States has no intention of invading that area. He will also see to it that there will be no invasion by the Netherlands, Thailand, or China. The general purport of the message is that by such steps peace can be maintained. But as you know, President Roosevelt made a proposal like this in a personal talk with Admiral Nomura last summer while Prince Konoye's cabinet was still in power, and it was rejected at that time as being of no value."

Admiral Kichisaburo Nomura, the Japanese ambassador to the United States, had been in charge of the protracted but now ending negotiations in Washington. General Tojo said, "Yes, I remember very well when the matter came up last summer. (While Tojo was war minister under Konoye.) I can't see that there has been any change. It would be impossible to save the situation on the basis of such a proposal. Does the president concede nothing more than that?"

"Not in this message."

"Then there is nothing that can be done."

The two men looked thoughtfully at each other, each deeply aware of the burden they shared. They had never been close friends. One thing they had in common besides limitless energy and devotion to work was their difficulty in developing close friendships. By virtue of being outspoken in their own views and impatient with the wrong-thinking of others, they both courted respect rather than popularity. Each had thereby won the respect of the other because up to now, their views about affairs of state had not greatly differed.

Togo said, "Ambassador Grew wanted to present the message to the Throne immediately and in person. That is out of the question, of course. But since I do believe it should be presented to His Majesty as quickly as possible, I have called Marquis Kido about it and asked him to arrange an audience for me. He suggested I discuss it with you. But he also said that on such urgent business a minister of state would be received in audience at any time, even in the dead of night."

"I have no objection to your taking the message to the Emperor," Tojo said, "but you should bear in mind that the planes of our task force may be at this moment on their way to Hawaii."

"I am well aware of it," Togo said. "What then should be the Emperor's reply to the message?"

Tojo said, "We had better decide that now."

Under the Japanese imperial system, the Emperor's reply to such a message would customarily be drafted by the government and merely approved by him. There being no reason to adopt a different procedure in this instance, the two men sat down immediately to compose an appropriate answer to the American president's telegram. It did not take them long. When they had finished writing it, Togo folded it and prepared to leave.

At the door, he said jokingly, "It's a pity to run around disturbing people in the middle of the night."

Prime Minister Tojo smiled. "It's a good thing the telegram arrived late," he said. "If it had come a day or two earlier, we would have had more of a to-do about it."

The two men bowed low to each other three or four times, then Togo hurried away. He had to return to his residence and change into formal attire for his dead-of-night audience with the Emperor.

DECEMBER 8,
1:25 A.M. IN TOKYO,
DECEMBER 7,
11:25 P.M. IN MALAYA

THE TROPICAL night air was humidly warm and the seas were pounding against the beach near Kota Bharu, capital of Kelantan Province on the northeast coast of the Malay Peninsula, 500 miles above Singapore. In the soft moonlight two miles offshore, three large Japanese army transport ships had just dropped anchor and the first troops of a 5,300-man, Twenty-fifth Army detachment under the command of Brigadier General Hiroshi Takumi were climbing down ladders into their landing boats, which pitched dangerously atop the six-foot waves.

Colonel Yoshio Nasu, who was to be the field commander of these troops when they reached shore, stood on the deck of one of the transports, the *Ayatosan Maru*, inspecting the men solicitously, checking their packs and rifles as they prepared to descend to the boats. Though he had been with them for only a short time, Colonel Nasu had come to know them personally as comrades, the way a Japanese army officer, unlike the officers of most other armies, was expected to know his men. While the concept of democracy was suppressed within the Japanese political structure, and had always been resisted by the army's political representatives and secret police as if it were as dangerous as communism, it was a concept which the army had adopted to a high degree, ironically, within its own structure. A good Japanese officer gave his leisure time as well as his duty time to his men. He listened to them, ate, drank, and sported with them, invited them to his home, offered them money from his own pocket when they needed it, tried to make them feel he was both a father and a close friend.

Colonel Nasu had not known these men until a few weeks before; until he joined this operation he had never been a combat officer. He had not been assigned to battle duty either in the 1931 Manchurian War or in the 1937 China "Incident," which was still in progress, and he had attained such a high post in the army's administrative structure he need not have been here at Kota Bharu tonight, preparing to take part in the first Japanese engagement of the war, had he not chosen to come. Indeed, it was only because of his powerful position that he had been able to secure this assignment. Colonel Nasu, at the age of 43, was chief of the War Ministry's personnel section. Filled with the Japanese soldier's characteristic eagerness to fight for his nation and his Emperor, he had ordered his subordinates to determine where the hardest battle was likely to take place if war came. When they told him it would probably be at Kota Bharu in Malaya, he had promptly assigned himself to the Takumi detachment as commander of infantry.

His shock troops were in their boats. There was nothing to do but wait for the bombardment which units of the second and third fleets, standing farther offshore, were scheduled to begin at 11:30 P.M., December 7, local time (1:30 A.M., December 8 in Tokyo). That was now just moments away. He was shouting last-minute instructions to the men in the boats when the boom and rumble of naval artillery from the rear told him the operation had begun. The first gun had been fired. Japan was at war.

The Japanese naval bombardment was quickly answered by furious salvos from British guns on shore and Nasu knew, as he watched the boatloads of men pull away from the ship, that they could expect a rough reception when they reached the beach, which was called, incidentally, the "Beach of Passionate Love." General Takumi, in planning the operation, had anticipated that the beach would be heavily mined, and that a line of enemy pillboxes at least three-deep, would begin a short distance inland. Since Kota Bharu was the natural northern gate to Malaya, and a base from which an invasion farther south could be outflanked, the British were known to have fortified it heavily. In addition to the expected shore defenses, there was a Royal Air Force field only about a-mile-and-a-half from the town. The airfield was, of course, Nasu's first objective as soon as he had won a beachhead. He could not guess how long that might take; the geography would also be a problem. Even when the troops reached the beach they would not actually be ashore, because the beach was on one of many islands formed by the mouth of the Kelantan River, which met the sea, not in one large stream, but in a network of smaller streams. For this reason the Takumi detachment had been equipped with rubber raft-boats. They might need them not only to reach the shore proper but also to get through the jungle which lay between the landing area and the airfield. The necessity of capturing this airfield and two others in the vicinity was another reason Kota Bharu had been chosen as the location for Japan's first engagement of the war. In addition, General Tomoyuki Yamashita, commander of the entire Malayan campaign (directed not only against Singapore and British Malaya but against Thailand and the other peninsula states as well) wanted to divert attention from his more sizable invasions scheduled to begin two hours later at Singora and Patani, 150 miles farther up the peninsula, within the Thai border.

It was time now for Colonel Nasu to climb down into his own boat, which was alreay loaded with 100 men. As it moved away from the sheltering bulk of the ship into the dangerous moonlight, he could see, too well for comfort, the silhouettes of other boats doing likewise. The moon was so bright the British gunners would be able to spot them easily as they approached land. Shells were already bursting around the first wave of boats, nearing the shores. The Japanese naval guns, firing at full speed, had not yet begun to silence the British.

Nasu's boat, moving in carefully, began to encounter the debris of other boats and floating gear and dead bodies, all of which proved the effectiveness of the British batteries. The wreckage and the number of bodies kept increasing until, close to the shore, where the constantly bursting shells lit up the sea, he saw so much raw, bloody human flesh floating on the surface he was reminded of watermelon. Several bullets punctured his own boat but it did not sink, and when he asked if anyone had been hit, the answers were all negative. A few abandoned boats were bobbing in the surf when his boat landed. The noise was awesome, and bullets were flying at the invaders in such furious volume that men had to dive for the sand, into which they burrowed their heads, then their shoulders, then their whole bodies.

As Nasu himself took cover, he was surprised to find that, instead of being frightened, he was somehow exhilarated. He had expected to tremble with fear when he experienced his first moments of combat, but he was as calm as if this were merely a maneuver, and he wondered at his strange reaction. He had only a moment to think about it. Two hundred men—two boatloads—were clinging to the ground around him and waiting for his orders. They had landed on a delta island which was, tactically, the worst point they could have chosen. They were dangerously exposed, and they were in a spot from which it would probably be difficult to reach the mainland and the British air base. That objective seemed infinitely distant to Nasu as he peered ahead into the darkness and saw a nasty tangle of barbed wire. Spotting a captain near him, he said, "See if you can cut that wire."

The captain took three steps forward and was thrown back two steps. He had detonated a land mine. Though it did not injure him, it proved to Nasu that the suppositions about mine fields were correct. There must be openings, however. When a defending force lays a mine field, it has to leave openings for its own movements. Despite the mines, the British artillery and machine guns, Nasu's men slowly inched forward, cutting more wire, looking for ways around it, burrowing under it until, at the expense of several lives, they found the gaps. Ahead of them they heard an English-speaking voice, presumably a British scout, shouting information back to the gunners. A Japanese machine gun fired a burst in the direction of the voice and it was not heard again. Though the Japanese casualties mounted, the survivors continued to press forward and even the wounded men tried to keep pace. One man, some distance from Nasu, ran at a British pillbox and plastered his body against its loophole so his comrades could rush forward and take it while he absorbed its fire.

A new force now entered the battle against the Japanese. Overhead, Nasu could hear the drone of airplanes. They did not attack the beaches. Worse than that, they were diving in to bomb the transport ships and the landing craft. Fire was visible on one of the ships, then another. It was absolutely imperative to outflank these British pillboxes and get to the air base from which those planes must be coming. But the British fought with such skill and tenacity, and they were so well dug in, it seemed they could never be outflanked. They could only be eliminated. One by one, the Japanese troops reached the pillboxes, spilled their blood around them, but gradually took enough of them to enable Nasu to change direction. He ordered the men in his immediate party to inflate their rubber raft-boats. When there were enough boats in the water, his whole group pushed silently off the delta island to head up the stream which seemed most likely to take them toward the air base.

Before they had traveled far, the gunfire around them abated and they realized they had indeed got past the enemy pillboxes. Colonel Nasu ordered a count of the men and found he still had 120 left of the 200 who reached shore with him. He felt pleased at their break-through, despite the losses. Now that they were past the beach they had at least a chance to stop those enemy planes he could still hear overhead. All they had to do was figure out the way to the air base through this dark, watery jungle.

DECEMBER 8,
2:45 A.M. IN TOKYO,
7:15 A.M. IN HAWAII

COMMANDER Mitsuo Fuchida's exhilaration continued to mount as the miles passed beneath him. In less than a half-hour, his flight of 183 planes, all fanned out behind him, should reach the northern coast of Oahu. From his 10,000-foot altitude, Fuchida looked down at the billowing layer of clouds below him and hoped it did not extend all the way to Hawaii. Visibility was one of his chief concerns. Another was American fighter planes. But where were they? He had expected the P-40s to attack before now, since he was convinced the Americans must, by this time, be aware of the Japanese task force. Whenever the P-40s did attack, he was ready for them, having assigned 36 of his Zero fighters to engage them. The United States couldn't possibly have much information about the new Zeros. Perhaps none at all. Those American pilots had an unpleasant surprise awaiting them. However good they might be, and he expected them to be excellent, they would find it difficult to cope with the new Zeros in their old P-40s.

Fuchida shuffled the papers in front of him and looked again at the mimeographed sheet he and Commander Genda had handed out the previous day to their pilots. Compiled mostly from information supplied by a Japanese pineapple-farm manager on Oahu, it showed the location of all the ships in Pearl Harbor as of December 6. The farm manager had forwarded the data to Tokyo by Western Union in telegrams ostensibly addressed to the owner of his pineapple farm. The "pineapples" to which the telegrams referred were actually ships in Pearl Harbor. But would all those ships still be there two days later? And where were the three American aircraft carriers which had been in the harbor a few days earlier? They were no longer there according to the report. Could they be lurking nearby in expectation of an attack? Fuchida hoped so because even though they presented the maximum threat to the success of the Japanese mission, he was confident that if they could be found, his men would manage to destroy them. Carriers, not battleships, were the prime targets of the attack.

Turning to his radio operator, Petty Officer Mazuki, he suggested they tune in a Honolulu radio station on which they could take a navigational reading and make sure their course was correct. Mazuki found a station which was playing American popular music. Fuchida did not know the tune. As his pilot, Lieutenant Matsuzaki, made a slight correction in course, followed by the entire armada behind them, the music ended and an announcer gave a weather report:

"There will be clouds above the mountains today, but the skies over Honolulu are clear."

A sunny December Sunday in Hawaii. Fuchida could recall, from his visit there 17 years earlier, what a warm and pleasant day that indicated. Sitting in the sun, swimming in the surf, trips up the Pali pass, through a forest of tropical greenery, to look down on the splendid view of Kaneohe and the windward side of the island. How many people had gone to sleep, six or eight hours before, planning such a Sunday? Their plans would soon be changed. Surprise attack was a danger one had to accept, living in the shadow of a huge naval base. His own family, his wife, Haruko, his eight-year-old son Yoshio, his four-year-old daughter Miyako, were living, at the moment, in the shadow of another great naval base, at Yokosuka, near the mouth of Tokyo Bay. It was not, however, the time to think about them. His wife knew nothing of the mission on which he had been sent, and hadn't even an inkling of where he was at the moment. This was as it should be. "The skies over Honolulu are clear." This bit of information eliminated one of his concerns. There should be no visibility problems.

DECEMBER 8,
SHORTLY BEFORE 3 A.M.

SITTING ON the *tatami* (straw mat) floor in a small Akasaka
hotel room, a cup of sake in hand, young, handsome Major Masahiko
Takeshita of the War Ministry personnel department gazed in continuing amazement at his superior officer, Colonel Joichiro Saneda.

"It is still difficult to believe," Takeshita said. "Pearl Harbor! Hawaii! I wouldn't have expected the navy to take such a gamble."

Colonel Saneda nodded and raised his cup of sake. "To the navy,"
he said.

"To a glorious victory," Major Takeshita added.

"And to His Imperial Majesty."

Though Major Takeshita drank the toast with a smile, he was not
as certain of victory as he appeared. A month earlier he had been one
of a number of leading young officers in the War Ministry who were
asked if they thought Japan should go to war against America. Takeshita had written, "We have no choice but to fight. If not, Japan will
be reduced to poverty for lack of oil."

Since the United States had frozen all Japanese assets in America,
and had banned the shipment to Japan of oil, other major sources of
oil would have to be developed, or the army and navy, indeed the
entire nation, would gradually be immobilized. If the United States
continued to withhold oil, then it would have to be got from Southeast Asia and the Netherlands East Indies. And if this made America
angry enough to fight, Japan would have to accept the challenge.
Otherwise, Japan would not only lose face, it would lose everything
it had won in the last 75 years. It would become again, as it had been
before the restoration of Emperor Meiji, a small, insignificant country. Yet, even as Takeshita had signed his name in favor of accepting
that challenge, he had felt no confidence in its probable outcome. It
would be difficult to defeat America. He knew that. Every career
officer in the Japanese Army knew that. Few if any, however, would
hesitate to fight.

Colonel Saneda poured more sake, and they continued to sip it
slowly. They were not drinking for pleasure. They drank simply to
pass the hours of tortuous suspense. At 10 P.M., almost five hours
earlier, Saneda had entered Major Takeshita's office in the War Ministry and, after glancing around to make sure they were alone, said,
"I suppose you know, it's war."

Takeshita had not quite known it. Though war seemed inevitable
to him, and he had sensed it must come soon, he had been told

nothing definite. And because the department to which he was now attached dealt only with army organization and regulations, he was not privy to any military plans or strategy.

"Before dawn," Colonel Saneda had informed him, "the army will launch attacks against Malaya, Thailand, and Hong Kong. And the navy will attack the Philippines, Singapore, Wake Island, Guam, and Hawaii. A full-scale attack on the U.S. Pacific Fleet in Hawaii."

It was astonishing news to Takeshita. After giving him a few moments to absorb it, the colonel had said, "I tell you this because it will be your duty to write the Joint Imperial Headquarters communiqué to announce the opening of hostilities. And I think you had better write it now."

Before leaving the room, the colonel had added: "Needless to say, it is also your duty to keep this absolutely secret. It will be several hours before the actual fighting begins."

Takeshita, after recovering from his initial shock, had found himself still surprised at his assignment, because the Information Bureau would ordinarily be expected to prepare such a communiqué. But high officials in the War Ministry had feared the secret might be leaked if it were entrusted to the Information Bureau. Takeshita was considered reliable, not only because he was well known to the general staff but also because he was the brother-in-law of one of the army's most prominent and best-loved officers, General Korechika Anami, who had been vice war minister from 1939 to April of 1941. General Anami was now commanding the Eleventh Army in central China.

Grabbing the nearest pencil, Takeshita had begun writing immediately: "Today, December 8, before dawn, the Imperial Army and Navy entered into a state of war with . . ." And upon finishing his communiqué, he submitted it to Colonel Saneda, who then undertook to put both the document and its author in a safe place for the next few hours. To avoid contact with fellow officers who might suspect something, the two men went down the slope from the War Ministry (which was located across the street from the Diet Building) to this small, little-known Akasaka inn where they could be incommunicado.

They had tried to sleep. Takeshita badly needed sleep. He had been on duty for more than 24 hours. (He hadn't seen his wife and eleven-month-old son, Masahiro, for almost two days.) But while his limbs and his eyes were tired, his mind was so crowded with astonishing information it would not rest. Finally he had glanced over at Colonel Saneda, who was equally wide awake. The colonel reached for the bottle of sake that had been brought to them and poured two small cups. Even sake could not touch them, however, at such a moment. After a few drinks, Major Takeshita looked at his watch.

Colonel Saneda said, "What time is it?"

"About a quarter of three."

The colonel stood up. "It shouldn't be long now," he said. "That's about 7:15 in Hawaii and 12:45 in Malaya. The war may already have begun. Let's go back to the office."

They returned up the hill to the War Ministry to await the moment when the news they had written would come true.

DECEMBER 8,
SHORTLY BEFORE 3 A.M.

A S F O R E I G N Minister Shigenori Togo's limousine drove smoothly down the hill from his official residence, and on through wide, quiet streets toward the Imperial Palace, he could look east in the direction of the Ginza district where the bright lights were now extinguished for the night, Tokyo being a city whose night life, though extensive and spectacular, did not continue into the late, late hours. How long would it be until those bright Ginza lights could shine again? Though the city did not yet know it, Tokyo would be blacked out every night henceforth. Togo's car, skirting the south bank of the palace moat, swung north through the outer gardens to the Sakashita carriage gate on the east side of the huge, walled establishment.

The Imperial Palace, in the very center of Tokyo, is an enormous, multistructured citadel about six miles in circumference, surrounded by deep, wide moats, and by 500-year-old stone walls, 100 feet high in some places. It was originally called Edo Castle after the little fishing village that would one day become Tokyo. Its construction was begun by a minor Japanese feudal lord several years before Christopher Columbus set out from Europe on the voyage that opened America. More than one hundred years later, near the turn of the sixteenth century, Edo Castle was taken by one of Japan's most powerful and astute feudal lords, Ieyasu Tokugawa, who was then in the process of consolidating the entire country under his absolute rule. For two-and-a-half centuries thereafter, until the unwelcome intrusion of America's Commodore Matthew Perry with his cannon-bearing fleet of black ships, the descendants of Ieyasu Tokugawa kept Japan under their absolute dominion and under almost complete isolation from the rest of the world. During that time, they also kept a long succession of Japanese emperors under almost complete isolation in the old Imperial Palace at Kyoto. Not until the American intrusion forced Japan to open its ports to the world did the Tokugawas' rigid feudal Samurai system collapse, thus clearing the way for the return to prominence of the ancient Imperial family. In 1868 Emperor Meiji, grandfather of Emperor Hirohito, moved his court from Kyoto to the enormous castle in the center of the now-imposing city of Edo (which he renamed Tokyo), and by emulating such Western nations as Great Britain and the United States, launched Japan into the expansive imperialistic era that was reaching its culmination this 1941 December night.

Togo's car, crunching the gravel of the palace plaza beneath its wheels, pulled up at the Sakashita gate where the guards were expecting him. Inside the parklike palace grounds, he proceeded left up a gradual incline to the Emperor's actual residence, a large, Japanese-style wooden mansion built by Emperor Meiji after he moved from Kyoto to Tokyo. Togo, dressed formally in a morning coat, was met at the door by an official of the Imperial Household Ministry who escorted him to the waiting room for high government officials, an enormous chamber furnished in Western style.

With the translated message from President Roosevelt in hand, Togo prepared to sit down in one of the comfortable armchairs while awaiting the call to his audience, but approaching footsteps indicated a chamberlain was already coming to summon him into the Emperor's receiving room. He was surprised when Marquis Koichi Kido entered the room. Marquis Kido, a small, balding man in middle years, with round, thin-rimmed glasses and a full black mustache, was the grandson of one of the nineteenth century aristocrats who helped bring about the restoration of the imperial family. Kido was also the most influential man in the Imperial Palace. As the Emperor's chief political advisor, it was he who, each time a cabinet fell, recommended, and therefore virtually chose, the next prime minister. He had chosen General Tojo as prime minister for what seemed to him an overriding reason—he was convinced that only Tojo had the strength to control the extreme war advocates within the army, that only Tojo would have the devotion and tenacity to pursue the Emperor's desires for peace. Having been awakened by the foreign minister's middle-of-the-night phone call asking permission to see the Emperor, Kido had come to the palace himself from his home in the Azabu district, about four miles away, to discuss President Roosevelt's message with Togo, and to make sure Togo's audience was arranged smoothly.

Kido glanced at the papers in Togo's hand. "What does Roosevelt's message say?" he asked.

"It makes no concessions," Togo said. "He simply demands again that we withdraw our troops from French Indochina. He promises that if we comply, the United States will not invade Indochina, or allow any of its allies to do so."

Kido shook his head and said laconically, "That's no use, is it? What's Tojo's opinion?"

"The same as yours," Togo said. "I've just come from discussing it with him. I think we're in agreement on how to handle the matter."

Before Marquis Kido had time to pursue the subject, if he wished to do so, a chamberlain entered the room and said to Foreign Minister Togo, "His Majesty is ready to see you now."

DECEMBER 8,
3:05 A.M. IN TOKYO,
7:35 A.M. IN HAWAII

AT 3:05 Tokyo time (7:35 in mid-Pacific) a touch of anxiety began to intrude upon Commander Fuchida's eager excitement. In just three or four minutes, his planes should be reaching Oahu, but the cloud cover was still so high (6,000 feet) his pilots might not see the island until they were directly over Honolulu, which would, of course, eliminate all hope of surprise. If surprise could be maintained, the dive bombers would open the attack by destroying on the ground as many planes as they could find at Hickam and Wheeler fields. Two minutes later, the torpedo planes would skim in above the waves (using a technique for shallow waters Fuchida and Genda had developed at Kagoshima Bay) to attack the battleships in the harbor. Then the Zeros would visit the airfields with an assortment of cannon shells and machine gun bullets. And finally the high-level bombers would drop their loads on the harbor area. But this plan could not possibly succeed if they failed to see the island before flying over it. If 183 planes were to appear suddenly in plain view over Honolulu, which the radio had reported to be clear, the time it would then take Fuchida to get his squadrons into attack position might be enough for the defenders to prepare themselves. Fuchida sighed with relief, therefore, and a smile broadened his slender face when, at 3:10 (7:40 in mid-Pacific), through a break in the clouds, he saw a long, white line of surf below. As if the gods were blowing away the clouds, they began to disperse now, and Fuchida could see enough coastline to determine his exact position. He was approaching Kahuku Point on the northern, windward side of Oahu. It was precisely where he wanted to be.

He would lead the flight toward the sparsely populated northwestern side of the island as far as Waialua, at which point, by prearranged flare signal—radio silence was to remain in effect until time for the attack order—the various squadrons would separate to seek out their assigned positions. Lieutenant Akira Sakamoto, with 25 dive bombers, would fly toward Wheeler Field in the center of the island. Lieutenant Commander Kakuichi Takahashi, with 26 dive bombers, would fly toward Hickam Field adjacent to Pearl Harbor, just west of Honolulu. Lieutenant Commander Shigeharu Murata, with 40 torpedo bombers, would drop almost to sea level and swing out around the southern coast. Fuchida himself, with 49 high-level bombers, would approach Pearl Harbor at 10,000 feet. And Lieutenant Commander Shigeru Itaya, maintaining his altitude with the 43 Zero fighters, would hover over the entire scene to engage any American planes that might threaten the bombers. Later, if possible, the Zeros would dive down to attack the smaller airfields.

Approaching the tiny coastal village of Waialua, Fuchida still saw no indication that the Americans had been alerted. The only planes in the air were Japanese. He opened his canopy, raised his flare gun, fired once—the signal for a surprise attack. Then he looked around to watch the various squadrons peel off behind him and separate from his level bombers. His own pilot, Lieutenant Matsuzaki, banked slowly toward the southeast. Fuchida, with 48 planes following him, crossed the rugged coastline far above Barber's Point and the mountains of northwestern Oahu and flew directly toward Pearl Harbor on the southern side of the island.

The clouds were all behind him now. In front of him, under a pale blue sky, lay the entire lower half of Oahu. Diamond Head in the distance. Honolulu on the near side of it, stretching for several miles between the mountains and the sea. Hickam Field, even closer, at the western edge of the city. And in the foreground, looking exactly like the six-foot square plaster model of it which he had been studying since October in the chief of staff's room aboard the *Akagi*, his prime target, Pearl Harbor, the home of the United States Pacific Fleet.

Although he had been expecting to find there a major part of that fleet, he could scarcely believe the view of it which greeted him through his binoculars. Eight battleships snuggled closely together at anchor, two by two, without a sign of life around them. No. Not eight but nine battleships, plus one heavy cruiser, ten light cruisers, an uncountable number of destroyers and other ships. It was not their presence, though, that he found so astonishing. He had expected to see a great many ships, but he had not expected to see them so cozily arranged. During his 25 years in the Japanese Navy, he had seen the German fleet assembled in Kiel harbor. He had seen the French fleet assembled at Brest. He had seen the Japanese fleet pass in review before the Emperor. But never, even in the most peaceful of times, had he seen a fleet anchored so vulnerably, with less than a thousand yards separating capital ships. Had the American Navy never heard about the Russian disaster at Port Arthur in 1904, when Japanese torpedo boats caught their ships bunched in the harbor?

The arrangement of ships in Pearl Harbor was too perfect to last. Fuchida decided there was not a moment to spare. Turning to radio operator Mazuki, he ordered him to transmit immediately the prearranged code signal for surprise attack: *"To . . . to . . . to . . ."*

Fuchida looked at his watch. It would now be 3:19 A.M. back home. It was 7:49 A.M. the previous day here in Hawaii.

DECEMBER 8,
JUST AFTER 3:10 A.M.

F O R E I G N Minister Togo entered the Emperor's receiving room, which was much smaller than the waiting room though no less elegant, and stood watching expectantly, in awe, for Emperor Hirohito's arrival. Though Togo had been privileged to meet His Majesty on numerous occasions, he still felt, each succeeding time, the same reverence he had felt the first time. The Emperor did not keep him waiting. After delaying just long enough to honor the imperial custom

of allowing his guests to precede him into a room, Hirohito made his
entrance, alone, and the door closed behind him.

Even in his Japanese Navy uniform the Emperor was not a figure
either of regal splendor or of military bearing. He was short and
slight. His feet pointed outward rather than straight ahead. His shoulders sloped. His chin was too small for his face, as was his mustache.
He wore rimless glasses. His right cheek twitched involuntarily. In his
smile there was no regal condescension but only gentle warmth, and
in his eyes there was a fatherly kindness which made him appear
older than his 39 years. He looked as if he would be more comfortable
wearing a suit or a kimono, but he had found it incumbent upon him
during recent years to wear either an army or a navy uniform at
conferences with government officials. If he appeared ill at ease, it
was perhaps because of his natural shyness, or perhaps because he
felt like a father about to hear the details of some new trouble into
which his children had fallen. He was, of course, already aware of the
general purpose of the foreign minister's visit.

Foreign Minister Togo bowed from the waist until his body was
bent forward at a 90-degree angle, then, after a suitably respectful
moment, stood erect. The Emperor waited.

"Your Majesty," Togo began, "a telegram has come, addressed to
you personally, from President Roosevelt. May I read it to you?"

The Emperor nodded, then listened with increasing sadness as
Togo read aloud the Japanese translation of the long message. The
American president apparently had a mistaken impression of the
function of a Japanese emperor if he thought a personal message to
him, even a message delivered much earlier than this one, could help
prevent war. Within the limits of his position as Emperor, Hirohito
had tried for several months, without success, to prevent it. But those
limits as he saw them were very restrictive. He had been taught from
earliest years that an emperor's duty was to reign, not to govern. The
prime minister and his cabinet were responsible for governing.
Though he might try to influence them, he believed he had no right
to direct them.

In the autumn of 1940, before Japan signed a Tripartite Alliance
with Nazi Germany and Fascist Italy during the premiership of
Prince Fumimaro Konoye, the Emperor had several times suggested
to the prince his opposition to it. And in the autumn of 1941, before
the imperial conference of September 6 which ratified the nation's
course toward war, he had summoned the army and navy chiefs of
staff, General Gen Sugiyama and Admiral Osami Nagano, to question
them about their hopes and intentions. He had asked Sugiyama how

long it would take to complete the south Pacific campaign which was then being planned. Sugiyama had said, "About three months," to which the Emperor had replied angrily, "When the China Incident began, you said it would end in a month. [At that time, in 1937, Sugiyama was war minister.] It has now gone on four years and has not yet ended." Sugiyama had said, "But the interior of China is huge." And the Emperor had answered with increasing heat, "If China is huge, isn't the Pacific Ocean even bigger?" At the conference the following day, the Emperor had broken all precedent, against the advice of Marquis Kido, by speaking up to the assembled ministers. The usual procedure at imperial conferences was almost ritualistic. The prime minister and his government came to read and conduct *pro forma* discussions before the Emperor of matters on which they had already decided and which they expected him to approve without question. The speeches of the prime minister and his cabinet members were always prepared beforehand in printed form and laid out on each desk. After they were read, the Emperor customarily indicated his acquiescence by leaving the room without saying a word. At the end of the September 6 discussion about breaking negotiations with the United States and preparing for war, Hirohito, to the amazement of all present, had cleared his throat and said, "I would like to read you a poem written by my grandfather, the great Emperor Meiji." And taking in hand a piece of paper, he had read:

> When all the oceans are brothers,
> Why must there be storm and strife in the world?

The implications of his grandfather's poem had been buried, however, in the nation's momentum toward war, a momentum which was now bigger than any one man, including the Emperor himself. When on October 17 he accepted Marquis Kido's suggestion that General Tojo be named prime minister, it was with the stipulation that Tojo disregard the September 6 imperial conference and pursue all possible avenues toward peace. But by October 17, all the acceptable avenues toward peace had apparently been closed and the country had moved inevitably, depressingly toward war.

When Foreign Minister Togo finished reading the telegram from President Roosevelt, he paused to await the Emperor's reaction. Finally, the Emperor said, "What kind of reply can be made to that?"

Implicit in the question was the Emperor's awareness that hostilities against America were scheduled to begin this very night. The action about to take place in the Hawaiian Islands would be the true reply to the president's message, yet a few suitable words, if such there were, would also be needed.

"Your Majesty may be aware," Togo said, "that President Roosevelt, last July, made a similar proposal which was rejected by Prince Konoye. French Indochina is, of course, only one of the subjects we have been attempting to negotiate with the United States. The president mentions none of the others. He offers no concessions to the Japanese viewpoint. Bearing all the circumstances in mind, Prime Minister Tojo and myself have prepared the draft of a reply from Your Majesty's government which we feel would be appropriate. With Your Majesty's permission, I shall read it."

The Emperor waited.

The foreign minister, bringing forth another sheet of paper, began to read: "Some days ago, the president made inquiries regarding the circumstances of the augmentation of Japanese forces in French Indochina to which His Majesty has directed the government to reply. Withdrawal of Japanese forces from French Indochina constitutes one of the subject matters of the Japanese-American negotiations. His Majesty has commanded the government to state its views to the American government also on this question. It is, therefore, desired that the president will kindly refer to this reply.

"Establishment of peace in the Pacific and consequently of the world has been the cherished desire of His Majesty for the realization of which He has hitherto made the government continue its earnest endeavors. His Majesty trusts that the president is fully aware of this fact."

The Emperor, without commenting on the obtuseness of what had been read to him, said simply, "That will do well."

Togo said, "Thank you for your graciousness, Your Majesty."

The two men looked at each other for a moment, both sharply aware of a whole set of circumstances to which neither had referred. Then Togo bowed deeply at the waist and waited while the Emperor retired from the room.

Returning to the waiting room, Togo asked a chamberlain where he might find Marquis Kido, but since the marquis was not to be found, Togo left the palace directly, escorted by the chamberlain down several hundred yards of red-carpeted corridors, all serene and tranquil. As he emerged from the palace grounds at the Sakashita gate, he gazed up at the heavens, full of bright stars, and felt as if he were bathed in a sacred spirit. It was now 3:25 A.M. Driving through the palace plaza, which was in utter silence like most of the sleeping city, he reflected upon the fact that the day which would dawn in a few short hours would be one of the most eventful in the history of the world, and that he himself had played a significant role in bringing this day's events to fruition. He believed that whatever might happen, he had labored for the sake of mankind and his country. And he was convinced that since his country's present course had been taken only after the search for alternatives was exhausted, that course must find ultimate approval in the judgment of Heaven.

DECEMBER 8,
3:23 A.M. IN TOKYO,
7:53 A.M. IN HAWAII

THE ONLY disappointment nagging at Mitsuo Fuchida as the attack began was the fact that there were no American aircraft carriers at Pearl Harbor. He had been told he would find none there. He was so impressed, though, with the importance of the carriers that he had pleaded for permission to go to sea and search for them, since his planes had enough fuel to fly out at least 150 miles from Oahu. Admiral Nagumo's chief of staff, Admiral Ryunosuke Kusaka, had vetoed Fuchida's plea.

"You must keep in mind," the admiral said, "that the attack on Hawaii is not the navy's main operation. Our mission here is only to neutralize the enemy fleet. The navy's primary objectives are in the southern seas."

Fuchida, aware that Kusaka reflected the thinking, not only of Admiral Nagumo but of Admiral Yamamoto, had abandoned his argument. And at this moment he would have to admit there were enough targets available, even without the carriers. He glanced left toward Wheeler Field in the distance, up on the high, red-earthed pineapple and sugar plateau near the center of the island. At any moment, Lieutenant Sakamoto's 25 dive bombers should be arriving at Wheeler, and there they were, peeling off from 12,000 feet, one after another, like swooping hawks, to plunge straight down toward the flight line where Fuchida could see tidy rows of planes looking almost infinitesimal at that distance.

At about 500 feet from the ground, the first dive bomber pulled out of its plunge. A moment later, a blossom of fire, not very large from so far away, erupted beautifully among the planes and scattered them in all directions. Fuchida and his crew shouted to the heavens. A second bomber pulled out of its dive above Wheeler and a second bomb exploded among the planes on the ground. Fuchida scribbled a message on a piece of paper and handed it to radio operator Mazuki who quickly transmitted it to the task force.

"Surprise attack in progress," it said. The time was exactly 3:23 A.M. in Tokyo, 7:53 A.M. here in Hawaii. A small cloud of smoke was beginning to form where the first bomb had struck.

Fuchida turned his head forward toward Hickam Field and Pearl Harbor. Lieutenant Commander Takahashi's 26 bombers were just beginning their dives. But not all of them seemed to be diving at Hickam. Some were descending upon the landing strip at Ford Island, a small aircraft base in the center of Pearl Harbor, where Fuchida caught sight of several gray-blue U.S. Navy planes he had not expected to see there. Good for Takahashi. He was using his head, altering his attack to meet the situation as he found it. Bursts of flame began to dot the Hickam flight line, then Ford Island, as Takahashi's bombers continued to descend.

At that moment, however, Fuchida's growing satisfaction was cut short as he saw Lieutenant Commander Murata's 40 torpedo bombers speeding in upon Pearl Harbor from the sea. They were flying directly toward the paths of the Takahashi dive bombers which were hitting Ford Island. Several of the battleships, the prime targets of the torpedo bombers, were lined up beside the island. If the dive bombers were to disrupt the torpedo bombers, the most important and most delicately planned aspect of the whole operation might fail. According to orthodox naval strategy, the torpedo bombers should not even have been included in the attack. The depth of Pearl Harbor was only 32 feet. No one had ever successfully launched aerial torpedoes in such shallow water. The Americans probably hadn't even entertained the possibility of torpedo-bombing when they planned their defense of the harbor. But at Kagoshima Bay, using the principle of stone-skipping on water, Fuchida and Genda had taught their pilots a technique in which the torpedo bombers would make their approaches just 39 feet above sea level, even lower than the tops of the ships they were attacking, and release their loads at full speed. To achieve accuracy, however, one would have to maintain a precision course. Could Murata's torpedo bombers maintain such an exact course with Takahashi's dive bombers plunging toward them?

The first of the torpedo bombers was now nearing one of the

battleships, getting closer and closer until, suddenly, just when it seemed almost too late, the plane pulled up in a steep turn to avoid collision. Its torpedo, if launched properly, must now be in the water, swimming along at its aggravatingly deliberate speed toward the target. In a few seconds, Fuchida would be able to see, even from this altitude, whether his revolutionary, shallow-water torpedo technique would succeed in actual practice. The seconds passed slowly. One, two, three, four . . . Then an explosive flash engulfed the side of the battleship and a burst of water shot into the air. Fuchida relaxed as the dive bombers cleared the area around the battleships and the torpedo bombers sped in, one after another, to hit their targets.

DECEMBER 8,
APPROACHING 3 A.M. IN TOKYO,
7:30 A.M. IN HAWAII

I N a midget submarine a few miles from the mouth of Pearl Harbor, Ensign Kazuo Sakamaki was becoming discouraged. It was now approaching 3 A.M. Tokyo time (7:30 A.M. here), and though he should long since have entered the harbor, he wasn't even near it. He was having dreadful gyroscope troubles.

Sakamaki was in command of one of the five, two-man midget submarines (78 feet long and 6½ feet in diameter) which had been released from mother submarines off Diamond Head eight hours earlier to invade Pearl Harbor and augment the Japanese aerial attack with their torpedoes, of which each carried two. Sakamaki did not know what had happened to the other four midget subs, but he hoped they were making better progress than he.

When he had launched his midget from its mother submarine, wearing his best uniform and carefully perfumed, he was so close to the Oahu shore that he and the one man who constituted his entire crew, Petty Officer Kiyoshi Imagaki, could hear jazz music from a party near Diamond Head. But only because of the young ensign's devotion to Emperor, country, and family had the sub been launched at all. Its gyroscope had been functioning so erratically it could not be trusted. Though Sakamaki knew this, he was determined to fulfill his mission. After sharply saluting the captain of the mother sub, he had lowered himself through the tiny hatch and carefully settled his miniature craft into the black waters. Immediately it had lurched almost onto its side. The trim was out of adjustment. Crawling back and forth through the narrow, front-to-back passageway, Sakamaki and Imagaki had spent the next hour shifting ballast and filling tanks with water. Finally, the ship had righted itself, freeing the two men to eat the boxed meal that had been prepared for them. Sakamaki drank a glass of sake, then clasped Imagaki's hand.

"To our success!"

"To our success."

Slowly they began to move forward. Though they did not know for certain that they were pointed in the right direction, they hesitated to raise the ship and look, because if the enemy were to spot them, it would end the navy's hope for a surprise attack. But after ten minutes of moving blindly through the water, Sakamaki decided he had to find out where he was going. He raised the ship until the periscope broke water, then peered through it.

Alas, they were going in the wrong direction, 90 degrees off course. The gyroscope was completely useless. Sakamaki's hands had now begun to perspire as he felt panic gripping him. "We must get to that harbor," he told himself, pointing his sub toward the lights at the harbor mouth. He and the other four midget submarine commanders had been instructed to slip inside the harbor during the night, then lay on the bottom until daylight, when they were to attack in conjunction with the Japanese air squadrons. But with this crippled ship, Sakamaki knew he was in trouble.

Time after time during the night he had tried and failed to find the mouth of Pearl Harbor. With the coming of dawn, he had hoped to do better. But unfortunately, when he looked toward Pearl Harbor, what he saw was two U.S. patrol vessels guarding the entrance.

Though his discouragement was deepening, Sakamaki was determined not to surrender to it. He must not even let his crewman see it.

"Have no fear," he said to Imagaki. "Now that we have come this far, it is our duty to get the job done. We shall somehow break through. Once inside the harbor, we'll send our torpedoes after an enemy battleship. If necessary, we'll ram a battleship. That's our mission. So cheer up."

Sakamaki did not take time to notice whether Imagaki was cheered by his words. Bringing the submarine to a depth of 35 feet, he pointed it directly toward the harbor mouth. The sun was now so bright he could see the white uniforms of the men on the patrol vessels. He could see also what type of vessels he faced. Each had four funnels.

"Just a couple of destroyers," he told himself. Bravely he continued toward them.

A few minutes later, the submarine was thrown into violent upheaval, and before Sakamaki was knocked unconscious by hitting his head against the hull, he heard the unmistakable boom of a depth charge.

When he regained consciousness several moments later, Sakamaki found smoke in the submarine. Reducing the engine to half-speed, he headed for the open sea until the smoke began to dissipate. He found that Imagaki was unhurt, and their torpedoes had not been damaged. With renewed determination he turned again toward the two destroyers at the harbor mouth. More depth charges were soon shaking the midget submarine, but this time they did not come so close. They came close enough, however, to damage the periscope. Sakamaki, unable to see where he was going, increased his speed in the hope that he could at least escape the destroyers. When the depth charges were far enough behind him, he decided to surface. Since he didn't know where he was going, he had no alternative.

He could not have chosen a better moment to expose himself. As his tiny vessel came up from the depths, a series of bomb explosions had turned all attention away from him toward Hickam Field and the interior of Pearl Harbor. The aerial attack had begun and columns of black smoke were beginning to rise.

"Look! They've done it!" Sakamaki shouted to Imagaki. "They've done it!"

With new determination, they prepared to submerge and grope once more toward the harbor mouth.

DECEMBER 8,
3:33 A.M. IN TOKYO,
8:03 A.M. IN HAWAII

PUFFS OF smoke, which looked small from 10,000 feet, began to multiply below as Mitsuo Fuchida ordered his own squadron of 49 level bombers into their bomb runs. But now a new danger arose. The

Americans, recovering quickly despite the damage they were absorbing, had begun to fire high-altitude antiaircraft guns, and with surprising accuracy. A plane on Fuchida's wing dropped its bombs prematurely, and when Fuchida looked toward it, at first in anger, he saw gasoline trailing from its wings. Both its bomb carriage and its gas tanks had been hit. Since Japanese planes were not equipped with self-sealing tanks, this one would have no chance to return to its carrier. The pilot, realizing his fate, peeled off and dove straight for one of the battleships below. Fuchida watched sadly as an American shell caught the crippled plane on the way down, causing it to explode in midair.

The antiaircraft fire continued to increase now, not so much from the battleships as from the cruisers and destroyers. Fuchida signaled a plane with a master bombsight to take the lead position, and his own plane pulled up close behind it. Suddenly, a shell exploded nearby, shaking his plane as if it were as light as a cherry blossom, and when the scare of the blast had passed, he realized they had been hit. A shell fragment had ripped a hole several inches wide in the fuselage and only a few inches from him. Fortunately, an inch was as good as a mile and the hole was not large enough to cause great concern, but when he turned to see what else might have happened, he noticed that the face of his radio operator had become pale.

"We've got a hole in the fuselage," Mazuki said, "and the rudder wire is damaged."

The fragment, in passing, had severed all but one strand of the rudder cable, and each time pilot Matsuzaki moved the controls, the strained wire sounded a mournful musical alarm. Yet the wire held, and the plane remained close on the tail of the sighting bomber as it approached the target. Fuchida fixed his eye on the plane in front of him to note the instant of bomb drop and waited impatiently. He was soon aware that they had overshot and no bombs had dropped. Then he realized why. A small cloud had come between the bombsight and the target. Banking toward Honolulu, the sighting plane swung around for a second run, and Fuchida's plane followed despite the increasing strain on the damaged rudder cable.

As Fuchida's squadron approached the double row of battleships again, an enormous explosion ripped one of the ships, sending a column of dark red smoke more than 3,000 feet into the air and creating a shock wave he could feel 10,000 feet high. Despite the smoke, however, the visibility was good enough to give him a view of the ships under attack and he was overcome by a sense of profound irony as he recognized one of the two ships his own plane was approaching. It was the *Maryland,* the same battleship he had visited in San Francisco harbor 17 years previously, and on which he had seen the catapult planes which made him decide to become a flier.

Despite fierce antiaircraft fire, the sighting bomber maintained a steady course, and as the squadron neared bombing position for the second time, Fuchida knelt down to watch through a small peephole in the floor, the descent of his own plane's bombs. Lieutenant Matsuzaki pressed the button at what appeared to be the precise moment, and the four bombs dropped in perfect pattern toward the *Maryland* and one other battleship right beside it. The ships were so far below, Fuchida began to wonder if the bombs would ever reach them. As the cluster of four grew smaller and smaller, he strained his eyes to keep them in sight. Soon they looked like four poppy seeds flying in formation. Then, as they disappeared altogether, he saw two bursts of smoke arise from the ship on the left. It was the *Maryland.*

"Two hits!" Fuchida shouted, leaping up from the hole in the floor. Pilot Matsuzaki and radio operator Mazuki filled the plane with their cheers. But not for long. A grating screech from the almost-broken rudder cable silenced all three of them and Matsuzaki, fully warned, limited the plane's maneuvers thereafter to the most gradual banks and turns, hoping desperately that the cable would hold.

Fuchida was now too busy to worry for more than a few minutes about the weakened cable. As the attack progressed, with his level bombers blanketing their targets in carefully-spaced groups of ten, he strained his eyes to see, through the increasing smoke and fire, the exact results of the continued bombardment. Several of the battleships had been hit, and dozens of planes lay broken on the ground, at Wheeler, at Hickam, at Ford Island, and, as he could see when his plane made a wide circle around Diamond Head, at Bellows Air Base on the eastern shore, which had apparently been hit by the Zeros. It was difficult to assess damage precisely because Hickam Field and the harbor were becoming obscured by the black smoke clouds that billowed upward from the stricken ships, planes, and buildings. To record the scene, he began taking pictures with a large, heavy hand camera which was mounted on a swivel but which had to be aimed over the side of the cockpit. The camera, in this situation, could see much more than the naked eye. But even with his naked eye, Fuchida could see enough. It was now only 3:50 A.M. (8:20 A.M. here), about a half-hour after the attack had begun, and the outcome of the operation was no longer in doubt. Even if no more damage were done, the raid was already successful beyond anyone's hopes. The time had come to send that message back to the task force.

He turned and gave the word to radio operator Mazuki, who stopped watching the almost-broken steering cable and began tapping out the prearranged code message that Admiral Nagumo on the *Akagi*, Admiral Yamamoto on his flagship in Japan's Inland Sea, and all the high government officials in Tokyo were awaiting: *"Tora . . . tora . . . tora . . ."* The word *tora*, in Japanese, means "tiger," and the message was based on an ancient Japanese proverb: "A tiger goes out 2,000 miles and returns without fail."

Fuchida was still circling the area, taking pictures, identifying the damaged ships, when he realized almost an hour had passed since the attack was launched. The first-wave planes had unloaded just about all of their bombs, and had nearly emptied their guns. Even now, only five or six American fighter planes were in the air, hardly enough to worry them. He ordered the first-wave planes to rendezvous at Kaena Point, on the northwest tip of Oahu, and at 4:30 A.M. (9 A.M. here) sent them back to the task force while he himself flew toward Barber's Point, to direct the second assault wave. Of the 183 planes in the first wave, all but ten had made the rendezvous.

Lieutenant Commander Shigekazu Shimazaki's 170 second-wave planes arrived on the scene chafing with frustration at having been omitted from the first wave. But it was not because they lacked skill that they had been held back. All the 550 officers and men in Fuchida's crews were so experienced and competent he made few distinctions among them. The 80 dive bombers and torpedo bombers in the second wave, under Lieutenant Commander Takashige Egusa, had been selected to attack aircraft carriers with 500-pound bombs. Since there were no carriers in sight, they would distribute these bombs among the battleships, while Shimazaki, with 54 level bombers, attacked the air bases and Lieutenant Saburo Shindo, with 36 Zeros, would cover and protect all of them.

Fuchida, after joining these planes above Barber's Point, began open radio communications with them, directing them specifically to their targets. It would not be as easy for them as it had been for the first wave. The Americans were alert now, and Fuchida was amazed at their quick reactions as the new attackers approached. The dive bombers and torpedo planes converging on Pearl Harbor were met by brutal barrages. And there were several more enemy planes in the air to harass the attackers. Nothing the Americans might do now, however, would change the outcome. Relentlessly bombs fell; ships shuddered under new explosions, and Fuchida, with his camera angled clumsily out the side of the cockpit and the wind whipping his face, recorded their distress as they burst into explosive flames, or keeled over onto their sides, or settled slowly to the harbor bottom. The success of the attack was beyond even his own belief. He was doubly thankful for the camera, despite its unwieldiness, because without pictures it would be difficult to make anyone believe the extent of the damage his planes had inflicted. He could count at a glance, despite the smoke and fire, at least four battleships either sunk or heavily damaged, and four others suffering some damage. No battleship was completely undamaged. Two cruisers showed signs of distress. Smoke arose from several transports and destroyers. And in the airfields within his view, the number of shattered planes had increased from dozens to hundreds as the second assault wave finished its business. Though there were still many targets, including oil-storage tanks, the basic, required objectives had been splendidly accomplished, and that was fortunate because the second-wave planes had used up their bombs.

At 5:20 Tokyo time (9:50 here) Fuchida ordered these planes to rendezvous off Kaena Point for their return to the carriers. The bombers were to go first, while the Zeros would wait long enough to eliminate any U.S. planes that might decide to follow and locate the task force. As his triumphant squadrons retired from the battle scene, Fuchida himself remained for one last look.

He took satisfaction from the fact that there were no fires or bomb hits in the city of Honolulu, though he was not surprised. His men were accurate. All the bases they had attacked, however, were covered with smoke and flame. Pearl Harbor itself was completely enshrouded by black clouds, and beneath that pall lay the remains of the proud U.S. Pacific Fleet.

DECEMBER 8,
SHORTLY AFTER 4 A.M.

C O L O N E L Sadao Akamatsu, one of Premier Tojo's four private secretaries, arose from his desk in the downstairs room which the secretaries sometimes used in the Tojo family quarters and took his coat from the hanger. He had decided he had better get back home for a short nap if he wanted to have any sleep at all before facing the busy day ahead of him. Akamatsu, who lived with his wife and three children in a little house about three minutes from the prime minister's official residence, had been awakened at 2:30, shortly after he went to bed, by a guard with a message from General Tojo. He was to come and give Foreign Minister Togo any assistance he might need in arranging an immediate audience with the Emperor. As it happened, Togo hadn't needed much help, but Akamatsu remained for more than an hour at the Tojo family house behind the official residence, just in case some problem might arise. Tojo himself had long since gone back upstairs to bed. The house was quiet, and even though war was scheduled to break out some time during the coming day, there wasn't much to be done at the moment.

Akamatsu put on his coat, left the house, and was walking along a footpath through the dark grounds when he saw the outline of a man approaching him. Up close he realized it was Navy Captain Empei Kanaoka, the prime minister's private secretary for naval affairs.

Akamatsu said, "What are you doing here at this hour?"

Kanaoka seemed excited. "The navy has just received a message," he said. "The attack on Hawaii has begun."

"Hawaii!" Akamatsu couldn't believe what he had heard. Hawaii was more than 4,000 miles away. It was the headquarters of the U.S. Pacific Fleet. "You mean the navy is attacking Hawaii?" Even though he was the private secretary to General Tojo in the latter's capacity as prime minister and as home minister, and had known him for twelve years, Tojo had never told him about any plans for such an operation.

Kanaoka said, "Before five o'clock we expect to have a message indicating success or failure."

When Akamatsu recovered from his shock, he said, "Do you want to go up and tell the general? I think he's asleep. He's been awakened once already tonight."

"No, let him sleep," Kanaoka said. "I'll wake him when we get something more definite."

Akamatsu decided it would be pointless to go home now. It was already after four. If the fighting had actually begun, there were many things to be done right away. With Captain Kanaoka, he returned to the secretary's room in the Tojo family house and went immediately to the telephone. He called Chief Cabinet Secretary Naoki Hoshino, then Tojo's other two private secretaries, Colonel Susumu Nishiura and Colonel Kenryo Sato, since it was obvious that all of them would be needed immediately. And after reaching them he called police headquarters. There were certain steps the police had to take about which they had already been instructed—notification of enemy embassies and stationing of guards around them, a roundup of enemy nationals and of a number of Japanese citizens who were potentially subversive, the tightening of surveillance over certain groups that might be dangerous to the war effort.

Shortly after Akamatsu completed his calls, the phone rang and Kanaoka answered it. The call was from the Navy Department. When Kanaoka put down the receiver he had a wide smile on his face.

"Now I'll wake up the general," he said. "The message has arrived from Hawaii. "Attack successful." Running from the room, he went up the stairs two at a time.

Colonel Akamatsu, exhilarated by the realization that war had finally come, felt nevertheless some trepidation about it. America would be a fearsome enemy. He wondered how General Tojo would feel when Kanaoka gave him the word that the fighting had begun. Akamatsu, who had known Tojo since 1929 when he was an officer in the regiment Tojo then commanded, had no doubts about his outward reaction. Tojo was a military man, after all. He did not shrink from the thought of war. He would receive the word calmly, but how would he feel in the privacy of his own heart about leading his country into a war of this magnitude? Akamatsu had the distinct feeling that Tojo, unlike many other generals, had not actually wanted war. He could not forget a poem Tojo had written and given to him in 1938, and which he still had on one of his walls at home. It said:

> The proper use of armies
> Is not to kill.

General Tojo, when he heard the knock at his bedroom door, sat up and turned on a light. "Come in," he called.

Captain Kanaoka burst breathlessly into the room. "The navy has received word from Hawaii," he said, "The attack there was successful."

Tojo's expression didn't change. While Kanaoka waited for some sign of elation or satisfaction, Tojo simply sat still in bed, looking thoughtful. Finally he said, "I'm glad to hear that. Has the report been sent to His Majesty?"

"I'll take care of it, sir, immediately."

Since Tojo had apparently nothing more to say, Kanaoka, somewhat deflated, excused himself. Surely the occasion called for much more excitement than the prime minister had shown.

General Tojo turned out the light and again settled down for what would be at best a short sleep.

DECEMBER 8,
5 A.M.

LOUD, happy confusion filled the large staff room of the battleship *Nagato*, anchored off the island of Hashirajima near Hiroshima, a notoriously easy-going port city on Japan's Inland Sea. The radio amplifier on the wall squawked with the sound of so many excited, competing voices that only occasional phrases could be distinguished. Messengers from the ship's communications room ran in and out, handing slips of paper to the eight or ten staff officers at the big, map-covered table in the center of the room. The messages were coming in batches now, and as they arrived, the officers would snatch them from the delivering hands to read them out in shouting voices which added to the din.

"Battleship *Pennsylvania*, direct hit!"

"Battleship *West Virginia*, sunk!"

"Cruiser *Helena*, heavy damage!"

"Battleship *Oklahoma*, capsized!"

Lieutenant Commander Yasuji Watanabe, who stood at the table compiling the score, had difficulty keeping pace. The reports had been coming in for more than an hour and a half now (beginning with the *"To . . . to . . . to . . ."* message from Commander Fuchida which, to everyone's amazement, was heard directly), and it was not easy to sort them out, spot the duplications, establish a true picture. Some of the early reports of the pilots above Pearl Harbor had come across the Pacific airwaves with such clarity they could be heard unmistakably over the amplifier. And at about twenty minutes after four, the officers in the staffroom had even heard an American radio voice shouting, "This is the real thing! Japs! Japs! Japs!" But shortly thereafter, the wave lengths had become jammed with so many voices that only the skilled operators in the communications room could sort them out, and Watanabe was toting the score now solely on the basis of the written messages the operators continued to send.

Standing quietly at the head of the table while all this noise swirled around him was Admiral Isoroku Yamamoto, the short, chubby, tan-skinned 57-year-old commander in chief of the Japanese fleet. Yamamoto's stern, solemn expression of an hour and a half earlier had softened, and his face was now the very image of calm expectancy. At moments he would smile slightly. Sometimes he would bend toward his chief of staff, Rear Admiral Matome Ugaki, who stood at his right side relaying details. Otherwise he remained quite still, watching, listening, waiting.

This was the most crucial moment in Yamamoto's remarkable naval career which had begun in 1904 when, as a young ensign, he was wounded in the leg and lost two fingers during Admiral Togo's epic victory over the Russian Navy. The attack against the U.S. Pacific Fleet in Hawaii was Yamamoto's strategy and his alone. The other ranking admirals in the Japanese Navy had looked upon it so fearfully and had opposed it so vigorously that he had been able to win approval for it only by threatening to resign. He had decided that if war came against the United States, the Japanese Navy would have to begin it with a massive blow against Hawaii. Japan could never gain her necessary objectives in the oil lands of Southeast Asia, he argued, as long as her fleet was in danger of being outflanked by the American fleet. He had insisted that the U.S. fleet would have to be neutralized, despite the perilous problems it would involve, and he had prevailed. Now he was finding out how well his strategy had worked.

Yet even if the Pearl Harbor attack had worked as well as it seemed, he could take only limited satisfaction from it; because much as he had insisted on its necessity in case of war, he had never wanted to put it into effect. Yamamoto had been for a long time openly on record against war.

As early as 1937, when he was vice navy minister, he had opposed the planned alliance with Germany and Italy despite the danger of assassination by right-wing army groups which favored such an alliance. He had said publicly at the time, "Japan should never be so foolish as to make enemies of Great Britain and the United States." When a reporter asked him, "Don't you think our gallant navy could defeat any other?" he had answered, "No, I do not." Army feeling against him became so intense, despite universal acknowledgment of his ability, that Admiral Mitsumasa Yonai, his friend and at the time his superior as navy minister, had suggested that he take on a police bodyguard. Yamamoto had declined. Yonai had then assigned the guard to him over his objections. But as Yamamoto continued to speak out against the stampede in the direction of war, the animosity of the extreme militarists toward him had increased until, in the summer of 1940, Yonai, who was then prime minister as well as navy minister, appointed him commander in chief of the fleet. "I sent him off to sea," Yonai later said, "because it was the only way to save his life." A year later, in the summer of 1941, when the then prime minister, Prince Konoye, asked Yamamoto about Japan's chances in a war against America and Britain, the admiral had said, "If I am told to fight regardless of consequences, I shall run wild considerably for the first six months or a year, but I have utterly no confidence for the second and third years. The tripartite pact has been concluded and we cannot help it. Now that the situation has come to this pass, I hope you will work for an avoidance of an American-Japanese war."

The war had come, however, despite his opposition, and six days earlier, at an audience in the Imperial Palace, Emperor Hirohito had charged him with the responsibility of leading the fleet into battle. From that moment forward, regardless of his personal feelings, he had looked upon himself as "the sword of my Emperor." On this day he was coming out of his sheath to plunge into that total, headlong, unreserved commitment which had been characteristic for more than a thousand years of the Japanese warrior.

Though the radio results were still arriving from Hawaii, his staff had enough information now to compile an astonishing list of sunk or damaged American ships. Lieutenant Commander Watanabe, after writing the list neatly on a sheet of paper, took it to the head of the long map table and handed it to him.

Admiral Yamamoto studied the list carefully:

> Battleships: 3 sunk
> at least 4 damaged
> Cruisers: 2 damaged
> Destroyers: 2 or 3 damaged
> Planes destroyed: in the hundreds.

The room became suddenly quiet as his staff watched for the commander in chief's reaction. He looked up from the sheet of paper, waited a moment, then, with a smile turned to the man who had handed it to him.

"Actually," he said, "it will be only half as good as you estimate."

For some time Yamamoto continued to watch impassively as new results, corrections, and confirmations kept coming in, but it was still too early for him to accept the outlandish reports they were getting. His staff officers could accept them because they were younger men who had not yet experienced actual war, and therefore did not realize how much exaggeration the heat of battle could produce. They would soon learn. Before the day ended they would be cutting their estimates down to a more reasonable size, but even so, it appeared certain now that this was to be a glorious victory for His Majesty, for the nation. A glorious way to begin this ominous war.

As he reflected on the way the war had begun, another anxiety began to nag at Admiral Yamamoto. Turning to Commander Shigeru Fuji, the political officer on his staff, he said, "The government's last declaration to the United States was scheduled to be delivered before our attack began. But I would like you to check it."

Fuji said, "I believe the note was delivered as scheduled."

Yamamoto said, "Nevertheless, I want you to check it."

DECEMBER 8,
6 A.M.

IN GROUPS of two or three, newsmen, with their pads and pencils, entered the information room at the War Ministry, where they stood in large clusters, waiting for the hastily called press conference to begin. Major Masahiko Takeshita, watching them, felt they must already have an inkling of what they were about to hear. As they talked to each other in restrained voices, expectancy showed in their faces and in their quick glances at each officer who entered the room. These reporters, though their newspapers were rigidly controlled by the Ministry of Information, and though they had been apprised only in general terms of the diplomatic crisis with America, had nevertheless been aware for many weeks of the imminent danger of war. And it must be apparent to them this morning that the time, 6 A.M., was too unusual and the atmosphere too electric for a routine War Ministry announcement. They could see their own excitement mirrored on the faces of the arriving army and navy officers.

It was a happy excitement that filled the officers, all of whom were aware now of the first word from Hawaii: "Very, very big success." When Takeshita had read this telegram from the navy in the code room of the War Ministry he had actually jumped with joy. But as he settled down to await further details, questions began crowding his mind. "Big success?" What could that mean? A few ships damaged?

Perhaps a battleship or a carrier sunk? Could it be possible? If they had managed to sink a battleship or a carrier, it would be a very big success indeed, but wasn't that too much to hope? And in the meantime, while the navy was enjoying its "big success" in Hawaii, how well was the army doing in Malaya? Though news of troop landings at Kota Bharu had arrived even before the news from Pearl Harbor, there was no word yet about the success or failure of the landings. Takeshita, envying his army comrades in that operation, prayed for their success. The army must not allow the navy to surpass it, especially since the army, with much greater fervor and enthusiasm than the navy, had realized the necessity and accepted the inevitability of the war.

Takeshita himself, unlike his dear friend and brother-in-law General Korechika Anami, had for several years supported ultrapatriotic groups, both military and civilian, which were demanding the establishment of a military government to prepare for an apparently inevitable clash with America. Though he had never felt confident of the outcome of such a clash, Takeshita was convinced that Japan could avoid it only at the expense of her self-respect. He had joined for this reason, as a young lieutenant, a prominent army faction called Kodo-ha—a group of officers devoutly religious, patriotic, and totalitarian, who insisted on the timeless ascendancy of the Divine Emperor and the absolute responsibility of the army to protect him by increasing the nation's strength. When Kodo-ha, in October of 1931, attempted a coup to establish a military government, Takeshita took part, and after the attempt failed, was "'punished" for it in a way that indicated the strength of Kodo-ha within the army. He was sentenced to three days house arrest, which he spent comfortably in the home of his regimental commander. Though the October, 1931 incident ended in failure, it had so intimidated the civilian government and the National Diet that the army, instead of suffering embarrassment for its inability to control its young officers, had emerged, in its role as protector of established authority, with more rather than less power in national affairs. Thus the attempted coup, while falling short of its goal, had done nothing to discourage a growing tradition of uprisings among young Japanese army officers.

Though Takeshita had severed his connections with the Kodo-ha faction in 1935, he had continued his efforts to increase the army's political power. Like several other young officers, he was a follower of Tokyo University Professor Kiyoshi Hiraizumi, a zealous nationalist and anticommunist. The rise of world communism in the 1920s concerned the Japanese Army as much as the threat of democracy, and led many officers to embrace Professor Hiraizumi's point of view. But it was not enough, in his view, simply to think properly about the inviolability of the Emperor and the ascendant role of Japan. He believed it was necessary to perform a deed worthy of one's beliefs. And the ultimate deed in support of the Emperor was to offer one's life.

A deep quiet came over the information room of the War Ministry as a naval officer arose to speak. Though Takeshita might wish an army man had been assigned to read this historic joint communiqué, he felt it was fitting that the honor should fall to the navy inasmuch as the navy had apparently struck the first hard blow of the war. As the newsmen raised their pads to take notes, he listened with increasing fervor to the reading of the words he had written:

"Today, December 8, before dawn, the Imperial Army and Navy entered into a state of war with American and British forces in the western Pacific. . . ."

War with America and Britain. Hearing his own words read aloud excited Major Takeshita even more than writing them because this public announcement made the fact official. Japan had finally taken the decisive step which had so long been needed. The country was actually at war against the two greatest powers in the world. As a soldier, he felt he could now face people on the street with renewed pride in the Imperial Army. The China Incident of the last four years had been, and was still, somewhat of an embarrassment to all Japanese soldiers because, despite a succession of advances, the army had not yet been able to conclude it victoriously. Chiang Kai-shek's Chinese puppet forces, though pushed back, were still intact and fighting after four years—another circumstance for which Japan could blame the United States. It was American support that maintained the Chinese resistance. It would not be so easy for America to continue helping the Chinese, however, if the Imperial Navy had actually achieved "a very, very big success" against the U.S. fleet in Hawaii this morning, and if the army succeeded in capturing Singapore and Hong Kong, as it seemed most likely to do. Perhaps the Americans and the British were not as strong as they pretended to be. The British were in deep trouble in Europe. Now the Americans might find themselves in even deeper trouble in Asia if the American Pacific Fleet had been badly damaged this morning. Perhaps Japan was on its way to a victory which would amaze the world.

But with the country now at war, why was he, a major in the Imperial Army, merely standing here, taking part in the announcement of it while so many of his friends were out fighting it? Like them, he had long since applied for transfer to a field unit and his wife, Reiko, had prepared for his departure from their comfortable home in the suburb of Mitaka, west of Tokyo. By this time, she must be wondering why he was still with her when so many others were gone. But she would never speak such thoughts. Reiko, whose grandfather had been a comrade of Takeshita's father in a nineteenth-century Samurai uprising, was the perfect wife for a Japanese soldier. She took loving care of their baby son, Masahiro, now almost a year old. She kept their house both clean and beautiful. And she asked no questions. As a well-trained Samurai wife, she was ever and always prepared, when her husband was away, to welcome him home, and when he was at home, to bid him farewell. In constant anticipation of farewell, she kept certain of his necessaries packed at all times. He sensed that deep in her heart she was thankful he had not yet been sent overseas, though she had never expressed herself on the subject. Whatever her feelings might be, however, Takeshita himself was chagrined to remain in Tokyo, and all the more so now that the fighting had begun. As he listened to the official war announcement that he had written, he thought about the often-repeated teaching of Professor Hiraizuma. It was not enough merely to believe in Japan's ultimate supremacy among nations. One had to perform deeds worthy of that belief. And what better deed could a man do than offer his life for the Emperor? Why hadn't his transfer come through? He would apply again, immediately, and keep renewing the application until it was accepted. As a staff officer in the powerful Military Affairs Bureau, he was not without influence in the War Ministry. He had no intention of sitting at a desk in Tokyo when so many of his colleagues were getting a chance to do great deeds in battle.

DECEMBER 8,
SHORTLY AFTER 6 A.M.

THE OFFICES of Prime Minister Tojo's secretaries, adjacent to his own office on the second floor of his official residence, were now alive with activity as phones rang and subordinates hurried back and forth, receiving orders, bringing information, making reports.

Colonel Sadao Akamatsu and Colonel Kenryo Sato, with their assistants, were sending special directives to the various government
ministries, ordering the inauguration of new, predecided wartime
regulations and making sure cabinet members had been informed of
a meeting scheduled for 7 A.M.

Chief Cabinet Secretary Naoki Hoshino and his aides were at work
on arrangements for the cabinet meeting and for the Privy Council
meeting which was scheduled later at the Imperial Palace. Even
more important, they were also going over the final draft of the
imperial rescript which would be issued sometime today in the name
of the Emperor, announcing officially to the Japanese people that
they were at war.

Captain Empei Kanaoka, Tojo's secretary for naval affairs, was on
the phone to the Navy Department, getting the latest word from
Hawaii. And Colonel Susumu Nishiura, Tojo's secretary for military
affairs, was on the phone to the War Ministry getting the latest word
from Malaya.

Colonel Nishiura was delighted to learn that the news from Malaya
was excellent. The units which landed at Kota Bharu, despite fierce
resistance, had already overrun several pillboxes in the surrounding
area. General Tojo, as an army man, would be pleased to hear this.
The navy seemed to be getting all the attention and credit up to now.

Nishiura, a tall, slender soldier with an erect Samurai bearing
which had been built into him by an army officer father and an army
officer grandfather, was now in his fourth year as an aide to General
Tojo and as an increasingly devoted companion-admirer. He felt the
prime minister deserved all the good news he could be given this
morning because these last few weeks had not been easy for him.
Until the first of December, when the nation's course was virtually
settled, Tojo had been torn between the Emperor, whom he loved
and who wanted peace, and the army, to which he had given his soul
and which wanted war. In order to keep faith with the Emperor and
continue his efforts for peace, Tojo had been forced to alienate the
extreme nationalists in the army, and large sections of the civilian
populace as well. Just this morning, shortly after arriving at his office,
Nishiura, while trying to eat a rice ball which was likely to be his only
breakfast, received a phone call from a right-wing journalist who
asked, as he had often asked before, when General Tojo was going
to get over his timidity and declare war on America. That fellow
would have a surprise coming to him when he turned on his radio
today. His point of view was one which a large part of the population
had come to share in the last month. Phone calls and letters demand-

ing war had been coming in every day by the hundreds and thousands. A member of the Diet had recently harangued Tojo from the floor and pleaded with him to heed the voice of the people. A retired major general, who knew Tojo but had been prevented from confronting him in person, had gone to Mrs. Tojo, representing a group of retired officers, and had accused him of preserving peace simply in the hope of maintaining himself in power. The officers had adopted a resolution urging him to declare war on America as soon as possible. Even Tojo's relatives were harassed in his name. A nephew at Tokyo's Waseda University was asked by a professor in class, "Why does your uncle keep procrastinating?"

More serious than any of this, however, was the evidence of a plot within the army, by belligerent young officers, to assassinate Tojo because he had not declared war. When Colonel Nishiura heard of it from trusted army friends, he hadn't doubted it for a minute. He knew well the attitudes of extremist groups in the army, and their willingness to eliminate any prime minister who displeased them. The fact that Tojo was himself an army man would not stop them. They felt a special hatred for "timid" generals. Nishiura, to protect Tojo, had immediately arranged to have Kempei (army secret policemen) stationed around the prime minister's official residence. Tojo, noticing them, had ordered them removed, whereupon Nishiura had instructed them to hide in the shrubbery within the grounds. Tojo had apparently not discovered this, though Mrs. Tojo knew about it. She made *udon* (Japanese noodles) for the hidden men every night. Very few things escaped the notice of Mrs. Tojo. One of her husband's subordinates, who felt the kind of wary admiration for her that Japanese men often feel toward women, had said of her, "She is too intelligent to be a wife."

The concern for Tojo's life within his circle of associates had made the previous day, December 7, a peculiar and uneasy one for his staff. Because pending military action had to be concealed from possible espionage agents, Chief Cabinet Secretary Hoshino and other aides had gone to play tennis on a public court, creating the impression that this was just an average Sunday. Only Colonel Nishiura and Colonel Akamatsu had remained at their desks, to take care of whatever problems might arise. As it happened, some problems did arise. In the morning, a Japanese soldier almost gave away the plans in Thailand by taking a diplomat into custody. Nishiura, at Tojo's behest, had sent a quick telegram of apology to Thailand promising to deal severely with the soldier. In the afternoon, a troop convoy on the way to Kota Bharu in Malaya, was spotted by a British plane. Though the plane was shot down, there was some fear that the pilot might have radioed this information before crashing. Unfortunately, nothing could be done about that.

Around four o'clock, quiet had settled over the official residence and Nishiura had begun to think he could at last relax. But just then a new and unexpected problem had arisen. General Tojo emerged from his family quarters wearing a homespun Western jacket with riding breeches and a crop. Nishiura decided this was carrying the just-an-average-Sunday theme too far. While it was desirable to convince possible espionage agents that Japan had no war plans, it was dangerous to do it so openly as to reinforce the same belief in the young army officers. If Tojo went horseback riding, he would make himself an easy target for them. Nishiura begged him to cancel his ride, and though Tojo was a man who seldom followed advice of caution, this time he did so. He settled for a short automobile ride with his family. When they returned, Nishiura had been able, finally, to relax.

Thinking this morning of the secret police still hidden in the bushes outside, Nishiura couldn't help smiling with satisfaction. Today's news would at least eliminate the need for them. Tojo would no longer have to be protected from the superpatriotic Japanese. He would soon be their hero. Now if only there were some easy way to protect him from the Americans . . .

Chief Cabinet Secretary Hoshino, whose position in the Japanese governmental system made him as powerful as any of the cabinet members themselves except the war and navy ministers and perhaps the foreign minister, had enough work this morning to tax even the extraordinary skill and efficiency which had prompted Tojo to choose him for the job. Though Hoshino, as the prime minister's top assistant, maintained quarters at the official residence, he had spent the previous night with his wife, Misao, and their two sons and a daughter at their family home in the nearby Koji-Machi district. When Colonel Akamatsu had called him out of bed to tell him the war had actually begun, he had felt, even though the news was no surprise, that the whole world was suddenly falling into a bottomless pit. The war was undoubtedly necessary, yet as he drove his car through the dark streets to work, he was filled with an uncomfortable apprehension about the days and weeks ahead. Neither he nor the prime minister knew as much about their new enemy, America, as they would like to know. He himself had never been in the United States. Tojo had once, in 1922, traveled across the country by train on his way home from a three-year sojourn as a military attaché in Germany, but it could not be said that he had more than an average person's knowledge of America, though he devoured whatever information he could get from the army and the Foreign Ministry.

When Hoshino arrived at the office and heard from Captain Kanaoka that the navy had affected a surprise attack on Hawaii (Tojo had kept this even from him), his apprehension had been tempered by amazement; he had run up to awaken the prime minister and report the development as if it were something Tojo hadn't known either. Tojo, after listening patiently, had said, "Yes, I've been awakened several times during the night, beginning at two o'clock when the foreign minister came to call." Hoshino, after hearing about the problem with the American ambassador and the Roosevelt telegram, had bowed out of the room to give Tojo a chance for another half-hour of sleep.

Hoshino's most delicate task this morning, after he had arranged for the cabinet meeting here at the official residence and then the Privy Council meeting at the palace, was to get the Emperor's rescript ready for approval by the Privy Council. Fortunately, a careful draft of the rescript was already completed. In fact, the drafts of two separate and opposite rescripts were completed. In November, when General Tojo still envisioned the chance of a settlement with America short of war, Hoshino had foreseen the possible need to use the Emperor's influence in persuading the extreme militarists to accept such a settlement. He had therefore directed one of his aides to write a peace, as well as a war, rescript. The peace rescript (the purport of which was that though Japan's position might be difficult, everyone should try to maintain national strength and international friendship) could now be burned. Provisional drafts of Imperial rescripts were always burned to preserve the impression that such documents emanated directly from the Throne. Actually, the writing of rescripts, when they were needed, was by custom, the duty of the chief cabinet secretary. It was one of a long list of his duties so important and impressive as to explain the great power the position bestowed. Besides drafting and promulgating documents and laws, Hoshino was responsible for appointments, promotions, and resignations of high officials, the fiscal accounts of the cabinet, the management of the general affairs of the cabinet, and the guidance of the Imperial Rule Assistance Association, which was now Japan's only legal political party.

Hoshino had been chosen for the job partly because of Tojo's long memory. The two men had met the first time by coincidence on a train in Manchuria during the autumn of 1935, when Tojo was commander of the Kempeitai—the army secret police—in China. Hoshino was there as chief of the finance ministry's national property section. They talked for three hours on the train without interruption; Tojo never forgot this perceptive young man he had met by chance. Hoshino had gone on to become, in 1936, secretary of the General Administration in Manchuria, then in 1940, after returning to Tokyo, the president of the government Planning Board. He had resigned from this high office six months before Tojo became prime minister and named him chief cabinet secretary.

As Hoshino waited for Tojo and his cabinet to arrive for their 7 A.M. meeting, he went over the war rescript once more with Shuichi Inada, chief of the general affairs section of the cabinet secretariat. It was Inada who had actually written the draft, and then, just the previous week, at Hoshino's direction, revised it. Hoshino felt now that Inada had done an excellent job. He was a master of the formal, almost Chinese-court style in which such documents were always couched. "We, by the Grace of Heaven, Emperor of Japan, seated on the throne of a line unbroken for ages eternal, . . ." As Hoshino went over the 600-word document, word by word, he noticed only a few small phrases that might be changed. He and Inada were already finished with their work by the time he heard the commotion in the hall outside that indicated General Tojo was now arriving. Satisfied with the rescript, he took a copy of it to the prime minister's private office, a huge room in the center of the second floor. Tojo was at his desk near the window, at the far end of the long, high-ceilinged chamber. He read the rescript so quickly that anyone unaccustomed to his speed might have supposed he had read it carelessly. Hoshino knew better.

Without comment, Tojo nodded his approval. He was in a thoughtful mood.

Hoshino said, "The cabinet meeting is set for seven."

Tojo nodded again, stubbed out a half-smoked cigaret and lit another as Hoshino left the room. Cigarets and coffee were Tojo's two most noticeable nervous habits. He drank an average of six cups of coffee a day in addition to tea during meals, and smoked an average of sixty cigarets. When his wife told him he should stop smoking, he would say, "Don't worry, it won't hurt me. I never inhale." He had reason this morning to smoke more than usual. He wished he had greater knowledge of America. He hoped the Americans were as committed to luxury and comfort as they had appeared to be during his short trip across the United States. He did not fear the possibility that Japan's Army would be outfought by the American Army. There were no soldiers in the entire world who could match the fighting spirit of the Japanese. He was less certain that Japan's industry and technology could keep pace with the famous American productivity, but he felt confident even in this area because the spirit of the Japanese worker would no doubt equal the spirit of the Japanese fighting man. Japan would win this war because Japan had to win it. Perhaps America could afford to lose, but for Japan, defeat would mean disaster. Japan was like a boy growing out of his clothing, like a farm family becoming too large for its few acres to support it. The population of these small islands was increasing so fast Japan had to find room for expansion. Where else should it look for room if not in other parts of the Orient, its natural sphere of influence? Japan had been so lazy during the two and a half centuries of Tokugawa rule that by the time Admiral Perry forced the country to open up, the Western powers had already grabbed much of Asia. These lands would have to be taken back from the West. The British would have to be ousted from Singapore, Hong Kong, even India, as the French had already been virtually ousted from Indochina. The Dutch had no right to the East Indies. The Americans had no right to the Philippines, nor did they have a right to continue propping up their stubborn puppet, Chiang Kai-shek, in China. All these greedy Western powers had to be driven from Asia, and it was Japan's sacred duty to accomplish it. Japan would either succeed or die fighting in the attempt.

Colonel Nishiura entered to report the army's progress in Malaya and Thailand, at which Tojo expressed his satisfaction.

"I understand you were awakened a few times during the night," Nishiura said.

Tojo smiled. "Several times, beginning at two o'clock. A message arrived from President Roosevelt to the Emperor, but it was too late."

Captain Kanaoka came in to report new details of the Hawaiian attack as well as other naval operations. Admiral Shigetaro Shimada, the navy minister, and other cabinet members dropped by to discuss the cabinet meeting. Then Hoshino put his head inside the door to say it was time for the meeting.

The cabinet members stood and cheered as the prime minister, dressed in military uniform, entered the large chamber across the reception room from his own office. It was exactly 7 A.M. General Tojo was a punctual man. The ministers resumed their seats at the huge round table in the center and their aides took places behind them. Tojo stood erect while they settled down.

"As you all must know," he said, "we are now at war." His voice, though naturally sharp and penetrating, showed no excitement. "Our army reports success at Kota Bharu in the Malayan Peninsula, and also in Thailand. But the operation about which you may want to hear is the navy's attack against Hawaii. Admiral Shimada will tell us about that."

The navy minister, who got along with Tojo so agreeably that other admirals were beginning to call him a toady and accuse him of neglecting the navy's interests, stood up and began to speak in a soft, quiet voice. "The navy's attack against Hawaii has no doubt been a great surprise to all of you," he said. "I am sure you understand it was necessary to maintain absolute secrecy about it. A very large task force, including six carriers, took part in the mission, and radio reports indicate great success. Pilots above Pearl Harbor say they have sunk several American battleships and have accomplished other good results. This is wonderful to hear, but I want to point out that it seems to us in the Navy Department that the damages to the enemy must have been overestimated. When we heard the report, we felt it was necessary to discount it to a certain extent. Even so, the news is great. The attack on the American fleet, which was the main purpose of our Hawaiian operation, has been accomplished."

Shimada spoke with such restraint that his disclosures were accepted by the ministers more solemnly than cheerfully. Naoki Hoshino, listening to him, was so impressed by his manner and so heartened by his words that he began to wonder if Japan might, after all, be able to defeat America. He had dreaded the war not only because he doubted his nation's capacity to win but also because his own personal background had been permeated with Western influences. He had been born in Tokyo's port city of Yokohama, where large numbers of Europeans and Americans lived. His father had been a minister in a Presbyterian church there, one of the first Japanese to become a Christian clergyman after Christianity was legalized during the reign of Emperor Meiji. In some ways, Hoshino's habits of thought were more Western than Oriental. He was a precisely logical man. He had always questioned Japan's chances in a war against the Western powers, though he had never said this to General Tojo, since Tojo was not in the habit of asking for his advice. He began to wonder now about his own reasoning. The war seemed to be starting very auspiciously. Perhaps Japan might sustain itself after all, at least until an opportunity arose for a negotiated peace.

General Tojo was speaking now of the imperial rescript, copies of which Hoshino's staff had hurriedly provided for each minister. Were there any comments on it? There were none. Tojo decided that though it was only 7:20, the business of the meeting was finished. There was no need to prolong it, but perhaps, on such an occasion, he should say a few concluding words. He was not addicted to unnecessary or lengthy speeches. He had once made a speech of only twenty words. His style was to present his message, strong and unadorned, then sit down.

He paused a moment and said, "At last the war has begun. There is no other way but to fight. We must announce this to the people."

He then turned and left the room. He had no time to waste in conversation with the ministers because, in addition to announcing the war to the people, he had to hurry to the Imperial Palace and announce it officially to His Majesty, the Emperor.

DECEMBER 8,
7 A.M.

A SUDDEN, loud, insistent pounding at the locked bedroom door of Otto Tolischus, in the house he had purchased next to the American Embassy, awakened him and routed him out of bed. A veteran newsman, 53 years old, Tolischus had come to Tokyo the previous February as the *New York Times* correspondent. Earlier he had been the *Times* correspondent in Berlin (he was a German-born, naturalized American) until he was evicted from Germany for writing a series of reports about the Nazis which won him a Pulitzer prize. On his arrival in Tokyo he had been told informally by a foreign ministry representative that if he repeated the kind of reporting he had done in Berlin, his stay in Japan would not be pleasant. Wrapping his robe around his short, rotund body, he opened the door to face four Japanese men in dark suits. It did not occur to him to be startled by their invasion of his home at seven o'clock in the morning. Though they bowed and smiled as they stalked into the room and surrounded him, he knew immediately they were plainclothes policemen. In the Japan of 1941 it was not surprising for the police unceremoniously to walk into private homes. That was why he kept his bedroom door locked.

"What is it?" he said, making no attempt to return their politeness.

His anger had begun to rise at the sight of them.

Their apparent leader said, "We are from the Metropolitan Police. Put on your coat. The procurator wants to see you."

At least they were not from the dreaded Kempeitai. But that was small consolation. For what possible reason could they be arresting him? A reporter filing dispatches daily could not imagine which stories might offend the Japanese police or censors. Only two weeks before, on November 26, Tolischus had been involved in an incident which still bemused him. Toshikazu Kase, the Foreign Office employee who acted as an interpreter and sometimes as a mouthpiece for Foreign Minister Togo, had called and arranged to meet him at the Imperial Hotel in the Marunouchi district near the Imperial Palace. When they met, Kase had said Togo wanted to present some Japanese views to the American public in the hope of forwarding the Washington negotiations which were then nearing a deadlock. Kase hoped Tolischus would send a dispatch to the *New York Times* explaining these Japanese views, which centered around three points. First, the Japanese formula presented in Washington on November 20 was Japan's last word and Togo hoped that in answering it, America would take this into consideration. Second, time was running short and the time element was more important than the exact nature of any formula. Third, Japan was willing to do everything compatible with decency to satisfy America on the Axis Alliance (the Tripartite Alliance between Japan, Germany, and Italy, which the American government abhorred). The next day, Tolischus, after obligingly writing the dispatch, took it for approval to Kase who changed a few words including the expression "compatible with decency," for which he substituted something more innocuous. He did not alter a Tolischus phrase crediting the story to "highest authoritative quarters." Kase asked Tolischus to telephone the dispatch in order to save time and assured him he would have no trouble with the censor. But when Tolischus called the censor he was told to submit his story in writing. Tolischus contacted Kase who eventually called back to say the dispatch would be cleared if it was credited to "diplomatic quarters" instead of "highest authoritative quarters." Tolischus, seeing this as a trick by the Foreign Office to put across its message while making it look as if it came from the American Embassy, had canceled the dispatch instead of changing it. There was no way to know now, however, whether the Kase incident, or some other one, equally innocent, had given rise to this early morning visit by the police. In Japan, police had never been limited by the concept of civil liberties or due process of law. It was easy, therefore, to overcome any temptation to argue with them, to demand justice, to ask them why he was being arrested, to talk to them about freedom of the press. They knew nothing about freedom of the press. There wasn't any of it in Japan. They might not even know the reason for his arrest. They might simply have been told to go get him.

Tolischus looked down at himself, wearing only a robe and slippers. "Will you give me time, at least, to dress and shave?"

One of them nodded. "You had better dress warmly. It is very cold outside."

Since they had been so agreeable about his dressing and shaving, Tolischus decided to try for a bit of breakfast. They didn't stop him. They were most cordial. Though he glowered at them, making no attempt to be pleasant, they smiled constantly as they drank his hard-to-get and preciously hoarded coffee.

Their leader spoke up warmly. "We are treating you like a gentleman."

Tolischus said, "I don't see why you shouldn't."

They were in such a happy mood his grumpiness didn't seem to affect them. Could it give them that much pleasure just to see him arrested? He examined the four men. None of them looked unfriendly. They kept glancing at each other with idiotically gleeful smiles on their faces.

One of them finally said to him, "I'll bet you don't know the big news."

Tolischus shook his head. "No, I guess I don't."

They were in no hurry to tell him. It was not until they had left his house, by the kitchen door, and crowded into a waiting taxi that one of them said, "There is a war between Japan and America, Britain, and the Dutch. Already there has been a battle. Manila, Singapore, and Hong Kong have been bombed."

It was not easy for Tolischus to digest this information, presented so abruptly, and accept the fact that it must be true. Even when war is half-expected, its actual beginning is like a blow to the stomach. He withdrew into his own private, depressing thoughts as the taxi moved through the awakening streets toward Akasaka, just to the west of the Toronamon district.

One of the men said, "You're a friend of Grew and Kase."

Tolischus wondered if that might be in some way incriminating. He decided he had better watch his remarks.

When they reached the Akasaka police station, the leader said, "Give me all your keys."

Without argument he obeyed. It was obvious now that they intended to search both his home and his office in an attempt to incriminate him. As the four policemen left the station, he was taken to a small, unheated room where he waited, under guard, for the outcome of their search.

DECEMBER 8,
7 A.M.

A T A N air base near Tainan in Formosa (which had been a Japanese colony since its conquest in the 1894–5 war with China), the crews of 192 land-based naval planes waited impatiently for the deep fog to lift so they could take off on what they assumed would be a war-opening mission against the Philippine Islands. Orderlies had passed through their quarters to awaken them at 2 A.M. (Tokyo time) for a scheduled 4 A.M. takeoff, but as four o'clock approached, so did the fog, and at takeoff time, the pilots, dressed for combat, stood by their airplanes, unable to see more than five yards in front of them.

Now, three hours later, they were still standing or sitting by their airplanes, looking at their watches, cursing the fog.

One of them, Flight Petty Officer Saburo Sakai, shouted through the impenetrable mist to one of the invisible pilots near him: "I think it's getting worse."

A disembodied voice answered, "How can you tell?"

"Now I can't even see my watch."

A bitter laugh echoed through the gloom.

Sakai was eager to get off the ground, not only because he coveted the honor of taking part in the war-opening attack but also because he loved flying more than anything else he had ever done. The affair between him and airplanes had begun hopelessly when, as a little boy on his father's one-acre Kyushu farm, he watched naval pilots from a nearby base fly overhead. Their speed enchanted him. To a farm boy, bogged down in the fields, such speed represented the ultimate freedom. But as the third of four sons in an impoverished Samurai family (the disestablishment of the Samurai class by Emperor Meiji in the late nineteenth century had reduced his grandfather to farming), he could hope for little more than to see, some day, an airplane on the ground. A charitable uncle in Tokyo had taken him there and put him in a Christian school. Overcome by homesickness, he had failed so dismally he was sent back home in disgrace. Eventually Sakai became an enlisted man in the navy, where he could, at least, realize his ambition to see airplanes on the ground. At night, he would secretly climb into them and pretend he was a pilot. After four years in the navy, his love of airplanes was no longer a secret. A pilot he met on the battleship *Haruna* encouraged him to try for flight training, and though he was almost excluded by the height minimum of 5 feet, 3½ inches, he kept taking the physical examination until, by breathing deeply and looking tall, he finally passed it.

Now a veteran of two and a half years as a fighter pilot in China, with 1,400 flying hours to his credit, he was a flight leader under the command of Captain Masahisa Saito, and was already considered by his superiors one of the most remarkable young pilots in the Japanese Navy. He had established the record for gasoline economy in Zero fighters, an accomplishment which helped account for the fact that this morning's mission against the Philippines could be launched from a land base almost 500 nautical miles away, in Formosa, thus freeing three carriers for duty elsewhere.

The three carriers had originally been assigned to the Philippine operation because it was considered impossible for Zeros to fly from Formosa to Luzon, engage in aerial battles, and return. The Zero was designed for flights of not more than six or seven hours. Under Captain Saito's direction, pilots like Sakai had proven, in exhausting test flights, that the plane was capable of much greater performance. They had developed so many techniques for saving gasoline that they could now undertake twelve-hour missions. Sakai had achieved his economy record by managing to keep his Zero in the air on less than 18 gallons per hour. Virtually ignoring his instruments, he flew as if the airplane were a physical part of him; he could feel the extent of its capabilities just as he could feel the strength of his own arm. He and his companions here in Tainan were among an elite group of Japanese naval aviators who could claim to be the best in the world. And during his two-and-a-half years in China, he had augmented his mechanical skills with the experience of uncounted combat missions.

He was ready now for the biggest mission of his life. He, Saburo Sakai, would soon have the distinction—if the damned fog would only lift—of taking part in the first act of a war against America. This would be nothing like the war in China. The American planes would be better, and so would the pilots. But he and his companions were ready for them and eager for the honor of being the first to face them. (They were, of course, unaware of events already taking place in Malaya and Hawaii.) It was beginning to seem though, that the moment would never come. The continuing fog was exasperating beyond endurance.

The loudspeaker system on the flight line crackled, indicating someone had turned it on and was about to speak. Sakai, like all the other pilots beside their airplanes, listened expectantly.

"Attention! Here is an important announcement," an amplified voice said "At zero-four-hundred hours this morning, a Japanese task force succeeded in carrying out a devastating surprise attack against the American forces in the Hawaiian Islands."

The immediate reaction to this announcement was the silence of shock. The Pearl Harbor secret had been guarded so closely that even these naval pilots, all of whom had friends on the Hawaiian mission, were completely unaware of it. When they began to comprehend the news, great shouts and cheers went up from one end of the flight line to the other. Men groped their way through the fog between planes to find companions with whom they could share reactions and speculations. A raid on Hawaii? From a task force? That meant carriers. Would they dare? And which carriers? How many? Who were the pilots? How could they have kept it so secret? Did he say "devastating"? That meant they had actually carried it off successfully. It was almost too good to believe.

Sakai embraced the first man he could find in the fog and they slapped each other on the backs as if they themselves had taken part in the Hawaiian raid. Then Sakai sobered and said, "But why are we cheering? While they attacked the enemy, we sat here on the ground."

He became abruptly aware now that he would not have the honor of taking part in the first act of the war. A wave of envious frustration consumed him. He shook a fist at the fog and cursed every vapor in it to avoid cursing those fellow navy pilots in Hawaii, whoever they were, who had already won for themselves the glory he had assumed would be his.

And when he was through cursing, another bleak reality occurred to him. By the time the miserable fog did lift, the Philippine defenses, because of the Hawaiian raid, would be fully alerted. Today's mission was likely to be the most difficult and perilous he had ever flown.

DECEMBER 8,
7 A.M.

HISATSUNE SAKOMIZU, a young official attached to the Japanese government Planning Board, gazed at the Tokyo street scene, but was too deeply occupied with his own disturbing thoughts to give much attention to the other people in the 7 A.M. Monday crowd hurrying to their jobs. Sakomizu himself was hurrying to the Tokyo Stock Exchange in the Kabuto-cho district in the center of the city, about a mile northeast of Ginza, at the behest of Finance Minister Okinori Kaya, under whom he had worked until November 1 when the Planning Board had asked for his services. Finance Minister Kaya had called him in the middle of the night, informed him of the war declaration about to be announced, and asked him, even though he was no longer in the Finance Ministry, to handle a financial matter of utmost delicacy and importance. Sakomizu was now on his way to try to fulfill Kaya's assignment.

An early morning news vendor was shouting, *"Senso! Senso!"* (War! War!) But though he waved his papers frantically at the faces in the passing crowds, nobody seemed to react to his astonishing news. It was as if people had not yet had time to comprehend the fact that war had actually come. Even those who bought papers from the excited vendor didn't seem to grasp what they were reading. They would glance at the banner story, which began, "Today at dawn, the Imperial Army and Navy entered into a state of war with . . . ," take two or three steps, stop to squint at what they were reading, then look up from the paper and hurry on about their business, their faces unchanged, as if they had stopped to glance at nothing more than an eye-catching advertisement. No one seemed to be discussing the news. The only words to be heard about it came from the vendor who kept shouting desperately, as if he could not endure the lack of response, *"Senso! Senso!"*

Sakomizu himself was no less shocked by the news than anyone else on the streets of Tokyo this chilly December morning. Despite Japan's aggravated disagreements with America, and despite the growing belligerence of the Japanese military establishment, he had been convinced that the crisis of the previous several months would ultimately be settled short of war. Having once spent a year and a half in New York working for an agency of the Japanese Finance Ministry, and having traveled between California and New York, he was sharply aware of America's awesome size and power, and he had always assumed Japanese military men were equally aware of it.

Despite the public fury aroused by ultramilitarist factions, he believed his nation's armed forces were controlled by sensible leaders, and he had enough faith in those leaders to feel certain they would never actually challenge the United States, however much they might feel provoked. It was a depressing disappointment to him to learn he had been wrong, especially since his father-in-law had been telling him for some time that he was wrong.

Sakomizu's father-in-law was a man who had reason to know. He was Admiral Keisuke Okada, for many years one of the most respected officers in the Japanese Navy, and from 1935 to 1936, the prime minister of Japan. Never militant himself, Prime Minister Okada had been saved from assassination by another man's courage in 1936 when a group of ultramilitant young army officers staged a bloody attempt at a coup d'état, which came to be known as the February 26th Incident.

After this abortive revolution, in which several high government officials were murdered, and in which Sakomizu himself helped save his father-in-law's life, the Japanese Army, despite the failure of the coup, or perhaps because of it, was able to increase its power and influence so sharply that Sakomizu, like most civil servants, found himself falling into closer and closer collaboration with the militarists. His father-in-law had not liked it. "Don't cooperate with them," Admiral Okada had kept telling him. When Sakomizu reflected this morning on how much more astutely than he the elderly admiral had judged the military, he also felt twinges of chagrin, but his dominant mood was depressive disappointment because, besides having to accept the fact that his country was now in an unpromising war, he felt compelled, as a loyal Japanese subject, to support the war with enthusiasm, however much he might deplore it.

His mission this morning was patriotic. It might also prove difficult. Finance Minister Kaya, having summoned him at 2 A.M. to his official residence in an old, Western-style house across the street from the Diet building, had said to him: "Even at this moment our navy may be attacking Hawaii. I'm sorry to tell you this. I'm afraid that when Japanese businessmen find out we've launched a war against America, they will become so alarmed the stock market will drop in the morning. If it drops, the enemy may think the Japanese people do not support the war. We must make sure that, however our businessmen react, stock prices will rise. That's your responsibility. I authorize you to do whatever is necessary."

When Sakomizu arrived at Kabuto-cho in Nihonbashi, brokers and their assistants were already hurrying into the triangular but round-faced Tokyo Stock Exchange building on the bank of one of the shipping canals that branch off the Sumida River. This peculiar building was an example of Japanese method in adapting Western classical architecture to the shortage of space in Tokyo. It was triangular because the ground allotted to it was triangular and all of it had to be used. The main entrance, at the point of the triangle just opposite a bridge over the canal, was rounded like a huge silo, with eight Doric columns and, sitting atop the columns, eight Romanesque statues sculpted by a Japanese artist. Sakomizu hurried to the president's office, a large, wood-paneled room with a beautiful parquet floor and fine leather overstuffed chairs. The president of the Exchange, Yahachi Aizawa, a dignified man in his middle years, showed by the expression on his face his concern about the war news even as he greeted the representative of the Finance Ministry.

"I have been sent here by Mr. Kaya," Sakomizu said, "to make sure the market rises today. He insists that it must not be allowed to fall. I'm sure you understand his reasoning under the circumstances."

Aizawa nodded. "We shall do everything possible."

With Aizawa's help, Sakomizu quickly assembled the most important men in the Exchange at the long table in the board of directors' room and asked for their advice. In addition to the president and vice-president of the Exchange, the chairman and subchairman of the Brokers' Association were also present. After very little discussion, they decided that the best psychological procedure would be to buy immediately a large block of stock in the Exchange itself, since this stock, called "Shinto," had long been regarded as a symbol of the market. In a rising market, the price of Shinto almost invariably rose. In a falling market, Shinto could be expected to fall. Sakomizu approved the brokers' suggestion and hurried to the balcony overlooking the huge buying and selling pit to observe the progress of their plan.

On the floor below him, almost a thousand men, brokers' representatives, Exchange employees, clerks and messengers, were milling around, waiting for the trading session to start. Sakomizu could sense no excitement in these men, though all of them must know by now that the war had begun. It looked like just an ordinary Monday morning.

Finally the market opened and Sakomizu watched closely as the transactions began. It did not take long for him to notice that there were too few transactions to raise his hopes. He knew the market well enough to observe unmistakeable signs of a dull, sluggish day ahead. Hoping fervently that the Brokers' Association plan would work, he watched the chairman of the association place an order for 20,000 shares of Shinto, then waited for the purchase to take effect. But nothing happened. Despite the purchase, the price of Shinto began to fall below the level of the previous Friday. Minutes passed without any encouraging sign. The pessimism in the pit was evident even in the balcony. Trading was slow. The blue-coated young men on the floor looked listless. Soon the general level of the market began settling into a gradual slump. Finance Minister Kaya's apprehension had been justified. Japanese businessmen obviously had little faith in a war against the United States of America.

DECEMBER 8,
7:30 A.M.

AS GENERAL TOJO'S limousine approached the Imperial Palace, the early morning sun was clear and the air cold. In the distance he could hear the sounds of bells announcing extra editions of the day's newspapers. Though he was accompanied by Colonel Akamatsu—in civilian clothes because he dealt with Tojo's civil rather than military functions—the two men exchanged few words. Tojo, pleased and surprised at the apparent extent of the Hawaiian success, dreaded nevertheless his imminent meeting with the Emperor, who had made his opposition to war so clear on so many occasions. When Tojo became prime minister in October, under the Emperor's charge to approach the American negotiations with a clean slate, he had felt there was still a chance for peace, though a slim one. Because he was to be prime minister, war minister, and home minister, he thought he would have more power than Prince Konoye, whom he was succeeding. But he had soon found that in his new eminence he had added more prestige than power. To the army, he was still just one of its generals, and he needed the army more than it needed him. In the Japanese governmental system—due to a concession made by army-dominated Prime Minister Koki Hirota after the frightening military coup attempt of February, 1936, only a general on active duty could be named war minister, and he had to be approved by the General Staff which could, therefore, end the regime of any prime minister simply by ordering the resignation of his war minister. This restriction ironically gave the war minister more power over the prime minister, to whom he was supposedly subordinate, than over the army, of which he was in titular command. Tojo, as war minister under army influence, had virtually forced the resignation of Prince Konoye. That might have shown him how little extra power was to be gained by adding to himself the duties of prime minister and home minister. His true power to govern resided in his continuing position as war minister. But this power could not long survive the displeasure of the army. Tojo had become acutely, uncomfortably aware of that in recent weeks during his efforts to extend the deadline for negotiations in Washington. Was the Emperor equally aware of it?

After walking the vast lengths of corridors which led to the waiting room for high officials in the Emperor's palace, Tojo arrived to find the army and navy chiefs of staff, General Gen Sugiyama and Admiral Osami Nagano there ahead of him. They too had come to report the opening of the war and the remarkable successes accompanying it. The chiefs of staff had independent access to the Emperor because in the Japanese system both services reported to him directly, not to the prime minister. They didn't report, however, in the sense of soliciting his desires or accepting his orders. Their usual procedure was simply to tell him what they planned to do, or what they had already done, and his usual procedure was to listen without comment. The Emperor had no agency at his disposal to investigate what the services were doing, nor did he envision himself as having the authority to supervise their operations. Even when the army informed him that it had launched the Manchurian war in 1931, and again that it had launched the China Incident in 1937, he had accepted these accomplished facts with resignation if not with approval.

This system would seem to make the chiefs of staff all-powerful, but in practice its workings were even more complex. Like the war minister, the chiefs, too, were dependent on the rest of the generals (or admirals) who, in turn, were deeply dependent on their own younger subordinate officers, most of whom were ultramilitant. The generals had become captives, not all unwillingly, of a now well-established tradition of young officers taking direct political action with their guns and swords, a tradition originally fostered by certain generals to increase the army's power over the government. The February 26, 1936, incident, for instance, in which the prime minister, Admiral Okada, narrowly escaped death, and which was not put down until Emperor Hirohito took personal charge and ordered the army to end it, was one of a series of disturbances in the 1930s, perpetrated by young officers but often encouraged by their superiors, which gradually heightened the country's right-wing, militaristic fever by eliminating or intimidating moderate leaders both in the army and in politics. Seven statesmen, including Viscount Makoto Saito, then lord keeper of the privy seal, were killed by the extremists in the February 26 incident. The Emperor's grand chamberlain, Admiral Kantaro Suzuki, a hero of the Russo-Japanese War, was left almost dead with four bullets in his body. And Prime Minister Okada was spared only because the soldiers assigned to kill him had mistakenly killed another man, his brother-in-law, instead.

In 1930, an extremist had murdered the then prime minister, Yuko Hamaguchi, because his government had accepted the terms of the London Naval Treaty which limited the size of the Japanese fleet. In 1931, the passionately nationalistic Kodo-ha army faction had failed in an attempted military coup only because a few key officers refused to take part. In 1932, a group of young navy officers and army cadets had murdered the then prime minister, Tsuyoshi Inukai, because he was one of the "evil advisers" around the Emperor. In 1933 and 1934, police arrested batches of young officers suspected of plotting coups against the government, but as the 1936 rebellion proved, these arrests did not deter the extremist groups. Even the generals themselves were unsafe. In August of 1935, Major General Tetsuzan Nagata, chief of the army's powerful Military Affairs Bureau, and himself an ardent nationalist who was suspected of supporting a previous coup attempt, was butchered by the Samurai sword of a lieutenant colonel who considered him not quite ardent enough. General Nagata had been a close friend of General Tojo, who was at that time in Manchuria. Each new outbreak served notice on moderate officers and politicians that another, more successful or at least more bloody one, might take place at any time. Everyone in Japan, from the Emperor on down, seemed to get the message. The succession of outbreaks by young officers, instead of discrediting the army, strengthened it. The government was forced to seek its protection, because if the army couldn't prevent the depredations of the young officers, there was no other agency that could hope to do so. By now, however, the generals having condoned, protected, and encouraged the extremists for so many years, had lost both the ability and the inclination to control them. The young officers and their factions had become so dangerous that it was healthier for a general to be popular with them than to be respected by them. Every general in the Japanese Army was aware of this, and many conducted themselves accordingly. Perhaps it was with the power of the young officers in mind that General Sugiyama had once said it was the duty of a general to comply with his staff, and that it was a bad general who relied on his own ideas. Sugiyama was already, in 1941, the army's most honored general, possibly because he could accept so readily the realities of army life. He was the only man who had held the army's three top positions—inspector general of military education, war minister, and now chief of staff.

At this moment General Sugiyama was easily the happiest man in the waiting room. Tojo, though he believed in the war, had not yet been able to overcome his guilt for disappointing the Emperor. Admiral Nagano, though he was elated at the news from Pearl Harbor, and had argued that the war must be launched quickly if at all, was nevertheless, like many other navy men, eaten by pessimism about the eventual outcome. General Sugiyama was not burdened by guilt or pessimism. He had once said, "If we are strong, the other side will back down." He was quite confident that as soon as the Americans tasted a few defeats, they would be ready for truly meaningful negotiations rather than the arrogant stalling tactics they had used against Japan since April.

The three men had just exchanged greetings when Marquis Koichi Kido entered the room. After coming to the palace in the middle of the night to facilitate Foreign Minister Togo's audience with the Emperor, he had returned home for a few hours of sleep, and had just now arrived back at the palace for what he knew would be a busy day. Because the Emperor had not wanted war, Marquis Kido had done everything he considered appropriate in an effort to avert it. The selection of War Minister Tojo as prime minister, had been, in his mind, the strongest possible move away from war, since Tojo had seemed to him the only man who might be able to control the extremists in the army. Though Kido's hopes in this direction had failed to materialize, he was not depressed about it. On his way to the palace this morning, as he reached the top of the Akasaka Mitsuke slope near the Diet building, he had gazed at the sun rising brilliantly above the city skyline and had decided that this rising sun was symbolic of his country's destiny now that it had entered war against the two greatest powers in the world. He had closed his eyes and prayed for the success of those navy planes which must already have completed their attack against Hawaii.

Anxious about the results of the attack, he was pleased, when he reached the palace, to find the prime minister and the chiefs of staff in the high officials' waiting room.

"What news have you had from Hawaii?" he asked.

Since this was a navy project, Tojo and Sugiyama turned to Nagano, who said, "The reports are so good we're afraid to believe them. Several ships sunk, including more than one battleship. And many, many airplanes destroyed."

When Marquis Kido heard this, he again closed his eyes in a prayer of thanksgiving. He felt that the gods had indeed come to the aid of his country.

A chamberlain arrived to tell the prime minister that His Majesty was ready to see him, and Tojo, with mixed feelings, followed his escort to the much smaller imperial receiving room which he had now come to know so well, but which he still entered with reverence. To him, the divinity of the Emperor was more than a legend; he saw in the Emperor a man who, by his own benevolence and quiet understanding, stood one step higher than anyone else. Tojo, speaking to his wife, had once said of him, "The Emperor has put divinity into himself."

As His Majesty entered the room, Tojo bowed deeply at the waist, then straightening himself to his usual erect bearing, examined the expression on the Emperor's face. It was a relief to notice that he appeared serene.

Tojo spoke slowly, respectfully. "When Your Majesty chose me to be prime minister in October, you directed me to begin with a clean slate as far as international relations were concerned. I feel I can say sincerely that I did so. But when the final note from Secretary Hull arrived on November 27, the situation changed abruptly. Your Majesty's government reached the conclusion that we would have to go to war against Britain and America. We have asked for your consent to do so and you have given it. We have been at all times sensible, however, of Your Majesty's great reluctance to resort to war."

The Emperor said, wistfully, "We have enjoyed a friendly alliance with England for so many years . . ."

Tojo nodded, "I am deeply aware of it, Your Majesty."

"And the British Royal Family treated me so magnificently during my journey there twenty years ago."

In 1921, when he was still the crown prince, Hirohito had made a grand tour of Europe which shattered precedent for Japanese royalty, and which left him with many memories he would always cherish, memories of a freedom which, as a Japanese prince and Emperor, he could never enjoy at home. When he visited England, King George and Queen Mary had taken him into Buckingham Palace and treated him as if he were one of their own sons. The king had even walked into his bedroom one morning, wearing slippers and without a necktie. "If there's anything you need," he had said, "just ask for it. I'll never forget how your grandfather [Emperor Meiji] treated my brother and me when we were in Yokohama. I've always wanted to repay his kindness. No geishas here, though, I'm afraid. Her Majesty would never allow it." Even more amazing than the informality of the king was the liberty allowed to the Prince of Wales, with whom Hirohito had played golf and attended a succession of public functions, and whom he quickly came to admire. The whole Royal Family had been a marvelous revelation to him. It was they who had introduced him to what was now his favorite breakfast: bacon and eggs.

Standing uncomfortably in his Japanese naval uniform, Hirohito mused for a moment about his warm memories of England, then quickly recalling himself to the duties of a Japanese emperor, put all such thoughts from his mind. He gazed sadly at Prime Minister Tojo who would now have to share with him the burden of a most difficult war. He could scarcely blame Tojo for failing to avert the war during his eight short weeks as prime minister. He himself had failed equally during sixteen years as emperor. He shook his head thoughtfully.

"I guess there was no other way."

Tojo, after a long pause, sensed that the audience was at an end. He was preparing himself for the farewell bows when the Emperor decided to mention another matter before he retired from the room.

"In the rescript," he said, "there is one personal feeling I would like to have expressed. I would like you to include words to the effect that it was not my will to start the war."

DECEMBER 8,
7:30 A.M.

AMBASSADOR Grew, having been awakened at 7 A.M. by an urgent summons from the Japanese Foreign Office, arrived at the official residence of Foreign Minister Togo at 7:30, the second time he had been there in seven hours. He might perhaps have been summoned even earlier but for the fact that the Foreign Office had trouble reaching him by telephone; the Tokyo Metropolitan Police had already cut the lines to the American Embassy. Had he been less hurried, Ambassador Grew might also have noticed, as he left the huge, white-walled compound of the embassy in the expensive Toranomon district, that it was surrounded this morning by an unusually large number of men. But Grew had a more important matter on his mind. He arrived at the foreign minister's residence full of hope that his requested audience with the Emperor had finally been arranged.

In the second-floor reception room which he had visited the previous midnight Grew was again greeted by Togo's interpreter, Toshikazu Kase, and together they waited uncomfortably for the foreign minister's entrance. When Togo came into the room, he wore the same formal dress he had put on for his audience with the Emperor, and not having slept all night (at 4:30 A.M., after returning from the Imperial Palace, he had been informed by a phone call from the Navy Ministry of the success of the surprise attack on Hawaii), he already felt the strain of what would no doubt be a very arduous day. He felt also the strain of anticipating a most difficult interview with Grew. The ambassador, though he did not yet know that Japan was now at war with his country, nevertheless wore a grave expression on his face. He had never found Togo a very prepossessing man; he found him this morning to be as formal as his attire and even more grim than usual. Grew did not receive from Togo's appearance, however, any impression of extraordinary developments.

Togo, taking equal notice of Grew's serious expression, and unaware that Grew was at least partially reacting to his own gravity, assumed the ambassador had heard on the radio the Imperial Headquarters war announcement. Expecting from the American some show of anger and vituperation, Togo began the interview in a self-protectively aggressive style.

Slapping down on a table a document which contained the Emperor's reply to President Roosevelt, he said in Japanese, speaking loudly to accommodate both his own vehement mood and Grew's distressing deafness, "In regard to the personal message of President Roosevelt to His Majesty, the Emperor, which you brought last night, I had an opportunity, after meeting you, to obtain the Emperor's opinion. The Emperor ordered me to transmit, through you, the following, as a reply to the president's message"

He then repeated the Japanese words he and Prime Minister Tojo had carefully composed: " 'Some days ago, the president made inquiries regarding the circumstances of the augmentation of Japanese forces in French Indochina to which His Majesty has directed the government to reply. Withdrawal of Japanese forces from French Indochina constitutes one of the subject matters of the Japanese-American negotiations. His Majesty has commanded the government to state its views to the American government also on this question. It is, therefore, desired that the president will kindly refer to this reply.

" 'Establishment of peace in the Pacific and consequently of the world has been the cherished desire of His Majesty for the realization of which He has hitherto made the government to continue its earnest endeavors. His Majesty trusts that the president is fully aware of this fact.' "

Though Togo had paused after every few words to give the interpreter time to translate, the purposeful obscurities in the message made it difficult for Grew to determine its exact meaning. Was this all the Emperor had to say in answer to such an urgent appeal from the president? It now seemed to Grew more important than ever that he press for a meeting with Hirohito.

"I shall, of course, transmit this message to Washington," he said, "but I should like also to call your attention again to my specific instructions, which are that I request an audience with His Majesty and discuss the president's message with him in person. Since relations between our two countries have now reached such a critical stage, I consider it more than ever essential that arrangements be made for a personal audience."

As Foreign Minister Togo stared up into the long, slender face of his visitor, a face that showed no sign of guile, it began to dawn upon him that Grew actually did not know war had started between the United States and Japan. Togo's position was, therefore, even more difficult and embarrassing than he had anticipated. Should he break the news, or should he, by saying nothing, keep this final meeting with the ambassador on the friendliest possible level? If the fact of war were to enter the discussion, it would become necessary to explain the delicate timing of the surprise attack on Hawaii. Admiral Nomura, the Japanese ambassador to the United States, had been instructed to hand Secretary of State Hull, at 3 A.M. Tokyo time (12:30 P.M. of the 7th in Washington) a notice announcing termination of the negotiations there. The attack against Hawaii had apparently begun before 3:30 A.M., Tokyo time. The interval was so short it would be difficult to explain. The navy should not have been so stubborn about making it a surprise attack. Togo had argued this matter heatedly during a war-planning conference on November 26. When he pointed out that notification should be made through usual procedures, Admiral Osami Nagano, the navy chief of staff, had said, "But we plan to make a surprise attack." And Admiral Seichi Ito, the vice chief of staff, had declared that the navy wanted negotiations with America to continue until after the first attack, in order to achieve maximum surprise. Togo, denouncing the navy's plan for a surprise attack, insisted that a war declaration would be absolutely essential to maintain Japan's good name among nations. At the next war-planning conference, Admiral Ito, speaking for the navy, agreed that the American State Department could be given a notification in Washington at 12:30 P.M. on the 7th, but it was to be a notification of the end of negotiations, not a declaration of war. Togo had then said, "Will there be a proper interval between notification and attack?" And when Ito assured him there would be, he had assented to the plan. It now appeared, however, that the interval had been embarrassingly short. It would be easier not to discuss the matter with Ambassador Grew.

Moving along to his second delicate purpose in summoning the ambassador, Togo handed him another, much longer document. "This is a copy," he said, "of a memorandum Admiral Nomura has already, I'm sure, handed to Secretary Hull in Washington. The memorandum, I am sorry to inform you, brings to an end the negotiations between your country and mine."

As he spoke, Togo was painfully aware that the memorandum fell short of the war declaration on which he had insisted at the November 26 conference. The war against America was, however, a war of self-defense. He had satisfied himself of that. Secretary of State Hull had sent to Japan on November 26 a note that was unquestionably an ultimatum. It demanded Japan's complete withdrawal, not only from French Indochina, but from the entire mainland of China. It demanded that Japan recognize and accept in China the enemy government of Chiang Kai-shek. It demanded that Japan sign a nonaggression pact, not only with Chiang, but with the United States, Great Britain, the Netherlands, and Thailand. And the only concession it made, if it could be called such, was that America, Britain, the Netherlands, and Thailand would renounce extraterritorial rights in China. Would it not have been national suicide for Japan to have accepted the terms of such a note? To fight against such impossible demands could not be called anything other than self-defense, and it was generally accepted among diplomats that a war of self-defense required no declaration. The United States had long ago asserted a policy that gave its president the right to exercise national self-defense at any time or place, and when an American punitive mission invaded Mexico without a war declaration in 1916, it had been explained as an act of self-defense. Taking all these considerations into account, Togo had decided it was quite reasonable to look upon a notice ending negotiations as the equivalent of a declaration of war.

Grew glanced quickly through the long document. It accused the United States of purposely delaying the negotiations between the two countries which had been in progress since the previous April, of refusing to make concessions, of insisting on unrealistic theories about relations between nations, of joining Great Britain and other countries in an attempt to dominate East Asia, and of plotting to destroy Japan's position in the world. "The earnest hope of the Japanese government to preserve and promote the peace of the Pacific," it declared, "has finally been lost." Under such conditions Japan could not but consider "that it is impossible to reach an agreement through further negotiations." This document, the ambassador decided, was the Emperor's actual answer to President Roosevelt's appeal. A breaking-off of negotiations. It did not lessen his determinatin to see the Emperor in person.

Looking down at Togo, Grew said, "It seems to me on reading this memorandum that it is more than ever important for me to see His Majesty in person. My relations with His Majesty have been at all times cordially proper. The heads of state of our two countries have always been extremely gracious in making themselves available, on important occasions, to each other's representatives. Am I to conclude from your present remarks that my request for an audience on this occasion is to be denied?"

Togo replied with equal firmness and formality. "If the purpose of your audience with His Majesty is simply to present the president's message in person, I feel it may be unnecessary, since His Majesty's opinion is as previously stated. However, I have no intention whatsoever of interfering with your desires. If you have something to add besides the personal message, I shall naturally give considerations." He paused, then asked, "Is there something else you wish to discuss with His Majesty in addition to what I have already presented him in writing?"

Ambassador Grew, bewildered by the foreign minister's impenetrable manner, studied him deliberately, then recognizing even though he could not comprehend Togo's absolute determination to keep him from the Emperor, decided he must give up, at least temporarily, his own resolve to gain audience. Shaking his head slowly, he said, "No, at the moment I have nothing additional to discuss with him."

Having secured this admission, Togo quickly brought the meeting to an end. He had no time to waste since he had already missed a cabinet meeting and was due at a Privy Council meeting, but his situation vis-à-vis Grew was now so equivocal he felt he could not say good-bye without a few friendly personal words. He took the time, therefore, to preserve his usual custom of walking downstairs with the ambassador, and before his farewell bow, he said, "In spite of the situation which has arisen, Mr. Ambassador, I wish to express my own appreciation for all of your efforts to preserve the peace."

Though Togo hoped this remark would be accepted as a gesture of warmth and friendship, his limitations in conveying such qualities led Grew to regard it as simply a formality, a polite little speech designed to soften the fact that Japan and the United States had reached a diplomatic impasse. As Grew entered his limousine to return to the embassy, he felt deep concern about this impasse, but also some degree of relief at having determined that nothing more serious had occurred than the breaking-off of conversations.

DECEMBER 8,
7:30 AM, NOON IN HAWAII

A S M I D D A Y approached in Hawaii, Ensign Kazuo Sakamaki and his one-man crew, Petty Officer Kiyoshi Imagaki, were still struggling, after repeated failures, to navigate their crippled midget submarine into Pearl Harbor. Though they hadn't come very close to achieving their goal, they had done well so far merely to remain alive in spite of the malfunctioning of their gyroscope, the loss of their periscope, and the peril of several depth charges dropped by the two American destroyers guarding the harbor mouth. One reason the sub had not been wiped out by depth charges was that, navigating blind underwater, Sakamaki did not always get near enough to the harbor entrance to attract the attention of the destroyers. But he and Imagaki had continued trying. They were now charging again in what they hoped was the direction of the elusive passage, and they were taking consolation from the fact that for some time they had not been attacked by more depth charges. Perhaps they had finally escaped the infernal destroyers.

If so, it was only to encounter new dangers.

A long, screeching, agonizing scrape, then a banging clatter like the sound of metal crashing against a wall, brought the submarine to a jolting stop. Had they hit bottom? Worse than that, Sakamaki concluded. Having absorbed most of the Japanese Navy's knowledge of the ocean floor around the Hawaiian coast, he decided they were stuck on a coral reef. Now he would have to call on all the strength of the little submarine's oversized engine, which, fortunately, was so powerful the craft could travel at 24 knots underwater. Sakamaki applied full reverse thrust and held his breath. Nothing happened. He gave the engine a rest, then tried again. The sub shuddered but did not move. Finally, on the fourth try, a slight scraping sound indicated it had moved at least a few inches. The scraping sound increased. The sweating faces of Sakamaki and Imagaki broke into wide smiles. They were moving backward at a rapid rate. They had escaped the reef.

They had only a few moments to celebrate before a hissing sound assailed them. Imagaki, after tracking it down, reported that the compressed air was leaking. So was the battery gas. And one of the torpedoes had also been damaged by the coral reef.

It was no longer possible for Sakamaki to conceal his discouragement. He could only superimpose upon it a renewed determination. He would not rest until he had torpedoed a battleship. He had no way of knowing, despite the smoke he had seen rising from Pearl Harbor, that most of the battleships there had been fairly well torpedoed by this time, and that the attack planes had long since returned to their carriers. Again, after a quick, dangerous peek above the surface, he adjusted his course toward the harbor mouth. Closer now than he had ever been, he began to feel a degree of confidence. During his few moments on the surface, he had seen no obstructions. Soon he would be inside the harbor at last, ready to launch his one undamaged torpedo.

While he waited tensely for the time to pass, however, the submarine was again drifting off course. And the next sound he heard was the now-familiar scraping of the hull against another coral reef. Once more he applied full reverse power, and once more he managed to pull back from a reef. But now, Imagaki reported a new calamity. The second torpedo had been damaged.

This was the worst development of all. The submarine was disarmed. Sakamaki could not possibly fulfill his mission. He had failed irrevocably. He had disgraced himself in his own eyes. Instead of dying gloriously as he had expected (since there was no hope of returning from a mission like this), he would now die in vain without ever repaying his *on*—his debt to the Emperor, to his country, to his ancestors, to his family, to the navy, to his friends. The whole pattern of obligations he owed to so many people and to so many institutions, simply for the privilege of being alive and being Japanese, would go unfulfilled.

Imagaki said, "What do we do now, sir?"

In a burst of anger, Sakamaki said, "The only thing to do is to plunge right into the *Pennsylvania!*" He was referring to the flagship of the U.S. fleet.

Imagaki said, "Yes sir."

"If we can't torpedo a battleship, we'll climb on deck and kill as many of the enemy as possible. Won't we?"

"Yes sir."

Again Sakamaki adjusted their course toward the harbor mouth.

DECEMBER 8,
8 A.M.

I T   W A S just eight o'clock when the thirty-two members of the Privy Council, including the prime minister and his cabinet, stood expectantly and turned toward the door of the east antechamber of the Emperor's palace, where they were assembled. The Emperor entered, impeccable in his naval uniform, and the whole roomful of people, in unison, reverently bowed from the waist. He walked silently to his table at the front and sat down. His face was without expression.

Near the Emperor, at the head of one of two long, facing tables, the president of the Privy Council, Yoshimichi Hara, and the vice-president, Baron Admiral Kantaro Suzuki, took their places, with the sixteen other councilors ranged beside them in descending order. Opposite them, at the second long table, sat Prime Minister Tojo and the thirteen members of his cabinet, all of whom were ex-officio members of the council. In front of each member was a copy of the imperial rescript which was one of the urgent matters on which the council would now be asked to vote.

The Privy Council, composed of a panel of distinguished imperial appointees, plus the prime minister and his cabinet, had the duty of ratifying all laws, treaties, and agreements before they became legal under the terms of the Japanese constitution. This gave the council a technical veto power over the government but it was a power that could rarely be exercised because the prime minister and his cabinet comprised almost half the council. The cabinet's voting power might be a fortunate circumstance for Prime Minister Tojo today because there were several members of the Privy Council, the two top officers in particular, of whose support he was not certain.

Council president Hara, sometimes regarded as an unofficial spokesman for the Emperor, had often made clear his opposition to war, and to the succession of moves which had led toward war. At an imperial conference September 19, 1940, just before Japan signed its alliance with Germany and Italy, Hara had spoken prophetically about the probable American reaction.

"This pact," he had said, "is a treaty of alliance with the United States as its target. . . . When Japan's position becomes clear with the announcement of this pact, she [the United States] will greatly increase her pressure on us, she will greatly step up her aid to Chiang Kai-shek, and she will obstruct Japan's war effort [in China]. I assume that the United States, which has not declared war on Germany and Italy, will put economic pressure on Japan without declaring war on us. She will probably ban the export of oil and iron, and will refuse to purchase goods from us. She will attempt to weaken us over the long term so that we will not be able to endure war. The president of the planning board [at that time Naoki Hoshino] has said that all available steps will be taken to obtain iron and oil, but the results are uncertain. . . . You cannot carry on a war without oil. The capital in Netherlands East Indies oil is British and American, and the Dutch government [routed by Germany's occupation of Holland] has fled to England; so I think it will be impossible to obtain oil from the Netherlands East Indies by peaceful means. I would like to hear the government's views on this."

General Tojo, at that time the war minister, had given Hara the government's views in his characteristically quick, succinct style: "As for the Netherlands East Indies," he said, "the government has a policy: It desires to obtain materials peacefully from there, but depending on the circumstances, it could use force."

Hara, though he had eventually given his approval to the Tripartite Alliance—it was customary for Japanese statesmen to vote for policies they opposed but could not defeat—had reiterated his reluctance as he did so. "We shall encounter many difficulties," he had said. "We cannot be optimistic about the possibility of an American embargo. Even though a Japanese-American clash may be unavoidable in the end, I hope that sufficient care will be exercised to make sure that it will not come in the near future, and that there will be no miscalculations."

Perhaps even more strongly opposed to war and apprehensive about it was the Privy Council's vice-president, the popular, 75-year-old naval hero, Baron Admiral Kantaro Suzuki. The son of a minor Samurai lord in the service of the Tokugawas, he was born in 1867, one year before the Meiji restoration, and therefore one year before his father was to lose his comfortable position. As soon as young Suzuki finished middle school he had entered the naval academy to begin a career which had included almost every honor the navy could offer. During Admiral Togo's climactic Battle of Tsushima Straits in the Russo-Japanese War, he had commanded a cruiser which sank two enemy ships. He had subsequently become commander in chief of the fleet, military adviser to the Emperor, navy chief of staff, and, on retirement in 1929, the Emperor's grand chamberlain, a post he still held when, in 1936, he was an almost fatal victim of the young militarists during the February 26 incident. About 40 soldiers had rushed into his official residence near the Imperial Palace at five o'clock that morning, determined to kill him because they considered him a bad influence on the Emperor. He had opposed the army's Manchurian war in 1931, and he had often been indiscreetly critical of the army, most of whose leaders he considered narrow in their viewpoints. Warned that the soldiers were coming after him, he had arisen from his bed and searched for his sword, determined to go down fighting in the Samurai tradition from which he had sprung, but since he had never before had occasion to use his sword, he couldn't find it, and therefore had to face the soldiers unarmed.

"Why are you doing such a thing?" he asked them as they burst into his bedroom.

One of them said, "We haven't enough time to talk about it."

Suzuki said, "Go ahead, then, shoot."

A corporal raised his pistol immediately and fired four bullets into him—one in the forehead which came out behind his ear, one in the left chest, one in the left thigh, and one in the groin. As Suzuki fell, the corporal knelt and was about to finish his job with a fifth bullet. He was stopped by one of his leaders, a captain who had twice met the admiral and so greatly admired him he suddenly lost his resolve to kill him. At this captain's order he was spared, and after several months recovered from his wounds, though he still carried a bullet in his groin.

After the February 26 incident, the Emperor, to show both his feelings for Suzuki and his displeasure with the militarists, had made the retired admiral a baron and appointed him to the Privy Council.

As Suzuki now gazed across to the opposite table where General Tojo sat with his cabinet, he reflected again on a long-held belief, that the military should never be allowed to have a strong voice in government. The army, with its militant young officers, its secret police, and its constant meddling in politics had brought the country to a war it had little chance of winning. In the past ten years the lack of control over the young army officers had been inexcusable. Though there were also a lot of young naval officers spoiling for war (Suzuki regarded this as a disease they had caught from the young army officers), there were not enough of them to intimidate the admirals the way the generals had been intimidated. It would be interesting now to see how successful these eager young warriors would be at intimidating the Americans and the British. The outlook was depressingly dismal. Most of the Privy Council members with whom Suzuki had discussed it agreed with him about that. But what were their options?

Council President Hara began the meeting by reading aloud the rescript which Chief Cabinet Secretary Naoki Hoshino had submitted. As he read, each member followed his own copy of the text. When Hara asked for comments after his reading, it was a mere formality. On a matter like this a discussion would not be expected, but one member, an elder statesman named Nariaki Ikeda, had a question to raise. He addressed himself to the second paragraph of the document which began as follows: "We hereby declare war on America and England . . ."

"All of us understand," Ikeda said, "that the official name of 'America' is 'the United States of America,' and as for 'England,' it is called 'Great Britain' or 'the British Empire.' So when we declare war against these countries, would it not be courteous to use their formal names, even though they are our enemies? To use abbreviations like 'America' and 'England' would be improper for a country like Japan, which puts so much emphasis on politeness and courtesy."

Ikeda's objection began a short argument, ever polite and courteous, about the phraseology of the paragraph. Though the man in whose name these words would soon be issued was present in the room, he was not invited to offer his views on the question. Foreign

Minister Togo spoke in defense of the rescript as it was. He said it needed no changes and others nodded their aggreement.

An elderly foreign affairs specialist named Kikujiro Ishi said, "No one could possibly take offense at the use of terms like 'America' and 'England.' We have used them before in official documents."

Ikeda was still not quite convinced.

General Tojo glanced at his watch as he listened to the discussion. These old men were vaguely reminiscent of that other group of elder statesmen, the *Jushin* (former prime ministers) whose questions he had been forced to answer at a meeting the Emperor insisted on holding for them just before the December 1 imperial conference at which the final war plans were settled. The Emperor had wanted to invite the Jushin to the conference itself, but that was one imperial request Tojo had firmly refused. He couldn't have a handful of deposed prime ministers disrupting one of the most crucial imperial conferences in the nation's history and then walking away with military secrets which only the fewest possible people should know. The Emperor had therefore invited them to a separate meeting at the palace and Tojo had patiently answered their questions about the impending war, without, however, confirming the fact that war was actually about to begin. At least, the Jushin had asked some important questions: Where will we get enough vital materials like oil? Can we endure a long war against the big powers? Will the morale of the people hold up? How would you plan to terminate such a war? That question was the most vexing of all. How could anyone be expected to have the answer to it? What could anyone say? Tojo was not very happy with what he had said, honest though it was. "The government will investigate the possibility of negotiating peace at a proper time through the Soviet Union or the Vatican. But we don't yet have a definite plan in which we are confident, so if any of you have a plan, please be so kind as to suggest it. If we succeed initially, we should soon secure enough strong positions to enable us to hold out in a protracted war. And of course we'll do everything possible to force China and Britain out of the war, thus weakening America's will to fight. This is the policy on which we shall proceed. But as of now we have no means in view to bring the war to an end. We shall have to work it out according to circumstances." When he had problems to solve like those the Jushin had mentioned, it was not easy for him to sit here this morning, on the first day of the war, listening to an argument about the proper names for 'America' and 'England.'

He shifted uncomfortably in his chair and glanced back at Naoki Hoshino who was listening attentively as the privy councilors argued.

Hoshino, though the rescript was his project, felt no displeasure or impatience with Ikeda's criticism of it. The elder statesman's attitude seemed to him very impressive. On a day when the amazing news from Hawaii put most people in a mood to celebrate, it was good to see someone insisting quietly but firmly that the rescript must not be issued until everything about it was absolutely proper. Ikeda was saying much more than his words indicated. He was saying, in effect, that whatever Japan did must be absolutely correct.

Finally, Ikeda was satisfied. There was no more discussion of the rescript's wording. Nobody mentioned the third paragraph in which the Emperor's personal feelings about the war might be discerned. As a result of his request to Prime Minister Tojo, that paragraph now read as follows:

To ensure the stability of East Asia and to contribute to world peace is the far-sighted policy which was formulated by our Great Illustrious Imperial Grandsire and Our Great Imperial Sire succeeding Him, and which we lay constantly to heart. To cultivate friendship among nations and to enjoy prosperity in common with all nations has always been the guiding principle of Our Empire's foreign policy. It has been truly unavoidable and far from our wishes that Our Empire has now been brought to cross swords with America and Britain . . .

President Hara spoke again. "In accordance with out constitutional duty," he said, "this council will vote on two questions: Do we certify that this nation is now legally at war with the United States, the British Empire, and the kingdom of the Netherlands? And do we approve His Majesty's most gracious rescript as it now stands? Both measures will be decided at once by voice vote."

Sitting near Hara, old Admiral Kantaro Suzuki listened with frustration and anger as the succession of "yes" votes moved around the room tow ird him from the lips of one member to another. Tojo's "yes" came loud and sharp. When Suzuki's turn arrived, only two votes remained unregistered—his own and Hara's. The whole thing seemed a pointless charade. The army had long since decided the entire matter, as well as the destiny of the country. Yet the charade must be neatly concluded. Every vote so far had been a "yes." There was no other choice. The planes were already bombing. The soldiers were already fighting.

Suzuki cleared his throat. "Yes," he said, in a voice still firm but definitely aged.

He turned to Hara, who also said "yes." It was unanimous. Japan was officially at war. Everyone turned toward the Emperor. Without a word, Hirohito arose and left the room.

DECEMBER 8,
SHORTLY BEFORE 9 A.M.

LIEUTENANT Matsuzaki, mindful of the possibility that his weakened rudder cable might break when he tried to land, waited for the other planes in the second wave to reach their carriers safely before he approached the *Akagi*. Aside from stragglers, therefore, Fuchida's plane was the last to regain the task force, which was easy to find now in the bright Pacific sunlight. So easy to find that Fuchida feared American planes might locate it at any moment. Matsuzaki brought his plane in gently, on a long, straight, shallow approach, and it came to a stop on deck without mishap.

Fuchida, descending from the plane, hurried to the briefing room where he found almost as much excitement as he had just seen over Pearl Harbor. The room was full of pilots, those of the second wave undressing from the flight they had just completed, while those of the first wave prepared for an anticipated third wave. All were shouting, laughing, trading experiences, counting their kills, happily describing the incredible desolation they had left behind them, while an intelligence officer passed among them, trying to compile some kind of comprehensive result from their exuberant and overlapping stories.

"How many planes did we lose?" Fuchida asked him.

"Ten from the first wave," he said. "We don't yet know about the second. There may be some more stragglers coming in."

"Only ten from the first wave?" Fuchida was happy to settle for that. Then he sobered. "But I'm afraid the second wave was not so fortunate."

A second-wave pilot, standing near him, shook his head in agreement. "There weren't many enemy planes in the air, but they were tough. They never stopped coming at us."

Fuchida said to the intelligence officer, "Have you had time to add up the results?"

"I haven't yet talked to everyone, but as of now, it looks like two or three battleships sunk, two badly damaged, and three slightly damaged. Two cruisers and three destroyers damaged, and about 250 planes destroyed. Does that sound possible?"

"It sounds even better than I had thought," Fuchida said, "but I wasn't as close as the boys in the dive bombers and torpedo bombers. Is that the report you get from them?"

"Yes sir."

"Then I believe it."

He called for order and was just beginning to quiet his men when the telephone rang. It was for him. Admiral Nagumo himself was on the line.

"I'm anxious to see you, Commander." Was there, perhaps, a touch of impatience in the admiral's voice? Was he annoyed because Fuchida had gone to see his pilots before reporting to him? "I'm eager to hear the results."

Fuchida, hurrying to the bridge, found Admiral Nagumo and his entire staff awaiting him. Fuchida's friend, Minoru Genda, with whom he had worked on the training and detailed planning for the raid, greeted him with a jubilant smile, as did most of the staff. Admiral Nagumo himself, more restrained, looked pleasantly expectant.

"I understand," he said, "you have a very successful operation to report."

Fuchida bowed. "Yes sir," he said, "Very successful." As he began to describe it in detail his voice rose slightly and his words poured out in an increasingly rapid stream. There were so many details, all so triumphant, he kept hastening from one to another in a headlong effort to get everything said before something slipped his mind. Nagumo and his staff listened carefully. After Fuchida finished describing the entire operation, and the scene at Pearl Harbor as he left it, he concluded, "But despite all we accomplished, there are still enough targets to keep us busy until nightfall. The oil storage tanks! They haven't even been touched. And they're so easy."

When Fuchida stopped, everyone waited through a long silence for Admiral Nagumo to speak. He said, simply, "Very good."

Another silence ensued while everyone waited for him to continue.

Finally, Fuchida said, "The men of the first wave are ready to take off immediately for a third wave, sir."

Nagumo said, "Tell me again how many ships you think you sank or damaged."

Fuchida said, "So far it looks like two or three battleships sunk, five battleships, two cruisers, and three destroyers damaged. Two hundred and fifty planes wiped out."

The elderly admiral, well pleased, nodded in cadence with Fuchida's list. When Fuchida finished, he said again, "Very good."

Fuchida began to get impatient. Valuable minutes were slipping away. He said, "Shall we prepare for the next wave, sir?"

Admiral Nagumo looked at him admiringly. "You seem eager to pursue the attack."

"Yes sir. I think we should repeat, repeat, repeat. There are many targets."

"How many battleships did you say?"

"Two or three sunk, five damaged. But there are all kinds of other targets. I think, sir, we should repeat again and again until dark."

Admiral Nagumo thought for a moment of the day's evident success, of the limits of his mission, and of the enormous responsibility for the task force under his command—perhaps the largest task force in the history of naval warfare. He looked squarely at Fuchida and said, "No, we shall not attack again." Then he turned and walked away.

Fuchida, astonished, stared into the faces of the other officers in the room. Some appeared to be as astonished as himself. Others, apparently resigned, shrugged as if they were not surprised at the admiral's decision. Fuchida slumped into a chair, crestfallen, then furious, and, as his anger subsided, deeply puzzled. How could a man as courageous and intelligent as Admiral Nagumo, a true Samurai, pass up such a magnificent opportunity?

Well aware of what Fuchida and many of his other officers were thinking, especially the younger ones, Nagumo returned and said to Fuchida, "How many enemy planes remained undamaged when you left?"

Fuchida said, "Because of the smoke, sir, I couldn't make an estimate."

Admiral Nagumo nodded knowingly.

Fuchida realized what was worrying him. He was determined not to lose any ships. A daring idea entered Fuchida's mind.

"May I suggest, sir, that we sail the entire task force up to within 50 miles of Oahu." Seeing the expression on the admiral's face, he hastened to explain. "If we go that close, our fighter planes can cover the fleet and the battle scene at the same time, while the bombers keep hitting whatever targets remain."

The silence which greeted Fuchida's suggestion made him realize he should not have offered it. He knew the traditional, orthodox navy dictum. Never sail a fleet up close to a fortified shore. And Admiral Nagumo was an orthodox navy man.

Nagumo said, once more, "No, we shall not attack again."

Fuchida, feeling empty now, tried but failed to think of more arguments. He looked around the room hoping for help from someone else; it was to no avail. He knew and all the others knew the admiral had made his decision. Fuchida sighed, shrugged in resignation. It would be a bitter disappointment to his men. But as he thought about Nagumo's attitude, he began to understand it. This operation had been conceived by Yamamoto; Nagumo had embraced it only with reluctance. Fuchida knew that. Nagumo considered it much too dangerous to the fleet. The entire task force could have been wiped out. Fortunately, the task force was still unscathed and its mission had been fulfilled beyond all expectations. The time had come to leave well enough alone, before the Americans managed, at last, to find them. There was a long war ahead, and the preservation of His Majesty's fleet was more important than the destruction of the enemy's oil tanks. Admiral Yamamoto would no doubt agree with Nagumo about that. Yamamoto had made it very clear that the Hawaiian operation was not the navy's primary objective. Yamamoto could not have dreamed that the Pearl Harbor raid would be such an overwhelming success. If only he were here right now, if only he could fly over Pearl Harbor at this moment, he might change his mind and make Hawaii a primary objective. Or if only Admiral Nagumo would get in a plane and go look for himself. Fuchida realized his own description could not do justice to the extraordinary scene he had witnessed. But even if Admiral Nagumo were to see it all for himself, would he not be that much more convinced they should retire with haste, since they had fully achieved their well-defined objective?

When Fuchida pondered the situation in this light, he could almost sympathize with Admiral Nagumo. But how could he ever explain that to the fliers awaiting him eagerly in the briefing room?

DECEMBER 8,
JUST BEFORE 9 A.M.

M R S . Katsuko Tojo had her husband's breakfast ready for him in the Japanese-style house which was their family home on the grounds of the prime minister's official residence. She wondered, however, if he would have time for breakfast this morning. He was probably swamped with work, and if the telephones in his office were ringing as often as the one here in the house, he must be getting short of patience. But of course he could be shielded from most of the calls in the office. Mrs. Tojo was beginning to wish she, too, could be shielded from the telephone. The calls were already coming in at such a rate it was difficult to get any work done.

She had not yet adjusted to the enormous changes which had come overnight. When she last saw her husband, before they went to bed in their separate rooms the previous night, his behavior was so calm and normal she was without the slightest inkling of the momentous events he must already have put in motion. Though she was acutely aware of the clamor for war, she had never heard her husband say war was about to start; and despite her sharp sense of perception, she had not guessed it from observing him. She hadn't been awakened by the unusual phone call he had received during the night, nor by his departure from the house and return, nor by the early morning visits of his aides. It was only when she got up and turned on the radio, after he had left for his office, that she found out the war had begun. She was not surprised, however, that he had said nothing to her about it. War was a man's business. The wife of a Samurai couldn't expect him to make her privy to such secret matters. And Hideki Tojo was every bit as much a Samurai as his father, who had arranged the match between them. The elder Tojo had joined the Imperial Army as a private in 1871, and in the process of rising to the rank of general, had fought for Emperor Meiji in the civil war of 1877 (a brief revolt by a Samurai faction against the Meiji evolution), the Sino-Japanese War of 1894-5, and the Russo-Japanese War of 1904-5. From father to son, the Samurai tradition had flowed like the course of history. Young Tojo was willful, brave, righteous, loyal, implacable, charitable to his subordinates, and almost as fanatically devoted to hard work as he was to his family. After he returned from his first combat duty, in the Russo-Japanese War, he had accepted willingly his father's choice of 19-year-old Katsuko as his bride. It was not a difficult decision. The daughter of a middle-class landlord in Kyushu, she had, thanks to her own insistence and her father's understanding, been allowed to come and study in Tokyo at one of the only two women's colleges in Japan at that time, the Nihon Joshi Giakoku. Though some young Japanese men might shy away from a woman so headstrong and intelligent she would insist on going to college, these fearsome qualities had not deterred young Tojo, especially after he took a good look at her. She was a beautiful girl, petite and slender, with high, swept-back hair over a serenely expressive face. It was because of a distant relationship to the Tojo family that she had gravitated toward it, eventually accepting the elder Tojo as a father-away-from-home. When he suggested she marry his son, she decided the prospect was attractive even though she hardly knew Hideki. He had been away from home for several years, as a military student, and then as a young officer. Before their marriage she met him only three times, always at parties, and never spent even a few minutes alone with him. A deep and continuing love had grown between them after marriage, however, and they now shared, in addition to their seven children, a common outlook on family life. She had accepted from the start all the traditional Japanese male prerogatives and her husband's natural habit of separating his career from his home. He had at the same time accepted her ideas about managing the home and the children. None of their children had ever seen them quarrel.

In the last eight weeks, since her husband's selection as prime minister, Mrs. Tojo had often wished there were room for the whole family in this house. It would be difficult to conceive of any other country as large as Japan where the prime minister would be unable to keep all his children under one roof. But in this house, pleasant though it might be, there simply was not room, and unlike some Japanese prime ministers, the Tojos could not afford to maintain a separate establishment. They were used to living on a general's pay, 550 yen ($126.50) per month, which was not quite enough for a large family, especially since Tojo had always been impulsive about giving financial aid to his men. When her husband first became a regimental commander in 1928, Mrs. Tojo had once had to slip out the back door and borrow 30 yen (about $7) from a neighbor because he was waiting to give it to a needy lieutenant at the front door. And several years later in Manchuria, when the wife of one of his men died in childbirth, he had brought the baby home, hired a nurse for it, and kept it for three months until it was old enough for transportation to the father's family in Japan. (By Japanese law, all children belong automatically to the father's, not the mother's family.) It was for such reasons that the Tojos could not quite afford another house in addition to what the prerogatives of office provided him. But though it was hardly ideal to have the family divided, it was a workable arrangement. Since the two oldest sons were married and had their own homes, only two daughters and one son were separated from their parents; and the war minister's official residence in which they lived—thanks to the fact that their father also held that post—was only three short blocks away. The two girls, Mitsue and Makie, were 24 and 18 years of age, old enough to take care of themselves, and the young son Toshio, now 16, was spending much of his time in Kyushu with friends as he prepared to enter military academy.

This left only the two youngest daughters, Yukie, 12, and Kimie, 8, underfoot—which was where they were at the moment, following their mother around, asking her questions about the war—which she couldn't answer, and about breakfast, which she couldn't answer either. Should she stop waiting for her husband and feed the children? Before she made the decision, he finally arrived.

Having heard the reports from the various battle areas, and having seen the Emperor and dispatched the technicalities of the Privy Council, General Tojo was in a cheerful mood, but it did not occur to him to mention any of these matters to his family.

His two little daughters ran to greet him and he put a hand on each of their shoulders. "Have you fed the pigs and chickens?" he asked.

The Tojos kept four or five pigs and a dozen chickens in a pen behind the house. Yukie and Kimie had the responsibility of taking care of them. Yukie, the older of the two girls, assured him the job was done.

"I hope you haven't taken any more of them across the street."

The girls giggled. He was referring to an instance when they had hidden some of the larger pigs at the foreign minister's official residence across the street because the time for slaughter was approaching. He sometimes teased them about the incident. He had not punished them for it. He seldom punished his children; when it was necessary he left it for his wife to do, but even then he didn't want her to do it in his presence. "Scold them when I'm not around," he had once told her. "When I see the children, I want to see them happy."

The two little girls took his coat and helped him out of his shoes, into his slippers. Mrs. Tojo said to him, "I was beginning to wonder if we would see you this morning."

He said, "I was beginning to wonder myself."

They sat down to breakfast immediately on the tatami-covered floor, at a low, Japanese-style table. A maid brought in the general's usual morning fare: *mizu* (a clear broth) with sugar and soy sauce in it, a black seaweed called *nori,* and eggs with *samma,* a pike-like fish. He ate quickly and with great zest.

Mrs. Tojo, curious about the war, but reconciled to her belief that it would be improper to ask questions about it, watched him in silence. She glanced out the window at the pine trees on the slope, glistening in the sun. The prime minister's official residence (as well as several other government buildings including the Diet building) was on the crest of the Miyakezaka hill. There were many old pines on the southerly slope at the rear of the Tojo house.

"It looks like a beautiful day," she said.

Tojo said, "Yes, but it's quite cold."

Through the pines she could look across at the American Embassy on another slope in the Toranomon district, about a half-mile away. What kind of breakfast would the people there be having this morning? She wondered if her husband intended to tell her anything about the war. There had been so little information on the radio.

"You seem to be in an excellent mood this morning," she said.

"Do I?" He looked up at her quizzically, then smiled. "I guess I feel relieved," he said, "now that all the decisions have been made and action has been taken."

She waited for him to continue but he said no more. When he finished eating, he arose quickly from the cushion on which he was sitting.

"I must get back to the office," he said.

Mrs. Tojo saw him to the door and, as he traded slippers for shoes, handed him his coat, which he put over his arm. There was no need to wear it since his office, in the main building, was only a few yards away. As she watched him go down the walk, she shared his evident relief at the fact that he would no longer have to bear the harsh pressures of the war advocates. She wondered what kind of day awaited him and what kind of future awaited the country. He seemed confident, and this made her feel confident, but within limits. There was a great difference in national power between America and Japan. Could Japan match America's ability to produce things? Evidently her husband thought so. He and the other people in the government had no doubt taken such matters into account. One couldn't help wishing, though, for a little more information. There were times when it was difficult to maintain the silence of a Japanese wife.

DECEMBER 8,
9:30 A.M.

A S Junnosuke Ofusa ran the two blocks from his home to the *New York Times* office near the American Embassy, he began to wonder why he was hurrying. What would he be able to do when he arrived? Ofusa's wife, Tamako, had awakened him a short time before to tell him what she had just heard on the radio—that Japan was at war with America. He was still asleep because he and his boss, *New York Times* correspondent Otto Tolischus, had worked until two o'clock in the morning, sending out a dispatch about the diplomatic crisis and preparing to cover a speech General Tojo was scheduled to make today before a mass meeting in Hibiya Park. It was obvious now that if Tojo made a speech in Hibiya Park today the *New York Times* would not be allowed to cover it, but Ofusa was anxious to get to the office anyway because he was worried about Tolischus. What would happen to his boss now that the Americans were enemies?

When Ofusa entered the *Times* bureau a half block down the street from the U.S. Embassy, he could see immediately that Tolischus was not there. Two plainclothes policemen were there, however, and the even-more-untidy-than-usual look of the place indicated they had already searched the drawers and files. Ofusa was neither surprised nor especially concerned at seeing them. As a Japanese citizen working for an American newspaper, he had been receiving visits from the police at least twice a week for the last three or four years. They were endlessly curious about the activities of Tolischus and of his predecessor, Hugh Byas, who had left Japan the previous March after Tolischus arrived.

The detectives smiled when they saw Ofusa. He recognized them since they were two who had often questioned him. They were not Kempeitai, but Tokyo Metropolitan secret policemen.

Though he was almost certain what the answer would be, Ofusa asked, "Where is Tolischus?"

"He's been arrested."

Ofusa was silent for awhile as he faced the two men, trying to decide what to ask them next. It seemed silly to ask them why Tolischus had been arrested. He was now an enemy alien. It might also be dangerous to ask them anything. Ofusa was fully conscious of his own equivocal situation.

"Can you tell me where he's been taken?" he said.

"He's under arrest," one of them repeated.

They didn't seem very talkative. Ofusa sat down at his desk, which had apparently been searched. Having nothing better to say, he asked, "Did Tolischus have breakfast?"

"No."

"Where can I send him a meal?"

One of them, relenting slightly, said, "Akasaka Police Station."

Ofusa picked up the telephone.

"Who are you calling?"

"Tolischus' cook. I just want to make sure he gets something to eat."

The detective nodded his permission. After talking to the cook, Ofusa hung up and sat looking at the two men. They had probably been assigned simply to guard the place. It was pointless to try to talk to them. They might not know any more than he did. But what should he do? He couldn't just sit there while his boss languished in jail. There must be some way to help him. A sudden idea came to Ofusa; he picked up the telephone again.

One of the detectives quickly turned on him. "Who are you calling now?"

"The American Embassy. I just want to notify them that Tolischus has been arrested."

The detective moved toward his desk. "If you try," he said, "you'll be arrested yourself."

Ofusa put down the telephone and shrugged.

The detective smiled. "You couldn't get through anyway. The line has already been cut."

Ofusa sat back in his chair and closed his eyes. He felt helpless and depressed. There was nothing he could possibly do for Tolischus. As he accepted this fact, it began to dawn on him that he had even greater reason to feel helpless and depressed. His country, which he loved, was actually at war with the United States, a country about which he had learned much during his ten years as a *New York Times* reporter. Because of his job he was privy to more information than most of his fellow Japanese, who knew only what they read in the strictly censored newspapers. He couldn't help feeling that disaster was about to strike. And he and his wife and two small children were right in the middle of it.

DECEMBER 8,
SHORTLY AFTER 10 A.M.

Y O U N G , tall Hisatsune Sakomizu, looking more like a college student than a special representative of the Finance Ministry, appeared out of place among the settled, middle-aged and elderly financiers in the board of directors' room of the Tokyo Stock Exchange. The one thing he had in common with these men was the expression of concern on his sharply handsome face. It was after ten o'clock and everyone in the room was worried about the continuing decline of the market.

Sakomizu, who had been sent to the Exchange by Finance Minister Okinori Kaya with instructions to do whatever might be necessary to make the market prosper on the first day of war, decided now that strong measures might be necessary. Turning to Exchange President Yahachi Aizawa, he said, "Do you see any indication that prices might rally?"

Aizawa said, "Not at the moment."

"It might be necessary then," Sakomizu said, "to settle the problem through the government's account." It was not a desirable solution because it would impose a further burden on the Japanese treasury, already overloaded with the expenses of war, and because it would leave the government with large blocks of stock in private corporations—stock the government did not want and which might be costly to liquidate.

Aizawa, to Sakomizu's surprise, put up his hand as if he were pushing back the very idea of the government entering the market.

"The market," he said, "depends on the protection of the government for its existence. And we stockbrokers depend on the market for our existence. The least we can do is to help the government now that the country is in need. We shall use our own accounts to settle the matter. We don't want to bother the government."

Sakomizu was so impressed by this patriotic and generous resolve that he leaped to his feet and shook Aizawa's hand. But the question remained whether the brokers, even with all their resources, could pump enough strength into the market to reverse the downward trend. He settled again into one of the plush leather armchairs and resumed studying the quotation board, which showed no inclination to rally. As the minutes passed, Sakomizu's apprehension increased. Could he depend on the brokers carrying the burden by themselves? Should he insist on a transfusion of government money? Had he already waited too long? These considerations were racing through his mind when he heard murmurs of surprise around him and looked up to see a new and sudden development on the quotation board. The drop in prices slowed dramatically. In a matter of a few minutes, the market was holding its own. Then gradually, and with increasing speed, prices began to rise. A babble of voices arose in the board of directors' room and smiles broke out on the faces of the assembled financiers as messengers began running into the room to talk to them.

Sakomizu was bewildered at the abrupt change in the atmosphere. Could the brokers have dumped enough money into the market to affect it as quickly and dramatically as this? No. It was not possible. The people around him were so busy now they seemed to have forgotten him. Grasping the nearest messenger by the sleeve, he said, "What's happened? What's causing the jump?"

The young man said, "Haven't you heard? Someone on the floor got a call from a friend in the Navy Ministry. They've attacked Hawaii and destroyed more than half of the U.S. fleet."

Sakomizu took a deep breath and said a prayer of thanks. As the stock prices continued to rise, it became more and more apparent that whatever the navy had done in Hawaii, he owed it a debt of gratitude since it had accomplished for him the job he had been assigned to do today. Japanese businessmen seemed suddenly to be less apprehensive about their country's chances in a war against the United States.

DECEMBER 8,
SHORTLY AFTER 11 A.M.

M R S . Yachiyo Nakashima sat up in bed at the Hosei-en Sanitarium in Higashi Murayama, a western suburb of Tokyo, thinking anxiously about her husband and two little daughters. While other patients listened with excitement to the latest radio bulletins about the war, she stared vacantly into space, her mind so full of troubles she had no room in it for news of naval attacks and troop landings. It was as if it were not enough to be suffering so severly from tuberculosis she had to be separated from her family. Now, with war, she must expect the aggravation of another problem which might soon prove even more severe. Yachiyo Nakashima, a Japanese girl, was married to a Nisei (a second generation American of Japanese descent), and though her husband had been in Japan for seven years, he had refused to renounce his American citizenship. On the contrary, he had repudiated Japanese citizenship although Japanese law would have permitted him dual status. In addition, he worked for an American company, the United Press news agency, which meant he would now be out of a job. And the Nakashimas' entire savings amounted to about 800 yen ($184). As the morning wore on, Yachiyo was becoming frantic because she hadn't heard from her husband since the war was announced and it was now almost eleven o'clock. Had he been arrested? It seemed quite possible. For some time the police had been visiting her regularly to ask her questions about his activities. Yet they refused to acknowledge that she was married to him. They had entered her in their records as a common-law wife because the Nakashimas had been married (in 1937) at the American Consulate. The marriage could not be valid, the police had told her, because her husband, having been born in Hawaii, had no Japanese family record. She was just about convinced the police had indeed arrested him when, at eleven o'clock, she looked up to see him approaching her bed.

Leslie Nakashima, a kindly-looking man, 39 years old, tried to wipe the worry from his expression as he gazed down at his wife whose pale face showed her own concern. He smiled as if this were just another day, and she returned his smile; but neither was able to deceive the other.

"I wasn't sure you could make it," she said.

"For awhile there, neither was I."

"The girls?"

"They're fine." The Nakashimas had a maid looking after their little daughters, Kazue, who was three, and Kay, who was just a year old.

There were many things she wanted to ask him. Had he talked to his boss? Had the police contacted him? Was there a possibility he would be deported, and if so would the authorities let her and the children go with him? She wasn't sure the doctors would allow her to travel even if the possibility arose. And if he was not imprisoned or deported, how would he find another job, being an American? "What's it like in the streets?" she asked.

"Our neighbors are celebrating," he said. "They're waving flags." The Nakashimas lived in Harajuku, a nice residential area near the Meiji Shrine on the west side of Tokyo.

"I hope they weren't nasty to you," she said.

"Not at all. It was strange. They weren't singing or shouting or making any noise. Just quietly waving their flags."

She looked up at him and smiled, took his hand and squeezed it. Despite her smile, he could see the questions on her face. How best could he answer them without increasing her worries?

"Apparently I'm not going to be arrested," he said. "The police were at the house for two hours. Five of them. They searched it from wall to wall, every inch. They took my typewriter and my camera but they didn't take me." Though they could, of course, come back and take him whenever they pleased, he felt no need to say that. There was at least a good chance that since they had not arrested him this morning, they intended to let him remain free, but he was not yet sure whether that would be an advantage or a hardship. If they did not arrest him, he would find himself trying to survive in Tokyo as an enemy alien. If they did arrest him, he could, as an American citizen, demand repatriation to the United States. But could he also demand it for his Japanese wife and two children? And even if it were approved, would Yachiyo's health permit her to travel? Would the United States allow her entry when she was suffering from tuberculosis? It was an insoluble dilemma which he could not bear to discuss with Yachiyo at the moment.

"You're looking good," he said.

Though she tried to smile she was near tears and her face showed it. "I assume your job is ended," she said.

"That's a safe assumption. They've arrested Bellaire." Robert Bellaire, the United Press bureau chief in Tokyo, had been taken by the police in the roundup of enemy aliens at 7 A.M.

Yachiyo Nakashima shook her head. "Leslie, what's going to happen to us?" she cried. "Will you be able to find a job?"

He put a consoling hand on her shoulder. "You know the proverb about the darkest hour," he said. "Of course I'll be able to find a job." But he wondered where.

DECEMBER 8,
NOON

T H E   S U N by midday had softened Tokyo's freezing cold, luring thousands of workers out of doors for their lunch breaks; in the Ginza especially, around the shops and department stores, the streets were even more crowded than usual. The comparatively few automobiles made their way slowly through the masses of bicycles, carts, wagons, trucks, and occasional rickshaws. *Tofu* (bean-curd) vendors blew their ocarina-like horns, sweet-potato vendors sang their mournful *"Yakiimo!"* and newspaper vendors jangled their bells in competition with each other. *Soba* boys, balancing trays stacked two feet high with bowls of Japanese noodles, weaved in and out among other cyclists, seeming never to spill a drop of their hot, soupy cargoes. Women in bright kimonos stared into the windows of department stores like Takashimaya and Matsuya, which displayed mannequins dressed in the "latest" Western fashions. But the majority of the people on the crowded sidewalks did not look as if they had come out to shop. They seemed to be there simply for the pleasure of mingling with others at this auspicious hour. The mood had changed markedly on the streets of Tokyo since early morning. The numbing shock with which most of the city's seven million people had accepted the first news of war had been replaced suddenly by elation at the news of immediate and amazing victories announced by the radio and newspaper shortly after 11 A.M. The Japanese were, without a doubt, the world's most adaptable people. Several times in their history they had embraced sudden changes so drastic as to alter their very style of life. During the eighth century, after becoming exposed to the vast wonders of China, they had radically disrupted their own culture to make it conform as closely as possible to the Chinese. And in the nineteenth century, after being forcibly opened to the invasion of Western culture, they had set out with desperate determination to absorb it also, at the expense of some of their own most venerable traditions. But while they had consciously accepted—often with great enthusiasm—the changes the West had thrust upon them, their transformation had been less smooth than it appeared on the surface. Japan, 88 years after the arrival of Admiral Matthew Perry, was still suffering from some degree of cultural shock and many Japanese harbored at least a subconscious resentment of the Western intrusion upon their culture. In 1934, the renowned Japanese novelist, Junichiro Tanizaki, writing about his country's Westernization, had declared: "I know as well as anyone that I am dreaming, and that, having come this far, we cannot turn back. I know that I am grumbling to myself and demanding the impossible. But there can be no harm if my grumblings are taken for what they are, in considering how unlucky we have been, what losses we have suffered, in comparison to the Westerner. The Westerner has been able to move forward in ordered steps, while we have met a superior civilization and have had to surrender to it, and we have had to leave a road we have followed for thousands of years." It was hardly surprising, then, if the Japanese felt a certain elation today at the news that they were so strongly asserting themselves against the West. Their elation manifested itself, however, not in cheers or shouts or arm-waving demonstrations, but only in happy smiles of surprise and satisfaction. Clerks and secretaries, businessmen and housewives milled about, wearing expressions of mingled wonder and pride as if they were all thinking, "There you are, that's the way we Japanese do it. One day of war and already we've beaten America."

Many of these people, however, when their minds encompassed more than the victorious moment, viewed the new war with sober uncertainty because they were already well acquainted with war and its hardships. For almost four years now the country had been inextricably bogged down in a war against China. Though the army called it an "incident" rather than a war because the Emperor had never dignified it with a rescript, it was nevertheless burdening the nation's economy so heavily that rice, sugar, and most other foods, as well as clothing, were strictly rationed. The average person on the street was beginning to look shabby because he had to wear snythetic fabrics too weak to endure normal laundering. And after long hours of work, he would go home to a small, flimsy, paper-windowed, unheated house only slightly more substantial than a shack. Despite the imposing concrete buildings in the business and government sections, most of Tokyo looked like a shanty town, with millions of tiny, unpainted wooden houses crowded so close together they seemed to lean on each other for support. If living conditions were this difficult already, how much more difficult would they now become with the nation, still embattled in China, going to war against such awesome opponents as Great Britain and the United States?

It was apparent to almost all of these people, however, that Japan had to fight the Western powers. Japanese newspapers for several months had been making this increasingly clear. The white nations of the West, which had been plundering Asia for more than a century, had now become even bolder and more aggressive in their attempts to enslave Japan. America, Britain, China, and the Dutch (the ABCD Powers) were engaged in a deliberate plan to encircle Japan and reduce it to insignificance. The white nations had always treated Japan with arrogance. Ever since Admiral Perry had arrived with his cannons and forced the country to accept him, Americans had been coming in and out of Japan as if they owned it. But at the same time they had passed a race-insulting immigration law to stop the Japanese and other Asians from going to America. The time had now come for the arrogant, bigoted Americans to learn that there was a limit to Japanese patience.

On the broad, main boulevard of the Ginza, men in business suits, working girls in smocks, women in kimonos gathered around the front of a radio shop which was beaming a newscast into the street over a loudspeaker:

"The Imperial Navy has attacked Hong Kong, citadel of British imperialism in China.... The Army of the Rising Sun has succeeded in making an initial landing on the coast of the Malayan Peninsula. ... The Navy has bombarded Davao in the Philippines ... Guam ... Singapore ..."

Everyone within hearing distance of the amplifier turned toward it and all other sound seemed to fade away as the crowd listened. With the announcement of each daring offensive action, people nodded, beamed, and waited breathlessly for the next. There were no cheers even when the newscast ended, perhaps because the excited announcer then informed his listeners that immediately thereafter, the Emperor's rescript would be broadcast. The very mention of the Emperor deepened the silence around the radio shop. Every head bowed forward in reverence, every eye looked toward the ground. The announcer paused before beginning this most delicate duty his profession could ever call upon him to render. In the reading of an imperial rescript, no miscue could be forgiven. An army lieutenant named Jiro Ushiroku had recently committed suicide because, in reading at a ceremony the Emperor Meiji's classic Rescript to Soldiers and Sailors, he had stumbled over one phrase. The radio announcer began enunciating with utmost care the imperial words officially issued in the name of Emperor Hirohito at 11:45, just 15 minutes previously:

We, by the grace of Heaven, Emperor of Japan, seated on the throne of a line unbroken for ages eternal, enjoin upon ye, our loyal and brave subjects:

We hereby declare war on the United States of America and the British Empire. The men and officers of our army and navy shall do their utmost in prosecuting the war. Our public servants of various departments shall perform faithfully and diligently their appointed tasks, and all other subjects of ours shall pursue their respective duties; the entire nation with a united determination will mobilize its total strength so that nothing will miscarry in the attainment of our war aims.

To ensure the stability of East Asia and to contribute to world peace is the far-sighted policy which was formulated by our great illustrious imperial grandsire and our great imperial sire succeeding him, and which we lay constantly to heart. To cultivate friendship among nations and to enjoy prosperity in common with all nations has always been the guiding principle of our empire's foreign policy. It has been truly unavoidable and far from our wishes that our empire has now been brought to cross swords with America and Britain. More than four years have passed since China, failing to comprehend the true intentions of our empire, and recklessly courting trouble, disturbed the peace of East Asia and compelled our empire to take up arms. Although there has been reestablished the National Government of China, with which Japan has affected neighborly intercourse and cooperation, the regime which has survived at Chungking, relying upon American and British protection, still continued its fratricidal opposition. Eager for the realization of their inordinate ambition to dominate the Orient, both America and Britain, giving support to the Chungking regime, have aggravated the disturbances in East Asia. Moreover, these two powers, inducing other countries to follow suit, increased military preparations on all sides of our empire to challenge us. They have obstructed by every means our peaceful commerce, and finally resorted to a direct severance of economic relations, menacing gravely the existence of our empire. Patiently have we waited and long have we endured, in the hope that our government might retrieve the situation in peace. But our adversaries, showing not the least spirit of conciliation, have unduly delayed a settlement; and in the meantime, they have intensified the economic and political pressure to compel thereby our empire to submission. This trend of affairs would, if left unchecked, not only nullify our empire's efforts of many years for the sake of the stabilization of East Asia, but also endanger the very existence of our nation. The situation being such as it is, our empire for its existence and self-defense has no other recourse but to appeal to arms and to crush every obstacle in its path.

The hallowed spirits of our imperial ancestors guarding us from above, we rely upon the loyalty and courage of our subjects in our confident expectation that the task bequeathed by our forefathers will be carried forward, and that the source of evil will be speedily eradicated and an enduring peace immutably established in East Asia, preserving thereby the glory of our empire.

The hundreds of people in front of the Ginza radio shop, their heads still bowed, their bodies stiffly unmoving, listened to the very end in a spirit of patriotic credulity, religious fervor, and total submission. Some prostrated themselves. Others wept in the fullness of their gratitude for the Emperor's august words. Hearing this proof of His

Majesty's own absolute confidence, who could doubt the outcome of Japan's righteous struggle?

After a solemn pause, but before the crowd had time to disperse, the radio announced that Prime Minister Tojo would now speak in response to His Majesty's gracious rescript. People raised their heads, since the prime minister did not command the same reverence and awe as the Emperor, but no one turned to leave.

In the second-floor film-screening room of the prime minister's official residence, about a mile west of the Ginza, technicians from NHK, the radio network of Nippon Hoso Kyokai (Japan Broadcasting Corporation) had their equipment tuned and ready as General Tojo marched into the room with a quick, short-stepped military gait, followed by an entourage of assistants. With calm assurance he sat down at a table in front of a microphone marked JOAK (the network's number one nationwide hookup), silently studying his script. Tojo's poise and public presence had increased markedly in the year-and-a-half since he hurried home from China to become war minister in Prince Konoye's cabinet. In those days, his hands would sometimes tremble as he read from his text at political functions. Today, as he prepared to read the most momentous speech he had ever delivered, he showed an outward calm that increased the confidence of everyone around him. At an engineer's hand signal, he began his address in an even, measured, noninflammatory tone:

Just now an imperial rescript declaring war has been granted. At this very moment our brave military and naval forces are defying death in the field of battle. In spite of all that our Empire has done, ardently desiring the preservation of the peace of East Asia, our efforts have ended in failure.

The Government has employed every means at its disposal in its endeavor to bring about a successful adjustment of Japanese-American relations. But the United States refused to make the least concession; instead, joining in league with Britain, the Netherlands, and Chungking, it demanded unilateral concessions on our part, such as unconditional and wholesale evacuation of our military and naval forces from China, nonrecognition of the Nanking Government, and the annulment of the tripartite pact between Japan, Germany, and Italy. Even then, we have continued to the last our efforts to reach a peaceful settlement. But the United States has shown no sign of reconsidering its own attitude. Should we submit to such imposition, the prestige of our empire would be compromised. It would mean not only a failure to settle the China affair, but it would also result in endangering the very existence of our empire.

Things having come to this pass, Japan is now obliged to go to war in order to surmount the present crisis and to defend itself and preserve itself.

On reading the imperial rescript, I am filled with awe and trepidation. Powerless as I am, I am resolved to dedicate myself, body and soul, to my country, and to set at ease the august mind of our sovereign. And I believe that every one of you, my countrymen, will not care for your life but gladly share in the honor to make yourself His Majesty's humble shield.

The key to victory lies in a faith in victory. For 2,600 years our empire has never known defeat. This record alone is enough to produce a conviction in our ability to crush any enemy, no matter how strong. Let us pledge ourselves that we shall never stain our glorious history but go forward to construct even a greater Japan of tomorrow. It is true that we have shown until today maximum measures of patience and endurance. But this is not because we sought ease and comfort, or because we feared the power and size of our enemy. It is only because we desired to preserve the peace of the world and prevent a calamity from befalling mankind. However, now that the enemy has challenged us and threatened the existence and prestige of our Fatherland, we cannot but stand up with resolution.

Our adversaries, boasting rich natural resources, aim at the domination of the world. In order to annihilate this enemy and construct a new order in East Asia, we should anticipate naturally a long war. At the same time it requires, needless to say, a tremendous amount of constructive energy. We must march toward surmounting every possible obstacle with firm conviction in the final victory. This is a heaven-sent opportunity to test the mettle of us Japanese of the Showa Era [the reign of Hirohito]. Only by undergoing this test successfully may we deserve the honor to be hailed by posterity as builders of Greater East Asia.

Happily at this moment the alliance with Germany and Italy, and the relationship of 'One-virtue-and-one-mind' which binds Japan with Manchukuo and China, are growing stronger than ever.

The rise or fall of our empire and the prosperity or ruin of East Asia literally depend upon the outcome of this war. Truly it is time for the hundred million of us Japanese to dedicate all we have and sacrifice everything for our country's cause. As long as this great spirit of loyalty and patriotism remains under the policy of Hakko Ichiu ['The Whole World under One Roof'], we have nothing to fear in fighting America and Britain. Victory, I am convinced, is always with the illustrious virtues of our sovereign. In making known these humble views of mine, I join with all my countrymen in pledging myself to assist in the grand imperial enterprise.

Having finished his speech, Tojo stood for a quick photograph, then headed immediately for the door. He hadn't time even to accept the good wishes of the radio men. He was already late for a speaking engagement before a businessmen's group, the Central Cooperative Council, at Tokyo Kaikan restaurant in Marunouchi. After that he was determined to get to the Meiji and Yasukuni shrines and report the news of the war to his ancestors. And he had to get back to his office, where an endless number of appointments and documents awaited him. It was the busiest as well as the most momentous day of his life.

In the Ginza, the people listening to the radio began to disperse, but not before hearing the latest word about the Imperial Navy's colossal victory against the American fleet in Hawaii. There was now a report that a U.S. aircraft carrier was among the ships that had been sunk. It was an amazing victory. One had to discuss it. Utter strangers turned to talk to each other. Who could have imagined that such a remarkable feat was possible on the first day of war? Japan was indeed a power with which the world would have to reckon, was it not? Why had so many people been fearful of a new war? Did they lack faith in the nation's leaders? Such people must be ashamed of themselves today. No one could doubt now that the men in power knew what they were doing.

The conversations were interrupted suddenly by a siren so startling that people at first did not recognize it.

Finally someone shouted, "Air raid!"

Though air raid rehearsals had been regularly scheduled for several years in Japan and everyone was accustomed to them, this warning came so unexpectedly, and at a moment of such great elation, that no one seemed to know what to do about it.

Then someone said in a rising voice, "It's not a rehearsal! It's real!"

The fact that the nation was at war bore down on people directly and personally now. The milling thousands began running for shelter. Within a few minutes, the Ginza subway station was more crowded than at rush hour.

Within a few more minutes, the alert ended. It had been a false alarm. But people were still looking warily toward the sky as they emerged from the subway station. One could not help feeling strange and uneasy to realize that bombs might drop at any moment.

DECEMBER 8,
1:30 P.M.

ONE HUNDRED ninety-two planes of the Japanese Navy's land-based Eleventh Air Force, having finally outwaited the morning fog to take off from Tainan, Formosa, were now approaching the Philippine Islands, several hours later than they had hoped to launch attacks there. Flight Petty Officer Saburo Sakai, leading a squadron of nine Zero fighters, had just rejoined the group after pursuing for several miles a suspicious formation of what turned out to be Japanese bomber planes on a training mission. As Sakai's fighters pulled back into place among the 75 other Zeros protecting the 108 bombers bound for Clark and Iba Fields near Manila, he was still fuming at the unknown fool who had led those training planes into such a critical area at so critical a time. But he quickly forgot this minor annoyance when he saw, far ahead, the dark coastline which he knew was northern Luzon. Moving closer and closer, he watched that almost black, forbidding darkness of the island emerge into a bright pattern of many-shaded greens. And as he followed the bombers protectively across the northern tip of the island, he looked down with wistful memories at the peaceful farm fields and rice terraces among the green hills and forests. His widowed mother and his brothers and sisters were no doubt at this moment working in their pathetic little family field near the town of Saga in Kyushu. His mother would be surprised and pleased if she could see him at this moment, flying bravely into battle against those big Americans. On one occasion when Sakai was twelve years old, his mother, called upon to mediate a quarrel between an older boy and himself, had said to his adversary, "You're bigger than Saburo. Why don't you beat him up?" Impoverished as she was, his mother never forgot that hers was a Samurai family. It was the duty of a proud Samurai mother to teach her son that he must be ready to accept battle. Sakai knew that now. At the time, however, he had been so taken aback by his mother's attitude, and so frightened of the bigger boy, he had run away.

Today, facing perhaps the biggest, most powerful adversary in the world, he felt no desire, not even the slightest inclination, to run away. He and his companions were, he was certain, the greatest fighter pilots in the world. And though it was possible his country might lose to America, he himself, and the men around him in their fast, new Zeros, would not lose to anyone. Especially not to these white Americans who looked down so condescendingly upon the Japanese. All of Sakai's previous combat experience had been against the Chinese. He would now be facing white men for the first time. They might be excellent pilots. He expected that, and he welcomed a chance to test his ability against them. But while they might be skillful, they were also so arrogant and bigoted they refused even to allow Japanese into their country. He could not help resenting them for that. He would show them quickly enough that in his Zero he was as big as any of them, and he would fight them as an equal. He would force them to acknowledge him as an equal however much they might wish to look down upon him.

The 192-plane attack force had now flown out over the China Sea. As it approached the Manila area, 192 pilots kept their heads moving back and forth in anticipation that American interceptor planes would appear at any moment. But even as they flew in across the coastline and divided into two groups (54 bombers and 34 Zeros destined for Clark Field, 54 bombers and 50 Zeros destined for Iba Field), they saw no American planes in the air.

Sakai and the eight Zeros under his command, assigned to protect the Clark Field group, flew on ahead of the bombers to be in position to drive off any U.S. planes which might attack them there. At his first view of the target, he stared in disbelief. He understood now why no American planes had yet attacked them. At least 60 bombers and fighters were lined up in well-ordered rows along the Clark Field flight line. Not only had the Americans failed to meet them in the air; they had even neglected to disperse their planes on the ground. The attack on Hawaii had taken place seven or eight hours previously. Hadn't they yet heard about it in the Philippines?

Sakai's nine-plane fighter group, with nothing else to do at the moment, circled the field at an altitude of 22,000 feet, expecting to find at least a few American defenders in the air. Finally Sakai spotted five U.S. fighter planes below him at 15,000 feet. Though he had been ordered not to attack until the bombers arrived, he signaled the planes on his wings to jettison their auxiliary fuel tanks and arm their cannons and machine guns in anticipation that they would now be attacked.

Ready for action, Sakai and his companions continued to circle the field, waiting impatiently for the Americans to come up after them. As soon as the Americans showed the first signs of attacking, Sakai would be free to disregard his stand-by instructions. But the Americans made no move to attack. Could they possibly be oblivious of nine Zero fighter planes sitting 7,000 feet above their heads? It was exasperating. How could a war begin if the Americans refused to fight?

At 1:45 P.M., the Japanese bombers, with the rest of the Zeros protecting them, appeared from the north and, seeing exactly the same view which had greeted Sakai a few minutes earlier, went to work immediately, dispersing with high explosives the planes the Americans had neglected to disperse. As Sakai watched the clusters of bombs erupt, he decided it was the most accurate bombardment he had ever seen. In the moments it took for those Japanese bombers to pass in review beneath him, the approximately sixty airplanes lined up on the ground virtually disintegrated. Hangars and other buildings flew through the air in chunks. Fires blazed upward all over the base. The Zeros were supposed, after the bombers retired, to drop down and strafe. Sakai wondered if there would be anything left to strafe.

When the bombers, still undisturbed, completed their destruction and turned for home, the 34 Zeros hovering above them followed them for ten minutes to make sure they were out of danger, after which the Zeros returned to Clark Field, lazily circling downward as their pilots watched the great air base burn beneath them. At 13,000 feet, Lieutenant Hideki Shingo, the squadron commander, gave the order to strafe.

Sakai, with another plane on each wing, plunged forward into a steep dive toward two B-17s which appeared to be, by some miracle, still undamaged. Leveling out just a few feet above the ground, the three Zeros fired long bursts of machine gun bullets into the huge, four-engine bombers, pressing in upon them until they were only a few feet away, then pulling up sharply into a steep climb to avoid collision.

When Sakai came out of this climb, separated now from his wing-men, he realized suddenly he had five American P-40s on his tail. The thrill of battle welled up in him, expanding his energies, sharpening his senses. At last he was in combat. The moment had come to teach these Americans what he could do and teach the P-40s what the Zero could do. Swinging into a left turn so sharp it was almost a skid, he then abruptly pulled the stick back as far as it would come while he pushed the throttle as far forward as it would go. The Zero, shifting into its special overdrive, climbed so fast it left all five P-40s behind it. Four of them, giving up the chase, swung to the right and disappeared into the huge clouds of smoke arising from the air field. The fifth made the mistake of spiraling to the left and separating itself from the others.

Sakai, seeing a potential victim, swung around to approach him from below and from behind.

The American, aware of his mistake now, went into a high loop, but Sakai's Zero, following him easily, closed the gap between them. At 200 yards, the P-40's belly came into Sakai's gunsight. A short machine gun burst established the range and ripped the P-40's vulnerable underside. Then Sakai's cannon, with one shell, knocked the canopy off the stricken plane, which suddenly lost its speed, hovered almost motionless in the air, and fell off to plunge downward, no longer an airplane but only a heavy, broken thing. Saburo Sakai had shot down his first American. It was the first U.S. plane to be destroyed in the air over the Philippines.

Unable to locate any more opponents, he rendezvoused with the rest of the Zeroes for the flight back to Formosa. In one attack, the Eleventh Air Fleet of which he was a part had destroyed between 40 and 50 of the 60 planes at Clark Field, and all of the 25 planes at Iba Field.

DECEMBER 8,
2:20 P.M. IN TOKYO,
6:50 P.M. IN HAWAII

I T   W A S twilight in Hawaii, 6:50 P.M., Sunday (2:20 P.M. Monday in Tokyo), when the ominous black hull of the Japanese submarine I-69, one of the five mother subs that had launched midget subs the previous midnight, broke water and came boldly to the surface near the Pearl Harbor entrance buoy. Since morning, the I-69 and the four other mother subs had cruised the waters around Oahu at periscope depth, hoping to recover the midgets, which, by now, had been gone long enough to accomplish their missions. But since none of the little subs had yet reappeared or even established radio contact with the mothers, anxiety about them increased by the hour. Finally, the I-69's captain, Commander Nobuyoshi Nakaoka, aware of the shattered condition of the American fleet, felt sufficiently contemptuous of its remnants to surface within sight of the still-burning naval base. Commander Nakaoka looked out of the conning tower of the I-69 just in time to see a now-familiar but still welcome sight. From the already shattered battleship row near Ford Island a new explosion arose, as impressive as any he had seen that day, and sent another huge column of smoke into the sky. Nakaoka continued to peer with satisfaction at the stricken base as the deepening darkness protected his submarine from view. The I-69 had been standing off Pearl Harbor for 30 minutes when a radio operator reported a message he had just received. It was from Lieutenant Masaharu Yokoyama, the skipper of one of the midget subs, and it was in the simple code they were to use in contacting the mothers.

It said only, "I have succeeded."

Because it was not a half-hour since the big explosion inside the harbor, and because the midgets were not supposed to contact their mothers before emerging from the harbor, Nakaoka felt a momentary hope that Yokoyama had escaped, but if he had still believed he could succeed in getting away, he would hardly have sent a message simply to report his success. Those three words, "I have succeeded," bore the mark of a man's final message to his Emperor, to his country, to his family, to his ancestors, to his comrades. Unfortunately, it was no longer realistic to hope that Yokoyama, or any of the ten midget submarine men, would never again be seen alive. It was comforting, however, to feel that at least one of them had succeeded in his mission.

While Nakaoka's I-69 and one other mother submarine waited at the mouth of Pearl Harbor in the diminishing hope of recovering Yokoyama, Ensign Kazuo Sakamaki, in his ill-starred midget, was off the eastern shore of Oahu, still trying to get to Pearl Harbor. He had kept his almost disabled craft on the move throughout the day, even though each new direction seemed to take him farther from his destination. His gyroscope was not functioning, his periscope had been destroyed, his compressed-air system had been damaged, his torpedoes had been disabled by collisions with coral reefs, and his crewman, Petty Officer Kiyoshi Imagaki, was weeping unabashedly. Sakamaki was no longer attempting to replenish the poor fellow's enthusiasm. He no longer had any enthusiasm to offer. Only his bitter frustration held back his own tears. But perhaps there was still a flicker of hope. The submarine had not stopped moving, at least, and if he could keep it moving along the shore, he was bound to reach that elusive harbor mouth eventually. Perhaps even now he was getting close. By this time it should be dark. Why not break surface again and see how he was doing?

When he looked out into the clear night he felt a sudden elation. There was Diamond Head, outlined clearly against the darkening sky. He had something to cheer about after all. Diamond Head and Pearl Harbor were only a few minutes apart. If Diamond Head was there, then Pearl Harbor should be . . . His hopes evaporated as a sudden awareness overcame him. There was Diamond Head, all right. But it was now on his left. If he were anyplace near Pearl Harbor, Diamond Head would have to be on his right. In exhaustion and despair he closed the hatch, flopped down on his bunk and went to sleep.

DECEMBER 8,
4 P.M.

BY midafternoon, about 200 foreign nationals, mostly American, British, or Dutch, had been arrested in Tokyo under provisions of Japanese antisubversive laws, and General Tojo, acting in his capacity as home minister, issued an anti-espionage regulation restricting the movements of all foreign nations. No foreigner would henceforth be allowed to enter or live in certain designated areas without a permit. No foreigner would be allowed to travel outside the area in which he lived. And all newly arriving foreigners would be given one day to register with the police. Violators would be subject to fines and up-to-three-month prison terms.

A spokesman for the Japanese Information Board, Tomokazu Hori, said in a statement to the press: "Japan will do everything in her power to crush enemies. But let us emphasize ... this is a war between states and not a war between individual nationals of Japan and the enemy countries. . . . The Japanese government will follow the policy of taking every possible precautionary measure ... to assure the safety of those nationals of the United States and the British Empire who are residing in Japan."

The four detectives who had arrested *New York Times* correspondent Otto Tolischus early in the morning entered the small, cold police station room where he was being held under guard and handed him a satchel which he recognized as having come from his home. When he opened it, he found it full of his own winter underwear. He wished he could put on a few layers of it right away. He was shivering.

The leader of the quartet of plainclothesmen said, quite formally and ceremoniously, "I detain you. You have violated paragraph eight of the National Defense Act."

Tolischus, having only a vague idea of the contents of this section of the Defense Act, looked puzzled.

The policeman quickly explained. "You sent political, diplomatic, and economic information to foreign agents harmful to Japan. That means penal servitude up to ten years."

Disquieting as Tolischus found this development, he was relieved, at least, to hear that he was not being charged with espionage or stealing military secrets.

"I am an accredited newspaper correspondent," he said, speaking slowly and carefully. "I work in that capacity with the knowledge, approval, and aid of the Japanese government. Every dispatch I have ever sent was news based on information from official Japanese government sources or from the Japanese press. Besides that, everything I've ever sent was passed by the Japanese censor."

His questioner brushed aside these remarks as irrelevant. "The foreign newspapers are all foreign agents," he said. "You know that, don't you?"

"No, I do not know that."

"And you did send out political, diplomatic, and economic information, did you not?"

"I did." It was pointless to deny that.

"Didn't you know that this was harmful to Japan?"

Tolischus decided that despite his anger he had better speak tactfully. "As I understand the Japanese Defense Act," he said, "it is meant to prohibit anyone from sending out secret information, or from sending out information secretly. It does not prohibit me from sending out news publicly announced in Japan. And I am not the one to decide whether an item of news is harmful to Japan. That's for the Japanese censors to decide. In every country where there are censors, the censor is responsible for what he passes, not the correspondent who wrote it. And I have never sent out any news which the censor did not pass."

His interrogator was not impressed. "We want you to sign a statement," he said.

Tolischus observed now that one of the other policemen had been taking notes. The coldness of the room was no longer noticeable. Tolischus realized he was only at the beginning of a long, hard, blood-warming session.

DECEMBER 8,
ABOUT 6:30 OR 7 P.M.

T H E streets of Tokyo were even darker tonight than they had been during all those blackout rehearsals of the last two or three years. But Maki Sakomizu, drawing her children in close for the walk, with her husband, from their house in Shinjuku (four miles west of the center of the city) to her father's house a few blocks away, realized it was not the intensified darkness that made this evening's atmosphere so oppressive. It was the certainty that this darkness would go on, night after night, with no end in prospect, while thousands of Japanese men and boys, some of them her own friends and relatives, would be dying needlessly in battlefields all over the Pacific. Maki Sakomizu was perhaps unusual for a woman whose family was Samurai, and who had married a man from a Samurai family. She hated war.

Despite her Samurai connections, she had come naturally to her antiwar sentiments. Her father, Admiral Keisuke Okada, even while he was an active naval officer, and later as prime minister of Japan in the middle 1930s, had openly opposed the nation's militaristic drift. In the famous February 26, 1936 incident, this opposition had almost cost him his life. But it had not stopped him from warning people, especially his son-in-law, Hisatsune Sakomizu, of the dangers of militarism.

Young Sakomizu, a career public servant who had become, one month earlier, a section chief within the government Planning Board, and whose position in the bureaucratic hierarchy was already so high he had been entrusted that morning with the task of making sure the stock market reacted favorably to the war news, could hardly afford to match his wife's outspoken opposition to war. But walking with his family through the dark streets to his father-in-law's home, he felt just as depressed as his wife. He stared intently through the gloom, making sure his eldest son and two daughters stayed close, then he turned to his wife and said, "We're fortunate, at least, that these children are so young."

The eldest son, Hisamasa, was nine. The two daughters, Tokuko and Takako, were six and three. The youngest son, Akio, was a four-month-old baby-in-arms.

His wife said, in a voice which lacked enthusiasm, "It's the one thing for which we can be thankful at a time like this."

"But I can't help worrying about them anyway," he said. "About all of us. If the country suffers, we all suffer." A war of such magnitude was certain to impose drastic hardships and deprivations upon a country of Japan's limited resources. Sakomizu, from his position within the Planning Board, could see only too well the limits of his country's resources, and having spent almost two years in America when he was attached to the Finance Ministry, he was equally aware of that country's virtually unlimited resources. This war against the United States would be, at best, a long and costly one; at worst, a disastrous one. Unless, of course, it was true, as many people said, that Americans lacked the unquestionable fighting spirit of the Japanese. Was it possible that the navy had actually destroyed 70 percent of the

U.S. Pacific Fleet in Hawaii this morning? And if so, would that discourage America, incline it toward an early peace settlement? One could hope so, but one had better not count on it. Such a huge, modern, and powerful country could absorb an endless number of hard blows. Would American cities be blacked out tonight, like Tokyo? A blackout in New York was hard to imagine. All those Broadway lights turned off, and all those remarkable New York restaurants dark. New York had seemed to him so civilized during his stay there. It was in a New York restaurant he had eaten raw oysters for the first time. Before he left Japan, in 1927, his mother had said, "Don't eat raw oysters." In Japan they were thought to carry typhus, but he had eaten them in New York and liked them. It was strange to think of New York being dark. It was just as strange, though, to look out at a completely darkened Tokyo. And so disheartening.

When they arrived at Admiral Okada's house, the servant who admitted them and set out slippers for them shook her head in warning as they took off their shoes.

This is not a good time to talk to the admiral," she said. "He spent all day pacing back and forth, mumbling, 'Stupid! Stupid!' Even when he went into the garden you could still hear him talking to himself. He acts crazy."

They found the elderly former prime minister pacing the living room like a bear in a cage. When he saw his son-in-law, he raised his hand in an impatient gesture. "They are so stupid!" he cried. "This cabinet will destroy our noble country. I feel sorry for His Majesty!"

Sakomizu said, "I didn't believe the military would go so far." He felt foolish now in front of his father-in-law who had been warning him for several years to stay away from the militarists. After Okada, as prime minister, came so close to death at the hands of fanatical soldiers in the bloody rebellion of 1936, he believed the militarists to be capable of anything.

At five o'clock on that memorable February morning, Okada's brother-in-law, Colonel Denzo Matsuo, who was staying with him at the prime minister's official residence, had aroused him to warn him there was a crowd of berserk soldiers outside, obviously bent on murder. Okada had not awakened easily because the previous night he had attended a party at the American Embassy given by Ambassador Grew, and as he was wont to do on occasion, he had drunk generously. But he became suddenly alert when 300 or more soldiers, led by three young officers, broke into the building, after killing four guards, and began running through the halls, looking for him. Okada and Matsuo, with seconds to spare, made it into the nearest bathroom and closed the door. It was obvious to Matsuo they could not remain hidden there, and since soldiers were now swarming over every part of the building, there was no escape. Realizing that he bore a facial resemblance to the prime minister, Matsuo made a sudden brave decision. "You stay here," he warned, and without hesitation he stepped out of the bathroom then ran through the house, drawing the soldiers' attention to himself. Within minutes, several of them had unloaded their guns into him, and while they examined his corpse, comparing his face to the pictures they carried of the prime minister, two maids found Okada and hid him in the bedding cabinet of a room near the kitchen. Sakomizu, who was then Okada's private secretary, reached the scene a short time later, having been forewarned by his wife that her father was under attack but that she had reason to believe he might be still alive. One of the soldiers, pointing to Matsuo's bullet-torn body on the floor, said to Sakomizu and to another of Okada's secretaries who was with him, "Is this Prime Minister Okada?" Looking down at Matsuo's remains, they both nodded sadly. "Yes, that's Okada," Sakomizu said, and pulled out a handkerchief, wiped imaginary tears from his eyes.

Later in the day, while the rebellion was still in flower, Prime Minister Okada had escaped from his official residence in the guise of a mourner accompanying what was presumed to be his own body.

As he sat down to dinner this evening with the Sakomizu family, the admiral was too distraught by the war even to notice his grandchildren. "Our country cannot win," he said. "It makes no difference how well the navy did today in Hawaii. We can't defeat America. And when we lose, what then will happen to the country, to the Imperial Family?"

He paused as if he thought his son-in-law might have the answer to that question, then went on talking. "And the navy! As a navy man I am shocked and disappointed. This war could not have started if the navy had opposed it with all its strength. Every admiral on active duty must know there is not enough oil to last two years. Why didn't they make an argument of it? Did they expect us old men in the Jushin to argue it for them? They must know Tojo pays no attention to us."

Okada, as one of the former prime ministers who comprised the Jushin, had attended the meeting arranged by the Emperor at the Imperial Palace ten days earlier during which General Tojo had reluctantly spoken about the national crisis and his government's determination to meet it. Seven other ex-premiers had been present at the meeting: Prince Fumimaro Konoye, Baron Kiichiro Hiranuma,

Baron Reijiro Wakatsuki, Koki Hirota, General Senjuro Hayashi, General Nobuyuki Abe, and Admiral Mitsumasa Yonai.

Though Sakomizu knew the Jushin had been called, he had not known exactly why. He said to his father-in-law, "What did Tojo tell you that day?"

"He told us Japan must be prepared to fight because otherwise we might be slowly strangled to death. To which I said the country should not be driven to a sudden crash because that would be even worse than slow strangulation. Yonai said we should not bankrupt ourselves now in an effort to avoid going broke in the future. But we may as well have been talking to ourselves."

"Does Tojo think Japan can defeat America?" Sakomizu asked. He wondered why Tojo, who seemed too intelligent to rush blindly into war, had not used the prestige of the Jushin to hold off the impatient militarists. But could Tojo have done so at this late date without endangering his own life? Even if he had been determined to avoid war, the belligerence within the army was now such an overwhelming force it may have deprived him of options.

Admiral Okada shook his head. "I don't know what he thinks. He told us it was not a question of our strength or ability to win. It was a question of being challenged. If a nation is insulted, then it must fight, whether or not it is prepared, whether or not it can win."

It was the traditional Japanese way of thinking. The bushido code of the Samurai. One might even admire it were it not for the fact that it was leading the country toward a possible disaster. Sakomizu gazed at his children, eating lustily as if this day were like any other, and the thought of their future brought tears to his eyes.

Admiral Okada was still talking about Tojo. "We asked him how he thought the war could be ended and do you know what he said? He said the government hadn't yet figured that out. He had no plan for terminating a war with the United States, so if any of us had suggestions on the subject, would we kindly submit them? Is that not stupid? And it is obvious now that he had already decided on war when he talked to us. We sat there thinking we were discussing only the possibilities which faced us. I left that meeting with absolutely no premonition that ten days later our navy would be attacking Pearl Harbor. Such a terrible thing to do to our country, our Emperor. So stupid! So stupid!"

The elderly statesman trailed off, shaking his head. He looked almost exhausted now, as if he had spent all his strength in anger. Sakomizu, feeling sorry for him, thought of his own father and wondered what he would say if he were alive today. His feelings perhaps would have been quite different since he had spent his life in the army, had been wounded during the Sino-Japanese War, had lost a leg in Manchuria. He had also lost his health there and died at the age of 56, having never recovered it. The army had been his father's entire world, yet Sakomizu himself, proud as he was of his father and of his Samurai background, had never felt any desire to be a soldier. He had instead, after graduating from Tokyo Imperial University in 1925, decided to go into public service, which was also acceptable within the Samurai tradition. He had never, of course, entertained any thought of going into business, which would have been quite unacceptable for a Samurai. His father had never tried to interest him in a military career. Yet after his father's death, on reading his diary, Sakomizu learned that he had always silently regretted his son's decision to forego the army. Sakomizu had felt badly when he discovered this. He had been an obedient son. Had his father asked him to go into the army he would have done so. He shuddered now, though, to think of what he might be doing at this moment if he had known his father's wishes. On this day, an army career appealed to him even less than usual.

DECEMBER 8,
AFTER 8 P.M.

New York Times correspondent Otto Tolischus was now in another taxicab, in the custody of another Japanese police officer, being driven through the blacked-out streets of Tokyo to a destination as yet unspecified. The cab drove northeast from Akasaka, past the Imperial Palace, in front of which one could see, despite the darkness, what looked like a great crowd of people sitting on their heels, heads bowed in the direction of His Majesty. After passing the palace and the familiar Marunouchi business district, where the buildings were limited by law to eight stories in height so they would not overlook the palace, the cab entered narrower, darker streets, unfamiliar to Tolischus, and in a short time he didn't know where they were. On all sides he could see the shadowy figures of soldiers standing guard. Every few blocks, the taxi would be stopped and challenged at military blockades. The officer sitting beside Tolischus would thrust his credentials under the flashlight that shone at them. "Metropolitan Police, transporting a prisoner," he would say, and the taxi would be waved along.

This policeman, unlike the others, seemed almost as depressed as his prisoner. Suddenly he said to Tolischus, "I am very sorry there is war between Japan and America."

Tolischus said, "You can't be any sorrier than I am." In one day, he had already had more than enough of the war. After his early morning arrest, he had undergone an afternoon of interrogation so intense and so unresponsive to facts or reason that it would sound like a comedy skit if it were put on the radio. It was not funny, though, if you were taking part in it, in the center of a cold, damp grilling room, with four policemen pressing down upon you. When they had taken notes on enough of his answers, one of them had compiled the material into what they called his statement and told him to sign it. Since it was in Japanese, they considerately consented to read it to him first in a verbal English translation, but this was so garbled he refused to sign it, thus giving rise to an outburst of fist-shaking and table-pounding that promised however much violence might be needed to persuade him. Finally he had compromised by writing out his own statement in English and signing that. When they read it, however, they insisted it was the same as theirs, and they badgered him until he had signed both documents. His personal cook was then graciously allowed to bring him his dinner, and afterward, before dispatching him on his cab ride through the dark streets, his questioners let him watch while they divided between themselves 1700 yen ($391) they had found in his house.

As the taxi pulled into the driveway of a large, cement-washed building about six stories high, Tolischus asked the policeman beside him, "Where are you taking me?"

"The Tokyo Detention Prison."

After passing through a succession of gates and barred doors, they entered a large, unheated hall which was crowded with other prisoners, some of whom Tolischus knew. Among them was Max Hill, chief of the Associated Press Bureau in Tokyo. He was wearing a faded blue prison kimono. Other foreigners stood around in various stages of undress, waiting to be questioned by officials or examined by prison doctors. There were also some Japanese prisoners who, Tolischus noticed, were subjected to thorough examinations, as if they were expected to stay awhile, whereas the foreigners received only cursory checkups, as if they were not considered permanent inmates.

Tolischus was relieved at this indication that his arrest was merely part of a general roundup of foreigners, prior to repatriation, and not the prelude to charges against him.

Hill, the Associated Press correspondent, when he saw Tolischus, made a quizzical writing sign with his hand, as if to ask whether Tolischus were being held for something he had written. Tolischus, his anger rising again at the indignities to which they were all being subjected, made no reply for fear, out of rage, he might say something he would be made to regret. After a short wait in the large hall, he was shoved into a tiny room, then called out again and told to strip for his physical examination. Shivering in the cold, he asked the policeman who had brought him to get him a blanket.

The policeman said, "I'll tell your assistant, Ofusa, to get you one tomorrow."

Tolischus said, "Why not tonight?"

"It's too late."

In any case, it was too late to spare him the misery of shivering through his medical processing. When he finished, he hurried back into his clothes and moved on to the deposit desk, where he was ordered to empty his pockets. His anger and frustration intensified at this demand because among the items in his pocket was 250 yen $57.50 he had managed to keep from the four policemen who arrested him. The last of his money went now, as well as his wallet and some work notes. He was allowed to keep only a toothbrush.

While he was still at the deposit desk, another American correspondent appeared—W.R. Wills of *Newsweek* and Columbia Broadcasting System. Wills, it seemed, had not yet been told what was happening. The two men were assigned to the same high, wooden tub for their compulsory prison-entry bath, and as they climbed into it, Wills said, "Looks like war."

Tolischus, startled, said, "It is war."

After arising, reluctantly, from the warm tub back into the cold room, Tolischus again dressed and moved along to the next stop, which was the bedding desk. Supplied with a slender mattress and a heavy prison quilt, he was escorted, finally, to his new residence— a tiny, frigid cell, dimly lit and already shaded for the blackout. In accordance with Japanese custom, he was ordered, before entering, to remove his shoes. His feet were destined to be no less icy than the rest of him.

Fully dressed, and without bothering even to examine his new quarters, Tolischus curled up under the quilt, seeking whatever warmth he could gather around him. But a moment later he almost forgot the cold as the heavy cell door clanged shut. Suddenly he knew for the first time what it felt like to be a prisoner. Only his rage saved him from the sinking sensation of horror. The whole Orient, the entire territory he had been assigned to cover, was suddenly in flames, and he was buried in a cell from which he could not report a word of the news.

DECEMBER 9,
1 A.M. IN TOKYO,
DAWN OF DECEMBER 8
IN HAWAII

AS DAWN approached in Hawaii, Ensign Kazuo Sakamaki, still navigating his crippled midget submarine in the waters off Oahu, found himself wondering once again exactly where he was going.

After abandoning, during the night, his 20-hour effort to steer the defective craft inside Pearl Harbor, he had set out for the small, nearby island of Lanai, not far from which the Japanese Navy had designated a location where all five midget subs were to rendezvous with their mother subs. Sakamaki was so exhausted and dispirited he had sailed all night on the surface with the hatch wide open, indifferent to the danger that the enemy might spot him. His one-man crew, Petty Officer Kiyoshi Imagaki, had finally gone to sleep. The submarine was moving slowly through the water despite the damages it had absorbed the previous day.

With the coming of the first faint light of dawn, Sakamaki's bewilderment increased because he found that he was now out of sight of land, but had no way of knowing whether he was heading toward Lanai. Even if, by chance, he were going in the right direction, would he live long enough to get there? He was now so dejected and defeated it scarcely mattered. There was nothing to do but continue until something happened.

Within a few minutes, however, a flicker of hope arose in him. He saw what looked like land ahead. Yes, it was land. Could it be Lanai? "We'll make it yet," he said to himself. "If we can just get there before full daylight, we'll be all right." Into his head came dreamy visions of repairing the submarine and returning to fight.

He shook Imagaki. "Wake up! We're approaching our rendezvous point. Let's see if we can get this thing to move a little faster."

Imagaki roused himself; they both took their positions and Sakamaki turned the gear to "Full Speed."

Instead of speed, the submarine produced vibrations. White smoke rose from the almost ruined batteries. At any moment they might explode but Sakamaki was given no time to reflect on such a possibility. Just then he heard a familiar scraping sound. The midget craft had hit another coral reef. Since this reef was only slightly below the surface, the sub came to a sudden stop, stuck fast upon it, fully exposed to any American ship or plane that might happen along. There was no possibility that its crippled engine could free it now. After quickly assessing the situation, Sakamaki realized this was the end.

Imagaki said, "What if the enemy sees us?"

Sakamaki said, "There is nothing to do but set the demolition charges. We can't let the sub get into enemy hands."

Both men had been well trained in the self-destruct procedures. They checked the explosives to make sure they were properly placed. They lit the fuse. And as soon as they were satisfied that it was burning properly, they scurried through the narrow passageway and up onto the deck. Sakamaki was surprised to see now that they had come within about 700 feet of shore before getting stuck. Could they swim that far? The waves were breaking high on the reef and angrily battering the little submarine. There was no time now, however, to worry about the height of the waves. At any moment, the ship would explode, and even before it exploded it might be attacked. From the dim sky above he could hear the sound of enemy planes.

"Here I go!" he shouted, and jumped into the churning water.

Coming to the surface, he turned in time to see Imagaki follow him. The sea was cold and the waves beat down on them. Sakamaki was conscious of swallowing great quantities of salt water as he thrashed his way through it to get away from the soon-to-explode submarine. One minute, two minutes, several minutes passed as he swam frantically.

Soon, a terrible realization overtook him. The ship should have blown up by now. Why hadn't it? Could the waves have splashed through the open hatch and doused the fuse? Or was the fuse simply slower than he anticipated? He should go back and see. He wanted to go back. Did he have the strength? He looked around for Imagaki but couldn't see him. He tried to shout. No sound came forth. A nauseating dizziness engulfed him and his consciousness faded away.

When Sakamaki awoke, he came to the gradual realization that he was in a bed, lying on a sheet, with a blanket over him. He opened his eyes. Standing by the bed was a man with a rifle. The man was wearing an American uniform. Through an interpreter, Sakamaki soon learned what had happened to him. He had been found unconscious on the northern shore of Oahu, near the Kaneohe Naval Air Station.

He was now America's Prisoner of War Number One.

DECEMBER 9,
JUST AFTER MIDNIGHT IN MALAYA,
AFTER 2 A.M. IN TOKYO

AT LAST they were out of the jungle; Colonel Yoshio Nasu felt he had put off an oppressive burden as his forward contingent of 120 men emerged into a clearing to find they had reached the edge of the British airfield near the town of Kota Bharu. Even the immediate prospect of another night battle with the British was preferable to the long day they had spent in the Malayan jungle and the crushing monsoon rainstorm they had absorbed throughout the evening. The thunderous cloudburst, which had begun pouring streams of water on Nasu and his men at about 8 P.M., and had only recently subsided, was not as unpleasant, nor had it caused as much delay, as the jungle itself. The rain could hardly make the men and their equipment any wetter than the steaming humidity had already done. One might even enjoy the coolness of the rain if one could overcome the fear of its awesome intensity. And though the water had fallen so thickly it was impossible to see more than a few feet ahead, the wrist compasses worn by Nasu and his officers had kept them moving, however slowly, in the right direction. But the jungle itself, with its oozing soil, its heavy, dripping, tangled vegetation, its biting insects and curdling wild animal sounds had been a hideous experience even to these veteran troops who had been told what to expect, and many of whom had faced greater dangers on Chinese battlefields. The training and tradition of the Japanese soldier helped prepare him to face death in battle, but there was no way to prepare a man adequately for the phenomenon of the jungle.

Colonel Nasu was still surprised at his own lack of fear in the face of death. Even though he was the descendant of many generations of Samurai warriors (his own father was killed in Manchuria during the Russo-Japanese War), he had never known until the beach-landing the previous night how deep a hold the Samurai tradition had upon him. He knew now the full meaning of the Samurai belief that "to lose everything, one can be calm." A Japanese swordsman always faced an opponent without a shield. His strength arose from the fact that he accepted death before the fight began. Free, therefore, of the burden of defense, he could devote all of his two-handed power, all of his concentration to his thrust. Having resigned himself to the ultimate loss, he could be calm.

As Nasu peered through the dark toward the hangar area on the other side of the airfield, he was conscious of a growing eagerness to get at the British again. Reorganizing his force, he began carefully the advance across the field, which was surprisingly quiet. Where were the airplanes which had done so much damage to the Japanese landing force? One of the troopships, the *Awagisan Maru,* had caught fire and sunk after 10 direct bomb hits plus a submarine attack. The *Ayotosan Maru,* from which Nasu had disembarked, was still afloat though it had been hit by six bombs. Nasu had been able to gather this from radio reports. But the planes which had attacked these ships did not seem to be here. Had they already moved on to other bases farther inland? Nasu was beginning to think the entire field had been abandoned when a sudden burst of rifle fire served notice that there was opposition ahead.

Nasu's men returned the fire and as they inched forward, on their bellies now, he expected a long, hard fight. His force was pitifully small for the task of taking an airport. He wished some of the other units from the beachhead had managed to join him, but he had no intention of waiting for help. His men were pouring forth a withering stream of bullets and pushing steadily forward as they fired. Though they might be outnumbered, they would soon give these British a taste of Japanese fighting spirit.

The battle was still only a few minutes old when Nasu began to wonder about these British. It was becoming apparent that there were not very many of them. No more than a hundred if one could judge by the volume of fire. And they had nothing here like those rugged beach defenses. Difficult as it was to believe, they were conducting only a rear-guard action, with small groups of men firing then falling back, attempting simply to delay the invaders. As the dark silhouettes of retreating men came into view, the Japanese troops began leaping to their feet to give chase. Watching this sudden rout, Nasu still found it hard to believe that the enemy had so quickly evacuated an airfield as important as this one. They were making a gift of it.

Within a few minutes, Nasu's men began bringing back prisoners at bayonet point, and he was surprised to see that only a few of them were British. Most were Indians fighting in the British forces. Why was the field so poorly defended? There was some confusion among the prisoners, but the impression they gave was that a false report of a pending Japanese attack had swept through the area that afternoon, causing a sudden rush to evacuate. Only these men had been left to stave off the Japanese, and some of them were now vanishing down a dark, narrow jungle road. One of Nasu's company commanders led his unit into the dangerous path after them. Surprisingly he encountered no traps. By the time he returned, with several more prisoners, the fighting had ceased, all the surviving defenders had been rounded up, and the area had settled into a deep silence, interrupted only by sharp, harsh Japanese voices giving orders to the captured men.

With caution, Nasu and his troops approached the buildings, but they encountered no opposition. The place actually was empty and the Japanese had been handed their first air base in Malaya. Colonel Nasu, after communicating this good news to General Takumi, gave the order to settle down for the night. It was approaching 1 A.M. After almost 24 rugged hours on Malayan soil, his men deserved their first sleep.

DECEMBER 9,
DAWN

AS THE light of dawn began sifting through the tall trees of the huge, forest-like Meiji Shrine park in western Tokyo, a strange procession of about a hundred men marched under the great Shinto arch within the park, along the avenue of approach to the shrine's main building. The men were wearing white hats, white kimonos, and white wooden clogs. Because frigid rain showers were pelting them on this cold December morning, most of them were also holding white umbrellas over their heads. Their group, which had marched to the shrine under the auspices of the Imperial Rule Assistance Association, was led by General Kuniaki Koiso, a prominent army officer now retired. Koiso, a short, dark-skinned man of late middle age with close-cropped hair, a pencil mustache and dimpled cheeks, could look back on a 30-year military career during which he held such positions as chief of the army's powerful Military Affairs Bureau, vice war minister, chief of staff of the Japanese Army in China, and a member of the Army General Staff. He had retired in July, 1940, after serving in the government as minister of overseas affairs. In 1931, while chief of the Military Affairs Bureau, he was a behind-the-scenes instigator of an unsuccessful army plot to establish an openly military government in Japan. He had little respect for civilian politicians; he loved the army as he loved his country. He was here at Meiji Shrine this morning to demonstrate this love.

As the strange procession moved out of the tree-surrounded walkway into the square, open compound in front of the main building, General Koiso marched proudly at the fore, leading his companions straight to the enormous, Japanese cypress-wood edifice built in 1920 to honor the great Restoration emperor who had died eight years earlier. It was a beautiful and impressive structure resembling a Buddhist temple more than a traditional Shinto shrine. Its pagoda-style bronze roof was as graceful as any of the roofs on the venerable temples of Kyoto, and the tall trees around it gave it an idyllic setting, remote from the noisy city streets which surrounded the park on all sides. Koiso and his companions walked up the wide flight of six steps leading to the front entrance, stopped, and in a traditional Shinto gesture, clapped their hands to call forth the soul of Emperor Meiji. After a moment of prayer, they then repaired to a nearby purification fountain for the unique aspect of the ceremony they were here to perform.

Putting down their umbrellas, they took up great handfuls, cupfuls and bucketfuls of water, with which they began splashing and dousing their bodies in a torturous orgy of self-abnegation. Within a few minutes, all of them were completely soaked and dripping as the virtually freezing water flew in every direction. Yet none of them shivered. None of them flinched under the stunning flood which they were pouring upon themselves. They were performing a ritual much respected in Japan—purification by cold ablutions.

The custom was an old one. From earliest days, Japanese men who aspired to high moral purposes had been pouring cold water over themselves on winter nights, or standing under frigid waterfalls to discipline their bodies and thereby elevate their souls. Many Japanese equated the ability to suffer bitter cold with the ability to suffer life's inevitable hardships. These men at the Meiji Shrine this morning, by dousing themselves with cold water, were signifying their eagerness to share the hardships of Japanese soldiers and sailors now fighting and suffering for their country.

General Koiso and his companions after they were thoroughly drenched, again turned toward the temple where they joined in a common prayer:

"May all the enemies of the august spirit of the Emperor Meiji capitulate quickly under the righteous strength of our great nation's armed forces."

Their prayer completed, these fervent patriots, the wet white cloth of their kimonos clinging to their benumbed bodies, bowed once more to the spirit of Emperor Meiji, then turned, descended the steps, and began their march away from the shrine.

Because the showers had not yet stopped, those who had come with umbrellas quickly reopened them to ward off the rain.

DECEMBER 9,
8:30 A.M.

MRS. SUMI Yokoyama, a young, attractive widow in her early twenties, was now starting the second week of her first job and she went to work each passing day with even greater enthusiasm than the day before. It was not surprising. A small-town girl from western Honshu who was married after finishing college and had lived with her parents since the death of her husband, she now suddenly found herself employed as the secretary of the most famous scientist in Japan—Dr. Yoshio Nishina, a man of such renown that the physics laboratory at the Institute for Physical and Chemical Research had been named after him. She had discovered that in addition to being famous, he was also polite and warm-hearted. She couldn't have found a better man to work for. After all, she had sought the job not so much because she needed it, but because she was a devoutly patriotic girl who wanted to do something useful for her country. How better could she spend her effort than by helping a scientist like Dr. Nishina?

She had been full of enthusiasm even before she reported for her first day at the big, campus-like compound of the Institute at Komagome in the northern part of Tokyo. And while her eagerness had increased day by day, this morning it knew no bounds because she was convinced that, with Japan now at war, a person like Dr. Nishina was more important than ever. He was the kind of man who might create wonderful new methods and inventions to help the war effort. Yesterday, after being awakened to the amazing news of war, she had gone to work in shock, from which it had taken her most of the day to recover. Now she had had twenty-four hours to comprehend and to adjust herself to the fact that the nation was actually fighting for its life on dozens of battlefields. She was filled with an overwhelming patriotism and zeal as she boarded the train on the Yamate Line at Shibuya en route to Komagome from her home in Setagaya. She did not doubt either the righteousness of Japan's cause or the irresistible strength of its arms, and neither did anyone else if she could judge by the excited, determined faces of the people pushing against her on the crowded train. Premier Tojo, in his radio speech the day before, had helped her understand why the nation was unable to avoid war. So had His Majesty in his wonderful rescript. And so had today's newspapers.

Premier Tojo had made it very clear that America had forced Japan to fight. Japan had been trying for months to negotiate but America had refused to make a single concession. How could America have the nerve to tell Japan to get out of China and Indochina? Why didn't America get out of the Philippines? And why was America helping Great Britain, China, and the Netherlands to encircle Japan? If Japan had given in to America, it would have become just another little country, as weak as it was before the Meiji restoration.

Today's Tokyo newspapers, having had time to recover from the shock of the war, offered several commentaries to help people like Sumi Yokoyama understand it, approve it, and take satisfaction from it.

Historian Ikujiro Watanabe wrote in *Nichi Nichi* that he had been hoping for peace up to the last minute, but he realized now that America's self-conceit, which had led it to make light of Japan, was like that of Czarist Russia at the time of the Russo-Japanese War. Watanabe also mentioned his feelings about the Imperial rescript:

It is not difficult for me to guess that the whole nation is filled with emotion in reading it and will be prostrate before the boundlessly gracious august mind. We do not fear war nor do we like it. We know there is something more dreadful than war. That is a mind which seeks a temporizing peace and lull. This will lead to a country's ruin. . . . Prior to the Russo-Japanese War, the Czarist court believed no country would dare declare war on Russia. The United States is likened to this. A Mukden Battle and a Battle of the Japan Sea, which decided the destiny of the Russo-Japanese War, will not be too distant. The U.S. apparently has been self-conceited in its wealth and strength, though the latter cannot be vouched.

Major General Yahei Oba, retired, writing also in *Nichi Nichi,* told his readers there was no longer any need to make arguments:

Look around. Once the Japanese Army moves, a surprise attack on the Malayan Penninsula is affected without delay, bombings on Singapore, Guam, and Wake Island are carried out successfully; and furthermore, Honolulu, lying far beyond the Pacific, is heavily bombed, sending to the sea bottom big warships. Moreover, an enemy ship was sunk in the eastern Pacific east of Hawaii. What striking adventures these are. Blood sacrifices at the outset of war. . . . These large-scale bombings have been unprecedented since history began. Even the German Luftwaffe has not dared such an epochal venture. Furthermore, all these air bombings were carried out with determination to sacrifice the lives of those who undertook the risks. We can but be moved heartily by this thrilling and grand determination. . . . Japan is, as it were, a coy maiden in ordinary times, but once orders are given, it acts with lightning speed.

The *Yomiuri* correspondent in Buenos Aires reconstructed with evident satisfaction the American reaction to the war. He assured his readers that his information had come from a United Press dispatch, though it might occur to some that he was giving this American news agency too much credit:

The United States government and people, especially President Roosevelt, received one of the biggest shocks of their lives when Japan attacked. Just before the Pearl Harbor attack, Roosevelt and Hull "were outlining the next step to be taken in order to make the Japanese nerve crack and they were positive the Japanese would give in."

When the news arrived, the President was unable to comprehend the full gravity. "He acted like one who had been stricken by palsy, his face pale with the immensity of the crisis he had invited."

The citizens of New York and Washington were speechless when the news was flashed over the air. . . . The situation at the White House and at the State Department was one of consternation, surprise, confusion, and paralysis of activity . . .

The news of the battle over the shores of Honolulu drained the blood from the face of President Roosevelt. At the press meeting on December 8, the hand in which he held a cigaret holder was continually shaking, and in a trembling voice he told reporters of the losses and casualties. . . . "The President looked like Napoleon when the latter first set foot on St. Helena."
. . .

The same correspondent in another dispatch, reported that planes of an unknown nationality, in a great formation, appeared over San Francisco Bay the previous night, then disappeared. Yomiuri also published an analytical article entitled "Economic Effects of Defeat," which pointed out a few of the side benefits to Japan of the first day's war action:

What is considered the most vital effect on America of the brilliant [Japanese victory] is, besides the loss of self-confidence, the loss of normal functioning of the American defense economics . . .

Having suffered this crushing blow at the outset, America can no longer wage a straight, capital-ship fight with the Imperial Navy, which means that all economic and political connections with the southwestern Pacific states have been completely severed. As a result of stoppage of defense raw materials, indispensible in war industries, the defense economics is bound to become crippled.

Japan's largest newspaper, *Asahi*, summed up as well as any the feelings of most Japanese people:

The die is cast. The Rubicon must be crossed . . . The imperial rescript and the statement issued by the government have made the people understand clearly the declaration of war. There is a limit to prudence and patience. Japan had devoted her best efforts to the last moment for the sake of peace. Japan is now punishing the Chungking regime [Nationalist China] that failed to understand the true intention of Japan in maintaining the stability of East Asia and has been uselessly resisting us. Japan is unable to understand why the United States and Great Britain have been aiding Chungking which is hostile to Japan.

As Sumi Yokoyama's train approached Harajuku, a vast, wooded park came into view on the left, and the conductor announced: "We are now passing the Meiji Shrine. I suggest we stand up and bow."

It had become customary, and therefore in fact compulsory, for people in trains, trams, or buses to rise and bow when passing the shrine. The same was true for those passing the Imperial Palace, or the Yasukuni Shrine, which was dedicated to all soldiers and sailors who had died for Japan in past wars.

It seemed especially appropriate on this second morning of a new war to bow in passing the Meiji Shrine. It was not easy on such a crowded train, but since these people were in the habit of doing it every day, they had devised the only possible technique. At the given signal, every torso bent forward in unison.

After the train passed Shinjuku, Tokyo's busiest station, the passenger load began gradually to thin out so that a person, instead of feeling like a match in a box, began to feel like a breathing human being, and eventually even an ambulatory one capable of darting hopefully for a seat, though there was small chance of getting to it ahead of someone else. As soon as the crowd had so depleted that there were seats for everyone and the ride was becoming quite comfortable, it was time for Sumi Yokoyama to get off, at Komagome. Walking the few blocks past little shops and restaurants from the station to the institute, she looked forward to what Dr. Nishina might have to say about the war. Was he as incensed as she was at America's arrogance? Did he have any plans for special scientific war projects? She had begun working for him so recently she did not yet feel she enjoyed his confidence; and she knew nothing about science, but she felt a surge of inner joy at the very likely possibility that this great man might be able to do something wonderful for the country.

In his new and not yet completely finished laboratory building on the grounds of the Institute for Physical and Chemical Research, Dr. Nishina, a short, portly, round-faced, energetic-looking man of middle age, paced impatiently as he talked to some of the younger scientists on his staff. They had vexing problems with their enormous new cyclotron which was to be as large as America's largest—the 200-ton atom smasher at the University of California in Berkeley. Japan had three cyclotrons, two here in the Nishina Laboratory, and one at Osaka University, substantiating the belief that the nation was at least number two in the field of nuclear research. It was useless, however, to have one of the two largest cyclotrons in the world if it couldn't be made to work properly. Its construction was not yet quite finished, and already it had developed complications.

Inasmuch as the laboratory's smaller cyclotron was operating nicely, Dr. Nishina's research was not at a standstill, but this machine, being small in size (23 tons), was incapable of the sophisticated projects he had planned for the larger one. Perhaps it was inevitable that a new apparatus of such great size would, at first, present problems. They would eventually be solved. He had an excellent staff, and since he himself had been originally an engineer, he was often able to help them with their difficulties. (He had become a nuclear physicist after graduation from Tokyo Imperial University in 1918, and had studied in Europe for six years under the great Danish scientist, Niels Bohr. During this period, Nishina and a colleague had developed a formula for scattering gamma rays which was a vital contribution to atomic research.) He sometimes became impatient, however, because it was annoying to lose time on purely mechanical troubles. What he needed was a few American technicians. Until recently there had been a completely free exchange of information between Japanese and American physicists. The Berkeley group had always been wonderfully cooperative.

"But I guess we can stop hoping for help from that direction," said Ezio Tajima, a brilliant young physicist whose time was being almost monopolized now by problems in connection with the large cyclotron.

Dr. Nishina smiled ruefully. "I'm afraid so." He took off his round-rimmed glasses and rubbed an eye. "I still find it hard to believe that this country could do anything so stupid as to go to war against America."

To speak this way in public would be like inviting imprisonment, even for a man as famous as Nishina, but he trusted the people on his staff and had always talked openly to them about the necessity for peace. Among scientists one had little need to be silent because there had always been general agreement that a war would be disastrous, both to scientific progress and to the welfare of the country. Most Japanese scientists, having studied abroad, were aware of their own country's physical and industrial limitations.

Tajima said, "How could the government have come to such a decision?"

"I think it was the army," Nishina said. "They've done it again, only worse than ever this time. Ten years ago they started the war in Manchuria without even informing the government, and they got away with it. Four years ago they started another war in China and they got away with that. But they'll never get away with this blunder. They just don't know anything about America. If they did, they would realize we haven't a chance to win. This is one war our stupid army will regret having started."

Heated by his feelings, Dr. Nishina had failed to notice the arrival of his new secretary, young Sumi Yokoyama, who stood with her mouth agape listening to his incredibily unpatriotic and misleading remarks. Was it possible that a famous man like Dr. Yoshio Nishina could believe that the war was a mistake, that it was the fault of the Japanese Army, that the Americans had been justified in making all those demands, and that they might even win the war? Didn't he know what had happened in Hawaii the day before? And in the Philippines and Malaya? Didn't he know that in 2,600 years Japan had never lost a war? Did he actually think the Americans could overcome the incomparable spirit of the Japanese people?

She went to her desk and sat down in a state of profound agitation. But surprisingly she felt no anger. She entertained no thought of reporting her famous employer to the police. She was simply overcome by the shock of finding that such a learned man could be so ill-informed, so wrong.

After his assistants had gone and she was alone with him she looked up hesitantly from her desk.

"Did you actually mean all the things you were saying when I came in?" she asked.

Dr. Nishina studied her closely and when he answered he spoke with care. "I'm afraid we are in for a very long and difficult war," he said.

"But we were forced into it."

"That may be true," he said. "Even so, it is ridiculous to go to war against America. I don't see how we can win."

Studying her face, he saw the pain he was inflicting upon her. Before she had time to answer, he quickly added, "But we are in it now and it can't be helped. If we work hard and fight hard, who can say what might happen? In any case, however we may feel, we must all do our best for our country."

Hearing her new employer speak this way, Sumi Yokoyama begin to feel slightly better about him.

DECEMBER 9,
7:30 A.M. IN HANKOW,
8:30 A.M. IN TOKYO

IN THE garden of his house near Bukan University in Hankow, China, Lieutenant General Korechika Anami drew back his long, powerful Japanese bow, called upon his mind for its customary concentration, and aimed an arrow at the straw target he had set up near the far wall. He held his aim longer than usual this morning before letting the first arrow fly. When he did let it fly, the arrow hit the target somewhat off center. That would not do. General Anami demanded much better of himself. Though his second arrow was closer, his third was off again. He knew why. His mind was occupied, not with the target, but with the war, with the auspicious successes of the first day of fighting, and perhaps also with a natural desire to be leading troops in battle rather than shooting these arrows at a bale of straw. His mixture of war excitement and personal restlessness was such that, though he was famous for his self-control, he could not quite achieve it today.

General Anami was the commander of the Japanese Eleventh Army, stationed in central China. Because he was headquartered in Hankow, a thousand miles north of the nearest military action at Hong Kong, he saw little hope that he would be involved in any immediate battles. He thus had even greater reason now than usual for his daily archery practice. It helped him work off his excess energies and control his frustration. Being a man who loved action, he had looked forward to his tour of duty here when he arrived the previous April, because at that time only in China was there an opportunity for action. But during his eight months here, he had conducted just one engagement against the enemy, and because the Japanese Army had yesterday assumed so many commitments elsewhere, he could foresee no new offensive campaigns in the interior of China for some time. He therefore could not help feeling impatient. His archery practice, however, was not simply a way to relieve this pressure, or to pass the time, or to provide exercise. It was, to him, one of the essential disciplines in sharpening his Samurai sensibilities. Anami, who traced his lineage to Samurai defenders against the Mongols in the thirteenth century, was himself the Japanese Army's most classic living model of a Samurai warrior. He was honored, respected, and even loved throughout the army, not because of any reputation for intellectual or military brilliance, but because of his Samurai qualities and his warm personality. His intellectual limitations had become evident in his youth when he failed the military academy entrance examination three times before his persistence finally won him admission. His academic record at the academy was only average and he won no awards at graduation. Yet his rigorous self-discipline, his open honesty, his absolute commitment to the army, his unique ability to lead his subordinates and to get along with his colleagues gradually earned him such a reputation as a soldier that, in 1929, he was named aide-de-camp to Emperor Hirohito.

From this prestigious assignment he arose to become chief of the army's Military Regulations Bureau, then chief of its Personnel Bureau, and, in 1939 (a year after his promotion to lieutenant general), vice war minister. It was after General Hideki Tojo became war minister that Anami was assigned to China as Eleventh Army commander.

When he came to China, he had left behind, in the suburb of Mitaka, west of Tokyo, a wife and seven children. He had no fear about their welfare, however, because his wife's younger brother, Major Masahiko Takeshita, lived next door. Takeshita was much devoted to the Anamis not only because he loved his sister but also because, like many other junior officers, he had developed a virtual reverence for the general himself.

Anami had brought with him to China his two most cherished physical implements of Samurai discipline—his bow and his kendo sword. He was expert both as a swordsman and as a marksman. But not this morning. After a disappointing half-hour of archery, he went inside to put on his carefully pressed uniform and, summoning his chauffeur, drove to his headquarters on the Bukan University campus.

When he reached his headquarters he found his staff (more than 200 people—mostly Japanese soldiers, but some Chinese clerks and stenographers) working calmly and diligently as usual despite the exciting war news. With the aid of this staff, Anami directed the three divisions (about 75,000 men) which comprised the Eleventh Army. He also exercised ultimate control over the Chinese civilian population of the Hankow area, which had been conquered by Japan as a result of an epic four-and-a-half-month siege in 1938, a year after the still-continuing "China Incident" began. Hankow was one of three industrial cities clustered on the banks of the Yangtze River about 1,000 miles from its mouth, near Shanghai. An indication of the width of that great river, even 1,000 miles from the sea, was the fact that 40 Japanese warships, including cruisers, were used in the siege of Hankow, and in 1941 important elements of Japan's China Fleet were still based there.

General Anami's first concern this morning was his control section, which was responsible for taking over British and American property in the Hankow region. At 7:30 A.M. the previous day, a few hours after the war began, Japanese military authorities throughout occupied China had seized enemy property. Anami had also arranged to have the British and Americans in his area assembled so he could speak to them.

"I want you to be calm," he had told them. "I promise that your safety will be guaranteed if you create no trouble. But if you do anything harmful to the Japanese cause, you will be put under strict control."

Later in the day, he had also arranged a gathering of the important Chinese in the area. To them he had said, "I think all of you understand the significance of this war. Japan's purpose is still the same as it has been—to establish a co-prosperity sphere throughout East Asia. I strongly urge you to put your trust in Japanese military power. And I caution you not to be agitated or tempted by enemy propaganda."

The officers in his control section made him feel this morning that his words had not been wasted. They informed him that the confiscation of enemy property was proceeding without incident. And no disturbances were reported among the Chinese populace. There seemed to be some small problem, however, among the local tobacco vendors. A delegation of them had come to headquarters and wanted to speak to the general. Since Anami was a cigaret smoker, he felt an understandable concern about the tobacco vendors.

"Show them into my office," he said.

When they were assembled in front of his desk, one of the vendors stepped forward.

"We have come to tell you that we are willing to close our shops," he said.

Anami was startled. "Why? Why should you close your shops?"

The vendor now looked surprised, as if the reason for closing were self-evident. "Because we sell mostly British and American cigarets," he said.

General Anami put up his hand to stop the man. "Do you think that matters to me?" he said. "There is no need for you to close your shops. I want you to remain open and go about your business as before."

After the happy tobacco vendors departed, General Anami sighed with relief. For a few moments, he had suffered an uneasy feeling. If the shops had closed, where would he have been able to buy American or British cigarets? He did not like Japanese cigarets.

Calling in his chief of staff, Major General Isamu Kinoshita, and a few of his staff officers, he said, "What's the latest war news?"

One of the officers said, "The navy has bombed Guam, Midway, and Wake Islands and destroyed most of the planes there. They expect to take Guam in a day or two."

"The navy had better be careful," Anami said. "While they're taking those American islands in the south Pacific, there is always a danger that American carriers might come down from Alaska or the Aleutians and make a surprise attack on us. What other news is there? How about Hong Kong?"

"Our planes have raided it and destroyed twelve of the fourteen British planes there. And, of course, the Twenty-third Army is still on the move in that direction."

This was the operation of greatest interest to General Anami at the moment. "I wonder," he said, mostly to himself, "what we could do to help down there?" Though Hong Kong was about 1,000 miles due south of Hankow, it was closer than any other active battle area. In some way the Eleventh Army should be able to make itself useful to the Twenty-third. Though Anami had a reputation as an excellent administrator, he simply could not reconcile himself to being a desk soldier. On the three occasions when he had led troops in battle, he had acquitted himself well. He had won a local skirmish with the Russians in Siberia in 1919. He had earned high praise for his part in the taking of Luan Castle in China's Shansi Province in 1938. And during his current China assignment, he had defeated 15 regiments of the Chinese Central Army at Chosa (southwest of Hankow) in September though he himself had only four regiments at his disposal. Why should it be his fate now to sit around handling routine administrative work when others were fighting? He would have to find some way in which to make a contribution. He was sharply conscious of a literal commitment he had expressed in a telegram to Tokyo the previous day, after the war was announced. The telegram was to Emperor Hirohito, whom Anami had come to know during his year as an aide-de-camp, and whom he worshipped both as a God and as a man.

"I will do my best and happily die for you," the telegram had said.

This was no idle promise. As a true Samurai, Anami would sincerely welcome the privilege of dying for his Emperor. It did not mean he had a wish to die. Like any strong, vital man, he dreaded death. He had thought about it often and deeply. A Samurai was taught to think about it, to come to terms with it, to learn to accept it as a fact with which warriors must always live. A Samurai was expected finally to reach the conclusion not only that life was a part of death, but that life and death were the same thing. General Anami had reached this conclusion. Because his life was dedicated to the Emperor, so, too, was his death.

DECEMBER 9,
SHORTLY AFTER 9 A.M.

T H E branches of the sacred black pine and camphor trees in the garden of the imperial sanctuary were decorated with strips of yellow and white cloth; mirrors hung from some of the strips. A mirror, in the Shinto religion, symbolizes one's ancestry. When one looks into a mirror he sees himself, which is to see his forebears. Hence, the mirror was one of three symbols of ancient Japan (the sword and a semiprecious stone shaped like a curved teardrop being the other two) which had become known as the imperial regalia. They represented the Yamato clan from which the Imperial Family had descended, and from which therefore, by extension, all of Japan had descended. Tradition held that the Yamatos, offspring of the Sun Goddess, had established ascendancy over other clans and founded the Japanese nation 2,600 years before. Chiefs of the Yamato clan had become, thereby, the high priests of Japan's ancient Shinto religion, and remained so, even to the twentieth century. The imperial sanctuary had been specially decorated this morning because the highest of Shinto priests, Emperor Hirohito, who occupied "the throne of a line unbroken for ages eternal," was expected to perform a special ceremony here, at which he would report to his noble ancestors their country's entry into another war.

Shortly after 9 A.M., the small group of invited guests began to arrive at the sanctuary, located in wooded grounds just within the moat which marked the southern boundary of the palace. Adjoining the sanctuary was the research center where the Emperor conducted the scientific studies in marine biology for which he was well-known. The Emperor's personal residence, the huge, wooden Kyoto-style palace built by his grandfather Meiji, was just a few hundred yards to the northeast along a path between two exquisitely landscaped lagoons.

Two of the Emperor's younger brothers, Prince Mikasa, an army officer, and Prince Takamatsu, a navy officer, were the first to take their seats in the pavilion which housed both the imperial sanctuary and the sanctuary of the gods. Then came Prime Minister Tojo with the members of his cabinet, Dr. Yoshimichi Hara, president of the Privy Council, and six former prime ministers—Prince Fumimaro Konoye, Admiral Mitsumasa Yonai, Koki Hirota, Admiral Keisuke Okada, Baron Kiichiro Hiranuma, and Baron Reijiro Wakatsuki.

Before the Emperor's arrival, court ritualists in priestly robes conducted a preliminary ceremony. With loud handclaps they called forth the spirit of the founder of the Japanese nation in 660 B.C., Emperor Jimmu (Kamu-Yamato-Iwarehiko-no-Mikoto), then the spirits of all the imperial ancestors. They also called forth, in the sanctuary of the gods, all the thousands of Shinto deities. Though Shinto had become in recent years the instrument of Japanese nationalism and militarism, it remained also what it had been since ancient times, a simple worship of deified natural phenomena, and of deified ancestors. Any part of nature—person, place, or thing—which inspired human reverence, wonder, or admiration, was worthy of such deification. This accounted for the fact that there were more than 110,000 Shinto shrines in Japan, each dedicated to its own god or gods.

Having called forth those gods and the spirits of the imperial ancestors, the court ritualists placed out for them offerings of food and sake. It was customary to make daily food offerings at Shinto shrines, and sake was considered to be much welcomed by the gods. After the offering, the chief court ritualist, Prince Kinteru Sanjo, intoned a Shinto prayer to all the gods and all the ancestors. With the last words of his prayer, the preliminary ceremony ended.

At exactly 10 A.M., His Majesty, dressed in an ancient ceremonial court robe, carrying a scepter in his hand, and looking somber, walked into the central pavilion, then into the inner imperial sanctuary where he took his seat facing his brothers and the rest of the audience.

A ritualist rang a bell, the loud, clear tones of which reverberated through the wooden building and through the sacred trees of the garden outside. As the bell sounds faded away and a reverent silence descended over the shrine, another ritualist stepped forward to hand His Majesty a branch from a sacred tree.

With this branch in hand, Emperor Hirohito stood up and turned to face the inner shrine. As he called upon the spirits of his father, Emperor Taisho, his grandfather, Emperor Meiji, and their unbroken line of ruling forebears, his voice, high-pitched and suggesting controlled emotion, began to increase in volume until it filled the pavilion. In stilted court language, similar to that of the previous day's rescript, he explained to the gods and to his ancestors the nation's decision to do battle, and its resolve to win. The small, select group of men in his audience could not help but turn their own thoughts inward as they listened to him.

The Princes Mikasa and Takamatsu, though both military officers, knew the deep regret with which their brother now spoke to their forebears, and they felt a warm sympathy for him as he accepted the weight of this new responsibility.

Prime Minister Tojo, listening to the man he revered above all others, was resolved that nothing would be allowed to stand in the way of the nation's victory, and that nothing must ever be allowed to disturb the Emperor's august mind.

Foreign Minister Shigenori Togo, aware now of an American radio report that the Hawaiian attack had begun about 40 minutes before Admiral Nomura delivered Japan's final note to the U.S. government, wondered if the Emperor had also heard about the report and how he would react to it.

Former Prime Minister Admiral Yonai felt deeply disturbed about the nation's war prospect as he listened to the Emperor's solemn words. And former prime minister Admiral Okada, of like mind, wondered what would happen to His Majesty when America began to demonstrate Japan's folly in challenging its enormous power.

Prince Konoye, whose prime ministry had ended only eight weeks before, was burdened by his inability to secure peace and his unsuccessful attempt to arrange a personal meeting the previous summer with America's President Roosevelt. Could this war have been averted if he had met the President? Konoye thought so. For a week during the previous August he had entertained bright hopes. The President had apparently approved a meeting and had even suggested a location, Juneau, Alaska. Both the Japanese army and navy had agreed to send representatives in the hope of finding a graceful way out of the China stalemate. But finally, President Roosevelt had declined the meeting. Why? Did the Americans not want peace? Or did they simply distrust Japan? Had the Japanese Army's occupation of southern Indochina hardened their feelings against Japan? Or had they already decided upon war as a result of Japan's alliance with Germany and Italy? When Konoye concluded that alliance the previous year, he had been convinced the union of Axis powers would be so strong as to scare America out of fighting. When Roosevelt decided not to see him, he realized what a bad miscalculation that had been. He realized also, at that moment, that his entire political career had been a failure. As he listened today to Hirohito's ritual words, he knew they were, in effect, a ratification of that failure, and he felt badly because Hirohito was not only his Emperor but his dear friend.

There was absolute stillness in the pavilion as the Emperor finished invoking the spirits of his ancestors. After pausing for a moment of silent prayer, he concluded, "We ask the Founder of this Empire (Emperor Jimmu) to grant His protection to our nation, which is now engaged in realizing the ideal that prompted its foundation."

Turning from the inner sanctuary, he glanced quickly at the men seated before him, then without allowing any expression to mar the repose of his features, walked out of the building.

T H E Japanese battleship fleet, led by Admiral Isoroku Yamamoto's flagship *Nagato,* moved majestically down the straits from its sheltered mooring place behind the island of Hashirajima toward the calm blue waters of the Inland Sea between Honshu and Shikoku. Two destroyers escorted the *Nagato* as the heavy dreadnought made its way between the green, hilly banks on each side of the narrow waterway. Behind the *Nagato* came five more battleships, all screened by destroyers, then two cruisers, the small carrier *Hosho,* also screened by a pair of destroyers, and, guarding the rear of the formation, two more cruisers. This powerful flotilla had gotten underway at noon after Admiral Yamamoto hastily decided that the Nagumo task force was apparently retiring from Hawaii and might need protection on its journey westward. Due to the necessity of radio silence, Admiral Nagumo's plans were not known precisely, but from limited information, Yamamoto had deduced enough to be concerned. At the same time, most of the officers on his staff had deduced enough to be infuriated.

As the fleet reached the Inland Sea on the way to the Pacific, there was a growing agitation among the officers in the staff room, and especially among those who professed the most passionate belief in air power—Captain Yoshio Miwa, Commander Akira Sasaki, and Commander Shigeru Fuji.

Just a short time earlier, the detailed report of the previous day's battle in Hawaii had arrived. To avoid betraying his position by using the radio, Admiral Nagumo, after all his planes returned and the Pearl Harbor damage was calculated, had given the report of the action to one of his destroyers, which had then sped as far as possible from the task force before transmitting the message to Yamamoto. The implications of the report were that Nagumo did not intend to strike Hawaii again, but rather intended to hurry immediately back to Japan.

Admiral Yamamoto, in sailing out to meet him, was reacting to the second implication, which could mean the task force had suffered damage.

Captain Miwa and Commander Sasaki, in the absence of any definite indication of damage, reacted to the first implication, which horrified them. There could no longer be any real doubt that Nagumo was retiring from Hawaii. The radio silence proved it. The radio would be crowded with voices if there were any new battle action. Why was he retiring without another attack? Was it not in the best tradition of naval strategy to keep pressing an advantage? It was no more than common sense to extend and enlarge a victory, make it as decisive as possible. Even a naval academy cadet would know that.

The senior staff officer, Captain Kamahito Kuroshima, himself a strong advocate of air power, was as concerned as the others about Nagumo's apparent strategy. "What disturbs me most," Kuroshima said, "is that he got none of their carriers. We have to get their carriers, but does Nagumo realize that? He's not a carrier man. He's a battleship man. I'm sure he thinks if you sink their battleships, you've sunk their fleet. If he really did as much damage to their battleships as he reported, he may feel he's accomplished his mission and he'd better get away before the Americans find him."

"What if they do find him?" Sasaki said. "He controls the air. He has the best fliers in the world."

"Even if their battleships caught him," Miwa said, "he could beat them off. Assuming they have that many battleships left."

Since there was strong gunnery sentiment on Yamamoto's staff, this view was not unanimously accepted. Despite the evidence of an overwhelming air victory against battleships in Hawaii the previous day, gunnery officers like Lieutenant Commander Yasuji Watanabe still preferred to believe that battleships could cope with airplanes. The battleships at Pearl Harbor had obviously been caught standing still. In the open sea, where they could maneuver, the situation would be different.

"It wouldn't be a bit different," Captain Miwa argued. "Wait and see what happens when our planes catch the *Prince of Wales* and *Repulse* off Malaya. They'll both be sunk."

Admiral Yamamoto and his staff were keenly aware of the arrival in Singapore a few days earlier of the greatest battleship in the British Navy, the new *Prince of Wales,* and the equally huge, fast battle cruiser, the *Repulse.* Since these ships were expected to menace the Japanese infantry landings at Kota Bharu and in Thailand, Japanese land-based naval planes were already searching for them along the eastern coast of the Malay peninsula. Perhaps because everyone on Yamamoto's staff was as eager as Miwa to see the two British ships sunk by these searching planes, none of his colleagues arose to argue, even against such a wildly hopeful prediction. There was only one man in the room who challenged him on it.

Admiral Yamamoto, who had been listening quietly to the argument, broke into a mischievous grin and turned to Miwa. "What makes you so certain of that?" he said.

Miwa said, "I'm absolutely convinced of it. We know airplanes can sink battleships. Our planes will sink both the *Prince of Wales* and the *Repulse.*"

Yamamoto was obviously enjoying himself. He shook his head emphatically. "I can't agree," he said. "They're both great ships. Our planes can't possibly hope to sink them."

The captain was now becoming carried away in his enthusiasm for air power. "You want to bet?" he said to his commander in chief.

Yamamoto, laughing, said, "Certainly. What will you bet?"

Miwa said, "Four dozen bottles of beer."

Yamamoto said, "I'll take you up on that," and still smiling, he left the room.

His departure ended the speculation about the *Prince of Wales* and the *Repulse,* but it did not end the discussion about whether Nagumo should again attack Hawaii. Miwa, Fuji, and Sasaki, aroused by the possibility of a complete knockout against the U.S. fleet, insisted that Nagumo should be sent back to exploit his advantage, and the entire staff basically agreed with them.

Watanabe, grabbing a piece of paper, said, "Let's draft a dispatch." Within a few minutes, everyone in the room had signed an order directing Admiral Nagumo to return for another attack against Pearl Harbor. The order then needed only two more signatures. Watanabe took it to Chief of Staff Rear Admiral Matome Ugaki, who also signed it.

Now it was simply a matter of getting Admiral Yamamoto's approval. Watanabe confidently took it to his quarters. But Watanabe's confidence began to waver when Yamamoto, after reading it, looked away thoughtfully for awhile before answering.

Eventually the admiral turned to smile at the excited, enthusiastic young gunnery officer whom he had elevated to his staff two years before, and with whom he played chess almost every evening after mess. Like a teacher speaking to a bright but impetuous student, he said to Watanabe, "If we sent this dispatch, Nagumo would still be unable to attack again. There is an old saying: 'Even thieves, when they have struck successfully and are loaded with booty, turn to trembling.'"

DECEMBER 9,
SHORTLY BEFORE 4 P.M. IN TOKYO,
2 P.M. IN MALAYA

T W O thousand Japanese troops, almost half of the Takumi detachment, were now gathered outside Kota Bharu, the capital of Kelantan Province on the east coast of British Malaya. As their field commander, Colonel Yoshio Nasu, ordered them to prepare for the advance into the town, he envisioned a hard battle for it. Though the British the previous night had surrendered a nearby airfield to his men without a fight, he did not expect them to give up so quickly this important municipality of 20,000 people. The ferocity of the battle for Kota Bharu's Beach of Passionate Love had instilled in him a high respect for British tenacity. The British units at the beach had not retreated. They had simply been wiped out. But the cost to the Japanese had been high—more than 300 dead and more than 500 wounded.

The 2,000 gathered here this morning comprised, however, a strong force. They had a battery of mountain guns and a battery of antiaircraft guns. They even had a company of engineers. Though they were not mechanized, they were extremely mobile. Having proven themselves by taking those fortified beach positions in one day, they were ready, and should be fully able to take the town. Nasu passed the word to his company commanders to advance, but with caution.

On the roads leading into the town from the north, they encountered some traffic in the other direction as Malayan refugees, loaded down with possessions, fled into the country. But Nasu was surprised at how few refugees there seemed to be. They did not clog the roads. They quickly scattered at the sight of his troops and the Japanese advance continued.

Nearing the edge of town, Nasu heard gunfire ahead and decided the battle was about to begin. But the firing died down quickly, and his men moved on. Only an occasional rifle burst could be heard to break the silence of the dense green countryside. As they reached the first houses, Nasu watched closely for some sign that the British were deployed inside, preparing a trap, but quick investigations by his men produced no enemy action and he began to think the British had left Kota Bharu as undefended as its airfield. Before he had gone another half-mile he was convinced of it. If there was to be a fight, it should have started by now. Instead, the streets were lined with Malayans, the town's inhabitants, none of whom seemed to expect violence. If the British forces were lurking someplace in the vicinity, these people would know it; they would not be on the street exposing themselves.

One other thing about these curious onlookers was a source of great satisfaction. They showed no hostility. Some were silent but some waved and smiled. They were, after all, Asians. Perhaps they welcomed the arrival of these fellow Asians to free them from the Western yoke.

It was shortly after 2 P.M. when the Japanese reached the center of Kota Bharu; their advance had now become a virtual parade. The British had indeed retreated to the south, leaving this clean, orderly city to the mercy of the invaders. As his subordinates went to work setting up a headquarters and arranging billets, Nasu asked himself what course he should take now. Should he immediately chase the enemy? Many of his men were fairly well rested, and they could travel at least 25 miles a day on foot. Any Japanese soldier could do that. Such hikes were a regular part of training. Some regiments on forced marches had proven that they could travel 25 miles a day for a month. Even at such a rate, however, Nasu's men might not catch the British, most of whom were probably mechanized. And if they did catch a large, strong British force, it might be disastrous. Perhaps it would be best to stop here and consolidate while awaiting orders from General Takumi, the commander of the detachment, and General Yamashita, the commander of the entire Malayan operation. The Kota Bharu invasion was, after all, only one part of what promised to be a long, hard drive for the whole peninsula from Thailand to Singapore. It had begun amazingly well. The landings of Yamashita's troops at Singora and Patani just above the Thai border had been virtually unopposed, and all of Thailand was now in Japanese hands after one day of war. But British Malaya would not be easy despite the enemy withdrawal from Kota Bharu. Yamashita's forces would soon be swinging south. It would be wise to wait for them. There would be plenty of opportunities to engage the British in the 500 miles of mountain and jungle that lay between here and Singapore.

DECEMBER 9,
5:30 P.M.

IN THE kendo gymnasium of Jikishin Dojo (the Direct Mind School) at Setagaya (a southwestern Tokyo suburb), about two dozen students, their faces carefully passive, sat absolutely immobile with legs folded back under them and hands on knees, around the edge of a wooden-floored arena about 25 feet square. They were watching one of their fellow students in a kendo match against the founder of the school, Sogen Ohmori, an acknowledged kendo master.

Ohmori and his student, gloved, masked, and with torsos padded, faced off in classical stance, pointing their thick bamboo swords directly at each other. They stood erect, watchful, flat-footed and perfectly balanced, narrowing their concentration in an effort to make themselves completely at one with their weapons. Their breathing deepened; hissing, rasping, fearsome sounds issued from their throats.

"Come," Ohmori said through his mask.

The student charged, swinging his sword, right, left, right, with all his strength. But wherever he aimed, however quickly he swung, the master's sword seemed always to be in the right place, warding off the blow.

Again they faced off. Again the student charged. One, two, three of his blows fell against the master's sword. Then a fraction of a second after the student's third unavailing blow, his frustration was intensified when the master's sword, too fast for his eye to follow, crashed with a startling whack against his leather torso shield.

Through instructor Ohmori's mask a faint smile was discernible as the student retreated.

"Come," Ohmori said again.

The student, once more on the offensive but changing his angles of attack, swung and swung again at close quarters. This time he seemed to find an opening. Quickly he moved to take advantage of it. Before his sword could score, however, he felt the jolting embarrassment of the master's sword coming down on top of his head mask.

The student's reaction was natural but disastrous. Tired and pressing hard, he forgot his training and began to flail desperately, leaving himself open to easy retaliation. His watching classmates now became embarrassed for him because herein lay his true defeat, which was self-defeat. Though he could not be expected to outscore a kendo master like Sogen Ohmori, he was expected to retain his self-control and composure, however badly he was being cudgeled. That was one of the important lessons of kendo. More than a sport, it was a discipline which had evolved from the exacting swordsmanship of the Samurai warriors, and which, therefore, demanded of its practitioners not only strength and dexterity but a certain way of life. Sogen Ohmori had not chosen lightly the name of this kendo academy when he founded it in 1934—Jikishin Dojo, or Direct Mind School. He taught his students more than kendo. It was his purpose to make them straight, devout, loyal, disciplined, concentrated, determined, patriotic, and thoroughly Japanese.

After administering a memorable lesson to his student opponent, Ohmori brought the day's kendo class to a close and sent his students off to their evening meal, which they themselves prepared. They had little time to eat because at 7 P.M., the evening lecture began.

On an ordinary night, Ohmori might read to them from ancient texts about warriorship, or instruct them in Zen Buddhism and proper conduct, instilling in them, at the same time, his own political beliefs, which were strongly nationalistic. Tonight he would speak to them mostly about their country, which had now finally, to his great satisfaction, stepped off the brink into war.

Though Ohmori was an ardent war advocate, a dedicated nationalist, a professional kendo master, a practitioner of the spiritual discipline of the Samurai, and a member of a famous Samurai family (his ancestors having been the feudal lords of Odawara, about 40 miles south of Tokyo), he had never been a soldier and, surprisingly, he was not a militarist in the sense of supporting the army's drive toward military dictatorship. He was a political activist and a member of the training department of the Imperial Rule Assistance Association. The association had been founded under the inspiration of Prince Fumimaro Konoye during his premiership in 1940 in the hope of providing a counterbalance to the army's political power. Ohmori believed that while the army was necessary for the accomplishment of Japan's international aims, some check should be imposed upon it to prevent it from exercising absolute internal control over the nation. He distrusted army officers, especially the young ultramilitants, whom he considered overly ambitious, self-centered and concerned with their own power rather than the country's welfare. He felt the young officers should be checked even though he approved of some of their moves. In 1931, he had been overjoyed by the Japanese invasion of Manchuria and at the same time horrified by the presumption of the army field officers who had launched a war there without government approval. He believed these extremists had created a barrier which isolated the Emperor from the people. He had joined the Imperial Rule Assistance Association because he had viewed it as an organization which might be able to break that barrier. Though he was still active in the association, he no longer held such high hopes for it. The army had prevailed and General Hideki Tojo had emerged as prime minister. Ohmori disliked Tojo because he regarded the general as the leader of the army's fascist element. Yet he favored the war into which Tojo had now led the country.

Ohmori did not, of course, intend to discuss his feelings about the army in front of his students this evening. He was well acquainted with the listening powers of the army's secret police force, the Kempeitai, and he knew that with the country at war, it was less prudent than ever to criticize the military. Because of his enthusiasm for the war, he was not even disposed to do so.

When his students were once more gathered for the lecture, he entered the room, dressed now in a traditional Japanese kimono, and surveyed their attentive faces as they sat before him, absolutely unmoving and silent. This was a handsome group of young men, mostly teenagers, their faces open and their minds receptive, already well-conditioned to his views and eager to hear his observations about the war. They did not expect his observations to be startling, unique, or even unusual. They knew him well enough to anticipate much of what he was likely to say. His views about war, politics, and Japan's place in the world were very much like their own, and like those of the great majority of Japanese. Yet he expressed himself so directly and with such force of conviction that after listening to him they always felt more certain of their own views. He inspired, elevated them; he made them proud of themselves, of their ancestry, of their country.

"Japan has now been at war for two days," he began. "I need not speak of the amazing progress of our navy and our army. You can all read the newspapers. Tonight I want to talk about why our country is at war against the United States and Great Britain, and why we should all be proud that our country has taken this daring step.

"First, we are at war because His Imperial Highness, the Emperor of Japan, has enjoined us to make war. We are Japanese and we are his children. If it is his will that we fight, then it is our will. That in itself is sufficient reason for us.

"Some of us, however, might wish to know why it is the will of our Emperor that we should wage war against these two great and powerful countries. We have all read the gracious imperial rescript issued yesterday. It makes His Majesty's reasons clear. Because America and Great Britain want to dominate the entire Orient, they now openly support our enemies in China. At the same time, America is rapidly expanding its military air bases in the Philippine Islands. Britain has strengthened its naval bases in Malaya and Hong Kong. On all sides, the Americans, British, Chinese, and Dutch are pressing against us. And America has even gone so far as to sever all economic relations with us, cutting off our oil and steel supplies in an effort to strangle us. It is to correct such evils that His Majesty has decided we must fight. We are struggling to eradicate the source of evil. We are fighting for the principles of right and justice. On this point, yesterday's imperial rescript is absolutely clear. Therefore, we must never lose this war. We cannot lose. We cannot surrender because the principles of right and justice can never be allowed to suffer defeat. We must fight until we win." Ohmori paused to give his students time to consider the implications of his words. Then he added with emphasis, "I want you never to forget what I have just said."

He turned his close-cropped head back and forth, surveying the intense expressions on his students' faces. Many of these youths would no doubt be called upon to face the enemy in battle before this war came to an end. They would be ready when called. He was certain of that.

"What is it exactly," he continued, "that we find so evil in the conduct of these Western powers? They constantly inform the world of their own goodness. And they never hesitate to admonish the rest of us. Most of you are perhaps too young to remember clearly the Manchurian War ten years ago. Britain and the United States castigated Japan for that war. But why did we take Manchuria? Because our population was growing at an explosive rate and we were short of food. Why were we short of food? Because those same countries were boycotting our products, applying every possible economic pressure against us. And while they criticized us for making Manchuria part of our empire, the Americans sat smugly in the Philippine Islands and Hawaii, which they had made part of their empire, and the British sat just as smugly in India, Malaya, Hong Kong, Australia.

"That was ten years ago. Did these Western powers ever come to admit their own hypocrisy? Not once. Instead, they've grown more overbearing each year. And finally, this year, America brought its arrogance to an absolute climax.

"In the spring, the United States handed Japan a list of impossible demands. Get out of China. Get out of Indochina. Get back to your own little islands and behave like a good little child. In the summer, when we refused to obey, the United States confiscated our assets in that country, refused to sell us any more oil or steel, attempted to paralyze us. And in the fall, while our government offered several concessions in an effort to avoid war, the United States refused to make a single concession on its side.

"But should we be surprised at this refusal by America to negotiate its differences with Japan? Not if we ask ourselves this question: What does America think of Japan? What do Americans think of us Japanese? We all know the answer. To them we Japanese are an inferior people. All Asians are inferior people. 'The Yellow Peril' they call us. They dislike us so much they've passed immigration laws to keep us out of their country. You know about those laws. I know about them. Every man, woman, and child in Japan knows about them. Is it surprising that we feel the way we do about America?"

Ohmori paused to control his emotion. Like most Japanese, he deeply resented the racial prejudice which had produced the Oriental exclusion laws in the United States. Though it was only an unspoken issue in the diplomatic relations between America and Japan, it was a much-discussed issue among the Japanese people and in the Japanese press.

"I don't know how all of you felt when you heard on the radio yesterday that the war had begun," Ohmori said in conclusion, "but as for me, I felt great relief. I felt we had come to an inescapable moment in history, and we had done what we had to do. And whatever the consequences might be, we were prepared to accept them."

When he finished speaking, there were no questions. It would be a breach of manners for any of these young men to speak up to one of his elders without invitation. After the lecture, the students of Jikishin Dojo bowed their heads and continued to sit perfectly still for a half-hour of meditation. Then they returned to their dormitory quarters, spread their *futons* (Japanese mattress pads) on the floor, and went to sleep.

DECEMBER 9,
6:30 P.M. IN SAIGON,
8:30 P.M. IN TOKYO

E I G H T E E N twin-engine bombers (Mitsubishi Type 96) and 15 Zero fighters of the Japanese Navy's land-based 22nd Air Flotilla stood ready for takeoff on the flight line of the Saigon airfield in southern French Indochina, an area which Japanese forces had occupied the previous summer in the move which prompted the United States to clamp its oil and steel embargo on Japan. Though the planes had been ready for several hours to take off from Saigon, they were held on the ground by conflicting reports as to the location of their assigned targets—those two proud giants of the British navy, the new, fast, overpowering battleship, *Prince of Wales,* and the equally fast battle cruiser, the *Repulse.*

These two great modern ships had been sent east to Singapore by British Prime Minister Winston Churchill, and had arrived just a few days before the war began, ready to protect Malaya against a possible Japanese invasion, and to show Japan that Great Britain, though pounded by Hitler in Europe, still had no intention to retreat from Asia.

The 35,000-ton *Prince of Wales* was one of England's two largest and finest warships, heavily armed with naval and antiaircraft guns, and generally considered unsinkable. The 32,000-ton *Repulse,* an older ship had been recently rebuilt to match the *Prince of Wales* in speed and armament. The Japanese Second Fleet under Vice Admiral Nobutake Kondo, which was protecting the army's invasion of northeastern Malaya, had no battleships strong enough to challenge either of these British dreadnoughts. Indeed, there was not a battleship in the entire Japanese Navy that would dare face them. When Admiral Isoroku Yamamoto had learned of their arrival in Singapore, he had exercised his only option by sending more planes to augment the 22nd Air Flotilla, under the command of Rear Admiral Sadaichi Matsunaga.

Early this afternoon, one of Matsunaga's reconnaissance planes had radioed back to Saigon a report that the two British warships, despite the previous day's Japanese invasions of the northeast coast of Malaya, were still sitting idly in Singapore harbor. But at 5 P.M., before the bombers and fighters had time to take off from Saigon, a Japanese submarine, the I-56, stationed outside Singapore, sent a conflicting report that the two ships had emerged at 3:50 P.M., and were proceeding northward toward the Kota Bharu beachhead. Be-

cause of the completely opposite reports, the reconnaissance plane
had been ordered by radio to hurry to Saigon with its photographs.
And the pilots of the 22nd Air Flotilla were now waiting anxiously in
the Operations building while the photos were being developed.

Twenty-three-year-old Lieutenant Sadao Takai, who was one of
those pilots, felt a special eagerness to get into action against the
huge British ships. Takai was a squadron leader in the Genzan Air
Group, one of the groups which composed the 22nd Flotilla. Two
nights earlier he had led his squadron toward Singapore in what was
scheduled to be the first bomb raid of the entire war, but a front of
enormous, close-packed thunderstorms had battered his planes so
severely they had been unable to hold formation, and the mission had
finally been canceled. This evening he was doubly anxious to erase
that frustration by taking off before a new front of thunderstorms had
time to form, yet he realized it would be unwise to launch a mission
so late in the day without confirming the location of the targets. And
he was too experienced a pilot to speculate as to whether the airplane
or the submarine report was most likely to be reliable. He knew that
neither a pilot's eye from high altitude, nor a periscope view from
three or four miles could be relied upon with confidence.

Takai and his fellow pilots pressed forward toward their commander, Admiral Matsunaga, as a photo technician came running
into the room with the reconnaissance plane's pictures.

Everyone fell silent while the admiral and his staff studied them.
There were, indeed, two huge ships in Singapore harbor.

Someone shouted, "Singapore, here we come!" and the excitement
in the room began to rise. When the scout plane report first arrived,
the depth of Singapore harbor had been studied and an attack
strategy had been developed similar to that which succeeded so well
at Pearl Harbor the previous day.

While the pilots set their minds on Singapore, however, Admiral
Matsunaga and staff continued to study the photographs. After a brief
consultation he looked up and called for silence.

"The two ships in the harbor are not the *Prince of Wales* and the
Repulse," he said, holding up the photos. "These are large transports.
I think we can assume the submarine report was accurate. That
means the British force is proceeding north toward our beachhead
at Kota Bharu. You men know your mission."

A stampede of running feet followed his words as the air crews
raced for their planes. At 7 P.M. in Saigon (9 P.M. in Tokyo) the 18
twin-engine bombers began speeding down the runway, each with
a single torpedo, weighing almost one ton, in its belly.

As Lieutenant Takai led his nine-plane squadron southwest toward Malaya in the last hour of daylight, he knew how difficult it would be to catch the British ships. His men were so well-trained, however, he felt they had an excellent chance. His own seven crew members had been flying with him for a year; they were ready for either day or night operations as were the rest of the men in the squadron. Each plane carried, in addition to the pilot, an experienced co-pilot, two navigators, two flight engineers and a radio operator, most of them were also qualified gunners. They were dedicated fliers and veterans of combat in China. Takai himself, a bachelor, had been devoted to flying since his graduation from Naval Academy in 1938, and his rise to the position of squadron commander had been remarkably quick, especially in view of the fact that he did not come from a Samurai family. His father was a government employee. Only one deep concern occupied the young lieutenant's mind as he and his country faced the hard realities of war against Great Britain and America. Just ten days earlier he had encountered sobering evidence of Japan's shortages in the necessities of war. His planes were blowing out tires so often in the tropical heat of Indochina that he had to send a transport plane back to Yokosuka Naval Base near Tokyo for a full load of new tires. The plane returned with only a half-load. No more could be spared, even for a bomber squadron in a forward battle zone. A few days later, Takai discovered another disturbing piece of information. In Indochina at the moment there was available only one torpedo per plane. The torpedo in the belly of his plane right now could not be wasted or jettisoned. He had to make it count because when it was gone he could not go back to the base and pick up another. He was confident, however, that if the *Prince of Wales* and the *Repulse* were found, they could be sunk, even though they might be the finest ships in the British Navy. And he realized they must be found quickly because unless they were destroyed, they would be turning their huge, 15-inch guns on the Japanese invasion fleet at Kota Bharu sometime tomorrow.

As Takai's planes flew south along the Indochina coast, cumulonimbus storm clouds rose up ahead of them, reminding him of his aborted mission against Singapore. Tonight he was determined not to turn back, however many storms they might encounter. Even if his formation were forced to scatter, his pilots were ready to go on individually in search of the British ships. Descending below the cloud level, they continued on course in tight formation, disregarding the turbulence which battered their planes.

A voice broke into the static on the radio and Takai's radio operator, listening carefully, picked up an order from Admiral Kondo, the Second Fleet commander. All available surface and air units, the order said, were to mobilize for night attack.

The Second Fleet, then, was also on the trail of the *Prince of Wales* and the *Repulse.* But did Admiral Kondo actually intend to challenge them with his underpowered force? He had two battleships, the *Haruna* and the *Kongo,* plus a supporting armada of cruisers and destroyers, but no carriers. None of his ships could match the fire power of the two British monsters. Admiral Kondo must be a very brave man to lead his fleet into such an engagement. It would be a shame to subject him to the consequences of his bravery. Takai and his men did not intend to let the surface ships beat them to the prize. They would simply have to reach the British ships ahead of the Second Fleet.

Unfortunately, however, as darkness fell, visibility continued to diminish, and though Takai presumed the British ships were sailing north off the coast of Malaya, he could only guess at their general location. He didn't even know the location of the Japanese fleet, and that worried him. The Japanese Navy had developed no dependable system to help its pilots distinguish friends from enemies at sea. Identification of warships, difficult in the daytime, was almost impossible at night, especially on gloomy, cloudy nights like this. Takai and the pilots in his formation, now flying at 1,000 feet to stay under the clouds, could see only a small area of ocean below them as they searched the waters between Indochina and the Malayan Peninsula.

They were still flying southward when they picked up a radio report from the second bomber squadron engaged in the search: "Enemy vessels sighted. We have dropped a flare bomb."

Each plane, in addition to its torpedo, carried four parachute flares to help light up the target in case of night attack.

Takai could hear the cheers of his crew behind him as he turned in the indicated direction and pushed his throttle all the way forward for maximum speed. The other squadron was already on the scene. It would be an unbearable disappointment to Takai if he were to miss this battle, after his earlier frustration in the cancelled Singapore raid.

Before his planes were close to the scene, however, his radio operator received a second message from the other squadron: "The vessel under our flare is the *Chokai.*"

The *Chokai* was a Japanese heavy cruiser, flagship of Vice Admiral Jisaburo Ozawa's Malaya Force, which was a component of Admiral Kondo's Second Fleet.

When Takai absorbed the new message, his reaction was not the disappointment one might expect. He was, instead, horrified. The theoretical danger of attacking a Japanese ship in the hazy darkness struck him now as a hideous and likely possibility. What would have happened if his radio operator had not, despite the static, picked up the second message? He shuddered at the image of himself trying to explain to his commanding offcer, Admiral Matsunaga, why he had torpedoed Admiral Ozawa's flagship.

He could sense the dejection of his co-pilot and the men behind him as everyone became aware of the problems now facing them. It was as if their task had been doubled. It was going to be just as difficult to miss their own ships as it would be to hit the British ships.

Another voice broke into the radio static and everyone listened carefully. This message was an order from Admiral Matsunaga: "Discontinue operation. All planes return to base."

A sudden outbreak of smiles and cheers greeted these words. Takai himself felt his tense muscles relax. Yet as he banked his plane and headed back toward Saigon, he was haunted by a terrible image. He could see the shells from the *Prince of Wales* and *Repulse* shattering ship after ship of the Japanese invasion fleet at Kota Bharu the next day.

MIDNIGHT
BETWEEN DECEMBER 9 AND 10

THE NIGHT was so dark that however many submarines the enemy might already have patrolling the Pacific near Japan, it was unlikely any of them could spot the blacked-out ships of Admiral Yamamoto's battleship fleet as it sped eastward to meet the carrier task force which had attacked Hawaii. Yamamoto and his chief of staff, Rear Admiral Ugaki, sat relaxing in comfortable chairs on the bridge of the flagship *Nagato* as midnight approached. Though they were facing each other at opposite sides of the helm, the darkness was so deep they could only vaguely discern each other's outlines. When they turned to look forward through the wide glass window, they could see nothing but black ocean ahead of them. They spoke only occasionally. Both men were absorbed in their own thoughts. It was the time of day when Yamamoto could try to forget his responsibilities and think of his wife and four children, at home in the Aoyama district of Tokyo, near the Meiji Shrine. He had last seen them a week before, when the Emperor had summoned him to Tokyo. When would he see them again? Such thoughts renewed in him his melancholy feelings about the war, which continued to depress him despite the apparent victory at Hawaii. How great a victory had it actually been, he wondered. Even after reading Admiral Nagumo's full and glowing report, he had not been able to dispel the fear that the results had been exaggerated. Before retransmitting the report to Admiral Osami Nagano, the navy's chief of staff, he had deleted most of the colorful details for fear they might be misleadingly optimistic. If the report proved accurate, his strategy had indeed worked far better than he had ever hoped. It would give Japan a year, possibly two years of grace before America could recover and begin closing in for the kill. Ultimately, of course, it would make no difference. One day the Americans would come, and when they did, the entire tragic foolishness of challenging them would be apparent to everyone. Meanwhile, there was nothing to do but fight with every weapon and every strategic device one could muster. Hawaii was a good start. What about the midget submarines, though? Had none of them survived? It was bitter to think of the ten brave men who had volunteered for that mission when they knew there was so little chance to return from it. At least that was one advantage in Japan's favor—the spirit and commitment of her fighting men, the depth of her warrior tradition.

At the sound of a door closing behind him, Admiral Yamamoto glanced around to see the shadow of a tall figure groping through the darkness toward him. As the man came closer, he decided it must be young Watanabe, his gunnery and logistics officer.

"Watanabe, is that you?"

"Yes sir."

"What is it?"

Watanabe was close now, standing beside the admiral but slightly to the rear. He turned on a tiny flashlight which was aimed at a piece of paper in his hand. The glow of the miniscule light, while leaving the room still dark, did slightly illuminate Yamamoto's features.

Watanabe said, "A message from His Majesty, sir."

Admiral Yamamoto, who had been sitting at ease, snapped to a sitting attention but said nothing.

Watanabe read the heading: "Appreciation from the Emperor."

Admiral Nagano had apparently gone straight to the palace upon receiving the full Hawaiian report. It was astonishing that His Majesty had reacted so quickly.

Watanabe continued. He was now reading the Emperor's words: "At the very outbreak of this war our combined fleet has displayed a brilliant strategy and fought bravely. At Hawaii it has heavily crushed the enemy's fleet and air strength. We have received a report of this signal achievement ourself. Moreover we extend our deepest praise to our fighting forces, officers, and men alike. If they strive harder and harder we foresee a magnificent future for our empire."

When Watanabe finished there was silence. Finally Admiral Yamamoto made a deep forward bow. He still said nothing. Watanabe, in the dim light of the flashlight he had forgotten to extinguish, could see tears trickle down the left cheek of the Navy's commander in chief.

Excusing himself, Watanabe left the bridge. On deck, there was no sound in the dark night except the throbbing hum of the great ship's engines.

DECEMBER 10,
6:20 A.M.

I T W A S no pleasure getting up so early on a cold, rainy morning to go to a meeting she would not enjoy, but since someone in the family had to go, Mrs. Maki Sakomizu set out, about 6:20, for the house a few blocks away where the meeting was to be held. This was a special Neighborhood Association meeting for the section of Shinjuku in which the Sakomizus lived. Such meetings were being held simultaneously by Neighborhood Association chapters in each city, town, and village throughout the country, and every householder in Japan was expected to be present or represented. Mrs. Sakomizu usually attended the association meetings, which were held monthly and on special occasions, because her husband Hisatsune, an official of the Finance Ministry, went to work early. Since this was true of many men, there was always a preponderance of women at the meetings.

When she arrived at the house in which this one was to be held, she noticed that a radio had been set up in the center of the front room. A man was turning dials, testing it. Apparently some high official would be addressing the meetings all over the country this morning on a nationwide network. She wondered who. It didn't really matter. One could guess the message. Now that we are at war, we must work harder than ever, tighten our belts, make greater sacrifices. Hadn't the Japanese people made enough sacrifices already? War was not new to them. They had been engaged in it constantly now for ten years, since the Manchurian invasion of 1931. For some time, such things as rice, sugar, matches, cigarets, soap, stockings, coal, and most canned goods had been rationed, and while many of these items were still available to people who could pay black market prices, they were much too expensive for anyone below the middle class. As for automobiles, refrigerators, washing machines, and such luxuries, only the very wealthy could afford them. Japan's heavy industry, for ten years now, had been geared, not to consumer goods, but to iron, steel, chemicals, and machinery, plus exports for foreign markets. Though wages and salaries had risen slowly, prices had more than kept pace. The Japanese people did not need a new war to acquaint them with austerity.

It was, nevertheless, an excited, smiling group that Mrs. Sakomizu encountered this morning at her Neighborhood Association meeting. Though they might not like the hardships they had been enduring, or the prospect of even greater hardships, most of them were in a state of euphoric elation from reading about the amazing victories during the first two days of war. They chattered gaily about the morning news. The British were retreating in Thailand. Hong Kong was said to be in confusion as the Japanese Army advanced southward toward it. And Germany was reported to be "electrified" at the speed and force of the Japanese Pacific "blitzkrieg." Sources in Berlin expected the Germans and Italians to "clarify their own positions" soon, which could only mean that they intended to declare war on America (though they hadn't yet made any promises to do so). These were exciting days in which to live, the greatest days in the history of the Japanese Empire. There was only one disturbing item in the news. A dispatch from Lisbon said that 25,000 Japanese nationals had been "arrested" by the Americans in the Philippine Islands. At the same time, in Bangkok, American, British, and Dutch nationals had been "put under the protection" of Japanese troops. One could sense from stories like this a great difference between American and Japanese treatment of captured enemy citizens. What would happen to those unfortunate Japanese in the Philippines?

The president of the local chapter called the meeting to order promptly at 6:30 because, as he announced, the Imperial Rule Assistance Association was about to bring them a special radio program. Everyone settled down on the straw-matted floor and listened, for the next half-hour, to a series of patriotic talks, with one speaker after another demanding of them greater effort, greater vigilance, greater commitment to the nation and to His Majesty, the Emperor. Despite the similarity of the messages, people listened to one after another with fervid attention, especially when the final speaker presented what he called the Imperial Rule Assistance Association's five point Code of Instruction for National Life:

"First, we must be strong," he said. "Japan is fighting at the risk of its national fortune.

"Second, we must beware of rumors and be careful not to be deceived by them.

"Third, remember that if you withdraw deposits from your bank unnecessarily, or if you are guilty of hoarding goods, you are commiting an act of treachery against the state.

"Fourth, in case of air raids or fires, the neighborhood units must work together in full cooperation.

"And fifth, do not be intoxicated by our brilliant war results. Be determined at all times."

Even Mrs. Sakomizu found herself responding with some enthusiasm. Here, at last, was advice the people around her badly needed. They all seemed to be intoxicated by the victories so far. She wished she could join them but she knew too much. Being the daughter of former Prime Minister Admiral Keisuke Okada, she had long since come to agree with him that it was suicidal to fight America. But why couldn't other people see this? Everyone was at least vaguely aware of the size and power of the United States. In a year, two years, three years, would these neighbors of hers still be holding meetings like this one, gossiping about the latest victories? She could hope so but she didn't think so.

As the program ended with the playing of "Kimigayo," the national anthem, everyone sprang to attention. Then everyone again settled down for the local business of the meeting. First came the collection of dues and the war bond allocations. Each householder was expected to pledge between five and ten percent of his income. When Maki Sakomizu's turn arrived, she made the pledge for her husband without comment. Next came a discussion of ration cards, and finally someone raised the question of procedures in case of air raids. Just the previous day, the city of Tokyo had begun issuing pamphlets on air raid precautions, but the primary responsibility, as everyone knew, rested with the neighborhood groups.

"If enemy planes attack the city and create large fires in our neighborhood, do we have enough water to fight them?" one of the men asked.

A few people smiled at the idea, and another man said, "How can the enemy attack Tokyo when he can't even defend Hawaii."

Most of the people, however, did not take the matter so lightly. They were not that much intoxicated with the victories of the first two days. The possibility of fire in their wooden city quickly sobered them; the discussion turned to such subjects as storage tanks and hand pumps. There were not enough hydrants, even in an area as prosperous as this, and there were not enough pumps, either. An effort should be made to find and buy more pumps, despite the cost. Even so, if enemy planes ever did succeed in breaking through the defenses and dropping their bombs, everyone would have to become a fireman. That much was certain. Tokyo was frightfully vulnerable to fire, as the 1923 earthquake had proven by completely devastating the city and killing 107,000 people. Modern Tokyo was only slightly less susceptible than the Tokyo of 1923. Fire drills would have to be intensified. Everyone would have to be trained. Each neighborhood would have to organize hundreds of people into bucket brigades.

Maki Sakomizu listened in silence as the discussion continued. She wanted to say something but what was there to say? The whole conversation seemed to her appalling. These people were not stupid, yet they seemed to have lost their perspective. They were seriously talking about hand pumps and bucket brigades to fight the kind of fires which would erupt in an air raid. Did they really think that a country with such pitiful resources could defeat America?

DECEMBER 10,
2 A.M. TO EARLY P.M.

BECAUSE a severe rainstorm had forced several Zero fighters to take refuge at auxiliary fields in southern Formosa on their return from Monday's Philippine raids, it was 10 A.M. Tuesday before they could all reassemble at Tainan, then refuel, rearm and take off for their next strike at Luzon. Flight Petty Officer Saburo Sakai, in a formation of 27 Zeros, was relieved as the flight progressed, to find no trace of the storm which, the previous day, he had escaped only by descending almost to the dark surface of the angry water. Fair weather would be important today because, after attacking any U.S. planes that might appear over Clark Field, the Zeros were to fly north to Vigan, on the western coast of Luzon, where the first Japanese infantry landing in the Philippines was scheduled to have begun at dawn.

It seemed unlikely, from the moment the 27 Zeros began circling Clark Field, that they would find any challenge there. After Monday's and yesterday's attacks, no healthy-looking planes could be seen on the burned-out air base, and no planes appeared in the air from elsewhere, but the Zeros, following orders, circled for a half-hour before turning north toward the infantry landing area at the centuries-old port city of Vigan. Flying peacefully above the Philippine mountains, Sakai began to wonder if he dared believe the evidence that, after only two days of war, American air power in the islands had already been eliminated.

Arriving over Vigan at 18,000 feet, the 27 Zero pilots looked down and saw, exactly where it was supposed to be, a landing force of one cruiser and six destroyers protecting four troop-transport ships. For 25 minutes Sakai and his companions circled lazily, more certain with each passing moment that the Japanese ships below them were in no danger. If no American planes had yet attacked a convoy of this size, it could mean only that the Americans had no planes left. This conviction, which kept growing in Sakai's mind, was suddenly routed when he noticed three expanding rings in the water near one of the ships. Though he was too high at 18,000 feet to have seen bombs explode, he was certain that only bombs could have caused such large water-rings. It was fortunate that none of the ships had been hit, yet even as he began searching the sky for the offending U.S. planes, he burned with guilt, shame, and anger at himself for not having seen the planes in time to drive them away. Scrutinizing the skies all around him and turning so far in his cockpit he was almost facing the planes behind him, he finally spotted, 6,000 feet overhead, flying southward at high speed, an American B-17 bomber, alone and unprotected.

Where, he wondered, were the other American planes. American air power over the Philippines apparently had not been eliminated after all. The presence of this bomber meant others must be nearby.

Perhaps the Amricans hoped they could get at the convoy by using one bomber to lure the Zeros away. They ought to know one bomber could not lure away all the Zeros. Maybe they were hoping, only, to create a momentary distraction. U.S. fighter planes might appear any minute now. But let them appear. Sakai had been waiting since Sunday for another encounter with the P-40s. He would not be shot down by one of them. He had promised himself that. He had made a vow that though he might some time be shot down by anitaircraft fire, or run out of gasoline and fall into the sea, he would not be shot down by another fighter plane. To the men with whom he flew, that was the ultimate disgrace. Never must he allow it to happen to him. Those American fighters could come when they pleased. He was ready for them.

It soon became apparent, however, that there were no American fighters to come, and that the lone bomber speeding away had actually been so courageous as to attack, without help, a convoy protected by a squadron of fighters. It was apparent also that the bomber might soon escape while Sakai and his comrades looked for its phantom escort. At an order from his squadron commander, Sakai and a group of Zeros suddenly turned to pursue it.

Since the B-17 was already several miles away, and since it was much faster than Japanese intelligence reports had estimated it to be, the pursuing Zeros had to fly at maximum speed to catch it. They were finally getting close to it, about 50 miles short of Clark Field, when Sakai and his companions were surprised to see three other Zeros, appearing as if by magic, swoop in to attack it from the side. The three Zeros, apparently from a group that had been assigned to hit Nichols Field near Manila, proved as ineffectual as they were sudden. After their initial firing runs, the B-17 moved on, untouched.

Sakai and six other Zeros in his group quickly joined these three, and the ten planes together assailed the Flying Fortress. But in the rarified air at its altitude (22,000 feet), the Zeros were difficult to control precisely, and all ten of them, attacking in succession, left their intended victim still undamaged. Sakai, chagrined at his own inaccuracy, could take consolation only in the fact that the B-17 gunners were equally inaccurate. Though they had maintained constant fire, they had done no more harm than the Zeros. Never before having encountered one of these awesome B-17s, he wished he had been given better intelligence about it. The Zeros, approaching from the side, all had miscalculated the airplane's speed, perhaps because it was so difficult to believe. For a bomber, and especially for such an enormous one, it was incredibly fast. But it must have a weakness.

Swinging around behind it to look for a vulnerable spot, Sakai decided at last he had found it. The plane had no tail turret. How could it protect itself against attacks from the rear?

At full speed he closed in on the B-17, aware that he must hurry, since they were now over Clark Field where American fighters, if there were any left, might come to help the beleaguered bomber. As he moved closer, two other Zeroes sped up to take their places on his wings, and the three planes flew in a virtual formation with the B-17, directly behind it. The big plane's pilot made it swerve from side to side like a dog trying to shoo away flies with its tail. The pilot's apparent strategy was to put the Zeros in view of his side-gunners, but it was to no avail since the gunners couldn't get enough time to aim.

Sakai had come as close now as he wanted to be. The bomber's right wing was centered in his gun sight. He pressed his trigger for a short burst of fire. Nothing seemed to happen. Then a few sheets of metal flew, like twisted paper, from the wing and, more important, a thin, white spray began trailing from the damaged area. Sakai, hoping to hit either the fuel or the oxygen system, shot a burst of cannon fire at the same spot, and another, and another. Suddenly, the thin spray was a full flow. The B-17 guns ceased firing and flames arose inside the fuselage. Sakai, pressing his trigger again, was momentarily infuriated to find he had run out of ammunition. He quickly realized, however, that it no longer mattered. Even as he retired from the attack, giving his wing men a chance to open fire, the unfortunate American plane went into a sudden dive toward the ground. Sakai, diving after it, grabbed a camera he had with him and began photographing its fall. He was amazed to see that, despite the plane's now disastrous condition, the pilot still maintained enough control of it so that at 7,000 feet, three men were able to bail out. A moment later, the plane, hopelessly aflame, plunged into a cloud and disappeared. Saburo Sakai had shot down his second American plane, this one piloted by a courageous flier whom Americans would soon be honoring posthumously as their first hero of the war—Air Corps Captain Colin Kelly.

While Sakai and his companions were attacking the B-17, the initial infantry landings on northern Luzon continued as planned, several other Zeros attacked the few planes to be found around Nichols Field, and a force of Japanese bombers devastated the Cavite Naval Base near Manila.

As a result of the day's operations over Luzon, Vice Admiral Nishizo Tsukahara, commander of the Eleventh Air Fleet, was able to report to Tokyo that American air power in the Philippines had been reduced almost to the point of elimination. These islands were now ready, far ahead of the most hopeful schedule, for a full-scale invasion by Japanese land forces.

DECEMBER 10,
1 P.M.

THE speakers' platform in front of the scoreboard at Koraku-en Stadium (in north-central Tokyo) was decorated with bunting. Along the stands were streamers which said:

"Smash America and Britain!"

"Let the Hundred Million of Us March Against the Enemy in One Blazing Ball of Fire!"

Actually, there were only about seventy million Japanese in 1941, but since the government was encouraging a higher birth rate (while complaining of a shortage of living space), there was a tendency among some people to refer to a projected hundred million as if it were already a fact. In any case, a disappointing portion of the populace had shown up for the "Smash America and Britain" Rally at Koraku-en Stadium this afternoon, even though it was sponsored and promoted by the Tokyo newspapers. The stands were scarcely more than half-full. Perhaps the intermittent showers had held down the crowd. Perhaps also the lack of any famous speakers on the program had kept people away. Japan's prominent officials felt no need to court the press by appearing at newspaper-sponsored events. It was more necessary, in fact, for the press to court the high officials, since they had absolute censorship powers. The cabinet information bureau, the army, and the navy had all sent representatives, however, and the navy had even sent a band.

Promptly at 1 P.M., the band marched onto the field playing the Naval March. Everyone stood and, as soon as the music came to a stop, turned to bow toward the Imperial Palace, which was about a mile south of the stadium. Then after a short, solemn prayer for the deceased heroes of the armed forces, and another prayer for a Japanese victory, the crowd sat patiently to hear short exhortations from several newspaper publishers, followed by longer ones from the principal speakers—Kiwao Okamura, a division chief from the cabinet information bureau, and Commander Hideo Hiraida, of Naval Intelligence.

"Just a few months ago," Okamura said, "I was in Honolulu, Hawaii. While I was there I met an elderly Issei (first generation Japanese immigrant to America). That man made an amazing prediction. 'Some time in the future,' he said to me, 'Japanese planes will come and they will attack the whole of Hawaii. I dream of the day when Japan will conquer all these islands.'"

After an interruption for applause, Okamura concluded: "What happened two days ago at Pearl Harbor makes this old man's dream come true."

Commander Hiraida, who followed Okamura, began his speech on a sobering note. "Despite our magnificent start," he said, "we must be prepared for great hardships and for a difficult struggle. We must accept the possibility that this war could last ten years."

Having put this warning dutifully into the record, he turned happily to a subject which seemed to belie it—the unparalleled accomplishments of navy fliers both in Hawaii and in the Philippines during the first two days of war. "The Japanese Imperial Navy," Hiraida promised in conclusion, "will continue to let action speak in proving to the world its superiority."

The crowd seemed now to forget the ten-year war warning with which he had begun his speech. A great cheer arose for Japan's invincible navy. Then a resolution was adopted in praise of both the army and navy. And at 3 P.M., the small crowd filed silently out of the big stadium. The event had been a disappointment to the Tokyo newspapers which sponsored it. They would have difficulties making it seem exciting in their next day's editions.

While the newspapers had been unable to draw a great crowd for their rally, however, the patriotic societies had no such problem. Despite the rain showers, 210,000 members of the Ex-Servicemen's Association were now marching resolutely, four abreast, toward Yasukuni Shrine, just north of the Imperial Palace. After assembling in the morning at Hibiya Park just south of the Palace, these men, some of them aged veterans of the Sino-Japanese and Russo-Japanese wars, had been marching through Tokyo all day, from shrine to shrine. But if they were tired, they tried not to show it now because they were finally approaching the climax of their entire demonstration—the visit to Yasukuni, where the souls of all Japanese soldiers and sailors went to be deified when they died for their country.

Yasukuni Shrine had been founded by Emperor Meiji in 1869 to commemorate distinguished statesmen as well as military men who died in the service of Japan. It had long since come to be revered, however, more as a military than as a civilian sanctuary.

The huge army of former servicemen, still marching erect in straight columns of fours, proceeded onto the parklike grounds and along a wide gravel lane lined with ginkgo trees which led them through two enormous Shinto *torii* (arches) to the wooden, bronze-roofed shrine itself. When the entire procession had finally arrived, and the 210,000 veterans were gathered before the shrine in seemingly endless but fastidiously straight military columns, each man clapped his hands three times. This was to call forth the deified souls of those who had died in Japan's several wars since the 1868 Meiji Restoration—the Sino-Japanese, the Russo-Japanese, the European, the Manchurian, and the Chinese, which latter was considered a war though it was still called only an "incident."

After summoning these deified souls, the whole assemblage knelt and 210,000 men bowed to the ground in homage. With pious fervor they prayed to former comrades-in-arms who had now become much more than that, who, by their courage and devotion to Japan had turned themselves into gods and earned the nation's highest honor —eternal residence at Yasukuni. The deification of battle victims was one of the more powerful factors in making Japan's warriors so willing to die for the country. It stirred a soldier's soul to realize that however ordinary he might be in life, he could become a god in death. And to these 210,000 retired soldiers at Yasukuni on the third day of a great new war, this ultimate reward for heroism was especially poignant because it had escaped them. It was not easy for them, kneeling before old friends who were now gods, to accept the fact that, their own military days being over, the new war would bring them no new opportunities for deification here.

DECEMBER 10,
11:30 A.M. IN MALAYA,
1:30 P.M. IN TOKYO

E N S I G N Masato Hoashi of the navy's 22nd Air Flotilla was becoming more and more frustrated as his head moved continuously back and forth, scanning the vast blue ocean beneath him. Hoashi was the pilot of one of the nine Japanese reconnaissance bombers which had taken off at 6:25 A.M. in an urgent effort to find the two huge British warships, *Prince of Wales* and *Repulse*. These ships had to be found because they threatened the Japanese invasion fleet carrying troops and supplies to the beachheads in northeast Malaya. The reconnaissance bombers, plus two other reconnaissance planes, had now been flying parallel search patterns for more than five hours, their throttles pulled back and their carburetor mixtures perilously lean, both to conserve fuel and to hold down their speed so they could not overlook their quarry by flying too fast. Ensign Hoashi was beginning to think they had already overlooked their quarry despite the care with which they flew their patterns. There was no sign of the two ships around the Kota Bharu landing sites in northern Malaya, and no sign of them near Singapore. As Hoashi flew northward on a return pattern, parallel to the Malayan east coast and about 50 miles out at sea, he couldn't help beginning to wonder if the British ships had withdrawn completely from the area. The weather was clear, the water peaceful. Though there was a British air base at the coastal town of Kuantan, less than 100 miles away, not a single enemy plane had yet been seen by any of the searchers. If the two warships were in the vicinity, wouldn't there be fighter planes covering them?

Hoashi was still cruising northward when all such questions and considerations were routed from his mind by the sight of two large, dark objects together with three or four smaller objects on the ocean's surface several miles ahead. Were these the British ships? Or were they Japanese ships also searching for the British ships? Hoashi's impatience grew as he waited for his plane to draw closer. It soon became apparent to him that the two large ships in the group were big enough to be the *Prince of Wales* and the *Repulse*. But of course, the Japanese battleships, *Haruna* and *Kongo,* both of which were in the area, were of comparable size. As Hoashi's plane drew nearer, he could see that these ships were proceeding southward. Was it not more likely that the British ships would be heading north toward Kota Bharu? He was close enough now for a good look. They were indeed battleships, escorted by three destroyers and followed by a supply vessel. They were traveling at high speed. But whose battleships were they? Approaching them head-on, Hoashi couldn't tell. Coming almost to within their gun range, he went into a gradual banking turn, confident that if he flew around them, getting a good side view through his binoculars, he would be able to identify them. The big ships were traveling in file, one behind the other at a distance of a little more than 1,000 yards. As his co-pilot took over the airplane's controls, Hoashi closely examined in profile, the first, then the second ship. A great smile of recognition spread across his face.

"There they are!" he shouted. "We've found them. I'm sure of it. Those are not Japanese ships!"

Turning to his radio operator he said, "Send this message back to headquarters: 'Sighted two enemy battleships. Seventy nautical miles southeast of Kuantan. Course south-southwest.'"

Now if only his plane had a camera he would be able to photograph this beautiful scene, but unfortunately there was a shortage of cameras in the Japanese Navy. Only one of the reconnaissance planes searching for the British ships was equipped to photograph them. Hoashi's plane was, however, carrying bombs. Should he attack? No, he had better not take the chance of being shot down until he was certain Admiral Matsunaga had received his radio message. Swarms of bombers would soon be arriving for the kill now that he had found the ships. The 22nd Air Flotilla had sent out 52 torpedo bombers and 34 attack bombers since morning, in addition to the nine reconnaissance bombers. Swarms of British fighter planes would also be arriving, no doubt, to attack the attackers. Perhaps he should drop his bombs, not on the ships themselves, but on the air base at Kuantan. If he could get to Kuantan early enough, he might be able to prevent some of those British fighters from leaving the ground.

Within a few minutes, Hoashi's radio operator leaned over his shoulder. "They got our message at headquarters," he said. "They just confirmed it."

Hoashi nodded. He took one more look at the ships he was circling. There was no doubt in his mind. Here were the great *Prince of Wales* and the *Repulse*. Banking his plane away from them, he headed northwest toward Kuantan on the Malayan coast with his load of bombs.

It was 12:20 P.M. when Second Squadron Commander Sadao Takai, leading his formation of nine torpedo bombers south toward Singapore, received Hoashi's radio report, relayed through headquarters. Takai's Second Squadron was following Lieutenant Commander Niichi Nakanishi's First Squadron. Since they were flying south, away from the reported location of the British ships, Takai, after sharing the good news with his crew, watched for Nakanishi's group to turn and reverse its direction, but the First Squadron, for some reason, continued south. Perhaps Nakanishi's radio operator had missed the message. Everyone was so near exhaustion now it would not be surprising. They had not returned to base from last night's fruitless mission until past midnight, and after having to make nervous landings on the blacked-out Saigon runway with armed torpedoes in the bellies of their planes, they had been forced to work hard the rest of the night in preparation for today's mission. They were now well into the fifth hour of this mission, having taken off at 7:55 A.M. Perhaps it was also exhaustion that had accounted for the strange behavior of the Third Squadron in Takai's group which, just a few minutes ago, had dropped all its bombs (nine 1,100-pounders) in a pointless and unsuccessful attack on a small enemy cargo vessel. Could the commander of the Third Squadron have supposed that little ship was a British warship? It was difficult to imagine. And now Nakanishi was still leading them south despite a message that the British ships were behind them. Takai was becoming bemused by all these strange procedures.

Minutes passed. Takai's fuel gauges indicated he was approaching the limits of his range, the point of no return. He called his radio operator.

"Nakanishi must have missed that message," he said. "Relay it to him and make sure he gets it."

As the operator was doing so, Takai decided he dared not wait any longer for Nakanishi to react. Banking into a 180-degree turn, he led his own squadron north. The First Squadron, seeing his move, also reversed course and fell in behind him.

At 1 P.M., when these two squadrons were still more than 100 miles south of Kuantan, low clouds began to form ahead of them. The thought of visibility problems was exasperating just when the enemy ships were expected to come into view at any moment. On the other hand, low, broken clouds might be advantageous once the ships were sighted. Takai's and Nakanishi's squadrons were heading northnorthwest at an altitude of about 8,300 feet. Anticipating battle, they moved into close formation, all pilots and co-pilots straining their eyes in search of their targets.

Three minutes after one o'clock, Takai saw a dark spot beneath a cloud about 25 miles straight ahead. Drawing ever closer, he eventually was able to make out two battleships, three destroyers, and another small vessel. The enemy ships. Or were they? Nakanishi seemed to think so. His First Squadron picked up speed and pulled ahead of the Second.

"Assume assault formation," the lieutenant commander ordered over the radio.

The two squadrons, still flying at 8,300 feet, were about eight miles from the naval force. Because it was standard procedure for the first squadron in a group to make the first attack, and against the largest ship, Nakanishi's nine planes went into a gradual dive, increasing their speed. Takai put his planes into a similar dive and led them toward the left flank of the task force since Nakanishi had chosen the right flank.

The first squadron, now circling at a distance of four miles, provoked a sudden and continuing antiaircraft bombardment from all the ships in the task force. Takai could see Nakanishi's planes between flashes of white smoke as shell after shell exploded around them. Takai's own planes had been fortunate so far. No shell had yet approached them, perhaps because he was keeping them, as much as possible, behind clouds. Darting from cloud to cloud, he held his binoculars in front of his face, just below eye-level, so he could raise them quickly to study the task force each time it came into view. It was moving south on a fast, straight course: a destroyer and the two big battleships in single file about 1,100 yards apart, flanked by two more destroyers, one on each side. The length of the white, narrow V-shaped wakes indicated great speed. Takai estimated it to be about 26 nautical miles per hour. If these were the British ships, why were they traveling south? Could it be that they feared a Japanese air attack and were trying to get back to Singapore? That didn't quite make sense. Big battleships should be better able to fight off air attacks in the open sea where they had room to maneuver. And as for the two big British battleships in question, they were apparently so powerful they didn't even fear air attacks. Otherwise why would they have openly advertised their recent arrival in the Far East?

Another mystery puzzled Lieutenant Takai as he peered through his binoculars. The second ship, which was his designated target, had a long, thin funnel of white smoke rising from it which one might almost think to be the result of a bomb hit except that Takai's and Nakanishi's squadrons were the only planes visible in the sky. Did this mean that some of the level bombers had already made their runs against the ships and had scored a hit? If so, they had already departed. Takai and his companions appeared to be at least the first torpedo bombers to reach the scene. There were no enemy planes in view. Takai, expecting British fighters to dive on them at any moment, had ordered his entire crew to keep searching the skies for them. None had yet appeared, despite the fact that at Kuantan, only about 75 miles away, there was an enemy airfield.

While the absence of enemy planes would simplify the attack, it nevertheless worried Takai because it raised again the question of whether these were actually enemy ships. Still circling, with the other planes of his squadron in attack formation behind him, he stared through his binoculars at the ship which was his intended target. It was a battleship. He had no doubt about that. It looked, from this distance, just like the Japanese battleship *Kongo*. Where was the *Kongo* right now? Where was the Second Fleet? Takai could not dispel the possibility that this might be part of it. The fact that these ships were filling the air with antiaircraft fire did not prove they were enemies. When ships were under attack they had to fight immediately and hope to find out later whom they were fighting.

Takai called to the cockpit the one man in his crew who was a trained observer. "Can you identify that ship?" he asked.

The observer studied the ship at which Takai was pointing. "It looks like our battleship *Kongo* to me, sir," he said.

Takai's agonizing uncertainty was mixed now with anger at himself. Three years earlier he had been a visitor on the *Kongo*. Why hadn't he studied it more closely? And why hadn't he learned to identify British warships instead of concentrating on American ships? About the *Prince of Wales* and *Repulse* he knew only what he had been told in Saigon during the previous week.

Takai's indecision was not diminished by a repeated flag signal from the third plane in his squadron: "Is this not our fleet?"

Lieutenant Commander Nakanishi and his First Squadron still didn't seem to think so. They were bearing down on the largest ship in the formation, which Takai hoped and prayed would turn out to be the *Prince of Wales*. His own squadron was now at 1,700 feet and had already passed the best point from which to begin a torpedo attack against the second large ship. The clouds were increasing and visibility decreasing. Takai decided there was only one thing to do. Despite the antiaircraft shells which had begun to burst all around him, he led his squadron out of the clouds so close to the task force he could almost look down on the second ship. He examined it closely.

"It is not the *Kongo!*" he shouted, and his crew echoed his happy cry.

His relief at the certainty that this must be the long-sought enemy gave way quickly to a new nervousness caused by excitement. He banked sharply and hurried back into the nearest clouds. Changing course to confuse the enemy, he led his planes in a dive to 1,000 feet, emerging from beneath the clouds in attack position, only a mile and a half from his target.

The enemy was obviously neither confused nor surprised. Only a moment after Takai's squadron appeared it was enveloped by a barrage of antiaircraft fire from battleships and destroyers. Takai's plane bounced and shook from the nearby explosion of shells as he pointed its nose toward the second ship, which, he decided, must be the *Repulse*.

The ship reacted quickly to the appearance of the planes, swinging into a hard right turn in an effort to make itself a smaller target by taking the attack from the front rather than the side.

Takai, descending almost to water level to get under the antiaircraft fire, pushed his throttles all the way forward to gain a top speed of more than 200 miles per hour, but even moving that fast he could not reach torpedo release range in time to attack from a broadside angle. The target became smaller and smaller as the ship's bow swung in his direction. There was nothing he could do about that now, however, and while it frustrated him, it did not surprise him. In such attacks, one expected a ship to be ready for the first plane if it had even two or three minutes to prepare, but in preparing for the first plane, it couldn't help leaving itself open to the following planes, which would arrive at intervals as short as fifteen or twenty seconds apart.

Takai's plane, skimming over the water on its bullet-like path toward the ship, attracted a series of antiaircraft explosions which jolted and shook it, but these explosions were slightly above it now and Takai was scarcely conscious of them as he went through the routine procedures in preparation for torpedo release. He had performed these procedures so many times in training he made the moves almost automatically.

The enormous ship loomed closer and closer on a collision course until he was so near that from his wave-top altitude he was actually looking up at it. With a hard jerk of his right arm he pulled back the torpedo-release mechanism. Then immediately, with both hands, he pulled back his control yoke to get the plane up over the deck of the ship and avoid hitting it.

Though the plane responded quickly, it missed the deck by only a few feet. Takai, who would have been satisfied even with inches, banked into a steep turn to get away as fast as possible.

When the antiaircraft explosions around him diminished, he decided he had achieved relatively safe distance. Easing his demands upon the overtaxed airplane, he put it into a gradual, circling bank in a clockwise direction; then, after deciding that no real damage had been done to it, nosed it upward into a cloud where he could relax.

His tense muscles began to loosen as he realized with satisfaction he had done his duty. He had performed a perilous deed for his country and he had survived. A feeling of relief was beginning to rise up in him when he heard running footsteps in the narrow passageway behind him and turned to see his observer approaching in some agitation.

"Sir! Sir! A terrible thing is happened!"

Takai waited expectantly.

"Our torpedo didn't release!" the observer shouted.

Takai felt as if the gods had just hit him on the head. That miserable torpedo which should by now have ripped a hole in the side of the British ship was still resting comfortably in the belly of his plane. Takai's anger and frustration were such that he had to catch firm hold of himself to avoid exploding. Heartsick, he reversed his course.

On the intercom, he addressed his crew: "We shall go in again at once."

Since all of the eight other planes in his squadron had now completed their torpedo runs, Takai would have to go in completely alone this time. After orienting himself once more to his target, he flew into a group of clouds quite near it, and came down through these clouds in so rapid a dive that when he pulled out, the ship was only about 1,500 yards ahead of him. He knew positively now that it was the *Repulse*. He was approaching it this time from the side, which gave him a good view of it, and gave him also an excellent target angle.

Pushing his throttles forward, he again skimmed the waves at top speed as the ship went into a quick turn away from him and its guns began to bark at him.

At 800 yards, he seemed to be flying through a wall of explosions; at 700 yards, he again checked the bomb-release mechanism; at 600 yards he stared up at the ship. Though it was in a turn, so that he was now approaching from a slight rear angle, he would still get a shot at its flank.

At 500 yards, he decided his position was right. This time he yanked the torpedo release even harder than the first time, and listened, above the noise of the shells exploding around him, for sounds from the bomb-bay. Though he heard no sound, he quickly felt a shock quite distinct from those caused by the explosions outside the plane. This was definitely the shudder a torpedo causes when it

drops from a plane. A wave of elation poured over Takai as he realized his torpedo was in the water. Though he might never know
whether he had scored a hit, he was confident that the direction and
angle were good. All he had to do now was to escape once more with
his life.

Putting the plane into overboost, he pulled it up sharply, and after
missing the deck of the ship again by just a few feet, flew away from
it at top speed.

At a safe distance, he eased back on the controls and reflected with
amazement that he had survived again. As if this reflection were an
invitation to collapse, he now felt himself begin to tremble and shake
so that he could not hold his hands steady on the controls.

His post-peril nervousness was forgotten when he heard Lieutenant Commander Nakanishi's voice on the radio: "Many direct torpedo hits. Lead battleship is listing heavily. Now it's returning to
normal position . . ."

Startled by this report, Takai looked back at the battle scene. In his
anxiety to release his torpedo, he hadn't noticed whether either of
the ships had been damaged, but he saw now, with a surge of satisfaction, that Nakanishi was right. The attack so far was a great success.
Big clouds of smoke were billowing from both battleships and still
more planes were arriving to torment them. But would the ships sink?
The *Prince of Wales* was reputed to be unsinkable. Though Takai
wished he could wait and see if it were so, he knew, after a fast glance
at his fuel gauges, that he didn't have time. Quickly reassembling the
eight other planes in his squadron, all of which had survived their
torpedo runs, he turned toward Saigon, 400 miles away. They would
have enough gasoline to get them home, but very little to spare.

Ensign Masato Hoashi, having bombed the British airfield at Kuantan on the Malayan coast, returned to where he had first spotted the
task force, about 70 miles offshore to the southeast, and found it,
several miles farther south, under full attack by the Japanese planes
he had alerted. Darting in and out of the clouds perilously close to
the beleaguered but still dangerous ships, he was able to observe
their rapid deterioration as the waves of attacking planes came,
struck and went. After a squadron of level bombers had scored the
first direct bomb hit (on the *Repulse*), two squadrons of torpedo
bombers (the Nakanishi-Takai group) scored the first torpedo hits on
the two ships. They were followed by squadron after squadron as
about 80 planes released their bombs and torpedoes.

By 2:15 P.M., an hour after the first four torpedoes exploded against
the flanks of the proud *Prince of Wales*, it was taking in water from

the effects of eight torpedo hits. Yet after listing for awhile, it had righted itself, perhaps because of skillful counterflooding by the crew, and was still sending up a fierce barrage of antiaircraft fire as two more squadrons of level bombers moved in at 8,400 feet to release their 1,100-pound bombs upon it. Several of these bombs scored direct hits, almost dead-center, and as Hoashi reported their explosions over the radio in a running account beamed back to headquarters, the heavy ship, which had already lost much of its speed, slowed even more drastically until its wake was little more than a ripple behind it.

The *Repulse*, which had absorbed its first direct bomb hit at least an hour-and-a-half earlier, was now a shattered mass of wreckage, still moving at a painfully slow rate, but unable to put up more than a token defense. It was no longer a worthy target.

Ensign Hoashi continued to hover over the scene as the last of the attack planes finished their work and departed. The *Repulse* could not possibly have more than a few moments to live. It settled slowly until its decks were almost awash, then in a dramatic upheaval, its stern rose high in the air. It became suddenly evident that the gunners stationed there had not, even now, given up fighting. Their guns continued to fire as the ship plunged out of sight.

The *Prince of Wales* was now almost derelict in the water, but it did continue to move at a funereal pace, and its guns kept firing even though the last of the planes which had destroyed it were now out of range. Suddenly the great ship was shattered by one more enormous explosion, as if its magazines had mercifully ignited to administer the *coup de grace*. The ship's forward motion stopped completely. It sat dead for a moment, then, in a rapid plunge, disappeared beneath the waves.

Ensign Hoashi had just witnessed a historic event. Japanese airplanes had today revolutionized naval warfare by proving something which even the great victory at Pearl Harbor had failed to prove—that the biggest, fastest, and best of battleships, operating under full power in ideal conditions on the open sea, were still no match for airplanes.

After watching the *Prince of Wales* sink, Hoashi looked up to see eight more planes approaching. Could they be Japanese? No. They had to be British fighter planes. Where had they been while the battle was in progress? Since Hoashi's was the only Japanese plane still on the scene, he decided this would be a good time to retire. Taking one last look at the approaching planes, he flew into a cloud, disappeared from their view, and headed back to base.

DECEMBER 10,
5:30 P.M.

THE PRIVY Council members were in their seats and Premier Tojo, at the head of one of the two tables, was shuffling papers in front of him when, at 5:30 P.M., Emperor Hirohito entered the east antechamber of the Imperial Palace. Everyone stood to make the usual bow from the waist; the Emperor took his seat facing the assembled company; the councilors sat down. Council President Yoshimichi Hara began the meeting as Tojo waited for the floor. It was a meeting which should not take long. Tojo and his cabinet had already decided, at a noon meeting of their own, what was to happen here.

When Hara finished, Tojo stood and read from a prepared text: "Two days ago, Your Majesty's government sent messages to the governments of Germany and Italy. These messages said, 'Today, Japan has entered into war against the United States and Great Britain. In accordance with the provisions of the Tripartite Alliance between Germany, Italy, and Japan, we now respectfully request that your government also declare war on the United States.'

"This morning," Tojo continued, "we received a reply from Germany and Italy. This reply makes four specific points. First, that our three countries must fight to the last for victory. Second, that none of the three should make peace separately. Third, that when victory is won, we shall all cooperate to found a New Order in the world. And fourth, that this communiqué goes into effect immediately, continuing as long as the Tripartite Alliance continues."

Tojo looked up from his text to study the faces of the Privy Council members. They seemed passive. This message from Germany and Italy, he pointed out to them, did not constitute a declaration of war. But it did, in his opinion, indicate the intentions of those two countries to declare war against the United States.

"In light of the circumstances," he said, "I have requested this meeting. I want to ask the Privy Council's approval of the following message from His Majesty's government to the governments of Germany and Italy: 'The government of Japan wishes to say, in reply to your government's message of December ten, that we hope the German Army will now make a positive move to the Near East. We can see a bright light ahead as a result of the cooperation between our three governments. For this, we thank Heaven.'"

Tojo stopped reading and looked across at council president Hara. "I now request a vote of approval by the council on this matter."

Hara nodded and the vote began. One "yes" followed another as the members spoke out in turn, dutifully making it unanimous. There were no comments. None were expected or solicited.

By 5:45, only fifteen minutes after the meeting began, the Emperor stood, received the bows of the assembly, and silently walked from the room.

Prime Minister Tojo collected the sheaf of papers in front of him and prepared to hurry back to his official residence. He was not altogether happy with the German-Italian message that had arrived that morning. Though it had made the point that Germany, Italy, and Japan must fight to the last for victory, and must not make separate peace, it had said nothing about Germany fighting the United States. Did Germany intend to continue fighting only against England and Russia, leaving Japan to fight the United States alone? Tojo could scarcely believe that Germany entertained such an idea. He hoped this message which the Privy Council had just approved would prompt Adolf Hitler to clarify his position.

DECEMBER 10,
EVENING, MESSTIME

T H E Japanese battleship fleet was now heading back toward Japan. After traveling westward at full speed through the night, Admiral Yamamoto had decided, late in the morning, on the basis of continuing radio silence from the Nagumo task force, that it had not run into difficulties, and must now be far enough from Hawaii to be out of range of trouble. In the afternoon, Yamamoto's staff, calculating that Nagumo must be within striking distance of the American Midway Island base, had drafted a dispatch ordering him to attack it, and Yamamoto had signed the dispatch, though without enthusiasm. The little atoll 1,500 miles northwest of Hawaii was not likely to be harboring enough planes or ships to merit the attention of a force as large as Nagumo's. But Yamamoto decided that if his staff was that impressed by it, Nagumo might as well drop a few bombs on it in passing.

Yamamoto was in a highly agreeable mood this evening as he joined his staff in the captain's quarters for mess. He was as delighted as he was amazed at the message from the navy's Twenty-second Air

Flotilla that they had actually succeeded this afternoon in sinking the two British warships, *Prince of Wales* and *Repulse,* off the coast of Malaya. With those ships gone, British naval power in the Far East was eliminated and the routes to Singapore and even India were wide open.

Because of the *Wales* and *Repulse* sinkings, this was no ordinary night at mess. Usually the conversation would get around within a few minutes to that most favored subject of men at sea—girls—and Yamamoto would listen with interest as well as amusement to the stories his officers would tell of their amorous adventures with geishas. Since they were earning good salaries (lieutenant commanders received a monthly base pay equal to $53, for instance; captains, $85; admirals, $126.50) and couldn't spend any money at sea, they could afford to be extravagant during the customary three or four days of anchorage each month. Yamamoto himself had a geisha friend at a house in Shimbashi near Ginza, a girl named Kikuji whom he had been seeing for about six years. And he had other geisha acquaintances because during his years as vice minister of the navy, he had, like almost every high official, attended many geisha parties in Shimbashi and Akasaka. Yet while he enjoyed the banter about girls, and sometimes, when in port, would even take members of his staff to geisha houses, he seldom talked to them about his own private life. His humor was quiet, but with these men of his inner circle, he was not the solemn, serious dignitary he seemed to the general public, nor was he the stern, stubborn, intractable man his army counterparts often thought him to be. He was, instead, a warm, fatherly man who enjoyed laughter and treated his subordinates as if he cared about them.

They were awaiting him eagerly tonight, and a great laughing cheer went up when he entered the room. Captain Yoshio Miwa was looking even more expansive than the others. It was he who had bet Yamamoto four dozen bottles of beer that Japanese navy planes would sink the *Prince of Wales* and the *Repulse.*

With a straight face, Yamamoto said to him, "Why are you looking so pleased this evening?"

Miwa said, "Didn't I tell you we would sink those ships?"

Yamamoto said, " 'We?' You talk as if you had helped sink them yourself." When the other men stopped laughing at Miwa he added, "I suppose now you want to collect your beer."

"We're all waiting for it," Miwa said, and with that, the whole staff roared agreement. As soon as the beer was brought in, the toasts were offered.

"To the Twenty-second Air Flotilla!"

"To His Majesty, the Emperor!"

"To victory!"

But as the meal progressed, Yamamoto's mood became progressively less buoyant, and after eating, when he played his usual five-game chess match with Lieutenant Commander Yasuji Watanabe, he was not quite up to his game. Though he was a quick player and would almost invariably win three games out of five, he was playing more slowly tonight and Watanabe was beginning to think he might even win this match for a change.

Finally Yamamoto looked up from the chessboard and Watanabe could see he was in a confidential mood. For some reason which Watanabe did not presume to understand, the admiral, who was 19 years his senior, often confided in him.

"In spite of this new victory today," Yamamoto said to him, "our success cannot possibly continue for more than a year." He was silent and thoughtful for awhile, then he added, "I feel great sympathy for the British commander (Vice Admiral Sir Tom Phillips) who apparently went down with the *Prince of Wales*. The same thing may happen to me someday in the not-too-distant future."

DECEMBER 10,
EVENING

ADMIRAL Mitsumasa Yonai, former navy minister and former prime minister now retired from public life, was not pleased to hear that there were reporters at the door of his home (in the Kojimachi district, near the Imperial Palace). He knew what they wanted—his reaction to the sinking of the *Prince of Wales* and the *Repulse*. That would be easy. But they wouldn't stop there. They would want to know also his feelings about the war. They would expect him to predict more victories. They would want him to say Japan was on its way to defeating America; what could he possibly say on that subject? He would rather say nothing. Yet he was a polite man. He couldn't simply turn the reporters away. He gave the nod and a servant opened the door to admit them.

The newsmen, after exchanging their shoes for slippers, filed into the traditional Japanese house and gathered in front of the retired statesman whom most of them had interviewed on previous occasions. From 1937 to 1940, Yonai had been navy minister in three successive cabinets. In January, 1940, he had become prime minister, heading the government until the army forced his resignation seven months later. He had never been popular with the army, having spoken too often and too freely against the drift toward war, and against the alliance with Germany and Italy. "The Japanese Navy," he had once said, "belongs to the Emperor. It is not for hire by Hitler or anyone else."

From his extraordinary height of more than six feet, he gazed down at the newspaper reporters through deeply circled eyes which testified to prodigious drinking habits. During his years in the navy, Yonai had become almost as famous for his alcohol capacity as for his qualities of leadership. A younger officer named Tameichi Hara who served under him on a cruiser in 1922 referred to him later as one of two great men he had met in the navy, the other being Admiral Kantaro Suzuki. Hara said that though he had never seen Yonai scold a man, the morale of the crew was extremely high because everyone was aware of being guided by one of the greatest leaders the Imperial Navy had ever produced. Hara was equally impressed by Yonai's judo skill—"none of us could throw him to the mat"—and by his drinking prowess. He recalled geisha parties at which Yonai would still be sitting "straight as a stoic Samurai" after drinking "almost as much sake as all the other guests combined." Through the years, Yonai had remained so fond of drinking that his once-handsome face was now slightly puffed; his unusually fair skin (which had earned him the nickname "White Elephant") had developed a pale reddish tinge, and the circles beneath his eyes were so deep they dominated his appearance. Besides drinking, he also read so widely (in Russian and English as well as Japanese) that he was considered one of the nation's best informed men. It was not his habit, however, to show off his learning. He was essentially a silent man, impressing people, in the Oriental tradition, not by argument but by the aura he created among other men. He stood still in front of the reporters, waiting for them to speak.

One of them said, "Could you tell us, sir, how you felt about the sinking of the two British battleships this afternoon? Were you surprised at such an accomplishment by the Imperial Navy?"

Yonai was indeed surprised. Despite his close association with the navy, and his intimate friendship with Admiral Yamamoto, he had not been informed of the offensive plans in Malaya. He hadn't even known specifically of the plan to attack Hawaii, although he had been aware for some time that such a possibility was under consideration.

"I really can find no words to thank our Imperial Navy," he began. Then he paused. He had better choose his remarks carefully. The country was now at war and his views about it were so well known the government and the secret police would scrutinize everything he said. He had once reminded his colleagues, during an argument against war, that the Japanese victories over China in 1904 and over Russia in 1905–6 had been won only narrowly despite their portrayal by the country's historians as smashing triumphs. And at the meeting of former prime ministers in the Imperial Palace ten days before the attack against Hawaii, he had made his feelings clear when General Tojo said it would be much better for Japan to be destroyed fighting than to accept ignominiously America's demands and economic sanctions. "Should we bankrupt the country quickly," Yonai had asked, "in an attempt to avoid bankrupting it slowly?" He saw no chance of defeating America. Just the previous day he had gathered several close and trusted friends here in his home to discuss the war. Despite the great victory in Hawaii, none of them thought Japan could win, and most of them thought the country would collapse within three years under American pressure. The only hope, they agreed, would be to bring about some kind of negotiated peace. These were precisely Yonai's own feelings. He hadn't better express them publicly, however.

"Our navy sank two British battleships," he continued. "It is an inevitable outcome. It is the result of the incessant training of our navy, the fierceness of which is beyond description. The navy had been fully trained against any situation and the enemy was unfortunate in meeting such a strong navy.

"The time has come for the Imperial Navy to display its full strength. To forestall enemy action is the cardinal principle of strategy, and our navy has achieved a remarkable success on this point. The war is won only with strong conviction for victory. The success of the navy so far is the result of its positive offensive spirit."

He was doing well. What else could he say? He hadn't yet mentioned his dear friend, Yamamoto. "As long as Admiral Yamamoto lives," he went on, "our navy is all right. I offer my hearty thanks and confidence to Admiral Yamamoto, commander in chief of the Combined Fleet."

That much, at least, he could say in complete sincerity. The navy and Yamamoto had done a splendid military job so far. He should go down to Iwakuni, assuming the fleet was in, and offer his personal congratulations to his old friend. There were many things about which he would like to talk to Yamamoto, and many dangers about which to warn him. Yamamoto must not be allowed to get intoxicated, like so many of his fellow countrymen, by these early victories.

Admiral Yonai, having paused, looked into the faces of the newsmen gathered around him. He could see they wanted something more. What was there to tell them? He knew what he would like to tell them, but it was out of the question. The most he could get away with would be a few words of carefully-tempered admonition. It was worth a try. "But the war has just begun," he resumed. "We must not be too elated over our victories. With the war prolonged, we cannot expect to go on without some losses. Even if a disadvantageous situation should occur, we must be fully convinced of our final victory. We must have confidence in the government and the army and navy. I, as a member of this nation, absolutely believe in our government and the army and navy."

That should be enough. He looked into the reporters' faces. They seemed satisfied. He smiled and bowed. They smiled and bowed. In a few minutes they were gone and he was able to relax. After that ordeal, it was time for a drink.

DECEMBER 11,
2:30 A.M. IN TOKYO,
5:30 A.M. IN WAKE ISLAND

IN THE pre-dawn darkness, Rear Admiral Sadamichi Kajioka stood clutching a rail on the bridge of his wave-tossed flagship, *Yubari,* an elderly cruiser which bobbed crazily in the rough sea just off the southern shore of Wake Island. Deployed around the *Yubari,* though blacked out so they could not be seen from shore, were the other ships of the task force under Kajioka's command—two more elderly cruisers, the *Tenryu* and the *Tatsuta;* six more destroyers, some of them even older than the cruisers; and two 12,000-ton transport ships carrying 500 naval troops plus all their supplies. It was Kajioka's assignment to capture this tiny American base 600 miles north of Japanese-held Kwajelein, but already he was encountering difficulties. His primary plan had been to send the troops ashore before dawn without naval bombardment and take the island in a surprise attack. Naval Intelligence had assured him he would find only about 400 Americans there, and most of them not soldiers but construction workers. As dawn approached, however, the prospects of a surprise attack had begun to dwindle because the waves were so high the transport ships were having trouble launching their troop-landing boats. Though Admiral Kajioka could not see this operation, he was getting the details of it by radio, and by light signals, which the transports dared to use because they were standing in closer than the *Yubari*, and could therefore shield their blinkers from the shore. The reports from the transports were relayed to the admiral by his staff officer, Lieutenant Commander Tei Koyama, and by the captain of the *Yubari*, Captain Masami Ben, both of whom were with him on the bridge.

Koyama, about to experience his first combat, was beginning to feel slightly impatient at the delay in landing the troops. "We don't have much more time," he said, "and the waves aren't getting any smaller."

Though there was no rain, the wind was high and the sea, as it approached the island surf, was churning up angry, white-capped ridges of water.

Admiral Kajioka continued to appear calm. At the age of fifty he was an experienced commander and a veteran of sea warfare, having served during World War I on a Japanese destroyer squadron in the Mediterranean, at that time as an ally of Britain and America. Despite his appearance, however, he was, in fact, somewhat disturbed this morning about several things. The war had come as a shock to him. Until he received his orders for the Wake attack about two weeks before, he had refused to believe Japan would actually challenge the United States. He was also disturbed by the shortness of time he had been given to develop a plan of attack and prepare his men for combat. The navy had simply presented him a map of Wake Island, a skimpy intelligence report, and a task force of almost obsolete cruisers and destroyers. The intelligence report was reassuring. It indicated that aside from the approximately 400 men on Wake, mostly construction workers, he would face little opposition. No shore batteries were mentioned and danger from the air was minimized. During the last two days, Japanese bombers from Kwajelein had been pounding the airstrip at Wake, but for today's landing operation his ships would have no air cover. He could only hope he wouldn't need any.

A man from communications arrived on the bridge of the *Yubari* with another report from the transports. As Lieutenant Commander Koyama read it, his ordinarily cheerful face turned grim.

"They've made no progress," he said to Admiral Kajioka. "The waves are overturning the boats as fast as they put them in the water."

There was no need for Kajioka to respond to this news. Koyama, who had known the admiral for a long time though he had been on his staff only since the previous August, was well aware that he would not be deterred by the loss of a few landing craft. However unhappy Kajioka might be about the lack of preparation for this assignment, he was nevertheless determined to fulfill it.

As dawn approached and the transports continued to fail in their attempts to unload troops, Kajioka simply dismissed his plan for a surprise attack under darkness and prepared instead for his secondary strategy, a daytime frontal assault. While the transports went on with their debouching efforts, he notified all other ships to stand by for bombardment of the island.

Dawn came up dismal and cloudy, but the clouds were not low enough nor the atmosphere dense enough to conceal the Japanese task force swaying in the waves offshore. Kajioka and Koyama, scanning through glasses the narrow beach which was their objective, could make out in the early morning light the figures of American defenders, darting back and forth in preparation for the invasion. Suddenly the attention of the two men was diverted skyward by the sound of approaching aircraft. Four little U.S. Navy fighters, quickly recognizable by their round, chubby fuselages as Grumman Wildcats, were coming at the task force from the direction of the island. The Americans apparently had a few planes left at Wake after all, despite the bombings of the two previous days. The Wildcat was so small a plane that the thought of four of them attacking a naval task force seemed laughable, yet it was not to be dismissed lightly when the task force had no air cover. The accomplishments of planes against ships in Hawaii and Malaya proved that. Two or three Zeros might be enough to drive them off, but Kajioka had no Zeros. Some of his ships didn't even have antiaircraft guns. Those that did were frantically taking aim at the oncoming planes which, having used the island to shield their approach, arrived over the Japanese task force only moments after they first appeared. Each of the planes, choosing a target, began spraying streams of machine gun bullets upon it. Men on the decks of the ships under attack scurried for cover and the planes passed on without doing any significant damage.

As the blue-gray, cigar-shaped Grummans circled for their second pass, all the antiaircraft guns on the Japanese ships opened up against them. They were not deterred. Flying straight into the fire, they bore down once more toward their targets, but this time their machine gun fire was light; Kajioka and Koyama could soon see why. These little fighters were carrying bombs, and they seemed to be diving directly toward the troop transports. As the bombs fell, a burst of flame arose from one of the transports. Because the fire seemed to be coming up from below decks, Kajioka watched it anxiously even though the ship did not appear to be in immediate distress. It was fortunate, at least, that these planes could carry only small bombs. Such a perfect hit with a sizable bomb could easily sink a transport.

The planes, having passed over, were swinging around for their third attack; as they closed in, Koyama could see that they had not yet released all their bombs. This time they also attacked one of the destroyers, the *Kisaragi*, which had moved in close to protect the transports. Despite all the antiaircraft fire the Japanese could muster against them, the four planes held their course unwaveringly. The bombs dropped away, and after the seemingly interminable moments of descent, one of them exploded on the deck of the *Kisaragi*, filling the air with noise and fire. It was obviously a direct hit, but hardly damaging enough to sink the ship.

Seconds later, however, another blast rocked the destroyer and Koyama glanced in alarm at Admiral Kajioka.

"Were there two bombs?"

"I don't think so."

A communications messenger arrived on the bridge.

Koyama said, "What happened to the *Kisaragi?*"

"I don't know, but a fuel tank has caught fire on the transport."

"See what you can find out about the *Kisaragi.*"

The stricken destroyer had become a cluster of explosions. Fires arose from her deck in series. And still the four little planes kept coming back.

Now a new and even greater peril arose. The sudden boom of shore batteries announced that the intelligence report had been wrong again. Within minutes, there were at least ten batteries firing, some from Kuku Point on the left, others from Peacock Point on the right. The planes continued to attack, the huge shore guns roared, the Japanese naval guns replied, and smoke began to fill the air as the battle reached full pitch.

It was not yet smoky enough, though, to hide the fate of the destroyer *Kisaragi*, which was disintegrating under the fury of its multiple explosions. There was no longer any possibility it could survive its troubles. It was already disappearing beneath the enormous waves when its last message was relayed to the bridge of the *Yubari.*

"We are sinking," it said. "The aerial bomb exploded a pile of depth charges stored on deck."

When this word reached Admiral Kajioka, he suppressed his anger at the stupidity of storing depth charges on deck. It was too late now to correct that mistake. The *Kisaragi* was gone.

Communications did, however, have one consoling piece of news to report. The fuel-tank fire on the transport had been contained. Kajioka had time only to nod his satisfaction. One of the planes, with machine guns ablaze, was heading straight for the *Yubari.* As the bullets spattered the deck with their metallic racket, the ship's antiaircraft guns opened up at point-blank range. But the plane did not fall. Skimming over the top of the *Yubari,* it banked and dove toward another target.

Shells from the shore batteries were splashing water around most of the ships now, and the other two cruisers, the *Tenryu* and the *Tatsuta* were suffering near misses close enough to inflict possible damage. Though all the cruisers and destroyers were returning the artillery fire, it was too much to hope they could knock out ten big shore guns. That was a job for aerial bombing. Kajioka knew now that he had been sent with a slingshot to do a rifle's work. Should he retreat? In three days of war, the Japanese Navy had scored a magnificent string of uninterrupted victories from Hawaii to Malaya. Did he want to be remembered as the admiral who suffered the first defeat? No, he must stay and fight despite the difficulties. There had to be a way of circumventing the shore guns and downing those pesky little planes. Should he swing around and attack the western or northern side of the island? Some of the guns might reach him even there. And he could land troops no place except on this narrow beach in front of him. But what made him think he could land troops here. Against these waves, he couldn't even put them in boats, and if he did manage that, how many of them would reach shore under the enemy's brutal artillery fire? Despite his determination to fulfill his mission, Admiral Kajioka could not suppress these considerations as time passed and his vulnerable ships kept firing futile rounds against the fortified shore positions. He was still trying to develop some new strategy when another setback assailed him. The destroyer *Hayate,* in full view between the *Yubari* and the shore, suffered a direct hit from an artillery shell. The blow was so severe it seemed almost to throw the ship out of the water. Kajioka watched in despair as it slowly began to sink before his eyes. There was no way, with his present force, to take this island. That was becoming more apparent by the minute. Though it was his duty to fight until death—his duty to the Emperor, to the nation, to his family, to his Samurai tradition —it was also his duty to the navy not to waste these ships and these men.

Without turning his eyes from the battle, he said to Lieutenant Commander Koyama, "We had better retreat. Send the order to disengage."

Koyama, despite his own bitter frustration, knew it would be cruel to protest. The admiral had obviously made the right decision, and it had not been easy for him. It would be insensitive and selfish even to talk about it. "How far back have you decided to withdraw?" he asked.

Admiral Kajioka still stared at the sinking destroyer *Hayate*. "To Kwajelein," he said, "until they send us some help."

DECEMBER 11,
AFTERNOON

C H I E F Cabinet Secretary Naoki Hoshino, with a smile on his face and a message in his hand, hurried into General Tojo's large, high-ceilinged office on the second floor of the prime minister's official residence. Tojo, at his desk, looked up, sensing something important from the quickness of Hoshino's step.

"It's happened," Hoshino said. "Here's the message from Berlin. Germany and Italy have declared war on the United States."

Tojo merely nodded and smiled, but his inner relief was much greater than this economical display of satisfaction would indicate. Though he was hardly surprised at the news, he was delighted to get it because, until this moment, he had not been completely certain of German intentions. While he admired the Germans (having spent almost three years in Germany shortly after the European War) he knew too much about Adolf Hitler's methods to be able to take him for granted.

Tojo could not discount Hitler's often-stated belief in the supremacy of the white, Aryan race. At an imperial conference before the Emperor in early November, Privy Council President Yoshimichi Hara (who often spoke for the Emperor) had made some chilling remarks about Germany and the other Western powers. We should always keep in mind, Hara had said, what might happen to relations between Germany, Great Britain, and the United States, all of whose populations belong to the white race, if Japan should enter the war. Hitler has said that the Japanese are a second-class race, and Germany has not declared war against the United States. If Japan takes positive action against the United States, will the American people adopt the same attitude toward us psychologically that they do toward the Germans? Their indignation against the Japanese will be stronger than their hatred of Hitler. The Germans in the United States are considering ways to assure peace between the United States and Germany. I fear, therefore, that if Japan begins a war against the United States, then Germany, Great Britain, and the United States will come to terms, leaving Japan by herself. We must prepare for the possibility that hatred of the yellow race might shift to Japan the hatred now being directed against Germany.

Tojo was aware that he hadn't quite been able to answer Hara's remarks on that occasion. "The government has not given up its earnest desire somehow to break the impasse in our negotiations with the United States," he had said, and he had freely admitted the problems confronting Japan: "If we enter into a protracted war, there will be difficulties. The first stage will not be difficult. We have some uneasiness about a long war, but how can we let the United States continue to do as she pleases, even though there is some uneasiness? Two years from now we shall have no petroleum for military use. Ships will stop moving. When I think of the strengthening of American defenses in the Southwest Pacific, the expansion of the American fleet, the unfinished China Incident, and so on, I see no end to difficulties." He had also admitted the racial problem: "I intend to take measures to prevent a racial war once war is started. I should like to prevent Germany and Italy from making peace with Great Britain or the United States by taking advantage of the results of our campaigns in the South Pacific. I think the sentiments of the American people are as the president of the Privy Council has indicated, and so I intend to take precautions."

It was true, however, that racial prejudice was not limited to the United States, which had gone so far as to prohibit the entry of Oriental immigrants. Racial prejudice was common in the West, and no one could deny that Hitler felt it. Yet it was now evident that

Hitler had not allowed his personal feelings, whatever they might be, to affect his Tripartite Alliance obligations.

Tojo said to Hoshino, "Have the Germans made the news public?"

"Hitler announced it in the Reichstag."

In that case, there could be no doubt about it. The Tripartite Alliance was now truly in full force and the world would soon feel that force. Though Hitler had taken two days to answer the cable Tojo and Hoshino had drafted on the first day of war, the delay was apparently no indication of uncertainty on his part. Or if it was, that uncertainty must quickly have been eliminated by the sudden, amazing accomplishments of the Japanese.

Hoshino said, "We'll have to draft a message from you to both countries. And I think you should also make a statement to the people. Is there anything special you want to say?"

Tojo thought about it carefully. Not much needed to be said. The Japanese Army and Navy were speaking eloquently in battles throughout Asia and the Pacific. The navy had ripped apart the U.S. fleet in Hawaii, and just yesterday had given the British fleet the same kind of treatment in the Gulf of Thailand off Malaya. The army was now well established on the Malayan peninsula and would surely take Singapore as soon as the troops could get there. The army had already taken Thailand, in just one day, and Hong Kong was under seige. Troops were landing easily on northern Luzon in the Philippines and on the island of Guam. Another American island, Wake, was under attack and the navy was beginning to talk about an invasion of Hawaii. Although such talk might be overly optimistic, it was not outlandish. If Hitler had ever doubted the fighting power of Japan, all these feats in less than three days must have dispelled his doubts. But there was no need to gloat over Japan's successes in a public statement.

"You should include something about the pledge between the three nations never to accept a separate peace," he said to Hoshino. "And make our intentions clear. The world is now divided in two, with the other side trying to maintain the status quo, and our side trying to create a new order. Point out that this will be difficult, but at the same time you should say something about our confidence in final victory." Tojo smiled. The astonishing successes of the first three days of fighting seemed to overcome his natural caution. "Yes, I think we can say now that we're going to win this war."

DECEMBER 11,
AFTERNOON

O N T H E aircraft carrier *Akagi*, flagship of Vice Admiral Chuichi Nagumo's task force, several pilots, in sweat clothing, ran lap after lap around the flight deck to keep in shape. Others lay in their bunks, reading magazines, dozing, or just waiting for evening, when there would at least be dinner and a movie to kill a few hours. Time was hanging heavy now as the task force continued westward toward home. If there were even some mail to read it would make the tedium more bearable, but of course there was none. Before leaving Japan, everyone in the task force had written letters to relatives and friends, and the letters had been sealed in a bag, to be kept at the Yokosuka Naval Base Post Office until after the Hawaiian attack was completed and there was no longer any danger of a security leak. Presumably, those letters had now been delivered, but no one would receive any return mail until at least December 23, the day the task force was scheduled to reach Hiroshima Bay.

December 23 was marked with a drawing of a big sake bottle on the calendar in the pilots' ready room because on that day they would also be allowed their first drinks since the task force sailed from the Kurile Islands November 26. Commander Mitsuo Fuchida had banned all liquor for the duration of the Hawaiian operation.

Fuchida was in the operations room now with several members of Admiral Nagumo's staff and with the flight commanders from the other five carriers, whom Fuchida had gathered on the *Akagi* to hear their full, final impressions of the Pearl Harbor raid, and to study any pictures they or their men had taken. He found to his surprise that many of the pilots had taken pictures with personal cameras, and all the pictures, as well as the reports of the flight commanders, confirmed without question the enormous damage reported the day of the attack. The pictures delighted him because they proved absolutely that his men were as skillful observers as they were fliers.

By the time this new replay of the attack was completed, Fuchida, most of the Nagumo staff members present, and all of the flight leaders from the other carriers were agreed on one point. Even now, three days after the attack, they should turn around and hit Hawaii again. All they had to do was convince the adamant admiral.

"Wait here," Fuchida said to the assembled company. "I'll go see if I can get him to meet with us."

Nagumo quickly and graciously agreed to come to the operations room, and when he heard and saw all the newly proven evidence of the success at Hawaii, especially the proof that about 240 U.S. planes had been destroyed, he once again expressed his delight. He was in such a good mood Fuchida decided the moment had come to get to the point.

He said, "After going over these reports and pictures, sir, almost all of us have come to the same conclusion. We think even now it is not too late to get at the carriers which escaped us. If we turned and struck Hawaii one more time, those carriers would be forced to come forward and meet us. By now the Americans have probably stopped expecting another attack. The carriers may even be back in Pearl Harbor."

Nagumo listened with patience. It seemed that in the last three days he had been buffeted constantly by orders and suggestions. There was Yamamoto's order the previous day to strike Midway Island, which they were then passing. (The task force had retired from Hawaii at a speed of 24 knots for 24 hours, then at 16 knots, on a course which took it about 400 miles north of Midway.) Yamamoto's order had made no sense. First of all, the weather was not good, but more important, Midway offered no worthy targets, Nagumo's staff had agreed with him about that. Even Fuchida, who was chafing with eagerness, had laughed at the Yamamoto order. But they did not seem able to understand the important considerations about Hawaii.

Nagumo said, "Do you think we could surprise the Americans again as we did Sunday?"

"Perhaps not," Fuchida admitted, "but surprise would be less important this time. Look at these pictures. We've destroyed their air power. Almost 250 planes."

"And they've had three days to replace those planes."

"Even so, we would still control the air."

Nagumo's face opened in a tolerant smile. "How many enemy planes got into the air against you?"

Fuchida said, "We counted fourteen."

"And how many of our planes did they shoot down?"

Fuchida could see the point the elderly admiral was trying to make. As they both knew, those 14 American planes, old P-40s, had accounted for 20 of the 29 planes the Japanese had lost. There was no longer any doubt among his own men about the skill and bravery of the American pilots. Those P-40s couldn't possibly match the Zeros in speed or maneuverability, but they had kept coming, even though they were far outnumbered. And that was despite the fact that the Americans had not been prepared for combat. They would be ready next time.

The flight leaders, unimpressed by Nagumo's caution, entered the argument on Fuchida's side, and the admiral had to handle all of them at once. Their eagerness did not sway him, however. During the Sunday raid, they had inflicted even more damage than he had hoped. Another raid could not possibly be productive enough to make it worth the risk; there were not enough undamaged ships left to hit. It was worthy of note that in the Sunday attack, the antiaircraft fire had begun almost as quickly as if there had been no surprise. Any new attack would cost far more than the 29 planes already lost. Radio reports indicated there were still at least 50 big, long-range bombers operating from Hawaiian bases, and there were also those elusive carriers, plus a whole fleet of submarines. One submarine had already attacked the task force since its departure from Hawaiian waters. Fortunately it had been beaten off, but if several were to attack at once, it would not be so easy to escape untouched, especially if, at the same time, the task force were within range of those land-based planes. Shore batteries and land-based planes were two dangers a fleet had always to avoid.

Finally Admiral Nagumo said, "We have destroyed perhaps 250 planes on the island of Oahu. You have the photos here. Very good. But what about the enemy planes on the surrounding islands? There are air bases on all the Hawaiian islands, and they all have planes. Many planes. We know that from the radio messages we keep intercepting. If we go back, we can expect those planes to attack the task force. They would have no trouble finding us this time. We went to Hawaii for one reason—to inflict so much damage on the enemy fleet that it will not be able to interfere with our progress in the South Pacific. Do you men think we should continue to risk the loss of our carriers even after we have accomplished that mission?" He paused. "I do not think so."

That ended the discussion. Nagumo thanked them and left the room. Fuchida dismissed the flight leaders and sent them back to their carriers. But Fuchida was still unhappy. He looked at his friend, Commander Minoru Genda, the task force operations officer, and shook his head.

"I guess we can't blame Admiral Nagumo," Fuchida said. "He's just doing what Yamamoto ordered him to do."

Genda, who had disagreed with Fuchida Sunday about the wisdom of a third-wave attack, nodded now as if he were more in sympathy with this observation.

"Yamamoto knows how much damage we did Sunday," Fuchida continued. "Why did he send us that ridiculous order to attack Midway? Why didn't he change his strategy and make Hawaii a primary objective? If we went back there, if we were allowed to attack in force, we could completely paralyze the U.S. fleet, not just cripple it."

Genda said, "One thing is obvious. Our next step should be to destroy those carriers we missed."

"And what better time than now, while the Americans are weak from the damage we've done?" Fuchida, frustrated and depressed, sat staring into space for awhile. "I was always an admirer of Admiral Yamamoto," he said finally, "but . . ." He paused, then went on as if talking to himself. "After Sunday, I began to think we might win this war. Now I'm not so sure."

DECEMBER 12,
MIDMORNING

JUNNOSUKE OFUSA sat at his desk in the *New York Times* office near the American Embassy feeling more like a caretaker than a reporter. There was nothing for a *New York Times* reporter to do in Tokyo these days, yet the now-imprisoned *Times* bureau chief, Otto Tolischus, had got word to Ofusa that he should "stay on the job until the money runs out." The *Times* kept a bank account in Tokyo to handle the expenses of the bureau. Ofusa, having obtained permission from the Finance Ministry to draw on this account, was paying himself his regular weekly salary. Within two months, the account would be depleted and in a way he looked forward to that because he disliked doing nothing. When the money was gone, he would have fulfilled the obligation Tolischus had put upon him by asking him to continue. But what would he do when the job expired? Sitting alone in the office he sometimes worried about that, even though it was not a reasonable worry. He was an experienced, well-known newsman and a loyal Japanese, despite the fact that he had worked ten years for an American paper. Someone would hire him when he finally closed this office, unless he were arrested in the meantime. That was a possibility he could not discount.

Besides the twice-weekly police questioning about his employers to which he had become accustomed during the last three or four years, Ofusa had also been receiving visits from the Kempeitai about three times a week since the American oil and steel embargo the previous August. A Kempeitai detective had once said to him, "We think Hugh Byas (Tolischus' predecessor) is a spy. We have the evidence." Ofusa, though filled with trepidation, had replied: "I'm his assistant. All his information comes through me, so I'm in the same church. If you arrest him you should arrest me. But if you do charge me with anything, please give me one chance to refute the evidence."

Ofusa could still recall the terror of that short interview. He had been so nervous he couldn't keep his feet still. Had the Kempeitai arrested him on spy charges, he would have been subject to capital punishment after a secret trial. But he had apparently said the right thing. They had not arrested him or Byas, and since the beginning of the war, four days before, they hadn't even gotten around to visiting him.

He was beginning to wonder about that when he heard heavy footsteps on the stairs outside the office.

The door opened and three detectives entered the room, all of them familiar to him from previous visits. One was from the Akasaka Police Station, one from the Metropolitan Police, and one from the Kempeitai. It was the latter he dreaded most. The torture methods of the Kempeitai were well known in Japan, which helped explain the remarkable cooperation the Kempeitai received from the public.

Ofusa's natural apprehension was at least partially relieved when he saw the ingratiating smiles on the faces of all three men.

"Good morning," they said. And one of them added, "How have you been?"

Ofusa said, "Fine, thank you."

The detective rubbed his hands together. "Cold out there today, isn't it?"

Ofusa nodded. "It is indeed." The day was clear but the temperature was only a few degrees above freezing.

The three men took off their coats and sat down as if they intended to stay awhile. What did that mean? Should he try to make conversation? The morning paper was in front of him. He could say, "Well, I see Germany and Italy have joined us against America." Or, "Well, I see our navy has shot down seventy-seven planes in the Philippines." But he said nothing.

One of them asked, "Are you keeping busy?"

Ofusa shrugged. "There's not much to do but I've been told to keep the office open, at least for awhile." Should he have mentioned that?

Would it provoke new questions about Tolischus? A useless concern. If they had questions to ask, they needed no provocation.

"What do you do all day?" another asked. "How do you occupy yourself?"

"It isn't easy, but I find things. And I read the papers."

"The news has been good, hasn't it?"

"Very good. Amazing."

Were they trying to get him to say something pro-American? Something anti-Japanese? Much as he regretted the war, and pessimistic as he was about it, Ofusa had no doubts about his commitment to Japan. He loved his country. Each week he bought as many defense bonds as he could afford. He was an active leader in his Neighborhood Association. It might be difficult to prove his loyalty, however, to these men. They were probably convinced he was an American spy, but at least they hadn't yet accused him. As they continued talking he became increasingly puzzled. They spoke only about general things, living conditions, the magnificent war victories, etc. They were very friendly.

Finally they stood up and one of them said, "You live right near here, don't you?"

"Just two blocks away. In Fukidecho."

"How's your wife? How are the children?"

Ofusa had a daughter, four, and a son only a few months old. It seemed inappropriate that these detectives should mention them. "They're both fine," he said.

"That's nice."

The three men had now moved to the door. Was this all they had to say to him?

"Well, it's been pleasant talking to you," one of them said.

Another added, "We'll be seeing you."

They turned and in a moment they were gone. Ofusa shuddered as the door closed behind them. With nothing but friendly words they had made him feel deeply uncomfortable. They had demonstrated the great talent of the Japanese police for keeping people confused, apprehensive, and untroublesome.

DECEMBER 12,
LATE AFTERNOON

A M O N G the hundreds of people outside the great Meiji Shrine on the east side of Tokyo—some kneeling on the cold ground, some standing, many carrying flags, all praying fervently for victory in the war—a murmur of excitement arose at the approach of a now-familiar group of men. Every day since the war began, people had been gathering thus at the Meiji and Yasakuni (soldiers' and sailors') shrines. Some of them had been rewarded previously, as they were today, by the appearance of this same company, headed by Prime Minister Tojo.

It was a small group. With Tojo were one of his private secretaries, Colonel Sadao Akamatsu; Navy Secretary Admiral Shigetaro Shimada; a few functionaries and only two plainclothes policemen. One of the surprising aspects of the Prime Minister's public appearances was the lack of concern about his safety. Though other secret policemen had been sent ahead to mingle with the crowd, there was no protective screen of men around Tojo as he briskly entered the square in front of the tree-enclosed building. Despite the ironic fact that he was coming from a cabinet meeting at which he had felt the need to promulgate a severe new wartime anticrime law, and despite a natural aloofness that made him uncomfortable in crowds, he could not conceive of himself being in personal danger as he mingled with the Japanese people. His popularity at this moment was so high there was no longer any concern, even among his associates, about the rumored prewar plots against his life by extreme militarists who had accused him of timidity. Japanese battle successes had been so spectacular in the first four days that Tojo was now regarded with reverence and awe by all segments of the populace, including the most belligerent.

People in the crowd, apparently wanting to get close to him but overcome by the diffidence so characteristic of Japanese when they encounter men of high station, pushed their children forward in place of themselves, so that Tojo, as he walked toward the temple, put his hands on the heads of one child after another. He did not allow them to detain him, however, until he had performed the worship which was his reason for coming here.

With his trusted friend Admiral Shimada and the rest of his company behind him, he hurried up the seven steps to the open front of the Shinto temple and, stopping at the central entrance, clapped his hands to gain the attention of the dieties enshrined there, including, of course, the Emperor Meiji. He felt a special reverence in the presence of Emperor Meiji, who had reigned until 1912, when Tojo was 28 years old, and who had become a symbol of benevolent wisdom to all Japanese. Standing before the soul of this deified Son of Heaven under whom he had been born and had lived almost half his life, Tojo felt that the old Emperor was transmitting to him directly his own power to make fair judgments and wise decisions. Long before he became prime minister he had developed the habit of coming here twice a month, usually on the first and the fifteenth, to recharge himself with the Meiji spirit, and to absorb Meiji wisdom. If he could but follow the old Emperor's guidance, he would indeed be able to lead Japan to victory, however rigorous and perilous the days ahead might be. Though Tojo did not delude himself into thinking the entire war would be as gloriously successful as its beginning, he was feeling each day, in the light of each new victory, more confident of eventual success. Today, Kowloon had fallen. Soon, Hong Kong and Singapore would be Japanese. The sinking of those two battleships Wednesday had virtually eliminated the power of the British Navy in the Far East. "Far East?" The very term was objectionable. Far from where? From England, where the expression had been invented to signify that the center of the British Empire was the center of the universe. Perhaps the English were no longer so certain of this. Though they and the Dutch might be able still to put together an Asiatic task force of sorts, they would not be able to withstand the overwhelming power of Japan's Combined Fleet. Yamamoto had calculated correctly. The U.S. fleet was now wallowing in distress at Pearl Harbor, and the oil of the Dutch East Indies was simply waiting for Japanese tankers to arrive and take it. For this, the old Emperor Meiji deserved most humble thanks. His spirit, his determination and leadership had made Japan the great, powerful nation it was today.

General Tojo's prayer completed, he turned from the temple to the hundreds of people watching him at the foot of the concrete steps which spanned the width of the building. He glanced at Colonel Akamatsu and Admiral Shimada, both of whom knew how uncomfortable he became in crowds. They could read his mind now as he prepared to go down among these people.

"It is for the Emperor that I have to do this," he said. "His Majesty is so far removed from his subjects, someone must act as his stand-in, and it seems to me that duty falls on the prime minister."

Shimada and Akamatsu both nodded, ready to share the duty with him. Few men were more loyal to Tojo than these two. Akamatsu, since the first time he served under Tojo in 1929, had considered him the most honest, righteous, diligent, and benevolent officer in the Japanese Army. Shimada had staked his reputation and his career on his loyalty to Tojo, and as a result, his career, ironically, was faring better than his reputation. Though he was now navy minister in Tojo's cabinet, thus enjoying one of the three highest positions his country could offer him, he was not highly regarded by either the navy or the army. Many of his fellow admirals distrusted him because they felt he had made himself an instrument of General Tojo rather than a representative of the navy, and because they thought he had surrendered too easily to the army's inistence on war. Some members of the army General Staff, on the other hand, had criticized him shortly before the war for supporting Tojo's efforts (inspired by the Emperor) to extend the negotiations with the United States. At a liaison conference on November 1, the army's vice chief of staff, General Ko Tsukada, had bluntly told Shimada to shut up when the navy minister suggested that talks with America continue until two days before the proposed beginning of war. There were times when Shimada seemed to have no one supporting him except General Tojo. However, that was enough.

As the three men descended into the crowd, Shimada and Aka-matsu pressed in protectively close to Tojo, but there was no need to protect him here. These people wanted only to smile at him, wave their flags at him, cheer him, touch him if they dared. He put his hand on an old man's shoulder. He rubbed a child's head.

"You must lead us to victory!" someone shouted.

"To victory!" said someone else.

Tojo's thin lips opened in a smile. "I'll try," he said, and everyone within earshot cheered. It was evident that they loved him, yet it cannot be said that Tojo was moved by their love. Popularity with the masses was not, in his view, an asset to be courted or overestimated. Just a day or so ago his wife had told him how happy she was at his sudden increase in public support. He had felt constrained to caution her. "When you have popularity, you feel strong," he had said, "and when you lose it you feel weak. But that is not as it should be. A man should never be moved by such a sentiment as popularity." Tojo, until the day the war began, had never been considered, by himself or anyone else, a popular man. He could not convince himself that because he was now enormously popular, he would always be so.

DECEMBER 13,
5 A.M. IN TOKYO,
3 A.M. IN MALAYA

A N O R D E R to halt was passed back through the long column of men moving silently in the darkness on the road south from Kota Bharu. The Takumi detachment, still more than 4,000-strong despite heavy losses in the Malayan invasion five days earlier, was now reaching the end of a twelve-and-a-half-mile forced march from Kota Bharu to the British airfield at Tanah Mirah. Colonel Yoshio Nasu, the detachment's infantry commander, called the halt because his men were now so close to the air base it was time to deploy them in attack formation. Though they had been on the road almost 15 hours, having been delayed several times because the retreating British had blown up most of the bridges along the route, there was no thought of a rest period before attacking the field. It had to be taken, not only to provide another sorely needed base for Japanese planes but also to eliminate the threat it posed against General Tomoyuki Yamashita's advance across the peninsula from Singora and Patani toward Jitra and Gurun on the west coast. Dawn was now less than four hours away. If there were any enemy planes still flying from Tanah Mirah, they must not be allowed to take off after Yamashita's armored columns, which were attempting to disrupt the enemy defenses in northern Malaya.

As the infantrymen took their positions for the final push through the dark jungle toward the airfield, the Takumi detachment's gun batteries (its only mechanized equipment) were wheeled into place and prepared for action if needed. Colonel Nasu was aware of the possibility that they might not be needed. Since the British had retired without a fight from the airfield at Kota Bharu, and from the town itself, they might also have retired from this airfield. But one could not count on such good fortune because from a British point of view it should be unthinkable to present ready-made airfields to the enemy without a struggle. There was something inexplicably peculiar about the British behavior in these first days of war. After the desperate battle for the beach at Kota Bharu, Nasu would have predicted that every inch of the peninsula would be fiercely contested. Since that first day, however, it had been difficult to find any British in the area around Kota Bharu, and reports from the west coast indicated they were badly organized there. General Yamashita was now trying to catch them in a two-pronged offensive. Before the Takumi detachment left Kota Bharu the previous noon, Yamashita's upper prong, from Singora, had already begun attacks on the towns of Jitra and Alor Star. The lower prong, moving quickly across from Patani on the road to Kroh, was more immediately threatened by air attacks from the Tanah Mirah field because it passed much closer to the Tanah Mirah area. This prong was racing so fast it was also slightly overextended and therefore possibly vulnerable. But if it could reach a point near the town of Gurun, where the road across from Patani met the Singapore road south from Jitra, it would isolate all the British forces in the north.

The advance units of the Takumi detachment were now rushing through the jungle and along the narrow roads of the rubber plantations toward the Tanah Mirah air base. Nasu and the main contingent, hurrying to stay close behind them, listened for sounds of fighting, but heard none. Nasu himself had almost reached the edge of the field before any sound other than the usual jungle noises broke the night air. From the cluster of airport buildings outlined against the dark sky ahead he heard a small explosion, then another and another. Were the advance units in some difficulty? Nasu and his men hurried forward, ready to support them.

When they reached the buildings, however, they were surprised to find most of their advance troops simply standing around, waiting for them, with nothing to do. The explosions, caused by booby traps, had wounded only a few men. And there were no enemy troops in sight. Aside from planting those pitiful little charges, the retreating British had done virtually nothing to inconvenience the arriving Japanese. The field was almost in working order despite some damage, probably inflicted, not by the British themselves, but by attacking Japanese planes.

Along the flight line, looking grotesque in the dark, were the ruined remains of British planes which had obviously been destroyed on the ground by bombs. It was comforting to see such proof of the accuracy and skill of Japanese pilots. Maybe that explained why these airfields were not being defended. Unlikely as it might seem, maybe the enemy had already lost all its air power in Malaya. Otherwise, how could two ships like the *Prince of Wales* and the *Repulse* have been caught without air cover only 70 miles offshore? Maybe the British were abandoning their airfields simply because they had no planes left to fly from them. The fields would not be abandoned for long. Japanese planes would soon be flying from them.

As Colonel Nasu inspected the airport he felt a warm satisfaction at helping turn over to Japanese fliers such a useful facility in such good condition. He was proud of these men in the Takumi detachment, proud of their bravery and their tireless tenacity. He was proud of the Japanese Army, to which he had devoted his life, proud of the navy, proud of his country and its magnificent accomplishments after five days of war. He had been in favor of war before it started. He had believed from the start that Japan would win and there was surely enough evidence now to support that belief. But the time to relax had not yet come. It was still a long way to Singapore.

Before Colonel Nasu settled down for a few hours' sleep, however, he received news that seemed to shorten the distance to Singapore. Word arrived that Jitra and Alor Star, on the west coast of the peninsula, were in Japanese hands. And the lower prong of General Yamashita's pincers was nearing Kroh. It seemed unlikely now that the British could hold out much longer in northern Malaya, where they had built their strongest defenses against invasion. There were few good natural defensive positions down the west coast highway toward Singapore. The Japanese might have to face some hard battles on the way, but the British, without air power, were in deep trouble. One could almost begin to envision the Japanese Army marching into the city.

DECEMBER 13,
7:30 A.M. IN HANKOW,
8:30 A.M. IN TOKYO

T H O U G H the wind was cold and snow flurries were falling, General Korechika Anami stood, as was his daily habit, in the garden of his house at Hankow, China, shooting arrows from his long Japanese bow at a straw target. This morning there was nothing wrong with his aim. One after another, the arrows clustered snugly around the center. Anami's concentration was exceptional today. No frustrations distracted him. He had thought of a way to employ usefully the now idle Eleventh Army, of which he was commanding general, and his mind was composed. Even the frigid cold of the snowy garden failed to reach him. Yet he would have to stop his target practice soon. It was almost time to go to headquarters. He would summon his staff immediately and disclose his plan. Perhaps he could now get his army on the move after all, but only if the plan proved as worthwhile and practical as it seemed to him. Much as he liked action, General Anami had no desire to seek it merely for his own satisfaction. He had never forgotten a charge his mother once made to him. "You must at all times control yourself," she had said. "Never let your subordinates die simply for your own glory." A thoroughly Samurai woman, his mother was still alive and vigorous at the age of 94. When Anami left for his first China duty in 1938 (she was then 91), she had written a poem about him:

> I don't think his parting is forever,
> But as his mother, I would like to go with him,
> Wherever he may go.

It was from his mother that he had learned to take seriously such mottos as: "Virtue is the best strategy in war."

As soon as he reached his headquarters on Hankow's Bukan University campus, General Anami called a meeting of his staff officers. The warmth between him and these men was evident from the ease and lack of constraint with which they entered his office and approached him. He was not overly talkative. He spoke to them only if he had something special to say. But he had an Oriental quality of making a person feel welcome without words. His officers felt a communion with him simply by being with him.

When most of them were assembled, he looked up casually and said, "I hope you're all coming to the party this afternoon." He had scheduled a farewell drinking session (he was quite fond of Japanese sake) in honor of a junior staff officer who was being transferred from Hankow. He intended even to see the man off at the airport the next day. Such gestures were natural to General Anami, which was one reason his men thought of him, not only as a general, but as a companion, a father, and a teacher. For a few years during his career he had been a teacher, first at the Central Military Cadet School, then, in 1934, as principal of the Tokyo Military Cadet School. His ways of teaching were modeled after the practical, exemplary methods of the Zen Buddhist masters, whom he admired, and the Samurai bushido masters whom he emulated. He had never been as strict with his students or his young officers, however, as he was with himself. He maintained discipline through warmth and persistence. He had once said, "If an officer gives affection, appropriate duty, and advancement to a subordinate, naturally the subordinate will serve faithfully and work hard."

As soon as his whole staff was assembled in his office, Anami arose and, with a dramatic gesture, announced: "I have decided to take offensive action in the direction of Bekisui."

Though the officers were obviously startled at this sudden development, since Anami had told them a few days earlier that the army wanted to avoid at this time any unnecessary campaigns in China, they showed no signs of being displeased at his intentions. After giving them time to recover from their surprise, he went to a map on the wall and began explaining both his purpose and his plan.

"Perhaps some of you have not yet heard the good news that came early this morning. The Sano Division [of the Twenty-third Army] broke through the British positions north of Hong Kong during the night and took Kyuryu."

He pointed on the map to Kyuryu, a Chinese mainland coastal city just above Hong Kong.

"I understand we have appealed to the Hong Kong garrison to surrender, but no one expects them to do so. If they continue to fight, however, they must get help from someplace. Now where is the one place from which the British in Hong Kong might hope to get help?"

He paused, but not to await an answer. It was a rhetorical question. With an emphatic gesture he pointed to Ojyukei, southwest of Hankow and northwest of Hong Kong, where the Chinese Fourth, Twenty-ninth, and Fifty-eighth Armies were encamped. Though these Chinese forces were positioned principally to checkmate Anami's Eleventh Army at Hankow, he had obtained some disturbing information about their movements.

"Intelligence reports indicate," he said, "that the Chinese already have at least one unit on the way to relieve the British at Hong Kong. If that is true, our duty is clear. To prevent the Chinese from coming in behind our Twenty-third Army at Kyuryu, we must threaten their flank. But in order to threaten them convincingly, we shall have to send a significant force. Therefore, I'm thinking of committing half of our Eleventh Army [more than 35,000 men] in a drive straight south toward Bekisui. That should put enough pressure on the Chinese to send them back to Ojyukei. What do you gentlemen think?"

Bekisui was on an almost direct north-south line between Hankow and Hong Kong. A large Japanese force there would pose a prohibitive danger to any Chinese column moving from Ojyukei toward Hong Kong. If the Chinese wished to get at the Japanese Twenty-third Army above Hong Kong, they would have first to defeat Anami's Eleventh Army. His planned move toward Bekisui was so eminently sound in the classic tradition of military strategy that his staff officers wasted no time in registering their enthusiasm for it.

They were as eager for action as he was, and here was a campaign that would be not only helpful to the Japanese forces besieging Hong Kong, but perhaps even essential to their success. Within a few minutes, General Anami's Eleventh Army headquarters was abuzz with activity as work began on the details of the move. Anami was suddenly happier than he had been for some time. He looked at his chief of staff, Major General Isamu Kinoshita, and smiled with satisfaction. Perhaps he would soon get a chance to take part in the war after all.

DECEMBER 13,
NOON

F O R E I G N Minister Shigenori Togo did not look forward to the luncheon he was about to give at his official residence—an event honoring the ambassadors of Germany and Italy, which countries had now joined Japan in declaring war against America. Though Togo felt obliged to welcome the help of these two Axis partners with a public show of comradeship, he undertook it reluctantly because his feelings toward the Germans were not friendly. In 1937 he had been appointed Japanese ambassador to Germany, but he found it so difficult to cope both with the Nazi government and the Japanese Army (an overpowering force in deciding his nation's foreign policy) that he lasted only ten months in Berlin. He disliked the Nazis and found the Germans unfathomable. "They cannot understand diplomacy," he told a friend. He was bitterly opposed also to the tripartite pact which the Japanese Army was then trying to arrange. "Japan cannot have serious negotiations with an upstart like Hitler," he said. The Japanese Army, which disagreed, soon arranged Togo's transfer to Moscow, where he served with somewhat more satisfaction for two years before returning to Tokyo and becoming, eventually, the foreign minister in Hideki Tojo's cabinet.

Togo greeted personally his 30 distinguished luncheon guests as they entered the elegant Western-style dining room of the foreign minister's official residence. German Ambassador Eugen Ott, tall, wide-faced, erect, and looking very pleased, strode strongly into the room followed by some of the top men on his staff. Togo bowed and smiled in what was, for him, an almost effusive welcome. He was by nature so austere, however, that even his most open smile was unlikely to make Ambassador Ott feel he had been enthusiastically received. Ott did not have to be very sensitive to realize Togo disliked him.

Italian Ambassador Mario Indelli, more expansive in personality than Ott, was given a correctly identical welcome when he arrived. While Benito Mussolini's Italy might be only a weak, junior partner of Adolf Hitler's Germany, Togo was too proper a diplomat to let it appear he was making distinctions. As soon as he had greeted all the invited guests, he quickly took his place at the long, large table between Prime Minister Tojo and the two ambassadors. Tojo had arrived on foot from his own official residence across the street with Chief Cabinet Secretary Naoki Hoshino. Among the other men taking their places at the white-clothed, flower-decorated board were Admiral Shigetaro Shimada, the navy minister; Teiichi Suzuki, president of the cabinet planning board; Masayuki Tani, president of the Board of Information; Admiral Osami Nagano, chief of the Navy General Staff; and Dr. Yoshimichi Hara with Baron Admiral Kantaro Suzuki, president and vice-president of the Privy Council.

As soon as the last dish was served and the waiters were pouring sake, Togo stood up abruptly to make his prepared speech. Anticipating a busy afternoon, he wanted to keep this luncheon as brief as possible. By the time he finished speaking and offering toasts, followed by Ott and Indelli doing likewise, it might be almost two o'clock. Perhaps it would be vain to hope they would keep their speeches short, but he could, at least, give them an example to follow.

"That Japan, Germany, and Italy concluded the tripartite pact on September 27 last year was due to their earnest desire to establish a new and righteous world order," he began. "However, the malicious interferences on the part of the United States and the British Empire against the moral aspirations of our three countries increased day by day, and there was no knowing when they would cease."

Togo's dislike of Nazi Germany had not led him to view the United States with sympathy. The conduct of the Americans filled him with moral indignation, a feeling for which he had great capacity since he saw himself as a man of unswerving reason and honor. The Americans, he felt, had been insufferably hypocritical in demanding that Japan give up its past gains and renounce all imperial ambitions while the United States was doubling the size of its navy, expanding its air bases in the Philippines, supporting Chiang Kai-shek in China, and interfering, politically as well as economically, throughout Asia. During the seven months of negotiations from April to November, President Roosevelt and Secretary of State Cordell Hull had forced Japan into one concession after another without making any concessions themselves. They had acted as if their main purpose were not to find a settlement with Japan, but to bring on war.

"It is quite natural, therefore," Togo continued, "that Japan has at last resolutely taken up arms against the United States and the British Empire for the sake of righteousness and justice."

German Ambassador Ott, sitting a few feet away, looked pleased. Righteousness was a concept not often mentioned in enterprises which his government embraced.

"It is the will of God that wrong cannot prevail over right," Togo concluded, "and therefore the ultimate outcome of the current war is very clear."

Ambassador Ott stood and led the applause.

Togo picked up his wine glass. "May I ask you gentlemen now to join me in drinking a toast to the brilliant future of the common war of Japan, Germany, and Italy; and at the same time, to the health of His Excellency, Fuehrer Hitler; His Majesty, the King of Italy and Emperor of Ethiopia; and His Excellency, Prime Minister Mussolini."

It was the beginning of a long round of toasts. After this first one, in which Togo included as many dignitaries as possible, he felt obliged to offer another for the two ambassadors. Then each of the ambassadors took the floor, making speeches and offering toasts to His Majesty, Emperor Hirohito, to Prime Minister Tojo, to their host, Foreign Minister Togo, to the wonderful people of Japan, to the people of Germany, to the people of Italy, to the friendship of all these people, to ultimate victory.

Togo drank sparingly. It was not his habit to drink very much at any time. His health was poor (he had suffered from a heart condition for several years) and his constitution was not strong. After drinking only a small amount of sake he could feel it. He had a taxing load of work to do when he returned to his office. Italian Ambassador Indelli was still offering toasts. "To His Imperial Majesty, Emperor Hirohito." Togo again wearily raised his glass. To His Majesty, yes, one offered not merely a toast, but everything. One's work, one's life, one's total self. But sometimes it could be difficult.

DECEMBER 13,
LUNCHTIME

UNITED STATES Ambassador Joseph Clark Grew, his wife, Alice, and their twelve guests were finishing lunch in the dining room of their elegant residence within the embassy compound. All the guests today, as was the case for the last five days, were members of the embassy staff. The Grews' social life had become rather restricted, yet they were making the best of it.

"What are you planning this afternoon?" the ambassador asked his wife. "Bridge again?"

"Yes, I think so," she said. "And you?"

"We're having a little golf tournament."

At such moments, life in the embassy seemed almost normal. The food was still quite good. Meat, fish, and vegetables were coming in daily. The Japanese servants were still on duty. And one could get the impression by glancing out over the Tokyo rooftops toward the prime minister's official residence and the Diet building on the opposite hill that life in the city was also following a normal pace. The ambassador's view from his house was, however, the only glimpse he was now permitted of life in Japan. Since Monday morning, the two-square-block American Embassy compound in the Toronamon district had been sealed by the police, and the 65 Americans inside were living in what had become a luxurious prison.

Ambassador Grew had not even realized his country was at war with Japan until midmorning, Monday, several hours after the fighting began. His meeting with Foreign Minister Shigenori Togo at 7:30 that morning had left him with the impression merely that negotiations were at a stalemate between the two countries. It was not until an hour after his return to the embassy that he was handed the press bulletin announcing the Japanese attack on Hawaii. It was 11 A.M. before a Foreign Office representative arrived with the following official notification:

Ministry of Foreign Affairs
Tokyo, December 8, 1941

Excellency:

I have the honor to inform Your Excellency that there has arisen a state of war between Your Excellency's country and Japan beginning today.

I avail myself of this opportunity to renew to Your Excellency the assurances of my highest consideration.

Shigenori Togo
Minister of Foreign Affairs

Eugene Dooman, the embassy counsellor, who was present at the reading of this letter, had asked the Foreign Office representative if it was because of the impending hostilities that Togo had been reluctant to see Ambassador Grew the previous night. The answer was: "Not at all. The Foreign Minister knew nothing about the attack on Hawaii until early this morning." Grew had been thereby reassured of Togo's innocence in the matter.

Immediately after this notification, the embassy had been officially sealed and its inmates had settled down to a new existence under police guard. Outside communication was completely suspended. The entire compound was searched and all radio equipment, for receiving as well as transmitting, was confiscated. Thereafter, the only news from the outside world came through the Japanese papers which were delivered regularly to Ambassador Grew, and which he did his best to interpret at daily briefings for his staff. The most immediate problem, housing, was solved by the simple expedient of overcrowding the two apartment buildings on the grounds to accommodate those who had been living previously outside the walls. The next problem, food distribution, was turned over to Second Secretary William Turner and Staff Translator Masaru Fujimoto, a Japanese-American who had been born in Seattle and educated at the University of California. Fortunately, a new shipment of canned goods had recently arrived from San Francisco, and Turner and Fujimoto had gathered it, with all other available supplies, at a central commissary from which each family drew rations to supplant the fresh foods supplied by the Japanese authorities. The only concern now was whether the canned goods would last until the time came for repatriation to the United States.

Because there was very little work to be done, everyone sought his own pastimes. The embassy library became more popular than ever before, and the community room, which had come to be known as "The Lido," filled up each day with bridge, poker, mah-jongg, and chess players. "The Lido" also had a phonograph, a piano, and a rack of magazines which most of the people had already read but to which some, out of boredom, were returning for a second look. Several of the staff members had asked the ambassador's permission to hold a Saturday night dance in "The Lido" this evening but he had vetoed the idea for fear the Japanese guards might think their American prisoners were taking the war too flippantly.

There was no reason to take the war flippantly, as Grew had pointed out at this morning's news briefing in the drawing room outside the library.

"Once again, everything we have to tell you is bad news," he said, before enumerating the top stories in the day's papers. The Japanese Army had announced that Kowloon was now occupied and that bombing raids were continuing against Hong Kong, Penang in Malaya, and the Philippine Islands. The navy had released an incredible summary of the first five days of war: Four battleships (U.S. and British), one carrier, one submarine, three small warships, and two other ships sunk; four battleships, four large cruisers, one submarine, five small warships, and five other ships damaged. The navy also claimed to have destroyed 202 planes; the army, 103. The Japanese government announced a new military treaty with the government of French Indochina. Tojo, Hitler, and Mussolini had exchanged congratulatory messages, and German submarines claimed to have sunk four British merchant ships in the Atlantic. There was also a Domei report from Shanghai which quoted a Chungking radio report which quoted a Reuters dispatch of the previous day from America which said New York City was bombed twice that morning. Was it possible? The report had come through such a comical succession of sources one might feel safe in disbelieving it. One might disbelieve any of the stories in the rigidly censored Japanese papers, but it would seem foolish to disbelieve all of them. According to every indication, the Japanese were indeed doing all too well, though it was impossible, behind these walls, to know exactly how well.

"The enemy seems to be gaining some remarkable victories," Grew had told the staff, "but don't lose heart. The pendulum swings. Our turn will come."

After the briefing, the ambassador had returned to his own sumptuous residence at the top of the tree-lined compound for lunch, and now that lunch was finished, he and his male guests went out to inaugurate a new pitch-and-putt golf course which they had laid out on the lawns. As the men departed, Grew's wife, Alice, a handsome, matronly woman in her middle years, was left to reflect upon her extraordinary situation while she awaited her bridge partners.

For Mrs. Grew, there was a special, personal irony in her imprisonment by the Japanese. She was the granddaughter of Commodore Matthew C. Perry, who had arrived in Japan in 1853, bearing a formidable demand from the President of the United States that Japan open its long-closed ports to American commerce. It was Mrs. Grew's grandfather more than any other one man who had forced the Japanese to adopt Western methods and institutions, including a modern military establishment and the policy of expansionism which had finally brought Japan to the fateful war on which it was now embarked. Viewed historically, Japan's newly launched conflict was a not-so-surprising outcome of America's insistence, conveyed by Commodore Perry, that the country end its two-and-a-half-century isolation and embrace Western ways. The Samurai aristocrats who governed Japan in the name of Emperor Meiji decided that since they were forced to westernize, they would be wise to do a thorough job of it. They sent thousands of bright young men abroad to study European and American science, technology, politics, military strategy, international relations—and they learned some fascinating lessons from the West. They saw how England had taken India, Australia, Malaya, and Hong Kong; how France had taken Indochina; how Holland had taken the East Indies. In 1898, they saw America take the Philippine Islands. Following these Western examples, Japan, too, began to reach out—toward the Russian-held islands to the north, toward the vast spaces of China and Manchuria to the east, and now, toward the oil-rich, Dutch-held islands to the south. Though the Western nations had made it clear that they did not like Japanese imperialism as well as they liked their own, the Japanese had already gone too far to back down without losing self-respect. They had decided to fight rather than meet America's retrenchment demands, and when the doors closed between the two countries, the grand-daughter of the man who opened them was one of the people caught on the wrong side.

While Mrs. Grew prepared for her bridge game, her husband and several members of his staff were outside, playing golf on a course the like of which none of them had ever before tried. About 80 yards long and 40 yards wide, the entire layout was on a slope so steep that one could purposely overshoot some of the uphill holes and count on the ball rolling back to the tin-can cups. The best golfers, like Robert "Chip" Bohlen, the embassy's Second Secretary, were quick to master this clever technique. The course offered one water hazard, the embassy swimming pool, which had no other use in this chilly December weather. Since there were not enough balls and clubs to go around, today's contestants had to do a lot of borrowing, especially from the ambassador, who loved golf and was well equipped for it. Until recently, he had often played with Japanese dignitaries at Tokyo country clubs. He had once played a memorable round with American baseball stars Babe Ruth and Lefty O'Doul when they visited Japan. They were amused at his croquet putting style until they noticed his accuracy. Unfortunately, his putting style was not much help to him today. On this course, luck was more important. But these were not lucky days for Ambassador Grew. He finished well back in the pack as Bohlen was ceremoniously declared the winner of the inaugural tournament.

As Grew shook Bohlen's hand, someone in the crowd said, "That's fine, but what's he champion of? We should give the course a name."

Someone else said, "Let's call it the Greater East Asia Black Sulphur Springs Championship Golf Course."

It was the perfect name as everyone quickly agreed. They had heard that the Japanese diplomats caught in America were now interned at the beautiful White Sulphur Springs resort near Washington. Anytime those diplomats wanted to trade quarters, these Americans were ready.

After the golf tournament ended and the laughter faded, Joseph Grew walked slowly up a curved path of stepping-stones through a small grove of trees to his personal residence at the top of the hill—a white house with tile roof and black ironwork trimmings. It was a beautiful house in which he had once taken great pleasure. He could take no pleasure in it now, nor in any aspect of his present situation. All the laughter of the golf tournament had been sadly hollow. It seemed almost sinful to laugh during days like these. Before going inside, he turned and gazed out at the vast expanse of Tokyo. Though not beautiful, it was an exciting city—at least it had been during most of his ten years here. He felt no excitement as he looked at it now. Only a deep depression. He liked the Japanese but they still baffled him. What could they possibly think they might gain in a war with America? How could they hope to win such a war? It had to end in tragedy, and this saddened him profoundly because in a way their tragedy was also his personal tragedy. For ten years he had been making every effort to maintain peace between the two countries. It was unbearable to watch all those efforts end in failure.

DECEMBER 13,
1 P.M.

AT 1 P.M., the crowd had already begun to gather in Hibiya Park, Tokyo's beautiful, 40-acre green at the south end of the Imperial Palace between the Marunouchi and Kasumigaseki districts. During the Tokugawa shogunate, the mansions of high feudal lords had stood on this land. In 1903, it had been opened to the public as a double-styled park, one section being of Japanese design, the other Western. It was into the more open, Western section that the crowd was pouring this afternoon. The occasion was a "People's Rally in Obedience to the Imperial Rescript," sponsored jointly by the Imperial Rule Assistance Association, the Tokyo Prefecture, and the Tokyo Municipality.

By 1:30 P.M., at least 30,000 people were packed together in front of the speakers' platform, waving placards and shouting "Down with the United States and England!" Animosity toward the two enemy nations had been increasing daily since the war began, perhaps because the Japanese newspapers could now be even more outspoken than previously against "the haughty Anglo-Saxons." The sins of America were most harshly condemned. Almost every day one of the newspapers would publish a new denunciation of the United States. A columnist in *Nichi Nichi* had written:

Who excludes us from the land of plenty by branding us undesirables? Who discriminated against goods made in Nippon? Who shackled us to an inferior naval ratio while reserving herself the right to build even a two-ocean navy? Justice, equality, open door. We have heard of these ideals from America for nearly half a century. And what has she done to us? . . .

The Japanese people felt encouraged now to express openly resentments many of them had long harbored against America.

Among the guests of honor at Hibiya Park on this clear but chilly December day were the German and Italian ambassadors, Eugen Ott and Mario Indelli (who arrived late, coming directly from the Foreign Minister Togo's luncheon for them), and Thai Ambassador Phya Sri Sena. After an opening address by Tokyo Prefectural Governor Jitsuzo Kasai, and a reading of the December 8 imperial rescript, former Prime Minister Senjuro Hayashi, a man with an erect bearing and a wide, handlebar mustache, was nominated as chairman of the rally. Then came the declaration of the meeting:

We are filled with trepidation by the imperial rescript which was granted to us. Our duty is to be wholeheartedly faithful. . . . Convinced that victory will be ours, we pledge ourselves to crush the United States and the British Empire for the purpose of attaining the objectives of this holy war.

The rally's principle attraction, Prime Minister Hideki Tojo, who also arrived late from Togo's luncheon, sat gazing out at the crowd as he awaited his turn to speak. Though Tojo felt physically safe mingling with people in public, he did not feel at ease in large popular gatherings. He had mixed emotions about that enormous, seemingly docile, but potentially dangerous entity—the Japanese public. As a Japanese soldier, and now as a statesman, he was not expected to be in any way influenced by what the people might desire. It was a government's duty to control them, to ensure their continuing loyalty and docility. Tojo, as a soldier, when he commanded the the Kempeitai in Manchuria, and now as prime minister, believed in controlling the public with a mixture of caution and unremitting firmness. Just this morning, at an emergency conference of prefectural police chiefs, he had said, "At this juncture, it is necessary to adopt a rigid policy for enforcement of regulations concerning speeches, publications, and rumors that might disturb the unity of public opinion."

Before the war began, he had taken a series of steps to make certain the public would give his government no trouble. He had arranged what he called "preventive arrests" by the fearsome Kempeitai of "Communists, rebellious Koreans, certain religious leaders, and others" who might be "antiwar or antimilitary." He had put "under observation and control" those patriotic nationalistic organizations which might "tend to be very excitable and rash." He had taken steps "to guide public opinion and exercise rather strict controls over it." And he had instructed the minister of justice to increase the penalties for certain crimes. Those stiffer penalties,which had been set only yesterday at a cabinet meeting, included capital punishment with no leniency for crimes of violence; life imprisonment for any burglary which caused injury; and ten years to death for robbery. Tojo had often spoken of his faith in the spirit of the Japanese public; he wanted every assurance that nothing would happen to undermine that spirit.

It was 2 P.M. when he stepped to the rostrum in Hibiya Park to address this 30,000-strong segment of the public.

"Upon receiving the imperial rescript on the promulgation of the war," he said, "the Imperial Army and Navy rose up to sweep away the unrighteous pressure of the United States and Britain. . . ."

The moment he finished that first sentence a roar arose from the crowd, so sudden and deafening it startled him. When the cheering finally abated, he continued.

"It has been more than 2,600 years since the Japanese Empire was founded, and Japan has never taken up arms with other aims than for righteousness and self-defense. . . ."

Another great wave of sound ascended from the throng. Again Tojo waited for it to die, but if he thought he could make a normal speech at this rally, he was soon disabused of the idea. These people had come, not to listen to him, but to adore him.

"The Japanese Empire, which hopes for the peace and development of East Asia, and the United States and Britain, both of which wish to place East Asia under their control, are incompatible. . . ."

Once more the thunderous sound erupted.

"Japan, however, with utmost patience and peaceful means requested the United States and Britain to make reflection. Despite Japan's endeavor, they never listened. . . ."

The cheering continued. Time after time he was saluted before he finally reached his conclusion.

"We must never be too elated over our victories. We shall never worry, even if the war should be prolonged. We shall endure any hardship and privation. We are convinced we shall be the final winners."

As Prime Minister Tojo finished speaking, he stared out for a moment at the huge, close-packed mass of shouting faces. He could not help being touched. It was difficult at a moment like this for him to maintain his usual wariness about the public. Never before had he been exposed to so intense a display of public adulation. To these people he was such an absolute hero they still continued cheering him after he stepped down from the rear of the platform and left the park. If this rally could be taken as a measure, he need not worry about the Japanese public's spirit or its enthusiasm for the war.

DECEMBER 14,
1:45 P.M.

MORE THAN 200 people had filled the small sanctuary of the Sengakuji Buddhist Temple (in south Tokyo near the Shinagawa Station), on the grounds of which the Lord Naganori Asano and the Forty-seven Ronin who gave their lives for him were buried. It was on this date, December 14, 1702, that the famous forty-seven master-less Samurai who had been Asano's retainers during his life, avenged his enforced harakiri by killing the man who caused it. And the Japanese were proving once again, as they did every December 14th, that they had not forgotten this chilling, true story of Samurai honor, loyalty, and commitment.

Outside the temple, spilling over its tree-covered grounds, were thousands of people who were here to pay their respects even though they knew they couldn't get in to attend the service. While the select 200 inside listened to lectures about moral aspects of the ronin story, then joined the Buddhist priests of Sengakuji in prayers before the forty-seven wooden tablets on which the ronin had left their names, the crowd outside bought fruit, incense sticks, toys, and souvenirs from the dozens of vendors who had set up stands. The fruit and incense would be placed at the graves of the ronin and their Lord Asano in the little wooded cemetery to the left of the temple buildings. Before midnight, when the temple closed, perhaps 100,000 people, many of them military men, would come to make offerings at the graves, and millions of others all over Japan would observe the day. The story of these forty-seven men was so remarkable it could almost explain by itself why the Samurai tradition had such a powerful hold on the Japanese imagination.

The compelling sequence of events began in 1701 when Lord Asano, the feudal ruler of Ako (on the Inland Sea coast of Honshu about forty miles west of Kobe) was insulted by another, more powerful feudal lord, Yoshinaka Kira, at Edo Castle, the headquarters of the Tokugawa shogunate which then ruled Japan. (Edo Castle later became the Imperial Palace when the Tokugawas gave way to the Meiji Restoration and Edo became Tokyo.) Infuriated by Lord Kira's affront, Lord Asano drew his sword, and though he was stopped before he could inflict more than a superficial forehead wound on his enemy, he was quickly ordered by the shogun's government to commit suicide. His crime had not been in seeking revenge for an insult. Such action was admirable for a Samurai. But he had drawn his sword in the shogun's castle, and for that offense he could retrieve his honor only by harakiri.

When Lord Asano's Samurai retainers learned of his fate and the circumstances surrounding it, forty-seven of them made a secret vow to wreak vengeance against the powerful Lord Kira, whom they deemed responsible. For more than a year they plotted their revenge which, because Lord Kira held a high position in the shogun's court, had to be undertaken with consummate guile. To conceal their intentions, the forty-seven men publicly disavowed the debt of loyalty which the Samurai bushido code demanded they pay to their dead master. They allowed their swords to rust. They began frequenting brothels and leading openly dissolute lives. One of them sold his wife into prostitution to help finance the cause. Another sent his sister to become a concubine in Lord Kira's home where she could gather useful information. Finally, on December 14, 1702, after waiting long enough to throw Lord Kira off guard, they stormed his home in Edo, and when he proved himself unworthy of his Samurai position by refusing to commit suicide, beheaded him with the very sword their Lord Asano had used to kill himself. Marching immediately to Sen-gakuji Temple where Lord Asano was buried, they laid the sword and Lord Kira's head before the grave of their dead master. Their leader, Kuranosuke Oishi, then made a speech which would thenceforth be studied diligently by generations of Japanese school children.

"We have come this day to do homage to you," Oishi said to his deceased lord. "We could not have dared to present ourselves before you unless we had completed the vengeance which you began. Every day we waited seemed like three autumns to us. . . . We have carried Lord Kira here to your tomb. And we have brought back this sword you prized so highly and which last year you entrusted to us. We ask you to take it and strike the head of your enemy a second time, thus to dispel your hatred forever. This is the respectful statement of forty-seven men."

Having accomplished the revenge which proved their loyalty to their dead master, the forty-seven immediately became public heroes. Their debt to Lord Asano was now paid. But in discharging it, they had abrogated their loyalty to the Tokugawa shogun, who sanctioned vendettas only if they were duly announced and registered with his government. As the forty-seven ronin were soon informed, they would have to erase this offense against the shogun if they wished to preserve their honor, and there was only one way to do it.

On February 4, 1703, all forty-seven men, ranging in age from 15 to 77, disemboweled themselves in a harakiri ritual near Sengakuji Temple, and were thereafter buried together on the temple grounds in a rectangular area just a few feet from the tomb of Lord Asano. They would be forever honored by the Japanese people because they had been faithful to the most important and exacting of Japanese traditions. Disregarding the disastrous costs to themselves and their families, they had accepted and satisfied each successive horrible obligation circumstances laid upon them.

When the service inside Sengakuji Temple came to an end at 2 P.M., the priests and the people who took part emerged and led a procession through the grounds to the gray stone slabs which marked the graves of the forty-seven men. The thousands of people waiting outside fell in behind the procession as it moved slowly past a museum full of ronin relics and past a stone, bowl-shaped well where the ronin had washed Lord Kira's head before presenting it at Lord Asano's grave. Finally, the priests, walking slowly in ceremonial robes, led the way up a set of steps into the fenced, rectangular compound where the graves of the forty-seven heroes had been laid out, in accordance with their order of precedence while serving Lord Asano. Thousands of people pressed in close to hear the priests intone Buddhist prayers commemorating the ronin. The ceremony at the graves was simple. Only a series of prayers. No speeches. These people needed no speeches about the ronin. They all knew that the forty-seven masterless Samurai represented what was best in Japanese manhood.

To non-Japanese, the ronin story might seem a horrible example of pointless revenge and needless bloodshed. To the Japanese it was powerfully moving, morally persuasive, nobly uplifting, and therefore in no way horrible. It was a story of fidelity to duty and loyalty to one's superior, both of which qualities were touchstones of the Japanese social system.

Perhaps equally important in 1941, the ronin story illustrated a characteristic highly cherished by the Japanese—willingness to accept the consequences of an act. When the Japanese were committed, it meant they were ready to accept whatever burden the commitment implied. Their Emperor, a week before, had committed them to a war which could have dreadful consequences before it ended. Some Japanese were already convinced of that. Yet it would never occur to any of them, schooled as they were in the same tradition as the forty-seven Samurai, that such a commitment, whatever its consequences, could be less than total.

DECEMBER 14,
11:30 P.M.

ZENJIRO OSAKI and his wife, Sumi, had retired early for the night in their family quarters above his corner shop at Bakuro-cho, Nihonbashi, not far from the very center of Tokyo. It was their custom to retire early because Osaki, a greengrocer, had to get up early. And during these cold December nights there was another incentive. One could get warm and comfortable wrapped snugly on the floor in a *futon* (Japanese floor mattress). Most Japanese houses were frigid in winter, not only because they were virtually unheated, but because their wooden walls were too thin to hold whatever heat might be generated by cooking, or by the little hibachi braziers which most people put under their low dining tables to take the chill off their feet.

Osaki, lying not quite asleep in his futon, was jolted wide awake about a half-hour before midnight when he noticed light flickering on the ceiling. In the short time it took him to react, the light was no longer flickering. It was glowing, and the entire room was illuminated by it.

Leaping to his feet, Osaki looked out the window to see fire rising from a Chinese noodle shop across the street in the next block.

Smoke and flames were pouring out of the noodle shop in such volume Osaki decided the whole neighborhood was in trouble.

"Fire!" he shouted, shaking his wife. "Fire! Fire! Get up!"

Knowing the speed with which fires could spread through Tokyo's close-packed, wooden houses, he decided he must evacuate his family immediately, even though the flames were now a half-block away and across the street. It was too narrow a street to afford him any comfort.

After arousing his wife, he pulled their two small boys (Minoru, five, and Zenzo, two) out of their futons and shook them until he was satisfied they were awake. In minutes, he and his family were dressed, though the children were still so sleepy they didn't yet seem quite aware that they were on their feet. A glance out the window told Osaki they had no time to spare, no time even to save the family valuables. The flames had already spread out from the noodle shop and were consuming houses in both directions. The house directly across the corner from Osaki was in full fire and burning brands were flying from it. The whole next block on the opposite side of the street was now a high wall of flame, and the heat was so ferocious Osaki could feel it through the flimsy walls of his house. He feared his house might ignite at any moment, spontaneously, from the heat alone.

"Get out!" he shouted to his wife over the roar and crackle of the flames. "Get the children out!"

And after one last, sad look at his possessions, he himself raced down the steep, narrow stairs into the street. So many people were milling about in their night clothes, both refugees from the fire and neighborhood spectators, that it took him two or three minutes to find his wife. She was standing with their older son, Minoru, shielding him from the heat of the flames.

Osaki said, "Where is Zenzo?"

A mask of fear spread across Sumi Osaki's already anxious face. "Isn't he with you?" she cried.

"Zenzo!" they both shouted, trying to make themselves heard above the roaring flames and the bawling children. Frantic, they rushed back and forth through the crowd, looking for their two-year-old son. No one had seen him.

Could he still be in the house?

Osaki looked up at a second-story window.

There, in the bright light of the fire, stood little Zenzo, his eyes blinking, his face showing his sleepy bewilderment.

Some of the flying fire brands were now hitting the Osaki house. Small patches of flame were beginning to appear on the dry, unpainted siding. In less than a minute, the whole house would be engulfed. A Japanese house could burn to the ground in less than ten minutes.

Osaki did not stop to think. Running back into his house, he raced up the stairs, found his two-year-old son still at the window, grabbed him in his arms and raced down the stairs. He emerged into the street and looked back in time to see his home and his shop blossom into flame, twist, crumple, and collapse like a burning piece of paper.

A clamor of bells and sirens announced the arrival of fire engines. Five or six of them. But it was too late for the firemen to help the houses in the block where the fire had started. It was also too late for them to save the Osaki house. The question now was whether they could save the rest of his block, whether they could prevent the fire from running completely out of control as many Tokyo fires had done in the past.

Tokyo's fire history was notorious. Time after time in the last 500 years it had been destroyed by flames, the most recent time being only eighteen years earlier, within the memory of Zenjiro Osaki and many other people here, when, after the great earthquake of 1923, a rampant conflagration eliminated three-fourths of the city and killed more than 100,000 people. Before that, in the days previous to the

Meiji Restoration, when Tokyo was called Edo, its fires were so frequent they had given rise to a famous Japanese saying: "Fires are the flowers of Edo." Fire protection in modern Tokyo was stronger than it had once been, but the bulk of the city was still a mass of inflammable houses. Every fire was a potential conflagration. And now, with the advent of war, there was an added danger, of which the authorities had taken cognizance just four days ago when Imperial General Headquarters published, in all the newspapers, a report on air defense:

Crack military and naval planes are now engaged in dealing thoroughgoing damage to enemy air and naval facilities over wide areas in the western Pacific. Judging by conditions at enemy air bases, and the strength of enemy air forces, the centers of Nippon are not in immediate danger of attacks by powerful enemy raiders. . . . But judging by the nature of aerial warfare, we ought to expect the entry of enemy air raiders through "cracks" in our air defenses. In the event of enemy air raids, the people should not lose their presence of mind and should cooperate with the authorities, remaining at their respective posts.

The people of Tokyo needed such assurances, as fires like this one in Nihonbashi proved. It was comforting to a fire-shy population to be assured that the enemy lacked the strength for more than token bombings, and that even if a few enemy planes did get through the defenses, the authorities apparently had plans to cope with them.

Those plans, however, would not help the Zenjiro Osaki family or the other families numbly watching the firemen fight this blaze which had already destroyed their homes. The fire had quickly moved to the house next to Osakis', and then to the house next to it, but there the firemen were making a stand and they seemed to be winning. Meanwhile, in the other direction, a broad business boulevard a block away had been a savior. Its width had kept the fire from crossing.

Though the skill, bravery, and energy of the firemen were remarkable, few people seemed to notice. Nobody in the crowd said much. The fire had done its work so suddenly everyone was still stunned. Zenjiro Osaki wondered what he would do now. His shop, his home, his furniture, all of his family's possessions except the clothes they were wearing had vanished before his eyes. He did have a pittance of insurance. It wouldn't be enough to cover the household goods. Osaki's anguish was so deep there was no way he could express it. On top of his other troubles, there was a danger that the army might take him. The thought of it was hateful. He had no interest in such a big event as the war. He didn't understand why it had to be. All he wanted was to go about his business and raise his family. But he was only 32 years old, and while he did have a family to support, he could not now claim that military service would be a hardship because he was a shopkeeper. He no longer had a shop to keep.

While Osaki's heart filled up with anguish, he felt no rage at what was happening to him. Anger would do no good. Fire was a force of nature. It was too big to resist. A person simply had to accept it, as he would have to accept army duty if called. It was not an Oriental characteristic to struggle against nature, against the inevitable. Westerners might try to conquer nature. Orientals bowed to it, and to the catastrophes it sometimes imposed. Instead of fuming in rage, one went to work and rebuilt.

Osaki had not, after all, lost everything. He still had his family. They had survived and they were well. They were no worse off than a lot of other people standing here beside him. Why should he feel sorry for himself? All he had to do was work and save and work and save. He was Japanese. Work held no terror for him. Work was the Japanese way of life. One day he would have another shop and another home. He looked down at his wife, Sumi, and tried to smile, She sighed, then, with an effort, returned his smile.

The fire was definitely contained now, but the whole block opposite the Osaki corner looked like a large vacant lot with several small bonfires burning on it. Only a few pathetic indications remained of the houses which had been there an hour before—blackened toilets, twisted metal household goods. In 45 minutes, a dozen homes had been completely consumed and two others virtually destroyed. Yet it could have been worse. While the occupants of the flattened homes huddled together disconsolately, many other people in the crowd, neighbors whose homes had been spared, could sigh with relief. Knowing Tokyo, they realized how fortunate they had been.

DECEMBER 15,
10:50 A.M.

A T T E N minutes before 11 A.M., the huge, black Mercedes Benz limousine of Emperor Hirohito, its imperial chrysanthemum emblem affixed to the radiator, came to a stop in front of the white, pyramidal-domed Japanese Diet building on the Miyakezaka hill, a half-mile southwest of the Imperial Palace. The motorcycle policemen escorting the car dismounted and took their positions to guard it.

On the sidewalk, the approximately 700 frock-coated members of Japan's parliament were standing at attention in orderly lines, waiting for the Emperor to arrive and open formally an extraordinary Diet session which was to begin at eleven.

The Emperor stepped down from his high-roofed automobile with an apparent diffidence which seemed to deny the grandeur of his position and of the bemedaled Japanese general's uniform he was wearing. He paused uncomfortably as the 300 members of the House of Peers, lined up on the right, and the 400 members of the lower House of Representatives, lined up on the left, bowed from the waist in unison. There was no ceremony outside. Passing quickly between the two ranks, the Emperor entered the building, accompanied by the speaker of the lower house, and followed by a retinue of royal princes and chamberlains, who had arrived in other cars. He went directly to a special room reserved for his exclusive use, where it was his custom to wait while the Diet members hurried to their seats in the meeting chamber of the upper house.

After five minutes, a period that had proven sufficient on previous occasions, he left the room, again in the company of the lower house speaker, and proceeded solemnly toward the meeting chamber, where all the members, some still breathing hard from their dash to get in ahead of him, bowed again as he entered. The speaker, after leading the Emperor to his throne on a raised dais behind the podium, walked slowly, himself, up another flight of stairs to the podium and announced that the Diet was now in session.

To the Emperor's right stood a group of his chamberlains. To his left stood the speaker of the upper house. The speaker of the lower house, at the podium, turned and bowed to His Majesty as a signal that it was time for his speech.

The imperial grand chamberlain ceremoniously walked up the steps to Hirohito's chair and handed him the speech, which the chief cabinet secretary's office had prepared for his delivery. In his rather high-pitched voice, Emperor Hirohito began to read:

We, in opening the Imperial Diet session with due ceremony, request each member of both the house of peers and the house of representatives to take notice: It is our great solicitude to contribute to world peace by ensuring stabilization of East Asia. Notwithstanding, both the United States and Great Britain dared to cause disturbance in East Asia, contrary to the desire of the Empire. Thus, the Empire has been forced to take up arms against them. We regret this deeply. It is our great joy that at this juncture the alliance with the friendly countries which have a common intention with our empire has become cemented more and more. The men and officers of our Army and Navy have manifested bravery and loyalty by doing their utmost everywhere. We herewith hope our subjects, in a firm conviction of ever victory and in their national unity, will enhance the national prestige at home and abroad by achieving quickly the objective of the war.

We hereby order the state ministers to submit to the imperial Diet budgetary measures and legislative bills urgently necessary in dealing with the situation. We hereby order you, in accordance with our wishes and in mutual unison, to fulfill the duties of helping the conduct of state affairs.

This last paragraph in the Emperor's speech was not meant to imply that the members of the Diet had any authority to make decisions about the budgetary measures or other affairs of state which were about to come under discussion. The Diet was a deliberative but not in any sense a law-making body. The aristocratic statesmen of the Meiji era, when they created it as a feature of the constitution of 1889, had been careful to give it the appearance but not the authority of a Western-style parliament. They believed the power to govern should be the exclusive province of a select group of well-educated, well-qualified aristocrats, and should not be limited in any way by public opinion. There was no reason, however, why the public should be deprived of opinions, or prevented from discussing them, so long as the government could feel free to disregard them. To the Meiji statesmen the establishment of a parliament seemed desirable because so many Western nations had parliaments. Hence they devised what seemed to them an ideal parliament—one whose members could talk but not act.

The members of the upper house, chosen from the Samurai aristocracy, were somewhat less serious about their positions than the members of the lower house, who were elected, but debate in both houses was usually undistinguished, perhaps because its futility was so evident. A parliament with no power could not easily attract brilliant men. In recent years, especially after the army's conquest of Manchuria, and the intimidating coup attempt of 1936, the Diet had become increasingly promilitary, with most of the members eagerly expounding the army viewpoint. The army had kept antimilitary members in check by criticizing and even threatening them in the newspapers, accusing them of conduct detrimental to the national welfare. On occasion, the army even rewarded favored members with gifts from a privy fund, but this was rare because the army was so much more powerful than the Diet it had no need to court the members. On the contrary, Diet members eager to ingratiate themselves with the army would lavishly entertain important officers in the geisha houses. The army had thus, quite easily, converted the Diet into an instrument for guiding public opinion.

When the Emperor finished reading his speech, he looked up at a huge chamberful of bowed heads. After a short, intense silence, the speaker of the lower house came down from the podium, approached His Majesty and took the speech from him. Then the speaker of the upper house came forward, bowed to His Majesty, and solemnly led him from the chamber. Emperor Hirohito having performed his duty and departed, the less formal proceedings were now ready to begin.

Prime Minister Tojo, who had been sitting in front with his cabinet ministers, arose, climbed to the speaker's platform, and began one of his characteristically short speeches:

I am profoundly impressed with the gracious address from the Throne. [He was overlooking the well known fact that one of his own assistants had written that address.]

In respectful response to the imperial wishes, it is my intention to overcome this difficult situation, unprecedented in history, by devoting my heart and soul to the service of the State, and thereby put His Majesty's mind at rest.

The body of Tojo's speech contained nothing he had not already expressed in previous speeches. He outlined the unsuccessful negotiations with America, listed the American proposals, accused America of rebuffing all of Japan's proposals, praised the performances of Japan's fighting men in the first week of war, and again assured the world that Japan would fight to the finish. It was neither an enlightening nor an arousing speech. Clearly, Tojo did not regard the Diet as a proper forum from which to announce important policies of state.

Foreign Minister Shigenori Togo, who followed him, spoke more heatedly.

Holding in contempt the real strength of our empire, the governments of the United States and Great Britain arrogantly took it for granted that they could easily compel Japan to submission with military and economic intimidations while prolonging the negotiations and strengthening their encircling positions against us. If we had acquiesced in such an attitude of the two governments, it would have resulted for Japan not only in the abandonment of the fruits of constructive effort spent in connection with the China affair ranging over four years, but in a menace to the very existence and the loss of prestige of our empire.

Having thus launched his attack on the enemy for their transgressions before the war, Togo then became the first to attack them for their conduct since the war began:

The American government is said to be propagating mischievous reports to the effect that Japan suddenly waged war without warning. But it is the American government itself that first provoked us by assuming a decisively warlike attitude.

On this score, Foreign Minister Togo was not so certain of his ground privately as he appeared to be publicly. A few days earlier he had mentioned to Prime Minister Tojo the American broadcasts accusing Japan of a sneak attack on Pearl Harbor without any war declaration. The timing of the delivery of Japan's final note was, of course, extremely difficult to explain. Tojo had suggested, with apparent seriousness, a rather unlikely explanation—that the Americans themselves had delayed the transmission of the final note. Togo had also felt obliged to report the matter directly to the Emperor, who might conceivably have learned of it for himself since he could hardly be forbidden, as were the Japanese people, to listen to the American radio. The Emperor had seemed to believe the American broadcasts. His anger had become more obvious by the moment as he listened to Togo's report. Togo could feel relieved now, as he delivered this part of his speech, at the fact that the Emperor had already left the Diet chamber. His Majesty's anger might have been renewed and intensified if he had heard this public charge that the American broadcasts were "mischievous." But it seemed necessary to Togo to make some answer to the broadcasts.

"When the American people stop to reflect," he continued, "they will realize the war is the fault of Roosevelt and Churchill. It is for Japan a war to free East Asia. Manchukuo supports it, French Indochina and Thailand support it. The Axis powers support it. Upon the outcome of this war depends the rise or fall of the Japanese Empire and East Asia, as well as the fate of the world."

The members broke into spontaneous applause by which Togo could not help being affected. He was not a public person. He did not delude himself as to the importance of this public response to his words, yet there was a certain satisfaction, a sense of accomplishment, at being able to command such a response in a situation as momentous as this one. The applause inspired him to greater fervor as he approached his conclusion.

"It is moreover expected to be a long war. Therefore the need is keenly felt for making a grim determination at home to bear any hardship or privation, with one hundred million people united as one man in iron-like solidarity, and also, for strengthening externally the alliance between Japan and her allies." As he reached his last sentence, he looked up from his text at the excited faces of the Diet members in front of him. "We shall, I firmly believe, ultimately attain a glorious victory."

The 700 members of Japan's parliament arose as one man in iron-like solidarity. They cheered, they clapped, they stamped their feet to demonstrate their support of the war. Had they been given the privilege, they would even have voted for it.

DECEMBER 15,
11 A.M.

OTTO TOLISCHUS looked up as the now-familiar wooden box was thrust into his cell. It must be 11 A.M. Lunchtime. Tolischus, the *New York Times* correspondent, who was one of the 270 American and British residents of Japan incarcerated when the war began, had learned, after a week of imprisonment, to tell time by the prompt arrival of his lunch and dinner at 11 A.M. and 4 P.M. Breakfast came each day about an hour after the dawn bugle call. Since it consisted only of warm soup, cold rice, and lukewarm tea, it wasn't exactly worth getting up for, but you had to be up anyway; an inspector came along, demanding a salute, a half-hour after dawn, so you ate the breakfast when it came simply because it was there and you were there and it gave you a way to pass the time.

The wooden lunchbox offered a slight variation in menu. Even before opening it, Tolischus knew that along with the inevitable cold rice it would contain cold radishes and other vegetables instead of warm soup and tea. He preferred even the breakfast to the lunch. The smell of Japanese radishes, a smell unique even among radish odors, tended to nauseate him.

After one week in prison it was becoming apparent to Tolischus that while he might not be tried for sending "political, diplomatic, and economic information" to such foreign agents as the *New York Times*, he could expect, nevertheless, a long stay in this tiny cell before repatriation to the United States.

(He was not aware of a statement issued the previous Wednesday by Premier Tojo, acting in his capacity as home minister. It warned the Japanese people to refrain from any conduct injurious to enemy nationals, even if Japanese citizens in enemy nations were reported to be mistreated. "The people of Japan, inherently kind and good-hearted, do not have to be told this by the authorities," the statement said. "The 270 American and British nationals who were taken into custody on declaration of war are now accommodated in school-houses and churches in Tokyo, Yokohama, Kobe, and other cities. Taking into account their different customs, the authorities have permitted them to bring their personal belongings and beds, and have installed heating facilities. They have also been given medical care and are permitted to purchase daily necessities from designated merchants. The Americans and the British have expressed their deep appreciation. The Americans are especially cheerful.")

After finishing his lunch, Tolischus stood up and read again a type-written notice which had been pasted to the wall that day, explaining the prison rules. They included one admonition with which he had not yet managed to comply. "Cultivate your spiritual nature," it de-manded. Tolischus, unfortunately, was still too angry to manage it. He had, however, worked out one method of helping himself endure his days. It was a routine of pacing the circumference of his tiny cell. He had found he could walk a parallelogram course by taking four steps lengthwise, then a quarter-turn followed by two half-steps crosswise, then a quarter-turn followed by another four steps lengthwise and two half-steps crosswise to complete the route. It was the only way he could move without stopping in such a confined space. He had already walked the route so often he had worn a hole in his sleeve from brushing against the rough prison wall and a hole in his trouser leg from brushing against the cot. But he had not yet learned to appreciate the privilege of occupying a cell which allowed this much walking space because he was unaware of the conditions under which some inmates were kept at the Tokyo Detention Prison. His cell had a wash basin with running water and a flush toilet. He could use the cover of the basin as a table and the cover of the toilet as a chair. He even had a window, though he couldn't look out because the glass was frosted. Some of the other prisoners, mostly Japanese but also a number of foreigners, were so tightly packed they had to sit all day on their knees and heels. In some of the cells, the toilet was an open, water-bearing trench along the wall.

Tolischus, as he paced his cell, reviewed over and over again the events of his stay in Japan, trying to decide whether he should blame himself for staying too long. Within recent months, many Americans in Tokyo had asked him if he thought they should get out and he had invariably advised them to leave. The increasing belligerence of the Japanese press and the aggressive attitude of the army had seemed more impressive than the government's statements about continuing the negotiations in Washington. Around the first of December, the Warner Brothers' film company representative had stopped him in a hotel lobby and asked him if he should evacuate. Tolischus had said, "Yes, by all means." Yet he had stayed himself. Should he have run? The more he thought of it, the more convinced he became that he could not have run, even if he had known he would go to prison for remaining. He was a newspaperman. He had come to Japan with his eyes open. He was here to get the news and as long as there was news of such importance to be covered, it was his duty to keep covering it. He had done the right thing, and therefore he had no complaint. This conclusion sustained his morale but it did not make it noticeably easier for him to avoid complaining. He couldn't quite reconcile himself to his jailers as he paced away the endless hours and days awaiting repatriation.

DECEMBER 15,
AFTERNOON

THE JAPANESE battleship fleet stood quietly at anchor in the still waters of Hiroshima Bay, hidden behind the lonely island of

Hashirajima. The ships here, unlike those at Pearl Harbor a week before, were not arranged in neat, close rows. The six battleships presently on hand (two of Japan's other four were with the Nagumo force and two were supporting the Malaya troop landings) had been placed at a distance from each other to take maximum advantage of the shelter the island offered, and to afford them maneuvering room if they should suddenly need it. Between and among them, always ready to help them, were the cruisers, the destroyers, and the auxiliary vessels. Sailors on the decks of the various ships went about their duties at such a leisurely pace they seemed not to know they were at war. On most of the large ships, paint crews were engaged in the endless job of spreading new coats of dark gray over the old coats of dark gray. Motor launches on routine ferry duty glided from ship to ship or from ship to shore. Along the shore was a railroad track, but when trains passed, none of the passengers could see the ships at anchor because, by government decree, blinds had to be drawn across all the windows on the seaward side to help maintain the fleet's security. This was an ideal place for anchorage. The straits between the islands of the bay offered protection from submarines. When ships needed repairs, they could reach Kure Naval Base within an hour. And there were no towns near Hashirajima to harbor possible espionage agents. The city of Hiroshima was far out of sight, several miles away.

The calm, leisurely external atmosphere of the fleet did not extend to the staff room of the flagship *Nagato,* where Admiral Isoroku Yamamoto was holding an intense session with his closest advisers. There were several matters of concern to him—the ease with which airplanes seemed able to sink battleships, the immediate and annoying though not insoluble problems at Wake Island, and the urgent need to formulate a plan for the second phase of the war.

He had at least taken steps toward handling the first two problems. It was quite apparent that if Japanese planes could sink American and British battleships, then American and British planes could sink Japanese battleships. He had therefore ordered a greater antiaircraft screen for the entire fleet. He could only hope now that the new guns he wanted would be quickly secured and installed, and that they would do the job. Naval warfare was changing so fast that even those who forced the changes could not themselves keep pace with the new developments.

As for Wake Island, Admiral Kajioka's need of more air support was so apparent now that Yamamoto had, earlier today, ordered Admiral Nagumo to detach his Second Carrier Division and Eighth Cruiser

Division for duty at Wake. The two carriers, two heavy cruisers, and four destroyers in this force ought to be able to take care of those four little American Wildcat fighter planes that seemed to be causing so much trouble to the invaders there.

In any case, the pitiful American defenders at Wake could not hold out for long. More important than this vexing little problem, and almost as immediate, was the need to develop a second-phase war strategy. After a week of fighting, the U.S. Pacific Fleet had already been badly crippled, the Philippines, without its protection, were isolated and destined for early occupation, British naval power in the Orient had been reduced to insignificance by the sinking of the *Prince of Wales* and the *Repulse,* and the whole south Pacific, perhaps even the east Pacific and the Indian Ocean lay helpless before the advancing forces of Japan. Since no one could have guessed that all this would happen so quickly, navy officials in Tokyo had only begun to think about which way to go next. But here in Hashirajima, the argument about future strategy had already reached a lively pitch. Some of Yamamoto's aides, headed by Rear Admiral Matome Ugaki, the chief of staff, favored a quick invasion of Hawaii. Others wanted to go south and take Australia. A few, including senior staff officer Captain Kamahito Kuroshima, proposed an intriguing idea, a move eastward to India and beyond.

Yamamoto, despite his feelings of urgency, listened with patience to all sides of the argument.

Admiral Ugaki spoke as if he had been staying up nights thinking about the problem. "We have no time to waste," he said. "At our present rate of advance, our first-phase offensive should be completed sometime in mid-March. That means we have to be ready by then to move in one direction or another. There is no hurry, of course, if we are content to go on the defensive. But when we go on the defensive, the enemy goes on the offensive. Is that what we want? Not I. In my opinion, we must maintain the initiative, and to do so we must act without delay. The question is, in which direction? I have not closed my mind. Like the rest of you, I have considered all three possibilities—Australia, India, and Hawaii. As of now, I must say I favor Hawaii. The most damaging blow we could possibly strike against the Americans would be to seize Pearl Harbor and deprive them of a base for their Pacific fleet. And this is the best possible time to move against Hawaii, while the defenses there are still disrupted. We shall never have as good an opportunity again. We have paralyzed their battleship fleet and we have a three-to-one advantage in carriers. But if we want Hawaii, we must move quickly. We must seize it before the Americans have time to reinforce it. Once those factories in the United States get up to full, wartime production, they will send out planes and weapons in such volume it will overwhelm us. Most of you have been in the United States. You know what I mean. But if we can take Hawaii and destroy the fleet before that happens, it might put the Americans in a mood to negotiate for peace and save us the uncertainties of a long war."

When Ugaki finished, there was a thoughtful pause before the reactions began. After a few short questions and remarks by other officers, Captain Kuroshima began raising some serious objections.

"It seems apparent that much of our success in Hawaii a week ago was due to surprise," he said. "We could not expect to surprise the Americans a second time. I have some strong reservations about a full-scale expedition against Hawaii. According to our intelligence, the United States has three divisions there. To defeat three divisions, we would need five or six. And since it takes 400,000 tons of shipping to transport one division, we would need two million tons for troops alone. Where would we get that many ships? Do you think the army would agree to such a plan?"

He allowed that question to stand for a moment, confident it would arouse no challenge. Most navy men agreed that the army gave the United States too little thought. To the army, Russia was still the principal enemy and Siberia was where the war should be fought. It was only because of the urgent need for oil that the army had consented to strike southward. The navy had good reason to doubt that the army would approve a serious move eastward to Hawaii.

"But let us assume," Kuroshima continued, "that we have the five divisions and the two million tons of transport shipping. Then it is our job to win control of the air over Hawaii, and to knock out the shore batteries so the troops can land. We can't depand on battleships against shore batteries. We know that. Can we depend on our planes? Do we have enough planes to knock out the shore batteries and to control the air at the same time? As Admiral Ugaki mentioned, we have a three-to-one superiority in carriers. But how much superiority do we have if you add their land-based planes to their carrier strength?"

Admiral Ugaki said, "I don't think we have enough information at this moment to make a determination. I still think we should study the possibilities."

Kuroshima said, "I think we should also consider going the other way, toward India. Look at the opportunities that would offer. The British Asiatic Fleet is sitting there, helplessly waiting to be destroyed. Once we dispose of it, we can walk ashore at Ceylon. All danger to our forces in the Dutch East Indies will be eliminated. India will immediately declare her independence from England and thank Japan for her liberation. And America's main shipping route to Russia will be cut. Without American aid, Russia can't possibly beat Germany. And once Russia is defeated, we shall have a direct link with both Germany and Italy."

Though this was an appealing concept, Admiral Ugaki had doubts about it. "While we are operating in the Indian Ocean," he asked, "what will the Americans be doing in the Pacific? We haven't yet eliminated the U.S. fleet. We have only crippled it. We haven't even touched the American carriers. Those carriers must be destroyed. While they're still intact, we cannot ignore them."

At this mention of the American carriers, a simmering frustration boiled up in Kuroshima. "Nagumo should have destroyed those carriers," he said. "If he couldn't find them at Hawaii he should have gone out looking for them instead of hurrying back here. They couldn't have been far away." He turned and spoke directly to Admiral Yamamoto. "Everyone is praising the Hawaiian operation but I do not consider it as much of a success as it should have been. Admiral Nagumo is not a carrier man. He doesn't understand air warfare. He's much too orthodox. I think he should be transferred from the carriers."

It was a daring remark for a captain to make, but Yamamoto had always encouraged his staff to speak freely. He gave some thought to Kuroshima's words before answering. Then he shook his head. "I can't transfer him. He's a proud old Samurai. If I transferred him, he would feel disgraced and commit harakiri."

After an uncomfortable silence, Yamamoto returned to the previous subject.

"The one thing on which we are all agreed," he said, "is that we don't have much time. We must quickly choose our course. Both of your plans present problems. The question is, Can these problems be solved? We are all familiar with the American Navy's theory that air control can be established just as well from bases on small islands as from carriers. Here in the western Pacific, and in the south Pacific, we have such bases, and we shall have many more of them when our first phase is completed. But the eastern Pacific around Hawaii is a vast area and we have no islands there. If we want to destroy the U.S. fleet, the best place to meet it is here, near our homeland, or in the south, where we could use our land-based planes as well as our carriers. But could we lure the U.S. fleet this far west? Even if we moved our fleet into the Indian Ocean, would the Americans dare move their remaining ships west under the threat of our land-based planes? That is a key question when we consider the Indian Ocean plan. On the other hand, if we move eastward, how can we lure the U.S. fleet out to meet us in mid-ocean, beyond the range of its land-based planes at Hawaii? I don't think we can get them out that far. Yet it is important, almost essential, that we meet and destroy the remainder of the American fleet. There can be no doubt that if we move against Hawaii, the U.S. fleet will be forced to challenge us. And it would be best to force the challenge soon, while the Americans are still weak. I agree with Ugaki about that, at least. I only wish it were as easy as it looks at first glance. Perhaps the Indian Ocean plan has even more potential. I think we should do a study of both. Does that seem sensible to all of you?"

After the nods and murmurs of general agreement, he said, "The next thing to decide, then, is who should conduct the study." He turned to Lieutenant Commander Yasuji Watanabe, who was his logistics expert as well as his gunnery officer. "How about you?" he said.

Watanabe was, of course, so honored at the nomination that he nodded eagerly.

"Then I think you should begin immediately," Yamamoto said. "It may take you a month or two." He had great faith in this young officer whose entire background had prepared him for his role as a naval warrior. Watanabe's father had been a steamer captain. His grandfather had been a sailing boat captain. His ancestors were of an old feudal family, the Hei Ke, who fought and lost an epic battle to another great family, the Genji, a thousand years earlier. After this battle, some of the Hei Ke had escaped from Honshu to Shikoku, where they became fishermen and sometimes even pirates, but almost always men of the sea. It was into this warrior clan with a thousand years of seagoing tradition that Watanabe had been born in 1903. Such a tradition was naturally enviable to a man like Yamamoto whose own father, though Samurai, was an impoverished school teacher in the little western Honshu village of Kushigun Sonshomura. Yamamoto, whose original name was Takano, had no social advantages with which to launch himself into the navy hierarchy. He had reached the top through ability and hard work. When he took the Naval Academy entrance examination in 1899, he ranked second among 300 applicants. After graduating with honors and suffering two wounds as a young ensign during Admiral Togo's destruction of the Russian Fleet in the Battle of Tsushima Straits, he had devoted himself so completely to the navy that he was 33 years old before he got around to approaching a go-between and choosing a wife. Meanwhile, at the age of 30, after his father's death, he had mitigated his social circumstances through the accepted Japanese custom of adoption. In a Buddhist ceremony he had been formally welcomed as a member of a prominent Samurai family, the Yamamotos, thus earning himself both a new name and a stronger social position. He still had reason, however, to admire and envy a man like Watanabe, who could trace his Samurai tradition back farther than a thousand years.

After the meeting, he took Watanabe aside and give him detailed instructions about the studies he was to conduct. Perhaps it would be a good idea to set up synthesized war games as tests for both the Indian Ocean and the Hawaiian plans. But as he spoke, he did not show great faith in the possibility of seizing Hawaii.

"It illustrates our ultimate problem," he said. "About a year ago, I wrote a letter to a man who was all in favor of war against the United States. In order to win such a war, I told him, it would not be enough just to take Guam, the Philippines, Hawaii, or even San Francisco. We would have to take Washington and dictate the peace terms in the White House." Yamamoto paused and smiled ruefully. "How do you think we'll ever manage that? I suppose we could send a submarine into the Atlantic and up the Potomac. Do you think that would be enough to conquer Washington?"

DECEMBER 16,
AFTERNOON

LESLIE NAKASHIMA took a Toyoko Line train from Shibuya, near his Harajuku home, to Denen Chofu, a southern suburb of Tokyo on the route to Yokohama. He had heard that his former boss, United Press bureau chief Robert Bellaire, was being held with other interned Americans at a girls' school there. The school, named Sumire Gakkuen, was not difficult to find since Denen Chofu was a small community. Nakashima was surprised, when he entered the main building, that there were no guards in sight. The place still had the appearance of a school rather than a detention compound. There was, however, a man at a desk with an official look about him.

"I understand you have an American named Robert Bellaire here," Nakashima said. "Would it be possible for me to talk to him?"

It was easier than Nakashima had supposed it would be. A few minutes later Bellaire appeared in the foyer dressed informally and looking surprised. He could hardly have been expecting a visitor. He and Nakashima shook hands warmly, each delighted to find the other in apparently good spirits.

Nakashima looked around toward a bench. "Can we sit down?" He still saw no guards. The two men sat and paused to survey each other before speaking.

Nakashima said, "It took awhile to find out where they were keeping you. Are they treating you all right?"

Bellaire shrugged. "I would say so, yes. They've got us in the girls' dormitory. We each have a room and a bed. It could be worse. How's your wife?"

"She's still in the sanitarium. She's worried, I'm afraid."

"I should think so. What's it like in Tokyo these days?"

"Well, the whole country's excited, of course, with one victory after another."

"They may as well cool off," Bellaire said. "No matter how many victories the Japanese win now, America will still win the war."

"I know that, though I wouldn't dare say it to anyone but you."

"Just sit tight and wait it out. You're all right, I gather. They haven't arrested you, anyway."

"No, they haven't arrested me."

"They got me about an hour after they announced the war," Bellaire said. He had been able to talk to an American Embassy man on the telephone from the home of Max Hill, the Associated Press bureau manager, who was also under arrest. "The Embassy hadn't even heard about the Hawaiian attack until I mentioned it on the phone. I wonder how much damage the Japanese actually did there."

Nakashima said, "One of the boys at the *Japan Times* called to tell me about it. I was still asleep. He said, 'The Japanese Navy has attacked Pearl Harbor.' And I said, 'The bloody fools! Do they think they can beat America?'"

Bellaire shook his head. "I guess they do." After a pause, he smiled and said with a laugh, "Well, anyway, what can I do for you, as if I were in a position to do anything for anyone?"

Nakashima felt no inclination to smile. He looked at Bellaire seriously and said, "I don't know what you can do, but I'm hoping you might be able to give me some advice. God knows I need some."

Bellaire sobered. "Having troubles? I was afraid you might." Bellaire was painfully aware of Nakashima's equivocal status as an American citizen of Japanese descent. To the Japanese government he would automatically be considered Japanese.

"I find myself in an impossible position," Nakashima said. "They say I'm Japanese so I can't get out of the country. But they also say I'm American so I can't get a job."

"Where have you tried?"

"I went to see George Togasaki at the *Japan Times.* He was very nice. He said he would try, but he'll have to ask police permission and you know what they'll say."

"You might have trouble getting onto a newspaper, all right. Where else could you go?"

"I went to Domei [the principle Japanese news agency] and talked to Ian Mutsu on the foreign desk. He was also very nice but he could think of only one solution to my problem." Nakashima paused for a moment reluctant even to mention this solution. "He said if I applied for Japanese nationality, he might be able to help me. Domei is looking for people, but I'm afraid they're not looking for Americans."

Bellaire was silent for awhile, fully aware that he himself, though imprisoned within these cold walls, was actually more free than his fellow American, Nakashima. Bellaire had only to sit it out uncomfortably until the two sides got around to repatriating each other's internees. Nakashima was not going to be that fortunate. Even if he were allowed to repatriate, what about his family? Bellaire, knowing that Nakashima's wife suffered from tuberculosis, could imagine the difficulties of trying to get her out of Japan and into America. But if Nakashima were to apply for Japanese citizenship, it might be disastrous for him later. It would probably mean the permanent loss of his American citizenship. And after this war, he would really need his American citizenship. It was an agonizing problem. What could one say to a man in such a predicament?

"I'm not sure what you can do," Bellaire said finally, "but I can't tell you to let your wife and children starve. I guess you'll just have to do whatever is necessary to make sure you and your family survive."

Nakashima said nothing. It was what he had expected to hear. It was the only advice Bellaire could possibly have given. There was no other solution. But even expecting it, Nakashima hated to hear it. There was something terribly final about giving up one's American citizenship.

DECEMBER 16,
AFTERNOON

AT HIS large, two-story home in the Myogadani section of north Tokyo, Admiral Baron Kantaro Suzuki was entertaining his old friend and classmate from naval academy days, Admiral Keisuke Okada, with whom he shared many memories and many points of view. After graduating from the academy, these two men, now in their seventies, had both served in the Sino-Japanese War and in the Russo-Japanese War. In the latter war, Okada was chief navigator of a cruiser which was sunk by a torpedo. Suzuki was captain of another cruiser which sank two enemy vessels. Both men thereafter rose rapidly in public life, Okada becoming, in turn, the navy's chief of warship construction, then navy vice minister, navy minister, and finally, in 1935, prime minister, while Suzuki became commander in chief of the fleet, then war councilor to Emperor Hirohito, grand chamberlain, and finally, vice chairman of the Privy Council, a position he still held.

Of all the memories they shared, the most compelling was the attempted coup d'état of February 26, 1936, when both came close to assassination by right-wing army officers. Though Okada escaped unhurt and Suzuki recovered in spite of four bullet wounds, each retained thereafter a profound distrust of the army and its methods. As they met this afternoon, both were conscious that this distrust had been deepened in them by events of the past two months. Admiral Okada, seated at a low table, sipped from a small cup of sake. Baron Suzuki, who drank only sparingly, sat nearby in a dark kimono, puffing at a long, thick cigar. He had a special passion for cigars. In the manner of old friends, the two sat silent awhile, thinking.

"When Tojo was chosen," Okada said, "I opposed it at the Jushin meeting. As soon as Marquis Kido suggested him, I pointed out that since the army had overthrown the Konoye cabinet, I wasn't sure it would be proper for the Emperor to name as the new prime minister the same war minister who had represented the army in deposing the old one. But Kido, I think, had already made up his mind. He said the army alone was not to blame for the end of the Konoye cabinet, and certainly Tojo was not to blame. Tojo was the one man, he said, who could control the army. So there was no point in pursuing the discussion. Kido recommended Tojo to the Emperor, and here we are in an idiotic war. The whole world can see now how well Tojo controlled the army."

Suzuki, who was less voluble than Okada, continued smoking his cigar. Finally he said, "I know so little about the details that brought us to war. We in the Privy Council are not told very much. I don't yet know what Matsuoka [Yosuke Matsuoka, foreign minister in the Konoye cabinet] promised Germany when he made the tripartite pact, or how much it influenced our policies. I only know he should have promised nothing. That alliance is a mistake we shall one day regret. Despite the German victories so far, I don't see how they can win the war."

"And I don't see how we can win," Okada said.

"The only hope is a stalemate. We might be able to negotiate if a stalemate develops, but that is not likely to happen for some time if at all."

"There is one thing we should be doing. We should be talking to people we can trust. Men like Yonai. We've got to find a way to depose the Tojo cabinet."

With all these victories, that will not be easy."

"But one day the victories will stop," Okada said, "and we must be ready when that time comes."

"Anyone who wants to depose the government will have to be very discreet."

"I know that."

As both men were sharply aware, the government was not simply Tojo. It was the army, and they both knew the fearsome power of the army, with its Kempeitai. In case they needed a reminder, however, they were about to receive one. Suzuki's daughter-in-law, Fumi, the wife of his only son, Hajime, came into the house from outside and asked if she could speak to him.

"I just talked to a lady across the street," she said, "and do you know what she told me? She pointed out a man standing in the alley over there. An obvious Kempeitai agent. She says he stands there every day, watching our house. He makes a note every time someone comes or goes."

Baron Admiral Suzuki's expression did not change as he listened to his daughter-in-law. He puffed again at his cigar, then glanced at Admiral Okada, but neither man showed any sign of disbelief or outrage. Here were two of the most famous, venerable, and honored men in Japan being told they were under surveillance by the army's secret police, yet neither was even surprised or angered. The omnipresent Kempeitai were simply a fact of life throughout the country. It would be pointless to get angry about them since nothing could be done about them. And it was hardly amazing that they should focus their attention on a former prime minister and the vice chairman of the Privy Council. Such men were considered especially dangerous, as Suzuki and Okada realized.

Suzuki put down his cigar and said to Okada, "Perhaps we had better change our meeting place." It was his only reaction.

DECEMBER 17,
1:30 P.M.

I N D R . Yoshio Nishina's office adjoining his laboratory at the Institute for Physical and Chemical Research in north Tokyo, the large console radio was on and his young secretary, Mrs. Sumi Yokoyama, was listening to the news.

"Domei reports from Lisbon," the announcer said, "that American naval authorities admit Japanese warships, for the last 24 hours, have been shelling the Hawaiian island of Maui, and also Johnson Island, which is 800 miles to the southwest. Domei reports from Saigon that the British forces in Malaya began a general retreat yesterday in the face of increasing pressure by Japanese Army units moving south toward Singapore. The Imperial Navy announced today that Nichols Field in the Philippine Islands was bombed again yesterday. Meanwhile, army units continue to crush the enemy on the principal Philippine Island of Luzon. The navy also released a photograph showing huge smoke clouds rising from Cavite Naval Base in the Philippines after a Japanese bombing attack. The Board of Information disclosed today that 1,500 Japanese citizens have been interned in the United States, while only 270 American and British citizens have been interned in Japan. To do their part in the Scrap Iron for Defense campaign, Tokyo firemen, in their traditional robes, are parading through the streets of the city with wagons, collecting metal objects of all kinds from patriotic citizens. The Welfare Ministry has announced that henceforth, a family must have a government permit to be allowed to employ more than one maid. But if this seems a hardship to you, consider the problems of our enemies. The British Food Minister has announced that in that country, which is suffering from severe food shortages, there will be no extra rations for Christmas . . ."

Miss Yokoyama's happy listening was interrupted by the entrance of Dr. Nishina, who seemed to be in his usual good mood. He was singing a well-known children's song called "Tetsudo Shoka," about the Tokyo-Yokohama railroad. He liked the songs of his childhood and often broke into spontaneous choruses of them. When he noticed her standing at the radio, he smiled and said, "Good afternoon."

She turned off the radio. "I was just listening to the news," she said. She wished he, too, had been listening. She hadn't yet forgotten her shock, the day after the war began, at overhearing him say the Japanese Army was stupid and Japan would lose the war. She wondered how he felt now, after ten days of uninterrupted victories all over the Pacific.

"Leave it on," he said, but she had already turned it off. He walked past her desk, which was separated by a cloth screen from the rest of his large, corner office room.

"I thought you might want to take a nap," she said. He kept a narrow bed by the window behind his desk, and though she had been working for him less than three weeks, she was already familiar with his habit of sleeping for a half-hour or so, when possible, after lunch.

"No nap today," he said. "I have to go to a meeting."

That surprised her. She knew of no meeting this afternoon. If he had something scheduled, she, as his secretary, ought to know about it. She said nothing. She couldn't expect him to tell her everything. She was still very new. Perhaps in time she would gain his confidence. He was such a nice man, with his comfortable, middle-aged ways, he didn't seem at all like the most famous and important scientist in the country. She couldn't help liking him in spite of the strange, unbelievable things she had heard him say about the war. Even the most brilliant men could sometimes be wrong.

Dr. Nishina gathered together some papers from his desk, stuffed them in a briefcase, and prepared to leave. On the way out, he stopped in front of her. "I'm not sure when I'll be back. It may be a long meeting."

As he looked down at her pretty face, he was still conscious of how he had shocked her with his remarks about the war. He would have to be careful of what he said to her on that subject. She would be happy, however, if she knew about the meeting he was now on his way to attend. He would have to be careful of what he said to her on that subject, also. It was ultra-secret.

DECEMBER 17,
2 P.M. IN TOKYO,
1 P.M. IN TAINAN

A T Tainan, Formosa, the pilots of the navy's land-based Eleventh Air Fleet were becoming restless. Since the third day of the war, they had not been able to find enough opposition in the skies over the Philippines to keep them interested. As the Japanese land forces continued their headlong advance toward Manila from numerous Luzon beachheads, the Zero fighters of the Eleventh Fleet were charged with protecting them from enemy aircraft, but for the last five days, there had been virtually no enemy aircraft left in the Philippines. In the first five days of battle, the Eleventh had wiped out America's air power there. Aside from routine flights during which they watched bombers drop load after load on Manila and Nichols Field, the fighter pilots now had almost nothing to do.

They could, of course, seek amusement in Tainan. A city of 90,000, it offered such tourist attractions as a temple honoring the pirate Koxinga who evicted the Dutch imperialists from Formosa in 1661, and the remains of an old Dutch fort which had proven too weak to prevail against the pirate. It offered also an endless number of Chinese restaurants, bars, and billiard halls frequented by pretty girls who liked aviators. Since many of the men preferred Chinese food even to the special rations they were given at the base (Japanese pilots, besides getting double pay, were also entitled to extra consideration in food and lodging), the Tainan restaurants were almost as popular with them as the bars and billiard halls, where the girls were. But much as they loved food, drink, billiards, and girls, these men loved flying more. They even loved combat, especially the victorious sample of it they had so far enjoyed against the Americans in the Philippines. Unlike most of the world's soldiers, who fought only because they had been taught to believe it necessary and they had been ordered to do it, the Japanese fighting man was characteristically eager for combat, eager to discharge, even with his life, his obligations to Emperor, country, family, and friends. The Samurai tradition had been so idealized and romanticized in Japanese society, despite the disestablishment of the feudal system by Emperor Meiji in the nineteenth century, that even the young men of the inferior classes, sons of business and professional men, farmers, and workers, though deprived of the distinction of being Samurai, could at least hope to honor their names by acting like Samurai. This was notably true in such elite groups as the Eleventh Air Fleet. The men of the

Eleventh, like those who took part in the attack on Hawaii, were completely dedicated professional fighters. They rarely stooped to the average soldier's traditional prerogative of complaining about food, lodging, or the restrictions of military discipline. But they were certain to complain if they were left out of an operation in which their companions were to take part. Friendly competition had developed among them, and no man could win honor by drinking, playing billiards, or spending his strength on girls. One did these things only to fill the hours between missions.

Flight Petty Officer Saburo Sakai was even more prone to restlessness than most of his friends since he did not drink, and since it was still an enthralling miracle to him, a poor Kyushu farm boy, that he could fly. On the ground, he found it difficult to keep himself occupied. Though he was an excellent billiards player, he would soon tire of the game. Though he loved Chinese food, he could not eat all the time. Though he wrote postcards to his family, he had little to tell them, since he was not allowed to mention where he was or what he was doing. "I am fine," he would write. "Don't worry about me." The mail service was slow. He seldom received answers.

Today he had come into Tainan for a Chinese meal, and afterward, as his associates left him to seek their various pleasures, had visited a Formosan couple, the Chuos, who had gone to extraordinary lengths in befriending him and several of his fellow pilots. Sakai had met the Chuos when he and some companions, finding the hotels too expensive, decided to rent a house where they would be able to relax in town. They had approached Mr. Chuo since his house was in a convenient location, but he had said, "No, I won't rent it to you. If you will make it your home, however, you are welcome to come here every day." Sakai had been so overwhelmed by this generosity he often visited the Chuos and they had become almost like parents to him. He spent hour after hour talking to Chuo's wife, Fumiko, who seemed to him the most brilliant woman he had ever met. But today he didn't feel like talking to anyone. After a short visit, he returned to the base and walked toward the flight line. In addition to his restlessness now, he was beginning to develop a dark expectation about the future. Idleness was an evil monster which poured unhealthy thoughts into his mind. Though he marveled at the courage of his country in challenging such a powerful nation as the United States, and at the brilliant strategies of the Japanese admirals and generals who had already won such amazing victories against the Americans, he could not yet, despite the growing list of victories, convince himself that Japan would win the war. Many of the victories, notably at Pearl Harbor and in East Asia, had resulted from surprise attacks. Henceforth it would not be easy to surprise the enemy. It was not even fair to do so. (He took satisfaction now from the fact that there had been no element of surprise in the first attacks by his group against the Philippines.) The victories might continue for awhile, but how could Japan defeat America? You had to invade a country to defeat it, and that was unthinkable. It had been enough of a miracle merely to attack Hawaii. San Francisco, Los Angeles, Seattle—those cities were a million miles away. Even an admiral as daring as Yamamoto could not include them in his dreams.

Sakai stopped at his Zero fighter, examined it with the automatic eye which a trained flier develops for his airplane, then laid a hand on the fuselage, lovingly, the way a cavalry officer might pat his horse. The dark thoughts began to recede in his mind. Great strategies were not for him to consider. This wonderful airplane was his concern, his only concern. He should not be standing here looking at it, idly touching it. He should be flying it against the enemy, for the glory of the Emperor, the nation, his family. He should right now be paying his debt to all of these, adding honor to his name. But why must he be so impatient? There were many battles to come. Had he not already shot two enemy planes out of the air, including a monstrous Flying Fortress? He would shoot down countless others. Though the enemy would be great, even greater would be his own fighting spirit, and the spirit of every Japanese warrior. He was certain of that. Perhaps through this spirit, Japan could attain victory.

He gazed up toward the nose of his plane, then higher, toward the sky, envisioning himself on the tail of an enemy fighter. The blood within him began to move and a slight smile crossed his face. For the moment, he could forget his restlessness.

DECEMBER 17,
2:30 P.M.

DR. TSUNESABURO ASADA, having arrived by train from Osaka, took a taxi to the large, elegant building of the Naval Club near Shiba Park in south Tokyo. As he entered the building and saw the faces of the officers in the lobby, he could not help noticing how proud and happy they looked, as well they might, in view of the navy's accomplishments during these amazing first ten days of war. Asada went up to a receptionist and mentioned a name—"Captain Yogi Itoh."

"Yes sir."

He was escorted along a corridor to an impressive-looking door. Entering it, he found himself in a wood-paneled conference room where about 20 men were already assembled. More than a dozen were naval officers of high rank. The others were scientists, all of whom he knew.

Captain Itoh, whom he also knew, came forward to greet him. He and Itoh had been fellow students at middle school. Itoh, after earning his doctor's degree, had gone on to become one of the navy's most highly respected and imaginative scientists. Asada, after earning his doctorate (at Tokyo Imperial University), had studied at the Institute for Physical and Chemical Research in Tokyo, then at the Kaiser Wilhelm Institute for Physical Chemistry in Germany, before returning to Japan to join the faculty of Osaka University, where he was now the chairman of the Physics Department.

Glancing around the room, Asada said to Itoh, "Has everyone arrived?"

Itoh said, "Just about. As soon as Dr. Nishina comes we'll start the meeting."

It was a meeting which Dr. Asada himself had inspired. Since 1937, he had been taking time out from his university work to deliver bimonthly lectures at the Naval Technical Research Institute in Tokyo, and at the Naval Aeronautical Research Institute in Yokosuka, about physical phenomena and scientific discoveries which might be applicable to military uses. Several times he had spoken of the findings of European physicists like Hans Strassman of Germany, who had learned of the enormous quantities of energy that could be produced from uranium. The navy had gradually become fascinated.

Having said hello to Captain Itoh, Asada went through the room greeting other friends and colleagues. Among them were Dr. Ryoichi Sagane, professor of physics at Tokyo Imperial University; Dr. Yasushi Watanabe, professor of electrical engineering at Tohoku Imperial University in Sendai, about 200 miles north of Tokyo; and Dr. Seishi Kikuchi, a fellow physics professor at Osaka University. Kikuchi was in charge of the 80-ton cyclotron at Osaka which was the largest of the three such machines now operating in Japan, though it would not be the largest when the giant, 200-ton atom-smasher in Dr. Yoshio

Nishina's Tokyo laboratory began working properly.

Asada, looking up to find that Dr. Nishina had now entered the room, went over to greet him. The two had been friends for many years. Both had studied under the distinguished physicist, Dr. Hantaro Nagaoka, at the Institute for Physical and Chemical Research, with which Nishina was still associated.

Since all the invited participants were now present, Captain Itoh, whom the navy had assigned to preside, quickly called the meeting to order.

"Before we begin," he said, "I would like to remind all of you once more that this is an absolutely secret meeting. Whatever is said here must not be discussed outside. Though I know you are all aware of that, it is so important I want to impress it upon you as forcefully as possible."

After allowing time for this warning to register, Itoh continued: "The Imperial Navy has called you gentlemen together because you are the nation's most advanced authorities in the field of physical research. I don't doubt that all of you have anticipated the reason for this meeting. We are here because the navy wishes to develop for the nation the use of atomic energy. Specifically, the navy wishes to develop an atomic weapon not only for the purposes of defense but also for the purposes of attack. We know, of course, that such a project will entail enormous labors, great ingenuity, and fearsome problems. What we want to know from you gentlemen is whether the project is feasible. If it is, we want to begin it immediately, and we want you to take part in it. Now, may we start by hearing some of your general thoughts on the subject?"

There was a deep silence in the room as all the navy officers turned to look expectantly at the scientists and all the scientists turned to look expectantly at each other.

Since no one else seemed ready to speak, Asada said, "If America were to develop such a weapon, it would be extremely dangerous for Japan. Therefore, as I have previously stated to some of you gentlemen, I feel we must, for our self-defense if for no other reason, find out if we can develop it."

One of the officers said, "Does that mean you think America can do so?"

Asada said, "I don't know. I think if we can do it, America can certainly do it."

The officer persisted. "All right, then, do you think we can do it?"

Dr. Asada shrugged.

Dr. Nishina said, "It will be very difficult, but I believe it is worth trying."

These were encouraging words from a man of Nishina's reputation. The naval officers seemed visibly heartened.

Dr. Kikuchi, who worked constantly with the Osaka University cyclotron, said, "It will take great stores of uranium, and we have very little."

"How much do we have?" Itoh asked.

Kikuchi looked at Nishina, who said, "At the Institute, we have several tons of uranium-bearing ore. This represents only a small amount of actual uranium. I understand that, in Shanghai, our army has about 800 kilograms (1,760 pounds) of uranium oxide from South Africa. I don't know whether that would be available."

Kikuchi said, "In any case, much more would be needed."

"And as you know," Nishina added, "there are no sources of uranium in Japan. Perhaps the navy, too, could get it in Africa."

One of the officers said, "Where, in Africa?"

"It might be available in Katanga."

"Then we'll get it. If the army could get it, we can get it."

That was the kind of spirit the navy liked. Enthusiastic smiles began to appear on some of the military faces, as if the procurement of uranium were the key to the entire endeavor and the delivery of it would solve all problems.

Asada said, "But even if you found an unlimited supply of uranium, nobody can promise to develop an atomic weapon. We still have three essential things to learn. We don't yet know how to concentrate the uranium isotope so its energy can be released. We haven't yet developed a mechanism to create a chain reaction. And we don't yet know the critical amount of the uranium isotope needed to sustain a chain reaction. Without a chain reaction, there can be no explosion. Without knowing how to create an explosion, we can't develop a weapon."

For a few thoughtful moments, the navy officers digested these sobering observations. Finally, one of them said, "Can these problems be solved?"

Nishina said, "Perhaps, eventually."

"Can it be done quickly enough to be useful in this war?"

"That is what we would have to find out. I don't think you should count on it."

Captain Itoh said to Nishina, "Will you be willing to take charge of the effort?"

Nishina looked startled. "Are you quite aware of how big a job it would be?" he asked.

Itoh nodded. "I'm aware, and the navy is aware."

"And how expensive?"

"The navy has the money."

"In other words, the navy is definitely ready to go ahead. Is that what you're saying?"

"Not only is the navy ready. We have already chosen a name for the project. We want you to know we consider it the navy's top priority research effort. We're calling it Project A."

Nishina thought for a moment. "Project A. And you want me to take charge of it?"

Itoh said, "We're counting on you."

"In that case," Nishina said, "I propose that we begin with a detailed study of the possibilities, then meet again to decide the best course. Does that sound sensible to the rest of you?"

There was a general murmur of approval. Itoh said, "How soon should we meet again?"

"It will take at least two months to study the problems."

Another officer said, "What about the Germans? Maybe they, too, are working on an atomic weapon. Could they help us?"

Asada said, "I doubt it. Most of Germany's atomic scientists happened to be Jewish, and they've been expelled from the country. Some of them have gone to the United States. In my opinion, only the United States has the potential to develop an atomic weapon."

One of the officers corrected him. "Japan and the United States," he said.

No one would argue against such a patriotic statement. Japan did, after all, have three cyclotrons in operation, plus a giant fourth one almost ready for use. Japan also had several exceptional atomic scientists. The possibilities were indeed worth exploring. On that note, the meeting ended. Project A was launched. The Japanese effort to develop an atomic weapon had officially begun, and Dr. Yoshio Nishina was in charge of it.

Dr. Asada hurried over to congratulate him. Neither man could match the apparent optimism of some of the navy officers. Both were aware of the enormous difficulties. Yet they felt some excitement about the project. Perhaps their spirit of scientific adventure was taking hold of them. Or perhaps it was the navy's enthusiasm. Asada, who had been as horrified as Nishina when he learned of Japan's entry into the war, realized now that his attitude was changing. The accomplishments of the navy in Hawaii and Malaya, the progress of the army in the Philippines and Malaya, had altered the prospects of war at least to some degree. Maybe Japan did have a chance to win. But only if the war were to be of short duration. In order to win at all, Japan would have to win quickly, before America's vast material superiority began to tell. He was certain of that. If Project A was to contribute to a Japanese victory, there was no time to waste.

PART II

AUGUST

1945

AUGUST 6,
8:16 A.M.

A T O P   T H E   Atago Hill, an area of relatively high ground just north of Shiba Park, the Japan Broadcasting Company's transmitting and monitoring center stood almost undamaged above the vast, fire-consumed wasteland visible from it in all directions on this clear, warm August morning. That wasteland, stretching for miles, was the corpse of Tokyo, devastated now by the waves of American bombers which had been showering incendiaries upon it since the previous November. So thorough were these bombers that even when they missed such important installations as broadcasting facilities, most Japanese refused to believe it was an oversight. If the radio station had been spared, it must be only because the Americans were hoping Japan would soon broadcast from it a surrender announcement.

The Americans, in their own broadcasts beamed to Tokyo, were now making daily demands that Japan capitulate. But there was no sign of impending capitulation in the activities at the Radio Center this morning. Most of the Japan Broadcasting Company's stations in Tokyo and in other communities throughout the country were broadcasting their regularly scheduled programs, and in the company's monitoring section, adjacent to the transmitting center, a corps of men (either too young, or too old or unfit for military service) sat as usual in front of powerful receiving sets, each listening to one of these outlets. The Japanese government had decided long ago that every station in the country should be monitored every minute it was on the air. If an announcer, even in some remote town, were to broadcast subversive or defeatist remarks, the authorities in Tokyo would know it immediately.

The large listening room of the monitoring section was, ironically, as quiet as a library. The long rows of radio sets, each tuned to a different station, could be heard only through the earphones of the men assigned to them. Aside from an occasional cough or the scraping of a chair leg, there was no sound. In dull, enervating stillness, the whole, vast roomful of auditors sat staring into space. Supervisors at

251

their desks looked as bored as the men at the sets, but were able, at least, to relieve their boredom by reading books or newspapers.

This placid, sleepy scene was altered slightly when the man who was monitoring the station at the southeastern Honshu port city of Hiroshima began tinkering with the dials on his receiving set. About an hour earlier, shortly after 7 A.M., this station and several others in the same area had gone off the air when Japan's radar network issued a warning that several enemy planes were approaching southern Honshu. At 8 A.M., however, the Hiroshima station had resumed broadcasting with the announcement of an all-clear signal. "Only three planes have been spotted coming this way," the newscaster had said, "but if they should appear over the city, it would be advisable to seek shelter."

That was a quarter of an hour ago. As the monitor assigned to the Hiroshima station adjusted his dials, a puzzled expression came over his face. He tried another adjustment and another. With a shrug, he took off his earphones and turned to his supervisor at a nearby desk.

"Hiroshima," he said, "seems to have gone off the air again."

It was 8:16 A.M.

AUGUST 6,
8:30 A.M.

D E E P within the huge, three-story, subterranean bomb shelter which had been the headquarters of the Japanese Imperial Navy since the destruction of the Ministry building by American airplanes the previous May, the ordinary Monday morning routine was proceeding as usual. The Naval General Staff's daily conference was in progress in a large room near the office of Admiral Mitsumasa Yonai, who was now the navy minister. Elsewhere throughout the bare, concrete-walled cellar, hundreds of staff officers and their aides went about their jobs, making personnel assignments, working out recruitment quotas, seeking ways to fill procurement needs, compiling new and increasingly dismal reports on airplane production, on ship repair problems, on food shortages, on enemy air raid damages, and on air defenses. The bomb shelter headquarters, in Kojimachi (less than a mile west of the Imperial Palace), was also the hub of the navy's Homeland Air Defense System, which still maintained the administrative procedures connected with resisting American attacks, even though such tactical measures as sending up fighter planes had now become virtually impossible. The Air Defense System's communication center received minute-by-minute reports of enemy plane movements from radar stations, patrol ships, and ground spotters. The officer in charge of the Homeland Air Defense, Commander Masatake Okumiya, could tell at any moment, from a large map which his staff constantly revised, how many enemy planes were approaching or flying over the Japanese mainland. It was information from which he could derive little satisfaction, however, since there was no way to repel those planes.

At about 8:30 A.M., Commander Okumiya was in the communications center on the middle level of the bomb shelter when one of his aides approached with an urgent expression on his face.

"There's an emergency phone call for you from Kure," the aide said. Kure Naval Base in southern Honshu, about 15 miles from Hiroshima, was one of the Japanese Navy's largest facilities. It was the principle maintenance and repair yard for the pitifully few Japanese warships which had not yet been sunk by the Americans. Commander Okumiya hurried to his desk to take the call.

The man on the phone at Kure was obviously in a state of some agitation. His voice was louder than necessary and he spoke rapidly.

"About fifteen minutes ago, there was a terrible flash over Hiroshima," he said. "Immediately afterward, a terrible, mushroom-like cloud rose into the sky over the city. Many people here heard a heavy roar, something like distant thunder. I don't know what happened there, but from the flash and the cloud it must have been something big. I tried to reach army headquarters by phone, but there is no answer. This is all I know right now. I'll send in the details just as quickly as I get them."

Commander Okumiya was puzzled. How could there be such a huge explosion in Hiroshima? Only a few enemy planes had been tracked over southern Honshu this morning. It sounded as if an army ammunition dump had exploded, but did the army have that much ammunition hoarded in Hiroshima? He said, "Do you know whether it was an air raid, or some other kind of explosion on the ground?"

The man in Kure said, "I don't know what it was. Only a few B-29s were seen, that's all."

"What's the weather like?"

"Fine."

"All right," Okumiya said, "call me as soon as you get more information."

After hanging up, Okumiya sat staring at the wall for a minute. A peculiar phone call, but a disturbing one. What kind of explosion could possibly cause a "bright flash" and a "tremendous cloud?" The whole story made no sense, yet it left him uneasy. He stood up and hurried directly to the room near Admiral Yonai's office where the Naval General Staff was meeting.

The admirals were discussing urgent naval problems. Okumiya waited for an opportunity to break in, then said, "Excuse me, sirs, but we have just received an urgent report from Kure about a peculiar explosion in Hiroshima which produced a terrible flash and a mushroom-like cloud. I can't figure it out. Do any of you gentlemen have an idea what might have happened there?"

The assembled admirals and their staffs looked up at him, then glanced at each other. Some of them shrugged. Some of them shook their heads negatively. None of them seemed very interested. In Hiroshima there was an army base, the headquarters of the Second Army Group which was responsible for all land defenses in southern Japan. But the navy had no facilities there. The admirals could hardly be expected to feel any vital concern about such a vague report. The navy had too many problems of its own these days to worry about peculiar explosions at army bases.

AUGUST 6,
8:36 A.M.

IN THE Railway Telegraph Center near the Tokyo Station, this was another slow morning. For several months now the day shifts at the center had been dull and inactive because daytime train travel had been virtually eliminated. American planes were in such complete control of the skies over Japan that a train traveling through the countryside during daylight hours would be inviting destruction by these deadly marauders. Japan no longer had enough trains, in any case, to operate on a full day-and-night schedule; those which were still in working condition ran at night. The daytime railway telegraph operators had, therefore, only a limited budget of messages to send and receive.

At about 8:25 this morning, however, the operators on duty were aroused from lethargy by a flood of messages from railway stations at Yano, Kaitaichi, Yoshiura, Hiro, Kure ... All of these localities had one thing in common—all were near Hiroshima. Their messages were frantic and confused, but they seemed to agree on one point—a remarkable explosion had just occurred in Hiroshima.

The telegraphers in Tokyo were puzzled. "If Hiroshima had that big an explosion," one of them said, "why hasn't the station there reported it?"

"We haven't heard from Hiroshima for a while," another man said. "Let's send them a query."

At 8:36 he tapped out the query. There was no answer.

AUGUST 6,
MIDMORNING

I N T H E spacious, wood-paneled center office on the second floor of the War Ministry (which had long since been moved from its old location near the Diet building to the hilly, landscaped grounds of the military academy at Ichigaya Heights in west-central Tokyo), General Korechika Anami, the army's best-loved officer and now Minister of War in the Japanese government, sat talking earnestly to the chief of staff, his old friend General Yoshijiro Umezu, and to Lieutenant Colonel Masao Inaba, chief of the Budget Section of the Military Affairs Bureau. As usual, they had an endless number of developing plans and problems to discuss this morning. A glance out the window of General Anami's office illustrated the major problem. From the prominent hill on which this huge, rectangular, tan-colored concrete building stood, he could look down directly on the Yotsuya area and beyond it for miles, to right, left or center, without seeing anything but devastation. The whole city was prostrate; the whole country was destitute. Most of the factories had been either obliterated by bombs or paralyzed by lack of workers and materials. The bombs had driven millions of workers from the cities. The population of Tokyo, for instance was down from seven million to less than four million. Until the workers returned, the factories could not possibly be reopened to supply goods the army needed, but how could the workers be induced to return to cities which had been leveled? Who would feed, clothe, and house them if they did return? The army, though it still had food stores for its own men, could not afford to feed the civilian populace. It was an endless, circular problem for which General Anami had no solution. It did not defeat him, however, because he still clung to a passionate conviction that there was one thing even more important than materiel—an indomitable spirit. If one were to ask him how long an army could go on fighting without factories to replenish its arms and equipment, he would say that a Japanese Army, dedicated as it was to His Majesty, the Emperor, could go on fighting as long as there were one man left with a weapon in hand. Neither he nor General Umezu had any inclination to stop fighting, despite the punishing blows Japan was now taking from America. They did not believe, however, that they were fighting aimlessly. They had struggled to keep the Japanese Army from collapsing, and they had decided carefully how best to use it. They were currently working out plans for the most momentous battle in Japan's long history—the defense of the homeland against an American invasion which was expected to begin within a month or six weeks. But their plans were being slightly delayed this morning by a strange and vexing circumstance. Supreme Headquarters in Tokyo had lost all communication with Hiroshima, the center from which the defense of southern Japan was to be directed.

Japanese military men agreed that the first American invasion thrust would be against the southern main island of Kyushu. At Second Army Group Headquarters in Hiroshima, detailed preparations were now in progress, under the guidance of Field Marshal Shunroku Hata, to push the invaders back from the Kyushu shores. It was not, in General Anami's opinion, a hopeless task. Though Japan's navy and most of its cities had been virtually wiped out, the army had carefully husbanded enough men and materiel for an expected climactic battle, and these men were ready to fight to their deaths for their sacred homeland. If the Americans were positively determined to occupy Japan at any cost, they might eventually do so at a horrendous cost. But Generals Anami and Umezu, like most army strategists, were convinced that once the Americans had tasted the welcome they were certain to receive on the shores and in the mountains of Kyushu, they would be forced to reconsider their demand that Japan surrender unconditionally. This welcome, however, was not yet quite ready for the Americans. There was still much work to be done in a very short time, and it was important to be in constant touch with Marshal Hata's headquarters in Hiroshima.

The silence from Hiroshima became more perplexing as the morning progressed. Radio, telephone, and telegraph contacts had all broken down at about the same time, shortly after 8 A.M. Then, shortly before 9 A.M., General Anami had received a telegram from the navy, informing him that an enormous explosion had occurred in Hiroshima.

The general and his aides found the telegram difficult to understand. "What could have exploded?" one of them said. "We don't have any big ammunitions dumps there."

"It could hardly have been an air raid. There were only a few B-29s in that area this morning."

"And how could an explosion knock out all communication? It might knock out the radio, or the telephone, or the telegraph, but not all three."

General Anami shrugged. He had so many other things on his mind he could not spend the whole day worrying about a communications breakdown. "Keep trying to reach them," he said.

The War Ministry's Communications Center was still trying, but without success. As eleven o'clock approached, there was still no word from Second Army Headquarters in Hiroshima, and the mystery continued to deepen. The Japan Broadcasting Company's monitoring center reported that Hiroshima's public radio station had gone off the air at 8:16 A.M., and the Railway Telegraph Center reported a series of vague messages about an explosion in Hiroshima, but nobody seemed to have any definite knowledge. General Anami was not the kind of man to be moved by rumors or vague reports. He was talking to General Umezu and Colonel Inaba about other matters when a messenger came in with a second telegram from the navy about Hiroshima.

This message informed him of a new conversation with the Kure Naval Base. The message quoted the conversation: "At 0815 hours this morning, immediately after two B-29s passed with high speed over the city, there was a searing flash, like a fantastic flash of lightning. It was followed by a sudden, roaring sound. In the next instant houses collapsed all across the city. It is as though a great steel fist had suddenly descended on Hiroshima. Fires broke out everywhere. Everything is all confused. The raging flames and the streams of refugees have made it impossible to get in touch with any place closer than Kaidaichi."

The town of Kaidaichi was about five miles from Hiroshima. General Anami was sufficiently alarmed to call in several officers, including General Seizo Arisue, chief of Army Intelligence. What did they think of this latest report from the navy? They agreed that it was time to get some definite first-hand information.

"Why don't we send a plane?" someone suggested.

A few minutes later a young officer was dispatched by plane and the high officials of the War Ministry returned to their ordinary duties. The Hiroshima puzzle would soon be solved. There was probably more rumor to it than truth. People were prone to exaggerate. But even if the city had suffered a terrible explosion, how terrible could it be? Hiroshima had been lucky for a long time. It had not suffered any severe air raids. What did the people there know about catastrophes? Tokyo and most of Japan's other cities had experienced thousands of dreadful explosions in the past few months. It was not easy for a person in Tokyo to get overly excited about a single explosion in a city 550 miles away.

AUGUST 6,
LATE MORNING

A T A small hotel in Nara, one of Japan's most historic cities (having been the nation's capital during the eighth century), Captain Mitsuo Fuchida, now the Imperial Navy's Air Operations Officer, was eating a late breakfast after completing an assignment at the navy's new Supreme Headquarters facility under construction in the mountains a few miles from here.

For the past ten days, Captain Fuchida had been in Hiroshima attending a joint army-navy liason conference at Second Army Group headquarters in preparation for the impending defense of Kyushu. The previous afternoon in Hiroshima he had received a phone call from his immediate superior, Admiral Shikazo Yanno, who was in Hyoshi, just south of Tokyo. "They're having some trouble with the communications system in the new headquarters," Admiral Yanno had said. "Fly over to Nara and tell them what we need."

Fuchida, leaving his assistant, Lieutenant Toshio Hashizume at their hotel, the Yamato, in the center of Hiroshima, had flown directly to Nara, where he worked far into the night and again for three or four hours this morning before solving the problems which concerned Admiral Yanno. The new navy headquarters here was to be almost completely underground and strong enough to withstand heavy raids by U.S. bombers, which had already destroyed the old Navy Ministry building in Tokyo. The army was constructing a similar facility in the mountains near Matsushiro in western Honshu. Fuchida, having finished his work at the navy facility, decided to eat a combined breakfast-lunch at his Nara hotel before returning to Hiroshima. He hated to have to leave Nara, with its beautiful old houses and temples which were still untouched by bombs. He had been born in this area and he considered it home. His wife, Haruko, and their two children were staying near here right now in his home village of Kashiwabara. He had sent them there when the bombings became too severe in Hyoshi, where he was presently based. He had been so busy since his arrival in Nara the previous afternoon he hadn't even been able to visit his family. He wished he could take a few days off to spend with them, but how could he rest when the whole navy, indeed the whole country was collapsing around him? A kimono-clad waitress, somewhat shabby but smiling prettily as if these were normal times, poured tea for him. He sat back and tried to relax a few minutes before leaving for the airport.

Fuchida's life had been hectic since that December morning in 1941 when he led 353 carrier planes in the historic attack against Pearl Harbor. He knew now what a pyrrhic victory that had been. Though it had cost the Americans four battleships, it had obviously hardened their will to fight, and it had taught them much more than it had taught the Japanese. The subsequent, relentless destruction of the Japanese Navy was proof of that, and Fuchida himself was carrying scars from the Battle of Midway which were a constant reminder of it. He could see now that the whole war had been settled at Midway, June 4, 1942. The Imperial Navy had never recovered from its disastrous defeat there, and from the loss of the four big carriers which went down that day.

Having been rescued miraculously at Midway and survived his wounds, Fuchida had taken part in the studies of a Battle Lesson Research Committee, then became a staff officer of the First Air Fleet and, now, air operations officer for the remnants of the Combined Fleet, which had been reduced to one battleship, four carriers, four cruisers and 28 destroyers, almost all of which ships were either crippled or immobilized by lack of fuel. As air operations officer, he was responsible for about 500 planes in usable condition, but none of these was available for daily use against the enemy. They were out of sight, hidden and hoarded for the day of the expected American invasion. Fuchida could hardly imagine a more frustrating job than the one he now held—air operations officer with no airplanes left to operate.

He was just finishing his late-morning meal when he received another phone call. Again it was from Admiral Yanno.

"Hiroshima has been hit by some kind of a terrible explosion," the admiral said. "Fly back down there and find out what's happened. All communications have been cut. Apparently it's something pretty bad."

Fuchida hung up and, with a sigh, headed for the airport.

AUGUST 6,
11:10 A.M.

IN THE Audience Hall of the Imperial Palace's Gobunko (Library Building), hidden among the tall trees of the Fukiage Gardens near the North Gate, Emperor Hirohito listened to the Lord Keeper of his Privy Seal Marquis Koichi Kido, who had been doing most of the talking during the 20 minutes they had been together. Kido was speaking of routine matters and it was not always easy to follow him because he spoke in extremely polite circumlocutions; he was so elaborate and proper in his choice of words he sometimes obscured his substance. The Emperor saw him just about every day, however, partly out of habit and duty (Kido had been privy seal for five-and-a-half years), partly out of affection, and partly, in recent months, because it had become openly certain that Kido was now of one mind with him on the subject of peace.

Kido's attitudes about war and peace had been sometimes difficult to follow. Before the war, he had maintained the friendliest relations with the military. He had looked with favor on the China "Incident," and on December 8, 1941, he had gazed at the rising sun and "thought it symbolic of my country's destiny now that we had entered war against the United States and England." Yet two months later, on

February 5, 1942, he had told Emperor Hirohito that Japan should negotiate a speedy end to the conflict by taking advantage of the capture of Singapore. The United States and Great Britain were grimly determined, he had said, and would not capitulate simply because Singapore had fallen. These 1942 remarks of Marquis Kido had so startled the Emperor (perhaps because they came at the time of Japan's greatest success in arms), that he had mentioned them a few days later to the then Prime Minister, General Hideki Tojo. He found Tojo unimpressed. And Kido himself apparently thought better of pressing the subject at that time. But in mid-June of this year, after the Emperor had made clear his own desire for peace, Marquis Kido had come forward with a peace "plan," which lacked details but which did, at least, satisfy the Emperor that the two were of like mind.

In addition to the colossal suffering throughout his country, Emperor Hirohito had sufficient personal reasons to favor peace by the summer of 1945. His daily schedule of conferences and military duties was rigorous. He was weighted down with the flow of army, navy, and government reports. On critical occasions, which were more and more frequent, he had to accept official callers in the middle of the night. His food was unpalatable since he insisted on limiting himself to army rations. And, on the night of May 25, he had suffered the disaster of seeing his personal palace burn to the ground. Though the Americans did not drop incendiaries within the Imperial Palace moats, they converted the surrounding areas into such tornadoes of flame (157,000 Tokyo dwellings were destroyed on May 25), that burning brands flew across the moats to ignite the old wooden imperial residence which had been built by Hirohito's grandfather, Emperor Meiji. Hirohito had thereafter moved into the Gobunko, where his quarters were makeshift but where there was, at least, a sizable airraid shelter.

As his privy seal continued to talk, the Emperor did his best to follow him, filling the pauses with an "I see," "I understand," or "Is that so?" whenever it seemed appropriate. Even when Marquis Kido stopped talking, the Emperor waited expectantly because there was something in the manner of this careful little man that indicated he had more to say.

Kido did, in fact, have another item on his mind, and he was debating now whether to mention it. He had heard from his military contacts that some strange and terrible explosion had struck Hiroshima. But he had no details. Should he mention this to His Majesty? The Emperor had often made it clear that nothing was ever to be withheld from him simply because it was too unpleasant. Maybe he should be told immediately, but what was there to tell him? The information was so sketchy it would be like reporting a rumor, and that would be unpardonable. In the Imperial Court there was one rule which should always be observed. Do not make partial reports to the Emperor. No, it would not be proper to tell him now.

Marquis Kido stood erect indicating he had no more to say. The Emperor observed him silently, then, accepting the cue, turned to leave the room. Kido bowed from the waist, presenting the dome of his bald head to the retreating Emperor, then bowed again as the Emperor disappeared through the door.

AUGUST 6,
NOON

T H E increasing paralysis that gripped the Japanese nation in August, 1945, could be felt in the prime minister's official residence near the Diet building, an office which, until less than a year before, had been a bustling center of activity. During the first three years of the war, under the premiership of General Hideki Tojo, and to a lesser degree under the premiership of General Kuniaki Koiso, both of whom were as deeply committed to the army as to the government, the prime minister's office had been the center from which Japan's war effort was coordinated. But on April 5 of this year, five days after American forces invaded the outlying home island of Okinawa, Baron Admiral Kantaro Suzuki, the 78-year-old naval hero who had recently become president of the Privy Council, was coaxed into accepting the premiership, and since he was a navy man, he soon found that though he might be the titular head of the government, he had little influence over the army, which, in effect, still controlled the country. The army's tendency to disregard Suzuki, plus the nation's progressively diminishing war activity, and Suzuki's own watchful-and-waitful, Oriental method of getting things done, had noticeably slowed the pace of business in the prime minister's office. The old admiral was neither inclined by temperament, nor allowed by the army, to assume dynamic leadership of the war effort as General Tojo had done. He found it difficult, in fact, even to discover from the army the day-to-day war situation. His chief cabinet secretary, Hisatsune Sakomizu, who had previously established some useful army connections when he was in charge of the First Section of the government Planning Board, was now forced to call on these unofficial and confidential sources in order to find out for Suzuki what the army was doing or preparing to do. Sakomizu had actually developed, within the War Ministry, a small but at least partially effective intelligence network. The Japanese government had thus come to a condition in which it was forced to spy on its own army.

Sakomizu who also cultivated other informants—newsmen, businessmen, civil servants—reported daily to Suzuki whatever pertinent information he was able to gather. Today, as noon approached, he had only routine matters to report. Walking downstairs from his third floor office (in which he was also living since his official residence and his private residence had both been destroyed by American bombs) he entered Prime Minister Suzuki's long, high-ceilinged private office chamber on the second floor to find the old man reading Chinese poetry while he smoked a cigar. Suzuki, who loved cigars, was forced by shortages now to limit himself to two a day. He observed no such limits to his indulgence in Chinese poetry, which he also loved and of which he had a scholar's knowledge. He tried to find some time each day to read from his vast and very valuable Chinese library.

When Sakomizu entered, a fatherly smile further broadened Suzuki's wide face. He entertained a paternal feeling for this young man whom he considered both trustworthy and brilliant. He had retained Sakomizu despite pressure from some of his own cabinet members who argued that such a critical position demanded an older man. The chief secretary of a Japanese cabinet was responsible for so many important functions he might almost be called the government's general manager. Suzuki knew it was not altogether because of Sakomizu's age (he was 45) that he attracted opposition. Sakomizu had been recommended for the position by his father-in-law, former Prime Minister Admiral Keisuke Okada, a known advocate of peace, and there was a general fear among bitter-end war advocates that Sakomizu shared his father-in-law's eagerness to get out of the war.

Suzuki, glancing at a piece of paper in Sakomizu's hand, said, "Is that the B-29 report?" From the day these giant American bombers began their raids on Tokyo the previous November, he had held them in awe. Now, nine months later, he regarded them as the ultimate weapon in the war. The B-29s by themselves, he believed, would completely destroy Japan if he did not soon get the country out of the war. But how was he going to manage this in the face of the army's unshakeable determination to continue?

Sakomizu said, "Nothing unusual. Last night they sent about 415 B-29s against us, mostly in Kansai and Chigoku (south central and western Honshu), although Maebashi (the capital of Gummu Prefecture, 70 miles northwest of Tokyo) was also hit. A two-hour attack by 130 B-29s. We apparently shot down seven and damaged three."

Prime Minister Suzuki had nothing to say. Seven B-29s was a pitifully small number to shoot down, but since neither the army nor the navy could any longer spare fighter planes to send up against them, it was gratifying that even a few of the monsters were being destroyed. In any case, the Americans were able to replace them so easily one would be foolish to think of Japan's thin network of antiaircraft guns as any real threat against them.

After a pause, Sakomizu continued: "The U.S. War Department has announced that 547,000 American troops have been killed, captured, or listed as missing in the war so far. Also, there are now 80,000 American workers on strike at various factories. Four thousand have just gone on strike at a B-29 plant in Cincinnati."

Suzuki shrugged. There were now so many B-29 plants in the United States, the closing of one of them would mean nothing. They had already done so much damage, and the U.S. Navy had so completely blockaded the Japanese islands that it would not even be necessary for American forces to launch their expected invasion. If the Americans were patient, they would have only to sit offshore in their huge armadas and wait for starvation to finish Japan. The daily food ration had already dropped to the bare subsistence level of 1,500 calories; there was only a little more than half as much rice in stock for civilians as there had been in 1941, and because of the blockade, there was no hope of replenishing it. American submarines and destroyers had reduced Japan's merchant fleet from an already inadequate six-million tons in 1942 down to slightly more than two-million tons now, and the surviving freighters were sinking day by day at a ruinous rate. With food imports down almost to zero, the whole population was already suffering from the primary effects of malnutrition —weight loss and fatigue. The general health situation was so precarious that the fire bombings of the cities might be said to have provided one benefit—the killing of rats, mice, lice, and fleas had sterilized huge urban areas, thus lessening the danger of epidemic. Tokyo, for instance, had shown no increase in typhoid or dysentery during recent months and that was most fortunate because medical facilities and supplies were virtually exhausted. There was also a water shortage for people remaining in the cities because leaky faucets in burned-out homes kept the pressure low.

Japan's three large urban-industrial centers, Tokyo-Yokohama, Nagoya, and Osaka-Kobe, had now reached such an advanced state of destruction that American pilots had to examine them carefully to find worthy targets. Great sections of Japan's smaller cities, including most of the industrial plants, had been wiped out and the American radio was now announcing in advance which of the surviving communities would be leveled next. During less than nine months of intensive bombing, more than 200,000 Japanese had already been killed and twice that many injured. In the single most severe attack of the war so far, the Tokyo fire bombing on the night of March 9–10, 125,000 people were killed or wounded, 268,000 dwellings were destroyed, and more than a million people were left homeless. Altogether, eight million Japanese were now homeless as a result of B-29 incendiary attacks. So many of these people had abandoned their jobs and moved to rural areas that even some of the factories which might have remained open were closed for lack of skilled workers. Only if the cities were rebuilt could these workers be induced to return, but construction facilities were so low that Prime Minister Suzuki did not even dream of such a solution. He could conceive of but one solution—an early end to this disastrous war which now threatened Japan's very existence. In spite of their current sufferings, however, were the Japanese even yet ready, less than four years after the overwhelmingly triumphant beginning of the war, to accept the kind of ending Suzuki envisioned? During the first six months of fighting, between December 1941 and June 1942, they had driven the Americans out of the west Pacific and the British and Dutch out of Asia. They had captured Guam, Wake Island, the Philippines, the Dutch East Indies, and Malaya. They had controlled the world as far south as Australia and as far north as the Aleutians; as far east as India and as far west as Midway Island, only 1,500 miles from Hawaii. Then on June 4, 1942, in the waters near Midway, the Japanese Navy had lost to the American Navy a battle so decisive it had turned the war around. From that day forward, the Americans had begun a slow but relentless drive westward across the Pacific, gradually destroying the Japanese Navy in a succession of air-sea battles, and taking island after island in a series of bloody invasions until now the U.S. fleet could sail up and down the shores of Japan bombarding its coastal cities without danger of retaliation. Suzuki was part of a small group of men within the Japanese ruling class who realized the hopelessness of the situation. These men were finally gathering the courage to try to bring the war to an end. They were not an organized group, however, nor were they confident of success.

When, on the previous April 5, General Kuniaki Koiso's post-Tojo government had fallen under the weight of the Okinawa invasion, and the former premiers who comprised the Jushin had nominated Suzuki as the next premier, he had been so reluctant to accept that Marquis Koichi Kido, had drawn him aside and said, "Japan's situation has become so critical that I must implore you to make a firm decision to save the nation." Like many of Marquis Kido's pronouncements, this one was so obscure as to be open to more than one interpretation. Suzuki interpreted it as a mandate from the Emperor, for whom Kido often spoke, not only to accept the premiership but to use the position in an effort to end the war. Dedicated as he was to the Emperor, Suzuki could not refuse such a mandate though it put him in a situation almost as difficult as the one he faced when he was shot four times during the famous February, 1936, army coup attempt. In accepting the premiership, he felt obliged to carry out what he considered the Emperor's "mission" to conclude the war, yet he did not know how to carry it out, nor did he even dare discuss it openly with anyone for fear the army might hear of it and attempt again to kill him. Faced with this dilemma, Suzuki, in his first address as prime minister, had said: "I, who am almost eighty years old, have tried throughout life to serve the cause of the country. Having, however, so far taken no active part in politics, I consider myself utterly unfit for the office of prime minister. It is only because of the grave situation that I have accepted the Imperial command. Now I stand at the head of this gallant nation, confident that though I fall at this, my last post of service, all you people, a hundred million strong, will march forward over my lifeless body to overcome the unprecedented crisis that confronts our Fatherland. . . ." At the same time, Suzuki was privately indicating to trusted associates, without making any open declarations, that he intended to work toward peace.

This double stance had created continuing difficulties for him, especially in the last days of July when he felt obliged to answer in some way the Potsdam Declaration of the United States, Great Britain, and China demanding that Japan surrender unconditionally. Admiral Mitsumasa Yonai, the navy minister, and Shigenori Togo, the foreign minister, both of whom were subtle proponents of peace, had argued that he should make no comment on the declaration. General Korechika Anami, the war minister, and the army and navy chiefs of staff, had argued that he should make a statement in support of the military's determination to continue fighting. Suzuki, in sympathy with Yonai and Togo, but cognizant of the army's power, had settled on a compromise resolution: "The government will make the attitude known in some form or other that it has no intention of accepting the Potsdam Declaration."

When Chief Cabinet Secretary Sakomizu was told to put that decision into effect, he arranged for Prime Minister Suzuki to answer a planted question on the subject at a press conference July 28th. During that press conference, Suzuki had said, "Since the joint declaration of America, Britain, and Chungking is a thing of no great value, it will only serve to re-enhance the government's resolve to carry the war forward unfalteringly to a successful conclusion. The declaration is simply an adaptation of the Cairo Declaration (an Allied statement of December, 1943, setting forth surrender terms for Japan). We have decided to *mokusatsu* it."

The word *mokusatsu* which Suzuki used meant in English either to "take no notice of it," "treat it with silent contempt," "ignore it," or "make no comment on it." If it meant the latter, it might convey the idea that the Japanese government was still considering what to do about the Potsdam Declaration. But most people, including the Japanese reporters at the conference, ascribed to the word one of the first three meanings, thus conveying in their stories the next day the impression that Japan had utterly rejected the terms of the Declaration. Inasmuch as Prime Minister Suzuki had never disavowed that impression, it was still accepted in Japan as the official government attitude. Though it was now nine days since Suzuki had made his statement of apparent contempt for the Allied demands, the American reaction to his remarks was not yet known.

After listening to Sakomizu's report, the aged prime minister said, "Has the Foreign Ministry received any word from Moscow?"

He was referring to a Japanese effort to use Russia as a mediator with the Western Allies. For three months, Japan's ambassador to Moscow, Naotake Sato, had been trying to lure the Russian government into a peace-making role.

Sakomizu said, "I understand Mr. Molotov (Russian Foreign Minister Vyacheslav M. Molotov) has agreed to see Mr. Sato the day after tomorrow. Molotov apparently returned to Moscow yesterday from the Potsdam conference."

Suzuki reflected uneasily upon this. He had reservations about the effort to mediate through Russia. It was, ironically, an army idea. "Have you arranged tomorrow's cabinet meeting?" he asked.

Sakomizu said he had done so. Cabinet meetings seemed like futile exercises in these frustrating days, yet the business of government had to go on. There was no shortage of problems to discuss.

"Is there anything else?" Sakomizu asked.

Suzuki said, "No, I don't think so."

Sakomizu was about to bow and leave when there was a knock at the door and a member of his staff entered the room. His expression indicated puzzlement.

"Domei has just sent us a very peculiar report from Okayama," he said. "Word has reached there that two or three planes attacked Hiroshima this morning and did enormous damage." Okayama was a city about 100 miles northeast of Hiroshima.

Both Suzuki and Sakomizu waited, expecting to hear more details. Finally, Sakomizu said, "Is that all you know about it?"

"That's all Domei seems to know."

"But what do they mean by 'enormous damage'?"

"They didn't say. Domei seems confused about it."

"It can't be that bad," Sakomizu said, "if there were only two or three planes." He turned to Suzuki. "Anyway, I'll see what I can find out about it."

Suzuki nodded. This vague scrap of information was the first word he had received about the incomprehensible development in Hiroshima. Though reports had begun coming in to the army and navy three-and-a-half hours before, no one had bothered to inform the prime minister.

AUGUST 6,
EARLY AFTERNOON

C A P T A I N Mitsuo Fuchida was still a hundred miles from Hiroshima, flying over the Inland Sea near Okayama, when he saw straight ahead, from his navy bomber plane, an enormous vertical cloud, slender and high with a dark billowing top, like no cloud he had ever before seen. So impressive was this cloud that it almost mesmerized him, reducing his vigilance against a deadly danger of which all Japanese pilots had now to remain constantly aware in the skies over their own country—the danger of free-roaming American fighter planes. Fortunately, there were none in the immediate vicinity. As Fuchida flew ever closer to the cloud, he became increasingly convinced that it was hovering directly over Hiroshima, and that the city had indeed been stricken by some extraordinary force. The thought of an atomic bomb passed fleetingly through his mind. The concept of such a bomb was not unfamiliar to him, yet the possibility of its actual existence was too remote for serious consideration.

When he was within a few miles of Hiroshima and the huge, jagged column of red-black-gray fumes loomed above him, he tried to contact by radio the tower of the Army Air Force field south of the city, where he intended to land. The tower did not reply.

As he flew over Kure and around the coastal hills to the east of Hiroshima and saw for the first time the delta valley with its six river-created islands on which most of the city was situated, he looked down through smoke and fire on a scene of devastation which made his memories of Pearl Harbor in 1941 fade into insignificance. Though his vision was limited by the dirty, fiery pall which still covered the entire area, he could see well enough to get the stupifying impression that the entire city of a quarter-of-a-million busy people from which he had departed only a day ago was simply not there any more. Huge fires rose up in all quarters, but most of these fires seemed not to be consuming buildings; they were consuming debris. The scene was so incomprehensible it benumbed Captain Fuchida's mind; nearing the airport, he selected a runway, followed a traffic pattern in which his was the only plane, and performed his landing procedures without any conscious awareness of what he was doing. When he landed the airport seemed to him dead and when he turned to taxi his plane back toward the tower, the reason became apparent. Though the airport buildings had not been obliterated, they had been demolished.

Thinking of his aide, Lieutenant Toshio Hashizume, whom he had left the previous day at the Yamato Hotel downtown, he alighted from his plane and looked around for transportation. There was none in sight. He would have to make the four-mile trip to the center of the city on foot.

At the airport exit he stopped short in horror. The road onto which he emerged was congested by a procession of dirty, bleeding, staggering, agonized people, all making their way in a slow, benumbed shuffle out of the city, like corpses walking to their own funerals. Many seemed able to continue only because they leaned upon each other for support. Some were naked, a fact of so little importance the others paid no attention to it. Some were hideously burned with blisters rising like bubbles from their dark, purple skin. Blood of varying shades, from fresh bright red to stale dark maroon spotted their clothing. Fuchida, in his clean naval uniform, stood at the edge of this pitiable mass with eyes and mouth wide open.

"What happened?" he finally shouted.

Some seemed not to hear him. A few looked up and shrugged or shook their heads then continued trudging south toward the sea. A few spoke.

"A terrible explosion. People say it was a bomb."

"Two planes came. Two bombs dropped but only one exploded. The other may explode any time."

"The whole city is burned. Nothing left."

"My whole family is dead. Everyone dead."

More than ever determined to get to the center of the city, Fuchida began making his way north against the flow of battered refugees, encountering one scene of agony after another. Scorched children by the side of the road, crying for their mothers. Traffic jams caused by people falling in the middle of the road to die. Corpses lying in the gutters, both left and right, some with people beside them, still trying to shake them back to life. And in every direction, shattered debris where buildings had stood the day before.

As Fuchida pressed northward he noticed that the buildings were more completely demolished and that the debris-burning fires were more widespread. The corpses were also more plentiful. He found a still-standing bridge over the Temma River (one of the seven finger-channels created by the Ota River when it deposited the delta soil of Hiroshima), and as he crossed it he could see that the water below him was filled with floating bodies. He continued in the direction of the Yamato Hotel, near the downtown area's best known landmark, the high-domed Industrial Promotion Hall.

He noticed now an increasing number of people vomiting as they groped their way along the streets. Perhaps they had been partially overcome by the smoke from all the fires, or sickened by the nauseous odor of burning flesh. To the north, he could see rain falling from the dark cloud which still hovered over the city. And as he walked, block by block, closer to the center of the city, he encountered greater and greater devastation. Occasionally he came upon soldiers or rescue workers trying to extricate people trapped in the ruins. He would stop and help, then ask questions, but he kept getting similar answers, which merely raised more questions.

"I don't know what it was. There weren't any planes that I heard."

"It was a bomb. It couldn't be anything else."

"It happened all at once. Only one explosion."

"It came down by parachute. Somebody saw it. And another one came down with it, but the second one landed in the mountains. Wait till that explodes."

"No more than two planes came over. Very high. Maybe three at the most."

Could it actually have been a bomb? A single bomb? If so, Fuchida's earlier thought about an atomic bomb had not been so absurd. But then, what about this talk of a second bomb having been dropped at the same time. That could not be ignored. Perhaps they were already doing something about it at Second Army Headquarters. What could they do about it, however, except to look for it? He was still finding it difficult to believe what he saw; he hadn't begun to figure out how to cope with it.

He now entered an area in which nothing at all remained except an occasional twisted skeleton of what had been a steel-concrete building. Here, there wasn't even much debris. Block after block was virtually flat as if the area had been laid out for subdivision and the streets had been put in but no one had yet built anything. Here there were fewer people also, but more bodies, and the stench of burning flesh was even more overpowering than it had been farther south. He was obviously approaching the very center of the disaster.

Because there were no street signs, nor recognizable landmarks, he was not certain of his exact location until, through the smoke and dust, he caught glimpses in the distance of the Industrial Promotion Hall's high, prominent dome. Though it was now only a skeleton dome, at least it was still standing. Perhaps some buildings in the center of the city had survived after all. Off to the east, he could see a very high industrial smokestack still standing, though the factory of which it was a part had apparently disappeared. An oddity. But if a brick smokestack could survive, was it not possible that the Yamato Hotel was still intact, and that Lieutenant Hashizume had lived through this thing?

For only a few minutes was Fuchida allowed to retain this hope. As he neared the hotel site, a gust of wind momentarily cleared the air in that sector, revealing to him that for at least a mile in all directions, maybe two or three miles, nothing remained. It was pointless to look for Lieutenant Hashizume at the Yamato Hotel. There simply was no such place.

Captain Fuchida stopped for a moment and closed his eyes. Suddenly he was very tired and utterly depressed. He had walked four miles through a scene so horrendous he could not even now comprehend it. He wished he could sit down, but he had to call Admiral Yanno in Tokyo. He had to get in touch with the army and see what had been done about those rumors of a second bomb. Wearily he trudged northward toward Second Army Headquarters. Perhaps he would find Lieutenant Hashizume there.

AUGUST 6,
AFTERNOON

Y O S H I H I R O Tokugawa felt a sinking sensation in his stomach as he approached the Agricultural Institute at Asakawa, a mountain community near Mount Takao, about 30 miles west of Tokyo. As a chamberlain in the Imperial Palace, Tokugawa had come here to ascertain the condition of a remarkable collection of marine life specimens which Emperor Hirohito had been gathering for twenty years. The collection had been sent here to save it from possible destruction after the Emperor's private palace, within the Imperial Palace grounds, burned down as a result of an American air attack in May. But while Tokugawa was still more than a quarter of a mile from the Agricultural Institute, he was disturbed to see that the building in which the Emperor's collection had been stored was no longer there. It appeared from this distance to have burned to the ground.

The Emperor's studies in marine biology afforded him his only relaxation from the cares of state. If his collection proved to be lost, it meant he had lost his most cherished possession. Tokugawa, anticipating such a possibility, felt it almost as deeply as if it were his own loss. Tokugawa loved Emperor Hirohito almost as he loved himself. And there was a degree of irony in this, considering the family backgrounds of the two men.

When Yoshihiro Tokugawa came to work as a chamberlain in the Imperial Palace in 1936, he was, in effect, taking a job in a castle his family had owned until just 68 years before. He was a prince in the great Tokugawa family which had maintained absolute rule over Japan for more than 250 years until the Imperial Restoration in 1868. During all those years, his ancestors, beginning with the guileful

Emperor Hirohito leads Japanese officers into the
shrine near Ise where, in accordance with religious
custom, he reported to his ancestors the details of
Japan's defeat by the Allies.
(Wide World Photos)

Marquis Koichi Kido
(courtesy of Kyodo Photo Service)

Admiral Isoroku Yamamoto
(courtesy of Kyodo Photo Service)

Shigenori Togo
(courtesy of Kyodo Photo Service)

eneral Hideki Tojo,
)ecember 8, 1941,
fter radio address to the nation.
ourtesy of Kyodo Photo Service)

Admiral Soemu Toyoda
(Wide World Photos)

General Yoshijiro Umezu
(Wide World Photos)

Professor Tsunesaburo Asada
(courtesy of Kyodo Photo Service)

Dr. Yoshio Nishina
(courtesy of Kyodo Photo Service)

Hisatsune Sakomizu
(courtesy of Mr. Hisatsune Sakomizu)

General Korechika Anami.
"I think the General came to say good-bye."
(courtesy of Mr. Masahiko Takeshita)

Masahiko Takeshita
(courtesy of Mr. Masahiko Takeshita)

warrior, Ieyasu, had kept Hirohito's ancestors silent and isolated in the old Imperial Palace at Kyoto. Had it not been for outside pressures, like the coming of Admiral Perry, the Tokugawas might still be ruling Japan and confining the nation, rigidly but peacefully, within its own shores. But they had been unable to stave off the Imperial Restoration, and when it came, the Emperor Meiji moved from Kyoto to Tokyo (then called Edo) to take possession of the headquarters of the Tokugawas, Edo Castle, which he renamed the Imperial Palace. Thus, the restoration was more costly to the Tokugawas than to any other Japanese. It cost them their power, their prerogatives, their castles; indeed, it cost them the entire country. All of this having happened only 39 years before Yoshihiro Tokugawa was born, he might have been expected to harbor at least a slight grudge against the beneficiary of his family's misfortune. Yet it was not in him to do so. More important than being a Tokugawa, he was a Japanese, and Hirohito was his Emperor. He could not equate his family's losses, or his own losses, against the Emperor's gain. The Emperor was like no other man. One loved him; one begrudged him nothing. In addition to this natural love of a Japanese for his emperor, Yoshihiro Tokugawa felt for Hirohito the love a man feels for a very dear friend. He rode with the Emperor, played golf with him, took walks with him. And he knew how much the Emperor's scientific research meant to him. It was not just a hobby. Hirohito had already published serious works on marine biology and hoped to resume his studies if this war would ever end. The loss of his specimen collection would be a severe setback.

Entering the grounds of the Agricultural Institute, Tokugawa rushed up to the first man he saw. Pointing at the ruins of the warehouse in which the Emperor's collection had been stored, he said, "What happened to that building?"

The man did not seem overly upset. "Where were you four days ago?" he said. "We had an air raid. Direct hit. Wiped that building out completely." With a sweeping gesture he indicated the totality of the destruction.

Tokugawa looked sadly into the ashes. "You mean the Emperor's entire collection is simply gone?"

The man's expression changed. "The Emperor's collection! Oh, that's another matter. You don't think we'd let that burn, do you?"

Tokugawa stared at him expectantly.

"We took all that stuff up to a mountain cottage where no air raid will ever reach it."

Suddenly, Tokugawa's breath came easily again. Twenty minutes later he was at that mountain cottage, counting the crates with a smile on his face. They were all there, all undamaged. He could return to Tokyo with a light heart. Perhaps it was ironic to take satisfaction in the knowledge that a collection of dead marine specimens was safe at a time when the whole country was being destroyed. Yet in days like these, a man did what there was to do. And he took satisfaction in whatever he might save.

AUGUST 6,
LATE AFTERNOON

GENERAL Korechika Anami, alone in his large, comfortable office on the second floor of the War Ministry, sat as erect at his desk as if he were on the parade ground. He was at all times erect, whether sitting or standing. He often said, "A straight backbone is good for a man's health." He had always lived by such maxims. "Virtue is the best strategy in war" was still his favorite. In many ways, Anami was the same straightforward, uncomplicated Samurai he had been when the war began. He still shot arrows at a target every day to intensify his powers of concentration, as he had done when he was commander of the Eleventh Army in China. He still practiced kendo swordsmanship and clung to such Samurai virtues as fidelity, tenacity, total commitment. They had stood him in good stead not only in China but later as commander of operations in western New Guinea, then as inspector general of Army Aviation, and now, finally, as war minister. It was because of these well-known virtues, because of his qualities as a gentleman, that Baron Admiral Kantaro Suzuki, when forming his cabinet the previous April, had requested him as war minister. But while Anami was still sustained by the same personal virtues that had made him loved and respected both outside and inside the army, he was now also beset by countless trying concerns.

Though the preparations against the expected Kyushu invasion were progressing reasonably well, and he still believed the army could repulse the first heavy thrust there, the preparations against a possible subsequent invasion of the Tokyo area were lagging badly.

There were also questions in his mind about the government of which he was a part. In June, General Hideki Tojo, now retired and living in the suburb of Setagaya, had come to warn him that while Admiral Suzuki talked about prosecuting the war, his real motives were questionable. And just within the last two months, some of Anami's most trusted junior officers, including his brother-in-law, Colonel Masahiko Takeshita, and Lieutenant Colonel Masao Inaba, both of the Military Affairs Bureau, had said they thought Suzuki was trying to stop the war. If they meant simply that Suzuki wanted peace, of course he did. Anami himself wanted peace. It was a matter of what one was willing to do to achieve it. He had said to them, "Suzuki is a man we can trust. We should respect him. He was a great fighting admiral. His courage is unquestionable. His faithfulness is a reality." But in the army, the grumbling against the Suzuki government persisted and he would have to be ready to cope with it.

Of even greater concern than Suzuki, however, was the Emperor himself. There was no doubt that he wanted peace. But again, what kind of peace? A peace which would eliminate the Japanese Empire, and thus eliminate him as emperor? It was against such a peace that Anami, as war minister, had a duty to guard; against such a peace that the army had a duty to fight.

Since he was busy with paper work, he did not look up immediately when his secretary, Colonel Saburo Hayashi, entered his office. Hayashi waited for the general to finish what he was doing. When Anami looked up, Hayashi said, "We now have a report from the Kempeitai on Hiroshima."

The Kempeitai had an office in the War Ministry.

"What have they found out?" Anami asked.

"It's not much, but it's not good," Hayashi said. They received a one-sentence wire from one of their men. All it says is: "A small number of bombers has turned the city of Hiroshima into a sea of flames."

"You mean they still don't know any more about it than that?"

"Apparently not."

General Anami shook his head. "What could be going on down there?"

AUGUST 6,
TOWARD EVENING

T H O U G H the day's work was done and Prime Minister Suzuki had retired to his home in Myogadani on the north side of Tokyo, Chief Cabinet Secretary Hisatsune Sakomizu was still at his desk on the third floor of the prime minister's official residence.

Sakomizu had, in fact, no place else to go. He was living in his office. On the previous April 13, his home in Shinjuku, and the nearby home of his father-in-law, Admiral Keisuke Okada, had both been destroyed by American incendiary bombs.

Because he had taken his position with the Suzuki cabinet just a few days earlier, he had then the good fortune to be able to move his family and himself into the chief cabinet secretary's official residence, near the prime minister's official residence.

On May 23, the chief cabinet secretary's official residence was destroyed by fire bombs. In the same raid, the prime minister's official residence was also attacked, but though the incendiaries fell like rain upon it, the firemen were ready and it was saved. Sakomizu himself had gone from window to window during the attack, pouring buckets of water down the outside walls. The next day, after sending his wife and five children to the country (the Sakomizus' fifth child had been born during the war, in 1943), he had moved his own pitifully few surviving possessions into his office, and there he could be found at almost any hour of the day or night.

He was cleaning up the odds and ends on his desk when one of his assistants brought in a new message about Hiroshima. This one was an official telegram from the superintendent general of the Chugoku (western Honshu) district.

The telegram said: "Hiroshima has been attacked by a small number of enemy planes with terrific damages. The bomb used by the enemy appeared to be of an entirely new type."

Sakomizu recalled now the Domei report which had come in at noon. Since then, the prime minister's office hadn't received a word about Hiroshima. Sakomizu had almost put the weird explosion story from his mind, assuming it to be just another rumor. But this could not be dismissed as a rumor. It was an official telegram. He decided to call the War Ministry. If the General Staff didn't yet know about it, they should.

AUGUST 6,
9 P.M.

SAIJI HASEGAWA, foreign editor of the official Japanese news agency, Domei, having finished his day's work, looked around the office for something else to occupy his time. He was not eager to leave because he had no place to go except the tiny room in which he slept at the Dai Ichi Hotel near the Shimbashi station. His home was in the southern suburb of Denen Chofu, and while he still went there on weekends to be with his wife and daughter, it was so difficult to get there as a result of the bomb raids on Tokyo that for several months he had been keeping a five-day-a-week room in the city. Until the previous May he had stayed at the world-famous Imperial Hotel in Marunouchi, across the street from Hibiya Park, but while the Imperial had withstood the great Tokyo earthquake of 1923, thanks to the genius of its architect, the American Frank Lloyd Wright, it had fared less well against American bombers. Though not completely destroyed, it had been damaged sufficiently in May so that Hasegawa was forced to find lodging elsewhere.

Since it was now 9 P.M., there simply wasn't much to do in the office. Most of his associates having gone home, there wasn't even anyone to whom he could talk. He might as well go back to the hotel and get some sleep. On his way out, he stopped at the traffic department. At least there was someone there to whom he could say good night.

"Another dull day," he said to the man at the desk. "Anything happening around the country?"

"Not much," the man said. "We got a report this noon that two or three B-29s had attacked Hiroshima and created a big explosion, but we've heard no more about it. Something strange down there."

Hasegawa shrugged. An attack by two or three planes didn't sound like anything which to get excited. He nodded, walked down the two flights of stairs to the ground floor, and emerged into the warm summer evening air. Since Domei was now housed in Hibiya Hall, a huge theater and public office building at the south end of Hibiya Park, he had only a few blocks to walk to the Dai Ichi Hotel. Domei had previously been in the Dentsu building in West Ginza, but on the afternoon of January 27, the first daylight B-29 raid of the war had destroyed it together with the entire Ginza, plus much of the business and night-club section surrounding it. On that occasion, the Shimbashi area around the Dai Ichi Hotel had also burned, but by a stroke of good fortune, the hotel itself had survived. And since the buildings around it were now gone, it had an excellent chance of continuing to survive. The American bombers didn't seem to think that a single building, standing alone, was a target worthy of their attention. There were, therefore, some isolated buildings and even a few clusters of buildings in central Tokyo still standing relatively undamaged amid the mile after mile of desolation.

Walking eastward toward the Ginza, Hasegawa had very little to see because the streets were blacked out as well as burned out. Though they were not deserted, neither were they crowded as they would have been on a prewar summer evening. Dimly visible people shuffled along, their heads down. Up close, one could see in the faint light the tired looks on the faces of the passersby, many of whom wore a drab, dismal costume which was called "the national uniform." For men it was a khaki suit with wrap-around leggings and a peaked, military cap. For women it was a bloomer outfit with baggy legs, quite like the traditional Japanese peasant garb. At the beginning of the war, the government had encouraged everyone to wear this uniform, but because of material shortages, it had never been made mandatory, and many people had thereby been able to avoid it.

In the debris-covered fields where stores and office buildings had once stood, tiny cooking fires were visible near lean-to shacks which people had built to house themselves. Many of the concrete burned-out buildings whose shells remained standing were still in use as makeshift shops and beer halls; outside the beer halls, long lines of men queued up, awaiting their turns to enter. Occasionally, a charcoal-burning, steam-driven bus would pass, crowded with people. These buses had been converted to steam because there was no gasoline to be had. They moved along steadily enough on level streets, but they were so underpowered that when they came to hills, the passengers had to get off and push.

Hasegawa, walking toward his hotel, was only minimally aware of this dismal but now-familiar scene around him. His mind was on his work, which is to say his mind was on the war. As foreign editor of Domei, he dealt with some aspect of the war every day. Almost every dispatch crossing his desk was related to it, and because he saw these dispatches before they were censored, he was much better informed than most of his countrymen. Though he understood the awful implications of the Potsdam demands, he was nevertheless alarmed at the Japanese government's apparent indifference to them because this was no time to increase America's fury. He knew the Suzuki government wanted peace. He had seen indications that the Japanese ambassador to Russia was trying to induce the Russians to negotiate a war settlement. Why then did the Japanese government refuse even to discuss this direct bid from the Allied powers? Did the government, or the army, actually think Russia could be trusted in such a situation? Though Russia and Japan had signed a nonaggression treaty five years earlier, Russia had already served notice that this treaty would not be renewed. It seemed to Hasegawa that Russia might strike a deathblow against Japan at any moment, yet Japan's leaders showed no sign of concern about such a possibility. Hasegawa wondered if these leaders would ever wake up to reality. The whole war proved that the men who controlled Japan lived in a fantasy world. He remembered an incident in England, a month before Japan entered the war in 1941, when he was the Domei London correspondent. He had attended a Mansion House luncheon at which Prime Minister Winston Churchill spoke. Though England was at that time taking terrible punishment from Japan's German allies, Churchill did not act like a man who anticipated defeat. Addressing himself pointedly to the Japanese diplomats and correspondents in the room, he had remarked that he liked Japan, that he had been fond of the country since childhood, and that he wanted therefore to give the Japanese some serious advice at a time when they seemed bent on making war against America. "Such a war," Churchill said, "would be decided by steel. According to your own statistics, Japan produces seven million tons of steel a year. The United States produces ninety million tons. Do you think that seven million tons of steel can defeat ninety million tons?"

Hasegawa had cabled a dispatch directly to Tokyo, quoting Churchill verbatim. A year later, in October of 1942, when he was repatriated with other Japanese citizens who had been interned in England, he learned that none of Churchill's remarks had appeared in any Japanese newspaper. And though they must have been reported to the government, they had obviously not impressed the men who ruled Japan. It was endlessly frustrating to be a Japanese newsman. The papers were constantly prevented from publishing unpleasant news of which the public should be aware. Yet even now, with the country almost prostrate, the papers were still allowed to print the most insanely dangerous nonsense. Today's *Yomiuri Hochi,* for instance, had said in an editorial that President Truman issued the Potsdam Declaration because there was a great cry for peace in the United States and he was trying to quell the storm of protest against American war losses, but the Potsdam terms were so injurious to Japan's pride they didn't deserve consideration. And a *Japan Times* editorial said the Japanese remained confident of their ability to smash any invasion, while the Americans were so war-weary their leaders had to be concerned about public dissatisfaction. Could the men who wrote those editorials possibly believe such things? If they wanted to see some real war-weariness, they had only to look out their windows, or walk down a Tokyo street as he was now doing.

When Hasegawa reached the elevated rail line which marked the western boundary of the Ginza district, he turned south and walked the last two blocks to the Dai Ichi Hotel. Glancing up into the clear, star-filled sky, he wondered if the American bombers would be coming tonight. They did not visit Tokyo as often now as they had a few months earlier. There was at least one advantage in living in a bombed-out city. After the bombers had destroyed almost everything around you, they gave you a rest while they went on to fresh targets. But they had now ravished almost all of Japan's large cities and were down to the smaller cities. At their present rate of destruction, they would soon run out of targets. What would they do then? Come back and pinpoint the spots they had missed? After a person had absorbed so much, he came to a point where he almost didn't care. The high, block-shaped shadow of the Dai Ichi loomed up in front of him now as he moved slowly toward it. He was in no hurry to get there. It would be nice if he could find some diversion but what was there? He had no intention of standing in line for a bottle of beer. Most of Tokyo's theaters were closed, and even if he were to find an open one, it was now too late. Here he was in what had always been the gayest section of the city; there was no gaiety now. It would be nice even if he could take a bath. That would be a pleasant way to end the evening, but baths were limited to once a week, and even then he had to bring scrap paper from the office to build a fire and heat the water. He stopped in front of the hotel, reluctant to go inside. For awhile he stared out into the darkness around him, wondering how much longer Japan would have to suffer this way before someone took the initiative and brought the war to an end. It was as if the country were so paralyzed it no longer had the energy even to say, "We give up." Nobody seemed to be alive any more. People simply got up each morning, performed their listless, routine motions all day, and lay down again at night. What else was there to do? Saiji Hasegawa turned and entered the hotel, went up to his room and lay down.

AUGUST 7,
2 A.M.

C H I E F Cabinet Secretary Hisatsune Sakomizu was sleeping fitfully in his office (which was now also his home) on the third floor of the prime minister's official residence when his telephone rang. Since it was not unusual for him in his job to be awakened during the night, he habitually laid out his futon near his desk so he could easily and quickly reach up for the phone.

This time it was a Domei News Agency reporter. "We just got a call from the monitoring center," the reporter said. "San Francisco Radio has broadcast a statement by President Truman about a bomb that was apparently dropped on Hiroshima yesterday. We don't know much about the bomb. All we heard was something about an explosion."

"I received a report of it last evening," Sakomizu said.

"It must have been an enormous bomb. Do you want to hear Truman's statement?"

"What does he say?"

"He says the Americans have dropped on Hiroshima a bomb more explosive than twenty thousand tons of TNT. Could that be possible? It's something called an 'atomic' bomb and it harnesses what they call 'the basic power of the universe.' It says here, 'The force from which the sun draws its power has been loosed against those who brought war to the Far East.' Do you want to hear more?"

"Yes, go on."

"Let's see—'It has never been the habit of scientists of this country'—meaning the United States—'or the policy of this government to withhold from the world scientific knowledge. Normally, therefore, everything about the work with atomic energy would be made public. But under the present circumstances it is not intended to divulge the terminal processes of production or all the military applications, pending further examination of possible methods of protecting us and the rest of the world from the danger of sudden destruction. I shall recommend that the Congress of the United States consider promptly the establishment of an appropriate commission to control the production and use of atomic power within the United States. I shall give further consideration and make further recommendations to the Congress as to how atomic power can become a powerful and forceful influence toward the maintenance of world peace.' Now listen to this. 'We have spent two billion dollars on the greatest scientific gamble in history—and won.' "

"How much?"

"Two billion."

"All right. What else does he say?"

"Here comes the worst part. 'We are now prepared to obliterate rapidly and completely every productive enterprise the Japanese have above the ground in any city. We shall destroy their docks, their factories, and their communications. Let there be no mistake; we shall completely destroy Japan's power to make war.'

" 'It was to spare the Japanese from utter destruction that the ultimatum of July 26th was issued at Potsdam. Their leaders promptly rejected that ultimatum. If they do not now accept our terms they may expect a rain of ruin from the air, the like of which has never been seen on this earth. Behind this air attack will follow sea and land forces in such numbers and power as they have not yet seen, and with the fighting skill of which they are already well aware.' "

After a pause, Sakomizu said, "Is that the end?"

"That's all. What do you make of it?"

"I want you to send me a copy of it immediately. Also, copies to the War Ministry and Foreign Ministry if they don't yet have it."

The reporter asked no further questions. In Japan there was no tradition of newsmen pressing government officials for information. However curious they might be about a development, they knew they had to be content with the information they were given.

Sakomizu did not go back to sleep after he hung up the receiver. The specter of an atomic bomb suddenly loomed large in his mind. Yet he still refused to believe such a weapon had actually been used at Hiroshima. He knew about the Japanese navy's Project A, which was launched in December, 1941, in an attempt to develop just such a weapon. Though the nation's greatest scientists had worked on it, the project had been abandoned after a year because it was obviously beyond Japan's capability to fulfill such a dream. When it was abandoned, all the scientists involved, including one of the world's most distinguished physicists, Dr. Yoshio Nishina, had agreed that not even America could hope to create such a bomb for years to come. It was inconceivable that the United States, while fighting a war in Europe and a war in the Pacific, could still have enough resources left over to undertake a two-billion dollar atomic bomb project. Yet the Americans were amazing people. They had already proven that. Could they actually have built an atomic bomb? Or was it just a large conventional bomb? Was President Truman simply making one more attempt to frighten Japan into surrendering? Sakomizu settled back into his futon and tried to get a little more sleep. It was a vain effort.

At 3 A.M., one of his aides rapped at his door. He had in hand an official announcement from the War Ministry that a new-type bomb had been dropped on Hiroshima.

AUGUST 7,
8 A.M.

M R S . Sumi Yokoyama had just arrived at her desk in the Institute for Physical and Chemical Research in north Tokyo when her telephone rang. It was a call for Dr. Yoshio Nishina, whose secretary she had been since a week before the war began, and as she might have expected, it was a call from the War Ministry. Dr. Nishina seemed to be conferring constantly with the army and navy these days about scientific matters. The famous physicist had no time left for his own research, especially since he had accepted the responsibility of coordinating various projects at science laboratories throughout the country. Most of Japan's important scientific institutions had until recently been located in Tokyo, but the bombings having forced their evacuation, they were now scattered in several smaller communities, some of them quite remote, which made coordination difficult. Only five staff members of the Institute for Physical and Chemical Research, including Dr. Nishina and his secretary, Mrs. Yokoyama, remained at the walled, parklike Tokyo compound in Komagome.

The Tokyo facility, though damaged by bombs, had not been demolished. Most of its staff and machinery had been transferred elsewhere simply because it was apparent that even more damaging attacks could come at any time. The institute's most impressive machinery, its two atomic cyclotrons, could not, of course, be moved, but inasmuch as Japan's secret Project A had long since been abandoned, the cyclotrons were no longer in use anyway. After Dr. Nishina and his Project A colleagues decided that neither Japan nor any other country could hope to create an atomic bomb for several years, they had concentrated their efforts on other hopeful enterprises, such as the refinement of radar, and the possible uses of cosmic rays and ultra-short waves. For some time they had hoped that ultra-short wave research might lead them to the development of a practical "death ray," and a large laboratory was built to house the "death ray" project, but it, too, had been abandoned, though the other studies still continued.

Dr. Nishina in his personal life had also felt the force of the war. His comfortable home just outside the walls of the institute had been destroyed during a fire bombing in April. His wife, Neiko, suffering from heart disease and neuritis, had gone to stay with her parents at Zushi, about 35 miles south of Tokyo; and his two sons, Yuichiro, 16, and Kojiro, 14, both such brilliant scholars they had been exempt from military duty, had been evacuated to a Kanazawa Prefecture school in western Honshu. Nishina himself now slept in a dormitory near the institute's compound, but he practically lived in his office. He was already there this morning when his attractive young secretary arrived.

Poking her head around the cloth screen which separated her desk from his, Mrs. Yokoyama said, "It's a call from the army. General Kawabe's office."

General Torashiro Kawabe was the army's vice chief of staff. When Dr. Nishina picked up the phone, he found himself talking to a colonel who was one of Kawabe's aides.

"General Kawabe asked me to call you," the colonel said, "because the city of Hiroshima has been hit by a new-type bomb and he wants to get your opinion of it. He wants to know what kind of bomb you think it is. We're sending a team to investigate. The general would like you to go along."

The colonel paused, waiting for a reaction to this request which, considering its source, was virtually a command. Nishina said, "Can you tell me anything about the bomb? How big was it? How much damage did it do?"

"According to some reports," the colonel said, "it just about wiped out the city."

A long silence ensued while Dr. Nishina digested this alarming news. Though the possibility that America had produced an atomic bomb seemed remote, he could not keep it from his mind, nor could he help supposing such a thought had also occurred to General Kawabe. On several occasions he had discussed with Kawabe the nature of atomic energy and the probability that one day an atomic bomb would be developed.

"When is the investigation team leaving?" Nishina said.

"Some time today," the colonel said. "We would like you to come to the War Ministry right away."

"I'll be there as soon as possible."

Sumi Yokoyama saw the worried look on Dr. Nishina's face as he put down the telephone. "What is it?" she asked. After three years and eight months as his secretary, she was so well established she didn't hesitate to speak up to him.

"The army wants me to go to Hiroshima," he said. "The Americans have apparently dropped a new-type bomb on the city."

She still did not understand why he looked so worried. The Americans had already dropped so many kinds of bombs she could see no reason to be that concerned about one more. Though she was privy to all of his business matters, she had only a minimal interest in the scientific aspects of his work. Knowing virtually nothing about the potentialities of atomic energy, she could not imagine why he should be as concerned as he appeared to be about a "new-type" bomb. He worried too much. She could see that. Though she had never argued with him about the war since that day right after it started when she overheard him say it was stupid, she knew, from some of his remarks, that he still felt the same way about it, and that he was now convinced Japan would be defeated. It still seemed to her he had too little faith in the spirit of the Japanese people. Admittedly the situation looked bad, but it would improve. Miracles did happen. Had he forgotten the "Divine Wind" which had, twice in the thirteenth century, buffeted the invasion fleets of Kublai Khan in the China Sea off Kyushu, and thus saved Japan from being overrun by Mongols? Somehow, Japan would also manage to repel the Americans when they came. Sumi Yokoyama was still confident of that. She did not discuss it with Dr. Nishina, however. He was so pessimistic it would be impossible to convince him. In spite of this, he was a good man, a brilliant man, a nice man. She enjoyed working for him.

"When do you leave?" she asked.

"They want me at the War Ministry right away."

She got up from her desk and, as she had done many times before, prepared to pack a bag for him.

AUGUST 7,
MORNING

CAPTAIN Mitsuo Fuchida, accompanied by Captain Yasukado Yasui whom he had encountered after his arrival in Hiroshima the previous afternoon, drove slowly in a commandeered truck up a winding mountain road just north of the city. They were out to investigate persistent rumors that another bomb had been dropped, also by parachute, by one of the planes which had dropped the horrendous bomb the previous morning. So many people had reported seeing the second bomb descend that they could not be ignored. By general agreement, it was supposed to have hit the ground someplace within this mountainous area Fuchida and Yasui were now searching.

If indeed there had been a second bomb, was it a dud, or had it been timed so that it might yet explode? In either case it must be found as quickly as possible. If it turned out to be a dud it would be of enormous value because it would almost certainly yield the secret of how the Americans had managed to create such an awesome weapon. But Fuchida and Yasui were becoming discouraged. They had already searched miles of mountain slope without seeing anything that looked like parachute cloth.

Coming to a lookout point on the narrow, sharply curved road, they stopped and alighted, moving their eyes systematically up and down, back and forth over the rough terrain above them. Though the foliage was thick, it was not thick enough to conceal a parachute. Turning around in the direction of the city, they gave the hillside below them the same thorough examination.

Fuchida said, "Do you think there actually was a second bomb?"
Yasui said, "I don't know."
Fuchida said, "There are so many rumors one doesn't know what to believe."

They stood silent now, their eyes raised a few degrees above the downslope in front of them so that they were staring once more, as they had several times this morning, at the incredible sight of Hiroshima. Yesterday's extraordinary cloud having disappeared, they could see the entire city, or what was left of it, and that was very little. For several miles in every direction from the city center, there was nothing at all except a few skeletons of what had been steel and concrete buildings. Even the fires were out now, there being nothing left to burn. During the night and early morning, as Fuchida walked around the flattened city, he had gone through one stage after another in his reaction to what he saw. First there was the paralyzing wonder at the total devastation, then the sickening horror at the unalleviated suffering—the moans of the wounded as they lay in the streets, their blistered skin, the jagged stumps of arms and legs, the blood and vomit, the stench of burning flesh, the piles of bodies in which the living had not yet been separated from the dead. After the horror came his realization that he must not succumb to it, that he was here to work and there was an endless amount to be done. The authorities in Tokyo were waiting impatiently to find out just what kind of bomb this was that could destroy a whole city. If he and Yasui could find a second one like it, they would have all the answers.

Climbing back into their vehicle, they resumed winding slowly up the mountain road. They were about five miles north of the city and becoming discouraged when they rounded a bend and suddenly saw in front of them, though at some distance from the road, a patch of rumpled, shiny cloth, unmistakably a parachute. It was draped over a clump of wild mountain shrubbery and its white nylon sheen gleamed in the sunlight as the breeze moved it. The two men leaped to the ground and ran through the brush toward it. But as they approached, they gradually slowed their pace, realizing their danger.

A few feet from the parachute, they peered carefully into the brush below it, following with their eyes the slender cords which converged on the ground. Attached to the ends of the cords was a metal cylinder about three feet long and a foot thick, with two black bands around it. Was this a bomb? It was bomb-sized, yet it did not look like a bomb and it certainly did not look like the kind of bomb that could level a city. On the other hand, how could one guess what such a bomb would look like?

Fuchida and Yasui took a few steps closer, then stopped to listen. Whatever the thing might be, no sound issued from it. Perhaps they were not close enough. It was frightening to be even this close. Yet if it were a bomb such as the one which exploded yesterday, and if it were timed to explode within the next few minutes, it would not matter how close they were. They might as well walk right up to it.

Fuchida approached and, taking hold of the parachute cords, slowly, carefully pulled the metal cylinder out from under the brush. Bending over it, he put his ear next to the casing. Still no sound. He touched the metal and found it warm, but perhaps that was from the sunlight which had filtered through the brush to it.

At one end was what looked like an opening, with a metal ring protruding from it. He touched the ring and pulled tentatively. To his surprise, whatever was inside the tube seemed unattached. He pulled harder and the contents began coming out. A whole set of instruments emerged, compactly arranged and connected by wires.

Fuchida and Yasui exchanged glances, each releasing the breath he had been holding. They knew now it was not a bomb. They could at least relax about the danger of being blown up at any moment. But what was it? What was the purpose of all these instruments bound together by wires? There was a clock. That was easy to recognize. And a thermometer. Then several other devices impossible to identify, and finally, a radio transmitter.

As soon as Fuchida saw the radio, he understood what he had in hand. "Do you know what it is?" he said. "It's an instrument to measure the performance of the bomb. They must have dropped it at exactly the same time, so the radio would send back whatever information they wanted when the bomb exploded." He shook his head in wonder. "Whatever made us think we could beat America?" He had thought so himself for a short while, after the astounding success of the attack he had led against Pearl Harbor on the first day of the war. But he had soon thereafter become discouraged at his country's failure to press the advantage won by that attack. And after the navy's catastrophic defeat near Midway Island six months later, in which he had almost lost his life, he had resigned himself to the certainty that Japan would lose. This incredible new bomb merely punctuated that certainty.

Carefully, the two men pushed all the instruments back into the tube, which they carried to their vehicle. In silence they began the depressing drive back down the mountain toward the desolate ruins of the stricken city.

AUGUST 7,
1:30 P.M.

AS FAST as his car would carry him, Marquis Koichi Kido, lord keeper of the privy seal, had returned from an official luncheon in his own home to his office at the Imperial Palace. Contacting the Emperor through one of the chamberlains, he had arranged for an immediate, urgent audience, for which he now hurried through the

Fukiage Gardens to the temporary imperial quarters in the Gobunko (library building).

The Emperor did not keep him waiting. At 1:30, His Majesty entered the makeshift audience hall.

Marquis Kido, bowing more hastily than usual, said, "Your Majesty, I have just returned from my home where I received a most alarming report through an army source. Yesterday morning, it seems, the city of Hiroshima was stricken by a bomb so enormous and so terrible it is difficult even to conceive."

The Emperor did not act surprised. He had, in fact, heard from his military aide the night before that some kind of explosion, perhaps from a bomb, had dealt a severe blow to Hiroshima. He was anxious, however, for the details. "Yes," he said. "What are the latest reports?"

"I understand," Kido said, "that the whole city has been destroyed. Perhaps 130,000 people killed or injured. And apparently by just one bomb. They say there were only a few airplanes. It must have been dreadful. And what is even worse, the Americans have apparently broadcast a statement by President Truman that it was an atomic bomb. You know, of course, what is meant by an atomic bomb. Is that possible? Could the enemy actually have used a weapon that would snuff out tens of thousands of lives in a single charge?"

The Emperor said, "Has all this been confirmed?"

"There is no longer any doubt about the damage," Marquis Kido said. "The suffering is indescribable. The army now has reliable reports about conditions in Hiroshima. But as to whether it was actually an atomic bomb, I don't think that has been established. The army seems to doubt it."

"You say the whole city was destroyed? And more than 100,000 people dead or injured?"

Kido nodded gravely, and as he looked up into the Emperor's face, he saw the anguish engraved there. He fervently wished that the duty of passing on this information to His Majesty had fallen to someone else.

Hirohito drew a heavy breath and looked away. He was silent for a long moment. Then he turned again toward Marquis Kido and said in a voice full of pain and resignation: "Under these circumstances, we must bow to the inevitable. No matter what happens to my safety, we must put an end to the war as quickly as possible so that this tragedy will not be repeated."

AUGUST 7,
2 P.M.

TWO LARGE twin-engine airplanes stood waiting in a camouflaged bunker at Tachikawa Army Air Base, 20 miles west of Tokyo,
as a convoy of military automobiles approached. In these automobiles
were the 20 men who composed the Japanese Army team assigned
to investigate yesterday's apparent disaster at Hiroshima. The team,
under the command of Major General Seizo Arisue, the dynamic
chief of the army's Intelligence Section, included also Dr. Yoshio
Nishina. General Arisue and General Torashiro Kawabe, the vice
chief of staff, had decided early in the morning that, since they now
had a reliable report stating "the whole city of Hiroshima was destroyed instantly by a single bomb," the possibility that the bomb was
atomic could not be ignored, and therefore any team of investigators
would have to include Nishina. Both generals were aware of the
atomic weapon project Nishina had directed for the navy at the
beginning of the war, and while they shared only a vague notion of
how an atomic bomb might work (the army had never attached high
importance to the military potential of such a remote and exotic force
as atomic energy), they knew of no other kind of bomb for which the
claim had been made that it might destroy a whole city. Hence, as
soon as Dr. Nishina had been summoned to the War Ministry at
Ichigaya Heights, the convoy of cars had sped away directly for
Tachikawa.

The drive had been fast and comfortable because the army still had
some cars in good condition, and inasmuch as there were very few
other cars on the streets, they encountered no traffic delays. Though
they did encounter an intermittent flow of people leaving the shattered city on bicycles and on foot (many of them laden with personal
possessions that indicated their intention to settle in the country),
such people showed their respect for army vehicles by pulling in
close to the sides of the road.

As soon as the convoy reached Tachikawa and the men on the
investigation team alighted from the cars, an air base officer drew
General Arisue aside.

"Sir, we have just received a report," the officer said, "that American bombers are now over Miyakejima heading toward Osaka."

Arisue accepted this news without a change of expression. Realizing what it meant, however, he decided he should discuss it with the
men accompanying him since half of them, like Dr. Nishina, were
civilians, and therefore not under his absolute authority.

Gathering them together, he said, "I've just received word that American planes are approaching Osaka. As you know, Osaka is almost directly on the route to Hiroshima. And if I judge the speed of American attack formations correctly, we should be reaching Osaka about the time they finish their bomb runs. As for myself, I shall take off immediately with my staff. But you civilians may wish to delay your flight. I leave that up to you."

Without awaiting their decision, Arisue and his army subordinates hurried to the plane assigned to them and took off for Hiroshima.

The civilians, left to make up their own minds about the perilous flight, stood on the runway, looking uncertainly at each other. Their plane, which was ready to go, seemed to be the only plane on this huge air base. If there were others, they had been carefully hidden from the American bombers which occasionally flew over to pay their disrespects, and the marauding American fighters, especially the recently introduced P-51s, which swooped down every day to spray machine gun bullets.

One of the civilians said, "Well, shall we take a chance?"

Dr. Nishina said, "Why not?"

Since General Arisue had taken off without hesitation, it would seem like an act of disloyalty to the country if they did less. In times like these, one could not think of one's self.

Dr. Nishina walked toward the waiting plane, and as he did, so did the others. The moment they were aboard, the plane taxied as fast as safety would allow toward the end of the runway. It taxied so fast it seemed as if it were already taking off. As the pilot obviously knew, there was no time to dawdle once he had left the protection of the camouflaged bunker. American fighter planes often came in at low altitudes and appeared without warning. They would enjoy catching a twin-engine transport-bomber preparing for takeoff.

AUGUST 7,
MIDAFTERNOON

A S T H E fifteen members of Prime Minister Kantaro Suzuki's cabinet gathered at the round table in their stately, paneled meeting room on the second floor of his official residence, the strange, "new-type" bomb which had hit Hiroshima was foremost in each of their minds. Few of them knew any details of the damage the bomb had done, but all were aware that the damage was great, and that the President of the United States had broadcast a statement that the bomb was "atomic." Was this true? And if so, what did it mean? What, exactly, was an "atomic" bomb? Only a handful of these Japanese statesmen understood the full possibilities of atomic energy. And only two were resigned to accept President Truman's assertion that America had developed an atomic weapon.

Admiral Mitsumasa Yonai, the navy minister, needed no further convincing. Reports from the Kure Naval Base near Hiroshima, and from such dependable navy observers as Captain Mitsuo Fuchida had so overwhelmed Yonai that he had this day written a secret memo to one of his aides: "Hiroshima destroyed by atomic weapon. This war is lost." Yonai's conclusion that the war was lost had not come just today, however. He had considered the war a hopeless cause even before it began. With the help of men like Admiral Keisuke Okada he had worked secretly to undermine the cabinet of General Tojo for almost three years in the hope of bringing the war to a negotiated end. And when he became vice premier as well as navy minister in the cabinet of General Kuniaki Koiso, who succeeded Tojo in July, 1944, he ordered an aide to conduct a confidential study of peace possibilities with special attention to the question of how the army might be induced to surrender. The results of this aspect of the study had not been reassuring.

Foreign Minister Shigenori Togo, who had held the same post at the beginning of the war until a quarrel with Premier Tojo forced him to resign, had also been convinced, long before the Hiroshima bombing, that Japan must sue for peace. When Suzuki asked him in April to join this cabinet, after Koiso's downfall, Togo had said he would do so only with the understanding that the Suzuki government would work for an early peace. Suzuki had been reluctant to speak even privately about an early peace because he was speaking publicly about increasing the war effort, but he had said to Togo: "So far as the prospects of the war are concerned, your opinion is quite satisfactory to me. And as to diplomacy, you shall have a free hand." Togo's acceptance of a post in Suzuki's cabinet was influenced to some degree by his feeling of responsibility for the part he had played in beginning the war. Though he was a chronic heart patient (his doctor had advised him just a month earlier to resign from the cabinet), he was determined to devote however much energy he had left at the age of 62 to ending this war which he had helped launch. As for his approach to peace, he had spoken at cabinet meetings in May about the advisability of dealing directly with America, but when the war minister, General Korechika Anami, speaking for the army, insisted on trying to negotiate through Russia if at all, Togo had acquiesced. He had little faith in the government of Joseph Stalin, yet, as General Anami had said at the time, in the words of a Chinese proverb, "When a bewildered bird enters a hunter's pocket, even the hunter will not kill that bird." Perhaps there was at least a modicum of hope in trying to negotiate peace through Russia. In any case. Togo was now hotly pursuing the possibilities through the Japanese ambassador in Moscow. But at the same time, he was more than ever convinced, since reading President Truman's statement this morning, that a direct approach to America was urgently necessary.

Premier Suzuki himself, as he entered the cabinet room, maintained his usual composure so well that an observer might wonder if this old man had any feelings at all about the apparently catastrophic bomb that had hit Hiroshima. Though his expression remained calm, he was, of course, deeply disturbed at this startling development. He had not yet satisfied himself, despite President Truman's statement, that the Hiroshima bomb was atomic. He did not intend, however, to say this to his cabinet. He didn't intend to express any personal opinion at all on the matter, or to present any policies for coping with it. Suzuki was well aware that his leadership arose, not so much from what he said or did, but from what he was. The men in this room honored him, even loved him as an old, almost legendary hero who had bravely faced death on more than one occasion in the service of the Emperor. To his cabinet ministers he was a moral leader whose very presence commanded respect, and whose guidance arose out of a sincerity within him that would accept no less from others. To Suzuki, on the other hand, his cabinet ministers were the most accomplished and trustworthy men he had been able to find, and therefore, the most likely to work out the policies needed to solve the nation's growing dilemma. His function, as he saw it, was not to try to provide them with answers, but to bring them together in such a way that between themselves they would find better answers than he could provide.

After bowing to the fifteen men at the round table, and to their aides who sat behind them, he took his place in his own high leather chair and, calling the meeting to order, turned to his home minister, Genki Abe, a bald, bespectacled man who, like most of the civilians in the room, wore the high-collared national uniform which all

Japanese men had been encouraged to wear.

"Mr. Abe," Suzuki said, "will give us a report on yesterday's development in Hiroshima."

Since the home minister was responsible for all local government and law enforcement, he was directly concerned with Hiroshima. "Yesterday afternoon," Abe said, "the director of the Police Bureau came to my office to report that an unknown type of bomb had been used by the Americans against Hiroshima. Because all communications had been broken, we could not obtain details at the time, but we have since ascertained that the damage to that city is beyond anything any of us has yet seen. Though the details are still sketchy, we have heard from dependable sources that Hiroshima is paralyzed. Almost all the buildings have been destroyed. A tremendous number of people have been killed. In a word, the city is completely ruined. And apparently it was all done by just one bomb, which is different from any type of bomb we now know."

After Home Minister Abe spoke, Suzuki called on Transportation Minister Naoto Kobiyama, then the chief of the Cabinet Planning Bureau, Tsukizo Akinaga, but neither of these men had any new details to add. Finally, Suzuki called on the man whose comments were most eagerly awaited, General Anami, the war minister. He would provide the army's reaction to this new bomb. As everyone knew, the army's attitude was the one most likely to prevail.

As the war conditions worsened, General Anami, the very model of Samurai rectitude, found himself in a position perhaps even more difficult than that of Prime Minister Suzuki. While Suzuki's loyalty could be directed singly to Emperor and country, the one being the same as the other in his mind, Anami felt deep obligations of loyalty to Emperor, country, army, and Suzuki; and he was painfully aware of the potential conflicts between these loyalties. His primary allegiance was, of course, to Emperor Hirohito, but how was he to handle the Emperor's obvious inclinations toward an immediate peace, which the army disapproved? As war minister, he owed an almost equal allegiance to the army, of which he was the highest representative. From the young officers on the War Ministry staffs to the senior officers on the General Staff, the men who controlled the army were determined not to accept a shameful surrender. Anami himself, though he had approved the tentative attempt to negotiate secretly through Russia, and though he had told his secretary, Colonel Saburo Hayashi, in July that he was thinking of peace, was staunchly opposed to surrender, and agreed with his army colleagues that serious peace proposals should be made only after Japan had inflicted signifi-

cant damage to the American invaders during the anticipated decisive battle for the homeland. Would the Emperor agree to this policy
when the decisive battle began and the casualties began to mount?
And would Prime Minister Suzuki agree? Though many young army
officers suspected Suzuki of a soft attitude about the war, Anami's
loyalty to the venerable naval hero—whom he had first met in 1929
when they were both aides to His Majesty—was as strong as his
admiration for him. When a group of young officers had suggested in
June that the army should overthrow the Suzuki cabinet and install
Anami as prime minister, the general had said to them: "I have
received a report that a certain section of the War Ministry is privately discussing possible new cabinet members in anticipation of an
Anami cabinet. They are stupid." His statement had quelled the
movement but it had not stopped the aggressive young officers in the
War Ministry, many of them Anami's own disciples, from referring to
Suzuki as a possible traitor. How would Anami be able to maintain his
loyalty to Suzuki if the aged prime minister did begin to weaken in
his resolve to prosecute the war? This question was more acute than
ever today as a result of the Hiroshima bombing.

Though General Anami had known since yesterday that something
was seriously amiss in Hiroshima, he did not know the extent of the
tragedy until, on his arrival at the War Ministry early this morning,
the vice chief of staff, General Torashiro Kawabe, told him of a
verified report that the whole city had been destroyed instantly by
a single bomb. When Anami heard soon thereafter about the broadcast statement by the President of the United States that the bomb
was atomic, he discounted this claim as did most of the officers in the
War Ministry. The bomb had apparently exploded in the air above
the city. Every military man knew that a bomb which exploded in the
air could do 200 times as much damage as one which exploded on the
ground. Perhaps the Americans had invented a proximity fuse which
would make a bomb ignite a certain distance from its target; if so, that
was hardly surprising. The Japanese had also developed such a fuse,
which they were holding back to use in the decisive battle for the
homeland. But while Anami discounted the claim that the American
bomb was atomic, he did not discount the damage it had apparently
done to the city, nor did he discount the damage it might do to the
already strained morale of the Japanese people. Throughout this
morning he had taken part in General Staff conferences on how to
cope with this new threat, whatever it might be. Because details from
the scene were still sketchy, General Seizo Arisue and a team of aides
had been dispatched to conduct a first-hand investigation, but until

their report arrived, a provisional army policy about the bomb would have to be promulgated. The General Staff had worked out this policy. It was now Anami's task to make Prime Minister Suzuki and his cabinet accept it.

"There can be no doubt," General Anami said, "that a sizable weapon has been used by the Americans at Hiroshima. But its exact size and effect can be determined only by a proper and thorough investigation. The army has already begun such an investigation. A team of experts, civilian as well as military, is at this moment on its way to the scene. Until these men send back their report, and we can determine precisely what happened, I believe we should exercise patience. Nothing should be said publicly about what may or may not have happened, and as little as possible should be said privately. There should be no announcement in the press at this time that the bombing of Hiroshima was in any way unusual."

When he finished speaking, a pause ensued, broken finally by the voice of Foreign Minister Togo whose impatience came through in spite of his apparent attempt to restrain himself. "Does the war minister believe," he asked, "that an event of such magnitude can be kept from the public?"

General Anami, constrained to defend the policy he had just outlined, said, "We do not yet know the magnitude of the event."

"But we do know that the city of Hiroshima was destroyed," Togo said. "And the President of the United States has announced that an atomic bomb destroyed it. His statement was broadcast to the Japanese people by the American radio. We can hardly keep that from the public."

"The fact that President Truman announced it does not necessarily make it true."

"Many people will believe it nevertheless. Does the army think it was not an atomic bomb that struck Hiroshima?"

"We do not yet know," Anami said. "First reports about any event tend to exaggerate it. All of us are aware of that. It may be that whatever happened at Hiroshima was much less damaging than we have been led to believe. It is difficult to conceive of a single bomb powerful enough to wipe out a whole city. I think we should all keep our minds open about the matter until we find out the absolute truth. Until we receive absolute evidence from our investigators."

Foreign Minister Togo, who considered General Anami a reasonable man, realized that in this situation it would not be easy to talk to him. On past occasions he had spoken quite frankly to Anami about a variety of subjects, some of them rather delicate—the danger of army interference in politics; the harm that could be and was often done by the Kempeitai; the impropriety of establishing a military cabinet. On all of these matters, General Anami had expressed full agreement with Togo. One might therefore expect him to agree today that the Hiroshima bomb had brought about a basic change in the entire war situation. Togo, as a diplomat, had read President Truman's statement so carefully he knew it had to be more than an idle claim. But Anami was not a diplomat. He was a soldier, the nation's leading soldier, and he was at this moment expressing the position, not simply of himself, but of the army. It would be fruitless to engage him in a frontal argument.

"I believe we have come to a time," Togo said, "when drastic new policies must be espoused. The condition of the entire nation is indeed critical. Our greatest cities have been leveled to the ground. Our food supplies have dwindled to such a perilous level that we must all dread the coming winter. We have no fuel to run whatever ships, automobiles, or machinery we have left. Most of our factories stand idle. And now, a new catastrophe befalls us. The situation calls for unusual measures. The enemy has gone far to destroy us. But the enemy has also made certain proposals which, properly explored, may lead to peace. Is it not possible that the time has come to explore the enemy's true intentions?"

Togo's words continued to fill the room after he finished. Everyone waited for Anami's reaction to these daring remarks which, however veiled, could be interpreted only as a bid to accept the hated Potsdam Declaration, to accept unconditional surrender.

General Anami, turning to Togo, looked at him with the clear, open expression which made so many people regard him as the epitome of the direct and guileless man of honor. He did not mention what Togo had just suggested. "It will be impossible to decide on policies," he said firmly, "until we receive a fuller report from Hiroshima."

Prime Minister Suzuki, who had listened carefully to the two men, realized that the army had now spoken the final word for the day. Taking a deep breath, he roused his heavy body from his chair and adjourned the meeting.

AUGUST 7,
5:30 P.M.

T H E twin-engine transport-bomber carrying General Seizo Arisue and his staff, having flown around Osaka to avoid American planes which were reportedly attacking there, approached Hiroshima from the Inland Sea at an altitude of about 500 feet, which gave the passengers a close view of the ground. As the plane banked around the coastal hills to the east, General Arisue was suddenly overwhelmed by the sight which lay before him. He knew Hiroshima well. Surely this was not Hiroshima. There was nothing here but a network of river tributaries branching out, between islands of scorched earth, on the way to the bay. As the plane flew directly over this hideous wasteland, he scrutinized it for signs of life. There was, he noticed, a dead tree with nothing else standing near it, and on a charred black branch of the tree he fancied he saw an equally black crow, but perhaps it was his imagination. Except for that skeleton of a tree he saw nothing; the deep, concentrated horror of the scene closed in upon him as his plane descended into it.

Approaching the army air field south of the city (the same field at which navy Captain Mitsuo Fuchida had landed the day before), General Arisue looked in vain for signs of activity. Pieces of planes were visible, scattered near the bunkers, some distance from the runways, and pieces of buildings lay sprawled near the aprons of the runways. The buildings which still stood appeared to be derelict. As Arisue's plane settled smoothly onto the runway, he looked out to the side and noticed that the grass was red, as if it had been toasted. When the plane came to a stop near what had been the operations building, no one came forth to welcome it. As the engines died, a deep stillness enveloped the passengers, and they sat, unmoving in their seats, stunned into silence by the enormity of what they had already seen.

Eventually, someone stirred and the ten men in the plane stood up, reached for their baggage, and numbly made preparations to alight. When they were all assembled on the ground, wondering where to go and how to find transportation, they were suddenly relieved to see, at last, a sign of human life. A man emerged from what looked like an air raid shelter and walked slowly toward them.

As he approached, General Arisue could see he was an officer, though his uniform was torn and soiled. Even from a distance it became obvious that he was not walking normally. He favored one side, and as he drew near, the reason became apparent. The side he favored was red and inflamed, while the other side looked quite normal. It was as if the man had been burned by a huge blowtorch while he was standing in profile to it. One hand, one arm, one side of his face and neck were burned, while the other half of him showed no sign of damage. Noticing a general (Arisue) in the arriving group, the injured officer walked up to him and saluted.

Arisue said, "What's happened to you? What kind of burn is that? What's happened to the whole city?"

The officer shook his head. "I don't know, sir. The Americans. . . . I don't know. Only two planes came over. Maybe three. They've got some new kind of bomb. The whole city. . . . Did you see it? The whole city, gone."

"But your face! How did you get such a burn? What makes the grass so red? You say two or three planes? Are you sure it was only one bomb?"

"There was only one explosion. An unbelievable blast. The ground shook. A bright flash burst out in all directions. It seemed to be near the center of the city. I didn't see the actual blast since I wasn't looking that way, but the flash of light I saw—and that seems to be what burned me—before I was knocked down."

"Are you saying there was a flash of light so hot it burned one whole side of you?"

"Apparently so, sir. You can see I'm not burned on the other side."

"How could that be?"

"I can only conclude, sir, that the flash of light is the dangerous thing when this type of bomb explodes. Everything exposed to the light gets burned, but anything even slightly covered is untouched. You notice, it's only where my skin was exposed. My face, neck, hand. Where my clothing covered me, I'm all right."

General Arisue, looking closely at the man's inflamed, flaking skin, shook his head in amazement.

"Everyone around here seems to be in panic," the injured officer continued. "They say there is no defense if the Americans use weapons like this. But you can see for yourself, sir, there is a defense. One has only to be covered when the flash of light comes."

These were amazing and encouraging words. General Arisue noted them carefully. Perhaps the situation was less desperate than it appeared. Yet one could not deny that a dreadful bomb had been dropped. This was a truly horrible weapon the Americans had developed.

Arisue said to the injured officer, "I want to see exactly what happened. Have you any transportation?"

The man shook his head. "I'm afraid not. We had only a few vehicles before the blast. I don't think any of them survived it."

"There must be some kind of vehicle around here."

"We have a motorboat that could take you across to Ujina. Maybe they could help you."

Ujina, the army port at Hiroshima, was about six miles from the center of the city, on the eastern side of the bay. Arisue recalled that it had looked fairly well intact when his plane flew over it on the way here. It was, indeed, the sensible place to begin. But what about Dr. Nishina and the other civilians in the second plane? They should have arrived by now. Perhaps they had been afraid to take the chance. He would give them a few minutes more.

After a half-hour, the second plane having not yet arrived, General Arisue gave up waiting for it. He couldn't continue standing around at this desolate airfield when he knew the General Staff in Tokyo was expecting a report as soon as he could get it to them. Boarding the motorboat which had been offered, he and his staff headed out into Hiroshima Bay toward Ujina. They quickly realized that their progress would be slow. Looking down over the side, they saw that the boat was plowing through masses of floating bodies.

AUGUST 7,
7 P.M.

IT WAS almost 7 P.M. before Mrs. Sumi Yokoyama, Dr. Yoshio Nishina's secretary, left her desk at the Institute for Physical and Chemical Research in Tokyo. She had stayed late not only because she had work to do, but because she entertained a vague hope that Dr. Nishina might call from Hiroshima, for which city he had left earlier in the day. This Hiroshima situation worried Sumi Yokoyama. What could have happened down there to make the army that concerned? She was not so surprised at Dr. Nishina's obvious concern. He had been in a pessimistic mood for a long time now, and recently he had said to her, "Very soon, the time will come to surrender."

Though she disagreed with him, she hadn't argued with him. She felt she would rather die fighting than surrender. In the end, Japan would win the decisive battle for the homeland. She was fully convinced of that. Everyone was talking about the final battle and preparing for it. Even the women and children. Members of the Women's Defense Corps were drilling several times a week with sharp bamboo poles. And there were groups of old men all over Japan doing likewise. The Americans would face more than they could handle when they tried to invade the home islands. But what had the Americans done now in Hiroshima? Had they actually developed an atomic bomb? It was unthinkable.

After clearing her desk and closing the windows, she left the building and walked through the tree-lined campus of the institute toward the front gate on the way to her "home." She hadn't far to go. She was staying now (as was Dr. Nishina) in a dormitory the Institute maintained just across the street from the front gate. She had moved into the dormitory after the Setagaya house in which she had lived was destroyed by American bombs during the May 25 air raid, the second most severe attack Tokyo had absorbed.

Just as she reached the front gate, Sumi Yokoyama was surprised to find herself confronted by Dr. Nishina, who was entering the institute compound, suitcase in hand.

"What happened?" she cried. "You can't have gone to Hiroshima and returned in so little time."

"We went part way," he said, "but our plane developed engine trouble and we had to turn back. We'll try again tomorrow."

"Then you still don't know what kind of bomb the Americans dropped down there?"

"No, but I have an idea."

Since he was walking toward his office, she took his suitcase and accompanied him. He was obviously tired and his face wore a grave expression. She worried about him. In the almost four years since she came to work for Dr. Nishina she had developed a daughterly regard for him. She wished he wouldn't work so hard. Every morning he was at his desk when she arrived and he seldom left it before midnight. When they entered the office now, he walked toward the desk.

"Why don't you sit down here in a chair," she said, "and I'll make you some tea."

He did so without argument. He was too weary to argue. When she returned with the hot water, he looked up and said, "Would you please bring me my slide rule?" The army that morning had supplied him with a few details of the bomb blast at Hiroshima. He decided to test these details against his own knowledge of atomic energy.

She brought him his slide rule and he began moving the bars back and forth, making calculations in his head while she busied herself preparing the tea. After pouring a cup for each of them, she sat back and watched silently while he continued working with the slide rule.

Finally he looked up at her in a quiet voice which was nevertheless filled with awe. "It's the atomic bomb," he said.

Though Sumi Yokoyama had little knowledge of atomic energy, she was vaguely aware of its awesome possibilities. She knew now, though she had not known it at the time, that Dr. Nishina had been involved in an attempt to develop an atomic weapon for Japan. His flat statement that the Americans were in possession of such a weapon, and had used it against Hiroshima, so overwhelmed her she could say nothing for some time. She recalled his recent remark, "Very soon the time will come to surrender." He had said that before he even dreamed the Americans possessed such a weapon. He was indeed a very wise man. Perhaps he knew much more than she about the country's true condition. Was it possible that she had been deluding herself? How could she overlook the fact that most of Japan's cities were in ruins, and that in recent months no Japanese planes ever seemed to challenge the hundreds and thousands of American planes in the sky every day? Suddenly, as if struck by a revelation, she knew the truth which until now she had refused to face.

She said, "This means, then, that we are in the final moment."

Dr. Nishina sat still, saying nothing. Eventually he stood up. "I'm very tired," he said.

Together, in silence, they walked to their separate rooms in the dormitory across the street from the institute.

AUGUST 8,
6 A.M.

T H E W A R M sun was already presenting the threat of another hot day when Leslie Nakashima alighted from a suburban train at Musashino, on the wide agricultural plain just west of Tokyo. Over his shoulder, as he headed out along a quiet country road was a sack of old clothing, mostly cotton garments for which he and his wife, Yachiyo, had bargained in Tokyo during the previous week. Nakashima was on his way to the farmhouse of the Miyamoto family, a source of vegetables without which he and his wife would now be perilously close to starvation. Each week he took this early-morning train ride an hour out of Tokyo with a pocketful of money (from the two jobs he held) and a sackful of old clothes. It was no longer possible to buy produce from the farmers with money alone. Though money was still welcome, commodities were a more dependable form of currency and clothing was the commodity which seemed most in demand among the farmers. Nakashima was therefore only one of many thousands of city people who made periodic trips to the country with all the old clothing they could manage to acquire.

Food was now so scarce in the cities that not even the unquestioning Japanese tradition of obedience to law was strong enough to keep people from dealing on the black market. The legal rice and vegetable rations were below subsistence levels. There were almost no fish to be had, since the Americans had virtually blasted the Japanese fishing fleet out of the water. And the rice in the legal market was of a quality so low no one would have eaten it before the war. To give it bulk, it was mixed with soy beans. But as Nakashima walked along this peaceful country road through the lush, green landscape, gazing at the endless fields of ripening rice, he found it hard to conceive of the desperate famine conditions gripping the country. When he thought of his weekly rice ration, however, he was brought back to reality.

Though it was not customary for men to make the country marketing trips, Nakashima had to do so because his wife, having suffered from tuberculosis for many years, was not strong enough to go. He had to take an early morning train because at eight o'clock he was due at the office on the first of his two jobs. He worked for the Domei News Agency from then until 3 P.M.; for the *Japan Times* from 4 P.M. until 9 P.M. Though the hours were long he could not complain, remembering, as he did, the days at the beginning of the war when, because he was a Hawaiian-born American citizen, and because he had worked for the American news agency, United Press, he couldn't get a job at all. Having a wife in a sanitarium and two little daughters to support, he had found it expedient to renounce his American citizenship in exchange for work. He wished now that he had been able to find some other solution to his problems, but it was too late for regrets. In times like these, one could only do his best to stay alive and keep his family alive. He had, at least, managed that, though he realized this morning that he had just come close to losing them. At the Domei office the previous day, he had heard some details of the Hiroshima bombing, about which the public had not yet been told anything. If the damage from this "new-type" bomb proved to be as heavy as the reports indicated, he had reason to worry gravely about his mother, who lived in Hiroshima, but he also had reason to marvel that his wife and daughters were still alive and safe. They had been in Hiroshima with his mother until two weeks earlier. In mid-July, his wife had sent him a letter from there saying she had found some people in Nagano Prefecture, near the west coast of Honshu, who would take care of the children, freeing her to come to Tokyo. She wanted to be with him, she said, despite the possibilities of bombing and starvation. He had therefore gone to Hiroshima, and on July 22, had managed to get his family onto a train so crowded they had to board it through a window, pushing the children in ahead of them. The following night, after 24 slow-moving hours, he had been tempted to get off at Fukui and look for a hotel room. His wife, realizing how difficult it would be to board another train, had insisted, fortunately, that they continue on this one. That night, the city of Fukui, where Nakashima had wanted to stop, was wiped out by bombs. After leaving the two children in Nagano Prefecture, the Nakashimas had made their way back to Tokyo, where they found, through a friend, the tiny house in which they were now living.

Nakashima had begun his vegetable trips to the country before his wife's return to Tokyo, while he was sharing a room in the home of a friend in the Ikebukuro district. He had established such a pleasant relationship with the Miyamoto family that he looked forward to his weekly visits with them. They had so many children and grandchildren that their need for clothing seemed almost inexhaustible. This morning, several of them, young and old, were on hand to greet him as he approached their modest farm cottage. Mrs. Miyamoto, called forth by a cacophony of voices, appeared at the door, and Nakashima soon found himself sitting cross-legged in front of a cup of tea, chatting about the war and the hard times. After the tea, the bargaining began.

He stood up and bowed, then opening his sack, produced the old clothing he had brought, laying the garments out, one by one, for inspection. Though most of them were already badly worn, he felt no embarrassment about that. His own clothing was also badly worn. Threadbare clothing was better than none at all. But it was not easy to judge Mrs. Miyamoto's reaction to what he had brought. Having welcomed him with a smile, she wiped all expression from her face when he began to display his offerings. After seeing his selection of shirts and pants and dresses, she countered it by laying out a selection of vegetables.

Nakashima waited, hoping she would add a few more melons and radishes to the pile. She seemed indisposed to do so. He produced money. She produced more vegetables, but still not enough to meet his needs now that his wife was living with him. He offered more money and again she added to the vegetable pile. It seemed now to be enough. He nodded his head to conclude the bargain. Mrs. Miyamoto returned his nod and smiled. Gratuitously, she added a few more vegetables to the pile in a culminating gesture of friendship. Nakashima thanked her, then put the vegetables in the sack from which he had taken the old clothes. He bowed and she returned his bow.

"I'll be back again next week," he said.

"We'll be here to welcome you," she said.

Slinging the sack of vegetables over his shoulder, he bowed again, to the whole family, and headed out along the same country road toward the Musashino railway station. A light breeze gently moved the trees. On all sides there were farmers working in the fields. There was no sound other than birdsong. The skies were clear. He hoped he would have the good luck to catch a train without a long wait. Then, if no American fighter planes swooped down to strafe the train, he might even get to work on time.

AUGUST 8,
MORNING

W H E N General Anami arrived, early as usual, at his War Ministry office, he found the morning newspapers on his desk, and the first thing that caught his eye was the regular monthly reprint of the imperial rescript issued December 8, 1941, the day the war began. On the eighth day of every month since then, each newspaper in Japan had reprinted this rescript at the top of its front page. The Emperor's words still stirred the soul of General Anami and heightened his sense of responsibility for the welfare of this man whom he loved above all others. "We, by the Grace of Heaven, Emperor of Japan, seated on the throne of a line unbroken for ages eternal . . ." Never in all the ages eternal had the throne been so threatened as now. Not even in the thirteenth century, when the Mongols were prevented from conquering Japan only by the intervention of the "Divine Wind" which blew their ships to destruction. If the Emperor and the nation were to be saved this time, it would take another such miracle, but General Anami could not count on the gods to provide it. He himself, as the highest officer in the Imperial Army, would have to find a way to fulfill the august words in the Emperor's 1941 proclamation:

. . . The situation being such as it is, Our Empire for its existence and self-defense has no other recourse but to appeal to arms and crush every obstacle in its path. The hallowed spirits of our Imperial Ancestors guarding Us from above, We rely upon the loyalty and courage of Our subjects in Our confident expectation that the task bequeathed by Our Forefathers will be carried forward, and that the source of evil will be speedily eradicated and an enduring peace immutably established in East Asia, preserving thereby the glory of Our Empire.

There were several other stories of interest in the morning papers. The Tobacco Bureau of the Finance Ministry had announced that the cigaret ration was being reduced from five to three per day. Anami liked cigarets as much as he liked sake. A new group of civilians had been organized in Tokyo to plant potatoes in some of the devastated areas of the city where buildings had once stood. Discouraging items. Anami scarcely took time to glance at them. He was looking for a specific story which he found several inches down from the top of the page. It bore a modest-sized headline:

40 P-51S RAID KEIHIN AREA

Led by one B-29, 40 P-51 fighters from Iwo Jima Island raided the southwestern area of the Keihin (Tokyo) District at 10:20 A.M. yesterday. The enemy planes machine-gunned and bombed military installations and then fled by way of Sagami Bay (south of Tokyo Bay) at 11:30 A.M. In this raid, some British planes of unidentified type took part for the first time.

Hiroshima was attacked by a small number of superforts at 8:20 A.M. Monday. The enemy dropped explosives and incendiaries. Damage is now being investigated.

Realizing the Hiroshima tragedy could not be ignored any longer, the army had decided the previous night to make this unobtrusive announcement of it. Perhaps more details would have to be released later, when the full story arrived from the scene, but in the meantime, Anami still favored saying as little as possible about it. The whole affair was becoming so worrisome he could not relieve his mind of it.

He called in an aide. "Haven't we heard anything yet from Arisue?"

"Nothing so far, sir."

"Let me know the minute we do."

Finally, in midmorning, a radio message from General Arisue was handed to him. (Though Arisue had dispatched it the previous night at the army transportation headquarters in Ujina, near Hiroshima, activities at this base had been so disrupted by the general confusion and by the inflow of dazed and wounded refugees that the communications section had not got around to transmitting it until morning.) As General Anami read the message, a dismal mood closed over him. He called in several other generals and certain of their aides, all of whom reflected the grim concern he showed in his face as he read to them what Arisue had to say:

Hiroshima totally destroyed by one bomb, a special bomb, a type never seen before. Opinions of survivors indicate we can cope with this new weapon. People directly exposed to blast were either killed or burned. But many not directly exposed show no signs of injury. Therefore burns can be prevented by covering body. Anything covered even slightly escapes burns. This means countermeasures are possible.

Many rumors circulating here. Some say same kind of bomb will hit Tokyo August 12. Advisable to be alert for such a possibility. Though it may be useless to dig more shelters at this late date, I suggest people be told to seek protection in shady places.

Dr. Nishina not yet here. Will begin scientific evaluation when he arrives. —Arisue.

For several moments there was only silence from the officers to whom General Anami read the message. Then, one of the generals said, "The whole city destroyed by a single bomb? I still can't believe it."

Another said, "It sounds as if Arisue was carried away by it, like everyone else."

"Was it an atomic bomb or was it not? We still don't know."

Finally General Anami said, "But we do know now at least one encouraging thing about it. There seems to be no doubt in Arisue's mind that we can develop a defense against it."

The officers around him were silent for awhile as if they were just grasping a thought which had escaped them until now. What was it

Arisue had said? "Anything covered even slightly escapes burns." That did sound promising.

One of the officers glanced again at the message, then looked up with a smile of relief on his face. "Maybe it's not as bad as we feared after all."

Another said, "At least we'll be able to tell people how to guard against it."

The gloom which seemed to have overcome everyone in the room gradually began to lift. The army had already found a way to minimize America's newest weapon.

AUGUST 8,
MIDMORNING

AFTER thinking for several days about an item of information he had heard from one of his students, kendo master Sogen Ohmori decided he should discuss it with someone well-placed in the army. The student, one of only five kendo trainees still attending Ohmori's Direct Mind School of Fencing in Setagaya, had been born in Manchuria and spoke Russian so well he was in charge of monitoring Russian radio broadcasts for the navy. He had told Ohmori of a Russian newscast which claimed the Japanese government was asking Russia to act as a peace mediator. That could only mean the government was preparing to surrender. Though one need not necessarily believe the Russians, it was possible, and Ohmori found it alarming. While he had never been a militarist, he had favored the war when it began and he still considered Japan's involvement to be righteous. Why should Japan be prevented from achieving its aims in Asia when its enemies, who were not even Asians, who excluded Asians from their own countries, were allowed to dominate or control China, the Philippine Islands, India, Malaya, and the East Indies? Did not the Emperor, in his rescript of December 8, 1941, say that the war was a fight for righteousness and justice? That being the case, there could be no surrender. Righteousness and justice were not qualities to be abandoned. They had to be defended to the end, just as the Emperor himself had to be defended to the end. His Majesty must never be subordinated to his enemies. Every man, woman, and child must be prepared to die to prevent that.

Ohmori knew to whom he should speak—a fiercely nationalistic officer in the political liaison branch of the War Ministry's Military Affairs Bureau, a man named Major Kenji Hatanaka, whom he had known for several years, and who was reputed to be a protégé of the war minister, General Korechika Anami. The fact that the navy had heard this Russian broadcast did not necessarily mean the army knew about it. Ohmori was sufficiently well-informed to realize that communication and cooperation between the army and navy were limited. In one respect, he had always favored the navy over the army. The navy was less militaristic, less likely to take over the country and establish a purely military dictatorship. But it was pointless to alert the navy about this apparent surrender threat. The navy authorities already knew it. They had no power, however, to prevent it. Only the army had such power. Ohmori, therefore, set out on foot from his home and school in Setagaya to visit Major Hatanaka at the War Ministry. Hatanaka, though a nationalist, did not seem to Ohmori an extreme militarist.

As Ohmori walked from Setagaya, a southwestern suburb which still had many houses standing (his own home and school had been hit but only slightly damaged by a bomb in May), toward the thoroughly bombed core of Tokyo, he passed through mile after mile of total desolation in which only the network of paved streets indicated that a city had once stood here. Within the Yamate Line, a railroad route circling central Tokyo, one could walk for miles and see virtually no buildings except the shacks people had put together by salvaging debris. Patches of weeds had popped up here and there, but in most places, the ground was a rusty brown.

As he approached the devastated Yotsuya district on his long walk, the Ichigaya hill loomed up ahead of him. Atop it, looking quite undamaged, was the modernistic concrete building which was once the military academy but now served as the War Ministry. After a reasonable wait at the guard gate, he was granted a pass and proceeded up the curving road to the top of the hill. Major Hatanaka greeted him warmly. He was a handsome young man with penetrating eyes and the intense, fiery appearance of a zealous missionary. Constant energy seemed to flow from him. He was already well known in the army for his enthusiasm, determination, and dedication. Among his friends were such influential young officers as the chief of his own section, Lieutenant Colonel Masahiko Takeshita, Colonel Okikatsu Arao and Lieutenant Colonel Masao Inaba of the Army

Affairs Section, and Major Hidemasa Koga of the Imperial Guards. General Anami, the war minister, had often praised Hatanaka's soldierly qualities.

"We haven't seen each other for some time," he said to Ohmori. "These days, everyone is busy."

"I don't like to take you away from your work," Ohmori said, "but I've heard something which I think you should know. Perhaps you do know it. The Russians are claiming on the radio that the Japanese government is seeking peace through them. Could that be true?"

"Yes, we know about it. I believe there have been some peace moves. The government is full of Badoglios."

The "Badoglio" to whom he referred was Marshal Pietro Badoglio of Italy who had been instrumental in unseating Premier Benito Mussolini and arranging his country's surrender to the Allies. In certain Japanese military circles, the name "Badoglio" had become synonymous with traitor.

Ohmori, horrified at this confirmation of the Russian broadcast, asked, "What is the army's attitude about it?"

"The army is very much opposed. And as for myself, I am adamantly against anything that even suggests surrender."

"I was certain you would be."

"The question is, how best to combat the Badoglios. I want to thank you for informing me of the Russian broadcasts, even though we, here, were aware of them. We're happy to know the Japanese people are behind us." Hatanaka paused, examined Ohmori closely, as if assessing him before continuing. "Some of us within the army are determined to prevent the Badoglios from betraying Japan," he said. "Are you in agreement with us?"

Ohmori nodded. "I am."

"Then there is something you can do. We need the help of a dedicated civilian group. A secret group. Well-placed people. Civil servants. Businessmen who deal with the government. Men who can influence government officials. Men who can bring us information about the government's plans. Could you organize such a group?"

"I see no reason why I couldn't."

"Excellent. Then we can work inside the army while you work outside it. And together we shall bind all of Japan firmly behind the Emperor. We shall make certain the entire nation is ready to protect His Majesty from his enemies. We must not surrender. Japan has never lost a war. Japan will not lose this war. We shall fight until we win."

There was a hypnotic quality to the fiery zeal with which Hatanaka spoke. One could see why he was so highly regarded in the army. Ohmori was deeply impressed. "I'll do everything I can," he said. Already he had in mind several people upon whom he could call. Influential people on whose feelings he could depend, and from whom he could get information. People who could make their views felt within the government. Bowing farewell to Major Hatanaka, he left the War Ministry in a better frame of mind than he had enjoyed for many months. There was still hope after all. There were still many people who felt as he did. If these people could organize their efforts, the Emperor would never be subjected to his enemies. The fighting power of Japan had not yet been broken. The army was still intact. The people, though they had suffered, still maintained their invincible Japanese spirit. And that spirit would yet prevail despite the physical power of the enemy. Ohmori's faith was suddenly renewed.

AUGUST 8,
NOON

FOREIGN Minister Shigenori Togo was clearing his desk in preparation for a visit to the Imperial Palace when the one-minute siren rang, indicating an air raid alert. He paid little attention. An alert did not necessarily mean an attack, especially in Tokyo where there was so little left to attack. But a few minutes later, as the clock on his desk approached noon, the one long blast was followed by five short ones, each about four seconds in duration, and this did indicate the probability of an attack. An alarm meant at least that American planes were getting close to the city. Togo's reaction was one of annoyance more than anything else. At all times he had so much work to do he could muster very little patience for anything or anyone that wasted his time. And today he was less patient than ever with such a routine delay as an air raid alarm because, after seeing the Emperor, he had to return quickly to his office to be on hand in case there was a message from Ambassador Naotake Sato in Moscow. This was a crucial day in the attempt to negotiate peace through Russia. It was the day Russian Foreign Minister Vyacheslav Molotov (back from the Potsdam conference since Sunday) had agreed finally to see Ambassador Sato. The purpose of Sato's appointment (at 5 P.M. Moscow time, 11 P.M. Tokyo time) was to secure Russian agreement to a Moscow visit by Prince Fumimaro Konoye, who had been Japan's premier until just before the war began, and who was now the chosen peace envoy in any possible negotiations through the Soviet Union. Togo was ill-at-ease about Sato's prospects of success today because he knew how difficult it was to deal with the Russians. He himself had once been ambassador to Moscow in the late 1930s. He feared that at any moment this afternoon he might receive another cable from Sato announcing that the meeting with Molotov had again been postponed, and asking for further instructions. Sato's recent messages had been so disheartening Togo had sometimes become impatient even at him. On one occasion when Sato cabled to announce a new delay, he had added gratuitously that in his opinion the only way Japan could end the war was by unconditional surrender. Togo, in some annoyance, had replied that if Japan wanted to surrender unconditionally, that could be done without Russian assistance. Part of his annoyance arose from the fact that basically he was in agreement with Sato's opinion. Yet since the attempt to negotiate through Russia had been launched, it must be pursued with vigor. Sato's meeting with Molotov, if it did take place, would give some indication whether this avenue of endeavor offered any chance of success.

With all these considerations crowding his mind, Togo reluctantly made his way downstairs to the Foreign Ministry's air raid shelter. Since the ministry was an old, wooden building, and not in the best of condition, it would be unwise to be caught in it if the Americans began dropping more of their incendiary bombs.

As Togo approached the shelter, the American planes (mostly P-51 fighters which were used as strafers and bombers because there were no Japanese planes for them to fight) had come in across Tokyo Bay and were almost upon the heart of the city. Escorted by B-29s which did their navigating for them on the flight from their Iwo Jima base, they divided into two groups, one heading south, apparently toward Yokohama or the Atsugi Air Base ten miles west of there; the other, however, heading directly toward the center of the undefended city. Togo could hear the drone of their engines as he hurried now to safety below ground. At least he would not have long to wait there. If they intended to bomb government buildings (of which so far only a few had been destroyed), the bombs would begin dropping within a very short time.

When, after several minutes, there was still no sound of bomb bursts, Togo became too impatient to remain in the shelter. He emerged into the bright sunlight of this warm August day in time to see the enemy planes continuing on toward the west, perhaps with the intention of strafing the Tachikawa Air Base 20 miles from the city—a favorite target. Togo ordered his automobile and was soon driven out through the Foreign Ministry's imposing stone and grill-work gate in the direction of the Imperial Palace. He had petitioned for an audience with Emperor Hirohito because he felt it was time someone said a few plain words to His Majesty.

Togo's automobile, entering the Sakashita gate of the palace, drove up the curving road past the Imperial Household Ministry, through the area burned out in May when the Emperor's personal palace was destroyed, to the library building in the Fukiage Gardens where the Emperor had set up temporary quarters. Here he was met by a chamberlain who said, "His Majesty is still in the shelter. He will receive you there."

Togo was not surprised. The all-clear signal after the disappearance of the American planes had sounded only a few minutes earlier. He followed the chamberlain along a winding path into a rather dense portion of the woods where they came upon a large, steel door set into a slope, hidden well by foliage and by overhanging pine trees. The door creaked slightly as the chamberlain opened it. Inside, they were met by another chamberlain who escorted Togo down a flight of stairs at least 50 feet deep and well into the hillside, then along a narrow passageway, through another steel door until they entered a sizable, though very plain, concrete-walled conference room. Togo had met the Emperor here on previous occasions. As he waited for him now, he reviewed in his mind what he planned to say to him.

When Emperor Hirohito entered the room, dressed in a military uniform, Togo made the customary bow from the waist, then set the urgent tone of his intentions by speaking immediately of the subject which had brought him here.

"Your Majesty is surely aware of the catastrophe which struck Hiroshima two days ago. It is no longer possible to doubt that the entire city has been destroyed. All accounts from the scene agree on that. And the President of the United States has announced that it was accomplished by a single bomb. An atomic bomb. Your Majesty, being a scientist, will understand that concept better than myself. In any case, eyewitnesses agree that only two or three planes were above the city when this took place, and that there was only one explosion. I consider it both foolish and dangerous to question the American assertion about the nature of the bomb when its power has been so well demonstrated. Whatever kind of bomb it may be, we have seen what it can do. And we must conclude that if the Americans have been able to produce one such bomb, they certainly have produced more. Yet the army still refuses to accept the American President's statement, insisting we do nothing until an investigation of the Hiroshima bombing has been completed."

Togo had been speaking so excitedly he was running short of breath. He paused, then looked directly into the eyes of his sovereign —eyes that seemed always to be filled with sorrow.

"Your Majesty," Togo continued, "I submit that we should not wait any longer. Most of our great cities have already been destroyed. At any moment, others may meet the same fate as Hiroshima. I believe, Your Highness, that as a result of what took place there, it is now all the more imperative that we end the war quickly. And I believe that the destruction of Hiroshima, horrible as it is, has given us an opportunity to take initiative in that direction."

Togo felt no fear in saying thus openly to the Emperor what he would not have dared to say publicly. On June 20, when Togo had a private audience to explain the peace overtures being made to Russia, the Emperor had said, in approval, that he desired the government to do all in its power to stop the fighting as soon as possible. And two days later, at an imperial conference of the Supreme Council for the Direction of the War (comprised of the prime minister, foreign minister, war minister, navy minister, and chiefs of the army and navy general staffs), the Emperor told the military members that although they had established the principle that the war must be fought to the absolute end, they should now consider other ways to cope with the nation's crisis. Though this was not perhaps as strong a statement as might be desired, it left no doubt in Togo's mind about the Emperor's personal views.

Having poured out the entire burden of his thought in one continuous stream, Togo fell silent now, awaiting the Emperor's reaction. Hirohito stood perfectly still, his hands at his side, his feet turned slightly outward. Though his face appeared at first glance impassive, Togo could read in his eyes his urgent concern about the nation's present dilemma. And in the facial lines which had developed during the three-and-a-half years since Togo used to stand before him as the first wartime foreign minister, Togo could read more than just the normal aging process. The Emperor looked like a man who had not had a carefree hour since the war began.

After a few moments' thought, Hirohito said, "I have been informed of the tragic fate of Hiroshima. I, too, feel everything possible must be done to prevent any further suffering among our people. I completely endorse your view. There is no way in which we can continue the struggle now that the enemy has begun to use against us a weapon of such devastating power. As you say, the tragedy of Hiroshima does give us an opportunity to sue for peace. We must not let this opportunity slip away. And we must not waste it in attempts to gain more favorable conditions. There is little prospect for success at this stage in bargaining for terms. We must simply take measures, concerted measures, to end the hostilities promptly."

Togo was so heartened to hear these strong, direct words that he found himself nodding eagerly as the Emperor spoke. It was exactly what he had wished to hear. But one question still remained. How could the army be brought to realize these personal wishes of the Emperor? And even if the army were brought to realize the Emperor's personal wishes, would it agree to surrender? The army, despite its loyalty to the Emperor as an institution, had many times disregarded his wishes as a person. One had only to recall the invasion of Manchuria, and six years later, the invasion of China, which the Emperor had never even acknowledged with a rescript.

Hirohito himself seemed to anticipate the question troubling Foreign Minister Togo. "Everything I have just said to you," he concluded, "I want you to communicate to Prime Minister Suzuki."

AUGUST 8,
SHORTLY AFTER NOON

Dr. Tsunesaburo Asada, wearing all the clothes he now possessed— shirt, pants, and a pair of *geta* (Japanese wooden clogs), stood staring wistfully into the ruins of his house in Motoyama, a residential suburb between Osaka and Kobe. This house, which had been completely destroyed in an air raid just three nights earlier (August 5–6), was the third of Dr. Asada's homes to be burned out since the intensive American air attacks began the previous November. He now owned no personal property except the books and experimental material in his laboratory at Osaka University, where he was still, as he had been when the war began, a professor of physics. Perhaps he would now have to move into his laboratory. He could think of no other place to go. Fortunately he had sent his family to a place in the country, near

Nara, and though he seldom saw them, due to the problem of finding transportation, he could at least feel fairly confident of their safety. It was also comforting to know they were getting enough to eat. He himself had recently been reduced, on occasion, to eating seaweed and the leaves of sweet potatoes.

Despite his losses, Dr. Asada did not feel like a defeated man as he stared into the ashes of this house in Motoyama. Though almost all of Osaka and Kobe, like Tokyo and the other large Japanese cities, had been virtually wiped out, he felt that Japan still had a chance to win the war. Because of his research and development work for the navy, he was fairly well informed about the military resources available for the anticipated decisive battle of the homeland, and he was reasonably confident that the invaders would be repulsed. Although there were no airplanes or fuel to spare in everyday dog-fights against the Americans, there were thousands of planes hidden in reserve for that final battle, and enough gasoline to put them in the air. In addition, Japan now had the proximity fuse, which heightened the effectiveness of bombs by making them explode 35 feet from their targets. There were already 15,000 of these fuses in storage, awaiting the invaders. Dr. Asada knew all about the proximity fuse because it was he who had invented it, in connection with the Kobe Steel Works, at whose laboratory he did much of his work. Since the failure of Project A, the atomic weapon program of which Asada had been one of the prime movers, he had devoted his energies to teaching and to other research-development programs, especially for the navy, with which he was still connected as a science adviser. It was through a joint effort of the navy and the Kobe Steel Works that he had been able to develop the proximity fuse.

He was still staring absentmindedly into the ruins of his house, thinking how fortunate he was that his wife, daughter, and two sons had been evacuated to the country, when he was surprised to hear 'the sound of music. Turning toward the street, he saw a man approaching with a portable radio.

The man said as he drew near, "Did you hear what the Americans have done now? They've invented a new type of bomb, and they've dropped it on Hiroshima."

Asada said, "Who told you that?"

"It was on the newscast. They said it did considerable damage."

As the man walked on, Asada thought fleetingly of the possibility that the "new-type" bomb had been atomic. It seemed unlikely. An atomic bomb would have done more than just "considerable" damage. He turned back to his own obliterated house, wondering if there might be any small items of value beneath he ashes. He was idly scattering little piles of ash with his geta when another man approached, an officer in naval uniform.

"Dr. Asada?" the man asked.

"Yes, sir."

"They're looking for you at the naval station."

Asada said, "My house has burned. I don't even have any clothing except what I'm wearing. When do they want to see me?"

"You've lost your house? I'm sorry. But they want to see you right away. A new kind of bomb has been dropped on Hiroshima. A very intensive type. The American radio says it's something called an 'itomic' bomb. I think they want you to go there and investigate."

Dr. Asada said, "Not 'itomic.' The word is 'atomic.'" The incorrect pronunciation had delayed momentarily his comprehension of what he had heard. He was almost through correcting the man before the enormity of the message began to register.

AUGUST 8,
8 P.M.

C H I E F Cabinet Secretary Hisatsune Sakomizu sat in his office on the third floor of the prime minister's official residence trying to clear his desk of the routine matters which had accumulated during the day. His progress was slow because he found it difficult to concentrate on this detail work. His mind was increasingly preoccupied and disturbed by whatever had happened at Hiroshima. When the first news of Monday's air attack there arrived, and even when he read the statement by the President of the United States that it was an atomic bomb which struck the city, he had remained skeptical. The possibility that America had actually been able to develop an atomic bomb during wartime seemed remote. But as he listened to Foreign Minister Togo's pointed questions to General Anami at yesterday's cabinet meeting, he had begun to reassess the possibilities. Togo, a most intelligent man, obviously believed President Truman. And while the army seemed not to believe him, it had issued a communiqué this afternoon which indicated that, whatever kind of bomb had hit Hiroshima, it was a fearsome one. Sakomizu read again the army communiqué, released at 3:30 P.M.:

In the attack made by a small number of B-29s on August 6, considerable damage was caused to Hiroshima city.

In this attack, the enemy used new-type bombs. Details are now under investigation.

The new type bombs ... were dropped by parachute and exploded before reaching the ground. A considerable number of houses in the city collapsed. The explosive power of the new bomb is now under investigation but it is considered that it should not be made light of.

If the army went so far as to say it "should not be made light of," it must indeed be an amazing bomb. In the months past, the army had been able to shrug off the most destructive bomb attacks as "routine" raids. But what disturbed Sakomizu even more than the army's equivocation was a British news agency story which the Domei correspondent in Stockholm had forwarded to Tokyo. It said that a Vatican spokesman had criticized America for using this new-type bomb. It must be a truly horrendous weapon if the Pope would go out of his way to condemn it.

While Sakomizu fell more and more deeply under the dismal spell of these considerations, a telephone call came for him, which he didn't feel like taking until he was told it was from the army transportation headquarters in Ujina, near Hiroshima. The caller was Dr. Yoshio Nishina, who, as Sakomizu was aware, had been sent by the army to investigate the bomb. (Though Nishina's plane had been turned back by engine trouble when he attempted to fly to Hiroshima the day before, he had managed to arrive there at 4 P.M. this afternoon, despite a squadron of P-51s which had attacked Tachikawa Air Base a short time before his takeoff.) With trepidation Sakomizu picked up the telephone.

Since the two men were well acquainted, there was no need for introductory remarks. Dr. Nishina said, "As you know, I've come down here to take part in the army investigation. But it seems to me I should also inform Prime Minister Suzuki of what I observe."

Sakomizu said, "When did you arrive there?"

"This afternoon."

"And what have you discovered so far?"

"What I've discovered is ..." Nishina's voice was so full of emotion he was finding it difficult to continue. "What I've seen so far is unspeakable. Tens of thousands dead. Bodies piled up everywhere.

Sick, wounded, naked people wandering around in a daze. The ground is simply flat where the city used to be. Almost no buildings left standing. . . ."

The full horror of the situation was bearing down now on Sakomizu. Others might have exaggerated the tragedy, but not Dr. Yoshio Nishina. "It's all true then?" Sakomizu said. "Hiroshima is completely wiped out?"

"Completely."

"But how did they do it?" The crucial question was coming. Sakomizu could no longer put it off. "What kind of bomb was it?"

Nishina said, "I'm very sorry to tell you this. Remember last year when we talked about an atomic bomb? I told you we had concluded that even America could not produce one for several years. But we were wrong. I must report to you that the so-called new-type bomb is actually an atomic bomb."

He was so near tears he had to pause for a few moments. Sakomizu could think of nothing to say to fill the pause.

Finally, Nishina continued. "We have always known American science and industry were very strong. But we didn't know they were this strong. They are even stronger than we can imagine."

After another pause, Sakomizu said, "Are you absolutely certain it was an atomic bomb?"

"I was virtually certain before I left Tokyo, especially after I visited the army Aeronautical Department laboratory this morning and saw some of the roofing tiles which had just been brought back from here. They were so completely melted no ordinary bomb, no ordinary fire could have done it. But the officers at the laboratory were still doubtful. Then this afternoon, when we arrived here and flew over the city before landing, I was even more convinced. Nothing less than an atomic bomb could have done so much damage. This is still only my opinion, you understand. There are those who may disagree. But tomorrow I plan to conduct some tests, and perhaps those who are now doubtful will then be convinced."

Sakomizu said, "Have you talked to any of the survivors?"

"When we landed," Nishina said, "I quickly questioned a number of people, but their stories were conflicting, so I went out to an island in the harbor where there is an antiaircraft battery. It seemed to me that antiaircraft gunners would have some training as observers. Also, they were far enough away so they weren't likely to be hysterical about what they saw. They confirmed the story that there were two B-29s. They said the bombing altitude was about 9,000 meters (29,000 feet). As soon as the bomb was released, the planes swerved sharply, one to the right, the other to the left, and flew away at full speed. No doubt they were well aware of their own danger when the bomb exploded."

Sakomizu had one more question. "You say there are some people who still don't believe it was an atomic bomb?"

"Some of the army officers here remain doubtful," Nishina said. "Perhaps that is why I felt I must call you personally. Please tell the prime minister for me it was truly an atomic bomb that destroyed Hiroshima."

When he finished talking to Dr. Nishina, Sakomizu sat at his desk for a few minutes, too stunned to move. Then, pulling himself together, he hurried to Prime Minister Suzuki's office. As he entered, the old man eyed him anxiously.

"You look as if you've received some news," he said.

"Very bad news," Sakomizu said. "I just talked to Dr. Yoshio Nishina in Hiroshima. He asked me to tell you that the city is truly destroyed, and that, beyond all doubt, it was an atomic bomb that destroyed it."

The aged prime minister seemed not to react at first. Then suddenly he got to his feet and began pacing behind his desk. "I want you to arrange a cabinet meeting for tomorrow morning at ten o'clock," he said.

"Yes sir."

"And I want you to write a speech for me. A speech proposing that we accept immediately the Potsdam conditions."

He stopped pacing and looked directly at his chief cabinet secretary. "This is the chance we have been waiting for," he said. "We now have an excuse to act. This is our chance to stop the war."

AUGUST 9,
4:30 A.M.

RIDING in one of the steam-driven cars assigned to the prime minister's office, Hisatsune Sakomizu had the dark, desolate streets of Tokyo virtually to himself as he chugged northward from the center of the city at 4:30 A.M. He was now on his way to Prime Minister

Suzuki's private residence in the Myogadani district to discuss a development which, in its impact, was comparable to the news that the Hiroshima bomb was atomic. An hour or so earlier, Seiji Hasegawa, the Domei foreign editor and an old school friend of Sakomizu, had called to tell him that Russia was now at war with Japan. Domei's monitoring center at Kawagoe City (about 35 miles northwest of Tokyo) had learned of this latest catastrophe from a Moscow radio broadcast which announced the text of the Russian declaration:

After the defeat and surrender of Hitlerite Germany, Japan became the only great power that still stood for the continuation of the war.

The demand of the three powers, the United States, Great Britain, and China on July 26 for the unconditional surrender of the Japanese armed forces was rejected by Japan, and thus the proposal of the Japanese government to the Soviet Union on mediation in the war in the Far East loses all basis.

Taking into consideration the refusal of Japan to capitulate, the Allies submitted to the Soviet government a proposal to join the war against Japanese aggression and thus shorten the duration of the war, reduce the number of victims, and facilitate the speedy restoration of universal peace.

Loyal to its Allied duty, the Soviet government accepted the proposal of the Allies and has joined in the declaration of the Allied powers of July 26.

The Soviet government considers that this policy is the only means able to bring peace nearer, free the people from further sacrifice and suffering, and give the Japanese people the possibility of avoiding the danger of destruction suffered by Germany after her refusal to capitulate unconditionally.

In view of the above, the Soviet government declares that from tomorrow, that is, August 9, the Soviet government will consider itself to be at war with Japan.

Even when Hasegawa read this statement to Sakomizu over the telephone, the latter could not at first believe it. He had been hoping to hear, through the Foreign Ministry, a different kind of news from Moscow. Japanese Ambassador Sato was to have seen Soviet Foreign Minister Molotov at 11 P.M., Tokyo time, to arrange for a Moscow visit by a Japanese peace envoy. "Are you certain your monitor heard the broadcast correctly?" Sakomizu asked Hasegawa. "The statement is quite simple," Hasegawa said. "It leaves no room for misinterpretation." When Sakomizu overcame his disbelief, a frigid fear took possession of him, followed by a wave of anger, then, finally, a sense of total despair. It seemed that all the forces of man and nature, including even the prime energy of the universe, were closing in together to crush Japan, to wipe it out entirely so that no person would remain on the entire earth who could say he was Japanese.

As soon as he finished talking to Hasegawa, Sakomizu called Prime Minister Suzuki who was asleep at his private residence. Suzuki told him to come immediately. Both men were aware that the Russian war declaration, involving as it did a serious failure in Japanese diplomacy, raised a grave question about the continuation of the Suzuki government.

When Sakomizu entered the prime minister's large, two-story house in Myogadani, he found Suzuki, already dressed in morning clothes, talking to Foreign Minister Togo who had arrived a few minutes earlier. Togo had already informed Suzuki of the Emperor's remarks the previous day.

"It is my opinion," Togo said, "that the war must now stop immediately."

Suzuki said, "That, of course, is also my opinion." But between the two men was the question of whether the army might still be unwilling to share this opinion. Suzuki turned to Sakomizu. "See if you can get Ikeda on the telephone."

The man of whom he spoke was Lieutenant General Sumihisa Ikeda, chief of the cabinet planning bureau, who had returned from Manchuria only three weeks earlier. Though he was asleep, he aroused himself and came to the telephone quickly when he learned that the prime minister was on the line.

Suzuki, after informing him of the Russian war declaration, asked, "Is the Kwantung Army (Japan's army in China) capable of repulsing a Russian advance?"

Ikeda could offer him no reassurance. "The Kwantung Army," he said, "is hopeless. Within two weeks, the Russians will occupy Changchu."

Changchu was Japan's major stronghold in central Manchuria. Suzuki said, "If the Kwantung Army is that weak, then there can be no doubt that the game is up."

Ikeda said, "The greater the delay in making the final decision, the worse the situation will be for us."

Suzuki could wish that all the generals in Japan shared this one's feelings about the matter. When he hung up, Foreign Minister Togo was impatiently pacing the floor.

Without bothering to ask what General Ikeda had advised, Togo said, "It seems to me the Supreme Council (for the Direction of the War) must meet immediately."

The prime minister nodded in agreement. He had scheduled a

meeting of the Supreme Council for the previous day, but had been unable to get all the members together. He turned to Sakomizu. "Don't give up until you reach every one of them. Tell them ten-thirty at my official residence."

Togo said, "I'll go myself, right now, to see Admiral Yonai (the navy minister). I feel confident that he, at least, will be in agreement with us."

After Togo's departure, the old prime minister looked at his young chief cabinet secretary and said, "Your worst fears have come to pass." Then, as if anticipating the question in Sakomizu's mind, which was the question of whether the prime minister and the whole cabinet had a duty to resign in a situation like this, he added: "I intend to let our present cabinet take the responsibility of seeing the country through the termination of the war."

So saying, he called for his hat and his automobile, then left home to go directly to the Imperial Palace.

AUGUST 9,
7:30 A.M.

E M P E R O R Hirohito was not surprised at the prime minister's request for a 7:30 A.M. audience. Since his chamberlains had been instructed to wake him, at any hour of the night when an important dispatch arrived, he was not even surprised at the news the prime minister brought. But he listened patiently while Baron Suzuki informed him that Russia was now at war with Japan, and outlined all the details available up to the moment. Though no cable had yet arrived from Ambassador Sato, confirming the war declaration by Russia, there could be no doubt that a state of war now existed. Russian armies had already moved across the border from Siberia to Manchuria. And in the opinion of the cabinet's planning bureau chief, the Kwantung Army would not be able to contain them, even for a short time.

After thus describing the situation, Suzuki paused and looked directly at the Emperor. "I have made up my mind," Suzuki said, "that we must now accept the Potsdam demands. We can wait no longer."

The Emperor, who was hoping Suzuki would say exactly this, nodded eagerly. "I am in complete accord with you," he said.

"But I am an old man," Suzuki said, "and I must frankly confess to you that I am not confident of my ability to bring this about. I do not know whether I shall be able to secure the unanimous agreement of the Supreme War Council and the cabinet. I know you are aware, Your Majesty, of the army's reluctance to seek peace at this time."

The Emperor nodded.

Suzuki hesitated. He was about to ask of the Emperor an unprecedented favor. He wondered if he dared do anything so unorthodox. Then he decided he must plunge ahead. There was no choice. "This morning, the Supreme Council meets," he said, "and this afternoon, the cabinet. In case I am unable to secure their agreement, I wish to request Your Majesty's assistance."

The Emperor looked surprised, but before he had a chance to answer, Suzuki resumed.

"Though I know that such a drastic measure is against all custom and usage," he said. "I beg you to grant me, please, your special help."

Emperor Hirohito gazed fondly at this old man who had long been one of his dearest friends and most loyal subjects. In 1936, after Suzuki was almost assassinated by army extremists, the Emperor had sent him flowers every day he was in the hospital, and after his recovery, had made him a baron and appointed him to the Privy Council. There was no question in the Emperor's mind about how he would answer the prime minister's extraordinary request.

"Of course I'll give you my assistance," he said.

Suzuki smiled and bowed gratefully. His hopes began to rise. He now had in mind a plan of action.

AUGUST 9,
10 A.M.

WHEN General Seizo Arisue awoke from a fitful night's sleep on a narrow cot at the army transportation depot in the port of Ujina, near Hiroshima, his mind was filled with images of the horrors he had seen the day before. The dead bodies, mangled and twisted; horse cadavers with feet in the air; bandaged adults moaning and children screaming in pain. He had gone on a tour of the city with Dr. Yoshio Nishina after the famous physicist arrived, and had listened to a scientific explanation of what had happened here. Nishina had pointed out a square piece of wood which was burned red on one side, but was unscathed on the other. "This could have been done only by an atomic bomb," Nishina insisted. Arisue was not a scientist. Though he sometimes had to deal with scientific matters as chief of Army Intelligence, he did not fully understand Dr. Nishina's observations as they traveled through the desolate city. Nor did he understand Dr. Nishina's warning that he would lose the white corpuscles in his blood if he remained long at the scene of the blast. He took a less pessimistic view of what had happened than did Dr. Nishina. As a military man, Arisue had to concern himself first with the question of countermeasures, and on that score he was fairly well satisfied.

After a meager breakfast (since the army was feeding refugees from its own reserves, an acute food shortage was in prospect), Arisue prepared for a meeting he had scheduled at 11 A.M. with Dr. Nishina and with army and navy experts. Then he turned on the radio to listen to the news. What he heard was an even more wrenching shock to him than the sight of Hiroshima in ruins. Russia had declared war on Japan. Suddenly, Arisue's plans changed. As chief of Intelligence, he was aware of, and had even taken part in the preparations for Japan's attempt to mediate peace through Russia. Though he had not actually expected that effort to succeed, neither had he expected it to fail so dramatically and disastrously. As a result of this development, he would have to get back to Tokyo immediately. But first he would drive to the army headquarters in the northwest suburbs of Hiroshima to talk to Marshal Shunroku Hata, commander of the Second Army.

Marshal Hata, one of Japan's two field marshals, was the man in charge of defending the island of Kyushu, just south of the main island of Honshu, in the anticipated climactic battle for the homeland. He had been out of town, fortunately, when the Hiroshima blast took place. He had hurried back to find his headquarters, on the outskirts of the city, battered but not shattered. When Arisue arrived, he was in his office. All the windows were broken. The plaster had fallen from the walls. The room was a shambles. But Marshal Hata, erect and straight-faced, greeted him almost as if nothing had happened. His uniform, though perhaps slightly threadbare, was well pressed. His little mustache was precisely trimmed. The hair still remaining on his semi-bald head was clipped short in the prescribed military style. He invited General Arisue to sit on a chair which had survived the blast.

"I'm sure you've heard the news about Russia," Arisue began.

Marshal Hata nodded.

"In view of it," Arisue said, "I fear I had better return to Tokyo without delay. Although I realize the importance of the investigation here, it seems to me that Russia's entry into the war is a far more serious matter than this new bomb the Americans have developed. What is your opinion, sir?"

Hata assured him he need not give way to despair about the new-type bomb. "I think things will fall into place," he said.

Under the circumstances, this was a most optimistic remark. Arisue waited for an enlargement of it.

"As I reported to Tokyo yesterday, it will be possible to defend against the bomb," Hata continued. "No doubt you noticed that people wearing white clothing suffered only light burns. And the same was true of people who were in shelters. Since the bomb exploded in the air, it did little damage to anything which was more than a foot underground. People don't seem to realize that it was fire which destroyed the city. What time did the bomb explode? About 8 A.M., just when most households had lit fires to prepare breakfast. I think that is what accounted for the destruction of Hiroshima, and for most of the burns people suffered. As a result of the blast, the cooking fires ignited the houses."

Arisue could not help being heartened as he listened to Hata. The marshal was expressing a point of view not unlike his own. He himself had said, in his first report to Tokyo, that countermeasures were possible. This honored and revered general in front of him was saying the same thing and more, in even stronger terms. It was gratifying to have one's opinion verified by a field marshal. When they were through talking, General Arisue felt reassured about the atomic bomb. He felt no less disturbed, however, about Russia's entry into the war.

"When are you leaving for Tokyo?" Marshal Hata asked.

"As soon as I can take off."

"Be careful of enemy planes."

It was a warning Arisue did not need. He was aware of the humiliating fact there were so many American planes over Japan a Japanese plane could fly only by sneaking through the sky.

AUGUST 9,
10:15 A.M.

WHEN General Yoshijiro Umezu, the army's chief of staff, and Admiral Soemu Toyoda, the navy's chief of staff, arrived at the prime minister's official residence for the 10:30 A.M. meeting of the Supreme Council for the Direction of the War, they found Chief Cabinet Secretary Hisatsune Sakomizu waiting with a document for each of them to sign. It was a petition which would permit the prime minister to summon the Supreme War Council, at an unspecified time, for a conference in the presence of the Emperor. According to Japanese governmental custom, which had the force of law, it was not permissible to convoke the Supreme War Council for an imperial conference without first obtaining the written agreement of the two military chiefs of staff as well as the prime minister.

"It's only a formality," Sakomizu said as he placed the letter of petition on the table in front of the two men.

If it was only a formality, it was not a thoughtless one. When Prime Minister Suzuki returned earlier that morning from the Imperial Palace, he had in mind a method of breaking the deadlock which was certain to develop, both in the cabinet and in the Supreme War Council, when he proposed an immediate acceptance of the Potsdam terms. His major concern was a deadlock in the Supreme War Council, inasmuch as this was the more powerful of the two bodies, being comprised, as it was, of the nation's four top military officials plus the prime minister and the foreign minister. Suzuki's plan involved help from the Emperor, who had expressed his willingness to help, but the plan could work only if there were an imperial conference at which the Emperor would be present. And it would be unheard of to call such a conference before the deadlock in the government had been broken. The purpose of an imperial conference was not to discuss undecided matters in front of His Majesty, but to inform him of matters upon which the members of the government had already decided. If a government could not come to unanimous agreement about a policy, it was time for that government to resign. But Suzuki was determined not to resign. He had resolved that his would be the last wartime cabinet. And he was prepared to adopt extraordinary measures to fulfill his resolve. Sakomizu, therefore, had the difficult task of persuading General Umezu and Admiral Toyoda, two men of independent mind, that they should sign a document which, according to governmental custom, ought not even be presented to them until some very difficult matters had been settled.

After reading the document, both Umezu and Toyoda had the same question. Why was he bringing it to them now?

"It seems likely," Sakomizu said, "that whatever you gentlemen decide during the Supreme Council meeting this morning, the cabinet will ratify this afternoon. In that case, it will be important to call an imperial conference without delay, which we can do only if we have your signatures. Since the circumstances are so extraordinary, I think it essential that we have this petition ready the moment we need it." He paused to watch their reactions. They appeared hesitant. Reluctantly, because it seemed necessary, he added, "I shall ask for your final agreements, of course, before I present the petition to His Majesty."

Umezu said, "Why don't you wait, then, and get our signatures just before you present the petition?"

"It may be difficult," Sakomizu said, "to locate you at that moment. You're both busy men. And even if you are available, I can't get your signatures by telephone. I would have to send someone to contact you in person, which would take time. Meanwhile there is always the possibility of an air raid or some other circumstance which could prevent us from reaching you. On the other hand, if you give me your signatures now, we can easily get your final agreement by telephone."

Though Umezu and Toyoda had raised a natural objection, neither man felt any strong reluctance to sign the document. There could be no imperial conference unless the Supreme Council and the cabinet arrived at a unanimous policy decision. It would be unthinkable to trouble the Emperor by exposing him to problems of state before they were settled. To do so would be to involve him in responsibility for the everyday affairs of state, which were, properly speaking, beneath him. On the other hand, if the Supreme Council and the cabinet did arrive at important decisions today, especially in the matter of how to cope with the Russian war declaration, there would be no reason to prevent an imperial conference. On the contrary, as Sakomizu insisted, there would be every reason to hasten it.

Admiral Toyoda, however, still looked skeptical. "You promise to get our final agreements before you use our signatures?"

It was a difficult moment for Sakomizu, who was accustomed to dealing candidly with people. Yet he did not feel any guilt about the equivocal position in which he found himself. Looking straight at General Umezu and Admiral Toyoda, he said solemnly, "I promise"

At such times, he decided, the fate of the nation was more important than either his sensitivities or theirs.

AUGUST 9,
10:30 A.M.

T H E L A R G E , concrete-walled, cellar-like air raid shelter at the prime minister's official residence was still fairly cool when the six members of the Supreme Council for the Direction of the War sat down at the conference table for the most important meeting since the war began. Though the surface atmosphere between them was friendly, the smiles on the faces of these six most powerful men in Japan concealed incipient conflicts between them which were certain to break out as soon as Prime Minister Suzuki took his intended position.

Standing at the head of the table, he began the meeting by making it clear tht he did not regard it as a routine session. "All of us are aware," he said, "of the magnitude of the developments which have overtaken our beleaguered nation in the last three days. The city of Hiroshima has been obliterated by a weapon which one of our own most distinguished scientists has confirmed to be an atomic bomb. We know not when another such bomb will fall on another of our cities. (There was already a rumor in government circles that Tokyo would be hit by a "new-type" bomb on the twelfth.) And in addition to this, we have learned during the night that we now face another overwhelming threat to our very existence—the armies of Soviet Russia. Gentlemen, I submit that in our nation's present condition, we have not the strength to meet these challenges. Taking into account the forces against us, I am convinced that it is no longer possible to continue the war." He stopped long enough to look directly into the faces around the table. "I believe we now have no alternative but to accept the Potsdam Declaration. I would like to hear the opinions of all of you on this subject."

Suzuki was certain to hear their opinions, of course, whether he wanted to hear them or not. His apparently pointless concluding remark was simply an outgrowth of the strategy he had evolved before the meeting, with Foreign Minister Togo and Chief Cabinet Secretary Sakomizu. "Don't bring them to a vote," Sakomizu had earnestly advised. "Let them talk, but don't let them come to any fixed decisions. Make certain the session ends in a fluid status." Suzuki was in full agreement. If his plan were to work, he would have to prevent the council members from making absolute commitments.

Suzuki's opening remarks had been so blunt, so lacking in the niceties and indirection of Japanese speech, that they were greeted by stunned silence. Finally, Admiral Yonai, the navy minister, and the one military man on whose support Suzuki felt he could depend, undertook to get the discussion started. "The matter which Prime Minister Suzuki has raised is an appropriate one," he said. "It is a matter we can no longer avoid. We're not going to accomplish anything here unless we speak out openly. Do we accept the enemy ultimatum unconditionally? Do we propose conditions? If so, we had better discuss them now."

After a short pause, General Umezu, the army chief of staff, said, "We can't yet speak with authority about the atomic bomb. We don't yet know the full story of what happened at Hiroshima. Our investigation is not complete."

Foreign Minister Togo said, "You know the city was hit by a weapon powerful enough to wipe it out. And that other cities may suffer the same fate at any moment. The President of the United States has assured us of that."

It was Admiral Toyoda, the navy chief of staff, who undertook to answer this. "Is it not reasonable to suppose," he said, "that President Truman's statement was intended simply to frighten us into a quick surrender? No nation, not even the United States, could have manufactured, during wartime, enough radioactive material to make the atomic bomb a weapon of widespread use. And even if the Americans did have a large stockpile of such bombs, world opinion would prevent them from using any more against us. Did you see this morning's newspapers? The Vatican has already criticized America for the attack against Hiroshima."

Umezu said, "We have also received a report from Marshal Hata (Field Marshal Shunroku Hata, army commander in Hiroshima) which indicates there are countermeasures against the atomic bomb, or at least methods of protection against it. There is no feeling at the War Ministry that the introduction of this weapon necessitates our surrender. And as for Russia's declaration of war against us, we don't yet know what it may mean in military terms. We haven't received any reliable information about possible Russian offensives."

Though Umezu seemed to be suggesting that there was still time to wait and see what might happen, no one took him up on the suggestion and he did not press it.

Admiral Yonai, who knew the minds of the other military men in the room, decided it would be pointless to get bogged down in an argument about the seriousness of the atomic bomb and the Russian war declaration. Everyone at this table knew how catastrophic they were. It was time to discuss the paramount question he had tried to introduce a few minutes earlier.

"I'm certain we agree on one thing," he said. "We all have a sincere desire to seek peace. The question to which we must address ourselves, therefore, is whether we should accept the Potsdam Declaration as it stands, or whether we should try to negotiate with the Allies in an effort to gain more favorable terms. There is, as we all know, one condition on which we must insist. Our national polity (political structure) and our Imperial system must not be destroyed. We are unanimous on that question, are we not?"

Everyone in the room nodded quickly. Whatever else might happen, the Emperor must remain on the throne of Japan and the continuation of his reign must be assured.

"Then the next thing to decide," Yonai continued, "is whether to insist on any other conditions. If so, what will they be? What are our attitudes on the question of disarming our forces, on the question of punishing war criminals, on the question of an Allied military occupation of Japan? The Potsdam Declaration threatens all these measures against us. Do we accept them? We can't just ignore them."

Foreign Minister Togo, though he recognized the truth in what Yonai had just said, wished, nevertheless, that such issues could be ignored for the moment because he felt there was time to discuss only the overriding question of immediate surrender. "We must act without delay," he insisted. "Japan's position becomes weaker with each passing hour. The only condition on which we can and must insist is the safeguarding of the Imperial family and the perpetuation of our Imperial system."

General Korechika Anami, the war minister, who had been listening until now, appeared ready to speak. Since he was perhaps the most powerful single individual in the room and in the country, everyone turned toward him. "It is my feeling and it is the army's feeling," he said, "that this proud nation must not yield so abjectly to its enemies. I, too, want peace. We all want peace. But if we are to make terms with the Allied nations, it must be on the basis of four conditions. Needless to say, the first is the guarantee of our national polity and the assurance that His Majesty will remain on the throne of Japan. But we must also insist, secondly, that our military forces be allowed to disarm and demobilize themselves; thirdly, that there be no allied occupation of Japan; and fourthly, that all war criminals will be prosecuted by the Japanese government."

By the time General Anami finished speaking, passion had arisen on the faces of both Prime Minister Suzuki and Foreign Minster Togo.

"You can't put in that many conditions!" Suzuki exclaimed heatedly. "You're deliberately trying to break up our efforts to negotiate."

Anami shook his head calmly. "I'm sorry you look upon it that way,' he said. "I simply believe that these are essential considerations."

Togo's astonishment was such that it took him a few moments to get hold of himself. The conditions just enumerated were so unrealistic and impossible of attainment he could scarcely believe that a man as sensible as Anami had uttered them. The explanation was quick in coming. General Umezu, having listened to Anami, nodded in agreement.

"I concur," he said, "in the war minister's opinion."

It was now evident to Togo that he had to contend, not just with these two men, but with the entire army. General Anami had stated not merely his own position, but a position decided upon, perhaps this very morning, by the General Staff.

Togo's consternation was increased when the navy chief of staff, Admiral Toyoda, said, "I, too, agree with General Anami."

Togo glanced toward Admiral Yonai, who could only shrug. Though he was the navy minister, he was not in control of the navy general staff. Togo could scarcely contain his exasperation. "It is now too late for such conditions," he said. "Japan's present situation is so precarious that if we were to make stipulations of the kind the war minister has offered the Allies would probably refuse to negotiate at all."

General Anami remained unruffled. "You speak of Japan as if we were a defeated nation," he said. "I must point out that we have not yet surrendered. We have not yet lost this war. And if the enemy attacks our home islands, he will do so to his sorrow."

"Do you think we have the strength to repulse him?" Togo asked.

Umezu answered him. "If we are fortunate, we might be able to drive the enemy back into the sea, though one cannot predict with any certainty what will happen in a battle. But even if the enemy does succeed in establishing beacheads, I am confident we can inflict prohibitive losses upon him."

Togo said, "This would be, however, only the first assault, and even so you admit that some of the attackers might be able to land. Then what about the second assault? By the time that comes, we shall have sacrificed most of our aircraft and munitions trying to stem the first assault. With nothing to replace our armaments, we'll be absolutely defenseless. At that point, we shall be unable to bargain even for the preservation of the Imperial House."

General Anami said, "We don't ask you to wait until then. We are all agreed that you should bargain now, but on the basis of those four important conditions."

"You are asking us to accept, not peace, but surrender," Umezu said. "Surely you realize that for Japanese warriors surrender is not permissible. The penal codes of both the army and navy provide heavy penalties for men who surrender. And even without penalties, our very traditions prohibit it. You know what we expect of our soldiers. They must fight until their weapons are useless, and even when they can no longer fight, the only honorable course for them is suicide. I doubt very much that our men at the battlefronts, all trained in this tradition, would meekly obey an order from us to surrender. Even if we do accept the Allied terms, we must accept them in the spirit of negotiations, in an effort to stop the war, not as an admission of surrender. To prevent incidents between their troops and ours, we must also have the right to make the proper arrangements. And we must be allowed to demobilize our men. We should insist on designating the time and place where the terms will be carried out in each area, and we must insist on the right to take whatever other precautions might be necessary to prevent outbreaks of violence."

Anami said, "We cannot surrender our sovereignty. It would be difficult for the people of Japan to tolerate an occupation of our country. We must do everything possible to prevent it."

"And if we cannot prevent it completely," Umezu said, "we should at least try to limit it to a few specific areas, outside Tokyo, with the fewest possible troops and for the shortest possible time."

The military men were arguing desperately now and sometimes repetitiously, but always with such determination that Togo was unable to shake them. As the second hour of the meeting passed, the air in the shelter, cool enough when they entered, became increasingly hot, stuffy, and also smoky from the cigars of the prime minister, the cigarets of the others. Umezu and Anami, with help from Toyoda, were now going through the Potsdam demands point by point, enumerating the difficulties of accepting them, and justifying their insistence on the four conditions. Finally, Admiral Yonai, the one military man who took a different view, decided no progress could possibly result from continuing the discussion.

"I would be happy to support the four conditions you present," he said to Anami. "They would be very advantageous to us if we could impose them. But unfortunately, we cannot. We are powerless. It is too late to take the position you gentlemen are taking. We have to accept the terms we can get. We have to accept the foreign minister's recommendations."

The effect of Admiral Yonai's remarks upon his military colleagues was not destined to be registered. Before anyone could answer him, one of Prime Minister Suzuki's aides burst into the room. As soon as he caught his breath he imparted to them a piece of appalling information which had just arrived.

"Nagasaki," he said, "has just been hit by a second atomic bomb."

The impact of this news brought an end to the deliberations of the Supreme War Council. It did not, however, alter the position of Generals Anami and Umezu, plus their naval ally, Admiral Toyoda, that peace should be sought only on the basis of their four conditions. The council was obviously deadlocked, three to three. Prime Minister Suzuki arose, but not to call for a vote. He simply adjourned the meeting. Since he had expected a deadlock, he was not unhappy about it. And he was rather pleased about one of the morning's developments. The two factions in the council had finally, for the first time, engaged in an open exchange of views on the subject of surrender. Perhaps some progress would come of it. But as he emerged from the underground shelter into the midday sunlight of Tokyo, he realized how little time he had to make his plan work. Hiroshima. Nagasaki. And what about the rumor that Tokyo was to be bombed on the twelfth? The rumor had reportedly come from an American pilot who was shot down and captured. One could no longer discount it. If there was any truth to it, Suzuki had only three days left. Would it be enough?

AUGUST 9,
7:30 P.M.

IN THE GARDEN of his Setagaya home on the southwestern outskirts of Tokyo, General Hideki Tojo, Retired, walked among the trees and shrubs he had planted when he had the house built during his most triumphant days as prime minster in 1942. It was a comfortable but not ostentatious Japanese-style house on the apex of a hill from which, on a clear day like today, one could see Japan's sacred Mount Fujiyama, about 50 miles farther to the southwest. Though the hill was only a modest slope, the people in the area called it "Pine Mountain" because, until recently, it had been crowned by thirteen huge old pine trees, all on the Tojo property. Only one of the pine trees remained now, Tojo having donated ten to the government to be used in the manufacture of a ship, and two more having been destroyed in the great incendiary air raid of May 25, which had also burned one corner of Tojo's house, and had eliminated a detached building in the rear that he used as a study. Despite his loss, Tojo felt fortunate when that raid ended and its fires subsided. He still had most of his house and garden. All but a few of the other houses in the neighborhood had been wiped out completely.

At the age of 61, Tojo looked lean and fit as he strolled among his surviving trees, mostly young maples, limes, plums, and persimmons. He was deeply tanned from working outside every day, trimming these trees and the hedges, tending flower beds, and more important, cultivating a large vegetable patch which provided a significant portion of his family's food.

Of Tojo's seven children, four, all daughters, were still at home. His two oldest sons were long since married with families of their own. His youngest son, Toshio, now a student at the military academy, expected to graduate in September. The oldest of the daughters, Mitsue, was 28; the youngest, Kimie, was just 12. Yukie, 16, had been drafted into industry and worked at a radar factory in the town of Kamata, an hour's streetcar ride from Setagaya. Makie, 22, was married to a handsome young Imperial Guards officer, Major Hidemasa Koga, whom Tojo had encouraged to court her three years earlier. Koga had brought his wife back to her father's house in June of this year because, with the country's military and political situation becoming more critical, he had decided to take a billet at the Imperial Guards headquarters just outside the Imperial Palace. Koga was a dedicated militarist, and like his father-in-law, he suspected the Suzuki government of plotting surrender. Tojo himself was so concerned about this possibility that he had gone to General Anami, the war minister, in late June and advised him to be careful because the cabinet of which he was a member was "questionable."

Aside from a few instances like this when he offered advice, either at the Imperial Palace or the War Ministry, Tojo was no longer active politically. He spent most of his time with his family. On nice days he gardened; on rainy days he read. He saw few of his old friends and associates, although some of them came occasionally to talk to him. Colonel Susumu Nishiura, one of his private secretaries when the war began, and now stationed in China with the Kwantung Army, had visited him in April during a short trip home and had brought him a rare gift—a whole carton of cigarets. Another of his former secretaries, Colonel Sadao Akamatsu, had been helpful to him since his retirement. After Tojo's resignation as prime minister in July, 1944, his popularity at the War Ministry had fallen so sharply he couldn't even get the use of an army car when he needed one. Akamatsu, angered at this, had spoken about it to General Anami. Thereafter, Tojo had no difficulty getting a car. Akamatsu was also in China now, stationed at Shanghai.

While Tojo worked or sat or strolled in his garden as he was doing at the moment, his mind, of course, dwelled very much upon the war. Though he was unhappy with its progress, he did not yet think it was lost. Much would depend upon the decisive battle for the homeland. This new American bomb, while it might be a factor, would not be decisive. Japan could still win if the government would take resolute action. He could not deny, however, that the country had reached a period of unparalleled crisis and that America had proven itself a fantastically powerful foe. He wished he had known more about America when the war began. He had hoped the Americans would not have much stomach for fighting, and as the early Japanese victories mounted, he had begun to think it might be so. For a time he had felt confident that if Japan could take all of southern Asia it would then be so rich in resources it could fight off any American attack until finally America would see the folly of continuing the war and would offer to negotiate. The confidence which he developed early in the war had depended on the assumption that Japan would have enough ships to carry those raw materials home from the conquered lands, that Japanese shipping losses could be held to less than 800,000 tons per year. But the shipping losses to American submarines and planes had actually averaged almost two-and-a-half million tons a year, virtually eliminating the merchant fleet.

While Tojo was still puttering and thinking in the garden, his wife put her head out the door of the house to say he had a phone call. It was a friend at the War Ministry. When he hung up, she could see he was concerned about something.

"What is it?" she asked.

"This morning," he said, "the Americans dropped another of their new-type bombs."

"Where?"

"Nagasaki."

"And . . . ?"

It was just like Hiroshima, I guess." Though Tojo did not yet know the details of the Hiroshima blast, his connections at the War Ministry were still good enough so that he had some notion of the disaster there. "And there's a rumor at the ministry," he added, "that the next one of those bombs will be dropped on Tokyo."

He studied his wife carefully. She showed no reaction.

"You and the girls have got to go to the country," he said. He had found a place not far from Tokyo where they would be welcome.

Mrs. Tojo shook her head firmly. "Not unless you go," she said.

"But I can't go. The Emperor may call on me at any time."

It was a conversation they had repeated on several occasions. It always ended the same way. Mrs. Tojo refused to leave her husband here alone.

"I think it may be true," he said, "that they will drop one of those bombs on Tokyo next. They say the information came from an American pilot who was shot down."

His wife seemed to pay no attention. "It's after eight o'clock," she said. "Time to go meet Yukie."

General Tojo looked at her for a moment but said no more. It was pointless to argue with her. She was a strong-willed woman. He took his hat and left the house, walking down the slope toward the Tamaden streetcar stop about ten minutes away. He didn't want his daughter walking home alone in the dark.

It was not yet quite dark when Yukie jumped down from the streetcar and ran over to him. At the age of sixteen, she was already a beautiful girl, even in the peasant pantaloons and coarse blouse of the national uniform she wore. Despite her long workday at the radar factory in Kamata, she looked fresh.

As she approached her father, she smiled and gave him a series of quick bows, which he returned. Then they walked in silence along the partially burned-out street toward home.

AUGUST 9,
9:30 P.M.

D E B A T E among the fifteen members of the prime minister's cabinet had become almost desultory, not only because the air in the meeting room on the second floor of the prime minister's official residence remained hot and humid even this late in the evening, but also because the cabinet had been in session (except for an hour's recess) since 2:30 P.M., and seven hours later, it seemed that everything which might be said had been said. Perspiration stood out on every face in the room, and on most of the faces, worry, impatience, or perplexity were also evident. The deliberation had been so fruitless thus far that no one seemed to know what to do next.

Foreign Minister Shigenori Togo had begun by outlining and advocating the position he championed during the morning meeting of the Supreme War Council. War Minister General Korechika Anami had then repeated basically the same position which he, General Umezu, and Admiral Toyoda had upheld that morning. (Umezu and Toyoda, the army and navy chiefs of staff, were not present at the cabinet meeting since they were not members.) After Anami spoke, Admiral Mitsumasa Yonai, the navy minister, had risen to disagree with the apparently unshakeable attitude of his military colleagues that Japan must either secure favorable peace terms or continue the war.

"There is absolutely no chance of victory," Yonai had insisted. "The foreign minister has stated the situation correctly. If the Allied nations will agree that our national polity be preserved and our imperial system retained, we should then accept the terms of the Potsdam Declaration immediately."

To this, Anami had responded hotly. "There is still an excellent chance of victory," he said. "The army is confident of its ability to inflict prohibitive losses on the enemy in the decisive battle for our homeland. If we put our total effort into this battle, we may be very pleasantly surprised at the outcome."

Yonai said, just as heatedly, "Our total effort is not enough. We have reached the end of our resources, both physical and spiritual. It is out of the question to continue."

For General Anami, Admiral Yonai was sometimes difficult to understand. The admiral was, after all, a military man, from a Samurai family. His navy record was splendid. He was intelligent, straightforward, and a most persuasive leader. He was a gentleman in the finest Samurai tradition, yet Anami could not escape the conclusion that he was timid because he had no stomach for seeing the war through to the end. Though this might be explainable to others on the basis of Yonai's opposition to the war from the beginning, such an explanation would not be enough to satisfy a man like Anami. Yonai was a warrior and his country was at war. The Samurai tradition demanded of him a total commitment which Anami felt he lacked. "There may be no certainty of victory," Anami conceded, "but it is also true that we are not yet defeated. And if we show ourselves determined to fight, we might still grasp life out of death."

Prime Minister Suzuki, listening to the two men debate, felt increasingly frustrated. Just as much a Samurai warrior as either of them, he well understood Yonai's position since it was also his own. There was no other sensible course but to end the war. Yet he could sympathize with Anami's apparent determination to fight on, even though he did not share it. Surrender had no place in the Samurai code. Surrender was, however, an absolute necessity for the nation. He had hoped Anami might recognize this fact and adjust himself to it, as he and Yonai had done. He expected from Anami a more reasonable attitude than he might have expected from some of the other men at the War Ministry. When he asked for Anami as his war minister, he had said to an associate, "Anami is the only high-minded military man I feel I can trust." It appeared now, however, that Anami might give him insurmountable trouble. Clearing his throat to get attention, Suzuki had interrupted the debate between his war and navy ministers to call on the other thirteen members of his cabinet for their views. He hoped that from listening to them he might get some idea as to how they would divide if the surrender issue came to a vote.

Home Minister Genki Abe, when called upon, had arisen to say that the morale of the people had declined greatly during the recent months of air raids and ever-shorter rations, but that the people still did not realize Japan was near defeat because from the armed forces the only news they ever heard was news of victories. If the Potsdam terms were accepted unconditionally, he insisted, an irate public might run amuck and begin assassinating cabinet ministers. Since Abe was in charge of the police, who would have to prevent such disorders if they were to be prevented, his appalling prediction could not be overlooked. Agriculture and Commerce Minister Tadaatsu Ishiguro followed Abe with another prediction—that the rice harvest this year would be the most meager in fifteen years. Transportation Minister Naoto Kobiyama said the American Navy made it impossible to count on Korea or Manchuria as continuing sources of food and supplies. And Munitions Minister Sadajiro Toyoda spoke of the pitiful conditions of the nation's industry, the closed factories, the lack of raw materials and parts, the rising absenteeism as workers fled from the bomb-torn cities.

Listening to his ministers, Suzuki had tried to gauge their attitudes; when they were finished, he felt that if the surrender issue came to a vote, he would have perhaps a two-to-one majority on his side. A majority was not enough, however. He would have to have unanimity. He had therefore recessed the cabinet for an hour, rather than adjourning it, and during that hour, from 5:30 to 6:30, he had gone with Foreign Minister Togo to the Imperial Palace, where they discussed in some detail with the Emperor the assistance they hoped he would give them. Having reconvened the cabinet at 6:30 P.M., Suzuki was simply biding his time now, listening to the repetitive debate which dragged along heavily as the hours passed. Soon, he decided, everyone would be sufficiently exhausted and it would be time for adjournment.

Education Minister Kozo Ota was speaking but no one seemed to be paying much attention as he reviewed the previous arguments, pointing out what everyone knew, that the cabinet was hopelessly deadlocked. Ota himself, Suzuki guessed, would divide on the side of Anami in case of a vote. Ota had been recommended for his cabinet post by Baron Kiichiro Hiranuma, who was now the president of the Privy Council, and a strong advocate of a fight-to-the-finish policy. Suzuki had included Ota in the cabinet as a concession to the most belligerent segment of the establishment. As Ota continued talking, he began to gain more attention, then gradually everyone was listening to him because he was speaking now, not about the question of surrender, but about the performance of the Suzuki cabinet since its inception. It was evident that he was not happy with the cabinet's accomplishments, either in the attempt to turn the tide of war, or in the attempt to negotiate peace through Russia.

Suzuki, who ordinarily sat back in his chair during cabinet sessions, sometimes even appearing to snooze through the more tedious deliberations, sat forward and listened to his education minister with rising concern. What was the man getting ready to say? There was only one conclusion toward which he could be driving, and unbelievable as it seemed, here he was, on the point of giving voice to it.

". . . this is a serious matter," Ota was saying. "I insist, the cabinet should tender its resignation because it has failed in its responsibility."

Suzuki put his hand down hard on the table and came immediately to his feet. "I am fully aware of our responsibility," he said, "but this is no time for the cabinet to argue responsibility. We must rather take steps to remedy the situation at hand."

Suzuki's quick, aggressive reaction had been necessary because it was true that under normal circumstances a cabinet which had suffered so many setbacks and which was now so hopelessly deadlocked would be expected to resign. Having resolved, however, to hold office until he managed to terminate the war, Suzuki was horrified at the possibility that this sudden, unexpected motion by a minor cabinet member might start a chain reaction which would destroy his government and shatter his peace plan.

There was no lack of attention now among the men seated at the big round table. The fate of the cabinet had been put in doubt and everyone knew it. Though the prime minister's statement had been quick and forthright, it might not be enough to save him. The outcome depended on the attitude of the war minister who was, in fact though not in title, the most powerful man in the room. Due to the Japanese government practice (firmly imposed by the army after the frightening military coup attempt of 1936) of restricting the post of war minister to generals on active duty, the army had, in effect, a veto power over any cabinet. If Anami wanted the cabinet to fall, he didn't have to bring the matter to a vote. He had only to tender his own resignation and make sure the army general staff refused to send Suzuki a new war minister. Since General Umezu, the chief of staff, was one of Anami's closest friends, and since Anami was regarded with personal reverence throughout the army, no one doubted that if he chose to do so, he could destroy the Suzuki cabinet at any time, and probably form a new, military cabinet with himself as prime minister. Was it possible that education Minister Ota's statement had been inspired by Anami as a first move toward taking over the government and imposing the war-continuation policy he seemed to be advocating? Ota was considered by many to be in sympathy with the army viewpont. Everyone turned toward Anami, realizing what it would mean if he agreed with Ota.

General Anami looked around the table and saw the expectancy on the faces of his cabinet colleagues. Many of them, it appeared, actually did expect him to resign. After glancing at Ota, who had raised the question, he turned deliberatedly toward the prime minister.

"I do not agree," Anami said, "with the opinion of Mr. Ota. In my opinion, the cabinet should not resign."

A faint smile crossed the face of the elderly prime minister. After a few more minutes of pointless debate about surrender, he adjourned the cabinet meeting. Though it was now 10 P.M. and he was exceedingly weary (having awakened at 4 A.M. to learn about Russia's war declaration), his day's work was not yet done. From the cabinet room he went directly to the office of Chief Cabinet Secretary Sakomizu, on the third floor of the building.

I think it is about time," he said, "to summon the members of the Supreme War Council."

He then walked downstairs to where Foreign Minister Togo was waiting for him. Together they left once more for the Imperial Palace.

AUGUST 9,
11 P.M.

C H I E F Cabinet Secretary Sakomizu, having arranged for the Imperial Palace to summon the members of the Supreme War Council for an imperial conference this very night at 11:30, sat in his office with some trepidation awaiting the reactions of the army and navy chiefs of staff when they received their unexpected notifications. The conference was to be held on the strength of the petition signed that morning by Prime Minister Suzuki, Army Chief of Staff General Umezu, and Navy Chief of Staff Admiral Toyoda. But the signatures of the latter two had been obtained by Sakomizu in exchange for a promise that he would get final approval of both men before actually scheduling an imperial conference. Sakomizu, acting for Prime Minister Suzuki, had, in fact, used the two men's signatures without securing their final approval.

Reaction from the military was quick. An officer in the Military Affairs Bureau at the War Ministry telephoned Sakomizu's office in a state of high agitation.

"General Umezu has just received a summons to an imperial conference of the Supreme War Council tonight," the officer said. "There must be some mistake."

"There is no mistake," Sakomizu said. "I have a copy of the order on my desk."

"But General Umezu says he has not given his approval for an imperial conference. How can there be an imperial conference when the council hasn't yet decided on a policy." The invariable purpose of imperial conferences was not to discuss issues but to inform the Emperor of policy decisions.

"General Umezu's signature," Sakomizu said, "is on the petition."

Unable to contend with this flat statement of fact, the army officer finally hung up, after which Sakomizu received a similar call from an officer at the Navy Ministry. Sakomizu had just completed this call, and was congratulating himself for having so quickly pacified both the army and the navy, when he heard a commotion in his outer office. It included the heavy sound of booted footsteps, the metallic sound of sword scabbards banging against furniture, and a jumble of loud voices.

He heard someone shout, "Where is Sakomizu!"

Before his secretary had time to answer, his office door burst open. Lieutenant General Masao Yoshizumi, chief of the army's powerful Military Affairs Bureau, rushed into the room, followed by several younger officers, all wearing their Samurai swords.

In Sakomizu's mind, terrifying images arose of another day, February 26, 1936, when young, extremist army officers in rebellion had stormed this same building to find and assassinate his father-in-law, Admiral Keisuke Okada, who was at that time the prime minister. Sakomizu himself had faced those officers, and by identifying another man they had killed as his father-in-law, had helped save Admiral Okada's life. The officers confronting him now seemed to Sakomizu no less agitated than those with whom he had been forced to contend nine years earlier.

General Yoshizumi, a balding, bespectacled man whose normal expression was rather kindly but who seemed now to be in a fury, rushed over to the chief cabinet secretary's desk. "Sakomizu, what is this all about?"

Sakomizu shrugged. "I don't know what you mean."

"You do know what I mean. By whose authority was this Supreme War Council meeting called tonight?"

"By the authority of the Emperor."

"But who signed the petition?"

"Prime Minister Suzuki, General Umezu, and Admiral Toyoda."

"General Umezu says he did not give his approval to such a meeting. How can the Supreme War Council meet before His Majesty when the members haven't even decided on a policy?"

"General Umezu's signature is on the petition," Sakomizu said. Though he tried to keep his voice firm, his fear was increasing by the moment as the younger officers with General Yoshizumi crowded around the desk, clanging their swords against it. There was genuine rage in some of these faces, and Sakomizu knew what the young extremists from the War Ministry were capable of doing when they were enraged.

One of them shouted, "We know what you're plotting! You're trying to force us to surrender!"

Another yelled, "Badoglios! You and Suzuki both! You're a pair of Badoglios!"

"What is the purpose of this meeting tonight?" General Yoshizumi demanded.

"It's just a routine meeting to give the Emperor a chance to hear the views of all the members."

One of the young officers shook his fist at Sakomizu. "That's a lie!" he charged. "You're plotting something. You're trying to betray us!"

"Who says the Emperor wants to hear the members' views?" General Yoshizumi pursued. "The purpose of an imperial conference is to inform the Emperor of a government decision, not to make him listen to arguments."

Sakomizu could not suppress a degree of sympathy for Yoshizumi. Under ordinary circumstances he might have adopted the same attitude. But the present circumstances were extraordinary. "The Emperor," Sakomizu said, "has apparently decided he wants to hear the arguments."

"Who told you that?" another officer insisted.

"Whose idea was it?"

"Badoglio! You're all Badoglios! It's a Badoglio cabinet!"

Sakomizu, unarmed and wearing his simple, drab national uniform, felt pitifully small and helpless in the midst of these bemedaled officers with their deadly hardware pressing up against his desk. He wished he dared say to them, "What's more important? The destiny of the country, or saving face for the army?" But he knew he had better say no more than necessary. The longer he continued talking to them, the more furious they became. If just one of them were to lose his temper completely, Sakomizu realized, his head might soon be rolling on the floor. One swing of a Samurai sword would be quite sufficient. Yet he could not get up and run. That would brand him a coward, and in addition would invite quick disaster. There was only one course of action open to him.

Rising to his feet and trying to look unafraid, he waved a piece of paper in his hand. "Gentlemen," he said, "here is the order for the imperial conference. It is now time to go to the Palace."

Turning toward the door, he walked slowly through the group of angry officers. None of them touched him.

AUGUST 9,
11:30 P.M.

ONLY THREE of the eleven men who gathered in the Emperor's personal air raid shelter under the Imperial Palace's Fukiage Gardens at 11:30 P.M. knew what to expect during the imperial conference of the Supreme War Council which was about to begin. Premier Suzuki, Foreign Minister Togo and Chief Cabinet Secretary Sakomizu had planned this extraordinary session carefully, and after the long cabinet meeting adjourned at 10 P.M., Suzuki and Togo had hurried to the Imperial Palace to get the Emperor's approval of their plan. Even Admiral Mitsumasa Yonai, the navy minister, was not privy to the prime minister's precise strategy, though he was an ally on the issue of surrender.

General Korechika Anami, the war minister, and General Yoshijiro Umezu, the army chief of staff, looked forward to the conference with growing suspicion as they walked, on this hot August night, through the dense foliage of the Emperor's garden to the steel door of the shelter. With them was Lieutenant General Masao Yoshizumi, chief of the War Ministry's Military Affairs Bureau, who was to act as the army's secretary at the conference. Yoshizumi, having just come from his confrontation with Sakomizu, felt certain that the peace faction was leading the military faction into a trap. He was still describing Sakomizu's suspicious behavior as the three men walked single file into the shelter, down the narrow stairway, and along an equally narrow hall to the conference room.

When they entered this room, 60 feet underground and into the hill, General Anami turned almost immediately to General Umezu and said, "What is Hiranuma doing here?"

He had not been informed that Baron Kiichiro Hiranuma, a former prime minister and now president of the Privy Council, would attend this meeting of the Supreme War Council. Though the Privy Council did have to ratify the decisions of the government before they became law, it was not proper to involve the privy councilors in the government's deliberations. It was becoming more apparent by the moment that Suzuki had some strategy in mind. Anami, who had to worry about the army's reaction to everything he did, would have liked not to be here tonight, but since the Emperor had summoned, there was no escape, even though the summons may have been procured by trickery.

The conference room was not large—eighteen by thirty feet—and because the shelter's air-conditioning machine functioned poorly, the air was already hot and humid. Narrow tables, covered with checkered damask cloths, had been arranged lengthwise, facing each other. At the head of the room, facing these tables, was another, smaller one for the Emperor. It was covered with gold damask and behind it was a plain screen. The steel beams of the shelter were exposed on the arched ceiling, but the walls had been paneled in dark wood. The air was so damp that drops of water stood out on the lacquered wooden panels. Everyone present was wearing either a full-dress military uniform or formal morning dress. Perspiration already showed on most of the faces.

The three army representatives took their places at the table which would be to the Emperor's left, where they found themselves flanked by the prime minister at one end and Sakomizu at the other. Sakomizu, who was there to act as secretary for the cabinet, sat next to General Yoshizumi, the secretary for the army. Though the sight of Sakomizu again brought anger to Yoshizumi's face, he made no reference, as he took his chair, to their confrontation a half-hour earlier.

Sakomizu himself was more concerned about the receptions he might expect from General Umezu (two chairs away on the other side of Yoshizumi) and Admiral Soemu Toyoda, at the other table. It would be understandable if both were angry at him for using their signatures without permission, yet neither man showed any sign of emotion.

At the head of the table, which would be to the Emperor's right, was Privy Council President Baron Hiranuma. Prime Minister Suzuki had invited him, at Sakomizu's suggestion, because if good fortune prevailed and favorable action was taken here tonight, it would be essential to have it ratified as quickly as possible by the Privy Council. In such case, Hiranuma's understanding and assistance would be most valuable. There was, however, a danger in asking him to attend. Neither Suzuki nor Sakomizu was certain he would embrace their views. An ultranationalist, he had always been a leader of the most belligerent segment of the Japanese aristocracy. It was Suzuki's hope that, however Hiranuma might feel now about surrender, he would favor it before this meeting ended.

Seated along the right-hand table from Hiranuma were Admiral Yonai, Foreign Minister Togo, Admiral Toyoda, Vice Admiral Zenchiro Hoshina, Director of the Bureau of Naval Affairs, who would act as the navy's secretary, and Lieutenant General Sumihisa Ikeda, director of the Cabinet Planning Bureau, who was prepared to answer any questions of detail that might arise.

On the tables in front of each man were copies of three documents—the Potsdam Declaration of the enemy nations, a summary of the Suzuki-Togo-Yonai position on the issue of surrender, and a summary of the Anami-Umezu-Toyoda position. By 11:45, everone in the room had glanced through the documents. Three minutes later, a sound from the corridor indicated that His Majesty was approaching. Most of the men in the room quickly raised their white handkerchiefs once more to their perspiring foreheads.

At 11:50, Emperor Hirohito, escorted by his military aide, General Shigeru Hasunuma, entered the room, prompting everone to arise and bow from the waist. After acknowledging the bows, Hirohito took his place at the small table set up for him. Though neatly dressed in an army uniform, he looked weary. His face was red and a few strands of his bristly black hair hung down, uncharacteristically, on his forehead. He had just finished listening to some final words of advice from his somewhat obtuse privy seal, Marquis Koichi Kido. He had also conferred with the prime minister and the foreign minister three times within the past seventeen hours. He was well briefed on the purpose of the meeting and he was prepared to do what the prime minister had asked him to do, but his heart was heavy because he would be doing something he had been told since childhood an Emperor should never do.

Baron Suzuki, standing at his place near the head of the table to the Emperor's left, opened the meeting by asking Sakomizu to read the Potsdam Declaration. This done, Suzuki arose again and said, "Your Majesty, we are now beginning the second meeting today of the Supreme Council for the Direction of the War. At a lengthy session this morning, we diligently discussed the question of whether our government, under the strain of the present difficult situation, should accept the terms of the declaration you have just heard. After three hours of debate, we could come to no conclusion. Thereupon, the cabinet was called into session this afternoon, but after almost seven hours of debate on the same issue, was unable to reach unanimity. Since a decision cannot be postponed any longer, I have asked permission to discuss the issue before Your Majesty, even though I realize it is unthinkable to take such a step."

Turning slightly toward Admiral Toyoda and General Umezu, whose unauthorized signatures he had used to bring about this conference, he added, "I wish to apologize for requesting Your Majesty to meet with us even though we are unable to inform you of any decision by the government. But I have done so because we have reached an apparently unbreakable deadlock."

After explaining the three-to-three division within the Supreme War Council, and the even more complicated division within the cabinet, where several courses of action had been suggested, Suzuki turned to his foreign minister. "I would like now to have Mr. Togo explain his views on the issue."

Togo stood and, with his quick precision, addressed himself at some length to the subject. "It is both humiliating and terribly difficult for Japan to accept the Potsdam terms," he began. "However, present circumstances compel us." He then proceeded to elucidate those circumstances, including the military situation, the destruction of the cities, the low morale of the people, the paralysis of industry, the danger of a Russian Communist invasion, and the unprecedented, unparalleled threat of the atomic bomb.

"It is with all of these inescapable factors in mind," he concluded, "that I urgently recommend our immediate acceptance of the Potsdam terms. And I wish to point out the danger of making our acceptance contingent upon too many conditions. If we try to impose several conditions, the Allied nations may reject all of them. I strongly suggest, therefore, that we stipulate only one condition—the safety of our Royal House and the perpetuation of our imperial system."

General Anami, listening to Togo, could scarcely contain himself. He was beginning now to grasp Suzuki's apparent strategy. The prime minister seemed to be taking advantage of the fact that it would be impolite to carry on a debate in front of the Emperor. Togo would present his proposal which was also Suzuki's proposal, then Suzuki would simply suggest that the other members of the council approve it, counting on the Emperor's presence, plus the Emperor's well-known desire for peace, to stifle discussion. Anami decided that such a strategy could not be allowed to prevail, even at the expense of a breach of manners. He had as much love and respect for the Emperor as any man, and the Emperor knew it. In his home were several gifts which testified to the Emperor's regard for him. He also desired peace as much as any man. But as the army's representative, he had more factors to consider than either Suzuki or Togo.

As Togo talked, Anami leaned toward General Umezu, on his left and whispered in his ear: "It begins to look as if there actually is a scheme afoot. Togo is presenting their plan. They've said nothing about presenting our plan. We can't let them get away with that. Perhaps we should stop discussing surrender terms and insist on an all-out continuation of the war."

As soon as Togo finished speaking, Suzuki arose quickly and asked Admiral Yonai, who was sitting beside Togo, to voice his recommendation. Anami was more certain than ever now of Suzuki's strategy. Yonai would agree with Togo. Then Suzuki would call upon the other navy representative, Admiral Toyoda, who, having heard the navy minister support the Togo plan, might hesitate to argue the matter in the Imperial presence. If Toyoda were to voice acceptance of the Togo plan, Anami and Umezu would be left alone, on the short end of a four-to-two division, and faced with the question of whether it would be at all permissible to argue before His Majesty what would then be clearly a minority position.

Admiral Yonai stood and, without preamble, said, "I agree with the foreign minister."

As Yonai sat down, General Anami leaped to his feet. "I oppose absolutely," he cried, "the opinions expressed by the foreign minister. I am convinced, in fact, that the only honorable course open to our government is to proceed resolutely with the prosecution of the war. If the people of Japan approach the decisive battle for our homeland with determination to show their full measure of patriotism, and to fight until none of us survives, then, Your Majesty, I am convinced that Japan can overcome the crisis facing her. I am confident we can drive back the invaders on their initial thrust and inflict prohibitive losses upon them because we shall be protecting our own sacred soil. What one of us would not fight fiercely for his own home? But even if the enemy repeats his thrusts and we cannot repel him, would it not be wondrous for this whole nation to be destroyed like a beautiful flower, leaving for the world's posterity only the great name of Japan and its brave, noble history? Would it not be glorious to be remembered as a people who refused to submit? Would it not be far better than surrendering ignominiously to our enemies?"

This romantic idea, uttered in the heat of emotion, was not, nevertheless, inconsistent with General Anami's Samurai attitudes toward death. To him, life and death were the same thing, the one being simply a continuation of the other. To a Japanese warrior, death was a much more acceptable prospect than surrender.

"But if we are not to follow so stern a course," Anami continued, "if we are to seek peace, let us insist that we seek it honorably."

He looked across the room at Admiral Yonai, then turned toward Admiral Suzuki. They were both military men. He would address his next question to them. "You speak of one condition," he said to Suzuki, "the condition that our Imperial House be preserved. But let me ask you—if the enemy refuses to grant that condition, would you say we should go on fighting?"

The old admiral stared at Anami for a moment, then shook his head vigorously in the affirmative. "Yes," he said. "If the enemy rejects that condition, we shall continue the war."

Anami turned to Admiral Yonai and received the same answer. "You admit," he said, "that we are able to continue fighting. And you stipulate one situation under which we should do so. You must, then, understand my attitude. I agree we should insist on the preservation of the Imperial House. But I say it is also necessary to insist that our military forces be allowed to demobilize themselves, that there be no enemy occupation of Japan, and that all war criminals be prosecuted by the Japanese government. These are the essential prerequisites to our quest for peace."

When Anami sat down, General Umezu arose immediately to agree with him. "The army," Umezu said, "is fully confident of its ability to deal the enemy a smashing blow. The Soviet declaration of war against us has indeed made our position less favorable, yet it does not force us to abandon our plans for the decisive homeland battle. To surrender unconditionally now would be to dishonor those thousands of men who have gladly fought and died for His Majesty. While I have no personal objection to seeking peace, I, too, insist that, at the very least, we hold out for the four conditions General Anami has enumerated."

Though Admiral Toyoda should have been the next to speak, he being the only member of the Supreme War Council who had not yet spoken, Prime Minister Suzuki chose not to call on him at this moment. If Toyoda were to take the floor directly after the two stirring pleas of Anami and Umezu, there could be little doubt that he would agree with them once again as he had done at the council's morning session. Suzuki appeared to overlook Toyoda, calling instead upon Baron Hiranuma who, as a nonmember, had a questionable right to speak. Since the president of the Privy Council was sometimes considered the probing voice of the Emperor, it seemed unlikely that anyone would try to stop Hiranuma from speaking, and it was doubtful that he would take as hard a line as the two army representatives. He was a difficult old man, of independent mind. In years past, he had been quite openly fascist, but the times had changed him to some degree. It was possible, even, that he might take strong exception to the army position.

Hiranuma's first words were not reassuring to Suzuki. "Before I express any opinion," Hiranuma said, "I would like to ask the foreign minister a question. Mr. Togo, whatever happened to our attempts to negotiate peace through Russia?"

Togo, completely unprepared for such a question, outlined briefly the Japanese diplomatic efforts to secure Russia's aid as a mediator.

"Then why did Russia declare war against us?" Hiranuma wanted to know.

To this question Togo responded by quoting from memory the Soviet war declaration. When he came to the Russian charge that Japan had rejected the Potsdam Declaration, Hiranuma interrupted him.

"Is it true," he asked, "that our government rejected the declaration?"

Togo decided not to go into the confusion surrounding the prime minister's July 28 statement about the declaration. "It is not true," he said.

"Then why did the Russians say it?"

Togo said, "It's all in their imagination."

Hiranuma went on, then, to the question of war criminals. Who would they be? He was aware that he himself might be considered a war criminal since he had been a strong advocate of a military pact with Germany and Italy during his short term as prime minister in 1939.

"I do not know which individuals will be classified as war criminals," Togo said. "But I do know we cannot avoid handing over such persons to the Allied powers."

On the question of demobilization, Hiranuma asked, "Is it at all possible that the Allies might allow Japan to disarm her own troops?"

"They would never permit it," Togo said flatly.

Hiranuma turned now to General Umezu and Admiral Toyoda. "Do the army and navy have any true confidence in their ability to continue the war?" he asked.

Umezu said, "The Supreme Command is prepared to exert its utmost efforts. We believe, for instance, that the enemy's use of the atomic bomb might be checked if proper antiaircraft measures are taken."

Toyoda said, "Heretofore, we have been preserving our strength for future use. We are now prepared to counterattack."

"Is there anything more you could do that you are not doing?"

"I think both in the army and in the navy we are doing our best under the circumstances," Toyoda said. He glanced at Umezu who nodded in agreement.

"That is no doubt true," Hiranuma said, "But it is now quite clear that your best is not good enough, and has not been good enough for some time."

This extraordinary criticism of the military left an uneasy silence in the room. Several men shifted uncomfortably in their chairs, perhaps due to their embarrassment at such brutal directness, or perhaps due merely to the difficulty of enduring the intense heat and dampness. Every face was wet and perspiration stains were spreading on most of the shirt collars. The high dome of General Umezu's bald head glistened with moisture. Mosquitoes buzzed in the air and two or three of the men made quick little moves to try to shoo them away.

Hiranuma, after questioning the military representatives at length, changed the subject. He said, "I am also concerned about public order. Though the people are loyal, there is danger that their loyalty might be undermined if the country is thrown into chaos."

Suzuki broke in to say, "I am in agreement with the president of the Privy Council. The government is very much alert to this problem. But the government will also have grave difficulty keeping peace if the war continues much longer."

Hiranuma nodded, then paused before resuming. He was ready now to put forth his opinions. "Basically, I find myself in agreement with the foreign minister's position," he said. "Of course, as everyone has stated, we must fight on if the national polity is threatened."

Suzuki felt a moment of relief. Hiranuma seemed finally to have come down on his side. But Hiranuma had not yet finished.

"On the other hand," he said, "if we also insist on the three conditions mentioned by the war minister, I do not believe we are necessarily doomed to failure. The foreign minister must do his utmost in this respect." Then, after addressing some remarks to the Emperor about his responsibility in such a grave matter, and offering some advice on how to word the government's reply to the Potsdam Declaration, Hiranuma sat down.

His listeners were now somewhat bemused. It was still not clear whose side he had taken. Though his questions had been hard and to the point, his opinion, when he finally stated it, had appeared to come down first on one side, then on the other. His conclusion had left General Anami's position undamaged. It was pointless now to hope Admiral Toyoda would defect to the surrender faction. He had a right to speak, however. Prime Minister Suzuki called upon him.

"I find myself still in support of the position taken by General Anami and General Umezu," he said. "We cannot say that victory is certain in the final battle for our homeland, but at the same time we do not believe we shall be positively defeated. If we negotiate with the enemy, it should be on the basis of General Anami's four conditions. And in the matter of demobilization, we must be especially firm. Unless we are allowed to disarm our own men, I cannot guarantee that the navy will accept demobilization."

After Toyoda finished, there was some restless squirming in chairs. What was to happen now? The council was still deadlocked after two hours. Suzuki's strategy for achieving unanimity had apparently failed, making him look foolish for involving the Emperor in it. The argument among the council members would simply have to continue at another meeting tomorrow.

Amid the silent speculation, the prime minister arose once more. "Every member of this council has now had an opportunity to speak," he said. "But after two hours of discussion here, and more hours of discussion at a previous meeting, we are still not in agreement. Three of us favor the proposal put forth by the foreign minister that we should accept the Potsdam terms on one condition—the preservation of the Royal House and the national polity. I include myself in favor of this proposal. However, the three other members favor the war minister's proposal that we stipulate four conditions before accepting the Potsdam terms. We are hopelessly deadlocked. But our nation is in a most difficult situation which permits no further delay. Therefore, I propose to ask His Majesty for his opinion on the issue, and I hope we shall accept his opinion as our own."

Before his listeners had time to react, Suzuki turned and walked the few feet from his table to the table at which the Emperor sat. Bending his body to a ninety-degree angle, the old man said, "I present myself humbly at the foot of the Throne, and I request Your Imperial Majesty's opinion as to which proposal should be adopted —the one stated by the foreign minister or the one containing the four conditions."

The shock which now overcame Suzuki's listeners was magnified by the fact that what he had done was unprecedented in modern times. Even the two men in the room who had been expecting his move, Togo and Sakomizu, were awed by it when it actually happened.

The Emperor himself was almost overcome by emotion at being so personally involved in a situation of such gravity and magnitude. He held the belief, instilled by the royal tutors who had guided his education from earliest youth (including General Maresuke Nogi, the army's most illustrious hero in the Russo-Japanese War), that an Emperor should reign but should not govern. During the twenty years since his enthronement, he had clung so firmly to this belief that he had never once ventured an official opinion on government policy. It would be improper to speak out, he felt, unless he were asked to do so. And no prime minister had ever asked him until now. This was, in fact, the first time he had ever heard a debate among the men who ruled the state. Suzuki had petitioned him to speak and he was prepared, but he was as nervous about it as his audience. His hands, clothed in white gloves, trembled slightly.

He was about to begin when he noticed that Suzuki remained standing in front of him. He nodded and said, "You may go back to your seat."

Suzuki, whose hearing was defective, cupped his ear and said, "Pardon?"

The Emperor put out his hand. In a soft, kindly, high-pitched voice, he repeated, "Go back to your seat."

As soon as the prime minister was settled, the Emperor arose and began slowly to speak as the men in front of him quickly bowed, then sat at attention.

"I have given serious thought to the situation prevailing at home and abroad," the Emperor said, "and have concluded that continuing the war can only mean destruction for the nation and a prolongation of bloodshed and cruelty in the world. I cannot bear to see my innocent people suffer any longer. Ending the war is the only way to restore world peace and to relieve the nation of the terrible distress with which it is burdened.

"I was told by those advocating a continuation of hostilities that by June, new divisions would be placed in fortified positions at Kujukuri-hama so that they would be ready for the invader when he sought to land. [Kujukuri was a beach area on the Boso Peninsula, the arm of land which jutted out to sea east of Tokyo and helped form Tokyo Bay.] It is now August and the fortifications still have not been completed. Even the equipment for the divisions which are to fight there is insufficient and reportedly will not be adequate until after the middle of September. Furthermore, the promised increase in the production of aircraft has not progressed in accordance with expectations.

"There are those who say that the key to national survival lies in a decisive battle in the homeland. The experiences of the past, however, show that there has always been a discrepancy between plans and performance. I do not believe that the discrepancy in the case of Kujukuri-hama can be rectified. Since this is the shape of things, how can we repel the invaders?"

One of the men in his audience had begun softly to cry, and though he was no doubt attempting to control himself, he could be heard by the others. With everyone's emotions approaching ultimate limits, his tears became contagious, and soon, several men were suppressing sobs as the droplets ran down their cheeks.

"I cannot help feeling sad," the Emperor continued, "when I think of the people who have served me so faithfully, the soldiers and sailors who have been killed or wounded in far-off battles, the families who have lost all their worldly goods—and often their lives as well—in the air raids at home. It goes without saying that it is unbearable for me to see the brave and loyal fighting men of Japan disarmed. It is equally unbearable that others who have rendered me devoted service should now be punished as instigators of the war. Nevertheless, the time has come when we must bear the unbearable.

"When I think of the feelings of my Imperial Grandsire, the Emperor Meiji, at the time of the Triple Intervention [an alliance between France, Germany, and Russia in 1895, forcing Japan to return territory won in the Sino-Japanese War], I swallow my own tears and give my sanction to the proposal to accept the Allied proclamation on the basis outlined by the foreign minister."

So strong was the emotional bond between the Emperor of Japan and his subjects that every man in the room was weeping by the time he finished, and as he arose to leave, the sobs were unrestrained. He himself wiped an eye with one of his white gloves before turning away. Escorted by his military aide, he walked quickly toward the door. Prime Minister Suzuki, gathering his strength, stood and faced the others. "I propose," he said, "that we make the Imperial opinion the decision of this conference."

The assent of the other five members could be taken for granted. After the Emperor had spoken, no one would rise to dispute him. As Suzuki had implied, however, by the use of the expression "Imperial opinion," the Emperor's words did not, in themselves, establish the policy of the Japanese government, nor did their approval by the Supreme War Council, which was only a quasi-legal body. The prime minister had asked the Emperor to summon the Supreme Council rather than the cabinet because he was aware that the Supreme Council, including as it did the military chiefs of staff, wielded the ultimate power in the state. It was the cabinet, nevertheless, which had the legal responsibility of accepting or rejecting the Emperor's opinion. Suzuki felt now that he would encounter no difficulty with his cabinet. General Anami was the key member, and since Anami, as well as the army's chief of staff, had bowed to the Emperor's will here in the Supreme Council meeting, he would do likewise in the cabinet meeting which must follow as quickly as possible. As soon as Anami expressed to the cabinet his acceptance of the Emperor's opinion, any other possible opposition to it would vanish.

The sobbing in the hot, damp air raid shelter increased for awhile after the Emperor's departure, then gradually diminished as the eleven men who had heard his hopeless words struggled to get hold of themselves. Within a few minutes they began to file slowly out the door, along the narrow hallway and up the narrow stairway.

As they emerged into the night air of Tokyo, which was only slightly cooler than the air in the shelter, the strain of the proceedings and of the rapidly deteriorating situation created an incident which no one could have anticipated. General Yoshizumi, still angry about the method Suzuki and Sakomizu had used to arrange the imperial conference, suddenly rushed at the prime minister.

"Are you happy now!" he shouted, trying to get at the old man. "Are you satisfied!"

General Anami reacted quickly, stepping between the two men.

Yoshizumi continued to shout. "You were false to your word, Suzuki!"

Anami took firm hold of his subordinate. "Be quiet, please," he said. "I understand your feelings, Yoshizumi."

Prime Minister Suzuki walked silently in the direction of his car.

AUGUST 9,
SHORTLY BEFORE MIDNIGHT

A S T H E blacked-out train approached Fukuyama, a middle-sized city about 65 miles northeast of Hiroshima, Dr. Tsunesaburo Asada could see ahead the glow of a great fire which lit up the sky. He knew what it meant. Tonight was Fukuyama's turn. The Americans were destroying the city, as they had promised on the radio to destroy all Japanese cities. The train would no doubt have to stop at any moment now and wait until the attacking planes departed. If, in the light of the fire, an American plane were to spot the train on the move, they could expect to be bombed and strafed immediately. The Americans seemed to enjoy a moving target, as if it were better sport. With train travel in the daytime now virtually out of the question, it was becoming hazardous even at night. Dr. Asada was increasingly surprised as the minutes passed and the train continued moving slowly toward the expanding fire which was eating at the core of the city. They were within the city now and so close to the fire they could see the flames. They could also hear, from the dark sky above, the roar of planes. Did the engineer not intend to stop at all? Did he think they dared continue right through the burning city?

Finally, in the wide switchyards near the Fukuyama station, the train did stop and a murmur arose among the passengers as they realized they were now almost directly below the attacking planes. They could only hope that since they were no longer moving they might not be spotted. The train was so tightly crowded that Dr. Asada, on his way to Hiroshima to investigate for the navy the "new-type" bomb that had exploded there, put his head out of the open window to get some air. Fortunately it was not an unbearably hot night, but with people jammed together as they were, the train was extremely uncomfortable anyway. The sixteen men in his party, plus their baggage and the heavy equipment he had prepared for the work he intended to do, were all condensed into a space big enough for six or seven people.

When he agreed the previous day to go to Hiroshima, the navy had assigned a group to go with him, including two doctors, a pharmacist, an engineer, a reporter, and ten enlisted men to do whatever heavy work might be necessary. These latter had already been useful, not only in carrying the equipment, but in elbowing their way onto the train. The equipment included an electrometer, an electroscope, and a Geiger counter which Asada had constructed at his laboratory the day before, in anticipation that he would find Hiroshima radioactive.

The American planes attacking Fukuyama seemed to be dropping mostly incendiaries. The whole center of the city was now aflame, and so was the ancient Fukuyama castle, to the north of the railroad station. Occasionally a high-explosive bomb would come down, adding a fearsome blast to the roar of the fires, and fighter planes were coming in low on strafing runs. Eventually, the railroad station itself ignited, and as the minutes passed into hours with the attack still continuing, Asada felt the helplessness and despair which he knew everyone around him must also be feeling. The flames surrounded them. The whole city of Fukuyama was ablaze. People could be seen running in all directions, trying to find a place the fire had not yet reached. The winds created by the fire were gusting, first one way, then another, and when they blew toward the switchyard, Asada could fell the hot blast on his face. Though the roar of the bombers could scarcely be heard now over the roar of the fire, the whistling of the fighters, as they came low to strafe, made everyone in the train freeze with fear. One of the planes came so close its bullets spattered against cars on a nearby track. Inside Asada's train, people tried to lower their heads and lean away from the windows, but they were so closely packed it was impossible for them to get any real protection except from the bodies of each other. There was silence as the strafing plane passed into the distance. Then there was a collective sigh. Then came more planes.

By 2:30 A.M., the center of the city was completely burned out, and while the outer areas were still in full flame, the fires had receded somewhat from the railroad yards. The station itself was now a mere skeleton and the planes were strafing less frequently. People on the train gradually began to relax, only slightly at first, then increasingly as the minutes passed. They began to talk.

"Do you think it's over?"

"Let's get this train out of here!"

"Whose idea was it anyway, to bring a train into the middle of an air raid?"

"They couldn't stop out in the country."

"Why not?"

"Another train might have come along in the dark and hit us."

"We've been here almost three hours. Aren't we ever going to move?"

"Not till all the American planes are gone."

At 3 A.M., the planes were apparently gone. Slowly the train began to move. Slowly it pulled out of Fukuyama, threading its way between the fires which still raged in the outer sections of the city, inching its way along as if to avoid the possible notice of any American fighter plane that might have lagged behind. Even an hour later, as the train continued at a painfully slow, stop-and-start pace toward Hiroshima, Dr. Asada could look back and see the sky aglow over the still-burning remains of Fukuyama.

AUGUST 10,
3 A.M.

PRIME MINISTER Suzuki brought the cabinet to order quickly as soon as all fifteen members had gathered at his official residence. He wasted no time in getting to the purpose of this unusual 3 A.M. meeting.

"The Supreme Council for the Direction of the War has just ended an imperial conference at the palace," he said. "At that conference His Majesty expressed the opinion that this government should accept the terms of the Potsdam Declaration with one stipulation—that our national polity and our imperial system be maintained. After His Majesty spoke, the members of the council decided to make his opinion the decision of the council. I wish to propose now that the cabinet do likewise, and I suggest that we vote on that motion."

While most of the members still sat in shock, Foreign Minister Togo arose and said, "There is a question as to how the single condition should be worded. The president of the Privy Council, Baron Hiranuma, who was present at the Supreme War Council's imperial conference, insists that the stipulation be stated in the following way, quote: 'with the understanding that the said declaration does not comprise any demand which prejudices the prerogatives of His Majesty as a sovereign ruler.' As you know, the approval of the Privy Council will be needed before any message can be sent to the Allied nations. I suggest that we accept Baron Hiranuma's phraseology."

Togo had already decided that he would not mention any reservations he himself might have about this phraseology. It was so strong it might cause trouble, yet there was no time to argue it. Since most of the cabinet members were still overcome by the circumstances in which they suddenly found themselves, no one took exception to the suggestion Togo had just made.

Suzuki stood and pressed his motion. Did the members agree that the government should accept the Potsdam terms with the one condition?

The prime minister was pleased to see that apparently everyone had raised his hand. But before his pleasure had time to become official, he realized it was slightly premature.

As the written motion was being passed around for signatures, Home Minister Genki Abe suddenly said, "I fail to see the necessity of signing this."

He was well aware of the necessity. Unless every cabinet member signed it, the document could not become official. But he felt an understandable concern. If the news of the surrender were to cause rebellion among the people or among the young officers, he might wish he were not one of those who had signed the surrender authorization.

For a few moments Suzuki feared he might have difficulty with the cabinet after all, despite General Anami's acceptance of the Emperor's will. But before the home minister's reservations had time to spread, help came from an unexpected source. Education Minister Kozo Ota, who had suggested only a few hours before that the cabinet resign, now said to Abe, "You must sign. The procedure is necessary."

Slowly, the home minister picked up his brush, dipped it into the ink, and affixed his signature. The government of Japan had taken its first official step toward surrender.

AUGUST 10,
6 A.M.

D A W N had already arisen when Vice Foreign Minister Shunichi Matsumoto entered Foreign Minister Togo's office with both the Japanese and the English texts of the note to be sent to the Allied nations. The English text, which was, of course, the one that would be cabled, had been prepared by Foreign Ministry translator Toshikazu Kase, the man who had acted as Togo's interpreter almost four years before, in the early morning hours of December 8, 1941, when American Ambassador Joseph Grew arrived with a telegram from the then President Franklin D. Roosevelt asking Emperor Hirohito to help preserve peace.

Togo, having had no sleep for more than 24 hours, looked even more pale and gaunt than usual. He did not seem, however, to lack energy. Quickly he read the English version:

In obedience to the gracious command of His Majesty the Emperor who, ever anxious to enhance the cause of world peace, desires earnestly to bring about a speedy termination of hostilities with a view to saving mankind from the calamities to be imposed upon them by further continuation of the war, the Japanese Government several weeks ago asked the Soviet Government, with which neutral relations then prevailed, to render good offices in restoring peace vis-à-vis the enemy powers. Unfortunately, these efforts in the interest of peace having failed, the Japanese Government in conformity with the august wish of His Majesty to restore the general peace and desiring to put an end to the untold sufferings entailed by war as quickly as possible, have decided upon the following.

The Japanese Government are ready to accept the terms enumerated in the joint declaration which was issued at Potsdam on July 26th, 1945, by the heads of the governments of the United States, Great Britain, and China, and later subscribed by the Soviet Government, with the understanding that the said declaration does not comprise any demand which prejudices the prerogatives of His Majesty as a Sovereign Ruler.

The Japanese Government sincerely hope that this understanding is warranted and desire keenly that an explicit indication to that effect will be speedily forthcoming.

Since the message had been drafted in accordance with Togo's precise instructions, he found no fault with it.

Matsumoto said, "I wish we did not have to use the wording 'prerogatives' of His Majesty, but I can't think of a better way to translate it." He had reservations about the entire message. He felt it should simply say, 'We accept the Potsdam proclamation. We understand that this acceptance will not affect the position of the Imperial household.' But it would be pointless to make that suggestion. The foreign minister would not be free to follow it even if he agreed with it.

Togo again scanned the text. "This is about as well as we can do," he said. "Send it through Switzerland. No. Send it through Switzerland and Sweden. That way at least one of the two cables should get through without delay. Have our minister in Berne forward it to the United States and China. And have our minister in Stockholm forward it to England and Russia." He handed the approved text back to Matsumoto. "And do it as quickly as possible."

AUGUST 10,
9:15 A.M.

YOUNG OFFICERS were already gathering in angry little groups along the corridors of the War Ministry when General Anami arrived, slightly later than usual this morning. Though he greeted them as if this were just another day, he was aware of their dangerous mood and he knew the reason for it. By now they must have at least a vague idea of what had happened during the night. It would not be easy for him, from this day forward, to handle these zealous, frustrated subordinates.

General Anami knew how they felt because he felt very much like them. Given his personal choice, he would never surrender. To a Japanese soldier even the word was abhorrent, and he was the very model of a Japanese soldier. He was also embarrassed because he had been outmaneuvered by old Admiral Suzuki the previous day in the arrangement of the imperial conference. It had been altogether a day of defeat, climaxed by the most sobering setback of all—the tragic words of His Majesty. They had been shattering words to hear, but because the Emperor had spoken them, they could not be ignored. General Anami, unlike some of his colleagues, had always believed there was one authority even higher than the army.

Entering his spacious office at the front and center of the second floor, he dropped his riding crop on his desk and called for the vice minister of war, Lieutenant General Tadaichi Wakamatsu.

"I would like you to arrange for a meeting of all the staff officers down to the rank of section chief," he said. "Have them assemble in the air raid shelter." If he intended to gather in one place most of the officers who controlled the Japanese Army, it had better be in a place where a well-aimed bomb could not eliminate all of them.

"At what time?" Wakamatsu asked.

Anami glanced at his watch. "The sooner the better. Make it 9:30."

The concrete-walled, vaultlike main room of the War Ministry's air raid shelter (located under the ground in front of the building, near the lip of the hill on which it stood) was crowded with generals, colonels, and lieutenant colonels when General Anami entered, accompanied by General Wakamatsu and General Yoshizumi, chief of the Military Affairs Bureau, the man who had threatened to attack Admiral Suzuki at the Imperial Palace.

The roomful of officers snapped to attention and Anami quickly put them at ease. General Yoshizumi began the meeting: "Last night, as many of you know, there was an imperial conference of the Supreme

War Council. General Anami, General Umezu, and myself attended. General Anami is here to speak to you about that conference."

The war minister stood silent for a moment, looking out at the faces of all these men he knew and loved, men who had depended on him to represent their cause and who were about to learn that he had failed. He began speaking to them quietly, restraining his own emotions.

"At a Supreme War Council meeting yesterday," he said, "the issue of accepting the Potsdam Declaration was discussed. General Umezu opposed it. Admiral Toyoda opposed it. I opposed it. The others favored it. But despite this deadlock, the council was summoned to meet in the Imperial presence last night. And at that meeting, His Majesty expressed his desire."

Throughout the room there arose a general "sssssssss" sound as many of the officers sharply drew in their breath—a characteristic reaction of Japanese men when they have just heard something astonishing.

General Anami continued. "His Majesty told us with tears in his eyes that he felt the time had come when we must bear the unbearable. It was his wish that we seek peace immediately. In compliance with his Imperial will, the Supreme Council, and afterward the cabinet, decided to accept the Potsdam terms on the condition that our national polity be preserved."

The room was in an uproar almost before he finished the sentence. General Anami stood patiently waiting for the chorus of "No! No! No!" to subside.

When relative quiet resumed, Anami said, "I don't know what excuse I can offer you. At the imperial conference, I insisted that we continue to fight. Then I insisted we could accept peace terms only if four essential conditions were met. But my powers of persuasion were not great enough. I'm sorry I have been unable to live up to your expectations. However, since the Emperor desires that the Potsdam terms be accepted, there is nothing that can be done. The important consideration for us now is to make certain the army acts in an orderly, organized manner. You must all disregard your own feelings and the feelings of the men serving under you.

"I want you also to bear one other important thing in mind. The war has not yet ended. The decision of the cabinet to seek peace was based on the assumption that the enemy will guarantee the preservation of our Royal House and our national polity. It is too soon to know whether the enemy will agree to this stipulation. The army must therefore be prepared either for war or for peace. But whichever it may be, you must all remember that you are soldiers. You must obey orders. You must not deviate from strict military discipline. In the crisis that faces us, the uncontrolled actions of one man could bring about the ruin of the entire country."

The silence which ensued was broken not by any of the high-ranking generals but by one of the younger colonels who arose and stood at stiff attention.

"The war minister has told us to obey him whether he orders us to fight or to surrender," the young colonel said. "Does this mean the war minister is actually considering surrender?"

The spirit of rebellion inherent in the question did not escape General Anami. His riding crop cracked like a whip across the top of the table at which he stood.

"Anyone who is not willing to obey my orders," he said, "will disobey them over my dead body."

AUGUST 10,
10:30 A.M.

LIEUTENANT Colonel Masao Inaba, chief of the budget sub-section of the Military Affairs Bureau, and sometimes speech-writer for General Anami, paid little attention to the air raid which was in progress when he emerged from the War Ministry shelter. He scarcely glanced up at the B-29s which were dropping incendiaries on the center of Tokyo. It seemed pointless for the Americans to bother hitting the city again. There was very little of it left to burn. Though Inaba could see a few fires from the eminence of Ichigaya Heights as he hurried toward the ministry building, he gave them no thought. He was concentrating now on something General Anami had said in the latter part of his bewildering lecture to the staff—the war had not yet ended. It was too soon to know whether the enemy would accept the Japanese government's one stipulation. The army must continue to be prepared for battle.

How could the army continue to be prepared for anything, Inaba wondered, after the news of the government's ignominious surrender bid became public? If the army were to maintain its aggressive spirit, it would have to be encouraged to do so in strong terms. There was an excellent possibility that the enemy would accept nothing short of complete surrender, in which case the army might yet realize its hope of fighting a decisive battle. Something should be done to make certain the army remained in fighting condition.

Inaba felt at this moment a desperate sense of urgency which was heightened by the fact that until today he had never considered seriously the possibility that Japan might be defeated. Even the advent of the atomic bomb had not convinced him that the enemy was unstoppable. The army was well dispersed and supplied with shelters. The civilians in the cities had adequate shelters available to them. And according to reports from General Arisue and Marshal Hata in Hiroshima, a person could protect himself against the bomb by dressing properly, especially by wearing white clothing.

Until this morning, Inaba had never doubted that the outcome of the war would be decided in the final battle for the homeland. He was certain that General Anami had felt the same way because he had accompanied Anami on a recent inspection tour of one of the few locations—Arioka Bay in southern Kyushu—where it would be possible for the enemy to land. Defenses there were so deep that Anami was convinced the first American wave would be decisively thrown back. It would take time for the Americans to prepare a second wave —time which might be used in negotiation. If such negotiations failed, the Americans would then face brutal resistance even against their second and third waves. Feeling this way, how could a man of such high quality as General Anami have spoken as he did this morning? Inaba was still far from satisfied by Anami's statement. A soldier of Anami's caliber could not have been speaking his own mind when he said the army should meekly accept surrender. He must have decided it was his responsibility to take the blame for the work of those three "Badoglios" with whom he was unfortunately associated in the government—Suzuki, Yonai, and Sakomizu. If General Anami had any fault at all, it was his lack of a political sense. He was too trusting. When Suzuki became prime minister in April, everyone had approved of the choice. He had made an admirable statement about the necessity of prosecuting the war to the very end. But in June, when rumors arose about the government seeking peace through Russia, and when it became apparent that those rumors were true, the younger officers at the War Ministry had quickly become convinced that Suzuki was a "Badoglio." No one, however, had been able to convince General Anami.

After dwelling upon these considerations for some time at his own desk on the second floor of the ministry building, Colonel Inaba went to the desk of his immediate superior, Colonel Okikatsu Arao, chief of the army affairs section of the Military Affairs Bureau. Colonel Arao, like most of the officers who had heard Anami's words, appeared to be still in a state of shock.

"In light of what he told us," Inaba said to Arao, "don't you think a statement should be radioed to our field armies, bouying them up and directing them to fight on with even greater determination? Especially the Kwantung Army. If they simply get a statement in Manchuria that Japan is suing for peace, they'll be so confused and discouraged the Russians will overrun them."

"That's an excellent idea," Arao said. "Why don't you go ask General Anami about it?"

Inaba hurried around the corner to the front corridor on which the offices of the high-ranking generals faced. When he entered the war minister's office, he found General Anami deeply involved in the detailed wording of the public announcement of Japan's peace bid. Anami had already engaged in several telephone conversations with the president of the government Information Board, Dr. Hiroshi Shimomura, with whom he completely agreed that the people should be informed of this startling development in such a way that the blow would be softened and their morale protected. He had very little time to listen to Inaba's suggestion that a message of encouragement also be sent out, under his signature, to the troops. But he liked the speeches Inaba had sometimes written for him. He had confidence in this young officer and he liked the idea of sending a message to the troops.

"Why don't you go write it," Anami said to him, "and I'll sign it."

Colonel Inaba hurried back to his own desk and went to work.

AUGUST 10,
LATE MORNING

T H E U . S . Navy Hellcat fighter-bombers, which had been attacking the town of Ito quite often lately, were now out of sight, having completed their morning raid. Their bomb bursts and machine gun racket had faded away. So had the equally frightening booms of the town's only antiaircraft battery, a loud and fearsome artillery piece which was, however, not much more effective than a fly swatter against the Americans.

With quiet restored, Naoki Hoshino, who now lived in Ito, had come out for his late morning walk. In early June, his Tokyo home having been destroyed during the great fire bombing of May 25, Hoshino and his wife, Misao, had moved to this pleasant spa on the Izu Penninsula, about 70 miles south of Tokyo and not far from where the American expedition under Commodore Matthew Perry had landed in 1853. There had been almost no reason for Hoshino to stay in the capital. When General Tojo resigned as prime minister, he had resigned as chief cabinet secretary, and though he was still a member of the upper house of the Diet, that body was now so inactive it made almost no demands upon him.

Here in Ito, life was relatively pleasant despite the recent plague of nuisance air raids. The surrounding farms had at least some food to offer. The hot springs were soothing, and the beach was beautiful. The people seemed more openhearted than in Tokyo, perhaps because their cares were not so heavy. But while they had not suffered hardships comparable to those of city people, they had seen enough of the war to feel it, and also to understand how badly it was going for Japan. Ito being located on the edge of Sagami Bay, which led into Tokyo Bay, it was very close to the route of Japanese merchant vessels as they tried to sneak in and out of Tokyo. In recent months, the townspeople often heard gunfire and explosions on the water, and from a hill near the town, they could see Japanese ships under attack by American planes, or by submarines which sailed fearlessly into the bay. The Americans must even have been able to send in minesweepers to clear paths for themselves. Several times Hoshino had stood on a hill with groups of townspeople and farm people, studying their reactions as Japanese ships went down under these attacks. They would watch silently awhile, then someone, gazing off across the bay in the direction of the huge Yokosuka Naval Base, would say, "Doesn't the navy have any ships they could send out to help?" No one would bother to reply because everyone, including the person who asked the question, knew the answer. It was not possible to deceive these people about the war. If the navy was unable even to save a ship approaching the mouth of Tokyo Bay, it would not be able to save the nation.

Hoshino, having been so deeply involved in the government at the beginning of the war, felt now a heavy sadness and regret as it became increasingly apparent that Japan was on the verge of defeat. He thought of his own role in the war. He had not, of course, made any of the decisions which led to it, yet he had been one of General Tojo's closest assistants throughout most of it. He wondered how Tojo felt about it now, and as he walked it occurred to him that there was still an important function for Tojo to fill if he were so disposed. Tojo had been the nation's leader when the war began. He had never tried to deny his responsibility for that. Would it not be fitting if Tojo were to come forward at this time and take the responsibility for ending the war? It was an idea which should be suggested to Tojo. Perhaps the thought had not occurred to him. Hoshino should go to Setagaya one of these days and discuss it with him. Yes, it would be worth doing, he decided. He would go as soon as possible.

As Hoshino continued his walk through the pleasant, sunny streets of Ito, he saw more and more people emerging from their shelters after the air attack. He was not prepared, however, for the strange sight which greeted him as he happened to approach the location of the town's only antiaircraft battery. The gun was silent now since the skies were clear, but gathered around it were several townspeople who were far from silent. They were gesturing excitedly at the soldiers who manned the gun. As Hoshino drew close, he began to get an inkling of the nature of the argument, yet it was so strange he could scarcely believe it.

"Don't shoot that thing any more!" one man was shouting at a bewildered officer.

"Take it away!"

"Get it out of here!"

A man on the fringe of the group, seeing Hoshino, turned to explain their feelings. "Before the army came and installed this thing," he said, "we never had any air raids here. Then they brought the gun, and one day when some American planes flew over, they fired it. That's when the air raids began. They've been attacking us ever since."

The other men were still shouting excitedly at the officer.

"Take it someplace else!"

"You're calling attention to us!"

"If you don't stop shooting at them, they'll destroy the whole town!"

The officer shrugged. "All right, I'll tell the army you don't want it," he said. "There are plenty of other places that need it."

AUGUST 10,
2 P.M.

LIEUTENANT COLONEL Masao Inaba returned to his desk after lunch feeling better. He had not only finished writing General Anami's exhortation to the Japanese armies in the field. He had also shown the statement to his immediate superior, Colonel Arao; to the chief of the Military Affairs Bureau, General Yoshizumi; and to the vice war minister, General Wakamatsu. Though they had suggested certain changes, they had basically approved of it, and with the changes now made, the statement was in the hands of Colonel Arao, who planned to see the war minister and get his approval that evening. General Anami, having left the ministry before Inaba finished the statement, was not immediately available to approve it.

Shortly after Inaba returned to his desk, his close friend and colleague, Lieutenant Colonel Masahiko Takeshita, came to see him with another friend, Lieutenant Colonel Tomomi Oyadomari of the ministry's information department. Takeshita, who had been in the War Ministry when the war began (it was he who had written the communiqué announcing it), had then served with the Fifteenth Army in the jungles of Burma before returning to Tokyo, where he was now in charge of domestic political liaison for the Military Affairs Bureau. Inasmuch as he was General Anami's brother-in-law, and lived next door to him in the suburb of Mitaka, he was considered one of the war minister's closest confidants.

Like most of the officers at the ministry today, Takeshita was in a morose mood. "Have you finished that statement to the troops?" he asked Inaba. "We want to get it on the air this evening." He and Oyadomari, both being concerned with army news releases, had been aware since morning that the statement was in preparation.

"It's finished," Inaba said, "but General Anami hasn't seen it."

"Who has seen it?"

"Arao, Yoshizumi, Wakamatsu."

"Did they approve it?"

"With certain changes, yes."

"It's not likely, then, that Anami will turn it down. Let's see it."

"I don't have it. I gave it to Arao."

"You must have a copy."

"Only my working copy, but that's been changed."

"Let's see it anyway."

Inaba, after rummaging through his wastebasket, came up with his original version of the statement and handed it to Takeshita, who read it quickly.

"Looks good," Takeshita said, Laying it on the desk, he began copying it. "What changes did they make?"

"Let's see." Inaba took the statement and read it aloud, enumerating the changes as he recalled them.

"Don't just tell me about them," Takeshita said. "Write them in."

"But we don't yet have Anami's approval."

"He did approve it in principle, didn't he?"

"That's true," Inaba agreed. "And it's only a statement to encourage the troops. Wakamatsu and Yoshizumi have both approved it. I don't see any reason why Anami would object to it."

"Hurry up and make the changes," Takeshita said. "We haven't much time before deadline."

AUGUST 10,
2:30 P.M.

SEVEN OF Japan's nine living ex-premiers, the Jushin, sat around the table of the cabinet room in the prime minister's official residence, listening to an explanation by Foreign Minister Shigenori Togo of the events of the previous night. Baron Admiral Suzuki, having opened this meeting of senior statesmen, sat back and listened while Togo outlined the reasons why the government was suing for peace—the abject condition of the nation, the atomic bomb, the Russian war declaration, and the will of the Emperor. Togo's usually calm, precise delivery was nearly broken by emotion when he recounted the Emperor's words to the Supreme War Council.

"And now, gentlemen," he concluded, "I shall gladly answer any questions you might wish to ask before you go to the palace." At 3:30, the Jushin were scheduled to meet the Emperor and hear from his own lips why he favored surrender.

Five of the ex-premiers in the room had nothing to say. Prince Fumimaro Konoye, Baron Kiichiro Hiranuma, Admiral Keisuke Okada, Koki Hirota, and Baron Reijiro Wakatsuki were all known to favor the acceptance of peace terms. (Two other ex-premiers were absent, Admiral Mitsumasa Yonai because he was an active member of the government, and Nobuyuki Abe because he was serving as governor general of Korea.) After a few hopeful moments when it began to look as if none of the Jushin would object to the decision of the Emperor and the government, General Kuniaki Koiso, who had been prime minister for nine months after the resignation of General Tojo in 1944, began shifting in his chair and impatiently clearing his throat.

"How will the Potsdam Declaration affect Japan's armed forces?" he asked the foreign minister.

It seemed an extraordinary question, but Koiso was an extraordinary man. For some time after the war began he had continued his practice of cold water ablutions at the Meiji Shrine as a way of participating in the hardships of the troops at the battlefronts. And when, in November of 1944, during his premiership, the B-29s dropped their first bombs on Tokyo, near the Imperial Palace, he had apologized to the Emperor for his "unforgivable negligence" in allowing the enemy to perpetrate such "arrogance and lawlessness." As a retired general, Koiso felt now that the army must receive prime consideration in any possible peace settlement.

Togo looked impatient at the question. The answer was as obvious as it was difficult to say. "If you have read the Potsdam Declaration," he said, "you must realize that complete disarmament of our forces is one of the terms."

"But that would be intolerable!" Koiso cried, leaping to his feet. "Soldiers of Japan have carried weapons by Divine Will for ages eternal."

"It is now the Emperor's will," Togo said firmly, "that we accept the Potsdam terms."

"You speak of maintaining the national polity," Koiso insisted, "but without an armed force, how can any government maintain the national polity?"

The foreign minister had no adequate answer to this, short of saying that the government would have to depend on the enemy's armed forces to maintain the national polity.

Koiso, blazing with indignation, said, "Under these conditions, it would be unpardonable to accept the Potsdam terms."

Since no one chose to answer him, he then subsided into his chair.

After a moment, Hideki Tojo arose. "I am in complete agreement with General Koiso," he said. "To accept the Potsdam Declaration will mean national suicide for Japan. The foreign minister seems to suggest that the enemy will protect for us our national polity. I see no reason to feel confident about this assumption."

Togo, who had been the foreign minister in Tojo's government when the war began, but who was no longer very friendly with Tojo, having left his cabinet in a quarrel over the administration of conquered lands, feared now that the nation's leader throughout most of the war was about to advocate a defiance of the Emperor's will.

Tojo's face was set in anger and he seemed ready to launch a bitter plea against surrender. But suddenly, as if overcome by a consideration which was beyond his powers to resist, the fiery little general paused and heaved a sigh.

"However," he concluded, "if it is His Majesty's wish that we accept the Potsdam terms, then nothing can be done about it. I have no more to say."

AUGUST 10,
MIDAFTERNOON

A T T H E Kure Naval Base hospital about 20 miles from Hiroshima, Dr. Tsunesaburo Asada was listening to one of the physicians describe what he had seen four mornings ago.

"There was a bright flash and a mushroom-like cloud arose, red in color. I decided it must have been an explosion at the army arsenal in Hiroshima. But it would take at least 10,000 tons of explosives to create such a blast, and I thought to myself, how could the army have that large a hidden stock when the navy is so short of explosives?"

Dr. Asada recognized that there was something at least slightly amusing in such an absurd manifestation of army-navy distrust at a moment like that, but right now he had neither the time nor the inclination to listen to any more stories. He had reached Kure about noon after a frightful train ride. He was eager to get to Hiroshima and see for himself what had happened.

"Have any other scientists arrived?" he asked.

"Yes, I believe Dr. Yoshio Nishina is here with a team of army investigators."

Having been associated with Dr. Nishina in the Japanese attempt to develop an atomic weapon, Dr. Asada was eager to talk to him now.

In three vehicles supplied by the naval hospital, he and his team of assistants, with all the equipment they could carry, made their way slowly, along roads still congested with refugees, toward the stricken city.

At three miles from the center of Hiroshima, they found that half the houses had been destroyed. At a mile-and-a-half from the center, almost all the houses were gone and the steel electric poles were bent. Though many of the wooden electric poles were still standing, the sides facing the downtown area were charred. All the wires had apparently disintegrated. There were no leaves left on the surviving trees, but there were leaf silhouettes on the trunks of these trees. Much more horrible to behold was the sight of hundreds and thousands of people, their faces looking like pork cutlets, still lying by the roadsides, alive but not yet picked up for treatment four days after the catastrophe. The stench was nauseous.

Approaching the central section, Dr. Asada stopped his vehicles at several locations to test with an electrometer for radioactivity in the soil. The trousers which the navy had supplied him for this expedition were so large he almost tripped over them when he walked, but he soon had a series of test results which confirmed what he had expected to find—that the soil was highly radioactive, and becoming more so as they neared the area of total destruction.

When he and his assistants reached what had been downtown Hiroshima, he knew they were now at the virtual epicenter because all around them, in an area more than ten blocks square, there was absolutely nothing. Whatever had been here—buildings, streetcars, automobiles, people—had either disintegrated or had been blown away. While Asada was staring numbly at this desolation, he saw another group approaching and quickly realized it was the army investigation team with Dr. Nishina. He hurried forward, bowing to his old friend and associate.

The two renowned physicists stood gazing at each other silently for almost a minute. Each man had tears in his eyes.

Asada said to Nishina, "Have you conducted any tests?"

Nishina said, "Not yet. We have no equipment."

"I've just tested the soil with an electrometer," Asada said. "You can imagine the results."

"Yes, I can imagine. Some of the army people still refuse to believe it was an atomic bomb, but we know better, don't we. It's a terrible thing to see. And I understand Nagasaki has also been hit by one of them."

"So I hear." Asada had been informed at Kure of the Nagasaki bombing. "And we have no means to combat it."

"Absolutely none."

They looked around for two or three minutes in all directions. Nishina said, "We shouldn't stay here much longer. We're just about at the epicenter."

Asada glanced at his watch. "I'm afraid you're right. I've been here almost ten minutes." Even at some distance from here, the radioactivity levels were dangerous.

The two men bowed before parting.

Asada said, "It looks as if America has succeeded in doing what we were unable to do."

"And it is much to our sorrow," Nishina said.

AUGUST 10,
4 P.M.

Dr. Hiroshi Shimomura, president of the Information Board, returned to his office after a tedious afternoon session with General Anami, Admiral Yonai and, for a short time, Foreign Minister Togo, working out the final phraseology of the government statement designed to prepare the public for peace. He was not unhappy with the statement. Though some might consider it vague, he regarded it as gentle and subtle. It began quite resolutely:

"The enemy's air raids upon Japan proper have recently become particularly fierce, and he is preparing for a landing operation. Our land, sea, and air forces are smashing his efforts everywhere. We are ready to crush the enemy at one stroke with the spirit of the whole fighting forces being the same as that of the Special Attack Corps." The Special Attack Corps was the kamikaze suicide corps. The first paragraph went on to condemn America's use of the "new-type" bomb and mentioned the Russian war declaration. "Our forces readily met the Soviet offensive," it avowed, "and will not allow their further advance."

"Yet we must recognize that the worst condition has now come," the statement concluded. "For defending the final line, for protecting the national polity and the honor of our race, the government is exerting utmost efforts, and at the same time expects that the people will also overcome the present difficulty to protect the polity of the Empire."

Dr. Shimomura, who had once been the editor of Japan's largest daily paper, the *Asahi Shimbun,* was satisfied that this statement (basically his own though Anami, Yonai, and Togo had offered suggestions) struck the exact tone needed at the present stage of the surrender negotiations. It was, he felt, firm without being aggressive. He had put into it what he considered a strong hint of surrender, thereby, he hoped, preparing people for peace without destroying their will to fight.

Shimomura had just entered his office when one of his assistants came running in with another document—a statement released by the War Ministry under General Anami's signature. Shimomura read this statement with growing consternation:

INSTRUCTION TO THE TROOPS
I declare to all officers and men of the Army:
The Soviet Union, pointing its armed might in the wrong direction, has invaded Japan. It is quite clear that its real aim is to conquer Greater East Asia, although it endeavors to justify its action. Things have come to such a pass it is pointless to say anything more on the subject. All that remains for us to do is to carry through to its end the holy war for the protection of the land of Gods.

We are determined to fight resolutely even if that involves nibbling grass, eating earth, and sleeping in the fields. It is our belief that there is life in death. This is the spirit of Great Nanko [an ancient exemplar of loyalty to the Emperor] who talked of being reborn seven times in order to serve the nation, or the vigorous fighting spirit of Tokimune [the shogun who directed the fight against the Mongol invaders in the thirteenth century] who warned against entertaining delusions and talked of pressing on vigorously with the work of crushing the ugly enemy.

All officers and men of the entire army without exception should realize the spirit of Nanko as well as the vigorous fighting spirit of Tokimune, and press forward actively to defeat and crush the haughty enemy.

WAR MINISTER KORECHIKA ANAMI

Shimomura dropped the statement on his desk and put his hand to his forehead. He was as puzzled as he was horrified at the words he had just read. Such a statement could destroy the peace efforts. What would the Americans make of it, coming as it did at the same time as the Japanese government's offer to accept the Potsdam terms? And even if the Americans didn't learn of it, what good would it do the troops? It would hardly prepare them for the coming of peace. Shimomura was doubly confused because he had just left General Anami. At no time during their two hours together had the general mentioned making any statement.

"Where did you get this?" Shimomura asked his aide.

"From the War Ministry. They've ordered all newspapers to publish it."

"Get me General Anami."

Shimomura was so upset he found it difficult to control his voice when he finally reached the war minister by phone. Anami had now arrived at his official residence around the corner from the Diet building.

"I've just read your statement," Shimomura said, "and I must say it is extraordinary. . . ."

Anami interrupted. "What statement?"

"Your press release. 'Instruction to the Troops.' "

Anami repeated it after him as a question. " 'Instruction to the Troops?' When did you receive it?"

"Just now."

Anami said nothing for a short time, obviously because he was listening to a man in the background whose voice Shimomura could hear but not understand.

Then Anami spoke again to Shimomura. "Ah, is that what you're talking about? Well, now I understand. Yes, please push it through somehow. Make sure it's published."

Shimomura started to protest, then caught himself. He knew the difficulties with which Anami had to cope at the War Ministry. Some of the young officers there were capable of murdering even their most beloved leader if they felt he was supporting a move toward peace. It was obvious Anami had not written the statement issued in his name. But it seemed to Shimomura that he had been afraid to repudiate the statement. Putting down the phone, Shimomura told his aide to prepare for release both the government statement and the war minister's statement.

AUGUST 10,
LATE AFTERNOON

I N T H E beautiful, green mountainous country at Yamato, about 15 miles southwest of Nara, Navy Captain Mitsuo Fuchida tried to forget the horrors he had seen in Hiroshima. Here, at the almost completed underground naval headquarters facility, with its clean concrete structures and shiny new equipment, one could almost feel that the war was only now starting, with the two sides even. The acute shortages of material which bedeviled the navy everyplace were less apparent at this sturdy, well-organized installation. Fuchida had come here again, at the behest of his commanding officer in Tokyo, Admiral Shikazo Yanno, to help hurry the final construction work in preparation for the impending transfer from Tokyo of the Supreme Naval Headquarters. In the decisive battle for the homeland, naval operations would be directed from here, while army operations would be directed from Matsushiro, in Nagano Prefecture, where the War Ministry was constructing a similar underground fortress.

The destruction he witnessed at Hiroshima had produced a numbing effect on Fuchida. Though he had seen it with his own eyes, he could not yet comprehend it. Having sent a report on the matter to Tokyo, including his opinion that only an atomic bomb could have done such damage, he tried now to put the whole subject of Hiroshima from his mind. Dreadful as it was, it could not be undone. And there was still a war to be fought. The question was, how to fight it. What could Japan do now to strike a useful blow in any direction?

While he was thinking in these terms, Fuchida received a phone call from a friend, Captain Toshiuki Yokoi, chief of staff of the Fifth Air Fleet which was stationed at Kanoya, near the southern tip of Kyushu. Captain Yokoi had been entertaining throughts similar to those of Fuchida. He found the Russian war declaration particularly infuriating.

"It was a dirty stab in the back," he said.

Fuchida agreed. "But what can we do about it?"

"I have an idea," Yokoi said. "Why don't we attack Vladivostok?"

"Attack Vladivostok!" Fuchida thought at first the man was mad. How could Japan go on the offensive anyplace, and especially against Siberia?

"Stop and think about it," Yokoi continued. "The army still has strong forces facing the Russians in Manchuria. And the last thing the Russians would be expecting is a drive north into Siberia. If the army made a move toward Vladivostok, we could send them air support from here. Why not? We've got several hundred planes hidden around here, waiting for the Americans to invade. But it's pointless to wait for the Americans. We can't beat them anyway. Why not attack against Russia? If we took Vladivostok it would be a significant victory."

As Yokoi talked, Fuchida, clutching at any hope that was offered, became more and more excited. "All right," he said finally, "I'm with you. It makes sense." He paused. "Now all we have to do is get the navy and the army to agree. Hold on while I call Yanno on another line."

While Yokoi waited, Fuchida put in a call to Admiral Yanno in Tokyo. When Yanno picked up the phone, Fuchida said, "I've just been talking to Toshiuki Yokoi in Kanoya, and he had a good idea. Why don't we attack Vladivostok?"

Without waiting for a reaction, Fuchida launched into an explanation of the strategy, but before he got very far, Admiral Yanno interrupted him.

"You can forget all that," Yanno said in a tired, dispirited voice which was totally uncharacteristic of him. "We've just received an order. There is to be no more aggressive action on any front."

"What did you say?" Fuchida was certain he had misunderstood.

"And also, Fuchida, you can stop what you're doing down there. You may as well come back to Tokyo as soon as you can manage it."

Fuchida was bewildered when he hung up. The tone of defeat and resignation in Admiral Yanno's voice had been strikingly obvious. Something dreadful must be happening in Tokyo. He picked up the other line and said to Yokoi, "I don't know what we're doing, but we're not attacking Vladivostok."

AUGUST 11,
8 A.M.

VICE ADMIRAL Zenchiro Hoshina, director of the Bureau of Naval Affairs, was about to enter the operations room in the Navy Ministry's underground air raid shelter for the regular morning staff meeting when Vice Admiral Takajiro Ohnishi, the vice chief of staff approached him.

"What are we going to do?" Ohnishi asked, in his customary, urgent tone of voice.

Though Hoshina knew what was on Ohnishi's mind, he answered noncommitally. "I don't know."

Ohnishi, who, as naval air commander in the Philippines the previous October had founded Japan's now famous Kamikaze, or Special Attack, Corps, still believed that, despite the Emperor's opinion, the nation should never surrender, and he assumed that Hoshina agreed with him. Hoshina did not agree. Having been present as secretary for the navy at the imperial conference two nights before, and having heard the Emperor personally express his opinion in favor of peace, Hoshina accepted without reservation the necessity to surrender. A close friend and admirer of the navy minister, Admiral Mitsumasa Yonai, he had in fact come to accept some time ago Yonai's belief that Japan could not win the war. It would be useless to say so, however, in front of a man as fanatically passionate as Admiral Ohnishi.

"How could His Majesty have come to such a conclusion!" Ohnishi exclaimed. "Surrender! Japanese warriors do not surrender. In our entire history this nation has never lost a war. And now they tell us that our own Emperor wants to surrender!"

Hoshina shrugged. "I was there and heard him say it."

Breaking away as politely as possible, Hoshina entered the operations room, where about ten admirals and an equal number of their aides were already assembled. Among the staff officers was Captain Yasuji Watanabe, who was now an assistant to Admiral Naokuni Nomura, president of the Merchant Marine Control Board. Watanabe, a member of Admiral Isoroku Yamamoto's staff when the war began, had brought Yamamoto's ashes back to Tokyo for a state funeral after the commander in chief of the Combined Fleet and architect of the Pearl Harbor attack was waylaid and shot down by American planes on April 18, 1943. (Because American cryptographers had broken Japan's top secret code system, Yamamoto's precise flight plans that day were known in Washington, and a squadron of 16 P-38 fighters was able to intercept him exactly on schedule as his plane approached Bougainville's Kahili airfield.) Captain Watanabe, who was Yamamoto's planning officer, had been scheduled to go on that fatal flight but Yamamoto had then decided to leave him behind because there were some staff problems which needed attention. After accompanying Yamamoto's remains back to Japan, Watanabe had stayed in Tokyo, where he was now in charge of dispatching and scheduling what was left of the country's merchant fleet. He had supplied a set of shipping statistics which Admiral Hoshina would read at this morning's meeting. Hoshina went over to check some of the figures with him, then sat down at his usual place near the head of the large table that dominated this damp, cement-walled catacomb-like room.

Within a few minutes, all the important personages had arrived and today's meeting of the Naval General Staff was about to begin. Admiral Yonai, though present, sat back in his chair. He usually attended staff meetings but seldom spoke. Admiral Soemu Toyoda, the chief of staff, who sat at the head of the table and presided, launched the meeting with a few remarks about the previous day's shocking developments.

"There were many ugly rumors circulating here at the ministry yesterday," he said. "I want to warn all of you that in these difficult days we must maintain the strictest discipline over our officers and men. The war has not yet ended. Bear that in mind. But bear in mind also that if and when the war does end, there must be no acts of indiscretion by navy personnel. As chief of staff, I intend to protect this country and maintain the honor of the navy. And I expect the cooperation of every one of you."

As he spoke, Toyoda glanced more than once at Admiral Ohnishi who represented, as he knew, the navy's greatest rebellion threat. The previous morning, after Toyoda and Yonai had issued a joint order which said essentially what Toyoda was saying this morning, he had gone from his office next door to Ohnishi's office and repeated the identical message in person. He did not want Ohnishi's fanatical young followers, especially among the kamikaze squadrons, to rise up and disgrace the navy. At the same time, however, Toyoda was full of sympathy for the Ohnishi point of view. He was still opposed to the kind of surrender course on which the Emperor and the government had embarked. In his mind the notion was developing that someone should try at least once more to persuade the Emperor against surrender. This was a notion to be discussed perhaps with the army, which seemed still eager to fight if one could judge by General Anami's public statement to the troops last evening. It was not a notion to be discussed with Admiral Yonai. Yonai, who would forbid it.

Admiral Yonai listened with approval to what Toyoda was telling the general staff. Yonai knew that when the surrender came, Toyoda would do everything possible to maintain discipline and order, even though Toyoda had opposed surrender at the meetings of the Supreme War Council. Yonai understood the pressures upon Toyoda to argue for continuation of the war. Not all of the belligerent young officers were in the army. The navy had its share, and they had a very persuasive, almost hypnotic leader in Admiral Ohnishi. Toyoda could not disregard these people. The threat of assassination was very real, and while Yonai himself was willing to live under it, as he had done in years past when he opposed the alliance with Germany and the moves toward war, he could not ask other men to take such risks.

After his opening remarks, Admiral Toyoda called on Admiral Hoshina for a report on the domestic situation. When Hoshina listed the previous day's enemy air raids against naval installations, there was very little reaction. Most of these facilities were attacked day after day by American planes from carriers a few miles offshore. At Hashirajima, near Hiroshima, where Japan's great naval fleet used to stand anchored, and from which place it had emerged to do battle in the waters of Hawaii, Midway, the Solomons, the Marianas, and the Philippines, only a few battered ships now remained, hidden in narrow straits between islands, with fake trees camouflaging their decks and superstructures. Though the Americans continued to attack Hashirajima, they could do little damage because there was so little left there to be damaged. Even the ships which were hidden there had no real value to the Japanese because there was not enough oil to operate them.

Hoshina's report about the current condition of the merchant fleet, compiled by Captain Watanabe, commanded more interest from the admirals around him. Merchant ships were now being sunk or damaged at the rate of 10,000 tons per day. In the previous month, 300,000 tons of shipping had been put out of commission, which meant that the country now had only 420,000 tons of cargo ships in operation, plus another 200,000 tons undergoing repair. At the present rate of loss, the merchant fleet would be totally eliminated in another two months. Even the small quantities of oil and rice from Sumatra and Malaya, iron and coal from China, and corn from Manchuria which were still coming in despite the blockade would soon be cut off.

The picture seemed totally dismal. Yet when Admiral Ohnishi arose to report on the navy's military situation, there was fire and enthusiasm in his voice. At every base, the vice chief of staff assured his colleagues, the officers and men were ready for the enemy to attempt his invasion. There would be no letdown because of peace negotiations. The war had not yet ended. Nobody knew whether the enemy would agree even to the single stipulation included in the government's surrender offer. The Special Attack Corps in particular were eager to fight, eager to sacrifice themselves in the decisive battle to save the homeland. Thousands of pilots were ready to take off from their hidden airfields and dash their planes against the ships of the invaders. The many explosive-laden small boats sequestered in the bays and rivers of Kyushu were waiting to dash out into the open sea and ram the enemy troop transports. The situation was not hopeless. Never had there been such an opportunity for brave young men to serve their country. He could only hope they would not be deprived of that opportunity. Even now it was not too late for Japan to win.

When Ohnishi finished, there was an uncomfortable feeling in the room. Neither the few admirals who agreed with him nor the majority who opposed him had any desire to go on record openly. Admiral Toyoda adjourned the meeting and the members of the Naval General Staff began drifting back to their offices, most of which were in the bowels of this large underground shelter. (The ministry building overhead was a mere shell, having been burned out during an air raid in May.)

Admiral Hoshina was almost at his office door when Admiral Ohnishi, who was walking behind, overtook him.

"Let me ask you something," Ohnishi said. "What did you think of the army's attitude toward the surrender proposal?"

Hoshina said, "Anami and Umezu were both against it."

"Do you think the army will continue the fight?"

"I don't know."

"I think they will," Ohnishi said. After gazing upward, dreamily, for a moment, he continued, "If twenty million people are ready to die for Japan, we can still win this war." It was a belief he had often and vigorously expressed in recent months. More than 1,200 of his kamikaze pilots had already died in suicide missions over the Philippines, Formosa, and Okinawa. He envisioned millions of Japanese soldiers, sailors, and civilians detonating themselves against the enemy in planes, in boats and automobiles, even on foot during the coming climactic battle for the homeland. Stepping closer to Hoshina, he spoke in a confidential tone. "Listen, why don't you talk to Admiral Yonai once more? Maybe it would still be possible to bring him over to our side. We can't surrender. We must continue the war."

Admiral Hoshina responded vaguely, leaving open the possibility that he would again discuss the matter with Yonai. The previous day, after the announcement that the government was seeking peace terms in compliance with the Emperor's will, there had been rumors in the Navy Ministry of an assassination plot against Yonai, whose influence in the cabinet and preference for peace were well known. Though it would be unfair to suppose Admiral Ohnishi had given rise to such rumors, some of his more extreme confederates among the younger officers might have done so. Ohnishi had great influence at all levels in the navy. He was dynamic and daring. He was well-loved by his men. That was why he was so dangerous. Hoshina hoped Admiral Yonai was sufficiently aware of the danger.

AUGUST 11,
MIDMORNING

B E H I N D   T H E closed doors of one of the smaller rooms in the War Ministry's air raid shelter, fifteen young officers, mostly colonels but a few majors, sat around a long table listening to Lieutenant Colonel Masahiko Takeshita who had called them together.

"What we're here to talk about," Takeshita said, "is something that must not be discussed outside, at least for the present. I know each of you, and I know how you feel about the events of the last two days. I also know how General Anami feels. He realizes now that the prime minister is acting strangely. He saw how Suzuki and Sakomizu tricked the Supreme War Council into the imperial conference night before last. He knows how they and Yonai and Marquis Kido have been influencing the Emperor. And he is very much disturbed, I can tell you." Inasmuch as Takeshita was General Anami's brother-in-law and frequent companion, his analysis of the war minister's feelings could not be discounted.

"Everyone wants peace," Takeshita continued. "General Anami wants peace. We all want peace. But we do not want the kind of disgraceful surrender which the Badoglios in the cabinet have talked His Majesty into accepting. They say they will insist on the one condition—that the national polity be preserved. That's nonsense. If we want to be certain that the national polity and the imperial system are preserved, we must insist on all four of the conditions for which General Anami and General Umezu have been fighting. We can't allow the enemy to disarm us and occupy the country. We can't allow him to imprison and kill anyone he chooses as a war criminal. If the enemy has that much power over us, he can do whatever he pleases to do; he can compel us to change our national polity in any way he wishes. And since it is not possible for foreigners to understand the unique national polity of Japan, you can be sure they will make us change our whole government to fit their own notions. The Potsdam Declaration says something about establishing a government based on the freely expressed will of the Japanese people. But we all know how easily the people can be swayed. It would not be difficult for the occupation forces to get the people to consent to the destruction of the imperial system. Do you agree?"

There was a general rumble of accord from his listeners, who included some of the most influential young officers in the War Ministry —among them, Lieutenant Colonel Masao Inaba, the author of the previous day's manifesto from General Anami to the troops, and Major Kenji Hatanaka, one of Takeshita's subordinates who was also one of General Anami's favorite protégés.

"We're all convinced something must be done to prevent the unthinkable disgrace which threatens this country," Takeshita resumed, "but the question is, what can we do? Major Hatanaka has worked out a plan which he has asked me to present to you. It's a plan which would establish a military government under the leadership of the war minister. Is there anyone here who disapproves?"

Though no one came forward to disapprove, there seemed to be some uncertainty. One of the officers asked, "How does the war minister feel about it?"

"I think I can assure you," Takeshita said, "that when the proper moment arrives, the war minister will be our leader."

The enthusiasm of the fifteen men in the room increased immediately. Their faith in General Anami was such that if he would lead them they felt anything might be possible. There were other problems, however.

"What about the Emperor?" one of them asked.

A hush came over the room as everyone waited for Colonel Takeshita's answer, but he was ready for the question. "I appreciate your feeling," he said. "If we continue the fighting until the war minister's four conditions for peace are met, we shall be temporarily disobeying the Emperor, and that is an awesome prospect. But as you know, Japan has had Emperors for more than 2,000 years, and in that time it has had many different kinds of Emperors, some strong, some weak. Let me ask you—if the Emperor Meiji were alive today, would he have wished to surrender?" It was a rhetorical question which needed no answer. "Unfortunately, our present Emperor is not strong, so we must do for him what he cannot do for himself. We must supply for him the strength and determination he lacks. In doing so, we might, as I say, be disobeying him temporarily. But it would be for his own welfare and the welfare of Japan. We would be acting in compliance with the wishes of his Imperial Ancestors. And that would constitute a wider and truer loyalty to the Throne."

"What you're talking about then," one of the officers said, "is a coup d'état."

"But a legal coup d'état," Takeshita insisted. "In a time of crisis, the war minister has the authority and even the duty to establish martial law. It's his responsibility to bring out the army and maintain order. Basically, that's what we're talking about."

There could be no doubt by this time that every man in the room was convinced. One of them said, eagerly, "All right, how do we go about it?"

Major Hatanaka, whose fierce zeal was evident in the burning intensity of his eyes, could restrain himself no longer. Though he had asked his commanding officer, Colonel Takeshita, to chair this secret meeting, the plan for the coup was his, and he wanted to explain it. Leaping to his feet, he cried, "What we must do is separate the Emperor from the Badoglios who have been advising him. First we have to take care of Suzuki, Yonai, Togo, and Kido. Once they're out of the way, we can talk to His Majesty and reason with him."

There was no disagreement about this, but exactly how was it to be done? Which of the generals in the War Ministry could be counted upon to take part? How many of them should even be informed of it? Which troop units should be used and how could the others be neutralized until such time as the coup was accomplished? What locations in the city would have to be taken? What was the best time to make the move? After a long discussion in which everyone participated, several important matters had been decided.

The time of the coup was to be no later than midnight of the thirteenth. It would be carried out by the authority of the war minister, General Anami, and it would involve the immediate cooperation of three other generals—Yoshijiro Umezu, the chief of staff, who was a close friend of Anami; Takeshi Mori, commander of the First Imperial Guards Division at the Imperial Palace; and Shizuichi Tanaka, commander of the Eastern District Army, which was the army corps responsible for the defense of the Tokyo area. Martial law would be enforced by the troops of the Imperial Guards and the Eastern Army, and after the Imperial Palace was taken, the Emperor would be restricted to a specific area within it, where he could no longer be influenced by peace agitators. Negotiations with the enemy would continue, but only on the basis of the four conditions set forth by the war minister. And if the enemy refused to negotiate, the war would continue to an absolute end.

When the discussion was finished and these plans agreed upon, the fifteen officers left the War Ministry bomb shelter quietly, two or three at a time. It would not be advisable just yet to draw attention to the fact of their meeting. Colonel Takeshita and Major Hatanaka, who were among the last to emerge, shook hands and smiled happily. They hadn't felt so hopeful in several months. They might yet save the nation. They had very few misgivings about their plan. All they had to do was convince the war minister that he should lead them.

AUGUST 11,
EARLY AFTERNOON

O U T S I D E Yaita Field, a secret Army Air Force facility in the mountains 80 miles north of Tokyo, Private Zenjiro Osaki, with a rifle on his shoulder and a revolver on his hip, paced back and forth monotonously along the fence. Though he was on permanent guard duty protecting the base, he didn't know the nature of the activities inside. There were rumors among his fellow guards that secret weapons or planes were tested here. None of these soldiers had any facts, however, to substantiate the rumors. They were completely separated from the vital functions of the base. They knew for certain only that it was an airfield, that they had to walk guard tours around its perimeter for hour after hour, day after day, and that they were to ask no questions about it.

Private Osaki disliked the assignment and he disliked the war. He had reasons enough. Since the war began, nothing had gone well for him. After the fire destroyed his home and shop in Tokyo's Nihonbashi district the night of December 14, 1941, during the first week of the war, he had been unable to reestablish his greengrocer's business. He had moved his wife, Sumi, and two sons into small quarters and had gone to work in another shop. In 1943, he had saved enough to move them again, into a new house built on the site of the 1941 fire.

But just as his situation seemed to be improving, he was drafted into the army. Then on March 10 of this year, the new house in which his wife and children were living was destroyed during Tokyo's most severe air raid of the war. And now, with his family evacuated to the country, where they were inaccessible to him, he found himself at this remote mountain air base, carrying a rifle back and forth, rain or shine, from morning until night.

There was very little about Japanese army life that Zenjiro Osaki liked. The hours were long. The rifle was so heavy it seemed to dig a groove into his shoulder. The food, a combination of rice and barley, was distasteful. And the pay, 5½ yen ($1.26) per month, was almost insulting to a man who had once been a shopkeeper. After two years in the army, Osaki was still, psychologically, a civilian. The Samurai tradition was not his and it did not stir him.

What bore down on him increasingly as he paced off his distance along the fence, turned, paced it off again, then again, then again, was the futility rather than the discomfort of his daily routine; and, by extension, the futility of whatever the air force was doing at this base, of what the whole Japanese Army was doing, of what Japan was doing. How long did it take a country to realize it was defeated? Even if some great secret weapon were being tested at this field, what good would it do? Who would manufacture it? There were so few factories left, and so few cities, it was ridiculous to think of putting new weapons to use. Even a private in the army could see that.

Osaki's job, however, was to walk this guard post, so he would walk it until he dropped from the heat. He didn't have to like it. He would do it because he was, after all, Japanese. And as he walked, he could comfort himself with one certainty. The war was not going to last much longer. Japan was getting ready to make peace with America. How did he know? He might be still a civilian at heart but he had developed one soldierly trait during his two years in the army. From small facts he could draw great conclusions. Two months earlier, he had been put on a list to be sent overseas. He had not yet been sent. This could mean only one thing. The fighting was about to end. He would bet on that. Meanwhile, he would keep pacing off his distance, doing his about-faces, and shifting his heavy rifle from shoulder to shoulder.

AUGUST 11,
MIDAFTERNOON

T H E War Minister, General Anami, stood erect before Emperor
Hirohito in the makeshift audience room of the Emperor's makeshift
residence, the palace library. Though the two men had been talking
for several minutes about routine army matters—personnel changes,
promotions, troop placements, fortifications—both had their minds
on a more critical concern, the surrender offer which the government
had sent to the Allies almost 36 hours before, but which had not yet
been answered. In General Anami's mind there was a strong apprehension that the delay was more than routine, that the Allies would
refuse to accept the one Japanese condition—preservation of the
national polity and the imperial system. Even if they did accept this
condition, he feared they might not honor it, and when he came to
the end of his routine business with the Emperor, he could not restrain himself from speaking about these worries. If the enemy was
to be given a free hand in disarming and occupying the country, what
guarantee would there be that he would honor any commitment he
might make in regard to the national polity. He was an enemy, after
all, not a friend. And however well disposed he might be, he could
not possibly understand the subtle workings of Japan's governmental
system. It was obvious, indeed, that he did not even care to understand. His propaganda placed all blame for the war upon the Japanese, and went so far as to blame His Majesty himself. Was it not
dangerous to put the nation, and the august Imperial House, helplessly into the hands of such an enemy? Would it not be wise even
now to reconsider the surrender offer and deny the enemy permission to occupy Japan? The country was not defenseless. In the event
of an invasion, the army and navy were both capable of striking a
hard blow against the enemy. This capability should be used in any
negotiation which might be conducted. There was no other way to
be certain the national polity would be preserved.

As always, General Anami argued passionately, directly, and simply. The Emperor could not help being charmed by him. Everyone
was charmed by him. Hirohito had seen many men grow in self-
importance and stuffy dignity as they arose in military rank, but
Anami seemed to be the same engaging, open, unaffected person
now he had been when he first came to the palace in 1929. Though
he had been at that time only a lieutenant colonel and an aide-de-
camp, it was already evident he would become an important figure
in the army, not only because he commanded respect as a living

embodiment of the ideal Samurai soldier, but even more important, because everyone liked him. Years and promotions had not changed him. His ingenuous warmth made a person happy in his company even when his arguments were impossible to accept.

It would be pointless to go over again all the reasons why Japan must surrender. Perhaps it was true that the army and navy could still strike a hard blow, but could they win the war? How had they done so far? Since 1942 when America began its counteroffensive, the Japanese armed forces had not been able to hold a single objective the Americans decided to take. The fighting spirit of the Japanese warrior, indomitable as it was, had not been able to withstand, in any Pacific campaign, the superior materiel of the enemy; and there was no reason to believe spirit would prevail on the shores of Japan. On the other hand, while America was an implacable enemy, it also boasted a tradition of righteousness which meant that any public promise it might make was likely to be honored. With a smile of assurance on his face, the Emperor said, "We feel certain about the safety of the national polity. Do not worry, Anami."

The war minister's reaction was one of startled silence, but not because of what the Emperor had said. Only because the Emperor had called him by name. His Majesty scarcely ever called him, or anyone else, by name. It was an overwhelming honor, one which Anami had never before received in the 16 years since he first enjoyed the privilege of being allowed in the Imperial presence. He was still basking in this honor when the Emperor spoke again.

"Was it necessary," the Emperor asked, "for you to release that warlike exhortation to the troops last night, when the government was awaiting an answer to our peace offer? Were you not acting contrary to the cabinet policy?"

Anami's joy at being addressed by name was jarringly replaced now by the awful shock of an Imperial rebuke. But to what was His Majesty referring? That statement Colonel Inaba had written yesterday? Was it so bad? Perhaps His Majesty had misunderstood its purpose.

Anami said, "Some kind of statement encouraging the troops was felt to be necessary, Your Majesty, because until peace actually comes, the army must be kept in readiness to fight."

The Emperor said no more on the subject. When General Anami left the palace, his feelings were in turmoil. He was still excited by the wondrous pleasure of hearing the Emperor call him by name. Yet he felt deeply chastened by the sting of His Majesty's reprimand.

AUGUST 11,
LATE AFTERNOON

THOUGH THE heat of the afternoon had begun to diminish, and the clean, country breeze felt good upon his perspiring forehead, Junnosuke Ofusa was becoming almost too weary to appreciate it. For seven hours he had been pedaling his bicycle through the green, agricultural Kanto Plain north of Tokyo, toward the little town of Tochigi in the foothills at the border of the plain. It was a trip he made every month to see his wife, Tamako, and their three children, all of whom he had sent there in 1943. His neighbors in Tokyo had laughed at him then for being so timid as to evacuate his family, and some had even called him a coward. His older daughter, who was six at the time, had cried because she was being forced to leave her schoolmates. But he thought he knew more about the Americans than most of his fellow Japanese, and he was convinced there would be air raids before the war ended. There had been times, throughout 1943 and most of 1944, during these long bicycle trips to see his family, when he regretted having evacuated them; he no longer regretted it. They had been spared the entire terrifying experience of watching the city go up in flames around them, and they were also getting enough to eat. He wished he himself could move to Tochigi with them, but the job he now had, as a translator for the *Nippon Times*, paid him 180 yen (about $40) a month, and while that was not as much as he used to make during those ten, happy prewar years when he was a reporter for the *New York Times*, it was, at least, enough to let him keep his family safe in the country.

He thought of his prewar boss, the *Times* Tokyo bureau chief Otto Tolischus, and wondered where he was now. The last time Ofusa had seen Tolischus was six months after the war began, when the police finally released him from Sugamo Prison and sent him to the detention center for repatriation to America. Would Tolischus return to Japan when the war ended? After his unpleasant experiences with the Japanese police, he could hardly be blamed if he chose otherwise.

On these weekends when he cycled to Tochigi, almost 50 miles from Tokyo, Ofusa would get up at 5 A.M., boil enough rice for breakfast and for a lunch on the road, then head north toward the suburb of Ueno from his tiny, three-room home in Fukidecho, near the American Embassy. His house and the houses around it had never been touched by fire, for which Ofusa thanked their proximity to the embassy, one of the few undamaged spots in the blackened city. Ofusa, like many Japanese, had developed an awesome respect for the accuracy of American bombers. Since everything more than a block or so from the large embassy compound had been leveled, he was convinced the embassy had been spared purposely by the ingenious Americans, and he could tell an eyewitness story which seemed to prove his point. On a cloudy day in May, when it could not have been possible to see the ground from an attacking plane, a flight of B-29s had nevertheless dropped a rain of incendiaries along a path leading directly to the embassy, but then, within a block of it, had swerved left, avoiding it. Though this might have been a stroke of luck, Ofusa didn't think so. He was persuaded that the Americans now had a device which allowed them to pick out landmarks through the clouds, and in a way he was glad of it, because by swerving when they did to avoid bombing the embassy, the bombers had also spared his house.

The first part of his trip to Tochigi was the most depressing. Until he passed through Ueno, on the north side of the city, there were almost no houses to be seen. The burned-out shells of brick buildings still stood here and there, with people living in them, and on all sides there were shacks, tacked together from debris. In front of these shacks he would often see small cooking fires, and people moving around slowly. That was one of the stranger features of Tokyo these days. The famous energy of the Japanese seemed no longer to exist. Most people moved around at a listless pace, as if they weren't sure where they were going. When he reached the more open suburbs, however, he came to some areas which looked almost normal, with clumps of houses intact and green patches around them. From here north, compassionate householders would come out onto the road to offer green tea to the steady stream of people leaving Tokyo for the country. The road was often so clogged with these refugees, plus their carts and household animals, it was difficult to cycle between them.

When he reached the city of Oyama, Ofusa experienced an upsurge of energy because, even though he had still a few miles to go, he felt that since Tochigi was the next town, he was almost there. Just north of Oyama he turned left and the terrain began gradually to change as he cycled toward the foothills of the distant mountains. Scattered in what appeared to be random arrangements among the rice fields were lovely, thatched-roofed farmhouses, sometimes with tile-roofed outbuildings. In the fields, farmers, and often whole farm families stooped laboriously over the inundated rows of rice plants. The last mile or so being uphill, Ofusa was out of breath and tired to the point of exhaustion as he arrived at the little cottage in which his wife and children were housed, but he tried not to show it as they came out to greet him. His wife, like most women in the country these days, wore the baggy trouser suit which had been adapted from the traditional female peasant costume, and which all Japanese women were encouraged to wear. As their little boy and two little girls swarmed around him, she stood back, bowing and smiling.

"Any news from the city?" she asked.

"Only rumors," he said. "The bomb which hit Hiroshima must have been dreadful. The Japanese government has sent a protest against it through Switzerland, whatever good that will do. And meanwhile, I hear another one like it was dropped on Nagasaki, though it hasn't yet been announced. There's also a rumor at the office that the government is seeking peace. I hope so."

"Do you believe it?"

"I don't know what to believe. I think peace has to come soon. The country has to surrender. There is also a rumor of a coup d'état by the army."

"Is that possible?"

"It's something to worry about," he said. "You never know what the army might do. But there are always rumors. I've stopped paying attention to them. What do you have to eat?"

His wife smiled. "Poor man, I'll bet you starve without a woman to cook for you."

"I'm better off than most people," he said. "At least I can take some extra food back from here every month. I don't know how other people in Tokyo manage. There just isn't enough food. If the war continues into winter, I'm afraid many will starve."

She shuddered. "Don't think about such things. Come in. Let me get your bath ready, then I'll feed you."

Ten minutes later, as she helped him into the deep, steaming tub, Junnosuke Ofusa could almost forget Tokyo and the misery he would again face when he returned there tomorrow. For a day at least he could lose himself happily in Tamako's tender care, in the delicious smells of whatever she was cooking, and in the happy sounds of his children's voices. If only those peace rumors would be true, he might soon again have his family with him every day instead of once a month. When the Americans returned, as they inevitably would, he might even get back his job with the *New York Times*. It was something about which he could dream, anyway.

AUGUST 11,
EARLY EVENING

T H E   H O U S E (around the corner from the Diet Building on the Miyakezaka hill) which was now the war minister's official residence, had been his deputy's office until recently, when the war minister himself took it over because American bombs destroyed his more imposing official residence nearby. This present office, at which General Anami was now also eating many of his meals and spending most of his nights, was a modest-sized but beautifully designed Japanese-style house, surrounded by well-kept trees and shrubbery. From the glass-enclosed corridor on the north side, it offered a full view of the wide moat, the slanted stone walls, and the magnificent trees of the Imperial Palace's still undamaged southern expanse. It also offered a full view, beyond the palace on both sides, of Tokyo's burned-out ruins.

General Anami, having returned from his audience with the Emperor at the palace, was sitting cross-legged at his low dining table, drinking a cup of sake after an early dinner, when his young brother-in-law, Lieutenant Colonel Masahiko Takeshita, arrived to talk to him. Unlike General Anami, who looked quite composed, Takeshita looked harried, and because he had lost weight in recent weeks, his somewhat threadbare uniform hung loosely on him. Anami poured him a cup of sake and the two men sat in silence for awhile.

Though they were next-door neighbors in the suburb of Mitaka, they saw little of each other there lately because neither was able to get home very often. Takeshita was billeted, with several other officers, at a large house the army had taken over in the Ochanomizu district north of the Imperial Palace. He saw his brother-in-law at the War Ministry almost every day, of course, and he often came here evenings to sit and drink with him. Both men held their liquor well. It was a matter of pride for a Japanese warrior to be able to do so.

Takeshita and Anami had first met in 1915 when Takeshita was only ten years old and his father, an infantry regimental commander, encouraged Anami, then a 26-year-old lieutenant in his unit, to court his beautiful daughter, Aya. From the beginning, the friendly, athletic, and soldierly officer who was destined to marry Takeshita's older sister was a hero to the ten-year-old boy, and when Takeshita grew into manhood, becoming himself an officer, he tried to emulate his brother-in-law, with whom he began to drink sake and practice kendo. After 30 years, Anami was still a hero to Takeshita. Tonight, however, the strain of recent events governed their companionship.

Anami knew the intensity of the fire and frustration consuming his brother-in-law and many of the other young officers at the War Ministry. He knew how perilously close they were to exploding, and being a Japanese soldier himself, he sympathized with their inability to accept the idea of surrender. But he also knew that such totally committed young men could become an uncontrollable force if they were not handled carefully. He would have to watch what he said to them and also what he said in public. He could not afford to let them get out from under his leadership.

Takeshita, in fact, had no desire to get out from under Anami's leadership. On the contrary, he planned to call on the war minister for further leadership so daring it was awesome to contemplate. This was not, however, the purpose of Takeshita's visit tonight. After a few perfunctory remarks, he got around to what he wanted to say.

"I've come here to apologize," he began. "You know that statement yesterday . . ."

"Which statement?"

"The manifesto to the troops."

"Oh, that!" Anami became suddenly sober. "This afternoon, His Majesty reprimanded me for it."

Takeshita was shocked. Though the Emperor might not be a strong man, he was still the Emperor, and it was dreadful to think of General Anami receiving a reprimand from him. Takeshita said, "I'm sorry. I'm very sorry."

"Why should you be sorry?"

"Because it was I who released the statement to the press. The blame should be mine. The situation yesterday seemed so urgent to me that I called in the reporters and handed it to them without your authorization. I had no right to do so and I want you to know I feel badly about it."

Anami was surprisingly magnanimous. With a gesture of his hand he said, "Don't let it worry you. "Shimomura [Hiroshi Shimomura, president of the Information Board] called me about it before he put it out and I asked him to go ahead with it. I was shocked, of course, when His Majesty rebuked me. He asked me if I didn't think it was contrary to cabinet policy. But I explained to him that it was necessary to encourage the troops because the army might still have to fight to the end. After that, His Majesty said no more about it."

Takeshita looked carefully at his brother-in-law in an effort to determine whether he was actually taking the whole matter as casually as he indicated. General Anami's facial expression was calm. He showed no signs of being upset. Takeshita thought of the coup d'état plans which he and some of his friends were formulating. Should he mention these plans now to the war minister? Takeshita decided to wait for a more appropriate moment.

When Takeshita stood up to leave the war minister's official residence, General Anami decided he would also go out. He called for his driver to take him to his family home in the western suburb of Mitaka. He had not seen his wife and children for several days and he missed them.

AUGUST 12,
1:30 A.M.

S H U N I C H I M A T S U M O T O, the vice minister for foreign affairs, chugged into the courtyard of the prime minister's official residence in his steam-driven automobile and leaped out of it before the driver had brought it to a complete halt. He was admitted to the building immediately and when he reached the third floor room which the chief cabinet secretary was using both as a home and an office, he found Hisatsune Sakomizu waiting for him with a freshly received copy of America's reply to Japan's August 9 surrender offer. The Domei radio monitoring station had picked up the message about a half-hour after midnight. A Domei reporter who had brought it to Sakomizu was still there when Matsumoto arrived. So was the Foreign Ministry's English language expert, Toshikazu Kase, whom Sakomizu had also called. Matsumoto could see deep disappointment and concern in the faces of all three of these men as he took the note and read it:

With regard to the Japanese Government's message accepting the terms of the Potsdam proclamation but containing the statement "with the understanding that the said declaration does not comprise any demand which prejudices the prerogatives of His Majesty as a soverign ruler," our position is as follows:

From the moment of surrender the authority of the Emperor and the Japanese Government to rule the state shall be subject to the Supreme Com-

mander of the Allied Powers who will take such steps as he deems proper
to effectuate the surrender terms.

The Emperor will be required to authorize and ensure the signature by the
Government of Japan and the Japanese Imperial General Headquarters of
the surrender terms necessary to carry out the provisions of the Potsdam
Declaration, and shall issue his commands to all the Japanese military, naval
and air authorities and to all the forces under their control wherever located
to cease active operations and to surrender their arms, and to issue such other
orders as the Supreme Commander may require to give effect to the surrender terms.

Immediately upon the surrender the Japanese Government shall transport
prisoners of war and civilian internees to places of safety, as directed, where
they can quickly be placed aboard Allied transports.

The ultimate form of government of Japan shall, in accordance with the
Potsdam Declaration, be established by the freely expressed will of the
Japanese people.

The armed forces of the Allied Powers will remain in Japan until the
purposes set forth in the Potsdam Declaration are achieved.

When he finished reading, Matsumoto let the piece of paper hang
listlessly in his hand. He could understand now why the others were
so gloomy. "... the authority of the Emperor and the Japanese Government to rule the state shall be subject to the Supreme Commander
of the Allied Powers ..." "... The ultimate form of government of
Japan shall . . . be established by the freely expressed will of the
Japanese people..." Would the army accept such clauses? Not likely.
Matsumoto read the note again without finding any new encouragement.

Sakomizu said, "It doesn't exactly promise to preserve the imperial
system, does it?"

"It doesn't seem to promise anything," Matsumoto said. "That
phrase about the people choosing their own form of government
could cause us a lot of trouble with the army. They'll argue that the
people might be persuaded to do without the Emperor."

"But is the Emperor included in the government?" Sakomizu suggested.

"I suppose we can argue that he is not included."

"The clause about the Emperor being 'subject to' the Allied commander seems to indicate an intention to let us keep the Emperor."

"The problem with that clause," Matsumoto said, "is the wording.
The army will explode over the idea of the Emperor being subject
to anyone."

Sakomizu could not disagree. He had now been visited twice by furious army officers who wanted four conditions attached to the peace bid. How would these officers react when they learned that America hadn't quite conceded even the one condition?

"Is it possible," Matsumoto wondered aloud, "that we could get the Allies to change that phrase?"

Sakomizu dismissed the hope. "Even if they were willing," he said, "it would take more time than we have. If we had to wait two days for another reply, our government would collapse."

"How could we translate it so it doesn't sound quite this bad in Japanese?"

Toshikazu Kase, the foreign ministry translator, suggested a rendering which would indicate in Japanese that the Emperor was to be "under the limitation of" the Supreme Commander of the Allied Powers."

"That may sound slightly better," the vice foreign minister agreed, "but will the army translate it the same way?"

Sakomizu said, "The army lacks good English translators. Maybe if you sent them your version quickly, they might accept it. But you would have to move fast because they will soon have this English version in hand, if they don't already have it."

"I'm afraid," Matsumoto said, "that they won't accept any translation."

"But I'm afraid," Sakomizu said, "we have no choice."

Matsumoto pondered the problem for several minutes as he paced the floor. "All right," he said finally. "Let's try to push it through as it is. I'll see if I can get Togo to accept it, and you see if you can get the prime minister to accept it."

As the two men parted, however, neither had any confidence that the army would accept it.

AUGUST 12,
6 A.M.

A F T E R finishing the light breakfast his wife had made for him, General Anami went upstairs to the bedrooms of his still-sleeping children to have one more look at them before he left the house. Of the seven Anami children, only four (two girls and a boy of school age plus a younger boy not yet five years old) were still at home. His oldest son was an air force technician. His second son, who had been an air force pilot, was killed during a 1943 air battle in China. When he learned the details of his son's death, Anami had written a poem in his diary:

> Though I have sacrificed my child to His Majesty,
> the Emperor,
> How can I forget my beloved son?
> Everyone feels sorry to see the leaves of a young
> tree fall before withering.

As he gazed down at his sleeping children, only lightly covered on their futons because the night had been warm, he realized how wise he had been to come out and see his family the previous evening. Already this morning he had received word from the War Ministry that the American reply had arrived and that it was far from acceptable. Today and the days ahead were going to be busy and difficult. At least he had been able to play with the children for a short time before they went to sleep last night—all except little four-year-old Koreshige who was sound asleep when he arrived home and was still sound asleep. General Anami bent to touch the child's cheek, then hurried downstairs where his wife, Aya, was waiting to say goodbye.

After 30 years of marriage and seven children, Aya Anami was still an astonishingly beautiful woman with small, delicate features and rich black hair which she parted on the right and combed straight across her head so that it framed her oval face. She was taller than average and slender. She moved gracefully. She said nothing as General Anami prepared to leave. The daughter of a Samurai, she was a quiet woman who asked no questions of her husband. Recently, she had spent very little time with him even when he was at home. It seemed that other officers and friends were always dropping in to see him. Last night, a group of his subordinates including young Major Hatanaka had come to see him and had stayed quiet late, discussing the country's terrible crisis and what should be done about it. Her husband was a troubled man, caught up in the difficulties of trying to keep several factions satisfied. She knew about his troubles. She heard him discussing them with others. Yet he never discussed them with her.

The general's car and driver were waiting when he and his wife emerged together from their home—a rather large, two-story, tile-roofed house which Anami had built in 1930 when he was a regimental commander. It was what was considered a standard-sized house for a regimental commander, comfortable but not ostentatious. Anami had never felt the need to enlarge it, or to buy a more imposing one when he became a general officer and an important figure in the army. The trees and gardens within its walls were carefully trimmed. At the back was his archery target, but he had no time this morning for archery. In the stucco wall on one side was a gate leading to the home next door of Mrs. Anami's brother, Colonel Takeshita. The two families spent so much time in each other's homes the gate might as well have been removed and thrown away.

As General Anami and his wife stood by his army car, he glanced across the street and shuddered inwardly. The whole area on the other side had been destroyed by bombs during a raid on a nearby airplane equipment factory. The flames had come within 40 feet of his house. He looked at his wife and smiled.

"Good-bye," he said.

"Good-bye," she said, and bowed.

He got into the car and, as it pulled away, waved through the back window. She raised her hand and returned his wave, wondering when she would see him again.

AUGUST 12,
8:20 A.M.

T H E A R M Y and navy chiefs of staff stood side by side facing the Emperor in the modest-sized room he was now using for audiences. General Umezu, bald and bullet-headed, looked sternly and coldly military at first glance, but on closer examination showed a friendly face with a mouth which seemed at all times ready to smile. Admiral Toyoda, close-cropped and fat-faced, with a nose almost as wide as his mouth and a little mustache separating them, looked, in his high-collared, black uniform, more like a theater usher than a naval officer. Umezu was their spokesman.

"No doubt Your Majesty has already had the opportunity to read the communication from American Secretary of State Byrnes [James

F. Byrnes] which arrived during the night in reply to our peace proposal. There is strong feeling both at the War Ministry and at the Navy Ministry, Your Majesty, that the enemy demands should be rejected."

As General Umezu talked, General Shigeru Hasunuma, the Emperor's chief military aide, stood in the background, listening passively. It was he who had arranged this hurried audience after being informed that the War Ministry was in turmoil. General Umezu, having arrived very early at his office, had walked into a hive of angry young officers. Measuring their mood, he had called Admiral Toyoda to sound out navy reaction to the Allied note. Together they had decided to inform the Emperor of the rebellious feelings with which the Allied demands were likely to be received by Japanese fighting men everyplace. Yet as Umezu spoke, there was none of the urgency in his voice that one might expect during a serious crisis.

"Your Majesty has surely noticed that the enemy note does not guarantee our national polity as we stipulated, nor does it promise to preserve our Royal House. It says the Japanese people will decide on our form of government, and as you know, the people are easily swayed. In addition, the note demands that until the people decide, Your Majesty is to be subject to the Supreme Commander of the Allied Powers. If such a clause is accepted, it is not possible to foretell the reaction of certain elements in the army and in the navy. For these reasons, Your Majesty, we petition you to reject the demands of your enemies."

The Emperor, who had watched Umezu closely as the general talked, gave no evidence of being perturbed. He was as well aware as both Umezu and Toyoda of the volatile nature of young Japanese military officers. He had been forced to step in personally to put down the coup d'état attempt of February, 1936. But the chiefs of staff would no doubt agree that the young officers could not be allowed to make the nation's decisions. Umezu's protestation did not seem very impassioned. It was as if he and Toyoda had come here simply to report the situation, or to impress the young officers by taking some kind of action.

The Emperor smiled at both men and said, "As you know, we have not yet received the Allied reply formally. When it arrives we shall study it well, and at that time we can probably make further inquiry about those points still in doubt."

Umezu and Toyoda bowed and prepared to leave the Imperial presence.

AUGUST 12,
10 A.M.

GENERAL ANAMI had finished talking to General Umezu about the reply from Secretary of State Byrnes and about the early morning appearance of Umezu and Toyoda before the Throne (of which Anami did not disapprove) when he heard a commotion in the hall outside his war ministry office. His secretary, Colonel Saburo Hayashi, who was with him, went out to investigate.

A moment later, a dozen officers from the Military Affairs Bureau came crowding into the room. They were led by Anami's brother-in-law, Colonel Takeshita, to whom Hayashi could hardly bar access. Takeshita's extreme agitation was evident on his face.

Waving a copy of the Byrnes note, Takeshita cried, "Have you seen the American reply that came last night?"

"I've read it," General Anami said.

"Well?" Takeshita, after waiting a moment for Anami to continue, asked impatiently, "What do you plan to do about it?"

"The cabinet meets this afternoon to discuss it."

"Discuss it!" Takeshita, who had expected Anami to be as furious as himself, and to show it, could scarcely endure the general's apparent calm. "What is there to discuss? You can't accept a surrender that would make the Emperor subject to his enemies."

General Anami stood up, his face indicating that he could see no point in carrying on a discussion like this with his brother-in-law while a dozen other officers listened. "That's something we shall have to decide at the cabinet meeting," he said.

Takeshita, aware now that Anami was trying to avoid going into the matter with him, suddenly lost his self-control. Pointing his finger at the war minister, he cried, "If you plan to accept these terms, you had better be ready to commit harakiri!"

There was not a sound in the room for some time after he finished. General Anami looked at Takeshita, seemed about to speak, then turned to his secretary, Colonel Hayashi, and said, "We had better go now."

In the car on the way to Anami's official residence, which was their destination, Anami sat silent for awhile, then said with a sigh to Hayashi, "That was a cruel thing Takeshita said to me. It is too much to tell me to commit suicide. Of course, I'm nearly sixty years old. I don't think it would be difficult for me to die. Perhaps for a young man like you it might be difficult, but not for an older man like myself."

Hayashi, who was not a friend of Takeshita and did not share his views, tried to steer General Anami away from the morbid thoughts which were apparently besieging him. "You still have a great duty to perform," Hayashi said. "The country is moving toward peace. However it may happen, the war is bound to end soon. And there are millions of our men scattered all over Asia and the Pacific. It will be your duty, sir, to disarm them and repatriate them. You should not think of committing harakiri until that is done. In my opinion, there is no reason for you to commit harakiri at all."

General Anami looked out the car window at the dismal ruins of the Kojimachi district through which they were passing. "I guess what you say is right," he said.

AUGUST 12,
NOON

N A V Y   M I N I S T E R Admiral Mitsumasa Yonai, who opposed the war (during a previous term as navy minister) even before it started, had resigned himself in the last year or so to the conclusion that it is impossible to end a war until the war is ready to end itself, that a certain inertia moves it along until it exhausts itself. During the last two or three days, Yonai had thought hopefully that the time had come. But today he was not so certain. The Allies' reply to Japan's surrender offer had further complicated an already delicate situation. He could imagine what was happening at the War Ministry this morning. He knew what was happening in the Navy Ministry's underground shelter quarters, and he was alarmed by it. The navy's young zealots, under the leadership of Vice Admiral Takajiro Ohnishi, the vice chief of staff, had accepted with bad grace two days ago the fact that Japan was suing for peace, but they had accepted it. There were signs today, however, that they might not accept a Japanese surrender under the terms demanded by the Byrnes note, with no specific guarantee that the national polity and the imperial system would be preserved. The emotional climate at the Navy Ministry this morning was so heated as to be almost combustible. Admiral Ohnishi was exhorting his followers to fight to the finish. During the last few days he had been difficult enough. At the meeting of the Supreme Council on the morning of August 9 (as vice chief of staff Ohnishi was admitted to such meetings), he had worn his sword and clanged it ominously. He had even approached the war minister, General Anami, and called Yonai a coward for favoring peace. Today he was even more rampant than usual. He had the young officers in such an uproar about the Byrnes note there was real danger of mutiny. And he was not alone in his recalcitrance among the navy's older officers. Admiral Toyoda, of all people, seemed on the point of joining the rebellious mob. A friend in the Imperial Household Ministry at the palace had informed Yonai of Toyoda's early morning appearance before the Emperor, with General Umezu, to plead for rejection of the Byrnes note. Yonai, who had not been informed of Toyoda's intention, was angered by this news. He had always considered Toyoda a friend and a man of quality. Like himself, Toyoda had spoken out against the war before it began, and he had refused the post of navy minister in General Tojo's cabinet. Though it might be understandable for Toyoda, as chief of staff, to oppose the navy minister, as he had done, in a Supreme War Council vote, it seemed unconscionable to Yonai that Toyoda had gone secretly to plead before the Emperor. Yonai was not a martinet. He had achieved leadership in the navy not because he demanded obedience but because he commanded respect. He was better educated and better read than any man in Japanese public life. His personality was engaging. His mind was quick and so was his body. No one in the navy had ever been able to throw him in a judo contest. No one in the navy had ever been able to outdrink him, either. He had become such a legend as a man that he could, under ordinary circumstances, maintain discipline simply by his presence. But the circumstances today were not ordinary. He decided he had better take stern measures.

Summoning Admiral Zenchiro Hoshina, the director of the Naval Affairs Bureau, he said, "I want you to go personally to Admiral Toyoda and Admiral Ohnishi and tell them to come here at once. It might be advisable also for you to come back here yourself and listen to what I have to say to them."

A few minutes later, when Toyoda and Ohnishi entered Yonai's office together, they found the navy minister (a big man, more than six feet tall) standing at his desk and staring down at them with bitter indignation.

"The behavior of the Navy General Staff in the last few days," he said, "has been execrable. Ohnishi, if you have anything to say about me, if you think I'm a coward, why don't you come and say it to my face? And what kind of impudence makes you think you have the right to walk into a meeting of the Supreme War Council wearing your sword? You have been acting lately in a way that is unforgivable."

Turning next to the chief of staff, Yonai continued: "And you, Toyoda, since when do you seek audience before His Majesty without informing the navy minister? By what right do you, in the name of the navy, and without consulting me, ask His Majesty to reject the Allied demands? The directive which you and I issued to all naval personnel two days ago (a directive demanding rigid adherence to the navy's discipline and the Emperor's desire in seeking peace) was intended to prevent just such behavior as this. It is inexcusable for you to have acted in such a way."

As Yonai finished, Toyoda remained at rigid attention, saying nothing. Perhaps he had made a mistake in going to the Emperor, but the pressure of Ohnishi and the younger officers had been so great he had felt that some such gesture was necessary. He had not told Yonai because he knew Yonai would forbid it. Yonai's anger now was understandable. There was no point in trying to answer him. The only thing to do was accept his rebuke. Still silent, Toyoda bowed deeply to the navy minister.

Ohnishi, at the same time, had reacted quite differently and surprisingly. A very emotional man, he had been caught quite off-guard by Yonai's assault upon him. All of his usual aggressiveness abandoned him and he burst into tears. "I'm sorry!" he cried, bowing his head. "I'm deeply sorry!"

Admiral Yonai sat down at his desk and looked up at the two men for almost a minute. Then, with a wave of his hand, he said, "That's all. You may go."

AUGUST 12,
2:30 P.M.

GENERAL Korechika Anami was in his War Ministry office preparing to leave for the 3 P.M. cabinet meeting when Colonel

Masahiko Takeshita arrived again with a sheaf of papers in his hand and a delegation of young officers behind him. Though their last meeting a few hours earlier had ended badly with Takeshita telling Anami he should commit harakiri if he planned to accept the demands of the Byrnes note, Anami showed this afternoon no indication of resentment against his younger brother-in-law. Takeshita was inclined to be impulsive, and like so many other officers in the army, he simply could not stomach the concept of surrender. Anami was disposed to be indulgent because in his heart he harbored the same feeling.

Among those with Takeshita now were Colonel Masao Inaba, Colonel Okikatsu Arao, and Major Kenji Hatanaka. When they entered the room, Anami was already on his feet and about to depart.

Addressing the war minister quite formally, and with his voice under careful control despite his high state of emotion, Takeshita said, "On behalf of the officers with me here, sir, and on behalf of many other officers, I would like to say that we deem it utterly inadvisable for Japan to meet the peace terms dictated in last night's note from Washington. We trust that you are as determined about the matter as ourselves. And we're confident that you will make your feelings known at the cabinet meeting this afternoon. We feel also that circumstances in the next few days may necessitate the enforcement of martial law. With this in mind, we think the Eastern District Army should be alerted so that troops will be available when and if they are needed."

Though Takeshita may have intended to continue and explain the entire plan for a coup d'état, Anami did not give him the opportunity. Nodding assent to what Takeshita had said so far, he turned to Lieutenant General Tadaichi Wakamatsu, the vice war minister, who had come in from his office next door to observe the proceedings.

"Colonel Takeshita has an excellent idea," Anami said to Wakamatsu. "Would you please see to it that the Eastern Army [which was responsible for the defense of the Tokyo area] is alerted?"

After issuing this order, Anami was about to make a quick departure when Takeshita spoke again.

"May I say one more thing before you leave, sir?"

"Of course."

"In order to prevent a disgraceful surrender," Takeshita declared, "we think it may be necessary to stage a coup d'état. We would then obtain from His Majesty an Imperial order to continue the war." Handing Anami one set of papers, he continued, "Here are the plans. We've worked them out in detail." Handing him another set of papers, he added, "and here is a petition signed by all of us, asking you to be our leader."

Before Anami could react to these papers which had been thrust upon him, another officer who had entered the room to watch, Colonel Hiroo Sato, chief of the war preparation section, spoke up to Takeshita. "I hope you men don't plan to do anything hasty," he said.

Major Hatanaka, who had been so agitated for the past several days that he found it difficult to contain his energy, turned on Colonel Sato savagely. "The trouble with this army," Hatanaka shouted, "is that there are too many Badoglios in it."

Sato lunged toward Hatanaka but other officers intervened. Anami then stepped forward and put out a hand to each man. "Come now," he said, "military men must trust each other."

During the awkward pause that followed, one of the officers standing near Takeshita whispered in his ear, as if prompting him. Takeshita, looking embarrassed, said to Anami. "We also want you to know we have faith in you, and we shall follow you whatever you decide to do."

Anami bowed gracefully, and before any more untoward incidents could occur, hurried to the door.

AUGUST 12,
3 P.M.

WHEN THE CABINET came to order for an informal session in its second-floor meeting room at the prime minister's official residence, Baron Admiral Suzuki began the proceedings by calling upon Foreign Minister Togo to read the note from American Secretary of State James Byrnes (which Suzuki reminded everyone had so far been received only informally) and to give his opinion of it.

After reading it aloud, Togo had to admit that the note was less than specific about the preservation of the Imperial system. "However, it is natural and to be expected," he said, "that the government, and therefore His Majesty to some extent, will be under the limitation of the Allied powers (he carefully used the Foreign Ministry's softened translation) until the Potsdam terms are fulfilled. This will not destroy or even change the Emperor's preeminent position among the Japanese people."

After passing quickly over the next two paragraphs, Togo came to the second crucial section of the Byrnes note—the demand that the Japanese people decide ultimately what kind of government they wanted.

"This provision, rather than making us uneasy, should actually reassure us," Togo insisted. "Who could believe that the Japanese people, given their choice, would choose anything other than the Imperial system?"

These were the best arguments Togo could muster and he presented them forcefully, in his aggressive, preemptory style. But were they strong enough to persuade the army? Every man in the room looked toward the war minister.

Since early morning, General Anami had been listening to people tell him he should reject the Byrnes note. In addition to the officers at the ministry, Baron Kiichiro Hiranuma, president of the Privy Council (who had earlier given weak support to the peace bid), had pleaded with him to hold firm. And one of the senior commanders in the field had exhorted him by telegram to resist "the temptation of enemy peace feelers and the negative thinking in the country." But if Anami was presenting the army position and Baron Hiranuma's position when he arose to speak, he might also have been presenting his own.

Quite calmly he began. "The foreign minister's remarks," he said, "do not alter the fact that the Allied demands as expressed in last night's communication would make His Majesty subject to the will of whomever they select as the supreme commander. In effect, the occupying forces would thereby have the ability to dispense with our Imperial system at any time. What else could they have in mind when they assert that the Japanese people should be given the right to choose their own form of government? It is not within our power to accede to this demand because we would be giving the Japanese people a privilege which is not ours to give—the privilege of dispensing with the Emperor. It should be clear to all of us that no one has the right to dispense with the Emperor because the Emperor is divine. He is a god. As long as there is a Japan, there must be an Emperor. We must therefore reject unequivocally these impossible demands. And this means we must reject not only the note they sent last night but also their insistence on occupying Japan and disarming our armed forces."

Togo realized now that he was in for a very difficult afternoon. He had not expected the divine right argument, which was almost impossible for a loyal Japanese to counter, nor had he expected Anami to take up again his earlier position concerning occupation and disarmament. Togo decided he had better ignore the divine right question and attack the other two.

"The offer of peace which we sent to the Allied nations two days ago," he reminded Anami, "contained only one stipulation because that was the Emperor's wish. If we were to send another note now with the additional stipulations you have mentioned, we would be showing disrespect for the Imperial wish. And we might also be eliminating the possibility of further negotiations with the Allies since they would surely accuse us of bad faith in our previous communication. I might also say, we in the Foreign Office have reason to believe that some of the Allied nations strongly advocate the elimination of our imperial system. This note from Washington indicates that America has not yet succumbed to that viewpoint. But if we persist in enlarging our demands, the Americans may then enlarge their demands."

Despite Togo's persuasiveness, General Anami was not prepared to abandon his position. The lines were now drawn, and as other cabinet ministers entered the discussion, it was merely to take one side or the other. With the exception of Navy Minister Yonai, who supported Togo, the others were not, to be sure, an important factor. Only two of them, Home Minister Genki Abe and Justice Minister Hiromasa Matsuzaka, wholeheartedly embraced Anami's view but several seemed strongly impressed by it. In any case, Anami alone, since he represented the army, had enough weight to balance the rest of the cabinet, and Anami could not be budged. Shortly after four o'clock, with the debate dragging hopelessly, Togo left the room to make a phone call to his vice foreign minister, Shunichi Matsumoto.

"The situation looks very bad," Togo said to Matsumoto. "At the moment I would say the atmosphere within the cabinet is against acceptance. Can you think of any new arguments I could use on them?"

As Matsumoto enumerated all the arguments he knew, Togo assured him he had tried each of them. "The only thing I can suggest, then," Matsumoto said, "is that you get the meeting adjourned. Don't let it come to a vote. Stall for time while we try to come up with some fresh ideas."

Togo returned to the cabinet room with the intention of following this advice.

General Anami was speaking again and he now seemed to be

pursuing a new strategy. He was addressing himself, not to the cabinet, but to the prime minister.

"I would like to remind you," Anami said to Suzuki, "of the Supreme War Council meeting in the Imperial presence two nights ago. Did you not agree at that time that if the Allied nations refused to guarantee the preservation of our imperial system and our national polity, you would support a continuation of the war?"

The prime minister, who until now had remained detached from the discussion, shifted uncomfortably in his chair. "Yes," he said, "I took that position."

"Do you feel that the note from Secretary Byrnes makes those guarantees?"

Suzuki sighed. Anami's question was not unexpected. Both Anami and Baron Hiranuma had argued this matter privately with him earlier in the day, and he could not deny that he found strong merit in their arguments. "No, I'm afraid the note guarantees nothing," he said.

Anami pursued his point like a prosecutor. "Then what is your opinion as to the course we must take?"

"I must admit that I personally find the note from Secretary Byrnes unsatisfactory," Suzuki said. "It does not promise the preservation of our national polity or of our Royal House. As a military man, I also find it unbearable to think of our armed forces being disarmed and disbanded. Under the circumstances, I feel there is only one thing to do. We must seek a clarification from the Allied nations. And if they refuse to make the necessary concession, we shall have no choice but to continue the war."

The shock of hearing Suzuki embrace this viewpoint left everyone momentarily numb. It had been generally assumed that the prime minister, who was one of the prime movers in the struggle toward peace, would favor acceptance of the Byrnes note despite any reservations he might have about it.

Foreign Minister Togo was the most astonished man in the room. Early in the morning Togo had gone to the Imperial Palace and learned from the Emperor that he favored acceptance. The Emperor had asked Togo to convey this to the prime minister and Togo had done so. It was unthinkable, it was infuriating to hear this indication that Suzuki was defecting from the imperial desire. Something had better be done quickly before the entire cabinet followed.

Leaping to his feet, Togo said, "I would like to make a suggestion." He paused long enough to get his anger under control. If he were to give freedom to his feelings, he would accomplish nothing. "The prime minister's remarks are worthy of careful consideration," he continued. "But at the same time, we cannot vote to pursue the war without regard to its probable outcome. Unless there is some prospect of victory, I remain convinced that it is essential to negotiate for peace. We do not, however, have to make a decision at this moment. Since the official communication from Washington has not yet arrived, I propose that we now adjourn this meeting and reopen it when that document does arrive."

There being no objection, Prime Minister Suzuki called the meeting adjourned, then left the room and went directly across the hall to his private office. He quickly discovered he was not alone. Foreign Minister Togo was at his heels. As soon as the two men were closeted behind the closed office door, Togo burst forth with what he had wanted to say during the cabinet meeting.

"How could you, of all people, take such a position?"he demanded.

The old man made a gesture of resignation. "General Anami was right. I did promise before His Majesty two nights ago that if the Allies refused to guarantee our Imperial system I would favor continuing the war."

"But you know very well the Emperor's own feeling." He said this morning he favors accepting the Byrnes note. Whether we like it or not, we have no alternative. The country is prostrate. The war cannot continue. If the cabinet now votes to try to continue it, I shall go again directly to His Majesty."

Without waiting for the prime minister to reply, the foreign minister stormed out of the room.

AUGUST 12,
4 P.M.

Dr. Tsunesaburo Asada, back in his physics laboratory at Osaka University after three days at Hiroshima, had just finished a detailed report on the nature of the bomb which hit that city when one of his assitants informed him he had a visitor, a naval lieutenant. Since Asada had prepared his report for the navy, he assumed the man must have been sent for some reason by the Osaka naval headquarters, but when his visitor entered the laboratory, Asada decided he had been mistaken. He didn't quite know this young man, yet the face was familiar.

"I used to be a student of yours," the lieutenant reminded him.

"Ah yes," Professor Asada said, suddenly remembering him quite well. He could even recall his last name. "Mr. Saito, isn't it?"

"That's right, sir."

Lieutenant Saito did not volunteer his first name and Dr. Asada did not recall it. He did recall, however, that Saito had been a chemistry student and had graduated from the university only a few years earlier.

"I see you're in the navy now," Asada said. "Are you stationed here in Osaka?"

"No sir, I'm an instructor at the naval academy."

"In that case," Asada said, "perhaps you witnessed the catastrophe down there." The Japanese naval academy was on the island of Etajima in the Inland Sea, not far from Hiroshima.

"I heard the rumble," Lieutenant Saito said, "and we all saw the cloud. That's what I've come to talk to you about."

Asada invited him to sit down and a girl brought tea. "I just returned from there myself," the professor said. "The navy is sending me to Tokyo tomorrow or the next day to report my findings to the General Staff."

"I'm on my way to Tokyo now," Lieutenant Saito said. "The commandant of the academy has sent me to present his report on the bomb."

A sudden chill came over Asada. "And what does your commandant's report contain?" he asked.

"In his opinion," Lieutenant Saito said, "the bomb was not atomic. It was a mixture of magnesium powder with liquid oxygen, in large amounts. He has decided that from a military standpoint, there is no reason to be unduly concerned about it."

Asada, having already witnessed the strong disinclination of military men to believe that America had actually developed an atomic bomb, could envision the naval General Staff in Tokyo believing this report rather than his own, which stated unequivocally that the bomb had been atomic. They were much more likely to believe a naval commandant than a mere physics professor.

"I conducted some very thorough tests in Hiroshima," he said, "and I found that four days after the blast, the entire city was still contaminated with radioactivity. You're a chemist. Tell me, could such a condition have been created by a magnesium detonation?"

Lieutenant Saito's wry smile indicated that he had now fulfilled the reason for his visit. "No sir," he said, "I do not think so."

Asada, suddenly aware and appreciative of the perception that had brought this young man to him, broke into an even wider smile. "I wonder if it would be possible," he asked, "for you to arrive in Tokyo with your commandant's report after I have submitted my report?"

"I think it would be possible," Lieutenant Saito agreed.

AUGUST 12,
LATE AFTERNOON

NAVY CAPTAIN Mitsuo Fuchida felt slightly more hopeful about the national crisis now than he had felt for the last three days. He had just emerged from the office of Vice Admiral Takajiro Ohnishi in the Navy Ministry's air raid shelter headquarters, and he was encouraged at having learned that at least one person of high rank on the navy General Staff was determined to prevent an ignominious surrender. Ohnishi had told him to hold himself in readiness and to pass the word among other naval officers that the war was not yet lost, nor was the country yet betrayed. There were plans afoot to save it.

Fuchida already knew of one plan—the coup d'état plot taking form in the army—and he believed the navy should join it. He had been horrified three days earlier when, on his return from Nara to Tokyo, he had learned of the government's surrender move. What about all the kamikaze pilots who had given their lives for Japan, and all the men he had seen go down in such battles as Pearl Harbor and Midway? "If those men were allowed to die in vain," he had said to his commanding officer, Admiral Shikazo Yanno, "then we, too, should die. We should fight until there is not one of us left." Unable to arouse Admiral Yanno, he had then gone to see an army liaison officer in the navy, and it was from this man that he had learned of the projected army coup. "If the army rises," Fuchida had promised, "I'll do everything I can to make sure the navy cooperates." The next day he had gone to the huge naval base at Yokosuka, and then to the naval air base at Atsugi, recruiting young officers to participate in the coup. Today he had been able to assure Admiral Ohnishi that everyone to whom he had talked was eager for action.

As Fuchida emerged from the concrete underground shelter, he stood still for a moment while his eyes adjusted to the light of the late afternoon sun. Another officer was approaching, and Fuchida could soon see, as the man drew near, that he was a rear admiral. The man waved and Fuchida suddenly recognized him. It was one of the Emperor's brothers, Prince Takamatsu, who was attached to the naval General Staff. Fuchida knew him well. They had been classmates and friends at the naval academy 25 years earlier.

Prince Takamatsu had an urgent expression on his face. He walked directly to Fuchida and took hold of his arm. "Fuchida," he said, "I hear you've been agitating for a coup d'état."

"Yes, indeed," Fuchida said eagerly. "You're with us, I hope. We must save the Emperor before it's too late."

Prince Takamatsu walked him a few feet away from the shelter entrance. "I have just come from a family meeting at the palace," he said. "My brother summoned us there because he felt it was necessary to speak to us. He told us frankly what his wishes are and he asked for our assistance. I want you to know, Fuchida, it is the Emperor's will that Japan accept the surrender."

This was a blow Fuchida could not have anticipated. It was inconceivable that His Majesty, whose very position made him immune to surrender, could actually wish to bow to his enemies. He was the foremost warrior in Japan. Yet he was also the Emperor. If this was his will, how could anyone oppose it? And if Prince Takamatsu said it was his will, it must be so. Takamatsu was not a man who could be false.

Trying to hold back tears from his eyes, Fuchida finally brought himself to rigid attention before the Emperor's brother. "Since that is His Majesty's desire," he said, "I shall obey it."

Prince Takamatsu smiled. "I'm happy to hear you talk that way. But what about all the officers among whom you've been agitating at Yokosuka and Atsugi? I'm aware of your activities in the last couple of days. Will you go back and tell them what I've just told you?"

Fuchida gulped. "They won't like it," he said, "but I'll go back and tell them."

AUGUST 13,
7 A.M.

DESPITE his feeling that he had scored heavily in yesterday's cabinet debate, General Anami was disturbed this morning. His success at the cabinet meeting had been so evident (especially his progress in swaying Prime Minister Suzuki), that he had gone, a few hours later, to visit one of the Emperor's brothers, Prince Mikasa, who happened also to be an army officer. It might still be possible, Anami hoped, to influence the Emperor's opinion about the Byrnes note by influencing Mikasa. He would use on Mikasa the same arguments he had used to such advantage on Suzuki. But any expectations he had of persuading the prince were soon shattered. Mikasa, having attended that afternoon's meeting of the Royal Family, knew exactly how the Emperor felt, and how strongly he felt, not only about Japan's present dilemma but about the army.

"Since the Manchurian Incident began [1931], the army has not once acted in accordance with the will of the Emperor," Mikasa had said to Anami. "It is most improper that you should still want to continue the war when things have come to this stage."

After absorbing these harsh words from the Emperor's brother, General Anami had gone to his official residence for the night, but he had been unable to sleep. Shortly after 3 A.M., he had thought of another idea that might influence the Emperor. Why not ask one of the army's two venerable field marshals to go to the palace and make an appeal to His Majesty? It would have to be Marshal Shunroku Hata, even though he was very busy in Hiroshima, directing relief work and trying to put together the pieces of his Second Army after the blast there. Marshal Gen Sugiyama was not so busy (he was in command of the First Army) but it was well known that he did not have the Emperor's confidence. He had been, indeed, as war minister and then as chief of the General Staff, one of the men most responsible for the Emperor's displeasure with the army. It had seemed to Anami that Hata was the very man to send to the palace, but it might be well to get another opinion. He awakened his secretary, Colonel Saburo Hayashi, and sent him directly to the home of General Umezu to get the chief of staff's opinion of the plan. Colonel Hayashi had returned with more discouraging words. General Umezu had said to him simply, "I am in favor of accepting the Potsdam Declaration." It was a shock to Anami who had believed that his close friend, Umezu, was deeply committed to continuing the war.

Now, at 7 A.M., Anami was on his way to the Imperial Palace to talk to the one other person who might possibly be helpful—Marquis Koichi Kido, lord keeper of the privy seal. Marquis Kido was living at the palace, in a room on the second floor of the large, pentagonal Household Ministry Building, where he also had his office. He had moved into the palace recently because he was convinced that the army saw him as perhaps the leading conspirator behind the peace movement and would therefore set out to kill him. He felt safe under the protection of the Palace Guards, who were part of the army to be sure, but who were presumably less loyal to the army than to the Emperor.

Passing through the Sakashita Gate of the palace, General Anami felt a pang of guilt as he glanced up to the left at the burned-out hillside where the Emperor's personal palace had once stood. The army's inability to protect His Majesty from the insulting loss of his palace was, to Anami, a sin which had to be redeemed.

Marquis Kido, wearing a traditional gray-black male kimono, was in his office when Anami arrived. His greeting was friendly. The two men had known each other since the early 1930s when Anami was a military aide to the Emperor and Kido was secretary to the previous privy seal.

"I've come to talk to you about the Byrnes note," Anami said. "I find it dangerously unsatisfactory. It guarantees nothing. If we accept it, I'm afraid it might mean the downfall of our nation. It seems to me we must by all means get the Emperor to reconsider his opinion and allow us to prepare for a final decisive battle. Pessimism in war never yields good results. If Japan will only make one last effort, strike one more hard blow, it may be possible to achieve peace on a more advantageous basis. That is my feeling, at least. What do you think?"

Kido had listened impatiently. He had made up his mind some time ago that Japan could not win the war, and he was in no mood to hear this kind of talk. "That just won't work," he said. "The Foreign Office has analyzed the Byrnes note very carefully, and after hearing Mr. Togo explain it, I cannot see why it should be considered so damaging to us. If it is people's opinions we need, we can get as many as we please, but we simply cannot go on gathering one opinion after another. We must abide by the opinions of the responsible authorities. There is no alternative."

Kido studied Anami carefully and decided the general was still not convinced. "Look here," he continued. "Suppose the Emperor does change his attitude. Suppose he rescinds the peace proposal of the tenth and issues a proclamation for a final, decisive battle. What would the Allied nations think? They would probably regard him as a fool or a lunatic. It would be unbearable to have His Majesty insulted that way. You may have your own ideas but I must do what I think is right."

General Anami seemed to be wavering now. There was resignation in his voice and even a slight smile on his face as he said, "I understand your position quite well. I knew you would say something like that. But I felt I must come to you because the atmosphere in the army is quite tense."

At the mention of the army Marquis Kido bristled. He had become quite impatient with it lately. "Don't talk to me about the army," he said, in a burst of pique. "The army is hiding in shelters while the people are exposed to air attacks. How can you carry on a war that way?"

General Anami was startled by these unkind words. Didn't Kido know that the people, too, had shelters? It was difficult to believe Kido could talk that way after he had seemed for many years to be such a good friend of the army. It was Kido, after all, who had recommended General Tojo, and later General Koiso as prime ministers. When he was himself the education minister in 1937, he had cooperated fully with the army in the effort to instill a military spirit in the youth of Japan. And as an adviser to the Emperor, he had, on occasion, preached caution when it seemed possible that His Majesty might take steps which would curb the army. Could Kido's attitude have changed that drastically? And why? Simply because the war was going badly? He had not complained when the war was going well. Anami felt chagrined and slightly foolish for having come here. He had lost more than he had gained by the conversation. He didn't want to get into a discussion about the army. He decided simply to say a few polite words and leave. When he bowed and retired from Kido's office, he was more disturbed than ever.

AUGUST 13,
8:45 A.M.

AS THE Supreme War Council convened in the stuffy air raid shelter of the prime minister's official residence, General Anami had reason to be uncertain about the alignment of votes this morning. There was a possibility that his position had gained the support of Prime Minister Suzuki, in which case he would have a four-to-two advantage in the six-member council, leaving only Foreign Minister Togo and Navy Minister Yonai in favor of accepting the Byrnes note. There was also, however, the possibility that General Umezu was about to abandon Anami's position (since he had told Colonel Hayashi during the night that he personally favored acceptance), and the further possibility that Admiral Yonai had influenced Admiral Toyoda in the direction of acceptance, all of which could leave Anami with no one on his side except, perhaps, Suzuki. He would soon see which of the possibilities prevailed.

Prime Minister Suzuki began the meeting by calling on Foreign Minister Togo who informed the council of a cable which had arrived during the night from the Japanese minister to Sweden. The cable reiterated the already familiar argument that Britain and Russia opposed retention of Japan's Imperial system, and that unless Japan quickly accepted the Byrnes note, America might do likewise.

"We should not reject the note," Togo concluded, "simply because it means that the Emperor would be, for a time, restricted by the Allied commander. We should consider the positive aspect that the Emperor would be assured of remaining on the Throne."

Admiral Toyoda was quick to answer this. "I have given the Byrnes note careful study," he said, "and I still read the same meaning into it. The Emperor would not only be 'restricted by' the Allied commander. His Majesty would be 'subject to' the Allied commander. We know what our true beliefs are about the acceptability of such a situation. We should not hedge. We should make our views clear to the Allies so there will be no doubt about the future status of the Throne. Why should the Emperor even have been mentioned in the Byrnes note? Why can't the Allied commander give his orders to the Japanese government?"

Anami could now feel reassured about Toyoda's support. But if he still hoped for help from Suzuki and Umezu he had better restate, forcefully, the position he had taken yesterday. Rising to his feet, he said once more that the note would have to be revised and clarified, that the sanctity of the Emperor was not a negotiable issue and must be guaranteed. The only way to guarantee it, he concluded, was to reject the Allied plan of occupation and disarmament.

Admiral Yonai argued impatiently that these matters had already been decided, and to make an issue of them now would be to oppose His Majesty's wishes.

Yonai's stand on the side of acceptance was no surprise, but Anamai was happy to see that Umezu arose to answer it.

"We are not arguing against the spirit of the Emperor's wishes," Umezu said to Yonai. "We are arguing about interpretations which must be clarified."

Anami felt relieved. However Umezu might feel, he would not desert the war minister's position. Anami still had, therefore, at least the three votes with which he had deadlocked the August 9 council meeting. Now what about Suzuki? Where did the prime minister stand this morning?"

Admiral Suzuki put aside a cigar he was smoking and leaned forward toward Umezu and Anami. "Does the military intend to upset our peace efforts by an endless discussion of the wording of the Byrnes note?" he asked. "Why can't we interpret the note as the experts at the Foreign Office see it?"

Anami's hope of a one-vote gain was dashed. Suzuki was again firmly with the peace faction and the Supreme War Council was again deadlocked at three-to-three. Though the debate continued, there was no sign of movement. At ten o'clock, some excitement arose when word came that the Emperor wished to see General Umezu and Admiral Toyoda immediately. Was he summoning them to ask that they vote for acceptance? If so, why had he not also summoned Anami? When they returned from the palace less than an hour later, those questions were answered. The Emperor had simply asked them to make certain that neither the army nor the navy would take aggressive action while peace negotiations were in progress.

This concern of the Emperor did not alter the alignment of votes in the council. The debate continued until after noon when the deadlock was still so hopeless that Prime Minister Suzuki adjourned the session.

AUGUST 13,
2 P.M.

BETWEEN the time the Supreme War Council adjourned and the cabinet was scheduled to meet, Chief Cabinet Secretary

Sakomizu hoped to get some rest. But about 2 P.M., his telephone rang. It was his old friend Saiji Hasegawa, the foreign editor at Domei news agency.

"The Americans got your message," Hasegawa announced cheerfully.

Sakomizu said, "How do you know?"

"San Francisco radio just broadcast a flash repeating exactly what we sent."

Sakomizu beamed for a moment, then suddenly groaned. "I'm happy they received it," he said, "but did they have to broadcast it?" He could imagine another delegation of furious army officers stampeding into his office as soon as the army monitors reported the San Francisco broadcast. This would be the fourth such visitation in four days and he was not sure how may more he could survive. On the night of the ninth and again on the morning of the tenth he had been put under duress by angry officers because he had used General Umezu's signature without authorization to arrange the imperial conference of the Supreme War Council. And just this morning the commander of the Kempeitai had come in person to warn him and Suzuki of dire results if the government actually surrendered. As Sakomizu knew, the Kempeitai was quite effective in bringing about dire results.

The message which he now expected would create new trouble was one he had sent shortly after noon through Domei. Deeply concerned about American broadcasts of the last two days which accused the Japanese of stalling and threatened more atomic bombs unless they capitulated immediately, Sakomizu had decided he had better get word to the United States that the Byrnes note was not being simply ignored in Tokyo. He had therefore asked Hasegawa at Domei to send out the following radiogram:

The Japanese government has decided in favor of peace. Delay in the formal acceptance of the Allied proposal has been caused by the fact that the cabinet is discussing procedures and technicalities.

He had sent the message through Domei because he knew the army would see it if he sent it through government channels. And Domei had apparently gotten it through unnoticed. He had not anticipated, however, that the Americans would give away his secret. There was nothing to do now but wait for the storm to descend from Ichigaya Heights.

Fifteen minutes later, it came. Several young army officers broke into Sakomizu's office with fists clenched.

"By what authority," one of them shouted, "did you send out a message that the Japanese government has decided to surrender?"

"You're a traitor!"

"Badoglio!"

When Sakomizu stood up to try to calm them he soon found he couldn't get in a word. They hadn't come to listen to him. Then it occurred to him that perhaps this was fortunate. He had no explanation that they would be likely to accept. He decided to say nothing and it was apparently a wise decision. After shouting at him for several minutes, they turned and left as quickly as they had arrived.

AUGUST 13,
MIDAFTERNOON

A M O N G the several hundred navy fliers gathered in the large auditorium at Oppama Air Base near Yokosuka was Lieutenant Saburo Sakai, who was now Japan's most honored living fighter pilot. Since December 8, 1941, when he shot down his first American victim over the Philippines, Sakai had shot down 63 others, including one who was now an American folk hero, Captain Colin Kelly. Sakai himself had been wounded so severely in air battle on one occasion that he was able to survive only by flying more than 500 miles over ocean water with several bullets in his body and head. As a result, he was now blind in one eye and walked with a limp. But he could still fly. He had not flown in battle, however, since the Iwo Jima campaign six months ago, in which he had shot down his last four American planes. He found it painfully frustrating now to watch the Americans fly over Japan, day after day, and not be allowed to pursue them. There were still some planes at the base, a few of them in excellent condition. Why could they not be used? For what were they being saved? It is often difficult for men of action to understand the strategies of their superiors who sit behind desks.

The commanding officer at Oppama, Commander Chiaki Matsuda, had called this meeting of all the pilots on the base perhaps with the intention of quelling some of the rumors which were circulating—rumors of surrender and of a possible coup d'état to prevent surrender.

"I've gathered you here," Commander Matsuda said, "first of all because I want to remind you that every one of you is an officer in the Japanese Imperial Navy. [Most were sergeants or petty officers. Japanese pilots were not given commissions for earning their wings.] I want you to be ready at every moment to maintain discipline among yourselves and among your men. You must hold yourselves constantly responsible for your deeds. You must at all times obey His Majesty, the Emperor. Remember, you are the finest pilots in the Japanese Navy. If this were not so, you would not be here. It is a great honor to be stationed at Oppama. And in the days ahead, I want Oppama to be an example to all other air bases."

He stopped and took a few steps forward from the podium to the edge of the stage. "Now I have unhappy news for you. The Japanese government, with the approval of His Majesty, has decided to accept the Potsdam Declaration. Within a few days, the nation will be forced to surrender. I feel as badly about this as all of you, but there is nothing any of us can do except to maintain discipline. I intend to make certain we do so. That's all."

There was no sound, no demonstration among the fliers—only a numb silence. Gradually they began to drift from the auditorium in twos and threes. The news was not absolutely startling. They had all heard the rumors. Yet it was a shock to hear them confirmed officially.

Lieutenant Saburo Sakai was so consumed by frustration his belly churned as he left the auditorium alone. He walked with eyes downcast toward the flight line. He wanted to be near his Zero fighter plane which was parked in one of the camouflaged bunkers. At last, the inevitable has come, he thought to himself. He had known for a long time that victory was impossible. But it was still possible to fight. Why were they no longer allowed to fight? There was at least enough gasoline available to send a few planes into the air. No doubt it was futile. In a day or two, the war would be over but that didn't stop the Americans from fighting. Every day, hundreds of their planes were still attacking Japan from Saipan, Tinian, Okinawa, Iwo Jima, and from the huge naval task forces which stood only a few miles offshore. It was a bitter, hateful experience for a flier to stand on the ground and watch these marauders fly overhead unchallenged.

When he reached the camouflaged bunkers, he nodded to one of the maintenance men, then patted the wing of his Zero and leaned against the fuselage. A friend of his who had also been at the meeting,

Ensign Jiro Kawachi, came along and, seeing him, stopped.

"Sakai," he said.

Sakai looked up but said nothing.

"I guess we haven't much time left," Kawachi said. "What if we were to go up on one last flight together. What do you say, Saburo?"

Sakai listened to him with growing interest. "We can't just quit this way," Kawachi continued. "We have to draw blood at least once more."

Sakai nodded. Good weather was forecast for tonight. The B-29s would surely come, and in such numbers they could be intercepted anyplace. The plan was already forming in Sakai's mind when he heard the drone of engines in the sky. From the south, an American B-24 bomber appeared, alone, at about 25,000 feet, heading toward the Yokosuka naval base. It was probably on a reconnaissance mission. The Americans were now flying daily reconnaissance missions over most of the large Japanese military installations. But whether it had come to bomb or to take pictures, it was still an enemy plane, a big, four-engine bomber, heavily armed. A worthy target.

Sakai looked at the B-24, looked at his Zero, then looked at his friend.

Kawachi's face lit up. "Shall we?"

Sakai said, "Let's do it."

Three minutes later they were off the ground and gaining altitude, Sakai in the lead, Kawachi on his wing. Once more, Saburo Sakai was happy, excited, exalted. The romance of the sky was in his soul. He felt he had been born to fly and to fight. The B-24 was still above him and at some distance from him, but when he gained altitude, he would be able to catch it. The Zero fighters were much faster than the bomber. It appeared now that the bomber pilot had seen the two Zeros approaching. Or perhaps he had simply completed his mission. Over Yokosuka, he went into a 180-degree turn and headed back south. It didn't matter. The Zeros would still catch him. Sakai was confident of that. But when he turned south in pursuit, he saw an unexpected problem ahead. A sizable bank of clouds was coming in off the Pacific and the American bomber was flying toward it.

Sakai pushed his throttle forward. Kawachi did likewise to keep up with him. But apparently the B-24 pilot was aware of them and had done the same. Though the Zeros were closing space, could they reach the bomber soon enough? The clouds were not far distant now. Sakai extended his Zero to maximum overdrive speed. He was almost within range. Against the background of the huge, white, billowy cloudbank, the bomber looked beautiful in Sakai's cannon sight. In just a few more seconds he could fire. Then suddenly the bomber began to look foggy, and a moment later it was not there at all. The B-24 had escaped into the clouds.

In total frustration, Lieutenant Saburo Sakai put his Zero into a banking turn as he, too, entered the clouds. After reversing his direction, with Kawachi still on his wing, he headed back toward Oppama.

AUGUST 13,
MIDAFTERNOON

O N T H E army motorcycle (with sidecar) which he usually had at his disposal, Major Hidemasa Koga of the First Imperial Guards Division was traveling from the Imperial Palace (where he was stationed) to the suburb of Setagaya to see his wife, Makie, who, with their 11-month-old son, was living now in the home of her parents, General and Mrs. Hideki Tojo. Koga had married Makie Tojo two years earlier after being at first reluctant about the match. He was then attached to General Tojo's staff (Tojo being at the time war minister as well as prime minister) and did not like the idea of marrying his commanding officer's daughter. But Tojo, impressed by the handsome young man's ability and soldierly qualities, had invited him to come and visit the family at the prime minister's official residence. After meeting Makie Tojo, Koga decided he did indeed want to marry her. In addition to being pretty, she was, as he later avowed to her mother, admirably meek and humble.

Because today was Makie's 22nd birthday, her mother, Mrs. Tojo, assumed when she saw her son-in-law pull up in front of the house on his motorcycle, that it was for this reason he had come. She soon realized that Major Koga had a deeper motive. Entering the house he went first to the front room on the left, a comfortable parlor which the retired General Tojo was now using as a study. Though Koga wanted to talk to his father-in-law, he did not stay when he saw that Tojo had a visitor. Hurrying to one of the rear rooms, he found his wife and baby son whom he picked up and embraced. The boy had seen so little of his father in recent months he showed no sign of recognition. Major Koga, having moved into the Imperial Guards headquarters at the palace, could find time only once every few days to ride his motorcycle out to Setagaya.

Holding the baby in his arms, he said to his wife, "Come with me downstairs to the air raid shelter. I want to talk to you in private."

When they reached the tiny concrete room below the house, Major Koga said to her, "If anything happens, I want you to take our son to my mother. [Koga came from a Kyushu family. His father had been a classmate of Hideki Tojo in military academy.] I think you should also take Yukie and Kimie (Makie's two younger sisters) with you. It will be safer in Kyushu. And when you get there, I think they should change their name to Koga." He anticipated that General Tojo's name might be difficult for his daughters to carry in the days ahead.

Having said this much, he reached out and took his wife's hand in a gesture of tenderness. "In stormy times," he declared, "I want you always to stay erect and proud. Never bow your head. Go forward." He paused, then resumed in an even more serious tone. "Do you have my hair and my fingernail clippings?"

By this time his wife knew what he was trying to tell her. Nails and hair, being the most time-resistant parts of the human body, are often kept in Japan as mementos of the dead. "I have them," she said.

"There are occasions," he said, "when a man must do his duty." She knew his feelings about the government's surrender plan, to which he was as deeply opposed as her father. She knew also he was likely to be involved in any movement to prevent it. He looked into her eyes then smilingly embraced her. "Come on, let's go upstairs."

They had been in the shelter for less than five minutes. When they emerged, Mrs. Tojo, a very intelligent woman who had quickly sensed the situation, was waiting for them.

Major Koga, in an apparently jovial mood, said to her, "Mother, have you put this house in order? We have our headquarters under control, but I feel that things are not yet in order in my own family."

Mrs. Tojo did not understand him. Before she could question him, he hurried again to General Tojo's study but the visitor was still there. He bid Tojo a very quick good-bye, then left the house and ran to his motorcycle. His wife, carrying their baby, and his mother-in-law rushed out after him to wave from the front gate.

AUGUST 13,
6:30 P.M.

T H E H E A T in the cabinet chamber and the debate were equally frustrating. Though all the windows in the large room were open, the air outside was as hot as the air inside. After more than two hours of argument among the cabinet members, perspiration stood out on every face and stained every collar. The argument had not, however, been fierce. It had been simply repetitious and stubborn. General Anami, polite and friendly as always, had nevertheless continued to assert that the Byrnes note was unacceptable because it guaranteed nothing. And while he had the support of only two other cabinet members (Home Minister Genki Abe and Justice Minister Hiromasa Matsuzaka) as opposed to ten or perhaps eleven favoring acceptance, his strength was such that he could still continue to keep the cabinet paralyzed.

Anami was, in fact, as weary of this situation as anyone else, yet he was also sensitive to more pressures than anyone else. He was aware of several disastrous possibilities which might materialize if he were to make the wrong move. He knew the Emperor's desires. He knew his own feelings, which he was able to control only by exercising all the Samurai self-discipline at his command. He also held a clear view of the emotional climate among key men in the army at this moment, and realizing that all emotions eventually cool, he was convinced he would serve no cause by standing up in front of his fellow cabinet members and bowing magnanimously to defeat. Time was what he wanted. Time offered a few possibilities which seemed to him at least more attractive than immediate capitulation.

Prime Minister Suzuki, cognizant that nothing was about to happen and that everyone needed a rest, called a short recess. He was not disposed to adjourn the meeting because he, too, was aware of time as a factor, and being sensitive to the dire threats beamed constantly at Japan by the American radio, he feared each wasted moment.

Before anyone had a chance to speak to Anami during the recess, he went, surprisingly, to the third-floor office of Chief Cabinet Secretary Sakomizu who had grown weary of the cabinet debate a few minutes earlier and had come upstairs to try to take a short nap. He was dozing on a small couch near his desk when Anami entered and asked if he could use the telephone.

Anami's call was to Lieutenant General Masao Yoshizumi, director of the army's Military Affairs Bureau, the man who had to be restrained from attacking Prime Minister Suzuki four nights earlier after the Emperor expressed his desire for peace. But since Yoshizumi was out of his office, Anami spoke instead to one of his aides, Colonel Okikatsu Arao.

"Is anything happening at the ministry?" Anami asked him.

"The situation is very tense but under control at the moment," Arao said. "Everyone here is counting on you. What about the cabinet meeting?"

"The cabinet is still in session," Anami said. "We're having a short recess at the moment."

"How is the debate going? Are you making any progress?"

"Surprisingly enough," Anami said, "I'm doing quite well. Several of the members seem to be coming around to our point of view."

Colonel Arao was so amazed as to be skeptical. "Is that really true?" he asked.

"Mr. Sakomizu is right here beside me," Anami said. "You can ask him if you wish."

Sakomizu, who had been almost asleep, was now wide awake and horrified. He held up his hands toward Anami in a gesture which said, don't get me mixed up in such a dangerous falsehood.

Anami, still talking to Arao, made a gesture indicating that Sakomizu should relax, that the conversation had nothing to do with him. "Yes, I would say the signs are quite encouraging," he said into the telephone. "Just make sure you keep all your men under control."

When Anami hung up, he looked at Sakomizu who was now sitting, dumbfounded, on the edge of the couch. Neither man said anything. Sakomizu, having suffered some anxious moments himself in his limited dealings with young army officers, sensed with a shudder the intensity of the pressure under which Anami was operating. The war minister stared at Sakomizu speculatively for a moment, then a conspiratorial smile broke across his very expressive face. He turned and left the room.

A few minutes later the cabinet reconvened, and after a short period of desultory debate, Prime Minister Suzuki, to the surprise of almost everyone, took the floor. He had decided there was no more time to waste.

"I would like," he said, "to ask for one more vote on this issue."

When the vote was taken, it yielded no surprises. Eleven members favored acceptance of the Byrnes note. Anami and two others opposed it. One man, Munitions Minister Sadajiro Toyoda, was still undecided.

Suzuki, who as presiding officer had not voted, then addressed the meeting. "When I first read the Byrnes note," he said, "I could not

imagine the Japanese government accepting it. I found it so unsatisfactory I was resolved to continue the war to the very end. I was
ready to burn the nation's bridges behind her valiant defenders.
After that, however, I read the note again and again. At last I came
to the conclusion that the Allied nations had not drafted it with any
sinister purpose in mind. I know, and all of you know, that His Majesty's heart cries out for one thing only—the end of the war, the restoration of peace. As prime minister, it is my desire to bow to the Imperial
will."

He looked around the room before continuing. "Therefore, I have
come to a most serious decision. I intend to report to His Majesty the
hopeless result of this cabinet meeting, and ask him once more to give
his gracious opinion."

With that, Suzuki adjourned the session. Like everyone else, General Anami was astonished. What could he do now to gain time?
There were many things he might do. If he were to resign, for instance, as the young officers at the War Ministry had often pressed
him to do, he would bring about the downfall of Suzuki's cabinet, the
almost inevitable result of which would be a new military government with himself as prime minister. Such a drastic course he was not
prepared to take. He decided simply to have a private conversation
with Admiral Suzuki, who had quickly left the room.

Anami gathered together the papers he had spread out before him
on the large oval table and handed them to an aide. Then he walked
across the hall to Suzuki's office. Though he was admitted immediately, he found that Suzuki already had another visitor, a naval officer.

"I'm sorry to interrupt," Anami said, "but I would like to make one
request of the prime minister."

Suzuki said, "Certainly, what would you like?"

"Would it be possible for you to wait another two days," Anami
asked, "before calling an imperial conference?"

Suzuki understood the nature of the war minister's concern. He also
appreciated the polite, unthreatening manner in which the request
was made. But his own decision had been taken and he feared the
consequences of delay more than he feared the wrath of young officers. "I'm sorry," he said, "but now is the time, General Anami. We
must not miss this opportunity."

The war minister listened, opened his mouth to say something else,
then thought better of it. He bowed, apologized again for interrupt-
ing, and left Suzuki's office.

AUGUST 13,
8 P.M.

G E N E R A L Anami returned to his official residence in time to change into a kimono and relax for a few minutes with his secretary, Colonal Hayashi, before the arrival, at eight o'clock, of a committee of conspirators from the War Ministry. He did not intend to tell them how the cabinet meeting had ended. He knew what their mood would be. Like every other general in the Japanese Army, he was sharply aware of the explosive tradition which had been allowed and even encouraged to develop among young officers during the previous 15 or 20 years. After the February, 1936, Incident (in which several statesmen were killed and Admiral Kantaro Suzuki was injured by rebellious young officers), Anami had been assigned to investigate its causes. One of the principle causes was provocation by older officers who understood the efficacy of terror in accomplishing political objectives. Each disturbance by young officers during the 1930s had increased the power of the army by further intimidating the populace and the politicians. At the same time, however, the generals themselves became uncomfortably aware that they had created a dangerous force just beneath them.

While Anami had never himself encouraged or used this force, he had now to deal with it, even in the person of his younger brother-in-law, Lieutenant Colonel Masahiko Takeshita. Until late 1935, Takeshita had belonged to the faction which perpetrated the 1936 Incident. He had broken with this group before it launched its coup d'état attempt, but the projected coup d'état in which he was now involved was a more serious matter than the previous one because of the country's present condition.

Takeshita was one of the five men who arrived at eight o'clock to be ushered into the war minister's study. Also in the group were Lieutenant Colonels Masao Inaba and Jiro Shiizaki, Major Kenji Hatanaka, and, acting for the first time as spokesman for the conspirators, the chief of their section in the Military Affairs Bureau, Colonel Okikatsu Arao.

As General Anami welcomed the five men, Major Hatanaka stepped forward impatiently. "I think you should be warned, sir," he said, "that there is a plot afoot to assassinate you if you keep fighting against the surrender. In my opinion, there should be more men guarding you."

General Anami smiled. "I believe I'm sufficiently well-guarded," he said. Then he turned to Colonel Arao, who had several sheets of paper in his hand. Arao was an officer highly regarded in the War Ministry. Anami had not known that he was involved in the plot.

"I've come here to submit a report," Arao began. "After careful study, we have concluded that the war should be continued until our national polity is absolutely assured. We think the only way to accomplish this is by means of a coup d'état."

Anami pointed to the papers in Arao's hand. "Is that the plan you have there?"

"Yes sir." Arao handed him a piece of paper which outlined the principle elements of the conspiracy. As Anami read, Arao explained.

"Although the Emperor has expressed a desire to surrender, it remains to be seen how much he was influenced by such men as Suzuki, Yonai, Togo, and Kido. We'll have to proclaim martial law, isolate the palace and imprison those four men. It goes without saying we count on your leadership. We must also have the cooperation of General Umezu [chief of staff], General Tanaka [Shizuichi Tanaka, commander of the Eastern District Army], and General Mori [Takeshi Mori, commander of the First Imperial Guards Division]."

"And when do you intend to put all this in motion?" Anami asked.

"At ten o'clock tomorrow morning." The original deadline, midnight tonight, had been abandoned because the conspirators had been unable, until now, to get hold of Anami when he had enough time to listen to them.

He glanced from one face to another and saw in each a tense impetuosity which seemed about to erupt. How was he to deal with these men? Not just these five but all those they represented. Emotionally, he was with them. He despised surrender as much as they did. He still had a tight hold on his emotions, however; they were agitated almost beyond control. He wished Suzuki had not been so impatient. He wished he could have another day or two during which to let everyone's feelings subside, but that was a pointless wish. He had to face the situation as it faced him.

"What about your communications setup?" he asked.

Colonel Arao was ready for the question. He went into detail about field phones, messengers, etc., but Anami's expression indicated he was not impressed.

"Your plan is very incomplete," he said.

"We'll change it, sir, in any way you decide."

"What we want," Colonel Inaba said, "is to have you take over as our leader."

Anami smiled ruefully. "I can well understand Saigo's feeling. On the other hand, I have offered my life to the Emperor." Takamori

Saigo was the reluctant leader of a conservative Samurai group which rebelled unsuccessfully in 1877 against the modernization policies of Emperor Meiji's regime.

Every man in the room, of course, had offered his life to the Emperor. It was for the Emperor that they were planning this coup d'état. They were determined to free him from the timid, corrupting influence of the people around him. When they heard Anami say he could understand Saigo's feelings, they decided he favored their coup.

"Does that mean, sir, you will lead us?"

"I'll have to think about it a little more."

The five men glanced at each other uneasily. How could they hurry him?

Arao said, "There's not much time, sir, if we want to launch the plan tomorrow morning."

Anami looked at his secretary, Colonel Hayashi, who stood in the background, listening. Hayashi, as Anami knew, did not favor the conspiracy. Turning to Colonel Arao, Anami said, "Why don't you come back at midnight. I'll talk to you then."

When the five officers left, he saw them to the porch. "Be careful," he said to them. "They [meaning presumably the peace faction] may be watching you tonight. I don't think you should all travel in one group."

The five men were deeply touched by this evidence of the war minister's personal concern for them.

When General Anami went back into the house, he found his secretary, Colonel Hayashi, looking worried and puzzled.

"How did you feel about all that?" Anami asked.

After a moment's hesitation, Hayashi said, "I don't yet know, sir, whether you approve or disapprove of their plan. As I heard it, from the background, I would say you gave them the impression you agree with what they're doing. If you don't agree, I think you'll have to tell them definitely. The people are beginning to hear rumors about the government accepting the Potsdam terms. The country is prostrate. Only sixty percent of the workers in the munitions factories are at their jobs. I think it's useless for the army to insist on continuing the war. The people simply won't follow us."

General Anami listened but did not reply. "Call Colonel Arao," he said, "and tell him I'll be coming to the ministry at midnight."

AUGUST 13
JUST BEFORE MIDNIGHT

W H E N G E N E R A L Anami and Colonel Hayashi reached the War Ministry, they found the place as alive as if it were midday. Several junior officers were hurrying along the halls with what looked like important papers in their hands. Others were conferring in groups of three, four, or five. There was in the atmosphere the same feeling of urgency one might expect during the final planning of a major offensive. Anami went directly upstairs to his second-floor office and summoned Colonel Arao, whose office was just down the hall and around the corner to the left. Arao came in alone. Anami invited him to sit in a chair near his desk. Colonel Hayashi had taken a chair closer to the back of the large, splendidly furnished office. The light was dim. Blackout curtains covered all the windows. Anami took out a cigaret, offered one to Arao.

"I've been thinking about your plan," Anami said. "These are difficult days, aren't they?"

"Yes sir, they are," Arao agreed.

"Whatever we do," Anami continued, "we must take into account the condition of the country and its present capabilities. We now have a situation in which our war production is less than sixty percent of what it should be. We're even having trouble manufacturing shells and bullets. With the cities burned out, the workers are abandoning their jobs. Food is already scarce and this year's rice crop doesn't look good. These are factors we must take into account."

"I'm aware of all that," Arao said.

"We must also keep in mind the welfare of His Majesty."

"That goes without saying."

"Whatever we do, we must not do it thoughtlessly."

"True."

"I must admit I have some serious doubts about the possible success of a coup d'état under these circumstances. It's a difficult undertaking."

Arao said nothing, waiting for Anami to continue.

Anami, having come to the moment when he might be expected to announce his decision, chose not to continue. He had said as much as he intended to say right now about the coup. He didn't feel it would be wise to say any more. After sitting in silence for awhile, he suddenly stood up.

"It's getting late," he concluded, "and I need some sleep. Tomorrow will not be an easy day."

Arao stood up, but knowing General Anami as he did, he chose not to ask the question which both men knew was foremost in his mind. Arao bowed and Anami dismissed him.

In the car on the way back to the war minister's official residence, Anami turned to Colonel Hayashi. "Well, I told him all those things you said to me. I wonder if he got the impression from it that I'm against the coup. I suppose he did."

"I suppose so," Hayashi said, not quite convinced.

AUGUST 14,
5:30 A.M.

T H O U G H   H E had not retired until long after midnight, General Anami was up shortly after 5 A.M., and by 5:30, he was in the garden of his official residence performing a Samurai discipline for which he was well known but for which he found too little time in recent months. He had his long Japanese bow in hand. Trying to free his mind of all else, he aimed it time after time at the straw target placed near the back of the delicately trimmed garden. It was not easy this morning, however, to group his arrows in the center of the target. Perhaps he had not practiced enough recently. Perhaps the problems bearing down upon him were too heavy for even so disciplined a man to put from his mind. After a short, indifferent performance, he hurried into the house and dressed for a 6 A.M. breakfast. He had a guest coming this morning, Marshal Shunroku Hata, who had flown up from Hiroshima to report to the war minister, and more important, to the Emperor, on conditions there.

Marshal Hata arrived promptly, and as the two men sat down at a low table in the dining room, General Anami's cook began serving them his usual breakfast—rice, soup, Japanese pickles, and black seaweed. They ate sparingly. Marshal Hata, whose Second General Army would be charged with the defense of Kyushu and all of southern Japan if there were to be a decisive homeland battle, was a slender, balding, close-cropped man with tight lips and a thin mustache. He had been General Hideki Tojo's choice for the premiership the previous April when Admiral Suzuki was appointed. Hata had been passed over either because of Tojo's support, or because there was resistance at the time against selecting an officer on active duty, or for both reasons. Anami got along well with him as he did with most people.

Anami asked him, "Is the damage down there actually as bad as the reports indicate?"

Hata's face clouded at the thought of it. "The city was wiped out," he said. "It is indescribably pathetic."

"Have you been able to get anything close to an accurate count of the casualties?"

"It's not yet possible," Hata said. "Many people who thought they had survived are now dying from radiation. It's quite horrible. Tens of thousands have died already."

Anami could scarcely conceive of such suffering, and even if it were possible to do so, it would not be permissible for him, as a soldier, to dwell upon it. His job was to weigh the military aspects of this new-type bomb. Was it, in military terms, irresistible? "Your preliminary report said there were ways to defend against it. Are you still convinced of that?"

Hata, after telling his dismal story of damages and casualties, became more reassuring when he talked about the military implications of the bomb. "We've established without a doubt," he said, "that people in white clothing were much less prone to burns than people in dark clothing. And people who were underground seem to have suffered no ill effects. Even vegetables like sweet potatoes, only an inch or so underground, were uncontaminated. I think the lesson is clear. If we wear white clothing and build more underground facilities, we can survive whatever they drop on us."

General Anami listened carefully, then said, "When you see the Emperor this morning, be sure you tell him that."

AUGUST 14,
7 A.M.

GENERAL Anami, after a depressing breakfast with Marshal Hata, arrived at his War Ministry office to find it overrun with young officers eager to meet the 10 A.M. deadline they had set for their conspiracy. In General Anami's name, they had even summoned to the Ministry General Shizuichi Tanaka, commander of the Eastern District Army; Lieutenant General Takeshi Mori, commander of the First Imperial Guards Division; and Lieutenant General Sanji Okido, commander of the Kempeitai. The conspirators did not seem to doubt that their plans were complete. General Tanaka and General Mori would cooperate fully as soon as the war minister spoke to them. Anami listened patiently as Colonel Okikatsu Arao described the preparations which had been made.

When Arao finished, Anami said, "What about General Umezu?" Arao said, "We are counting on you to speak to him."

Umezu, being the chief of staff, could not be and had not been ignored in the planning, but because he was less approachable than Anami, and because he was a close friend and considered to be a follower of Anami, the conspirators had decided the best way to reach him was through Anami.

"Let's go see him now," Anami said to Arao.

Umezu's office was just down the hall, between Anami's office and a luxurious sitting room at the corner which was reserved for the Emperor to use on the rare occasions when he visited the ministry. Umezu was at his desk when Anami and Arao arrived.

"I'm sure you're aware that some of the officers feel the need for a coup d'état," Anami said. "Colonel Arao would like to tell you all about it."

Inasmuch as the projected coup had been incubating for the last three days just a few feet down the hall in the Military Affairs Bureau, and also inasmuch as Umezu kept in close, constant communication with Anami who had known of the coup since its conception, the announcement of it this morning was hardly news to the chief of staff. He listened quietly as Arao explained the details. He was as eager as anyone in the War Ministry to find a means of avoiding total surrender. The previous night, he and the navy's chief of staff, Admiral Toyoda, had held a long meeting at the prime minister's office with Foreign Minister Togo and Chief Cabinet Secretary Sakomizu, trying unsuccessfully to induce these men to change their minds about accepting the Allied terms in their present form. If Arao and his associates had developed any brilliant new methods for handling the situation, he wanted to hear them.

After Arao finished talking, however, Umezu's reaction was both quick and negative. "I couldn't possibly give my approval to anything like that," he said.

Anami said nothing, and since it would not be proper for a colonel to ask the chief of staff to explain himself, Arao also said nothing. Umezu eventually decided to fill the silence with at least a short elaboration.

"First of all, the plan is not well conceived," he said. "If for no other reason, I would oppose it because it is doomed to failure. But even more important, it calls for the use of soldiers inside the sacred ground of the Imperial Palace. That would be a sacrilege."

Arao looked helplessly at Anami, who seemed to have no difficulty maintaining his composure. Standing up, he said to Arao, "Well, you now have the chief of staff's reaction. Perhaps we should go back to my office so you can explain it to the others."

When they returned to Anami's office, he himself announced to the conspirators swarming there, "The coup d'état will have to be abandoned. The chief of staff disapproves of it."

After an initial uproar, the force of General Anami's personality prevailed. The conspirators, in sullen silence, filed out of his office.

Back in the Military Affairs Bureau, where most of them had their desks, they huddled in small groups, The prevailing mood was anger, not against General Anami but against General Umezu. One of the conspirators, Lieutenant Colonel Masataka Ida, offered a theory about the possible reason for the chief of staff's unexpected stubbornness.

"Umezu had a long meeting last night," Ida informed his associates, "with Suzuki, Togo, and Sakomizu. The Badoglios have won him over to their side."

While most of the conspirators continued to talk bitterly about General Umezu, one of them, perhaps the most determined and impassioned of all, Major Kenji Hatanaka, gradually withdrew into himself. The lack of the chief of staff's support did not, in his mind, lessen the need for a coup d'état. He wasn't yet ready to abandon the project.

General Anami, meanwhile, had not deluded himself that the hours ahead were likely to be quiet and uneventful. General Mori of the Imperial Guards, General Tanaka of the Eastern District Army and General Okido of the Kempeitai, having been summoned by the conspirators for an appointment with the war minister, were still waiting to see him. He called them into his office.

"I think all three of you realize," he said to them, "that the next day or two will be very critical for our country. I want each of you to be even more careful than usual. Keep tight control over your men. Don't let anyone get out of line. And take every security precaution you consider necessary."

After these three generals had left, he arranged to have all the senior section chiefs in the War Ministry gathered for another meeting. He would tell them essentially the same thing.

AUGUST 14,
7 A.M.

W H E N T H E people of Tokyo awoke August 14, they were startled to find that on this hot, summer morning their flattened city looked as if it had been hit by a snowstorm. The scorched ground was covered by a blanket of paper leaflets dropped by American planes during the night.

Among the many people who read these leaflets was Marquis Kido. At 7 A.M., when he arose from his futon in the room he now occupied on the second floor of the Imperial Household Ministry, a court chamberlain showed him one of the slips of paper which littered the palace grounds as well as the rest of Tokyo. After a quick look at the leaflet, Kido was stricken with consternation. It said in simple Japanese:

To the Japanese People:
Today we come not to drop bombs but to inform you of the answer of the Allied countries to the conditions of surrender which your government has made. On August 8 (August 9 in Japan) the Japanese government proposed peace talks to the Allied countries. This was not only the will of the government of Japan but also the will and the strong desire of the Emperor. That is why we are dropping these leaflets. The Japanese government must decide whether to seek peace or continue the war. We are certain that if you read the two documents below, you will see how your nation can be brought to the end of war.
[The text of the Potsdam Declaration and of the conditional Japanese peace note were inserted here.]
We Allied countries understand that Japan is preparing to accept the Potsdam Declaration which was signed July 26, 1945, but to this declaration your country has posed a condition—the preservation of the Emperor's right as ruler of the nation. We Allied countries prohibit any such rights to the Emperor. We want you to understand this fact and we want an early reply.

Ultimately the national polity will be decided by the freely expressed will of the people. The soldiers of the Allied countries will stay in Japan until every provision of the Potsdam Declaration has been accomplished.

Kido envisioned with horror the reaction of soldiers and young officers throughout Japan when they saw this leaflet. Until now, the government's surrender efforts, though widely rumored, were not actually known in the army except to the select group centered around the War Ministry. The danger of a coup d'état would become extreme as soon as the troops learned the truth. Kido called the imperial library, in which the Emperor was living, and made an appointment to see His Majesty, who had been up for some time. Hirohito, for many years an insomniac, was finding it difficult to sleep at all during this critical period.

After the Emperor had read the leaflet, Kido, who had a tendency to speak in paragraphs, said, "It is my concern, Your Majesty, that when the troops read this leaflet, they will become enraged, making a military coup inevitable and the execution of our planned policy very difficult. It will bring about the worst possible situation for the nation."

The Emperor did not disagree. The leaflet unquestionably posed a threat to the surrender plans. It was more than ever essential now for the government to hasten its efforts.

"My advice, Your Majesty," Kido continued, "is that you remain firm in your resolution to secure peace. I recommend that you summon the members of the Supreme Council for Direction of the War, and the members of the cabinet to an imperial conference at which you might restate your feelings about peace."

The Emperor said, "I would like you to contact the prime minister and make arrangements toward that end."

Kido had no difficulty contacting the prime minister since Admiral Suzuki had arrived at the imperial library a few minutes before and was waiting to see the Emperor. When Kido emerged from the imperial presence, he found Suzuki in the next room.

"Have you yet been able to arrange a convocation of the Supreme War Council?" Kido asked him.

A harried expression crossed the face of the old prime minister. "I've been trying," he said, "but I'm having a hard time. The army wants me to wait until this afternoon at one o'clock and the navy wants to postpone it without setting any specific time. [The two chiefs of staff, General Umezu and Admiral Toyoda, had expressed these attitudes in a conversation the previous night with Foreign

Minister Togo.] My position is quite difficult."

"I do not doubt that your position is difficult," Kido said, "but we have no time to waste. Did you see the leaflet the American planes dropped during the night?"

"I haven't read it," Suzuki said.

"It confronts us with an exceptional new danger because it includes Japanese translations of our offer and of the Allied demands. When that leaflet falls into the hands of the troops, we shall be thrown into a chaos beyond hope of salvaging. I have just spoken to His Majesty on this very subject and he agrees that we should summon the Supreme War Council and the cabinet forthwith."

Suzuki said, "I told the cabinet yesterday that I intended to ask His Majesty once more to express his opinion. That's why I've come here this morning. Though I'm terribly sorry to bring His Majesty such troubles, the attitude of the army and navy in the last three days has convinced me there is no other course. I intend to ask his Majesty to call another imperial conference. Would you like to talk to him with me, in joint audience?"

Kido said, "Though there is no precedent for a joint imperial audience with both the prime minister and the lord keeper of the privy seal, I shall arrange it immediately."

AUGUST 14,
10:20 A.M.

LIEUTENANT Colonel Takeshita, his excitement suddenly renewed, was rushing in an army staff car from the War Ministry at Ichigaya Heights to the prime minister's official residence near the Diet building. A few minutes earlier, two of General Umezu's aides had come into Takeshita's office with what sounded like good news. The chief of staff had apparently changed his mind about a coup d'état, or perhaps he had been misunderstood earlier. They reported that he was not completely opposed to it after all. There was still hope if only Takeshita could quickly get hold of the war minister. But General Anami, after his meeting with the senior section chiefs, had hurried off to a cabinet meeting.

When Takeshita reached the prime minister's official residence, he brushed past the guard and hurried up the stairs to the cabinet room on the second floor. Even as he ran, he felt a rather empty stillness in the building. The only sound he heard was the pounding of his own boots on the wooden steps. Approaching the second floor he was surprised to find the door of the cabinet room open. Looking in, he saw that the room was empty. But a cabinet meeting had been scheduled. He was certain of that because General Anami had said so and General Anami did not lie. Takeshita asked a passing clerk where the cabinet was meeting.

"The cabinet members just left for the Imperial Palace," the clerk said. "There's to be a joint imperial conference for the cabinet and the Supreme War Council."

Takeshita was filled with alarm. He knew the prime minister was trying to arrange an imperial conference but he thought it had been delayed at least until afternoon. If the Emperor had summoned both the cabinet and the Supreme War Council, it could only mean that he was about to reiterate his desire to accept the Byrnes note. Takeshita felt he must reach General Anami and get the coup d'état started before the Emperor spoke.

Running back to his staff car, he sped down the hill to the palace, only about a half mile away, and talked his way past the guard at the Sakashita Gate. For an officer of his rank, and with his impressive identification, it was not difficult to gain entrance. Once inside, he had no problem finding his way to the library in the Fukiage Gardens, where the Emperor was now living. Takeshita was well acquainted with the curving, tree-lined roads which criss-crossed the palace grounds. The imperial conference would probably be held in the Emperor's air raid shelter. He went there directly.

Running along the path through the pine woods, he reached the metal door of the shelter to find it barred by troops of the Imperial Guards Division. There was no question of talking his way past these men.

"You can't go in," one of them said firmly. "There's an imperial conference underway."

Takeshita, discouraged but not yet ready to give up, sat down in the cool shade of the tall pine trees to wait for the meeting to end and General Anami to emerge.

AUGUST 14,
10:30 A.M.

IN THE hot, humid, badly air-conditioned shelter beneath the Fukiage Gardens, twenty-five dignified men sat staring at the water-soaked walls and at each other, all aware that their nation's crisis was now approaching a climax which few of them had envisioned. For the last five days, most of these men, at meetings of the cabinet and the Supreme War Council, had been deadlocked in what was perhaps the most horrendous and bewildering debate of all time—the question of how to end a war that had already brought unprecedented destruction on their country, and the question of whether they should bow to a new kind of bomb which had the apparent capability of wiping out a whole nation of people. They had been arguing for five days about what might turn out to be a matter of national suicide. And they had not yet settled the matter.

In addition to the prime minister, the fifteen members of his cabinet and the two Supreme War Council members who were not also cabinet members (General Umezu and Admiral Toyoda), seven other men were here for this crucial meeting—Baron Kiichiro Hiranuma, president of the Privy Council; General Sumihisa Ikeda, chief of the cabinet planning board; Naoyasu Murase, director of the Legislative Bureau; Kingo Machimura, superintendent-general of the Tokyo Metropolitan Police; General Masao Yoshizumi and Admiral Zenchiro Hoshina, directors of the army and navy military affairs bureaus; and Hisatsune Sakomizu, chief cabinet secretary.

When they were summoned by the Emperor at 10 A.M. for a 10:30 imperial conference of the cabinet and Supreme War Council, most of them had been so surprised they were caught without the formal morning attire usually required for appearances before the Throne. Some, because the day was so hot, were even without neckties, which they had to borrow from secretaries or associates; a few, like Home Minister Genki Abe and Chief Cabinet Secretary Sakomizu, were wearing the high-necked, khaki national uniform. Fortunately, the Emperor had stipulated that informal wear would be acceptable. Most of the cabinet members were notified of the conference at the prime minister's official residence, where they had gathered for a scheduled cabinet meeting, and had come to the palace together in a convoy of official cars. The only two in formal dress were Prime Minister Suzuki and Foreign Minister Togo, both of whom had been aware that the conference was to be called.

As the twenty-five men sat waiting for the arrival of the Emperor,

Sakomizu felt the tension of two special concerns which occupied his mind. He was worried about the suitability of an imperial rescript on which he had been working, with the help of his staff, for three days and nights. Since the preparation of imperial rescripts, when needed, was a responsibility of his office, and since he envisioned an immediate need for one, he had written what he thought would fit the occasion he anticipated, but the situation within the government was still so fluid he wasn't yet certain that the occasion he anticipated was going to arise. He was worried also about the condition of the prime minister. Suzuki was an old man, no longer accustomed to the pressures he had learned to endure years earlier as a naval officer, and at no time practiced in the kind of controversy which had swirled around him during the last five days. This morning he had seemed quite vague about the procedures he should follow today, and even after winning the Emperor's cooperation in calling the conference, he had not thought to put on paper what he should say when the conference began. Sakomizu feared he might become confused and thus weaken his argument.

At exactly 10:55, Emperor Hirohito entered the room wearing an unadorned army uniform and followed by his chief military aide, the elderly General Shigeru Hasunuma. As everyone stood and bowed deeply, the Emperor sat down in a straight-backed, wooden chair at the same small, cloth-covered table he had used for the conference of the Supreme War Council the night of August 9. Behind him was a gold screen. General Hasunuma took a chair in the corner to his right. The members of the meeting sat in rows of chairs facing the Emperor, with the prime minister, war minister, navy minister, foreign minister and two chiefs of staff at the front.

When Prime Minister Suzuki arose to speak, Sakomizu was immediately relieved. The old man was forceful and to the point.

"His Majesty has called this conference," he said, "so that we may discuss in his presence the note from American Secretary of State Byrnes, and so that those who dissent from the majority view about accepting the Allied terms may express their opinions." After explaining in a few words the issues which had deadlocked the cabinet and the Supreme War Council since the Byrnes note arrived, he turned to the three men in the front row who had maintained the deadlock. "I would like now," he said, "to ask General Umezu, Admiral Toyoda, and General Anami to explain their positions. General Umezu?"

General Umezu, who knew the Emperor's mind and did not entertain much hope of changing it, began by apologizing to His Majesty for the unfavorable turn the war had taken. Then in a few words, he summed up his position and concluded, "If our imperial system cannot be preserved, I believe we must be ready to sacrifice the entire nation in a final battle."

Admiral Toyoda, who spoke next, saw an opportunity to impress upon His Majesty some considerations which the surrender faction might not have presented to him. First he enumerated point by point what was unacceptable about the Byrnes note. The Japanese people must not be subjected to the humiliation of foreign occupation. The Japanese army and navy must not be subjected to the humiliation of disarmament. The Japanese Emperor must not be subjected to the will of a foreign commander. In rising passion, he said, "Though we cannot guarantee victory by continuing to fight, we are ready to fight. The whole nation is ready to engage in a decisive battle for our homeland. We are prepared for suicide warfare. We are all willing to die for His Majesty. Why then are we not prepared to do something less difficult—tell the Allied nations that the demands they make are not acceptable in their present form? Why should we not press for further negotiation on these demands? Why should we not stipulate once more that they clearly guarantee the preservation of our unique, imperial system?"

Toyoda's plump, round face was covered with beads of perspiration as he sat down. When General Anami arose, everything had already been said. He was brief.

"At the very least," he said, "we should press for clarification of the Allied terms. If the enemy refuses to negotiate further with us, if he will not even listen to our demands that His Majesty remain untouched, then it would be better for us to fight on, because we do have, even now, a chance to win."

There were tears in General Anami's eyes when he looked at the Emperor. Realizing that this man whom he loved above all others disagreed with everything he was saying, he decided he could not continue. Bowing toward the Emperor, he suddenly sat down.

Prime Minister Suzuki arose slowly from his chair as an even deeper stillness settled over the already quiet room.

"I believe there are no other dissenting arguments to present," he said. "I wish to apologize, Your Majesty, for bringing before you once more a divided government. And I beg you once more to give us your august opinion in this matter."

The Emperor was sitting erect at his table, his face covered with perspiration. He raised a white kerchief and dabbed his forehead, then lowered his hand to his lap. Several strands of his hair were uncharacteristically out of place, falling forward toward his eyes. He seemed not to notice this. Clearing his throat, he sat forward on his chair.

"I have listened carefully," he said, "to all the arguments against Japan's acceptance of the Allied reply as it now stands. My own opinion, however, has not changed. I have studied the conditions prevailing in Japan and in the rest of the world, and I believe that a continuation of the war promises nothing but additional destruction. I have also studied the terms of the Allied reply, and I have come to the conclusion that they represent a virtually complete acknowledgement of our position as we outlined it in the note we sent a few days ago. In short, I consider the Allied reply to be acceptable."

He glanced toward the three men who opposed acceptance. "I realize," he continued, "that there are those of you who distrust the intentions of the Allies. This is, of course, quite natural, but to my mind, the Allied reply is evidence of the peaceful and friendly intentions of the enemy. The faith and resolution of the Japanese nation are, therefore, the paramount considerations.

"I fully appreciate how difficult it will be for the officers and men of the army and navy to surrender their arms to the enemy and to see their homeland occupied. It will be just as difficult for me to issue the order that this be done, and to deliver so many of my trusted servants into the hands of the Allied authorities so they may be tried as war criminals. I am aware also of the willingness of the people to sacrifice themselves for their nation and their Emperor. But I am not concerned with what happens to me. I want to preserve the lives of my people. I don't want them subjected to further destruction. If the war were to continue, the whole nation would be reduced to ashes. How then could I carry on the wishes of my imperial ancestors? If the war ends now, the nation still has a chance to recover.

"The decision I have reached is like the one forced upon my grandfather, the Emperor Meiji, at the time of the Triple Intervention. As he endured the unendurable, so shall I, and so must you." In his address to the Supreme War Council five days earlier, Hirohito had made the same reference to the interference by France, Germany, and Russia in 1895, which compelled Japan to return territory taken in the war against China.

He paused now and let his eyes travel over all the men assembled before him. "It is my desire that you, my cabinet ministers, accede to my wishes and forthwith accept the Allied reply. It is not an easy task to end the war and restore the country. It will take much time, but if the people of Japan cooperate like a family, we shall be able to accomplish it. And I myself shall cooperate with the people in their efforts.

"I cannot express the sorrow I feel when I think of all who have been killed in the battlefields and in the homeland, and when I think of their bereaved families, I am filled with anxiety about the future of those who have been injured, or who have lost all their property or their means of livelihood. I shall do everything in my power to help them.

"Inasmuch as the people of Japan are unaware of our deliberations, I know they will be deeply shocked when they hear of my desires. If it is considered appropriate, I am willing to go on the radio and explain the matter to them personally. The troops, in particular, will be dismayed at our action. The war minister and the navy minister may not find it easy to persuade them to accept it. I am willing to go wherever necessary to explain it to them.

"I now request the cabinet, therefore, to prepare at once an imperial rescript which I shall broadcast to the nation, announcing the termination of the war."

Without awaiting a reaction, he arose and quickly left the room, followed by his military aide. After his departure, the twenty-five men he left behind relaxed all their efforts at self-control. The air was filled with gasps and sobs. Heads were bowed and there were tears in every eye. It was several minutes before anyone left his place. Finally, the prime minister moved toward the door, then the others. Without any conversation, still wiping tears from their eyes, they walked single file through the narrow corridor of the shelter and up the stairs which led them outside, into the pine-covered Fukiage Gardens.

When Anami emerged, his brother-in-law, Colonel Takeshita, was waiting for him. Though Takeshita obviously wanted to talk to him, Anami, still sobbing, was in no condition at the moment to talk to anyone. Right behind him was General Umezu, who had reportedly changed his mind about a coup d'état, but he, too, was weeping and looked as if he were in no mood to talk now.

Takeshita watched the procession of tearful men walk slowly to a convoy of palace cars which were waiting for them. As they drove away from the front of the library building, he jumped into his own staff car and followed them to the Imperial Household Ministry where they transferred to their official cars. He continued following Anami's car, which, like the others, went directly back to the prime minister's official residence.

Takeshita had been deeply shaken by the emotional condition of the cabinet and war council members as they came out of the Emperor's bomb shelter. It was evident to him that as a result of whatever the Emperor had said to them, they were on the verge of accepting the disastrous Allied surrender terms. Everything possible must be done to stop them. He was determined to talk to the war minister at least one more time.

AUGUST 14,
12:20 P.M.

THE CABINET members, returning to the prime minister's official residence for a formal vote on the question of accepting the Emperor's judgment, found when they arrived that Admiral Suzuki's chef had prepared a lunch for them. If, despite their deep depression, any of these men were experiencing hunger at this moment, they were quickly relieved of it when they saw what there was to eat —whale meat and black bread. The only virtue of whale meat, even in these days of acute food shortage, was that it could be obtained with relative safety, despite the American Navy, in waters close to the northern Japanese island of Hokkaido. As for bread, it was one Western innovation which few Japanese had ever learned to favor.

The prime minister seemed able to stomach more of this meal than anyone else, perhaps because, while he had just undergone an intensely emotional experience, he had also gained the most important objective he had ever undertaken and could thus find more reason to relax than at any time in the past week.

General Anami picked politely at his food. Though he had regained his outward composure, he had no appetite. Anguish was still upon him as were guilt and frustration. He felt a desire to take on himself the blame for the failure of the entire army, the entire nation. He could no longer sit here at this table pretending to eat. Getting to his feet, he made his way out of the room and down the hall to the toilet.

On the way, he saw his secretary, Colonel Hayashi, who was awaiting his pleasure. "Come with me a minute," he said to Hayashi. "There's one more thing about which I want to ask your advice."

The two men went into the toilet together, and as they stood side by side, Anami said, "The Emperor has spoken and we have no choice but to seek peace. But I understand from the intelligence section that there is a large American task force just outside Tokyo Bay. What do you think of the idea of striking one hard blow against that task force and then proposing peace?"

Though Hayashi understood the frantic frustration attacking the war minister at this moment, he was, nevertheless, horrified at the proposal. "I think it would be a terrible mistake," he said. "In the first place, the Emperor has expressed a desire to end the war immediately. And in the second place, though there is a rumor of a large American task force just south of Tokyo Bay, it hasn't been confirmed by the Air Patrol."

Anami did not answer these objections. Though he couldn't overcome his belief that the enemy would ease his peace terms if Japan were to stage just one more impressive show of strength, he was no longer prepared to argue the point even with his own secretary. When both men were finished in the toilet, he said, "Well, my brother-in-law is waiting for me in the foyer. I must go talk to him."

Colonel Takeshita accompanied General Anami to a small room where they would have at least some privacy. Knowing Anami well enough to be able to read his intentions in his face, and not wanting to hear those intentions openly expressed, Takeshita began talking quickly to forestall them.

"General Umezu," he said, "has changed his mind about the coup."

Anami was startled. "Where did you hear that?"

"He told some of the officers on his staff."

Though this was news to Anami, he didn't argue it.

"That means there is still hope for our project," Takeshita proceeded. "Inaba and myself have drawn up a new troop employment plan. Even Sato helped us." (Colonel Hiroo Sato, a few days earlier, had been so opposed to a coup d'état he had almost come to blows over it with Major Kenji Hatanaka.) Takeshita produced a copy of the plan, which Anami scanned quickly, then returned to him.

"It's too late," Anami said. "The Emperor has spoken and they're now preparing a rescript which will end the war."

Feeling weary and helpless, Anami sat down while the younger Takeshita paced nervously in front of him, trying to think of a usable idea. Takeshita said, finally, "It's not too late. There is one thing you could still do. Resign."

It was reasonable to suppose, even at this hour, that if Anami were to resign, the cabinet would fall immediately, thus paralyzing the machinery of surrender at least until another cabinet could be formed. And since the army would not be likely to approve a new cabinet unless Anami were its prime minister, there was no doubt that Takeshita's suggestion had a certain attractiveness. Anami seemed for awhile to be considering it seriously and wavering toward it. This was not, of course, a new idea, many young officers having favored it in early summer when they became disenchanted with Admiral Suzuki's policies, and one older officer having suggested it just this morning as a means of forestalling the surrender. On every previous occasion Anami had rejected the idea because he felt it would be an act of personal disloyalty to the man in whose cabinet he was serving.

After some hesitation, he rejected it now for additional reasons. "Even if I were to submit my resignation at this point," he said, "the other cabinet members would simply go ahead and carry out the Emperor's wishes without me. But worse than that, I would never again have the cherished privilege of meeting His Majesty."

Takeshita was about to continue his argument when he looked into his brother-in-law's face and saw how deeply serious this last remark had been. To Anami the Emperor was much more than a divine symbol. He was a living god. Though it might be permissible to pray to God and try to induce him to change his mind, it was not permissible, after God had announced his absolute wishes, to disregard him. Takeshita said no more. Taking friendly leave of the war minister, he left the building and returned, disconsolate, to the War Ministry.

AUGUST 14,
12:45 P.M.

AN ADDITIONAL concern struck General Anami after his brother-in-law left the prime minister's official residence. Colonel Takeshita would quite naturally be returning now to the War Ministry to break the bad news to his fellow conspirators. Anami decided he had better be there to speak to these men himself when they learned what was happening. If he hurried, he would have just enough time to say a few words to them before getting back to attend the 1 P.M. cabinet meeting.

When Anami arrived at the ministry, he could see that the news had preceded him. Some young officers were weeping in the corridors. Others were storming and raving that the war must continue, that the Badoglios must be eliminated. Takeshita had already told them the worst. They had been awaiting him because they knew he had sped off for one last talk with Anami. They had not known until Takeshita's return, however, that another imperial conference had taken place this morning and that the Emperor had again insisted on immediate surrender. They were still in the throes of this ghastly revelation when the word spread through the huge building that Anami himself had now returned.

As he walked into the building and up the stairs, he could see enough evidence of chaos to convince him that if these young men were to be kept in line, he would have to take hold of them immediately. It was his intention to call them together and talk to them, but he quickly realized he didn't have to call them together. As soon as he entered his office they began flooding in on him. Was it all true? Had the Badoglios actually won over the Emperor? What next? Could His Majesty be saved from them?

Anami had always been so approachable that they completely forgot military formality and battered him with their questions as if he were not the war minister but simply one of them. Standing at his desk, he held up his hands to quiet them.

"It is all very true," he said. "This morning, His Majesty again expressed his desire for an immediate surrender. This afternoon, the cabinet will ratify his wishes and an imperial rescript will then be issued, ending the war. If you want to know what I'm going to do, I intend to accept and obey the will of His Majesty. And as I stand here in front of you, I order every one of you to do the same."

The shock was enough to establish silence in the room. If any men here were inclined to disobey, they were still too deeply stunned to show it.

"The Imperial Army," he continued, "must act in complete accordance with the Emperor. Japan will now face difficult times and so will all of you. I've heard some of you speak of committing harakiri. A man should never commit harakiri before accomplishing his duties. Every one of you has duties still to perform. However hard your lives may be, even if you do actually have to eat dirt and sleep on the ground, you must all live on and do your best to protect the nation."

The principal conspirators, hearing these words, reacted each in his own way. Colonel Okikatsu Arao felt saddened but somewhat relieved. Though he had consented to act as spokesman for the plot, he had never been convinced that it would work.

Colonel Masao Inaba felt an intense bitterness toward peace-advocates Suzuki, Yonai, and Sakomizu (especially the latter whom he considered the instigator of the surrender move), but he was not as surprised as his companions at Anami's words. He had felt since morning that the coup attempt was doomed.

Colonel Takeshita, who knew Anami better than any of the others, noted with sorrow that when the general spoke of living on to protect the nation, he had said "you" rather than "we." Takeshita had not forgotten that he himself, in a moment of passion a few days earlier, had said to Anami, "If you plan to accept [the Potsdam terms], you had better be ready to commit harakiri."

Colonel Masataka Ida was the only man in the room who had anything to say when Anami finished. "Will the war minister explain why he has changed his mind?" Ida asked.

"Yes, I shall explain," Anami answered. "When I heard the Emperor's words, when he spoke with tears in his eyes of his sorrow at having to see the army and navy surrender to the enemy, when he asked all of us, like himself, to endure the unendurable, I could no longer oppose his will. Now that the Emperor has expressed himself, we have no choice but to obey him." Anami paused for effect before repeating something he had said a few days earlier. "Anyone who disagrees will have to do so over my dead body."

The room was silent for a short time, then one man broke into uncontrollable, hysterical sobs. It was the man who had originally conceived of the coup d'état—Major Kenji Hatanaka.

AUGUST 14,
1 P.M.

A D O Z E N high officers, mostly admirals, had gathered at the Naval Research Institute in the southern Tokyo suburb of Meguro to hear Dr. Tsunesaburo Asada report on the Hiroshima disaster. Though Dr. Asada had arrived in the city from Osaka in midmorning, the meeting of the institute could not be scheduled until 1 P.M. because of the time it took him to travel the eight miles from Tokyo station to Meguro. The station had been so badly damaged by bombs that most of its facilities were disrupted and arrivals were sometimes delayed almost as long as departures. On his way to Meguro by subway and streetcar, he noticed the expressionless silence of the people around him and the people in the street. Everyone moved at a pace much slower than he had ever seen in Tokyo. There was almost no conversation. It seemed to him there was resignation, even indifference in most of the faces, but no bitterness or despair. Most of the passing vehicles were trucks, which swerved constantly to avoid the potholes and cracks in the streets caused by bombing.

Fortunately, there was at least some rice and tea for him when he reached the institute, a high-walled compound where most of the navy's fundamental as well as technological research was conducted. While he ate hurriedly, the naval dignitaries assembled in the office of the institute's director, Vice Admiral Sakae Tokunaga. The meeting was conducted by Vice Admiral Ryutaro Shibuya, chief of the Naval Materiel Command, who quickly called upon Asada.

The distinguished physicist described the condition of Hiroshima and explained the bomb which destroyed it in terms which were scientific and technical, never emotional or sentimental. Convinced that it was crucially important to make these men accept his findings, he concentrated on the military considerations of the Hiroshima explosion, and later the Nagasaki bombing, which had proved that America had more than one such weapon.

"We still have much to learn about what has happened in Hiroshima and Nagasaki," he concluded, "but there is one thing we were able to determine with absolute certainty. The bombs which destroyed those cities were atomic devices. In a shorter time than any of us anticipated, American scientists have discovered how to release the awesome power of the atom."

Since most of the officers present were concerned with the navy's technical needs, he had not oversimplified his report. He assumed they could understand him. Expecting, nevertheless, that they would have questions, he stood waiting for their reactions after he finished. But for several moments there were no questions and when they did come they were mostly about minor, technical points, so limited in scope that he began to wonder if these men had, indeed, grasped the enormity of what he had just told them.

Finally, Admiral Shibuya, the chairman of the meeting, thanked Asada for the thoroughness with which he had undertaken his investigation. Shibuya had been somewhat aware of atomic possibilities. Though he had not been involved in the navy's Project A, he had taken part in a 1934 navy study to determine whether the theories of German-American physicist Albert Einstein and/or Italian physicist Enrico Fermi might lead to the manufacture of a super weapon. The conclusion reached by Shibuya's group in 1934 had been negative and he had not had time since then to keep pace with advances in the field of nuclear theory. He found himself somewhat bewildered, therefore, in trying to evaluate Asada's report. Yet he had to evaluate it since it would be his responsibility to guide the navy's efforts to counteract this new weapon. (Shibuya and the other officers at this meeting, since they were not headquartered in the Navy Ministry, had not yet heard, at 1 P.M., about the morning's events at the Imperial Palace.) As he listened to Asada, Shibuya had been trying to think of a way for Japan to meet this new crisis.

"It seems to me from what Dr. Asada has told us," he said, "that there is only one thing for the navy to do. I think we must gather together all the best scientists in Japan and intensify our research so that within the next six months or so, we can manufacture our own atomic bombs. In the meantime, we shall have to develop a method of dropping such bombs on American cities."

Dr. Asada, who was appalled by the impracticality of this suggestion, answered it politely. "It is my opinion," he said, "that we do not have the knowledge at this time to develop such a bomb."

One of the other officers answered his objection. "But why can't we develop the knowledge? That would be the purpose of bringing together the scientists. If the Americans can do it, so can we."

Asada was not called upon to counter this supposition because still another officer arose with a further suggestion.

"The place to gather the scientists," he said, "is the new underground facility at Matsushiro, where they would be safe from American air raids." The Matsushiro facility to which he was referring was the huge, concrete system of fortresses, now almost complete, in the western province of Nagano, that had been built for the army and for the Emperor. Asada noticed that most of the officers at the meeting reacted favorably to this idea. And so, apparently, did Admiral Shibuya.

"I think we should get to work immediately," he said, bringing the meeting to a close. "And at the same time, we should advise everyone to wear white clothing for protection against the heat rays of these bombs."

Dr. Asada shrugged. He said no more.

AUGUST 14,
2:30 P.M.

OF ALL the War Ministry conspirators who had heard General Anami's 1 P.M. demand for loyalty, the man who felt least bound by it was, ironically, Major Kenji Hatanaka, a young officer considered to be among the war minister's most loyal disciples. Having been reduced to near hysteria by Anami's dismal words, Hatanaka had now sufficiently recovered his self-control to be back in action, pedaling a bicycle from Ichigaya Heights to the Dai Ichi building across the street from the Imperial Palace in Marunouchi, where the headquarters of the Eastern District Army was located. Still determined to execute a coup d'état, he wanted to talk to the Eastern Army's commander, General Shizuichi Tanaka.

Surprisingly, Hatanaka felt no disloyalty to General Anami or to the Emperor as he continued despite Anami's direct order, to foment rebellion. Like many of the young officers at the ministry and some of the older ones, he had been for several years a follower of Tokyo University's intensely militaristic and nationalistic Professor Kiyoshi Hiraizumi who taught that one could be loyal to the Imperial institution even while disregarding the current Emperor if one could be certain that the current Emperor was taking the wrong course or falling under the influence of unsuitable advisers. Hatanaka was absolutely certain that, due to unsuitable advisers, Emperor Hirohito was taking the wrong course and his regard for the Emperor was such that he firmly intended to show his loyalty through disobedience. If this meant he had also to disobey the war minister, whom he revered, that, too, would be quite proper since Professor Hiraizumi taught a corollary to the effect that if one found it necessary to disobey the Emperor, it would be equally proper to disobey any superior officers who might stand in the way. Though such a daring action might bring death to one who performed it, at the same time it would bring honor if his survivors knew that his motives were good.

In Japanese history there was a long tradition of honorable disobedience from which Hatanaka could draw inspiration. During the feudal era, and to a lesser extent even during the Meiji period, it was common for farmers to demonstrate against oppressive landlords, and though these farmers were often executed for performing acts which could not be tolerated within the social structure, they were also very much admired for their courage and for the rectitude of their cause, however hopeless it might have been. Hatanaka was so convinced of the rectitude of his cause, despite the war minister's apparent defection, that he was quite willing to die for it, and in the hour-and-a-half since General Anami's remarks about accepting the Emperor's will, he had found that several other officers shared his resolve. He hoped General Tanaka would feel the same way.

When he reached the Dai Ichi building, one of the many handsome, still undamaged Marunouchi office structures facing Hibiya Park and the palace plaza, he ignored the elevators and raced up the stairs to the Eastern Army's sixth-floor headquarters. At the door of General Tanaka's office, he was confronted unexpectedly by one of the general's aides.

Hatanaka decided it might be best to adopt an air of authority. "I'm here to speak to General Tanaka," he said.

"Your name, please, Major?"

"I think you know my name. Major Kenji Hatanaka of the Military Affairs Bureau."

The aide was evidently stalling. Hatanaka had been here several times in the last few days trying to get General Tanaka to commit himself in favor of the coup. Though Tanaka had not yet agreed to help, neither had Hatanaka given up on him.

"About what do you want to speak to the general?" the aide asked.

"That is a private matter between the general and myself."

"But I can't let you walk into his office without knowing what you want."

Hatanaka raised his voice. "I didn't come here to discuss anything with you," he said. Putting his right hand on his sword, he took a step forward.

The aide, putting his hand on his own sword, stepped between Hatanaka and the door to the general's private office.

Hatanaka began shouting now. "I do not intend to leave here without seeing the general." He took another menacing step forward.

General Tanaka, in his office, heard the raised voices and opened the door. When he saw who was causing the commotion, he spoke quickly and coldly before Hatanaka had a chance to open his mouth.

"What are you doing here?" the general demanded. "No, don't tell me. I know what's on your mind. I don't want to hear it. Get out, immediately. Go."

Hatanaka, having snapped to attention from force of habit when the general appeared, stood frozen in place as Tanaka scowled at him. Confronted by the general, who was immaculately dressed and wore a very imposing handlebar mustache, the slender, nervous major was not impressive. Though he opened his mouth to speak, no words came out. As the general turned away from him, Hatanaka saluted in what turned out to be a rather comic gesture. A moment later, the general had disappeared back into his office and Hatanaka was left standing there, with his hand at his forehead, facing the aide, who still had his hand on his sword.

With as much grace as he could muster, Major Hatanaka swung around and glumly left the office. It was a severe blow to lose all hope of Eastern Army support, but it was not a decisive blow. He would simply have to count on the Imperial Guards. Perhaps he might yet be able to enlist Lieutenant General Takeshi Mori, commander of the First Imperial Guards division. There were several Guards officers on whom he knew he could depend, including General Hideki Tojo's son-in-law, Major Hidemasa Koga.

AUGUST 14,
3:30 P.M.

T H E W O R K of the cabinet had been proceeding so slowly and tediously since the afternoon meeting began that General Anami had finally decided, about 2:30, that he had better excuse himself and go for a short time to the War Ministry where some pressing matters awaited him. There was very little the cabinet could do now until its chief secretary, Hisatsune Sakomizu, had finished preparing the two imperial rescripts which would be required—one for the Japanese public, the other for the armed forces. Early in the cabinet meeting, General Anami and Admiral Yonai, the navy minister, had received a message from the Emperor asking them if they thought he should make appearances before the troops to help keep them under control. Yonai had said, "I will guarantee the good behavior of the Imperial Navy." And Anami had said, "I speak for the army." The only other matter of importance so far settled by the cabinet was the "surrender" note which the Foreign Ministry would be sending to the Allied powers. In addition to a surrender note, it was a note of caution suggesting that the occupation forces use tact to avoid incidents with the highly emotional Japanese troops. The note asked hopefully that the Allies limit their areas of occupation and allow the Japanese forces, especially those overseas, to disarm themselves.

Since this note was Foreign Minister Togo's idea, Anami was not closely concerned with it. Discovering that there was very little for him to do at this point in the cabinet meeting, he had politely taken his leave with the promise to return as soon as he was needed, and he now arrived at his War Ministry office to make sure the army was carrying out the preparatory demobilization orders he had already issued, mostly by telephone, to his subordinates.

His first concern was a meeting between himself and the army's five other highest ranking officers, all of whom, fortunately, were in Tokyo today. In his office he gathered Chief of Staff General Umezu; commander of the First General Army, Field Marshal Gen Sugiyama; commander of the Second General Army, Field Marshal Shunroku Hata; commander of the Air General Army General Masakazu Kawabe; and Inspector General of Military Education, General Kenji Doihara.

The session with these men was short, and though somber, quite agreeable. After a discussion of the mechanics of demobilization, Anami said, "We all know what we must do now, and I'm confident that each of us is ready to do it. I have here one other matter which I think the six of us might consider. My aides have prepared a short statement of loyalty to His Majesty that perhaps all of us might want to sign. I shall read it to you: 'The Army will act, to the last, in accordance with the Imperial desire.' That's all there is to it. I, myself, will be glad to sign it."

So saying, he picked up a brush and affixed to it his character, after which he quickly notarized it with his seal. He handed it to the others who, in turn, did likewise. Since there was nothing more about which to talk (or about which anyone felt like talking), this meeting ended and Anami prepared for the next.

About thirty officers, including most of the senior section chiefs and some of their staff members had been gathered in the conference room adjacent to Anami's office. Among those present were the vice war minister, Lieutenant General Tadaichi Wakamatsu; director of the Military Affairs Bureau, Lieutenant General Masao Yoshizumi; director of the Military Personnel Bureau, Lieutenant General Hiroshi Nukada; and director of the Military Regulations Bureau, Major General Yoshio Nasu.

For General Nasu this was an especially poignant moment because it was he who had led the infantry attack in Malaya which began the war. When Nasu, then a colonel, waded ashore with his troops against the British guns of Kota Bharu at 1:25 A.M., December 8, 1941, he was preceding the navy's Pearl Harbor attack by two hours. Having thus taken part in the army's first act of the war, he was now about to take part in the total demobilization which would be its last act.

Also present when General Anami entered the conference room were several of the younger staff officers who had planned the coup d'état he had vetoed three hours earlier. His brother-in-law, Lieutenant Colonel Masahiko Takeshita was sitting at the rear. Near him were Colonel Okikatsu Arao and Lieutenant Colonel Masao Inaba. A few feet from them, still looking flushed and deeply agitated, his uniform drenched with perspiration, was young Major Kenji Hatanaka.

General Anami stepped up onto a small dais at the front of the room and gazed at the faces of these men, for most of whom he had a deep, personal affection. What would happen to them when the army dissolved and they found themselves at the mercy of the enemy? Would they all be imprisoned as criminals for their part in the war? And if not, how would they adjust to their new lives as civilians, especially in a country which could offer nothing but hardships for several years to come? None of them had ever been anything other than soldiers. How would they earn their livings? Such questions were too bewildering to ponder, especially when there was a more immediate question which had to be settled—the loyalty of these men to the Emperor.

"All of you are aware of what happened last Friday," he began. "His Majesty asked his government to accept the enemy's Potsdam proclamation with the stipulation that our imperial system be preserved. And with that provision we in the army agreed. But at the time, no one could say for certain what the future held, whether Japan would soon be surrendering, or whether we would have to go on fighting. Our ultimate decision still depended on the enemy's reaction to our offer. For this reason I then ordered all of you to await developments but to hold yourselves in readiness and be prepared for either eventuality.

"However, the situation has now changed. Our course has become clear and definite. Four hours ago the Emperor commanded that Japan accept the enemy's terms. He offered to come here and speak to you himself, in order to make sure the army obeys his command. I said that would not be necessary. I speak for the army and I have promised His Majesty that the army will remain loyal to him. The army, like the rest of the country, must obey the Emperor's commands. That is Japan's only hope of salvation. The Emperor is convinced that the Allied nations will allow us to preserve our national polity, and he has expressed that conviction to the field marshals.

Accordingly, Field Marshals Sugiyama and Hata, Generals Umezu, Doihara, Kawabe and myself signed a pledge just a few minutes ago, to guide the army in accordance with the Imperial desire. I don't want any officer in this army to presume that he know better than the Emperor and the government what is best for the country."

Having delivered this message in clear, simple, forceful terms, he paused to let it sink in, then resumed in a softer tone. "I agree that conditions today are extraordinary, but remember that obedience is still one of the chief virtues of a soldier. The future of Japan is no longer in doubt, but neither will it be an easy future. You officers still have a duty to perform, and you cannot absolve it through death. Your duty is to remain alive and to help your country along the path to recovery."

On this note he finished. Once more, as Colonel Takeshita observed, he had spoken of "your duty" rather than "our duty." The implication was melancholy but it could not be questioned. If General Anami were to kill himself, even after forbidding his subordinates to do so, he would be acting in the most acceptable Samurai tradition. He was not, after all, just a soldier in the ranks. He was the commander of a defeated army. For a thousand years or more, in the wars between Japanese feudal lords, losing generals had gained honor despite defeat by committing harakiri.

After the general finished his remarks and left the room, most of his listeners sat for a few minutes in stunned silence. Takeshita was not the only one who had drawn an inference from his last words. Gradually the men stood up and returned, one by one, to their own offices.

Takeshita, who was one of the last to leave, felt someone tug at his sleeve as he walked down the hall, and turned to find Major Hatanaka behind him. The major was trembling slightly and Takeshita could see he was on the point of tears.

"We must carry on for his sake," Hatanaka said. "We and only we can do it."

"Do what?"

"We have to go ahead with the coup."

Takeshita looked at him in wonder. Was he serious? After studying his face, one couldn't doubt it. "You'd better forget it," Takeshita said. "It's hopeless."

"We've got to do it," Hatanaka insisted. "I'll talk to you later." And with that he turned, running down the hall to talk to someone else.

AUGUST 14,
4 P.M.

LIEUTENANT Colonel Masataka Ida, his uniform rumpled, his hands trembling, but with an exalted expression on his face, entered the office of the Military Affairs Bureau and surveyed the desultory activities there. Instead of going to his own desk, he walked over to a window where several men were staring out at a bonfire of documents in the courtyard of the War Ministry. Enlisted soldiers, supervised by a noncommissioned officer, were feeding additional papers to the flames as fast as they could be consumed.

Ida, who had boldly asked General Anami at the 1 P.M. meeting to explain his sudden change in attitude, had not attended the 3:30 meeting in the conference room from which some of his colleagues had just returned. He had been sitting alone in the ministry bomb shelter, composing his thoughts about the nation, about the army, about himself.

Now, after watching the bonfire for a few minutes, he cried out, "That's it, burn it all! Destroy every document! Then there will be only one thing left for us to do—destroy ourselves! Every one of us, every officer in the Imperial Army must cut his stomach open! How else can we apologize to the Emperor for our failure? How else can we make our names immortal? How else . . ."

Colonel Ida's dramatic exhortation was still pouring out of him when Major Hatanaka entered the room. Hearing Ida, he stopped to listen. When Ida finished and, feeling suddenly self-conscious, walked over to his own desk, Hatanaka followed.

Ida was puzzled when he looked up at Hatanaka. The major, usually meticulous about his appearance, looked unbelievably sweaty and dirty. (Ida did not know about the bicycle trips Hatanaka had taken through the hot, dusty streets to the Eastern Army headquarters and the Imperial Guards quarters.) At the same time, Hatanaka had such an excited, enthusiastic expression on his face one might think he hadn't been told what was happening to his beloved country and his beloved army.

"Colonel Ida, I'd like to talk to you," he said, "but not here. Let's go up on the roof where we can be alone."

A few minutes later, they were pacing back and forth on the hot, graveled tar of the ministry's roof. Though the building was only three stories high, it afforded an excellent view of the city because it was situated on the crest of the Ichigaya hill. It seemed miraculous that American bombs had not obliterated it. During daylight air raids, some of the officers liked to stand on the roof defiantly, watching the waves of bombers pass overhead, dropping their loads. Though several nearby buildings had been destroyed or damaged, the ministry remained intact, partly because, of course, it had always been afforded maximum fire protection. If they chose to look into the distance, Ida and Hatanaka could see mile after mile of burned-out Tokyo before them in every direction, much of it so completely flattened that the checkerboard street patterns were visible. Neither man paid much attention to this, however. They had seen it all before.

"I heard what you were saying downstairs," Hatanaka began. "Do you really think we should all kill ourselves?"

"It's the only correct thing to do," Ida said.

"But do you think it would work?"

"Why not? I'll bet at least a fourth of the officers in the army are ready to do it."

Hatanaka was skeptical. "I doubt if you'll get any more than that, and it's not enough. No. Your plan is beautiful, but it won't work."

"All right, then, what would you do?"

"I've been thinking about it," Hatanaka said, "and I've decided I want to demonstrate my loyalty as a Japanese even if it means that some people might call me a traitor. I would rather fight the enemy than put my Emperor and my country into his hands."

Colonel Ida was astonished. "You mean that even after the Emperor has spoken and General Anami has ordered us to obey . . ."

"Heaven may favor either side," Hatanaka continued. "That is something no human being can predict. But judgment is always affected by action, and if the mainspring of action is wholehearted loyalty, then why need the man of action feel ashamed even if he fails? No one can see the future until it is past but everyone is free to act in accordance with his own conscience."

Ida was amazed at the major's persistence. "Do you have a plan of action?" he asked.

"Yes, sir, I have. We must occupy the Imperial Household Ministry and cut off the palace from all outside contact. We must concentrate our efforts on helping the Emperor preserve Japan. I've already established liaison with the Imperial Guards. The preparations have begun. Even if we start with only a few officers, the whole army will soon follow. I have no doubt that we shall succeed. Heaven favors our cause. Will you join us, Colonel Ida?"

When Ida failed to answer, Hatanaka added, "Don't you think this is a more beautiful plan than cutting open your belly?"

"It would be more beautiful if it succeeded," Ida said, "but General Anami says a coup d'état has no chance of success. The Emperor is determined to end the war."

"But if you believe, as I do, that Japan is eternal and indestructible, you must make one final attempt to change the Emperor's mind."

"If the coup were to fail and a civil war resulted, what would happen to Japan then?" Ida asked. "No, I think the army has to obey the Emperor's decision. Then if some of us chose individual solutions, it won't endanger the country." He stopped, turned to Hatanaka and adopted a philosophical tone. "I'm afraid your plan is doomed to failure," he said. "A fire on which water has been poured will not burn again. That's the way of life."

Hatanaka was not to be put off easily. He needed all the support he could find, and since Ida had apparently resolved anyway to sacrifice his life, he was an ideal recruit. "You talk about us failing," Hatanaka said. "How do you know the surrender plan will succeed? The enemy has not promised to preserve our national polity if we surrender."

"That's true," Ida admitted. "The Emperor's plan may fail, but your plan is certain to fail."

A pained and slightly impatient expression came over Hatanaka's face, making Ida realize the desperate dedication of his younger colleague. Though Ida was only a year older, he did outrank Hatanaka, and at this moment he experienced a fatherly feeling which, combined with the exaltation of his own decision to commit suicide, made him resort once more to philosophical eloquence. "The tide of time is flowing against us," he said in lofty cadence. "that is why I intend to commit suppuku. [An elegant word for harakiri.] Let the world bear witness that I do not tamely lower this fist I have raised against the enemy. Instead, I take my sword in hand and cut open my belly."

Hatanaka was still thinking of more practical matters. "I've already received assurances from several Imperial Guards officers . . ."

Ida held up a hand to stop him. "I admire your spirit. Hatanaka. I admire it more than I can tell you. Perhaps I even envy it. So I say to you, go ahead with your plan. I won't try to stop you. But I won't join you, either. No. I have decided to die tomorrow." He extended a hand. "Farewell, Hatanaka."

The young major shook his head, bowed, and turned away. He couldn't afford to waste any more time on Colonel Ida.

AUGUST 14,
5:30 P.M.

A F T E R four-and-a-half hours of deliberation within the cabinet, one crisis had been resolved but another was now arising. General Anami, upon receiving a phone call from the War Ministry, had insisted that the Privy Council be called upon to approve the decisions the cabinet was in the process of making. When Chief Cabinet Secretary Sakomizu and Legislative Bureau director Naoyasu Murase argued that the constitution did not require a Privy Council vote, Anami had eventually and agreeably conceded. Now, however, he was proving more stubborn about the wording of the imperial rescript which would end the war.

Sakomizu and his staff, with the help of a language expert, had worked for three days on the rescript, and had then reworded it extensively this afternoon to make it comply with the Emperor's remarks at the morning imperial conference. The wording was a delicate matter not only because the subject of this rescript was momentous and because the Emperor planned to break all precedent by reading it himself on the radio, but also because it had to be written in the style of the Japanese imperial court—an archaic style full of Chinese characters, references, and constructions. No one could write an imperial rescript without a knowledge of Chinese literature. Sakomizu, in the last three days, had become grateful to his father for insisting that he study Chinese in school. That training had suddenly assumed a new importance to him. Yet in a situation of such gravity, he was not completely confident of his own linguistic abilities. For this reason he had called in a specialist in Chinese literature, a man named Tadaatsu Yasuoka, whom he still had sequestered in the prime minister's air raid shelter. He planned to keep Yasuoka there until the rescript was approved.

The cabinet was now deliberating about Sakomizu's draft of the rescript but had changed only a few words when General Anami raised the first serious objection to it. Having said nothing while other cabinet members quibbled over a word here and a phrase there, he now said, "I would like to point out one sentence which I must say I find unacceptable. Half way into the second paragraph, you will notice the sentence, 'Despite the best that has been done by everyone—the gallant fighting of military and naval forces, the diligence and assiduity of Our servants of the State, and the devoted service of Our one hundred million people, the war situation grows more unfavorable to us every day, . . .' " He put aside the mimeographed copy from which he was reading. "I could not sign my name to such a statement," he said. "I would then be declaring that many recent announcements by Imperial Headquarters were lies."

The veracity of army and navy communiqués was one of the most whispered issues in Japanese daily life—whispered because no one, not even cabinet members, dared discuss it openly. The Kempeitai had proven that prominence in public life was no assurance against imprisonment. In early May, the army's secret police, who for many years had inhibited free speech among the general public by threat of dire consequences, arrested and incarcerated 400 well-known public figures, including a high-court judge and a former ambassador (who would one day become prime minister), Shigeru Yoshida, for speaking out in favor of peace. Even now, on what might be the last day of the war, there was only one cabinet member who dared answer General Anami on this subject. Navy minister Yonai, whose own department had falsified war news to such an extent that even the battle of Midway was publicized as a victory, felt compelled at this moment to resist whatever strategy the war minister might be developing.

Admiral Yonai rose to his feet and suggested that General Anami should put from his mind the unfortunate communiqués of Imperial Headquarters. "Japan is on the verge of destruction," he said heatedly, "and we all know it."

General Anami showed no annoyance at the passion with which Yonai spoke. In a soft, even voice, he said, "We have not yet lost the war, as this rescript draft would seem to indicate. It is simply that the situation has not turned in our favor."

Yonai could not conceal his exasperation. "We have lost battle after battle, including the battles for Okinawa and Burma. Are you speaking now of a last-ditch battle for the homeland? We shall lose that, too. We have been defeated. We have been clearly defeated."

"We have lost battles," Anami admitted, "but we have not yet lost the war. The navy may be convinced that we have lost the war. The army is not so convinced."

It seemed to Anami that his true motives in resisting Sakomizu's phraseology should be clear at least to some of the cabinet members. He had still to bear in mind the pride of the Imperial Army's officers and men. He had already experienced enough difficulty keeping the young officers under control. They might yet erupt if they were to hear the Emperor say, in effect, that they had lost the war. Surely Admiral Yonai, being a military man himself, could understand this problem, yet he showed no sign of it. Admiral Suzuki should also understand it but he sat back in his chair saying nothing. Anami felt he had no choice but to keep insisting, politely, upon a change, without explaining his reasons, which were too delicate for a Japanese general to admit openly.

"I suggest," he said, "that instead of saying, 'The war situation grows more unfavorable to us every day,' we say, 'The war situation has developed not necessarily to Japan's advantage.'"

Yonai was equally insistent. It seemed to him the sentence Anami favored was so ridiculous under the circumstances it would make the Emperor sound like a fool. "The sentence as it stands," he said, "reflects the true situation."

Anami said, "I cannot accept it."

The meeting lapsed into silence. Sakomizu, at a table behind the main table, glanced at his watch. It was now approaching six o'clock, the hour at which the Emperor was expecting to record the rescript. The Japan Broadcasting Company had a crew of technicians standing by at the Imperial Household Ministry, in the palace, waiting for the Emperor to arrive and read into their microphone. After a short consultation with Information Bureau director Hiroshi Shimomura, Sakomizu left the room and called the Imperial Household Ministry to announce the delay.

The chamberlain to whom he spoke said, "I understand, but can you give me some idea when it will be?"

"Let's reschedule it for seven o'clock," Sakomizu said hopefully.

As he was returning to the cabinet room, he encountered Admiral Yonai, who was on his way to the washroom.

"Don't give in to the army," Yonai said to him. "Hold out for your wording."

Sakomizu shrugged. It was not for him to give in or hold out. He had no vote in the cabinet, nor was he certain he would choose to fight Anami over such a matter even if he did have a vote. Minor word changes would not alter the real meaning of the rescript. And he could see how adamant about the issue Anami had become. For several days he had feared, from one crucial moment to another, that the war minister might suddenly resign, thus disrupting all the peace efforts. It was still not too late for this to happen.

AUGUST 14,
7 P.M.

W H E N T H E cabinet resumed after a short recess, most of the members were anticipating glumly a continuation of the stalemate between the war and navy ministers over the wording of one clause in the rescript—". . . the war situation grows more unfavorable to us every day . . ." The war minister wanted it changed to ". . . the war situation has developed not necessarily to Japan's advantage . . ." The navy minister, before the recess, had insisted that the original wording was the one which fit the circumstances. During the recess, Admiral Yonai had made a short trip to the Navy Ministry to make sure the situation there was under control, and on the way back he had brooded over this disagreement which separated General Anami from himself. Though he had never been close to Anami, they had worked well together in the cabinet until the question of surrender became critical. At one time in June, under the stress of growing frustration at the government's inability to get anything done, Yonai had decided to resign, but had then changed his mind only because Anami had prevailed upon him to remain. He had a high regard for Anami's character despite their disagreements. He was exasperated by this present disagreement, however, because it seemed to him it had arisen simply from the army's desire to save face. He was tired of the army's sensitivities about its own feelings. It had never shown much sensitivity about the feelings of others. He himself had more than once been under threat of death by young army officers and he was aware that many of them right now would like to see him dead. They hated him for his resistance to the war before it started, and they hated him for his current espousal of the peace efforts, nor was he the only person involved in the present situation who had reason to be impatient with the army. Prime Minister Suzuki had survived an actual attempt by army officers to assassinate him nine years earlier. And even the Emperor must still remember many occasions when the army disregarded his feelings. The army had launched the Manchurian war in 1931 and the China Incident in 1937 without bothering to consult the Emperor or the government. And it was the army that had insisted most stubbornly on launching this hopeless war against America. Why couldn't the army stand up and take its share of the responsibility? But General Anami, unlike some of his colleagues, was not the kind of man who would deny a responsibility. Why then was he maintaining this ridiculous pretense that Japan had not lost the war? Was it to assuage the feelings of everyone else in the army? Or was it simply to insure against the very real possibility of rebellion among the young officers? It suddenly occurred to Admiral Yonai that he had hit upon the reason for Anami's stubbornness —a reason which Anami would not, of course, be able to explain.

As soon as Prime Minister Suzuki called the cabinet to order for its evening session, Admiral Yonai stood up and said, "On the question of the phrasing of that sentence we've been discussing, I would now like to see it revised in accordance with the war minister's desires."

Anami looked up at him and as their eyes met Yonai felt there was true understanding between them. Yonai then glanced across the room at Chief Cabinet Secretary Sakomizu whom he had encouraged just an hour before to resist Anami's amendment. The astonishment on Sakomizu's face seemed to say, "How could you knuckle under so easily after insisting that I remain firm?" There would be no need to explain this, however, to Sakomizu. He would eventually understand.

Prime Minister Suzuki, who sometimes seemed to be doing nothing, inserted himself quickly when he heard Yonai's concession. "Let it be done," he said.

When Admiral Yonai sat down, General Anami arose to speak. "There is just one more revision," he said, "that I would like to request."

The room fell silent as everyone contemplated the appalling possibility of another long, tedious argument over wording.

"I call your attention," he said, "to the section of the rescript which begins: 'We are always with you, Our good and loyal subjects, relying upon your sincerity and integrity.' It is not possible for us to know what will happen to our country and our Emperor under enemy occupation. That will be up to the Allied nations. But we do know, and I think we should register the fact that while he was able to do so, Emperor Hirohito kept faith with his ancestors and his responsibilities. I would like to suggest, therefore, that we insert the following words at the beginning of that section: 'Having been able to save and maintain the structure of the Imperial State,' We are always with you, and so forth."

Sighs of relief passed through the room. This was a revision about which no one should argue.

Prime Minister Suzuki said, "Let that also be done." And it was settled.

Sakomizu grabbed his copy of the final draft and rushed from the room. He had to send the revised text as quickly as possible to the Imperial Palace and he had also to prepare it for the official signing by the cabinet. Since the Japanese language, with its thousands of characters, many of them from the Chinese, did not lend itself to the use of typewriters, even that job would entail perhaps a two-hour delay while the entire document was being recopied by hand. Sakomizu hurried to a room downstairs where calligraphers and mimeograph operators were waiting.

The cabinet now moved on to the next order of business. When should the imperial rescript be released to the public? The Emperor was still standing by, ready to record it for radio as soon as it reached him. But it was now too late to hope it could be released today.

Foreign Minister Togo said, "I propose the broadcast be scheduled for 7 A.M. tomorrow. Any undue delay might be to the detriment of the country."

As soon as Togo finished speaking, the cabinet learned that General Anami's objections had not yet ended. "Impossible!" he cried. "We haven't yet issued orders to our troops overseas. And before that, we must take measures to make certain those orders will be obeyed. It will take time to persuade all those men to lay down their arms. I suggest, therefore, that the Emperor's broadcast be delayed at least until day-after-tomorrow."

Yonai immediately said, "We can't afford to wait that long." And once more an argument began.

It was beginning to look as if the cabinet meeting itself might last until day-after-tomorrow. Fortunately, Hiroshi Shimomura, director of the Information Bureau, had a compromise to offer.

"If the broadcast were at 7 A.M.," he said, "it would not, in my opinion, be completely effective because many people, especially farmers and factory workers, would be starting their day's work and therefore out of touch with their radios. In addition, we would have no time to inform the public that the broadcast was scheduled. On the other hand, if we postpone the broadcast too long, there might be violence. With so many rumors circulating we could have serious unrest. I suggest, therefore, that the best possible time would be the lunch hour tomorrow. Throughout the morning, we can broadcast announcements alerting people to listen at noon."

Everyone turned to Anami. After a moment's hesitation, he nodded in agreement.

Prime Minister Suzuki stood up. "Will the war minister make sure," he asked, "that advance notice of the broadcast is given to all the front-line troops?"

"I'll do my best," Anami said.

Without pause, Suzuki said, "The meeting is recessed until the

rescript is ready for signing." He turned and quickly left the room
before anyone had time to raise new questions.

AUGUST 14,
7:30 P.M.

K E N D O master Sogen Ohmori was at his Direct Mind School of
Japanese Fencing in Setagaya when the telephone rang. He answered it to find himself talking to Major Kenji Hatanaka who was
even more excited tonight than usual. During the last week, since
their meeting at the War Ministry, Ohmori had talked to Hatanaka
almost every day. After Hatanaka's suggestion that he form a civilian
group to help the military resist surrender, Ohmori had gone to work
so enthusiastically that he now had a loose-knit organization of about
100 men who were ready to support an attempted coup d'état. More
important than the number, however, was the fact that most of them
were in positions of some influence. They were newspapermen, businessmen, government employees, aristocrats, and even a few Diet
members. They had been gathering information of all kinds, which
Ohmori had passed on to Hatanaka, and they were ready to take
action in the streets as soon as they received the word from the War
Ministry. Most of them owned Samurai swords or pistols and
Hatanaka had promised to provide them more adequate arms at the
right time.

After listening to Hatanaka's first few words on the telephone,
Ohmori concluded that the right time was going to be tonight.

"You had better alert your people," Hatanaka said. "We're getting
ready to move. The Emperor declared for peace this morning and the
cabinet is preparing a surrender rescript which he plans to read on
the radio. The Badoglios are to blame for it. General Anami couldn't
stop them this time. But we still plan to stop them. Are you with us?"

"We're awaiting your orders," Ohmori said. "What do you want us
to do?" He had a sudden, grim vision of himself manning a barricade
with a bayoneted rifle in hand.

"We don't want you to do anything at the moment," Hatanaka said.
"Just be ready when we call on you. The beginning is up to us. The

first thing we have to do is prevent that rescript broadcast and isolate the Emperor from the Badoglios. As soon as we accomplish that, we'll have plenty for your group to do."

"Just let us know," Ohmori said.

Hatanaka, having completed his message, hesitated a moment. "There is one other thing I would like to ask of you," he said.

"Yes?"

"If we fail tonight, will you try to explain to the people what we were trying to do?"

"You won't fail," Ohmori declared. It was inconceivable to him that the government could get away with anything so outrageous as surrender.

AUGUST 14,
7:45 P.M.

E M P E R O R Hirohito's chief military aide, General Shigeru Hasunuma, was in his office at the Imperial Household Ministry, talking to several of his subordinates, when two young Imperial Guards officers entered the room. Hasunuma, who did not know either of them, was puzzled by their visit. He listened as they talked to one of his aides.

The first to enter, a handsome young major, stepped forward and said, "We've been told that His Majesty plans to record his broadcast this evening. Can you tell us what time the recording will be made?"

Between Hasunuma and his aide there was an exchange of glances which did not escape the young major. Addressing himself to the general, he said, "We're staff officers of the Imperial Guards Division, and we want to make sure the Guards are ready if needed."

Neither Hasunuma nor his aide said anything.

The other Guards officer stepped forward. 'Has the recording already been made?"

Hasunuma's aide said, "No, not as far as we know. We don't know anything about it."

"That's hard to believe," the Guards officer insisted. "You must know something about it."

His companion put out a hand to restrain him. "They're telling the truth," he said. "Let's go."

After they had saluted and left the room, General Hasunuma said, "Who are they?"

Another aide who had been listening said, "I think one of them is Major Koga."

That did not identify him for General Hasunuma. "Who is Major Koga?" he asked.

"He's a staff officer in the Guards Division, as he said, and he's also General Tojo's son-in-law."

AUGUST 14,
8 P.M.

O N   T H E way to the War Ministry from his official residence, General Anami said to his secretary, Colonel Saburo Hayashi, "How do I go about resigning my position?"

To Hayashi, this was an indication that the war minister, though he had accepted the decision to surrender, did not want his name publicly associated with it. "I believe it takes just a written notice," Hayashi told him. "I understand all the members of the General Staff are planning to resign."

They drove on in silence. Though the city was blacked out, there was enough moonlight to silhouette the grotesque shapes of the ruined buildings they passed. The August heat was so intense that even the breeze created by the car's movement offered no relief.

When they arrived at the ministry, Hayashi was astonished to find that the sentries at the front gate had left their posts. Anami, to whom such a situation would be inconceivable even a few hours earlier, gave no indication now that he so much as noticed it. As his car drove up the winding interior road he said nothing. The car stopped at the front of the main building and they entered to discover that the halls were empty and deathly quiet; their footsteps echoed as they hurried up the stairs. There seemed to be no one left here at all. It was as if, when word of the surrender leaked out, everybody at the War Ministry had decided to be someplace else by the time the enemy arrived.

Reaching his own second-floor office, the war minister sat down and went through a pile of communications, military orders, memoranda, and letters which had accumulated on his desk, signing some, initialing others, throwing a few away. The paperwork of surrender was almost as voluminous as the paperwork of war. When he finished these pressing matters, he began going through his drawers, discarding other papers and mementos.

Hayashi, watching him, said, "Is there anything I can do to help?"

"No, but if you could get hold of Lieutenant Colonel Takeshita, I would appreciate it. Tell him I'd like to see him."

Hayashi went down the hall and around the corner to the Military Affairs Bureau but found no one there. When he returned to say so, Anami asked, "What about Colonel Arao? Did you see him?"

Arao, Takeshita's commanding officer, had his desk in the same room. "He's not there either," Hayashi said.

Unable to find either man, the general took up a pen and himself wrote a message to be cabled to all Japanese troops under his name and the name of General Umezu, the chief of staff. After outlining the facts of surrender and ordering absolute compliance, he wrote:

... The Emperor has made his decision. The army expects you to obey that decision and make no unauthorized moves that would put to shame the glorious traditions of the Imperial Army and its many distinguished military services. You must behave in such a way that you need never fear the judgement of posterity, and it is expected that your conduct will enhance the honor and the glory of the Imperial Japanese Forces in the eyes of the entire world . . .

The minister of war and the chief of staff dispatch this order with grief in their hearts, and they expect you to appreciate the emotions of the Emperor when he himself broadcasts the imperial rescript terminating the war at twelve noon tomorrow.

This message finished, General Anami took another piece of paper and wrote out a short letter of resignation which he put into his pocket. Since the cabinet was to meet at 9:30 and sign the rescript, he had a few minutes to sit and relax. As the time approached when he had to leave, Colonel Arao arrived. Anami stood up to greet him.

"I was looking for you, Colonel," he said. "There is something I would like you to do for me. I don't want any of our young officers to commit any foolish or heroic acts. No suicides. Understand? The country needs them, and I want them to go on living. You can help if you will."

"Yes sir, but how?"

"Talk to them. Tell them what I said. Find jobs for them. Maybe you can get them into the police force."

"And what about those of us who are older?" Arao said.

Anami, obviously understanding that he himself was included in Arao's question, did not answer it. He walked away and stared at the blacked-out window for a few moments, then turned again to the tall, muscular colonel.

"Japan will recover," he said. "Our people work hard. And even if the army can't play a part in what's to come, the men in the army can do so. That means you, Arao. That's what I want to say to you. Preserve your energies for the work that lies ahead. You'll find it rewarding." He nodded in punctuation, then smiled. "I've got to go now. The cabinet is about to meet again."

On his desk was a box of cigars which he had taken from one of the drawers. He picked it up, looking around for a piece of wrapping paper. Since there was none in sight, he began wrapping it in a newspaper from the wastebasket. He had almost finished when he stopped and let the paper fall away. Opening the box, which was almost full, he extracted two cigars and gave them to Arao.

"I want you to have these," he said.

Finishing his job of wrapping, he buckled on his sword, looked down to check the appearance of his uniform, and prepared to leave.

AUGUST 14,
9:40 P.M.

G E N E R A L Anami, arriving a few minutes late for the 9:30 cabinet meeting at the prime minister's official residence, took from his pocket the letter of resignation he had written and gave it to his secretary, Colonel Hayashi, as they entered the building.

"Will you please hand this in for me," he said. "You'll have to find out exactly how it's done."

As Anami hurried up the stairs to the second-floor cabinet room, Hayashi went to the office of the cabinet's general affairs section. To the man at the desk he said, "Quite frankly, what I have here is the war minister's resignation. He just asked me to submit it, and I would like to know the procedure."

"You needn't be in any hurry about that," the man said. "The entire cabinet will be expected to resign in a bloc tomorrow."

"Oh, in that case . . ." Hayashi shrugged, went upstairs, and reported this information to General Anami, who was sitting in the cabinet room with Admiral Suzuki and about two-thirds of the members, waiting for the others to arrive.

Anami said no more about resignation. He did say, however, "Will you please have two sheets of hanshi [a special white paper] ready for me?"

Hayashi, who could imagine the use for which the paper was intended because he was familiar with Samurai death rituals, felt a deep chill run through him.

It was almost ten o'clock by the time the full cabinet had assembled for the formal rescript signing. The patched and pasted sheet of heavy paper which lay on the table in front of the prime minister was no doubt the untidiest imperial rescript ever promulgated. After the calligraphers had prepared two copies of the document as approved by the cabinet, it had been hurried to the Imperial Palace, where the Emperor had requested five additional changes. Though none of them was major, they would, under ordinary circumstances, have necessitated recopying the entire text, but since this would have entailed another long delay, it was decided simply to make the changes on strips of paper to be pasted over the original. The document the cabinet was about to sign therefore displayed a rather tattered dignity which perhaps befit the occasion. Emperor Hirohito had already signed it and his seal had been affixed.

The prime minister, calling the cabinet to order, wasted very little time on words. "We all know why we are here," he said. "I shall be the first to sign."

Wetting a brush with black ink, he wrote carefully, with a slightly quavering hand, the characters which spelled the name "Kantaro Suzuki." After affixing his seal, he pushed the document along the table to Admiral Yonai, the navy minister, who was the second to sign. After Yonai came Justice Minister Matsuzaka, then the war minister. General Anami signed quickly with only a glance at the melancholy document, then handed it on to the next man. There were some people in the room who, until that moment, had still expected Anami to reject surrender.

AUGUST 14,
10:20 P.M.

A M O N G the hundreds of people jammed into the 10:30 train for Nagoya at Tokyo Station, Dr. Tsunesaburo Asada was the only one who knew the war was over. After his report to the navy on the effects of the atomic bomb in Hiroshima, he had made a similar report to the Home Ministry. In the early evening, when he went to the Navy Ministry to ask if anything else was expected of him, he found most of the officers there in tears. "The Emperor has ordered us to surrender," one of them told him. Another said, "You had better get out of Tokyo tonight. There'll be trouble here tomorrow when the news is announced." They assigned an enlisted man to take him to the station.

At 8:30, when he reached Tokyo station, which was now a shell with only the four walls standing, he found that the Nagoya train, though not scheduled to leave for another two hours, was already so full it would be impossible to get aboard. Not only were the aisles and seats and spaces between the seats stuffed tight with people; so were the overhead luggage racks. Men were even standing on the tops of the backs of the seats. Since this train was the only one scheduled to go south tonight in his direction, toward Osaka, he was about to abandon hope of escaping Tokyo before morning when suddenly the sailor who was escorting him fell upon the discovery that the very last car was reserved for the navy. Asada was soon ensconced in it comfortably next to a man he could not see because of the almost total darkness.

As 10:30 approached, Asada was beginning to relax. In a few minutes he would be on his way home. But it now occurred to him, quite joltingly, that he no longer had a home, it having been destroyed by bombs the night of August 5. He had been so busy in the last few days he hadn't had time to think about that. But sitting in this blacked-out train on what he knew to be the last night of the war, he decided that the loss of his home, the third home he had lost to the bombers within the last year, was not so important. He was going home even though he didn't have a home, and the war was over and as soon as he could find a place to live he would be able to bring his family in from the country and have them with him. They would all start a new life together. The whole country would be starting a new life. Since it was not comfortable to think of the possibilities and limits of that new life, he tried to put it from his mind and think only of the happy fact that the war was ending. He was tempted to say to the unseen man sitting next to him in the dark, "Do you know that the war is over?" but he hesitated and then decided against it. The man would be unlikely to believe it since it had not yet been announced, and if he proved to be the wrong kind of man, he might even report to the police that Asada was spreading defeatist rumors.

Asada settled back in his seat and was pleasantly nurturing his secret when he looked down the aisle to see a man approaching with a tiny flashlight which he played back and forth, apparently in search of a seat. When he reached Asada, he still hadn't found one. Asada could see, in the glow of the tiny light, that the man was wearing a naval officer's uniform. Asada, who was wearing an open shirt and a pair of pants he had borrowed from the navy because all of his clothing had been burned with his home, realized that he was now in for some trouble.

The officer playing the tiny flashlight on him said, "Civilians aren't allowed in this car. It's reserved for the navy."

Asada said, "But I'm on an assignment for the navy."

"That makes no difference. You're a civilian. You're not supposed to be in this car."

"I tell you, I'm working for the navy. And there's no room in the other cars."

"Then you'll just have to get off the train. This car is for navy officers."

Asada began wearily to grope in the dark for his things. He was about to stand up and give the intruder his seat when the unseeable man next to him said, "Stay where you are." To the officer in the aisle waiting for Asada's seat, he added, "Leave him alone."

The officer in the aisle immediately became furious. "This car is not for civilians," he cried. "Who are you to tell me I can't take a seat from a civilian?"

As it happened, the man sitting in the dark next to Asada also had a tiny flashlight. He turned it on and pointed it at his own shoulder, which bore the ensignia of a navy captain. The officer in the aisle was obviously outranked. He moved on without a word. Dr. Asada thanked the unseen captain sitting beside him. The wheels of the train squeaked and it lurched ahead. His seat was safe at least until the first stop which would probably be Yokohama. If he were lucky he might even reach Osaka sometime tomorrow night, despite the inevitable delays. It might even be possible for the train to travel in the daytime tomorrow, if the American fighter planes had stopped strafing. He wished he could see the man beside him. He must be a nice man, Asada decided, to have done what he did for a stranger.

Asada wondered whether he should tell the man the good news that the war was over. Though he was tempted, he decided he had better wait a little while.

AUGUST 14,
10:50 P.M.

T H E S I G N I N G of the document and several items of miscellaneous business having been completed by the cabinet, only one thing now held up the official promulgation of the imperial rescript announcing Japan's surrender. During the meeting the cabinet had agreed that 11 P.M. would be the time of promulgation, and since that was still ten minutes away, the members sat waiting in virtual silence. They stared at the walls, fidgeted nervously, or began gathering up the papers on the table in front of them. Several had tears in their eyes. Perhaps the most outwardly composed was General Anami, who sat up straight in his chair with no emotion showing in his face.

At a table behind the large, round cabinet table, Chief Secretary Sakomizu sat looking at his watch. Outside in the hall were various members of his staff awaiting the official word which they would then convey, each in accordance with his special assignment, to the Imperial Palace, the Foreign Office, the army, navy, police, and other agencies. The newspapers would be informed later.

When the second hand of his watch indicated 11 P.M., Sakomizu stood up and said, "Gentlemen, the imperial rescript is now in effect."

As if to kill the impact of this dramatic moment, an air raid alarm sounded, the first since four days before, when the Americans had instituted a bombing pause to encourage the surrender movement. No one in the cabinet room showed much interest either in the alarm or in Sakomizu's announcement. The dominant feelings were emptiness and exhaustion. The members remained at their places, little inclined to move or talk, as Sakomizu opened the door and hurried out to put his staff in motion.

AUGUST 14,
11:05 P.M.

EMPEROR Hirohito, immaculately dressed in an army uniform, had been waiting several hours for the cabinet to finish its deliberations and technicalities so that he could record his rescript for radio. When word arrived at his temporary residence in the imperial library that the rescript was now official, he wanted to get into his Mercedes Benz automobile immediately and travel through the darkened palace grounds to the Household Ministry, where the recording was to be made. He could see, however, that the chamberlain who was to accompany him, Sukemasa Irie, was holding back for some reason.

Finally, Irie said, "Your Majesty, the air raid alarm of a few minutes ago is still in effect."

Hirohito, a man who had shown patience beyond measure throughout his twenty-year reign, was running short of it now. One more of America's atomic bombs could wipe out another hundred thousand of his people. "I would like to go anyway," he said.

"May I advise," Irie asked, "that we wait in the shelter at least until we have some indication of the enemy's targets?" He could not bring himself to express openly his concern that the one man who had the power and prestige to guide Japan to peace might be killed on his way to do so.

The Emperor, studying the chamberlain's face, understood what was in his mind. "We had better go to the shelter," he agreed.

AUGUST 14,
11:05 P.M.

VICE MINISTER Shunichi Matsumoto at the Foreign Office had waited with trepidation since noon for the cabinet to make the surrender official. Like Foreign Minister Togo and most of the senior officials at the ministry, he expected more atomic bombs to fall on Japan very soon, and he especially feared the next one might hit Tokyo, wiping out both the Emperor and the government, thus depriving the country of the only institutions capable of making peace.

Since there was no way even to estimate how many of these bombs the Americans might have, Matsumoto believed the prudent course was to assume they had as many as they needed, and that the next one might arrive at any moment.

With this in mind, he had written, shortly after noon, a message, to be sent through Switzerland and Sweden, to the four Allied powers. Though his staff was standing by, he was so eager to cable this message that he had begun answering his own phone in the hope, each time, that the call would be from the prime minister's office.

Finally, about five minutes after eleven o'clock, he received the call for which he was waiting. The surrender was now official. He sent an aide to dispatch immediately the cablegram he had written in anticipation many hours earlier. The message read:

Communication of the Japanese Government of August 14, 1945, addressed to the Governments of the United States, Great Britain, the Soviet Union, and China:

With reference to the Japanese Government's note of August 10 regarding their acceptance of the provisions of the Potsdam Declaration and the reply of the Governments of the United States, Great Britain, the Soviet Union and China sent by American Secretary of State Byrnes under the date of August 11, the Japanese Government have the honor to communicate to the Governments of the four powers as follows:

1. His Majesty the Emperor has issued an Imperial Rescript regarding Japan's acceptance of the provisions of the Potsdam Declaration.

2. His Majesty the Emperor is prepared to authorize and ensure the signature by His Government and the Imperial General Headquarters of the necessary terms for carrying out the provisions of the Potsdam Declaration. His Majesty is also prepared to issue His commands to all the military, naval and air authorities of Japan and all the forces under their control wherever located to cease active operations, to surrender arms and to issue such other orders as may be required by the Supreme Commander of the Allied Forces for the execution of the above-mentioned terms.

There was, perhaps, an indication that Japan had not changed its order of priorities in the ironic fact that while the cabinet had used ten hours and engaged in considerable debate preparing the Emperor's message to the powerless Japanese people, Matsumoto had written in less than an hour, without discussion or debate, this message which was of comparable importance to the Emperor's since it was addressed to the powerful enemy. It was the Foreign Office cablegram, not the imperial rescript, which promised to turn off the tortures Japan was enduring.

AUGUST 14,
11:15 P.M.

THE Prime Minister had already left the cabinet room and those few ministers who remained were preparing to leave. Most of them were stuffing papers in brief cases or bidding each other good night. General Anami, who had sat quietly for several minutes after the meeting ended, stood up now, attached to his belt the sword he was wearing tonight, a long, Samurai blade which he seldom wore, then put on also a pair of white gloves which gave him a quite formal appearance. He picked up the newspaper-wrapped box of cigars he had brought with him from the War Ministry and walked over to Foreign Minister Shigenori Togo, one of his principle adversaries during the surrender debates.

Bowing politely, Anami said, "I have seen the foreign minister's note to the Allied powers about the occupation and disarmament, and I am grateful beyond expression. [he was speaking, not of the note just dispatched to inform the Allies of the Emperor's surrender rescript, but of the note written earlier in the afternoon asking the Allies to limit their occupation and to let the Japanese forces disarm themselves.] If I had known the matter would be handled so well, I would not have said some of the things I said in the heat of debate."

Togo in return bowed stiffly and spoke precisely. "Though I resisted proposing those points as conditions for accepting the Allied terms," he said, "I did not object to presenting them to the Allies as the desires of the Japanese government."

Anami said, "I am most grateful to you."

"At any rate," Togo said, "everything has worked out all right."

The two men smiled, bowed again to each other, and parted.

General Anami, with his box of cigars still tucked under his arm, and his hat in hand, walked across the hall to the door of the prime minister's office, which was closed. As soon as he knocked, the door opened. Admiral Suzuki, sitting at his desk near the far end of the long room, looked dreadfully tired and at least as old as his 79 years. With him was his son, Hajime, who often helped him as a personal secretary; Cabinet Minister (without portfolio) Heigoro Sakurai; and Chief Cabinet Secretary Sakomizu. All three of these men stood when the war minister entered.

"I beg your pardon for disturbing you," Anami said, walking quickly to Suzuki's desk.

The prime minister stood and the two men faced each other across the desk.

Anami opened the conversation in a soft voice, but quite formally. He had prepared his words and wanted to deliver them carefully. "Since the problem of ending the war arose, I have expressed many opinions contrary to yours. I have represented the army. I may have expressed myself too strongly at times but my intentions were always to assist the prime minister to the best of my ability. I fear that as things worked out, I was not always successful and I troubled you very much. I would like to apologize for that. I would like you to realize that my chief aim has always been the preservation of the national structure. I had no other purpose. Please believe me."

Suzuki walked around from behind his desk and put a hand on the war minister's shoulder. Although the old admiral did not admire the army, he had admired and trusted Anami since they first met many years earlier at the Imperial Palace when Suzuki was grand chamberlain and Anami was a military aide to the Emperor. Anami's recent conduct as the most powerful member of his cabinet had not diminished Suzuki's regard for him. Even during these last days of controversy, Suzuki had been convinced that while Anami had to maintain the army's viewpoint, he had been in his heart an advocate of peace and an ever-faithful follower of the Emperor. Suzuki knew that at any time, Anami could have disrupted the peace efforts by resigning. The fact that he had not resorted to such a tactic was proof enough of his loyalty. Suzuki had never, of course, even privately, asked Anami to express his personal feelings about peace, nor had Anami ever asked Suzuki to do so, even in the earlier days of the cabinet when Suzuki was publicly advocating a fight to the finish. It would be unfitting for Oriental gentlemen to approach each other so openly. Yet each of these men felt he understood the other.

"I do believe you," Suzuki said. "I'm grateful for the frankness with which you expressed your opinions and I know your only motivation was love for your country."

Anami said, "I worry about His Majesty."

"You can put your mind at rest about the Emperor's welfare," Suzuki assured him. "His Majesty goes to pray at his ancestral shrine every spring and every fall."

Tears came to Anami's eyes. "Yes, you are right, I believe he will be safe." After a moment's pause, he brought forth the box of cigars in its pathetic newspaper wrapping and gave it to the prime minister. "I want you to have these," he said. "They came from the southern front."

For a moment he put his hand on Suzuki's shoulder. Then he stepped back, saluted sharply, and turned to leave.

Sakomizu, also an admirer of the war minister, did not want to see him disappear so abruptly.

"Just a moment, sir," he said. "Let me walk with you." The two men went down the stairs together and out to Anami's car which was waiting in the front driveway. They said nothing. Each smiled and bowed warmly.

After watching General Anami drive away, Sakomizu returned to the prime minister's office. Admiral Suzuki looked up at him and said, "I think the war minister came to say good-bye."

AUGUST 14,
11:25 P.M.

IN THE MOONLIGHT outside the Imperial Household Ministry, Emperor Hirohito alighted from his automobile to be met by Information Bureau director Hiroshi Shimomura, who escorted him into the huge, rambling structure. Despite the blackout, the heavily-curtained building was well-illuminated inside, thanks to the fact that the palace had its own power generator. The Emperor, conducted by Shimomura and followed by Chamberlain Sukemasa Irie, hurried to the imperial administration room on the second floor, where a sizable group of chamberlains and radio technicians, dressed formally despite the insufferable heat, had been awaiting him for several hours. After all these men had bowed from the waist, the Emperor looked around, saw the microphone in the center of the room, and walked toward it.

"How loud should my voice be?" he asked.

Shimomura said, "Your normal volume will be ideal, Your Majesty."

"Shouldn't we have a test before we begin?" the Emperor suggested.

Shimomura was now confronted with a problem. Though a test would be useful, one could not ask the Emperor to undergo such an inconvenience.

One of the chamberlains solved the problem. He said, "Mr. Toda [Yasuhide Toda, another chamberlain] has a voice similar to His

Majesty's voice. Perhaps Mr. Toda would read a few lines for a test."

Toda stepped forward, and after he had read several lines of a newspaper article into the big, standing microphone, one of the radio technicians, most of whom were now in an adjoining room with their equipment, came to the door to announce that the voice level was satisfactory. The presence of the Emperor was such an inhibiting factor that the technician spoke with a strained formality which sounded awkward, probably because it was the first time he had ever felt compelled to choose his words so carefully.

The Emperor now stepped up directly to the microphone, which was adjusted to his height. He held in front of him the heavy piece of white paper which was his copy of the imperial rescript.

Shimomura, who was wearing white gloves, raised his right hand and brought it down sharply as a signal to begin.

The Emperor, in a high-pitched voice which he nevertheless kept lower than usual, began to read in clear tones with convincing emphasis: "To Our good and loyal subjects—After pondering deeply the general trends of the world and the actual conditions obtaining in Our Empire today . . ."

When he had finished reading the approximately 650 words of the rescript, he looked around anxiously. "Was it all right?" he asked.

Shimomura relayed the question to the chief radio engineer who was so awed by the Emperor's presence that his reply was barely audible. "There were no technical errors," he said, "but a few words were not quite clear."

Shimomura now faced another problem. One could not ask His Majesty to repeat the reading.

This time, the Emperor himself relieved the situation. "It seemed to me my voice was pitched too low," he said. "I would like to do it again."

Once more he stepped close to the microphone and Shimomura gave the starting signal. This time, the Emperor's voice seemed slightly too high and there was a degree of tension in it. He also left out one word. About halfway through the reading, tears came to his eyes. Soon, others in the room began to cry.

When the Emperor finished his second reading, he said, "I fear that was not very good. For one thing, I think I omitted a word. I am quite willing to do it a third time."

A Household Ministry official went into the other room and asked the chief engineer, "Are you ready to do a third recording?"

The chief engineer, thinking he had been asked if a third recording was necessary, and acutely aware that it was not proper to make the Emperor keep repeating his performance, said, "I don't think we need one."

Meanwhile, Shimomura had conferred hastily with Imperial Household Minister Sotaro Ishiwatari and Grand Chamberlain Hisanori Fujita. All three agreed that it would be tactless to accept the Emperor's offer of a third reading.

Shimomura said to him, "It was quite satisfactory, Your Majesty."

Shimomura then bowed deeply and everyone in the room did likewise. Emperor Hirohito, accompanied by Chamberlain Irie, left the room and the building. In his car on the way back across the palace grounds to the library which was now his home, he said nothing.

As soon as the Emperor left the Household Ministry, a discussion began as to where the recordings should be kept until broadcast time the following noon. One of the chamberlains said to the radio men, "Why don't you take them back to the station with you?"

Several of the radio men registered disapproval of that idea. "They'll be safer here," one of them said. The army knows about the broadcast. If there is any trouble before morning, we're certain to have visitors at the station."

"It would also be disrespectful to the Emperor," another of the radio men insisted, "to keep the recordings anyplace but here in the palace."

By this time, the recordings were ready. Two of each reading had been placed in flat, round cans. Unfortunately, the tops of the cans did not fit, so the chief of the ministry's general affairs section, Motohike Kakei, produced a pair of khaki-colored cotton bags into which he put them. They were now in his hands and no one seemed to want to take them from him, but he knew of no hiding place where he would consider them safe. He took them, therefore, to Chamberlain Yoshihiro Tokugawa.

Tokugawa took the records into a room which was used only infrequently by a lady-in-waiting to the Empress. In one corner of the room was a small safe to which he had the key. After locking the recordings into the safe, he concealed it by piling a stack of papers around it in such a way that they looked as if they were simply old documents being stored there.

AUGUST 15,
SHORTLY AFTER MIDNIGHT

L I E U T E N A N T Colonel Masataka Ida began to wonder what he
was doing here. He had been waiting for some time, with Major
Hatanaka and two other conspirators, in the reception room of General Takeshi Mori's office at the Imperial Guards headquarters near
the northwest corner of the palace grounds. He was getting tired of
watching Major Hatanaka pace back and forth, his fists clenched,
muttering feverish oaths.

"What's the general doing in there!" Hatanaka exclaimed in a voice
which was bitterly impatient but not loud enough to be heard
through the wall. "Why doesn't he come out and see us? We have no
time, no time at all!"

Ida wondered what could have possessed him to arouse himself
from sleep and come with these men. Hadn't he made it clear to
Hatanaka when they talked in the afternoon that he preferred suicide to rebellion, that no coup d'état could succeed unless General
Anami supported it? Yet when Hatanaka and his close associate,
Lieutenant Colonel Jiro Shiizaki had found him in the War Ministry
room where he was sleeping, he had allowed them to talk him into
coming here on the supposition that he, being older, would be better
able to persuade the commanding general of the Imperial Guards
Division to join the insurrection. "General Mori was one of my teach-
ers at War College," Hatanaka had said. "He thinks of me still as an
immature boy. And Major [Hidemasa] Koga is also too young, though
the general thinks highly of him. But if you will talk to him, Colonel
Ida, I'm sure the general will come around to our point of view, and
when he does, we can't fail." So here was Ida, getting ready to help
talk a general into a conspiracy which he wasn't quite sure he had
joined himself. Fortunately, with the intense and voluble Major
Hatanaka on hand, he would not have to do much talking.

Finally, about a half-hour after midnight, Ida, Hatanaka, Shiizaki,
and the fourth man in their company, an air academy captain named
Shigetaro Uehara, were told that General Mori would now see them.
When this word arrived, Ida was astonished to see that Hatanaka,
who had been pacing back and forth impatiently during their long
wait, did not even intend to see Mori.

"You talk to the general," he said to Ida. "I'm sure you can win him
over. I have something else I must do right away." Pulling Captain
Uehara with him, he departed in haste, leaving Ida with only Shiizaki,
to support him in his discussion with Mori.

When Ida and Shiizaki entered the general's tiny office, they realized quickly that he had made them wait, not because he was in conference, but because he obviously didn't want to see them. He had with him only his brother-in-law, Lieutenant Colonel Michinori Shiraishi, a Second Army staff officer who had come to Tokyo from Hiroshima twenty-four hours earlier with Marshal Shunroku Hata. The general and his brother-in-law had no doubt been merely chatting while the four conspirators waited in the reception room. The brother-in-law now stood behind the general's desk as the interview began.

Ida said, "General Mori, we have come to ask your help. We think there is still a chance to save Japan from an ignominious surrender. We believe that with the support of the Imperial Guards, we could yet free the Emperor from the people who are influencing him and . . ."

"Are you asking me," General Mori interrupted, "to use my men in an unauthorized operation? I have no permission from the Eastern Army to send my men into such an action."

"But we are convinced, sir, that the Eastern Army will be with us as soon as General Tanaka [Eastern Army commander] sees that we have had the courage to act and that we are destined to succeed."

General Mori was not quick to answer, and when he did answer, he spoke in a slow, deliberate style which was exasperating to anyone in a hurry. "I've been in the army, in the service of His Majesty and of our country for a long time," he began, "and I've learned many things." After this prologue, he continued on at such length, expounding the things he had learned, that Ida began shifting in his chair. Gradually, the general branched off into his philosophy of life and Ida realized helplessly that this meeting was to be not a discussion but a monologue. Since it was worse than improper to interrupt a general, Ida waited for a pause that might conceivably be taken for a stop.

"If you'll allow me to explain our plan, sir," Ida eventually interposed, "I think you'll see it is quite practical. In the beginning, we need only the support of your Guards Division. With the help of your men, we can quickly isolate the Palace and arrest the Badoglios to stop them from influencing His Majesty. When the palace is secure and people like Suzuki, Yonai, Kido, and Togo are in custody, the government will fall immediately. By that time, General Tanaka and the Eastern Army will be with us. All we'll have to do then is declare martial law and establish a military government."

General Mori again deliberated at length before answering. "I understand what you're trying to do," he said. "But I could not decide lightly to join you. I would have to think about it very carefully."

Ida was suddenly encouraged. "You do agree, then, that the plan is practical? The only problem, sir, is that we have so little time. We need your answer as quickly as possible."

"Indeed," the general said. "But as you must realize, no cause was ever helped by a wrong decision. And I feel there is only one way I could be certain to reach the right decision. I would have to go and pray at the Meiji Shrine."

Ida opened his mouth to speak but did not know what to say. Another hour-and-a-half could be wasted while General Mori took a trip to the Meiji Shrine. Yet one could not tell a man it was unnecessary or unimportant for him to pray. One could only hope he would pray quickly. Ida stood up, bowed, and saluted. "I understand your feeling, sir," he said. "We'll be here to talk to you when you return."

AUGUST 15,
A HALF-HOUR AFTER MIDNIGHT

L I E U T E N A N T Colonel Masahiko Takeshita was asleep in the big, hilltop Ochanomizu mansion (about a mile northeast of the Imperial Palace) which was now an army officer's billet. He was awakened abruptly by the excited voice of Major Kenji Hatanaka who had just come bursting into the room.

"Takeshita! Takeshita! Come on, get up!" Hatanaka called out as he approached. Bending down to shake Takeshita by the shoulder, he said, "Hurry! I have to talk to you!"

As soon as Takeshita aroused himself enough to comprehend what was happening, he whispered, "Hold your voice down! Quiet! Can't you see there are two other men asleep in this room?"

Hatanaka, after aiming a flashlight around the dark room, said, "Come on, then, get up. We can talk outside."

Though outranked by Takeshita, who was also four years his senior, Hatanaka could speak to him freely and familiarly because they had been friends for many years, since 1929, in fact, when they met while both were attending the ultranationalist lectures of Professor Kiyoshi Hiraizumi at Tokyo University. Together they had taken the professor's course in Japanese history, and had thereafter become close companions. It was in this course that they had first heard Hiraizumi expound the theory that though the Emperor, as a divine symbol, had the right and the duty to reign over the country, he was not empowered to govern it. This theory, which even the Emperor himself had been taught as a small boy, was very much in Hatanaka's mind tonight.

Rising grumpily to his feet, Takeshita followed Hatanaka out into a corridor whose shoji screens opened onto a southern view of the city. Since the hill on which the house had been built was sizable, and since the almost full moon had risen high in the sky, they had an eerie, depressing view of the vast landscape of ruins Tokyo had become. This house was the only one left in the neighborhood and one of the few substantial houses still standing as far as the eye could see in the direction of the city's center.

Though Hatanaka had always been a highly emotional man, Takeshita had never seen him as fully aroused as he was tonight. "We're on the move!" he exclaimed. "I tell you, we're on the move! We've already got the Second Regiment of the Imperial Guards with us. That's your regiment, isn't it? (Takeshita had once been the flagbearer of the Imperial Guards, First Division, Second Regiment.) They're inside the palace grounds now, the whole regiment, waiting for orders from us. We plan to take over the palace at 2 A.M. That's only about an hour-and-a-quarter from now. I've got to hurry. Colonel Ida has joined us, and he's at the Guards headquarters at this very moment, persuading General Mori to join us. We're really ready, Takeshita, but we also need you. Come on. Join us."

Hatanaka's transcendent fervor almost overwhelmed Takeshita, who was, even without this exhortation, emotionally disposed to take part in a coup d'état. When the original conspiracy had begun four days earlier, it was he who had gathered together the most likely participants and it was he who had chaired their first meeting. It would be difficult for him to stand idly by while even a small handful of those original conspirators tried to carry through the plan. But would it not be equally difficult, and also foolish, to embrace a conspiracy which had no chance of success?

He looked sadly into Hatanaka's burning eyes. "Why can't you reconcile yourself," he said, "to the fact that it's all finished? All hope has ended. We can't stage a coup d'état after we've failed to get any of the four generals we needed."

"We couldn't get them because they're bewildered," Hatanaka insisted. "The men at the top are so bewildered the whole army is bewildered. Nobody so far has known what to do. But we know what to do, and if we show the others, they'll soon follow us. Once we've created a real emergency situation and declared martial law, the whole army will be with us."

"Not General Anami," Takeshita said. "He gave his word to the Emperor when he signed that rescript, and whatever happens, he'll stick to it."

Hatanaka studied Takeshita closely in the pale light of the moon. "That's exactly why I've come here to talk to you," he said. "You're the one man who can still talk to General Anami and explain the true situation to him. Go to him, Takeshita. You don't have to ask him to join the coup. Just ask him if he will join us after we succeed. That's all we need. Go ahead. Talk to him. You can convince him."

Takeshita was scarcely listening to Hatanaka now because the mention of General Anami had brought back to his mind those two meetings the previous afternoon when the war minister had spoken to his subordinates about the future as if he himself would not be a part of it. Did he actually intend to commit suicide? If so, when? Surely not tonight. Yet why not tonight? This might be the most fitting time, the last chance before the Emperor read his dismal rescript to the people of Japan.

"Will you do it?.' Hatanaka persisted. "Will you join us?"

"Takeshita said, "No, I tell you, I can't join you. It's completely pointless. There's no chance of success."

"There is if you join us."

"It's impossible."

"It's not impossible!" Hatanaka cried. "There's still time if we hurry. Please! I beg you to join us!" He had become so impassioned there were tears in his eyes. "Our plans are all set," he said. "Who can stop us? The government can't stop us. The cabinet can't stop us."

Takeshita, against his better judgement, was tempted to agree, but there were people who could stop the coup and he knew it. Either General Mori of the Imperial Guards, or General Tanaka of the Eastern Army could stop it. The Emperor himself could stop it. When Takeshita thought of all the overwhelming factors against the coup, his better judgment began again to take hold of him. "No, I just can't do it," he said to Hatanaka, "and I wish I could talk you out of doing it."

Hatanaka stared at him morosely. "Is that your final decision?"

"That's my final decision."

Hatanaka sighed deeply and his shoulders slumped. "In that case," he said, "we'll have to go ahead without you." He turned and hurried toward the door, then looked back. "Maybe after our plan succeeds," he said, "you and General Anami will join us. You'll still be welcome."

Takeshita again reflected about General Anami. "Wait a minute!" he called to Hatanaka. "I'm coming with you." Running back into his sleeping room, he hastily put on a uniform. When he rejoined Hatanaka, the young major had a euphoric smile on his face. "Are you coming with me to the War Ministry," he asked, "or are you going to see General Anami?"

"You know very well where I'm going," Takeshita said as they went outside to the army automobile in which Hatanaka had come. "Take me to the war minister's official residence."

AUGUST 15,
1 A.M.

W H E N Lieutenant Colonel Takeshita arrived at the exquisite Japanese house on the Miyakezaka hill which was the war minister's official residence, he encountered, outside the entrance, a single army policeman whose face showed signs of deep concern. The moment he saw Takeshita, whose identity he knew, his expression brightened.

"I'm glad you've come," he said.

Takeshita was admitted by a middle-aged maid whose face was a study in consternation. "You don't know how relieved I am to have you here," she said. "I had no idea what to do."

"Where is the general?" Takeshita asked.

She pointed to the front room, which was the principle room in the house. After replacing his shoes with slippers, Takeshita went to the door of the room, rapped, and opened it.

He heard General Anami's deep voice from inside. "Who's there?"

"It's I, Takeshita."

"Takeshita! Why did you come?" There was a note of annoyance in the general's voice.

Takeshita took two or three steps into the room and stopped.

Anami was sitting on the tatami floor at his low, Japanese-style desk. On the desk were some pieces of white paper. In his right hand, he held a writing brush; near his left was a bottle of sake with a tiny drinking cup.

Seeing that his younger brother-in-law had hesitated to come forward, he added, with a conspicuous lack of his usual grace, "Anyway, come on in."

As Takeshita approached the desk, he decided, after a quick glance, that the paper was hanshi, the use of which indicated that Anami was writing something important. Though Takeshita was quite convinced now that this dear friend and relative-by-marriage was preparing to commit harakiri, he said nothing about it, waiting for Anami himself to speak. The war minister looked so calm and so healthy it was difficult even now to believe the unmistakable signs that he planned to kill himself.

"Sit down," Anami said. "But first, call the maid."

When the maid entered, with an only slightly less worried look on her face than Takeshita had seen a few minutes earlier, Anami sent her to the kitchen for two large glasses. He had decided that the traditional, thimble-sized sake cup was not adequate for this night's thirst. While awaiting her return, he folded some of the papers on his desk and put them in a small cabinet. The room, rather large by Japanese standards (about fifteen feet square), was dimly illuminated. A few feet from where the two men sat was the general's futon which the maid had already laid out for the night, with a mosquito net around it, suspended from the ceiling. In one corner were a kimono stand and a sword rack.

As soon as the tall glasses arrived, Anami filled two of them with the sweet rice wine and handed one to Takeshita.

"You probably know," Anami said, "that I've intended for some time to commit seppuku. I've decided to do it tonight."

Takeshita said. "I didn't know you had definitely made up your mind until I heard you speak this afternoon at the ministry." He had assumed for some time that if the war should be lost, Anami, as war minister, and as a devoted Samurai, would commit suicide to atone for the army's failure. The two men, however, had not discussed it. "I won't try to stop you, of course," he added, "but can't you postpone it to a later day?"

Anami's expression brightened at these last words. "You won't try to stop me. Fine. I'm glad to hear that. When I heard you outside, I was afraid that was why you had come. Since I was mistaken, I bid you welcome. Drink."

Both men raised their glasses, after which Anami said, "You came, actually, at a very opportune moment. We shall have a chance to talk."

They talked at length about the war, the army, the future, their families. General Anami felt that Japan had placed herself in a most difficult position. He was not dissatisfied with the way the army had fought, nor with his own job as war minister. He had done his best even though he was willing to take the responsibility for the failure. The army, too, had done its best, but the job had been too big. The future would be bleak for some time, yet Japan would recover. Their children would live to prosper, and even Takeshita himself, unless he decided foolishly to follow Anami's example, would see good days before he was old. He was, after all, only forty. A young and able man. He would be responsible now for two families. Could he accept such a responsibility? Takeshita could and would.

Thoughts of Kenji Hatanaka's desperate last-minute conspiracy crossed Takeshita's mind and he was tempted to tell Anami about the young major's continuing efforts to foment a coup d'état. But why should Anami be asked, at this hour of his death, to concern himself with such a hopeless escapade? Hatanaka's frantic intrigue seemed trivial now compared to the fact that this man whom Takeshita had loved and revered since boyhood was actually about to kill himself. Though Takeshita had sometimes thought of the possibility that Anami might one day kill himself, and had even thought abstractly of the possibility that, as a Japanese soldier, he himself might under certain circumstances do the same, he found now that the abstract speculation had nothing like the impact of the impending fact. The realization that this was his last conversation with his beloved brother-in-law overwhelmed him with sadness. It was dreadful to know that Korechika Anami would be dead before the night ended. It would be improper, however, to try to deprive him of the privilege, to argue that he, too, should live on as he had ordered other officers to do. Anami was not in the same situation as his subordinates. He was the war minister, and had an obligation, therefore, to accept responsibility for the entire army. He was also a man who made ultimate demands upon himself. It was fitting that he should make the ultimate gesture of the defeated Japanese general. But did he have to do it immediately?

"Why must it be tonight?" Takeshita asked. "I understand your decision to commit seppuku, but why can't you postpone it a few days?"

"My father's anniversary is the fourteenth," Anami said. (The Japanese observe death anniversaries not so much by month and year as by the day of the month on which a loved one died.) "I know it is now past midnight, so it's no longer the fourteenth, but I've dated my will on the fourteenth, and that's as close as I can come. My son's anniversary is not until the twentieth."

"Why can't you wait at least until then?"

Anami's face clouded and for a moment he seemed near tears. "The Emperor will read that rescript on the radio at noon tomorrow," he said. "I could not bear to hear it."

He refilled Takeshita's glass, then refilled his own. He was drinking quite heavily. Trying to find something lighter about which to talk, he said, "You might be amused to know I had my vitamin injection tonight the same as any other night. When the maid brought it, I could hardly say I wouldn't need it because I was about to die. Could I, now?" He laughed.

Takeshita did not respond to the laughter. "When I came in," he said, "you were writing something. Did I interrupt you?"

"No, I had finished," Anami said. He drank more sake, then sat silent for a few moments. Impulsively, he reached into the cabinet by his desk and took out two sheets of papers he had put there when Takeshita arrived. He read them to himself, then, after a hesitation, handed them to Takeshita.

On the first piece of paper was a Japanese-style poem, written in Anami's clear, generous handwriting:

> Having received great favors
> from his Majesty, the Emperor,
> There is nothing more for me to say
> in the hour of my death.
>
> KORECHIKA
> The night of August 14
> The 20th Year of Showa.

On the other sheet was a three-line acknowledgement of his responsibility as war minister:

> Believing firmly that our sacred land will never perish,
> I, with my death,
> humbly apologize to the Emperor for the great crime.
>
> KORECHIKA ANAMI, Minister of War
> The night of August 14
> The 20th year of Showa.

"Showa" was the term used to designate the reign of Emperor Hirohito, who was enthroned in 1925. The "great crime" to which Anami referred was basically the crime of defeat and surrender, but it also included the army's habit of ignoring the Emperor's wishes, a habit of which Anami had been made acutely aware by the Emperor's brother, Prince Mikasa, who has said to him three days earlier: "Since the Manchurian Incident, the army has not once acted in accordance with the Imperial wish." Though Anami had not been involved in the Army's 1931 decision to invade Manchuria, or its 1937 decision to invade China, or even its subsequent insistence on attacking America (he having been in China at that time), he felt keenly now, as a result of Prince Mikasa's remark, the guilt of all these offenses against the Emperor.

As Takeshita read and reread the poem and the apology, Anami poured more sake and continued to drink. Though Takeshita was profoundly affected by what Anami had written, he could think of nothing to say about it. He handed back the sheets of paper.

"If you drink too much," he said to Anami, "you won't be able to hold the sword steady."

"A man should drink before cutting his belly," Anami said, "because alcohol makes the blood come faster."

AUGUST 15,
2 A.M.

GENERAL Takeshi Mori, commander of the First Imperial Guards Division, who had spoken of praying at the Meiji Shrine in an effort to decide whether to join Major Hatanaka's coup d'état conspiracy, was not destined to visit the shrine tonight or ever again. He now lay dead on the floor of his office in the Guards' headquarters. Blood still flowed from a bullet hole in his chest and from several sword cuts on his torso. Near him lay the decapitated body of his brother-in-law, Lieutenant Colonel Michinori Shiraishi, who had died trying to defend him. Shiraishi's corpse, from which blood was still spurting, had been slashed so deeply that chunks of flesh fell away from it. Near his severed head lay his unavailing sword. The walls closest to General Mori's desk were spattered with blood.

Also in the room, standing near the two victims, were Major Hatanaka with a pistol and Captain Shigetaro Uehara with a Samurai sword. Seated near a corner, looking dazed, was Lieutenant Colonel Jiro Shiizaki. Lieutenant Colonel Masataka Ida was at the door, and behind him was Colonel Kazuo Mizutani, General Mori's chief of staff.

Hatanaka, white-faced and trembling, saluted first the body of General Mori, then the body of Colonel Shiraishi. Uehara did likewise.

Hatanaka, turning toward the door, muttered, "There was just no time. There was no time to argue."

It was now 2 A.M., at which hour the coup d'état was scheduled to begin.

Hatanaka and Ida stood facing each other for a long, uncomfortable moment. It seemed to Ida that with two men dead, the coup d'état attempt had, in effect, begun, and there was no choice but to carry on with it. He wondered if Colonel Mizutani, whom he had been trying to recruit for the conspiracy, would now try to stop it.

"I had better go to Eastern Army headquarters," Ida said.

Hatanaka, with tears in his eyes, said, "That's a good idea." It had suddenly become more important than ever to secure the support of General Shizuichi Tanaka, the Eastern Army commander.

Colonel Mizutani said to Ida, "I'll go with you."

As the two men hurried away, Hatanaka sent for the two Imperial Guards staff officers who were most deeply committed to his plot— Major Hidemasa Koga and Major Sadakichi Ishihara. He had already asked them to prepare a division order which he had hoped General Mori would sign. When they arrived at the general's office, Koga had with him several copies of the document.

Hatanaka met them in the hall. "We have to act quickly now," he said. "General Mori is dead."

While Koga and Ishihara were overcoming their shock at seeing the two bodies on the floor, Hatanaka got right to work. First, a facsimile of the dead general's signature had to be added to each copy of the document. Then he found the general's seal in his desk and stamped each copy. "Imperial Guards Division Strategic Order No. 584" was now ready to be dispatched to each of the key regimental and battalion commanders. The "order" was as follows:

August 15
0200 hours.

1. The Division will defeat the enemy's scheme; it will protect the Emperor and preserve the national structure.

2. The commander of the First Infantry Regiment will occupy the East Second and East Third garrison grounds (including the vicinity of the Eastern District Army strategy room) and the vicinity of Honmaru Baba [the "honmaru" is the inner citadel of the palace], thus guarding the Imperial Family in this sector. The commander will also send a company of troops to the Tokyo radio station and prohibit all broadcasts.

3. The commander of the Second Infantry Regiment will use his main force to guard the Imperial Family in the Fukiage district of the Imperial Palace.

4. The commander of the Sixth Infantry Regiment will continue present duties.

5. The commander of the Seventh Infantry Regiment will occupy the area of the Nijubashi Gate and prevent outside contact with the Imperial Palace.

6. The commander of the Cavalry Regiment will order a tank force to Daikan Avenue (near the police station) to await further orders.

7. The commander of the First Artillery Regiment will await further orders.

8. The commander of the First engineers will await further orders.

9. The commander of the Mechanized Battalion will guard the Imperial Palace at its present strength.

10. The commander of the Signal Unit will sever all communication with the Imperial Palace except through Division Headquarters.

11. I shall be at Division Headquarters.

GENERAL TAKESHI MORI
Division Commander

Major Hatanaka had now begun his move to take over the Japanese government and liberate the Emperor from the influence of the "Badoglios."

AUGUST 15,
2 A.M.

GENERAL Anami and Colonel Takeshita, still drinking sake at the war minister's official residence, heard what sounded like a gunshot from the direction of the Imperial Palace. Anami turned to Takeshita with a look of surprise on his face.

Takeshita stood up and went out onto the side porch, looking down the hill toward the palace. Though it was about a half-mile away, the night was so hot and the air so still the sound of gunfire could easily carry that far. Takeshita wondered if this was the start of Major Hatanaka's coup attempt. He listened for a few minutes but heard no more.

When Takeshita went back into the house, he found General Anami waiting with an inquisitive expression. "I think it was a gunshot, all right," Takeshita said, "and it sounded as if it came from the palace." He wondered if he should tell Anami about Hatanaka's intentions. Why not? It was now too late for the war minister to get excited about it or try to stop it. And he did have a right to know what was happening.

"I suppose I should tell you," Takeshita said, "that Hatanaka has not given up on the coup d'état. He's getting ready right now to occupy the palace. He still thinks he can overthrow the government and continue the war."

"He still thinks that does he?" Anami was unimpressed. "Whom does he have behind him?"

"I guess he has at least some of the Imperial Guards."

"Is that so?" Anami shrugged. "He can't possibly succeed. General Tanaka will never agree to it. The Eastern Army will not take part."

Though he had now consumed much more sake than he was accustomed to drinking. Anami showed it only in his complexion, which had somewhat reddened. He looked calm and he was in perfect control of his faculties. Taking up the writing brush once more, he said, "I want to leave some messages for friends," and he began to list them. When he came to the cabinet ministers he named one after another until he came to Admiral Yonai.

"Yonai!" he exclaimed. "Kill him!"

Takeshita was startled. Though many army officers hated Admiral Yonai because of his antiwar attitudes, Takeshita had never heard Anami criticize the navy minister. Whenever Anami's subordinates spoke ill of Yonai, Anami had defended him, despite the fact that Yonai often sided with the opposition in cabinet debates. Early in the summer when Yonai wanted to resign from the cabinet it was Anami who convinced him he should remain. Was it possible that despite all this, Anami shared with other army men a hatred of Yonai? Takeshita, after studying Anami's face, decided that was not the case. Anami didn't want anyone to kill Yonai. No doubt he was just momentarily annoyed at the recollection of Yonai's opposition to the army during the last few days.

Anami, changing the subject, said to Takeshita, "I'd like to ask a favor of you."

Takeshita said, "Whatever you wish."

"If I do not succeed in killing myself, will you help me? Will you be my second? I doubt that it will be necessary, however. I think I'm quite capable of it."

Takeshita silently accepted the responsibility.

The maid entered to say that a Captain Uehara was outside. Takeshita, recognizing the name of one of Hatanaka's co-conspirators, went out to see him.

Uehara was in high spirits. He had changed his uniform so that there was no sign of blood on him. "Major Hatanaka sent me," he said, "to tell you the plan is proceeding as scheduled."

Takeshita was not that easily convinced. "Do you mean," he asked, "that General Mori has agreed to it?"

Uehara was momentarily flustered. "Actually, no, he didn't agree. He had to be killed. But in spite of that, everything is proceeding as we hoped."

Takeshita received this news without comment.

Uehara said, "Have you any message for Major Hatanaka?"

Though Takeshita knew now that he would never have for Hatanaka the kind of message he wanted, it seemed pointless at this moment to say so. "I have nothing for him yet," he said.

Dismissing Captain Uehara, he went back inside to General Anami, who still sat erect on the floor, with legs crossed.

"Who was that?" Anami asked.

Takeshita said, "It was one of Hatanaka's men. He says they've killed General Mori."

General Anami took a long time before responding. Eventually he said, "There's one more crime for which to apologize to His Majesty."

AUGUST 15,
2:30 A.M.

G E N E R A L Shizuichi Tanaka, commander of the Eastern District Army, had decided to spend the night at his headquarters in the Dai Ichi building across the street from the Imperial Palace; he wanted to be immediately available if trouble developed. He was sitting in his office with very little to do when his chief of staff, Major General Tatsuhiko Takashima entered the room. Takashima had just talked to Colonel Mizutani and Lieutenant Colonel Ida, who had arrived a few minutes before with news of the astonishing developments at the palace. Mizutani, who was General Mori's chief of staff, had described his death, while Ida had argued that the army must now unite behind Major Hatanaka. After listening to both of them, General Takashima had hurried to General Tanaka.

"There seems to be serious trouble at the palace," Takashima said. "Some of the Imperial Guards are in revolt and General Mori's chief of staff says he's been killed."

General Tanaka leaped to his feet and reached for his sword. "I'd better get over there and stop it."

Takashima was horrified. "What are you planning to do? Just walk into the midst of it?"

"I'm not afraid," Tanaka said.

"But if they've actually killed Mori, they won't hesitate to kill you. And then what good will you have done?"

Takashima's argument was so sensible Tanaka could not ignore it. He put away his sword and said, "I guess it would be better to find out first what's going on over there."

Takashima said, "I'll make some phone calls." He turned to leave the room. "And I'll also arrange for a company of men to go with you if you do decide to go."

Tanaka said, "All right, but hurry."

AUGUST 15,

3 A.M.

CHAMBERLAIN Yoshihiro Tokugawa was asleep in his room on the first floor of the Imperial Household Ministry when one of the younger chamberlains, Yasuya Mitsui, burst in upon him and awakened him. In an excited whisper, Mitsui announced, "The Imperial Guards are in revolt. They've taken over the palace and cut the telephone lines."

Tokugawa was not completely surprised. Having noticed suspicious moves by some of the Guards officers in the last few days, he had gone to General Mori and asked if the Guards could be trusted in case of emergency. Though the general had assured him he need not worry, Tokugawa had not been fully reassured. It appeared now that Mori had been wrong. Donning a kimono, Tokugawa took a flashlight out into the hall where he encountered, by chance, Imperial Household Minister Sotaro Ishiwatari and four members of his staff. Ishiwatari confirmed the alarm.

"They've apparently blocked all the gates," he said. "I just tried to leave the palace by the Inui Gate [on the northwest side] and they wouldn't let me out."

It occurred to Tokugawa that since Ishiwatari was one of the more important advisers to the Emperor, and therefore a likely candidate for assassination by the rebels, he was, in fact, fortunate that they had not held him at the Inui Gate. Perhaps the guards there had not known who he was.

"You'd better come with me," Tokugawa said. "I know a place where no one is likely to find you." After returning to his own room to get a set of keys, he led Ishiwatari and his four companions to a room used by ladies-in-waiting to the Empress. In this room he opened a cupboard behind which was a secret passageway to an underground chamber of which very few people in the palace were aware. When Ishiwatari and his party were comfortably installed in this hiding place, Tokugawa said, "You should be safe here, but just as an added precaution, lock the door when I leave and don't open it unless you hear five knocks."

Tokugawa then made his way back up the narrow stairs and through the cupboard to the first floor of the ministry building. He wondered if he had hidden the imperial rescript recordings in a safe enough place. The soldiers were certain to come searching for them. He couldn't think of a safer place in which to put them. He wondered also if Marquis Kido, lord keeper of the privy seal, had found a place to hide. Since he was the Emperor's chief political adviser, the rebels were certain also to come searching for him.

AUGUST 15,
3:20 A.M.

M A R Q U I S Koichi Kido heard an insistent knock at the door of his room on the second floor of the Household Ministry and opened it to find chamberlain Yasuhide Toda with his hand raised, ready to knock again. "You had better get out of here right away," Toda warned. "The Guards have rebelled and they're in control of the palace."

"So, it has finally happened," Kido said. "Just as we feared it might. But what fools they are. They can't stop the surrender now."

"Whether they're fools or not," Toda said, "they have guns and they can kill us."

Kido, mindful of the February 26, 1936, attempted coup d'état in which several statesmen were killed, said, "All right, I'll come with you, but where can we hide?"

"In the doctor's office," Toda said. "You can pretend to be a doctor."

As they were groping their way through the darkened halls, Kido suddenly tugged at Toda's arm. "I've got to go back to my room," he said. "I've left some papers there that I don't want the soldiers to find."

Rather than waste time arguing, Toda returned with Kido and together they began tearing up documents, which they flushed down the toilet as fast as the toilet would flush. When they had disposed of the most important papers, Kido consented to leave the rest, and the two men again went down the dark hall to the infirmary. As soon as he had shut Marquis Kido into this room, Chamberlain Toda hurried off to assure Chamberlain Tokugawa that the lord keeper of the privy seal was safe.

"Where did you hide him?" Tokugawa asked.

"In the infirmary."

"They could easily find him there," Tokugawa said. "We'd better go get him."

A few minutes later, Marquis Kido was again moving through the halls of the vast ministry building, this time behind Tokugawa's flashlight. Eventually, they reached the same room into which Tokugawa had taken the household minister and Kido was soon hurrying through the same cupboard down the stairs to the underground chamber in which Ishiwatari was hidden. Tokugawa felt now that he could relax somewhat. If the rebellious soldiers were unable to find Kido, Ishiwatari, or the rescript recordings, what could they do? They could, perhaps, try to get hold of the Emperor, himself, but no, it was inconceivable that they would go that far.

AUGUST 15,
SHORTLY AFTER 4 A.M.

CHAMBERLAINS Tokugawa and Toda moved silently through the dark palace grounds, avoiding the sentry posts of the rebellious soldiers as they made their way from the imperial library to the Household Ministry building. They had gone to the library to allay their nagging concern for the Emperor's welfare. Having found his quarters serene, they were now returning to the ministry, which was far from serene. As they approached the building, they could see the dark shadows of soldiers outside it. Fortunately, the chamberlains were much better acquainted with the huge, rambling structure than were the soldiers; they therefore managed to slip into an inconspicuous entrance without being seen.

Inside, however, they could hardly avoid being seen. Every two or three minutes, soldiers would come running along the halls, up and down the stairs, in and out of rooms, looking for Marquis Kido, for the rescript recordings, or for the Emperor's seal with which Major Hatanaka and Major Koga hoped to forge Imperial orders. Chamberlain Toda went upstairs to his office while Tokugawa went to the office of the Emperor's military aides to report that the Emperor was safe. After talking to the military aides, who were, like everyone else

in the palace, prisoners of the rebels, Tokugawa left their office to go
to his own room. He was walking along the second-floor corridor as
inconspicuously as possible when he heard from behind a sharp command: "Halt!"

He turned to find an officer and an enlisted soldier approaching
him. Both were armed.

The officer said to the soldier, "Bring him along."

The soldier, relaying the order, said, "Hurry up! Move."

Tokugawa did not obey. He stared coldly at the soldier and the
officer.

The soldier, after glancing at the officer, began to prod Tokugawa
with his rifle. "I said move!"

Tokugawa, being the descendant of a line of Samurai shoguns so
strong they had been able to rule Japan for 250 years, refused to be
pushed around by rebellious troops. "What are you trying to do?" he
demanded. "I don't have to go anyplace with you."

"You will obey orders," the officer informed him. "We want to
question you."

They were outside the administration room in which the rescript
recordings had been made. More soldiers and officers emerged from
this room, and from other rooms along the corridor, to gather around
this slender, bespectacled aristocrat who seemed to think he could
defy them.

"If you have any questions to ask," Tokugawa said, "ask them right
here."

"Where is the Emperor's seal?" one of them demanded.

"And where is the rescript recording?" another added.

Tokugawa, standing erect, said, "How would I know anything like
that?"

"I'll bet you do know," one of his questioners insisted. "You're a
chamberlain, aren't you? I'll bet you also know where Kido is hiding."

Tokugawa, glancing from one of these men to another, realized he
did not recognize any of them. None of them recognized him, either,
nor did they suspect that they were talking to the only man in the
entire palace who knew the answers to all their questions.

"I don't know what you're talking about," he said.

One of the officers who had been listening said, "Don't bother with
him any more. If he won't answer questions, kill him."

"That's right," cried one of his companions. "Kill him!" And a
chorus of "Kill him!" arose from the surrounding troops.

"Go ahead, kill me," Tokugawa shouted at them, "but I don't know
what good that will do you."

His outburst quieted them. One of the officers said, "He's right. His blood would only rust our swords."

Most of the rebellious soldiers began drifting away to resume their search for the recordings, the Imperial seal, and that well-known symbol of evil advice to the Emperor, Marquis Kido. But one lieutenant continued to detain Tokugawa. This young officer seemed suddenly compelled to justify what he was doing. Japan must not surrender, he declaimed. The Emperor was being misled. The army had to save him from the people around him. To free him it might be necessary to disobey him temporarily, but this did not in any way indicate disloyalty. Surely, an Imperial chamberlain could understand that much. "Why aren't you on our side?" the lieutenant concluded. "What kind of a Japanese are you, anyway?"

By this time, two more men had stopped to listen. Tokugawa's answer was more than one of them was willing to take. "I'm the kind of Japanese who serves the Emperor," Tokugawa said, "and that's what I'm trying to do . . ."

He got no farther. A fist flew out and caught him flush on the right side of the jaw. His eyeglasses went flying down the hall as he crumpled to the floor.

AUGUST 15,
4:30 A.M.

A N   A R M Y truck and several smaller vehicles pulled into the driveway of the prime minister's official residence on the Miyakezaka hill near the National Diet building. As these vehicles came to a stop, a swarm of soldiers and a few school-aged youths leaped to the pavement in the faint, predawn light. They were armed with rifles, knives, and swords. On the truck were two light machine guns which several of the soldiers lowered to the ground and placed in position facing the building. These men, from Yokohama, were under the leadership of a Captain Takeo Sasaki who had heard about the impending surrender and had concluded that only the assassination of the prime minister plus certain members of his government could save the country from such a disgrace. At Sasaki's direction, the machine guns began announcing their arrival with a tattoo of bullets against the side of the three-story structure.

Chief Cabinet Secretary Sakomizu, asleep on the sofa in this third-floor office-residence, was awakened by the rain of bullets, but not sufficiently awakened to comprehend from whence they were coming or what they were hitting. "Don't the Americans know the war is over?" he wondered sleepily. "When will those awful air raids stop?" Before he had much time to reflect on this subject, he began to grasp the fact that one of the bullets he heard had hit the outside wall of his room. He sat up suddenly, as did his younger brother, Hisayoshi, who happened to be staying overnight with him.

"What could that have been?" Sakomizu said to his brother. "I don't hear any airplanes."

Hisayoshi Sakomizu went to the window and looked out. When he turned away from the window, his complexion was fading to white. "It's the army attacking us," he said.

In Hisatsune Sakomizu's mind arose the vision of February 26, 1936, when he had helped save his father-in-law, Admiral Keisuke Okada, the then prime minister, from assassination by army officers in this very building. It was fortunate that on this occasion Prime Minister Suzuki was not here. He had gone, after the late night cabinet session, to his private residence in the Myogadani district of north Tokyo. The chief cabinet secretary, leaping to his feet, put on his clothes and ran from floor to floor, trying to determine the exact situation and making sure no one had been hit by bullets, some of which were now coming through the windows.

To each person he encountered, he said, "When the soldiers break in, don't resist. We can't fight them. We have no guns."

He was repeating this injunction to several people on the ground floor when one of them said to him, "Don't worry about us. They're not after us. It's the prime minister and yourself they'll want to kill."

Here was an observation Sakomizu could not gainsay. He was mindful of the several occasions during the last few days when angry officers had threatened to kill him if the government were to surrender. Whoever these soldiers outside might be, they were most likely, when they found that the prime minister was absent, to choose his chief assistant as a substitute victim.

"You had better get out of here while you can," one of Sakomizu's aides suggested.

A maid said, "They've got the whole building surrounded."

Bullets were now hitting the outside walls from all directions; the shouting voices of the soldiers could be heard above the din.

Another of Sakomizu's aides warned, "They'll be storming the doors any minute. You'd better hurry."

There was a passage through the cellar by which Sakomizu might escape, but he felt he couldn't go just yet. "i have to call the prime minister and warn him," he said. "They may go to his house when they find out he's not here."

One of his assistants said, "I'll do that. You get out of here."

Accompanied by two policemen and his younger brother, Sakomizu hurried down into the basement and through a concealed underground passage which brought them to an opening just outside the wall of the rear garden. His brother and one of the policemen emerged first to make certain the way was clear.

"Come on," the policeman said. "There's no one in sight."

Sakomizu, deciding it would be wise to look nonchalant, lit a cigaret. When he came out into the open, near a clump of shrubs, he was smoking casually and walking at an easy gait as if he were on an early morning stroll. Unfortunately, he concentrated so hard on the cultivation of this casual air that he failed to notice a large sheet of corrugated tin in his path. As he stepped on the tin, it produced such a clatter he thought he was hearing gunfire. Dropping both his cigaret and his nonchalance, he broke into a run and kept running for two blocks, until his brother and the policemen caught up to him.

"One of you look back," Sakomizu gasped, "and see if they're chasing us!" He would have done so himself but he was still so frightened he wasn't sure he could turn his head.

"There's no one coming," his brother assured him.

The four men slowed to a walk, and as they caught their breath Sakomizu decided they had escaped at least the immediate danger. In a few minutes they would reach the nearby home of an old friend whom he could trust. There, he could relax. But not completely. As they walked along, they saw on the street a litter of leaflets which, though Sakomizu didn't know it, had been dropped during the night by angry naval pilots from Atsugi Air Base west of Tokyo. The headline on the leaflets said:

> Suzuki and Sakomizu
> Must be Killed.

A block farther on, they saw a wall poster which said:

> Kill Suzuki, Okada,
> Konoye, Sakomizu!
> They are Japan's
> Badoglios!

Sakomizu decided that for a while, at least, he had better stay out of sight.

AUGUST 15,
SHORTLY BEFORE 5 A.M.

H A J I M E   S U Z U K I , the only son and sometimes secretary of Prime Minister Suzuki, was awakened by the telephone downstairs at his father's imposing, two-story house in Myogadani. When he answered the phone, the caller at the other end, whose voice he did not recognize, said, "Soldiers are here attacking the prime minister's official residence. Get Admiral Suzuki away from his house immediately. They'll be there soon."

Behind the voice on the telephone, Hajime Suzuki could hear loud sounds of confusion, but before he had time to ask questions, the connection was broken. He dropped the phone and ran through the house shouting: "Everybody up! The army is in revolt! They're coming after us!"

Despite his noisy alarms, when Hajime Suzuki reached his father's second-floor room, the old prime minister was still asleep.

Admiral Suzuki, having completed only six hours earlier the monumental task of leading Japan toward peace, was now sleeping the deep sleep of a man who could fully relax for the first time in several months. Even the threat of imminent death did not quickly arouse him. He was 79 years of age. His life work was done. He had faced death several times before. Why should he bother now to run from it? Hajime Suzuki was not interested in discussing such questions. He raced to the closet, grabbed some clothing and helped his father dress. But because the old man refused to get excited about the danger, it took fifteen minutes to get him ready to leave. When the prime minister and his son arrived downstairs, everyone else in the house was ready to depart. The chauffeur was on his way to the car in the narrow, hillside street at the side of the house, and the ten policemen assigned to guard the prime minister were all standing by, awaiting developments. Suzuki's wife (Hajime's stepmother), who had helped save the admiral's life when he was wounded almost mortally in 1936, came from her own room to take his arm. With her on one side of him and his son on the other, he walked as quickly as possible out through the garden to the corner gate. It was light now and the chauffeur was already trying to start the car when Suzuki reached it. His wife and son got into the back seat with him. While the driver continued his efforts to start the engine, one of Suzuki's secretaries who also acted as a bodyguard, and a nephew of Suzuki named Takeshi Suzuki, got into the front seat.

The driver tried again and again to start the car. The engine refused to turn over. The driver's neck began to redden and show perspiration. He muttered to himself, it's the gasoline! Terrible gasoline! It just won't spark!"

Inasmuch as this was the prime minister's automobile, the gasoline was, of course, the best available in Japan, but during the recent days of privation, even the best was so inferior one could not depend upon it. Anyone so fortunate as to have a gasoline-burning car, however, could not complain. The wood-burning steam cars, also reserved for only a privileged few people, were far less dependable. To compensate for the low quality of the gasoline, the chauffeur usually parked the car on the downgrade when he brought Suzuki to his personal residence. It was then possible to start it by coasting down the hill on the side of which the Suzuki house stood. The previous night, however, when the chauffeur brought Suzuki home after the final cabinet meeting, he had thoughtlessly parked on the upgrade. Once more he pressed the starter and once more the car failed to start. With increasing urgency, annoyance, frustration he kept trying. The minutes passed. The car still did not start. The grinding sound of the strained battery became weaker and weaker. It was quite apparent that the car would not start.

The policemen assigned to guard the prime minister stood around the car, watching the efforts to start it.

"Why don't we push it while you turn it around facing downhill?" one of them suggested to the driver.

Still sweating over the starter, the driver seemed not to hear him.

Another policeman sensibly pointed out, "We can't turn it around. The street is too narrow."

The driver, finally accepting the fact that he couldn't start the car, looked around and realized there were almost a dozen able-bodied policemen on hand.

"I'm afraid we'll have to ask you fellows to push us uphill," he said.

Fortunately, they did not refuse. But before they began, Mrs. Suzuki, in the back seat, realized she had forgotten to bring her husband's formal morning wear. He would be seeing the Emperor today. He could not go to the Palace improperly dressed. A maid, who was also watching the efforts to start the car, rushed back into the house to get the clothing Mrs. Suzuki wanted. Through all this, Suzuki himself sat serenely, saying nothing.

As the ten policemen leaned into their task of pushing, the prime minister's big limousine began slowly to move up the narrow street to the first corner, where it turned right, still uphill, in a northerly direction away from the center of the city, whence the rebellious soldiers would be coming. By the time the puffing, sweating policemen reached the middle of this block, they had brought the car to the summit of the hill. With one final push, they released it to the downgrade, and as it rolled away from them, waited anxiously to hear it start. Gradually, the car built up speed. The driver let out the clutch. The engine coughed, sputtered, coughed again, and finally ignited. Prime Minister Suzuki was on his way to the presumed safety of his younger sister's home in the Hongo district, about two miles to the southeast.

When the policemen returned the block-and-a-half to Suzuki's house, they realized how close he had come to assassination. The truckload and several carloads of soldiers from Yokohama under Captain Sasaki had now arrived, and they were swarming around the place. The policemen prudently stood back and watched as Sasaki's men searched for the prime minister.

AUGUST 15,
SHORTLY BEFORE 5 A.M.

M A J O R Hatanaka and his two principal co-conspirators, Major Hidemasa Koga and Lieutenant Colonel Jiro Shiizaki, were at the Imperial Guards' command post inside the palace planning their next move with Colonel Toyojiro Haga, commander of the Second Guards Regiment. Haga had joined the conspiracy and committed his regiment to it because he had believed Hatanaka's assurances that General Anami, and the whole Eastern Army under General Tanaka, were ready to join it as soon as the palace was secured. Hatanaka and

Haga were now in the throes of a dilemma because, despite an exhaustive search of the Household Ministry building, their men had not yet found the rescript recordings, the Imperial seal, or Marquis Kido, whom they considered one of the arch villains of the surrender movement.

As the four officers talked, they were startled to hear a telephone ring. Hadn't all the lines in and out of the palace been cut? No. Hatanaka remembered suddenly that he had ordered one line to be left intact—a private line to Eastern Army headquarters, through which he hoped to communicate with General Tanaka at the proper moment.

Colonel Haga, who answered the phone, had difficulty understanding the voice at the other end. The connection was not good.

Finally, the voice came through clearly enough: "This is Major General Takashima at Eastern Army Headquarters. Can you hear me?" General Takashima, General Tanaka's chief of staff, was taking advantage of the fact that someone in Eastern Army headquarters had discovered the line was open.

"Yes, sir," Colonel Haga said, "I can hear you now."

After Haga had identified himself, the general said, "Are your men involved in the attempt to take over the palace?"

"Yes sir," Haga said. "I'm in command of the Second Regiment."

"Under whose orders have you committed your men to that action?"

"Under orders from General Mori."

"Listen carefully," Takashima pursued. "Are you aware that General Mori is dead?"

"Yes, sir." Major Koga had told Colonel Haga that their commanding general was dead, but had not revealed the circumstances.

"Do you know how General Mori died?"

"No, sir."

"He was murdered by some of your colleagues. Do you hear me? You can go to his office if you want to see his body. The orders you think you got from him were forged. You must disperse your men, Colonel Haga. All the insurgent troops in the palace must return to their barracks. And I want you to send couriers here immediately for new orders." The connection was still bad. Static crackled on the line. "Have you heard everything I just said?" General Takashima demanded.

Though Colonel Haga had heard enough to get the gist of it, he was so bewildered he couldn't answer. Takashima repeated his message. Haga still said nothing.

Takashima, concluding that Haga was afraid to talk, asked, "Is someone there behind you?"

"Yes sir. Major Hatanaka is here."

"Let me speak to him."

When Hatanaka picked up the phone he did not wait for the general to begin the conversation. "This is Major Kenji Hatanaka," he said. "I beg the chief of staff to understand our position. Our men are eager to . . ."

"I do understand your position," General Takashima broke in, "and I want you to know your position is hopeless. You're completely alone. The Eastern Army will not join you. There is no way in which you can succeed. You may hold the palace, but only temporarily. You're surrounded. You can hope for no outside help. You have already been defeated. So listen to me carefully, Major. Don't make any more rash decisions. Don't sacrifice any more lives in a futile cause. I respect your private feelings. But remember, you are an officer in the Imperial Army. You must obey the Emperor. Can you hear me?"

"Yes, I hear you, General."

"Then do as I tell you to do."

"Let me think, General, let me think!" There was an element of frenzy now in Hatanaka's expression and in his voice. "I have just one request to make of you, sir. Before the Emperor's rescript is broadcast, may we have ten minutes on the radio to explain our position. Only ten minutes, General, to talk to the Japanese people, to give them the reasons for what we've done and explain what we hope to do. We would need only ten minutes, sir. That's all we ask of the Eastern Army."

"But your position is untenable," General Takashima persisted. "Can't you understand that? It's hopeless. The only decent thing for you to do now is make sure no one else gets killed."

Major Hatanaka put down the telephone without replying. He looked bewildered now as he faced Colonel Haga, who felt both foolish and furious at having allowed himself to be so beguiled.

"Is it true, then," Haga demanded, "that you or some of your men killed General Mori?"

Hatanaka's failure to answer was enough to convince Haga, whose fury was so great he could scarcely contain it. "I see now," he said, glancing also at Major Koga and Lieutenant Colonel Shiizaki, "why General Anami hasn't come. He never said he would come. You've lied to me about the whole thing!"

Hatanaka still had nothing to say. The two men stared fixedly at each other for a few moments. Then Colonel Haga shouted: "Out! Get out! Get out of here right now!"

Major Hatanaka, without a word, turned and left.

AUGUST 15,
5:10 A.M.

I N T H E new sunlight of what promised to be another hot, humid day, General Shizuichi Tanaka, accompanied by two subordinate officers, drove up to the Imperial Guards headquarters near the northwest corner of the palace. They arrived in time to see the First Guards Regiment (about 1,000 men) lined up in formation and ready to march.

General Tanaka's car, showing his command emblem, came to a stop beside the officer in charge of the Guards unit, a colonel. One of Tanaka's aides jumped out of the car and called the entire unit to attention.

"His Excellency, the commander of the Eastern Army!" he shouted.

When Tanaka emerged from the car, sporting the handlebar mustache which had become famous throughout the Japanese Army, the colonel in charge of the Guards recognized him immediately and saluted.

"Where are you taking these men?" the general demanded.

"Into the palace, sir."

"By whose order?"

The colonel looked puzzled. "General Mori's order, sir. Division order number 584."

The general said, "Come with me," and preceded the colonel into the headquarters building. "I want to inform you," he said, "that the orders under which you were about to march were forged. The officers attempting to seize the palace are conducting a completely unauthorized, intolerable operation. They have murdered General Mori and disobeyed the wishes of His Majesty. I intend to suppress them immediately. Now, from whom did you receive this Division Order Number 584?"

"From one of our staff officers, sir. Major [Sadakichi] Ishihara."

"Where is Major Ishihara?"

The colonel pointed toward the next room. "I think he's in his office."

Major Ishihara looked stricken when he was brought forth to face General Tanaka, whose reputation filled many people with fear. Before taking charge of the Eastern Army, he had served two tours of duty as commander of the dreaded Kempeitai, and in 1944, when civilian unrest became a problem in the occupied Philippine Islands, he had been sent to suppress it. His methods were not gentle. He wasted no time, however, terrorizing Major Ishihara. "Put this man under guard," he said to the colonel, "and send your regiment back to the barracks."

Having thus neutralized almost half of the rebellion's potential strength, General Tanaka put a phone call through to Colonel Toyojiro Haga, commander of the Second Guards Regiment, whose troops were in the palace, at the very center of the rebellion, even though he himself was now disillusioned with it. Haga was still at the command post in the palace. Tanaka ordered him to come immediately to the Inui Gate at the northwest corner.

When Tanaka's automobile reached the Inui Gate, just a few hundred yards from the Imperial Guards headquarters, he was challenged by the heavily armed sentries, but as soon as his identity was established, these men, who had been told by their officers to allow no one inside, bowed to his higher authority. The huge double doors opened slowly, creaking on their hinges, and Tanaka looked for the first time into the palace grounds, where confusion seemed to reign. There were soldiers manning machine guns along the road, soldiers running back and forth, and soldiers standing around as if they didn't quite know what was happening.

Out of this scene came Colonel Haga, with a contingent of his subordinate officers, marching to the gate where Tanaka stood facing the machine guns. The general was not pleased to have all these weapons pointed at him.

When Haga saluted, Tanaka said, "I believe my chief of staff told you on the telephone that General Mori is dead."

"Yes, sir."

"I am now the commanding general of the First Imperial Guards Division. Is that clear?"

"Yes, sir."

"I believe General Takashima also told you on the telephone to disperse these men and get them back to their barracks. Why haven't you done so?"

"I've given the order, sir, but the men are spread throughout the palace. It may take a little time."

"It must not take any longer than necessary. I want you to send runners to every unit."

"Yes, sir."

"And get these machine guns out of here immediately. They're an insult to His Majesty."

"Yes, sir. Right away."

Though General Tanaka's manner was severe, there was no doubt in his mind now about Haga's loyalty. Haga's face showed the mixture of fear and respect that Tanaka wanted to see. When he saluted and returned to his automobile, he knew the rebellion was broken.

AUGUST 15,
5:20 A.M.

G E N E R A L Anami, after winding a white cotton band around his waist, had put on a simple white shirt to which he pinned one medal. Lieutenant Colonel Takeshita was still with him in the front room of the war minister's official residence, and so, now, was Lieutenant Colonel Masataka Ida, who had finally abandoned his affiliation with Major Hatanaka's attempted coup d'état.

General Anami, running his hand fondly over the soft material of the shirt, said, "This was given to me by the Emperor when I was his aide-de-camp. He had worn it himself. I can think of nothing I prize more highly. I intend to die in it."

He then went to a closet and brought out a dress uniform, onto which he pinned all his decorations. After he had folded the uniform carefully, he laid it in an alcove.

Turning to Takeshita, he said, "When I am dead, will you drape my uniform over me?"

Takeshita nodded.

Anami then took out a photograph of his son, Koreaki, the army pilot who had died in air battle over China, and laid it on top of the uniform.

Takeshita said, "Have you any message for your family?"

Anami said, "Tell my wife I am very grateful to her and I have absolute confidence in her. She has done well." He continued to talk about his family until he was interrupted by another visitor at the front door. The maid came in to announce that General Okido, commander of the Kempeitai, wished to speak to the war minister.

Anami turned to Takeshita. "I don't want to see Okido," he said. "You go talk to him but don't let him into the house."

After Takeshita left the room, Anami said to Ida, "Will you go watch the back of the house for me? I don't want anyone coming in."

As soon as he was alone, Anami picked up the two sheets of paper on which he had written his final poem and his apology to the Emperor. Then, with a short, dagger-like sword in hand, he went out onto the corridor-porch facing the Imperial Palace, the moats and trees of which he could see in the early morning light. He was determined that at least this last act of his life would be performed in the Japanese way. A man like Anami, devoted to Japanese traditions, could not escape the feeling that the power of the West had stripped his country of almost everything it once held dear. Since the invasion by America's Admiral Perry, Western science, Western technology, Western thought, the Western way of life had increasingly weakened or superseded much of Japan's long-honored life style. Western technology was so irresistible it had even forced Japan to abandon the highly codified martial behavior of the Samurai and make war in the Western way. Now Japan was about to absorb the ultimate disgrace of losing in the Western way. Surrender was not a Japanese but a Western tradition, and it was the one Western tradition Anami could not bear to accept. Instead, he was about to embrace a still-honored Japanese tradition which would save him from having to witness it. Descending to the porch floor, he adopted the proper position with his torso erect and his legs folded back under him. He laid the two sheets of paper beside him and drew the short sword from its sheath. Holding it tightly in his right hand, he plunged it deep into the left side of his belly. When the sword was in as far as it would go, he ripped to the right and upward. As his blood spilled forth, he removed the sword and with his left hand placed it at his neck, seeking the carotid artery from which, as he knew, the blood would flow most quickly.

At this moment, despite his agony, he heard footsteps within the house.

"Who is it?" he called out.

His secretary, Colonel Hayashi, appeared on the porch, having entered the front door past Takeshita, who was still there talking to

General Okido. When Hayashi saw what was in progress, he respectfully retired from the porch and went back to the front door where he spoke to Takeshita.

Going immediately to the porch, Takeshita found General Anami sitting in a pool of blood as he tried to find his carotid artery. Anami's pain was so intense that his torso, though still rigidly straight, had begun to sway forward and backward. He seemed unable to find the exact part of his neck into which to plunge the short sword.

Takeshita said, "Shall I help you?"

Anami said, "No. Leave me."

Takeshita went into the garden where he sat for awhile with Ida, who was now sobbing uncontrollably. When Takeshita returned to the porch, General Anami was still sitting erect. The floor was saturated with blood, which was now pouring also from the war minister's neck. The two sheets of paper beside him were stained with dark red blotches.

Takeshita, bending close to him, whispered, "Aren't you in agony?"

When he received no reply, he bent even closer. Anami was still breathing. Picking up the sword, which had fallen to the floor, Takeshita plunged it deeply into the other side of his brother-in-law's neck. Anami's body swayed, then fell forward.

AUGUST 15,
6 A.M.

PRIME MINISTER Suzuki, after arriving safely at the home of his younger sister, Mrs. Yoshiko Okamoto, in the Hongo district (not far from his own home which he was forced to flee), had settled down for what he hoped would be a few hours of sleep. Only two responsibilities were left to him now before his retirement from public life —a short radio speech to be broadcast after the imperial rescript at noon, and then the formalities of resignation. He needed some sleep before the time came to undertake either of these duties.

While the old man tried to sleep, apparently safe from the soldiers who were out to assassinate him, his son, Hajime, continued to worry about them. Had they ever arrived at the family home in Myogadani. Finally he decided to telephone home and ask one of the maids or guards if there was still cause for alarm.

When he called the number, a man answered. Probably one of the policemen guarding the house. "Well, we've made it safely to the Okamotos," Hajime said. "Is there anything happening there?"

The voice at the other end said, "You say you're at the Okamotos? Is this Kantaro Suzuki's son?"

Hajime Suzuki, suddenly aware that he was talking to one of the soldiers, put down the phone. It would be easy for them to find out where the Okamotos lived. He realized to his horror that he had given away his father's hiding place.

Fifteen minutes later, the old prime minister was again dressed, in his car and on the move, this time to the home of his brother, retired General Takao Suzuki, who lived in the Shiba district on the south side of Tokyo.

AUGUST 15,
SHORTLY AFTER 6 A.M.

CAPTAIN Takeo Sasaki and his rebellious troops had now searched the Suzuki family home in Myogadani so thoroughly they were quite convinced the prime minister was not there. It was possible, however, that a secret hiding place had been built into the house. If so, there was one easy way to smoke him out. Sasaki ordered his men to soak the house with gasoline they he had brought from the Yokohama army base at which most of them were stationed. Recalling that Admiral Keisuke Okada, the prime minister during the 1936 army rebellion, had escaped death by hiding in a mattress cabinet, Sasaki made sure that all the closets were well doused.

When the house was sufficiently soaked with gasoline, everyone was ordered out. Torches were tossed in through the windows and Prime Minister Suzuki's private residence was soon in flames.

The ten policemen assigned to guard the house stood by and watched. Someone called the fire department, but after the firemen arrived, they, too, stood by and watched. They wanted no trouble with the soldiers, nor did they lack sympathy for what the soldiers were doing. As the fire commander said after one of the soldiers informed him that Suzuki was bringing the country to surrender, "If he's a Badoglio, he deserves to have his house burn down."

AUGUST 15,
7 A.M.

MRS. Aya Anami had been up for some time. She was in the kitchen of her suburban Mitaka home preparing breakfast for her children, but she was thinking of her husband. She was troubled about him. That was nothing new, of course. She had been worrying about him for several weeks, and especially during the last ten days or so. She hadn't even seen him for three days. Since his appointment as war minister the previous April, his responsibilities had been so heavy she was satisfied if he managed to get home two or three times a week. She was boiling rice when she heard the telephone ring and went to answer it. She recognized immediately the voice at the other end. It was her younger brother, Masahiko (Colonel Takeshita). He sounded serious.

"Aya," he said, "The war is over. The Emperor will announce it to the people at noon."

"Oh?"

He paused while she absorbed that much of his message. "I must also tell you, Aya, that your husband has committed seppuku."

"Oh." In her voice there was neither exclamation nor question. She was simply acknowledging what he had said. Aya Anami was the wife of a Samurai and the daughter of a Samurai. She was not expected to display her emotions openly, even to her own brother.

"The general is not yet dead," Takeshita continued, "but he is unconscious. He is not suffering."

"Shall I come immediately?" she asked.

"No. Wait there until we send a car for you."

"I'll be ready," she said. There was nothing more to say. She put down the telephone and went upstairs to change clothing.

AUGUST 15,
ABOUT 11:30 A.M.

G E N E R A L Anami's body, dressed in his uniform and covered with a quilt, was laid out in one of the rear rooms of the war minister's official residence. Mrs. Anami sat nearby on the tatami floor. The house was full of army officers who had come to pay their respects. A few government officials had also come and gone. In a short time, the general's body would be taken to the War Ministry for cremation.

As Mrs. Anami sat vigil by the corpse, one of the officers she had seen on duty at the front door came back to talk to her. He had a look of surprise on his face.

"Admiral Yonai is outside," he said. "Should I allow him in?"

Mrs. Anami arose to her feet. "I'll come out and welcome him," she said.

All the army officers in the house reacted with amazement when they heard that Admiral Yonai had come. Many of them hated him, not only because he had been a peace advocate but also because he had resisted unification of the army and navy. He had always feared that the army would swallow the navy if the two were joined. Though he and Anami had worked well together in the cabinet until the peace controversy shattered their rapport, the antipathy of most army officers against the navy minister was so strong he had been forced to accept a bodyguard as protection against army extremists. It was difficult to envision him appearing in the midst of his enemies on such an emotional occasion, just after they had lost their most beloved hero. He was standing at the front door unaccompanied, however, when Mrs. Anami arrived there to greet him. He hadn't even brought his bodyguard. An extraordinarily tall man, he towered above the army officers who were also standing near the door. Instead of his naval uniform, he wore a dark civilian suit.

He bowed deeply to Mrs. Anami and she bowed to him. After asking him to enter, she led him back through the narrow corridor to the mourning room.

Admiral Yonai, with head bowed, stood over General Anami's body for a few moments. Then he went to his knees and sat down on the floor, gazing fixedly at the general's face, which looked serene now despite the agony he had suffered.

After several minutes, Yonai arose, bowed to Mrs. Anami, and walked from the room. He had not said a word. As he left the house, the army officers near the door, though many of them were his bitter enemies, watched him with grudging admiration.

Yonai's secretary was waiting for him at his car. As they drove away, the navy minister said of Anami, "We have lost a very valuable man."

AUGUST 15,
NOON

A S T H E H O U R of noon approached, every Japanese citizen with a radio available to him sat next to it, awaiting an event so momentous that most people wondered if they had heard correctly the announcements of it which were broadcast throughout the morning. According to these announcements, the people of Japan would hear on radio at noon, for the first time ever, the actual voice of the Emperor. Never before had Hirohito or his father, Taisho, the two emperors whose reigns fell within the era of radio, spoken in person over the air. If it was true that the people were about to hear Emperor Hirohito's voice for the first time, what might they expect him to say? Would he announce that Japan had retaliated for the bombings of Hiroshima and Nagasaki by dropping a new-type bomb on Washington? Would he exhort the populace to even greater efforts and sacrifices now that Russia had joined the war against Japan? Could it be that the enemy had landed, or was about to land, on the sacred soil of the homeland and the Emperor wanted to remind all of his subjects that they had a duty to fight until death? These were among the possibilities widely considered and discussed by the Japanese at home and the troops who would be listening overseas. The one possibility almost no one discussed was that the Emperor might announce Japan's surrender.

At exactly noon, a Japan Broadcasting Corporation announcer named Nobukata Wada opened his microphone and said, "A broadcast of the highest importance is about to begin. All listeners will please rise."

After giving seventy million people enough time to come to attention, the announcer continued: "His Majesty, the Emperor, will now read his imperial rescript to the people of Japan. We respectfully transmit his voice."

The national anthem, "Kimigayo," issued forth from millions of radios. When the music stopped, a short pause ensued, after which the entire nation listened for the first time, in awe, to the voice of the man who was revered as a god.

"To Our good and loyal subjects," the Emperor began. "After pondering deeply the general trends of the world and the actual conditions obtaining in Our Empire today, We have decided to effect a settlement of the present situation by resorting to an extraordinary measure.

"We have ordered Our Government to communicate to the Governments of the United States, Great Britain, China, and the Soviet Union that Our Empire accepts the provisions of their Joint Declaration. . . ."

Alone in a small room of the air raid shelter at the imperial library within the palace, the Emperor listened to his own recorded voice on the radio. Though he felt deeply the frustration of defeat, he felt also a certain relief at knowing that this ruinous war was finally coming to an end. Until a few minutes before noon he had been attending, in the same room where he had twice during the last week spoken out for peace, a meeting of the Privy Council, which had convened this morning to ratify officially the surrender. The council session had recessed when the hour of the broadcast approached. After the broadcast, the council would reconvene and complete a formality which, on such a day as this, did not seem very important. Meanwhile, the council members, with Prime Minister Suzuki and Foreign Minister Shigenori Togo, sat around a radio the royal chamberlains had provided for them, listening tearfully to the Emperor's words.

". . . To strive for the common prosperity and happiness of all nations as well as the security and well-being of Our subjects is the solemn obligation which has been handed down by Our Imperial Ancestors, and which We lay close to heart. Indeed, We declared war on America and Britain out of Our sincere desire to ensure Japan's self-preservation and the stabilization of East Asia, it being far from Our thought either to infringe upon the sovereignty of other nations or to embark upon territorial aggrandizement. But now the war has lasted for nearly four years. Despite the best that has been done by everyone—the gallant fighting of military and naval forces, the diligence and assiduity of Our servants of the State and the devoted service of Our one hundred million people, the war situation has developed not necessarily to Japan's advantage, while the general trends of the world have all turned against her interest. . . ."

The entire Japanese population, closer in number to seventy million than 100 million, was now transfixed by a shock almost as paralyzing, for the moment at least, as the atomic bomb. Were people's ears deceiving them? Was His Majesty actually saying that the war had ended and Japan had surrendered? Though his language was elegantly euphemistic, its meaning could hardly be denied. The families in front of their radios at home, the crowds listening to amplified speakers on the streets in front of shops, the office workers at their desks, the factory workers at their benches, the government workers gathered in auditoriums, the farmers in their villages, the soldiers and sailors in their barracks began looking at each other in rigid astonishment.

". . . Moreover, the enemy has begun to employ a new and most cruel bomb, the power of which to do damage is indeed incalculable, taking the toll of many innocent lives. Should We continue to fight, it would not only result in an ultimate collapse and obliteration of the Japanese nation, but also it would lead to the total extinction of human civilization. Such being the case, how are We to save the millions of Our subjects; or to atone Ourselves before the hallowed spirits of Our Imperial Ancestors? This is the reason why We have ordered the acceptance of the provisions of the Joint Declaration of the Powers. . . ."

At the home of friends in Setagaya, kendo master Sogen Ohmori felt first mortified, then horrified as he listened to the radio. Up to the moment the Emperor began speaking, Ohmori had been comfortably certain there would be no broadcast. Major Kenji Hatanaka having assured him on the telephone the previous night that the army was taking steps to prevent surrender, Ohmori had felt supremely confident that at noon, the radio announcer would inform the public the Emperor's address had been canceled. Whatever the army wanted was what the country would do. When Ohmori arrived at the home of his friends, he was tempted to let them know there would be no broadcast, but noticing that they had already dressed formally to be in proper attire when they heard the Emperor's voice, he decided he would remain silent to avoid disappointing them. Now that His Majesty's voice was actually coming from the radio, and Ohmori realized that the army had not been able to prevent the surrender, his mortification turned to horror then despair. Everyone else in the room was weeping. He felt tears come to his own eyes.

"... We cannot but express the deepest sense of regret to our Allied nations of East Asia, who have consistently cooperated with the Empire toward the emancipation of East Asia. The thought of those officers and men as well as others who have fallen in the field of battle, those who died at their posts of duty, or those who met with untimely deaths and all their bereaved families, pains Our heart night and day. The welfare of the wounded and the war-sufferers, and of those who have lost their homes and livelihood, are the objects of Our profound solicitude. The hardships and sufferings to which Our nation is to be subjected hereafter will be certainly great. We are keenly aware of the inmost feelings of all of you, our subjects. However, it is according to the dictate of time and fate that We have resolved to pave the way to peace for ten thousand generations by enduring the unendurable and suffering what is insufferable. . . ."

In the railroad station of the small town where the train from Nagasaki to Tokyo had stopped, Dr. Yoshio Nishina, listening with his fellow passengers to the Emperor's voice, thought about the "hardships and sufferings" the country must now endure, and they were monstrous to contemplate. Yet could they be worse than the wartime hardships the country had already suffered? It would be possible now, at least, to work toward constructive rather than destructive goals. Rebuilding the country would be a more exciting challenge than fighting a hopeless war. The atomic bomb, the results of which he had just seen both at Hiroshima and Nagasaki, was a terrifying weapon, yet there was something magnificent in the fact that the Americans had been able to harness the atom. They had proven it could be done. They had opened up a new world of possibilities. Dr. Nishina wondered if the cyclotron at his Tokyo laboratory was working properly. Out of his hideous experiences at Hiroshima and Nagasaki some fresh ideas were forming in his mind. The more he thought about the challenge of the days ahead, the more eager he was to get back to work. There was a saying that work was the religion of Japan. Work would be its salvation.

"... Having been able to safeguard and maintain the structure of the Imperial State, We are always with you, Our good and loyal subjects, relying upon your sincerity and integrity. Beware most strictly of any outbursts of emotion which may engender needless complications, or any fraternal contention and strife which may create confusion, lead you astray and cause you to lose the confidence of the world. Let the entire nation continue as one family from generation to generation, ever firm in its faith in the imperishableness of its divine land, and mindful of its heavy burden of responsibilities, and the long road before it. Unite your total strength to be devoted to the construction for the future. Cultivate the ways of rectitude; foster nobility of spirit; and work with resolution so you may enhance the innate glory of the Imperial State and keep pace with the progress of the world."

As the Emperor's voice faded after his last words, and the radio remained silent for several moments out of respect for him, the almost universal reaction throughout Japan was a matching silence followed by outbursts of uncontrollable weeping and sobbing. When, after another playing of "Kimigayo," people began leaving their radios, their movements were slow, listless, automatic, unthinking. The nation was in a state of shock so deep that full comprehension still eluded almost everyone. Even the members of the Privy Council, who had known what the Emperor was going to say, were overwhelmed by his edict as they resumed their meeting to ratify it. At the war and navy ministries, where his message was also expected, the officers gradually overcame their sieges of sobbing and resumed the task which had occupied most of them before the broadcast—the burning of documents.

In every Japanese city, people began coming out of their houses, wandering the streets aimlessly, prostrating themselves in prayer at Buddhist shrines and Shinto temples. Everywhere, the sky was clear, the sun was bright, and the August heat was intense, but few people noticed it now. When friends met, they would stand gazing numbly at each other for several minutes before speaking.

At Shimbashi railroad station, a woman said to a teen-aged boy, "I heard there was to be an important broadcast at noon. What was it?" The boy bowed his head and mumbled something in a subdued voice. The woman, unable to grasp the enormity of his reply, said, "What! What!"

On a train from Tokyo to Kamakura, an army sergeant said to a private in the seat beside him, "There was something hidden behind that rescript. There must be something hidden. They're pretending to end the war, but actually they will lure the enemy onto the shore and then we'll attack. I'm sure of it."

At the Tokyo office of *Nippon Times,* an English language newspaper, Junnosuke Ofusa and the men around him sat silent at their desks for some time after the broadcast ended. Then an editorial writer leaped to his feet with shouts of joy and began throwing paper into the air. He was one of the newspaper's several Japanese-Americans who had been in Tokyo when the war began and had been refused repatriation to the United States because they were considered Japanese. His mood was contagious. Soon, others joined the celebration. The editorial writer, said, "Now we can forget all that nonsense we've been writing." Another man said, "And we can stop worrying about the Kempeitai." Ofusa, who was Japanese, felt numb. He continued to sit at his desk, staring straight ahead. Though he was delighted to know the war was over, the thought of the future bewildered him. He wondered if he had any chance of getting back his prewar job with the *New York Times* when the Americans arrived.

At Western Army Headquarters in Fukuoka, on the island of Kyushu, several army officers decided to execute a group of captured American B-29 fliers in retaliation for the destruction of Japanese cities. Selecting sixteen men from the local prisoner-of-war camp, they took them into a wooded countryside and, in a display of the savagery which had become so common during the war, hacked them to bits with Samurai swords.

On the other side of Kyushu, at Oita Naval Air Base near Beppu, Vice Admiral Matome Ugaki, who had been Admiral Isoroku Yamamoto's chief of staff and had almost been killed with the Combined Fleet commander when American P-38 fighters ambushed their two planes in 1943, decided now that the time had come to follow the revered Yamamoto in death. Ugaki, as commander of the shattered Fifth Fleet, was in charge of all the kamikaze squadrons which had been hidden on Kyushu in anticipation of the American invasion. Leading an eleven-plane formation, he took off from Oita on what he called the last of the suicide flights. Far out at sea, the eleven planes disappeared into the water without attacking any U.S. ships.

In the public plaza of the Imperial Palace at Tokyo, near the beautiful Nijubashi (Double Bridge), thousands of people gathered either to show their sympathy for the Emperor or to seek comfort from being near him. Some stood with their eyes closed in prayer. Some sat with their legs drawn up under them and their heads bent so far forward they touched the graveled ground. A few sang the national anthem or shouted "Banzai" cheers for His Majesty. Many wept. Upon this scene came Hiroshi Shimomura, director of the Information Bureau in the Suzuki government. Getting out of his car, Shimomura looked at the people near the Nijubashi then fell to the ground, weeping. He gazed up toward the palace and tried to say, "Your Majesty, forgive me!" but only the first two words came out. He was weeping so hard he wondered if he would ever again be able to weep.

On the other side of Nijubashi, within the palace at the edge of a grove of trees, lay the body of Major Kenji Hatanaka. At 11 A.M., he had fired a bullet into his own forehead. Near his body lay that of his associate, Lieutenant Colonel Jiro Shiizaki, who had cut open his belly with a sword.

At the Imperial Guards headquarters on the other side of the Palace lay the body of the Guards' commanding officer, General Takeshi Mori, who had died resisting Hatanaka's attempted coup d'état. Near Mori's body lay that of Major Hidemasa Koga, son-in-law of General Hideki Tojo. Koga, after the failure of the coup attempt in which he took part, had opened his belly in the design of a cross.

At the War Ministry on Ichigaya Heights, everyone came to attention as the body of General Korechika Anami arrived from the war minister's official residence. Prior to the cremation ceremony, which was scheduled for twilight, his remains were placed in a special room where a continuous procession of officers and men filed past, paying homage to the army's most loved general and one of Japan's most highly respected public figures.

AUGUST 15,
1 P.M.

GENERAL Hideki Tojo, who had listened to the Emperor's familiar voice in the company of his wife and four daughters at their Setagaya home, sat silent for some time afterward, engulfed by waves of anguish and despair. What had gone wrong? Was there anything he could have done, as the prime minister under whom the war began and for two-and-a-half years thereafter, to have prevented this disaster from overtaking the Emperor, the country, his own family, and himself? Could he have worked harder or planned better? Could the people have fought harder or with more spirit and determination? Would it have made any difference against the awesome power of America? It was difficult for a Japanese general to acknowledge that physical strength could overcome spiritual strength. The army had always preached, and had even based important military calculations on the belief that the fighting spirit of the Japanese soldier would compensate for whatever material or numerical advantage a foe might have. The Japanese fighting men had not lacked spirit in battle. No one could accuse them of that. Nor had the civilian populace which stood behind them. Japan had not been outfought. It had simply been overwhelmed. Those great early days of the war, the greatest days in the history of the Empire, when Japan was all victorious, when Tojo himself was a national hero and could speak in person to His Majesty at any time he wished—those days seemed now a dreadful delusion. Just three years later, the country was in ruins, the empire was lost, and Tojo himself would no doubt be accused of war crimes as soon as the Allied armies arrived. Everything had been lost. Nothing was left. Except the Emperor. That was one consolation, at least. Japan still had its Emperor. And its people. And there still remained the beautiful islands themselves. There was, then, something left. Had not His Majesty spoken on the radio about the imperishableness of this divine land?

Tojo turned to his wife, Katsuko, and their four daughters, all of whom continued to sit, stunned, in front of the radio. "You heard what His Majesty asked of you," he said to them. "Until today, every one of us had to be ready to sacrifice himself for the country. But from this moment on, we must do everything possible to restore the country. It may be more difficult than sacrificing ourselves, but I want all of you to do your best."

Mrs. Tojo, listening to her husband, noticed that he had not included himself when he told them to do their best. She wondered what course he would choose if the Americans came to arrest him. But even this terrifying possibility did not linger in her mind. She felt empty. At moments, she seemed about to lose consciousness. When she heard her husband speak, she simply nodded.

The telephone rang. Everyone was startled. Tojo got up and left the room to answer it. A few minutes later, he called for his daughter Makie, the wife of Major Hidemasa Koga.

When Makie came to him, Tojo said, "They're bringing your husband home in an hour. Are you prepared?"

Makie Koga said, "Yes, I'm prepared."

AUGUST 15,
3:35 P.M.

B A R O N Kantaro Suzuki, wearing the formal attire his wife had remembered to bring when they fled from their home to prevent his assassination that morning, stood before Emperor Hirohito in the makeshift audience room of the imperial library. The old admiral looked tired. The young Emperor looked thin and pale. Suzuki, as the prime minister in the last days of the war, had presided over one of the most momentous debates in the history of mankind—a debate to decide how a nation, already reduced to rubble and approaching starvation, should react to the incalculable new force of atomic power; a debate to decide a question of possible suicide for an entire people. Hirohito, by settling that debate, had also made it possible for Suzuki to lay down the burden of his office. Suzuki was now no longer prime minister. He had just submitted to the Emperor his resignation and that of his cabinet. With the formalities of their meeting completed, the two men gazed at each other warmly. Both were close to tears.

The Emperor said, "You have had a most difficult thing to do, Suzuki, and you have done it well."

The old man, hearing the Emperor say these kind words about him, and even call him by name, felt that his life was complete. He had met many crises during his long naval and political career. He had narrowly escaped death on several occasions. Today he was convinced that his continuing survival had not been accidental, that this one awful duty now finished had been waiting for him always at the end of his destiny. By fulfilling this last duty, he had proven to himself that there had been a purpose in his life. But he still felt one great disappointment in himself vis-à-vis the Emperor, and though he had already apologized for it in his letter of resignation, he wished to do so in person as well.

"Your Majesty, there is nothing I so deeply regret," he said, "as the fact that I twice had to invoke your help to do what I should have been able to do myself."

The Emperor smiled at him. "Don't be troubled about that, Suzuki. You have done your work well."

INDEX OF NAMES

ABOUT THE AUTHOR

THOMAS M. COFFEY is also the author *Agony at Easter*, the story of the Irish rebellion of 1916. He has been a newspaperman and television producer on the West Coast and a writer for NBC News in New York. During World War II, he was an American Air Force pilot in the Pacific. He has lived in Europe and in Japan, where he researched the story of *Imperial Tragedy*. He is now at work on a story parallel to *Imperial Tragedy* — a study of the American experience in World War II.